Advanced Accounting

Author: Paul M. Fischer, William J. Taylor, Rita H. Cheng

 CENGAGE
Learning·

Australia · Brazil · Japan · Korea · Mexico · Singapore · Spain · United Kingdom · United States

Advanced Accounting: ,

Advanced Accounting
Paul M. Fischer, William J. Taylor, Rita H. Cheng

©2016 Cengage Learning. All rights reserved.

For product information and technology assistance, contact us at
Cengage Learning Customer & Sales Support, 1-800-354-9706

For permission to use material from this text or product,
submit all requests online at **cengage.com/permissions**
Further permissions questions can be emailed to
permissionrequest@cengage.com

This book contains select works from existing Cengage Learning resources and was produced by Cengage Learning Custom Solutions for collegiate use. As such, those adopting and/or contributing to this work are responsible for editorial content accuracy, continuity and completeness.

Compilation © 2017 Cengage Learning

ISBN:978-1-337-44876-5

Cengage Learning

Cengage Learning is a leading provider of customized learning solutions with office locations around the globe, including Singapore, the United Kingdom, Australia, Mexico, Brazil, and Japan. Locate your local office at:
www.international.cengage.com/region.

Cengage Learning products are represented in Canada by Nelson Education, Ltd.

For your lifelong learning solutions, visit **www.cengage.com/custom.**

Visit our corporate website at **www.cengage.com.**

Brief Contents

Chapter 1

Business Combinations: New Rules for a Long-Standing Business Practice

Learning Objectives

When you have completed this chapter, you should be able to

1. Describe the major economic advantages of business combinations.

2. Differentiate between accounting for an acquisition of assets and accounting for an acquisition of a controlling interest in the common stock of a company.

3. Explain the basics of the acquisition model.

4. Allocate the acquisition price to the assets and liabilities of the acquired company.

5. Demonstrate an understanding of the tax issues that arise in an acquisition.

6. Explain the disclosure that is required in the period in which an acquisition occurs.

7. Apply the impairment test to goodwill and adjust goodwill when needed.

8. Estimate the value of goodwill. (Appendix)

Business combinations have been a common business transaction since the start of commercial activity. The concept is simple: A business combination is the acquisition of all of a company's assets at a single price. *Business combinations* is a comprehensive term covering all acquisitions of one firm by another. Such combinations can be further categorized as either mergers or consolidations. The term *merger* applies when an existing company acquires another company and combines that company's operations with its own. The term *consolidation* applies when two or more previously separate firms join and become one new, continuing company. Business combinations make headlines not only in the business press but also in the local newspapers of the communities where the participating companies are located. While investors may delight in the price received for their interest, employees become concerned about continued employment, and local citizens worry about a possible relocation of the business.

The popularity of business combinations grew steadily during the 1990s and peaked in 1998. From then until 2003, activity slowed considerably, with the dollar amount of deals falling even more than the number of deals. From 2003 to 2007, there was a steady rise in deals and the dollar amount of acquisitions. By 2009, the number of deals and their value fell to roughly half of their 2007 levels. Exhibit 1-1 includes the Merger Completion Record covering 1999 through 2009. The data include all acquisitions in which a U.S. company was involved as either a buyer or seller. The drastic change in business combinations can be attributed to several possible causes, such as the following:

♦ The growth period prior to 2002 reflects, in part, the boom economy of that period, especially in high-tech industries. There was also a motivation to complete acquisitions prior to July 1, 2001, when FASB Statement No. 141, *Business Combinations,* became effective. FASB Statement No. 141 eliminated the pooling-of-interests method. Pooling allowed companies to record the acquired assets at existing book value. This meant less depreciation and amortization charges in later periods. When the alternative purchase method was used prior to 2001, any goodwill that was recorded could be amortized over 40 years. After 2001,

Exhibit 1-1
10-Year Merger Completion Record: 1999–2009

10-Year Merger Completion Record: 1999 to 2009				
Year	No. of Deals	% Change	Value ($bil)	% Change
1999	9,248	—	1,423.1	—
2000	8,974	–3.0	1,786.3	25.5
2001	6,423	28.4	1,155.4	–35.3
2002	5,685	–11.5	626.7	–45.8
2003	6,269	10.3	526.9	15.9
2004	7,350	17.2	866.4	64.4
2005	8,249	12.2	1,012.2	16.8
2006	9,141	10.8	1,431.3	41.4
2007	9,575	4.7	1,808.1	26.3
2008	7,917	–17.3	999.2	–44.7
2009	5,514	–30.4	703.1	–29.6

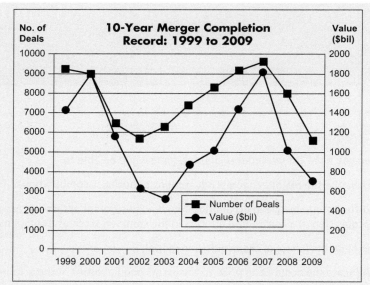

Source: Mergers and Acquisitions Almanac, February 2010, p. 31.

FASB Statement No. 141 required goodwill impairment testing, which meant there was a risk of a major goodwill impairment loss in a future period.

♦ The decline in acquisition activity could also be attributed to the soft economy during the post-2001 period. The high-tech sector of the economy, which had been a hotbed of combinations, was especially weak. Add to it the increased scrutiny of companies being acquired, as caused by the accounting and business scandals of the period, and the motivation to acquire was lessened.

♦ Aside from broad-based accounting infractions, specific allegations of precombination beautification arose. It became clear that adjustments were made to the books of the company being acquired to make it look more valuable as a takeover candidate. This included arranging in advance to meet the pooling-of-interests criteria and making substantial write-offs to enhance post-acquisition income. In the fall of 1999, it was alleged that Tyco International arranged to have targeted companies take major write-downs before being acquired by Tyco. This concern caused a major decline in the value of Tyco shares and led to stockholder suits against the company.

♦ The steady increase in acquisition activity after 2002 could be attributed to a growing economy and stabilization in the accounting method used.

♦ The steep decline in activity since 2007 is likely a result of the deep recession during that time period. With improvements in the economy during 2010, business acquisitions have accelerated.

♦ Acquisitions per year have been fairly level since 2010. For an updated count of activity, do a computer Internet search using "Thomson-Reuters Mergers and Acquisitions Review" and select the latest quarterly report.

ECONOMIC ADVANTAGES OF COMBINATIONS

1

OBJECTIVE

Describe the major economic advantages of business combinations.

Business combinations are typically viewed as a way to jump-start economies of scale. Savings may result from the elimination of duplicative assets. Perhaps both companies will utilize common facilities and share fixed costs. There may be further economies as one management team replaces two separate sets of managers. It may be possible to better coordinate production, marketing, and administrative actions. The U.S. Federal Trade Commission defines six types of mergers. They are:

Backward Vertical Integration. This is a deal where a company moves down the production–marketing cycle by acquiring a supplier of products or services it provides.

Example: The acquisition of Smith International by Slumberger. Smith International is a provider of drilling bits and fluids to the oil industry. Slumberger is an oil field service company providing a range of services to oil companies including drilling of oil wells. The transaction was stock for stock and will likely be a tax-free exchange for investors (to be explained in a following section).

Forward Vertical Integration. This is a merger where a company moves up the production–marketing cycle by acquiring a company that uses its products.

Example: The acquisition of Healthvision Solutions, Inc., by Lawson Software. Lawson is a provider of software solutions including healthcare applications. Healthvision provides integrated healthcare technologies directly to healthcare organizations. This was an acquisition for cash.

Horizontal Merger. This is a merger of companies that offer similar products or services and are likely competitors in the same market space.

Example: The huge drug store chain, Walgreen Company, acquired the New-York-based drug store chain of Duane Reade Holdings, Inc. This cash acquisition quadrupled the number of stores Walgreen has in the metro New York area.

Product Extension Merger. This is a merger where the acquiring company is expanding its product offerings in the marketplace in which it already sells products and/or services.

Example: R. R. Donnelley & Sons Company acquired, for cash, Browne & Company. Donnelley provides integrated communication services for a wide range of customers. Browne provides critical capital markets communications.

Market Extension Merger. This merger increases the geographic market coverage of the same products or services already offered by the acquiring company.

Example: First Energy acquired Allegheny Energy. Both companies are power companies. The acquisition expands First Energy's market in Pennsylvania and extends its market to include portions of West Virginia, Maryland, and Virginia.

Conglomerate Merger. Example: This is an acquisition of a firm in an unrelated line of business. In effect, the acquiring firm has a portfolio of investments. Some have said that a conglomerate is similar to a mutual fund in its purpose to maximize returns over a range of companies.

Thomas H. Lee Partners acquired for cash CKE Restaurants, Inc. CKE owns the Carl's Jr. and Hardee's quick service restaurant chains. Thomas H. Lee Partners businesses include information services, lending, publishing, music, and consumer products, including Snapple.

Tax Advantages of Combinations

Perhaps the most universal economic benefit in business combinations is a possible tax advantage. The owners of a business, whether sole proprietors, partners, or shareholders, may wish to retire from active management of the company. If they were to sell their interest for cash or accept debt instruments, they would have an immediate taxable gain. If, however, they accept the common stock of another corporation in exchange for their interest and carefully craft the transaction as a "tax-free reorganization," they may account for the transaction as a tax-free exchange. No taxes are paid until the shareholders sell the shares received in the business combination. The shareholder records the new shares received (for tax purposes) at the book value of the exchanged shares.

In early 2014, Iberiabank Corporation filed a form 8K with the SEC which provided the following information concerning its merger with Teche Holding Company:

> On January 12, 2014, IBERIABANK Corporation ("IBKC") the parent company of IBERIABANK, entered into an Agreement and Plan of Merger (the "Merger Agreement") with Teche Holding Company ("TSH"), the parent company of Teche Federal Bank. Under the Merger Agreement, TSH will merge into the IBKC (the "Merger") after which Teche Federal Bank will merge with and into IBERIABANK. Each outstanding share of TSH's common stock will be converted into the right to receive 1.162 shares of IBKC common stock at the effective time of the Merger (the "Exchange Ratio") plus cash in lieu of any fractional interest. The Exchange Ratio will be adjusted if the market price of IBKC common stock on the NASDAQ

Global Select Market during the prescribed measurement period to the merger falls below $55.80 or rises above $68.20, pursuant to the formula set forth in the Merger Agreement. All TSH stock options, whether or not vested, will be cashed out and shares of restricted stock will become fully vested in connection with the transaction and will be exchanged for shares of IBKC common stock like the other shares of TSH common stock.

The Merger is intended to qualify as a tax-free reorganization for federal income tax purposes. The Merger is expected to close during the second quarter of 2014. If the Merger is not consummated under certain circumstances, TSH has agreed to pay IBKC a termination fee up to $5,000,000, and IBKC has agreed to pay TSH a termination fee of up to $4,000,000 in certain circumstances.[1]

Further tax advantages exist when the target company has reported losses on its tax returns in prior periods. Section 172 of the Internal Revenue Code provides that operating losses can generally be carried back two years to obtain a refund of taxes paid in previous years. In an effort to stimulate the economy, Congress enacted a special 5-year carryback for 2008 and 2009 operating losses. Should the loss not be offset by income in the allowed prior years, the loss may be carried forward up to 20 years to offset future taxable income, thus eliminating or reducing income taxes that would otherwise be payable. These loss maneuvers have little or no value to a target company that has not had income in the two prior years and does not expect profitable operations in the near future. However, tax losses are transferable in a business combination. To an acquiring company that has a profit in the current year and/or expects profitable periods in the future, the tax losses of a target company may have real value. That value, viewed as an asset by the acquiring company, will be reflected in the price paid. However, the acquiring company must exercise caution in anticipating the benefits of tax loss carryovers. The realization of the tax benefits may be denied if it can be shown that the primary motivation for the combination was the transfer of the tax loss benefit.

A tax benefit may also be available in a subsequent period as a consolidated tax return is filed by the single remaining corporation. The losses of one of the affiliated companies can be used to offset the net income of another affiliated company to lessen the taxes that would otherwise be paid by the profitable company.

REFLECTION

- Business combinations may have a wide range of economic advantages to a firm including vertical and horizontal integration, market and product expansion and diversification as a conglomerate company.

- Potential sellers may be motivated by the tax advantages available to them in a business combination.

2

OBJECTIVE

Differentiate between accounting for an acquisition of assets and accounting for an acquisition of a controlling interest in the common stock of a company.

ACQUISITION OF CONTROL

Control of another company may be achieved by either acquiring the assets of the target company or acquiring a controlling interest (typically over 50%) in the target company's voting common stock. In an *acquisition of assets*, all of the company's assets are acquired *directly* from the company. In most cases, existing liabilities of the acquired company also are assumed. When assets are acquired and liabilities are assumed, we refer to the transaction as an acquisition of "net assets." Payment could be made in cash, exchanged property, or issuance of either debt or equity securities. It is common to issue securities since this avoids depleting cash or other assets that may be needed in future operations. Legally, a *statutory consolidation* refers to the

---

1 Iberiabank Corp (IBKC) form 8-K filed with SEC on January 13, 2014.

combining of two or more previously independent legal entities into one new legal entity. The previous companies are dissolved and are then replaced by a single continuing company. A *statutory merger* refers to the absorption of one or more former legal entities by another company that continues as the sole surviving legal entity. The absorbed company ceases to exist as a legal entity but may continue as a division of the surviving company.

In a *stock acquisition,* a controlling interest (typically, more than 50%) of another company's voting common stock is acquired. The company making the acquisition is termed the *parent* (also the acquirer), and the company acquired is termed a *subsidiary* (also the acquiree). Both the parent and the subsidiary remain separate legal entities and maintain their own financial records and statements. However, for external financial reporting purposes, the companies usually will combine their individual financial statements into a single set of consolidated statements. Thus, the term "consolidation" may refer to a statutory combination or, more commonly, to the consolidated statements of a parent and its subsidiary.

There may be several advantages to obtaining control by acquiring a controlling interest in stock. The most obvious one is that the total cost is lower, since only a controlling interest in the assets, and not the total assets, must be acquired. In addition, control through stock ownership may be simpler to achieve since no formal negotiations or transactions with the acquiree's management are necessary. Further advantages may result from maintaining the separate legal identity of the acquiree company. First of all, risk is lowered because the legal liability of each corporation is limited to its own assets. Secondly, separate legal entities may be desirable when only one of the companies, such as a utility company, is subject to government control. Lastly, tax advantages may result from the preservation of the legal entities.

Stock acquisitions are said to be "friendly" when the stockholders of the acquiree corporation, as a group, decide to sell or exchange their shares. In such a case, an offer may be made to the board of directors by the acquiring company. If the directors approve, they will recommend acceptance of the offer to the shareholders, who are likely to approve the transaction. Often, a two-thirds vote is required. Once approval is gained, the exchange of shares will be made with the individual shareholders. If the officers decline the offer, or if no offer is made, the acquirer may deal directly with individual shareholders in an attempt to secure a controlling interest. Frequently, the acquirer may make a formal *tender offer.* The tender offer typically will be published in newspapers and will offer a greater-than-market price for shares made available by a stated date. The acquirer may reserve the right to withdraw the offer if an insufficient number of shares is made available to it. Where management and/or a significant number of shareholders oppose the acquisition of the company by the intended buyer, the acquisition is viewed as hostile. Unfriendly offers are so common that several standard defensive mechanisms have evolved. Following are the common terms used to describe these defensive moves.

Greenmail. The target company may pay a premium price ("greenmail") to buy back its own shares. It may either buy shares already owned by a potential acquiring company or purchase shares from a current owner who, it is feared, would sell to the acquiring company. The price paid for these shares in excess of their market price may not be deducted from stockholders' equity; instead, it is expensed.[2]

White Knight. The target company locates a different company to acquire a controlling interest. This could occur when the original acquiring company is in a similar industry and it is feared that current management of the target company would be displaced. The replacement acquiring company, the "white knight," might be in a different industry and could be expected to keep current management intact.

Poison Pill. The "poison pill" involves the issuance of stock rights to existing shareholders to purchase additional shares at a price far below fair value. However, the rights are exercisable only when an acquiring company purchases or makes a bid to purchase a stated number of shares. The effect of the options is to substantially raise the cost to the acquiring company. If the attempt fails, there is at least a greater gain for the original shareholders.

---

2 FASB ASC 505-30-25-4, *Equity-Treasury Stock—Recognition* (Norwalk, CT , 2010).

Selling the Crown Jewels. This approach has the management of the target company selling vital assets (the "crown jewels") of the target company to others to make the company less attractive to the acquiring company.

Leveraged Buyouts. The management of the existing target company attempts to purchase a controlling interest in that company. Often, substantial debt will be incurred to raise the funds needed to purchase the stock; hence the term "leveraged buyout." When bonds are sold to provide this financing, the bonds may be referred to as "junk bonds," since they are often high-interest and high-risk due to the high debt-to-equity ratio of the resulting corporation.

Further protection against takeovers is offered by federal and state law. The Clayton Act of 1914 (Section 7) is a federal law that prohibits business combinations in which "the effect of such acquisition may be substantially to lessen competition or to tend to create a monopoly."

The Williams Act of 1968 is a federal law that regulates tender offers; it is enforced by the Securities and Exchange Commission (SEC). Several states also have enacted laws to discourage hostile takeovers. These laws are motivated, in part, by the fear of losing employment and taxes.

Accounting Ramifications of Control

When control is achieved through an asset acquisition, the acquiring company records on its books the assets and assumed liabilities of the acquired company. From the acquisition date on, all transactions of both the acquiring and acquired company are recorded in one combined set of accounts. The only new skill one needs to master is the proper recording of the acquisition when it occurs. **Once the initial acquisition is properly recorded, subsequent accounting procedures are the same as for any single accounting entity.** Combined statements of the new, larger company for periods following the combination are automatic.

Accounting procedures are more involved when control is achieved through a stock acquisition. The controlling company, the parent, will record only an investment account to reflect its interest in the controlled company, the subsidiary. Both the parent and the subsidiary remain separate legal entities with their own separate sets of accounts and separate financial statements. Accounting theory holds that where one company has effective control over another, there is only one economic entity and there should be only one set of financial statements that combines the activities of the entities under common control. The accountant will prepare a worksheet, referred to as the *consolidated worksheet,* that starts with the separate accounts of the parent and the subsidiary. Various adjustments and eliminations will be made on this worksheet to merge the separate accounts of the two companies into a single set of financial statements, which are called *consolidated statements.*

This chapter discusses business combinations resulting from asset acquisitions, since the accounting principles are more easily understood in this context. The principles developed are applied directly to stock acquisitions that are presented in the chapters that follow.

REFLECTION

- Control of another company is gained by either acquiring all of that firm's assets (and usually its liabilities) or by acquiring a controlling interest in that company's voting common stock.

- Control through an acquisition of assets requires the correct initial recording of the purchase. Combined statements for future periods are automatically produced.

3

OBJECTIVE

Explain the basics of the acquisition model.

EVOLUTION OF ACCOUNTING METHODS

Prior to the issuance of FASB Statement No. 141 in 2001, two methods were used to account for business combinations. These were the purchase method and the pooling-of-interests method. The *purchase method* usually recorded all assets and liabilities of the company acquired at fair value. The purchase method was the primary method in use. However, under some circumstances, the pooling-of-interests method was allowed. The *pooling-of-interests method* recorded the assets and liabilities of the acquired firm at their existing book values. This method was intended to be applied to business combinations that were a "merger of equals." Specific criteria existed as to combinations that would qualify. Ninety percent of the stock of the firm acquired had to be received in exchange for the shares of the acquiring firm. All shareholders of the acquired firm had to be treated equally. Numerous other criteria also attempted to guarantee a fusion of existing owners rather than a takeover of one company by another. In the end, some companies engaged in a series of equity transactions prior to the combination so that they would be able to meet the pooling criteria. Pooling allowed the carry over of book values to the acquiring firm. That resulted in greater future income because of typically lower depreciation and amortization charges on assets. Pooling did not result in new goodwill being recorded. At that time goodwill was amortized. Thus, pooling also led to greater income in the future since there would be no goodwill amortization.

FASB Statement No. 141 eliminated the pooling method. Assets and liabilities acquired in a pooling of interests, that began prior to the effective date of FASB Statement No. 141, were allowed to continue as originally recorded. This means that current-era financial statements still include assets and liabilities of a firm acquired in a pooling that were initially recorded at their book values on the acquisition date.

The purchase method required under FASB Statement No. 141 focused only on recording fair values for the portion of the assets and liabilities acquired in the purchase. The accounts of the acquired company would only be adjusted to full fair value if the parent company acquired a 100% interest in the acquired firm. If, for example, the purchasing company bought only an 80% interest in the acquired firm, accounts would be adjusted by only 80% of the difference between book and fair value. Thus, in an 80% purchase, an asset with a book value of $6,000 and a fair value of $10,000 would be recorded at $9,200 ($6,000 book value plus 80% × $4,000 excess of fair value over book value).

The new *acquisition method* included in FASB Statement No. 14lr (now included in FASB ASC 805), issued in 2007, requires that all assets and liabilities be recorded at fair value regardless of the percentage interest purchased by the acquiring company (provided that the interest purchased is large enough to constitute a controlling interest). In the above example, the asset illustrated would be recorded at the full $10,000 fair value even though the acquiring company only purchased an 80% interest in the company that owns the asset. The acquisition method also eliminated the prior practice of discounting of fixed and intangible assets to a value less than fair value. This would happen under the purchase method when, in a rare case, the acquiring firm made a "bargain purchase." A *bargain purchase* occurs when the price paid for a company is less than the sum of the fair value of its net assets (sum of all assets minus all liabilities).

Applying the Acquisition Method

The four steps in the acquisition method are as follows:

1. Identify the acquirer.
2. Determine the acquisition date.
3. Measure the fair value of the acquiree (the company being acquired).
4. Record the acquiree's assets and liabilities that are assumed.

Identify the Acquirer. In an asset acquisition, the company transferring cash or other assets and/or assuming liabilities is the acquiring company. In a stock acquisition, the acquirer is, in most cases, the company transferring cash or other assets for a controlling interest in the voting common stock of the acquiree (company being acquired). Some stock acquisitions may be accomplished by exchanging voting common stock. Most often, the company issuing the voting common stock is the acquirer. In some cases, the acquiree may issue the stock in the acquisition. This "reverse acquisition" may occur when a publicly traded company is acquired by a privately traded company. The appendix at the end of Chapter 2 considers this situation and provides the applicable accounting methods.

When an acquisition is accomplished through an exchange of equity interests, the factors considered in determining the acquirer firm include the following:

1. Voting rights—The entity with the largest share of voting rights is typically the acquirer.
2. Large minority interest—Where the company purchases only a large minority interest (under 50%) and no other owner or group has a significant voting interest, the company acquiring the large minority interest is likely the acquirer. Determination of control could be based on domination of the decision-making process to obtain the related economic benefits.
3. Governing body of combined entity—The entity that has the ability to elect or appoint a majority of the combined entity is likely the acquirer.
4. Terms of exchange—Typically, the acquirer pays a premium over the precombination market value of the shares acquired.

Determine the Acquisition Date. This is the date that the acquiring firm makes payment by transferring assets, issuing stock, and assuming the liabilities of the acquired company. Normally, this is also the legal closing date. The closing can, however, occur after the acquisition date if there is a written agreement that the acquirer obtains control of the acquiree.

The acquisition date is critical because it is the date used to establish the total fair value of the company acquired, and it is usually the date that fair values are established for the assets and liabilities of the acquired company.

Measure the Fair Value of the Acquiree. Unless there is evidence to the contrary, the fair value of the acquiree as an entity is assumed to be the price paid by the acquirer. The price paid is based on the sum of the fair values of the assets transferred, liabilities assumed, and the stock issued by the acquirer. If the information to establish the fair value of the acquiree is not available on the acquisition date, a *measurement period* is available to ascertain the value. This period ends when either the needed information is available or is judged to not be obtainable. In no case can the measurement period exceed one year from the acquisition date.

Specific guidance as to what may be included in the price calculation is as follows:

a. The price includes the estimated value of contingent consideration. Contingent consideration is an agreement to issue additional consideration (assets or stock) at a later date if specified events occur. The most common agreements focus on a targeted sales or income performance by the acquiree company. An estimate must be made of the probable settlement cost and that amount is included in the price paid. The measurement period is available to refine the estimated value.

A contingent agreement that would require the issuance of stock is classified as either a liability or equity. Subsequent to the measurement period, agreements that create a liability are remeasured and the changes are included in the income of the subsequent period. Agreements classified as equity are not remeasured. Generally, an agreement is classified as equity if the settlement is to be in shares (or shares or cash at the option of the acquirer). However, even if the settlement is in shares, the agreement is considered a liability if:

1. It is a fixed amount known at the time of the purchase.
2. It is an agreement to make up for a decline in the value of the acquirer's shares.
3. It is an amount that varies on something other than the fair value of the acquirer shares.

To qualify as equity, the agreement would have to be the grant of additional shares based solely on the performance of the acquiree company. The agreement could be fixed as to the number of shares or could base the settlement on the value of the shares used for settlement. There would be no adjustments for the change in the estimated value during the duration of the agreement. Guidance for the classification of contingent consideration as a liability or equity comes from FASB ASC 815-40-25-1 through 28.

b. The **costs of accomplishing the acquisition**, such as accounting costs and legal fees, are not included in the price of the company acquired and **are expensed**. In the period of the acquisition, the notes to the financial statements must disclose the amount of the acquisition costs and state the line item expense on the income statement that includes these costs. (3) Where the consideration used is the stock of the acquirer, **the issue costs may also be**

expensed or they can be deducted from the value assigned to paid-in capital in excess of par, but they are not included in the price paid.

Record the Acquiree's Assets and Liabilities That Are Assumed. The fair values of all identifiable assets and liabilities of the acquiree are determined and recorded. *Fair value* is the amount that the asset or liability would be bought or sold for in a current, normal (nonforced) sale between willing parties. Fair values are determined following the guidance of FASB ASC 820, *Fair Value Measurement and Disclosure.* FASB ASC 820-10-35-37 to 54A provides a hierarchy of values, where the highest level measurement possible should be used. The hierarchy is as follows:

◆ Level 1—Unadjusted quoted market value in an actively traded market. This method would apply to actively traded investments and to inventory.

◆ Level 2—Adjusted market value based on prices of similar assets or on observable other inputs such as interest rates. This approach might apply to work-in-process inventory and plant and equipment that sells in an organized market.

◆ Level 3—Fair value based on unobservable inputs, such as the entities' best estimate of an exit (sale) value. The value of plant and equipment, not normally sold in an active market, would likely be calculated under this approach.

There are a few exceptions to the fair value rule that will be discussed. The sum of all identifiable assets, less liabilities recorded, is referred to as the fair value of the net assets. The identifiable assets never include goodwill that may exist on the acquiree's books. The only goodwill recorded in an acquisition is "new" goodwill based on the price paid by the acquirer. The fair value recorded for the net assets is not likely to be equal to the fair value of the acquiree as an entire entity (which is normally equal to the price paid).

Goodwill. Goodwill results when the price paid exceeds the fair value of the acquiree's net identifiable assets. The excess of the fair value of the acquiree over the values assigned to net identifiable assets is "new" goodwill. The goodwill recorded is not amortized but is impairment tested in future accounting periods.

Bargain Purchase. A bargain purchase occurs when the fair value assigned to the net identifiable assets exceeds the price paid. When this occurs, every effort should be made to revalue the amounts assigned to net identifiable assets to eliminate the difference. If, after reconsideration of the fair values, an excess of fair value of the net identifiable assets over the price paid still exists, the excess is recorded as a "gain" on the acquisition by the acquirer. Disclosure for the period of the acquisition must show the gain as a separate line item on the income statement or identify the line item that includes the gain. Exhibit 1-2, the 2014 Ralph Lauren Corporation, Consolidated Statements of Income, includes a "gain on the acquisition of Chaps." The note, just below the income statements, explains the calculation of the gain.

Exhibit 1-2
Ralph Lauren Corporation
Consolidated Statements of Income

	Fiscal Years Ended		
	March 29, 2014	March 30, 2013	March 31, 2012
	(millions, except per share data)		
Net sales	$ 7,284	$ 6,763	$ 6,679
Licensing revenue	166	182	181
Net revenues	7,450	6,945	6,860
Cost of goods sold[a]	(3,140)	(2,789)	(2,862)
Gross profit	4,310	4,156	3,998

(continued)

Other costs and expenses:			
Selling, general, and administrative expenses[a]	(3,142)	(2,971)	(2,916)
Amortization of intangible assets	(35)	(27)	(29)
Gain on acquisition of Chaps	16	—	—
Impairments of assets	(1)	(19)	(2)
Restructuring and other charges	(18)	(12)	(12)
Total other costs and expenses, net	(3,180)	(3,029)	(2,959)
Operating income	1,130	1,127	1,039
Foreign currency losses	(8)	(12)	(2)
Interest expense	(20)	(22)	(24)
Interest and other income, net	3	6	11
Equity in losses of equity-method investees	(9)	(10)	(9)
Income before provision for income taxes	1,096	1,089	1,015
Provision for income taxes	(320)	(339)	(334)
Net income	$ 776	$ 750	$ 681
Net income per common share:			
Basic	$ 8.55	$ 8.21	$ 7.35
Diluted	$ 8.43	$ 8.00	$ 7.13
Weighted average common shares outstanding:			
Basic	90.7	91.3	92.7
Diluted	92.0	93.7	95.5
Dividends declared per share	$ 1.70	$ 1.60	$ 0.80
[a]Includes total depreciation expense of:	$ (223)	$ (206)	$ (196)

See accompanying notes.

Ralph Lauren Corporation
Consolidated Statements of Comprehensive Income

	Fiscal Years Ended		
	March 29, 2014	March 30, 2013	March 31, 2012
	(millions)		
Net income	$776	$ 750	$681
Other comprehensive income (loss), net of tax:			
Foreign currency translation adjustments	52	(93)	(50)
Net realized and unrealized gains (losses) on derivatives	(27)	(13)	32
Net realized and unrealized gains (losses) on available-for-sale investments	(5)	4	1
Net realized and unrealized losses on defined benefit plans	—	(1)	(2)
Other comprehensive income (loss), net of tax	20	(103)	(19)
Total comprehensive income	$796	$ 647	$662

Chaps Menswear License Acquisition On April 10, 2013, in connection with the transition of the North American Chaps-branded men's sportswear business ("Chaps Menswear Business") from a licensed to a wholly-owned operation, the Company entered into an agreement with The Warnaco Group, Inc. ("Warnaco"), a subsidiary of PVH Corp. ("PVH"), to acquire certain net assets in exchange for an aggregate payment of approximately $18 million (the "Chaps Menswear License Acquisition"). Warnaco was the Company's licensee for the Chaps Menswear Business. The Company funded the Chaps Menswear License Acquisition during the first quarter of Fiscal 2014 with available cash on-hand.

(continued)

The Company accounted for the Chaps Menswear License Acquisition as a business combination during the first quarter of Fiscal 2014. The acquisition cost was allocated to the assets acquired and liabilities assumed based on an assessment of their respective fair values, as follows (in millions):

Assets acquired:	
Inventory	$ 30
Accounts receivable	19
Licensed trademark intangible asset	9
Total assets acquired	58
Liabilities assumed:	
Accounts payable	(22)
Other net liabilities	(2)
Total net liabilities assumed	(24)
Fair value of net assets acquired	34
Consideration paid	18
Gain on acquisition[a]	$16

(a) Represents the difference between the acquisition date fair value of net assets acquired and the contractually-defined purchase price under the Company's license agreement with Warnaco, which granted the Company the right to early-terminate the license upon PVH's acquisition of Warnaco in February 2013.

The licensed trademark intangible asset was valued using the excess earnings method, discounting the estimated after-tax cash flows associated with the Chaps-branded men's sportswear licensed trademark as of the acquisition date, factoring in market participant-based operating and cash flow assumptions. The reacquired licensed trademark intangible asset was amortized over a nine-month period through December 31, 2013, representing the remaining term of the prior license agreement that was terminated in connection with this acquisition.

The operating results of the Chaps Menswear Business have been consolidated into the Company's operating results beginning on April 10, 2013. Transaction costs of $3 million were expensed as incurred and classified within SG&A expenses in the consolidated statement of income for Fiscal 2014.

Prior to FASB 141r, there was an extraordinary gain when the price paid exceeded the total of only current assets minus all liabilities. Under current rules, there is an "ordinary" gain when fair value of the net identifiable assets exceeds the price paid.

REFLECTION

- The acquisition method records all accounts of the acquiree at fair value. Any goodwill on the acquiree's books is ignored.

- An acquisition cost in excess of the fair value of the acquiree's net identifiable assets results in goodwill.

- An acquisition cost less than the fair values of the acquiree's net identifiable assets results in an ordinary gain being recorded by the acquirer.

4
OBJECTIVE

Allocate the acquisition price to the assets and liabilities of the acquired company.

VALUATION OF IDENTIFIABLE ASSETS AND LIABILITIES

The first step in recording an acquisition is to record the existing asset and liability accounts (except goodwill). As a general rule, assets and liabilities are to be recorded at their individually determined fair values. The preferred method is quoted market value when an active market for the item exists. Where there is not an active market, independent appraisals, discounted cash flow analysis, and other types of analysis are used to estimate fair values. There are some exceptions to the use of fair value that apply to accounts such as assets for resale and deferred taxes.

The acquiring firm is not required to establish values immediately on the acquisition date. A measurement period of up to one year is allowed for measurement. Temporary values would be used in financial statements prepared prior to the end of the measurement period. A note to the statements would explain the use of temporary values. Any change in the recorded values is adjusted retroactively to the date of the acquisition. Prior-period statements are revised to reflect the final values and any related amortizations.

The procedures for recording the assets and liabilities of the acquired firm are as follows:

1. **Current assets**—These are recorded at estimated fair values. This would include recording accounts and notes receivable at the estimated amounts to be collected. Accounts and notes receivable are to be recorded in a net account that represents the probable cash flows; a separate valuation account for uncollectible accounts is not allowed. All accounts share the rule that only the net fair value is recorded, and valuation accounts are not used.

2. **Existing liabilities**—These are also recorded at fair value. For current contractual liabilities, that is likely to be the existing recorded value. For estimated liabilities, a new fair value may be used in place of recorded values. Long-term liabilities will be adjusted to a value different from recorded value if there has been a material change in interest rates.

3. **Property, plant, and equipment**—Operating assets will require an estimate of fair value and will be recorded at that net amount with no separate accumulated depreciation account.

4. **Existing intangible assets, other than goodwill**—These will also be recorded at estimated fair value. The valuation of these items, such as patents and copyrights, will typically require the use of discounted cash flow analysis.

5. **Assets that are going to be sold rather than used in operations**—Such assets are *not* recorded at fair value. They are recorded at net realizable value and are listed as current assets.

6. **When the acquiree is a lessee with respect to assets in use**—The original classification of a lease as operating or capital is not changed by the acquisition unless the terms of the lease are modified as part of the acquisition. The acquiree has no recorded asset for assets under operating leases. If, however, the terms of the lease are favorable as compared to current market rent rates, an intangible asset would be recorded equal to the discounted present value of the savings. If the lease terms are unfavorable, an estimated liability would be recorded equal to the discounted present value of the rent in excess of fair rental rates.

EXAMPLE

The acquiree is a party to a 5-year remaining term operating lease requiring payments of $1,000 per month at the start of each month. The current rental rate for such an asset on a new 5-year lease would be $1,300 per month. Assuming an annual interest rate for this type of transaction of 8%, the calculation would be as follows:

Payment	$ 300 (excess of fair rent value over contractual amount)
n	60
Rate	8%/12
Present Value	$14,894 (beginning mode)

An intangible asset, Favorable Operating Lease Terms, would be recorded and amortized over five years. The effective interest method of amortization should be applied.

If the acquiree is a party to a capital lease, the asset would be recorded at fair value as would the liability under the capital lease.

7. **When the acquiree may have acted as a lessor**—Again, the classification of the lease is not changed unless the terms are changed. For operating leases, the acquiree has the asset recorded on its balance sheet. The asset is recorded at fair value, and it is not impacted by the terms of any lease applicable to that asset. If the terms of the operating lease include rental rates that are different than current rental rates, an intangible asset or estimated liability is recorded. An intangible asset would be recorded for favorable lease terms, and an estimated liability would be recorded for unfavorable terms. Note that the lessor terms are favorable when the contract rental rate exceeds fair rental value, and terms are unfavorable when the fair rental value exceeds the contract rate. The value of the intangible asset or estimated liability uses the same procedure as illustrated for the lessee above.

If the lease is a capital lease, the acquiree has no asset recorded other than the minimum lease payments receivable account. This account would be remeasured at the discounted present value of the payments at the current market interest rate for such a transaction.

EXAMPLE

The acquiree/lessor has a minimum lease payment receivable on its books at $178,024 (96 beginning-of-the-month payments of $2,500 at 8% annual interest rate). If the current market rate of interest for this transaction is 12% annual, the fair value of the minimum lease payment receivable would be calculated and recorded as follows:

Payment	$ 2,500, beginning of the month
n	96 months
Rate	12%/12 = 1%
Present Value	$155,357 (This is the amount of the minimum lease payment receivable that would be recorded.)

8. **Intangible assets not currently recorded by the acquiree**—Identifiable intangible assets must be separately recorded; their value cannot be swept into the "goodwill" classification. An intangible asset is identifiable if it arises from contractual or other legal rights (even if it is not separable) or is separable. For example, the acquiree may have a customer list that could be sold separately and has a determinable value. The acquiree cannot record the value of this self-developed intangible asset. However, this value must be estimated and recorded as one of the assets acquired in the acquisition.

FASB ASC 805-20-55 provides examples of intangible assets that are identifiable. They include:

- Marketing-related intangible assets including trademarks, trade names, service marks, collective marks, and certification marks
- Internet domain names
- Customer-related intangible assets including customer lists, order or production backlog, customer contracts and related customer relationships, and non-contractual customer relationships
- Artistic-related intangible assets including plays, operas, ballets, books, magazines, newspapers, musical works, pictures, and video materials
- Contract-based intangible assets including licensing, royalty and standstill agreements, advertising, construction, management, service and supply contracts, construction permits, franchise agreements, operating and broadcast rights, servicing contracts, employment contracts, and use rights
- Technology-based intangible assets including patented technology, computer software and mask works, unpatented technology, databases, and trade secrets

9. **Research and development assets**—The fair values of both tangible and intangible research and development assets are recorded even where the assets do not have alternative future uses (the usual criteria for capitalization of R&D assets). Where the assets included in the acquisition have value only for a given project, the assets are considered to have an "indefinite" life and are not amortized until the project is completed. Upon completion, the useful life is to be estimated and used as the amortization period. The assets are to be expensed at the completion or abandonment of an unsuccessful project.

   Tangible and intangible R&D assets that are used for multiple R&D projects are separately recorded and are amortized based on the projects served by the assets.

10. **Contingent assets and liabilities**—This refers to contingent assets and liabilities possessed by the acquiree on the acquisition date and must not be confused with contingent consideration that is part of the acquisition agreement. The fair value of a contingent asset or liability is recorded at its fair value on the acquisition date, if such a value exists. The measurement period allows added time to estimate these values.

    If a fair value does not exist on the acquisition date, guidance for estimating the value comes from FASB ASC 805-20-25-20. Two criteria must be met for an estimate of the contingent asset or liability to be recorded:

    - Information available by the end of the measurement date indicates that it is probable that an asset existed or a liability had been incurred as of the acquisition date. It is implicit in this condition that it must be probable at the acquisition date that one or more future events confirming the existence of the asset or liability will occur.
    - The amount of the asset or liability can be reasonable estimated.

    Examples of contingent assets would include possible bonuses, refunds stemming from tax disputes, and possible favorable outcomes of lawsuits. Contingent assets can not be recorded except as a part of a business acquisition. Contingent liabilities include pending claims such as unfavorable lawsuits, warranty costs, premiums and coupons, and environmental liabilities.

11. **Liabilities associated with restructuring or exit activities**—The fair value of an existing restructuring or exit activity for which the acquiree is obligated is recorded as a separate liability. To record a liability, there must be an existing obligation to other entities.[3] The possible future costs connected with restructuring or exit activities that may be planned by the acquirer are not part of the cost of the acquisition and are expensed in future periods.

12. **Employee benefit plans**—The asset or liability under employee benefit plans is not recorded at fair value. Instead, a liability is recorded if the projected benefit obligation exceeds the plan assets. An asset is recorded when the plan assets exceed the projected benefit obligation. The same procedure is applicable to other employee benefit plans.

13. **Deferred taxes**—Some acquisitions will be structured as nontaxable exchanges as to the acquiree. In such cases, the acquirer must continue to base deductions for amortization or depreciation of acquired accounts on their existing tax basis. A deferred tax liability is recorded for added estimated taxes caused by the excess of fair value depreciation over book value depreciation. A deferred tax asset is recorded for estimated future tax savings.

    The acquirer would also record deferred tax assets or liabilities for temporary tax differences, such as using straight-line depreciation for financial reporting and an accelerated depreciation method for tax purposes.

    The acquirer will also record a deferred tax asset for any operating tax losses or investment credit carryovers acquired from the acquiree.

    Taxation issues are considered in the "Tax Issues" section of this chapter.

Applying the Acquisition Model

Let us assume that the Johnson Company to be acquired by Acquisitions, Inc., has the following balance sheet on the October 1, 2017, acquisition date:

---

3 FASB ASC 420-10-25-2, *Exist or Disposal Cost Obligations—Overall—Recognition* (Norwalk, CT , 2010).

Johnson Company
Balance Sheet
October 1, 2017

Cash	$ 40,000	Current liabilities	$ 25,000
Marketable investments	60,000	8%, 5-year bond payable	100,000
Inventory	100,000	Total liabilities	$125,000
Land	30,000	Common stock ($1 par)	$ 10,000
Buildings (net)	150,000	Paid-in capital in excess of par	140,000
Equipment (net)	80,000	Retained earnings	185,000
		Total equity	$335,000
Total assets	$460,000	Liabilities plus equity	$460,000

Note 1: A customer list with significant value exists.
Note 2: There is an unrecorded warranty liability on prior-product sales.

Fair values for all accounts have been established as of October 1, 2017 as follows:[4]

Account	Method of Estimation	Fair Value	
Cash	Book value	$ 40,000	
Marketable investment	Level 1—Market value	66,000	
Inventory	Level 1—Market value	110,000	
Land	Level 2—Adjusted market value	72,000	
Buildings	Level 2—Adjusted market value	288,000	
Equipment	Level 1—Market value	145,000	
Customer list	Level 3—Other estimate, discounted cash flow based on estimated future cash flows	125,000	
Total assets			$ 846,000
Current liabilities	Book value	$ (25,000)	
Bonds payable	Face value (adjusted with premium/discount)	(100,000)	
Premium on bonds payable	Level 2—adjusted market value, using market-based interest rate applied to contractual cash flows	(4,000)	
Warranty liability	Level 3—other estimate, discounted cash flow based on estimated future cash flows	(12,000)	
Total liabilities			(141,000)
Fair value of net identifiable assets			$ 705,000

Recording the Acquisition. The price paid for the company being acquired is normally measured as the sum of the consideration (total assets) exchanged for the business. This would be the sum of the cash, other assets, debt securities issued, and any stock issued by the acquiring company. In a rare case, the fair value of the company being purchased may be more determinable than the consideration given. This could be the case where stock is issued that is not publicly traded and the fair value of the business acquired is more measurable. The basic procedures to record the purchase are as follows:

◆ All accounts identified are measured at estimated fair value as demonstrated above. This is true even if the consideration given for a company is less than the sum of the fair values of the net assets (assets minus liabilities assumed, $705,000 in the above example).

---

4 FASB ASC 820, *Fair Value Measurement and Disclosure* (Norwalk, CT, 2010)

◆ If the total consideration given for a company exceeds the fair value of its net identifiable assets ($705,000), the excess price paid is recorded as goodwill.

◆ In a rare case where total consideration given for a company is less than the fair value of its net identifiable assets ($705,000), the excess of the net assets over the price paid is recorded as an ordinary gain in the period of the purchase.

◆ All acquisition costs are expensed in the period of the purchase. These costs could include the fees of accountants and lawyers that were necessary to negotiate and consummate the purchase. In the past, these costs were included as part of the price paid for the company purchased.

Examples of Recording an Acquisition Using Value Analysis. Prior to attempting to record a purchase, an analysis should be made comparing the price paid for the company with the fair value of the net assets acquired.

◆ If the price exceeds the sum of the fair value of the net identifiable assets acquired, the excess price is goodwill.

◆ If the price is less than the sum of the fair value of the net identifiable assets acquired, the price deficiency is a gain.

1. Price paid exceeds fair value of net identifiable assets acquired.
   Acquisitions, Inc., issues 40,000 shares of its $1 par value common stock shares with a market value of $20 each for Johnson Company, illustrated above. Acquisitions, Inc., pays related acquisition costs of $35,000.

Value Analysis:

Total price paid (consideration given), 40,000 shares × $20 market value	$ 800,000
Total fair value of net assets acquired from Johnson Company	(705,000)
Goodwill (excess of total cost over fair value of net assets)	$ 95,000
Expense acquisition costs	$ 35,000

	Dr.	Cr.
To record purchase of net assets:		
Cash	40,000	
Marketable Investments......................................	66,000	
Inventory	110,000	
Land..	72,000	
Buildings	288,000	
Equipment	145,000	
Customer List	125,000	
Goodwill..	**95,000**	
Current Liabilities.......................................		25,000
Bonds Payable.......................................		100,000
Premium on Bonds Payable		4,000
Warranty Liability		12,000
Common Stock ($1 par, 40,000 shares issued)		40,000
Paid-In Capital in Excess of Par ($20 per share × 40,000 shares less $40,000 assigned to par)		760,000
Dr. = Cr. Check Totals.......................................	*941,000*	*941,000*
To record acquisition costs:		
Acquisition Expense	35,000	
Cash		35,000

2. Price paid is less than fair value of net identifiable assets acquired.

Acquisitions, Inc., issues 25,000 shares of its $1 par value common stock with a market value of $20 each for Johnson Company, illustrated above. Acquisitions, Inc., pays related acquisition costs of $35,000.

Value Analysis:

Total price paid (consideration given), 25,000 shares × $20 market value	$ 500,000
Total fair value of net assets acquired from Johnson Company	(705,000)
Gain on purchase of business (excess of fair value of net assets over total cost)	$(205,000)
Expense acquisition costs	$ 35,000

Entries to record the purchase and related costs are as follows:

	Dr.	Cr.
To record purchase of net assets:		
Cash	40,000	
Marketable Investments.	66,000	
Inventory	110,000	
Land.	72,000	
Buildings	288,000	
Equipment	145,000	
Customer List	125,000	
Current Liabilities.		25,000
Bonds Payable.		100,000
Premium on Bonds Payable		4,000
Warranty Liability		12,000
Common Stock ($1 par, 25,000 shares issued)		25,000
Paid-In Capital in Excess of Par ($20 per share × 25,000 shares less		
$25,000 assigned to par)		475,000
Gain on Acquisition of Business		**205,000**
Dr. = Cr. Check Totals	*846,000*	*846,000*
To record acquisition costs:		
Acquisition Expense	35,000	
Cash		35,000

The gain must be reported as a separate line item in the income statement of the acquirer in the period of the acquisition. Notes must include an explanation of the reasons that allowed the gain to exist.

Recording Changes in Value During Measurement Period

During the measurement period, values assigned to accounts recorded as a part of the acquisition may be adjusted to better reflect the value of the accounts as of the acquisition date. It is possible that new assets and liabilities that existed on the acquisition date may become known during the measurement period; they must also be recorded as part of the adjustment. Changes in value caused by events that occur after the acquisition date are not part of this adjustment. They would usually be adjusted to income in the period in which they occur.

The values recorded on the acquisition date are considered "provisional." They must be used in financial statements with dates prior to the end of the measurement period. The measurement period ends when the improved information is available or it is obvious that no better information is available. In no case can the measurement period exceed one year from the acquisition date.

Let us return to the earlier example of the acquisition of Johnson Company in exchange for stock with a total value of $800,000. Assume now that the values assigned to the buildings, customer list, and warranty liability are provisional. The 2017 financial year will include the income statement accounts for the acquired, Johnson Company, starting as of the October 1 acquisition date. The values and resulting adjustments to income for 2017 and projected for 2018 are as follows:

Account	Provisional Value	Depreciation/Amortization Method	Recorded in 2017 (3 months)	Projected for 2018 (full year)
Buildings	$288,000	20-year straight-line with $48,000 residual value. $240,000/ 20 years = $12,000 per year, $1,000 per month	$3,000	$12,000
Customer List	125,000	5-year amortization, calculated monthly. $125,000/5 years = $25,000 per year, ¼ annual amount for 2017	6,250	25,000
Warranty Liability	(12,000)	Debited as repairs are made	3,500	7,000

Better estimates of values for these accounts become available in early 2018. The new values and revised depreciation/amortization are as follows:

Account	Revised Value	Depreciation/Amortization Method	Adjusted Amount for 2017	Amount to Be Recorded in 2018
Buildings	$320,000	20-year straight-line with $50,000 residual value. $270,000/ 20 years = $13,500 per year, $1,125 per month	$3,375	$13,500
Customer List	150,000	5-year amortization, calculated monthly. $150,000/5 years = $30,000 per year, $2,500 per month	7,500	30,000
Warranty Liability	(18,000)	Debited as repairs are made	3,500	10,000

The recorded values are adjusted during 2018 as follows:

	Dr.	Cr.
Buildings ($320,000 new estimate – $288,000 provisional value)	32,000	
Customer List ($150,000 new estimate – $125,000 provisional value)	25,000	
Warranty Liability ($18,000 new estimate – $12,000 provisional value)		6,000
Goodwill (sum of above adjustments)		51,000

Goodwill would normally absorb the impact of the adjustments to all other accounts since it is the difference between the price paid and the values assigned to identifiable net assets. Had there been a gain on the original acquisition date, the gain would be adjusted at the end of the measurement period. Since the gain was recorded in the prior period, the entry to adjust the amount of the gain would be made to retained earnings. If there is goodwill but the increase in net assets is greater than the amount of goodwill, a gain would be recorded for the balance of the adjustment.

The depreciation/amortizations for the prior period must also be adjusted retroactively. The entry made in 2018 would be as follows:

	Dr.	Cr.
Retained Earnings (net adjustment of $375 + $1,250)	1,625	
Accumulated Depreciation—Buildings		375
Customer List		1,250

The comparative statements, which include 2017, would include the revised amounts. The revised depreciation and amortization amounts ($13,500 and $30,000, respectively, for 2018) would be recorded in 2018.

Recording Contingent Consideration

Let us again revisit the acquisition of Johnson Company. This time, we will assume that the acquirer issued 40,000 shares of stock with a market value of $800,000. In addition to the stock issue, the acquirer agreed to pay an additional $100,000 on January 1, 2020, if the average income during the 2-year period of 2018–2019 exceeds $80,000 per year. The expected value is calculated as $40,000 based on the 40% probability of exceeding an average income of $80,000 and having to pay the added $100,000. The revised value analysis and recording of the acquisition would be as follows:

Value Analysis:

Total price paid:		
Stock issued, 40,000 shares × $20 market value	$800,000	
Estimated value of contingent payment	40,000	$ 840,000
Total fair value of net assets acquired from Johnson Company		(705,000)
Goodwill		$ 135,000
Expense acquisition costs		$ 35,000

Entries to record acquisition and related costs are as follows:

	Dr.	Cr.
To record purchase of net assets:		
Cash	40,000	
Marketable Investments	66,000	
Inventory	110,000	
Land	72,000	
Buildings	288,000	
Equipment	145,000	
Customer List	125,000	
Goodwill	**135,000**	
Current Liabilities		25,000
Bonds Payable		100,000
Premium on Bonds Payable		4,000
Warranty Liability		12,000
Estimated Liability for Contingent Consideration		**40,000**
Common Stock ($1 par, 40,000 shares issued)		40,000
Paid-In Capital in Excess of Par ($20 per share × 40,000 shares less		
$40,000 assigned to par)		760,000
Dr. = Cr. Check Totals	*981,000*	*981,000*
To record acquisition costs:		
Acquisition Expense	35,000	
Cash		35,000

If during the measurement period, the contingent consideration was revalued based on improved information, the estimated liability and the goodwill (or gain in a bargain acquisition) would be adjusted. For example, assume that within the measurement period the estimate was revised to $50,000, the adjustment would then be as follows:

Goodwill ($50,000 new estimate – $40,000 provisional value)	10,000	
Estimated Liability for Contingent Consideration		10,000

If the estimate is again revised after the measurement period, the adjustment is included in the income of the later period. If the estimate was revised to $65,000 after the measurement period, the following adjustment would be recorded:

Expense, Increase in Estimated Contingent Consideration Payment	15,000	
Estimated Liability for Contingent Consideration		15,000

Contingency agreements can include other factors than an earnings target including market share or research milestones achieved by the acquired firm. The acquired firm may be concerned with the future value of the shares it receives from the acquiring company. In such a case, there may be a contingent agreement to issue additional shares to make up for a fall in the price of the stock issued in the purchase.

In general, contingent consideration agreements require the recording of a liability, and its subsequent adjustment through income as demonstrated in the preceding example. There may be cases where the contingency is to be settled by issuing additional shares of stock and the agreement qualifies as equity based on the requirements listed on page 10.

Assume that in the preceding example, the $100,000 potential contingent payment was to be settled by issuing additional shares with a value of $100,000 such that the agreement qualified as equity transaction. Assume that the expected value was again $40,000. The entry to record the purchase would be the same as that above except the $40,000 entry crediting the "Estimated Liability for Contingent Consideration" would be replaced with the following credit:

Paid-In Capital Contingent Share Agreement 40,000

Contingent share agreements, classified as equity, are not subject to re-estimation and remain at their originally recorded value until settled. The following entry would be made if the agreement required 4,000 shares (worth $25 each) to be issued:

Paid-In Capital Contingent Share Agreement 40,000
    Common Stock, $1 par 4,000
    Paid-In Capital in Excess of Par 36,000

If the contingency provision is not met, the $40,000 would be transferred to paid-in capital as follows:

Paid-In Capital Contingent Share Agreement 40,000
    Paid-In Capital in Excess of Par 40,000

Accounting for the Acquisition by the Acquiree

The goodwill recorded by the acquirer is not tied to the gain (or loss) recorded by the acquiree. The acquiree records the removal of net assets at their book values. Recall the initial example of the acquisition of Johnson Company for $800,000 (on pages 16 and 17). The excess of the price received by the seller ($800,000) over the sum of the net asset book value of $335,000 ($460,000 assets − $125,000 liabilities) is recorded as a gain on the sale. In this case, the gain is $465,000. The entry on Johnson's books would be as follows:

	Dr.	Cr.
Investment in Acquisitions, Inc., Stock	800,000	
Current Liabilities	25,000	
8% 5-Year Bonds Payable	100,000	
Cash		40,000
Marketable Investments		60,000
Inventory		100,000
Land		30,000
Buildings (net)		150,000
Equipment (net)		80,000
Gain on Sale of Business		465,000
Dr. = Cr. Check Totals	*925,000*	*925,000*

The only remaining asset of Johnson Company is the stock of Acquisitions, Inc. Johnson would typically distribute the stock received to its shareholders and cease operations.

R E F L E C T I O N

- The acquirer records all accounts of the acquiree company at fair value on the acquisition date, but adjustments are allowed during the measurement period.

- The acquisition cost includes the estimated expected value of contingent consideration.

- The acquiree removes the book values of the accounts transferred and records a gain or loss on the sale.

TAX ISSUES

5

OBJECTIVE

Demonstrate an understanding of the tax issues that arise in an acquisition.

In some acquisitions, the acquiree may have operating losses in periods prior to the acquisition. The acquirer may be able to carry these losses forward to offset its income taxes payable periods after the acquisition. This is a "deferred tax asset" to which value will be assigned. The sale of a business may be structured as either a taxable or nontaxable event, which means the seller pays taxes on any gain in a taxable exchange but defers the taxes on a gain in a nontaxable exchange. If the exchange is taxable, the acquirer records all accounts at fair value for tax purposes and gets depreciation and amortization deductions based on the fair value of the assets on the acquisition date. There may be some differences in the tax basis and recorded financial accounting amounts. If the exchange is nontaxable, the acquirer will base future amortization and depreciation on the book value of the acquiree's accounts on the acquisition date. This leads to deferred tax assets or liabilities that need to be recorded on the acquisition date.

Tax Loss Carryovers

Tax law provides that an existing company with a tax loss may first carry the loss back to the previous two years to offset income and thus receive a refund of taxes paid in the preceding years. If the loss exceeds income available in the prior 2-year period, the loss can be carried forward up to 20 years to offset future income and, therefore, reduce the taxes that otherwise would be paid. As mentioned earlier, Congress has extended the carryback period to five years for losses incurred in 2008–2009. Our examples will use a 2-year carryback period. The acquired company may have unused tax loss carryovers that it has not been able to utilize due to an absence of sufficient income in prior years. This becomes a potential benefit for the purchasing company. Tax provisions limit the amount of the net operating loss (NOL) available to the acquiring company to discourage business combinations that are motivated primarily by tax loss carryovers. The purchaser is allowed to use the acquired company's tax loss carryovers to offset its own income in the current and future periods (but not prior periods) subject to limitations contained in Internal Revenue Code Section 382.

The value of the expected future tax loss carryovers is recorded as a deferred tax asset (DTA) on the date of the acquisition. It is, however, necessary to attempt to determine whether there will be adequate future tax liabilities to support the value of the deferred tax asset. The accountant would have to consider existing evidence to make this determination. If it is likely that some or all of the deferred tax asset will not be realized, the contra account Allowance for Unrealizable Tax Assets would be used to reduce the deferred tax asset to an estimated amount to be realized.[5] This may have the practical effect of the contra account totally offsetting the deferred tax asset. The inability to record a net deferred tax asset often will result in the consideration paid for the NOL carryover being assigned to goodwill. This occurs because the price paid will exceed the value of the net assets that are allowed to be recorded.

---

5 FASB ASC 740-10-30-5, *Income Tax—Overall—Initial Measurement* (Norwalk, CT , 2010).

EXAMPLE

Bergen Company had the following book and fair values on the date it was acquired by Panther Company:

Account	Book Value	Fair Value
Cash	$ 30,000	$ 30,000
Accounts Receivable	80,000	80,000
Inventory	100,000	120,000
Land	140,000	200,000
Building (net)	250,000	465,000
Equipment (net)	50,000	75,000
Patent	0	50,000
Accounts Payable	(90,000)	(90,000)
Bonds Payable	(100,000)	(100,000)
Net Assets	$ 460,000	$ 830,000

Assume that the price paid for Bergen Company is $1,000,000. Bergen Company has tax loss carryforwards of $200,000.

The value of the tax loss carryforward is calculated as follows:

Losses that may be carried forward	$200,000
Applicable tax rate	× 40%
Potential tax savings	$ 80,000
Adjustment for amount not likely to be usable	(30,000)
Net value of tax loss carryforward.	$ 50,000

Value Analysis:

Total price paid:	
Stock issued, 50,000 shares × $20 market value	$1,000,000
Fair value of net assets acquired	(830,000)
Net value of tax loss carryforward.	(50,000)
Goodwill	$ 120,000

The entry to record the acquisition is as follows:

	Dr.	Cr.
To record purchase of net assets:		
Cash	30,000	
Accounts Receivable	80,000	
Inventory	120,000	
Land.	200,000	
Buildings	465,000	
Equipment	75,000	
Patent.	50,000	
Deferred Tax Asset	**80,000**	
Goodwill.	**120,000**	
Valuation Allowance for Deferred Tax Asset.		**30,000**
Accounts Payable		90,000
Bonds Payable.		100,000
Common Stock ($1 par, 50,000 shares issued)		50,000
Paid-In Capital in Excess of Par ($20 per share × 50,000 shares less $50,000 assigned to par)		950,000
Dr. = Cr. Check Totals	*1,220,000*	*1,220,000*

If there is a decrease in estimate for the valuation account within one year of the acquisition date, goodwill is reduced for the same amount. Thus, if within one year, the valuation account were lowered by $20,000 (from $30,000 to $10,000), Goodwill would be credited for $20,000 as follows:

Valuation Allowance for Deferred Tax Asset	20,000	
Goodwill		20,000

However, if the adjustment is caused by events that occur after the acquisition, the credit would be to the current provision for taxes.[6] Changes in the valuation account after the 1-year period result in an adjustment to the tax provision for the period in which the new estimate is made.

Tax Values in an Acquisition

There may be limitations on amounts that can be assigned to certain accounts even in a taxable exchange. For example, a fixed asset may have the following values:

Book value on the books of acquiree	$75,000
Estimated fair value for financial accounting	90,000
Basis required at acquisition for tax purposes	50,000

This would occur when the company used straight-line depreciation for financial reporting, but used accelerated depreciation for its tax returns. The asset would still be recorded at the fair value of $90,000, but a deferred tax liability (DTL) would be recorded for the lost tax deductibility equal to the tax rate (40%) times the excess of the fair value over tax value calculated as follows:

Fair value	$90,000
Tax value	50,000
Excess not deductible	40,000
Tax rate	× 40%
Deferred tax liability	$16,000

The DTL would be amortized over the depreciable life of the asset. Assuming a 5-year asset life and straight-line depreciation, the annual tax impact using a 40% tax rate would be $3,200 ($16,000/5 years), which would be recorded as follows:

Deferred Tax Liability	3,200	
Current Tax Liability		3,200

Goodwill, while not amortized for financial reporting purposes, is amortized straight-line over 15 years for tax purposes.

Nontaxable Exchange

In a nontaxable exchange, the acquirer is limited to deductions for amortization and depreciation based on the book values of the acquiree on the acquisition date. Despite this, all accounts are still recorded at full fair value, and deferred tax liability or asset accounts are recorded as follows:

Difference	Results in:
Fair value of identifiable asset exceeds book value	DTL
Book value of identifiable asset exceeds fair value	DTA
Fair value of liability exceeds book value	DTA
Book value of liability exceeds fair value	DTL

---

6 FASB ASC 805-740-45-4, *Business Combinations—Income Taxes—Other Presentation Matters* (Norwalk, CT , 2010).

EXAMPLE

To understand the impact of a nontaxable exchange, consider an example of the acquisition of Book Company for $1,500,000. The consideration was 50,000 shares of $1 par value shares of the acquirer company. The market value of an acquirer share was $30. The tax rate is 40%. Fair values are compared to the tax basis of Book Company as shown below.

Column	1	2	3	4
Account	Fair Value	Tax Basis	Fair Value in Excess of Tax Basis (Col. 1. – Col. 2)	DTA (DTL) (–40% × Col. 3)
Cash	$ 100,000	$ 100,000	$ 0	$ 0
Accounts Receivable	150,000	180,000	(30,000)	12,000
Inventory	200,000	160,000	40,000	(16,000)
Land	200,000	150,000	50,000	(20,000)
Building	600,000	450,000	150,000	(60,000)
Equipment	300,000	200,000	100,000	(40,000)
Copyrights	100,000	2,000	98,000	(39,200)
Accounts Payable	(250,000)	(250,000)	0	0
Bonds Payable	(315,000)	(300,000)	(15,000)	6,000
Net Identifiable Assets	$1,085,000	$ 692,000	$393,000	$(157,200)

Value Analysis:

Total price paid:		
Stock issued, 50,000 shares × $30 market value		$1,500,000
Fair value of net assets acquired	$1,085,000	
DTL.	157,200	
Net identifiable assets less net DTL.		927,800
Goodwill		$ 572,200

The entry to record the acquisition is as follows:

	Dr.	Cr.
To record purchase of net assets:		
Cash	100,000	
Accounts Receivable	150,000	
Inventory	200,000	
Land.	200,000	
Buildings	600,000	
Equipment	300,000	
Copyright	100,000	
Goodwill.	**572,200**	
DTL		**157,200**
Accounts Payable		250,000
Bonds Payable.		300,000
Premium on Bonds Payable		15,000
Common Stock ($1 par, 50,000 shares issued)		50,000
Paid-In Capital in Excess of Par ($30 per share × 50,000 shares less $50,000 assigned to par)		1,450,000
Dr. = Cr. Check Totals	*2,222,200*	*2,222,200*

While the DTL is recorded as a single amount, each component would be realized separately. The amount applicable to accounts payable would be realized as the accounts are collected; the amount applicable to inventory would be realized when the inventory is sold. The amounts applicable to the land would be deferred until the land is sold. All other amounts are amortized over the life of the accounts to which the DTA/DTL pertains.

R E F L E C T I O N

- The acquisition may include a tax loss carryover from the acquiree which results in the recording a deferred tax asset (DTA).

- In a taxable exchange, the values used for taxation may differ from those assigned in the acquisition. Typically, lower book values will be used for depreciation in future years. This results in a deferred tax liability (DTL).

- The acquisition may be a nontaxable exchange, which means the book values will be used for taxation and fair values will be used for financial reporting. Because book values are usually lower than fair value, this also results in a DTL.

REQUIRED DISCLOSURE

6

OBJECTIVE

Explain the disclosure that is required in the period in which an acquisition occurs.

Substantial disclosure requirements for an acquisition occur during the reporting period. These requirements are detailed in FASB ASC 805-10-50-2 and can be summarized as follows:

a. The name and description of the acquiree.
b. The acquisition date.
c. The percentage of voting equity interest acquired.
d. The primary reasons for the acquisition and the factors that contributed to the recording of goodwill (if any).
e. A qualitative description of factors that make up the goodwill recognized.
f. The acquisition date fair value of all types of consideration, including cash, other assets, contingent consideration, and debt and equity instruments issued.
g. Detailed information concerning contingent consideration, including a description of the arrangements and the range of outcomes.
h. Details concerning acquired receivables, including gross amount, fair value and the expected collections.
i. Disclosure showing amounts recorded for each major class of assets and liabilities. For the acquisition of Johnson Company for $800,000 in stock on pages 16 and 17, the disclosure information would appear as follows:

Current assets	$216,000
Property, plant, and equipment	505,000
Intangible assets subject to amortization	125,000
Intangible assets not subject to amortization	0
Goodwill	95,000
Total assets acquired	$941,000
Current liabilities	$ 37,000
Long-term debt	104,000
Total liabilities assumed	$141,000
Net assets acquired	$800,000

j.   Information on assets and liabilities arising from contingencies.
k.   The goodwill that will be deductible for tax purposes.
l.   Goodwill assigned to reportable segments (if any).
m.   Information concerning transactions between the companies that are not recorded as part of the acquisition.
n.   Disclosure of acquisition costs and issue costs associated with the transaction. This includes identifying the line item of the income statement that includes the acquisition costs.
o.   Any gain resulting from the acquisition. The gain is to be disclosed as a separate line item on the income statement. The reasons for the gain must also be disclosed.
p.   The fair value of the noncontrolling interest and the method used to value it.
q.   The gain or loss on prior investments in a step acquisition. A step acquisition is where a controlling interest is purchased in stages (explained in Chapter 7).
r.   Publicly traded firms must disclose the following performance measures:

1.   Revenue and earnings of the acquiree since the acquisition date
2.   Pro forma revenue and earnings had the acquisition occurred at the start of the reporting period
3.   If comparative statements are issued, pro forma revenue and earnings for all prior periods for which comparative statements are issued

Exhibit 1-3 is a complete example of the disclosure required for an acquisition during the reporting period. It is the 2012 acquisition of Pringles by the Kellogg Company. It includes the required pro-forma disclosure.

Exhibit 1-3
Note 2
Goodwill and other Intangible Assets
Pringles® acquisition

On May 31, 2012, the Company completed its acquisition of the *Pringles*® business (Pringles) from The Procter & Gamble Company (P&G) for $2,695 billion, or $2,683 billion net of cash and cash equivalents, subject to certain purchase price adjustments, which resulted in a reduction of the purchase price by approximately $15 million to $2,668 billion net of cash and cash equivalents. The acquisition was accounted for under the purchase method and was financed through a combination of cash on hand, and short-term and long-term debt. The assets and liabilities of Pringles are included in the Consolidated Balance Sheet as of December 28, 2013 and December 29, 2012 and the results of the Pringles operations subsequent to the acquisition date are included in the Consolidated Statement of Income.

The purchase price allocation, including the allocation to reportable segments, was completed during the quarter ended June 29, 2013 when the valuations of fixed assets and intangible assets were finalized resulting in a reallocation from that reported as of December 29, 2012 of goodwill between the Company's reportable segments. Prior year amounts were revised to reflect these changes as of the date of the acquisition, resulting in reductions to goodwill and the foreign currency translation component of other comprehensive income (OCI) of $15 million as of December 29, 2012.

During the quarter ended September 28, 2013, the Company recorded an immaterial correction of an error to the purchase price allocation for Pringles that was outside of the measurement period, which resulted in an increase to other non-current liabilities, goodwill and non-current deferred tax assets of $15 million, $13 million and $2 million, respectively. The goodwill of $13 million was allocated to our operating segments as follows: Europe, $10 million and Asia Pacific, $3 million.

The final acquired assets and assumed liabilities include the following:

(millions)	May 31, 2012
Accounts receivable, net	$ 128
Inventories	103
Other prepaid assets	18
Property	317
Goodwill	1,319

(continued)

Other intangibles:	
Definite-lived intangible assets	79
Brand	776
Other assets:	
Deferred income taxes	23
Other	16
Notes payable	(3)
Accounts payable	(9)
Other current liabilities	(24)
Other liabilities	(75)

Goodwill of $645 million is expected to be deductible for statutory tax purposes.

Goodwill is calculated as the excess of the purchase price over the fair value of the net assets recognized. The goodwill recorded as part of the acquisition primarily reflects the value of providing an established platform to leverage the Company's existing brands in the international snacks category, synergies expected to arise from the combined brand portfolios, as well as any intangible assets that do not qualify for separate recognition.

For the year ended December 28, 2013, the Company incurred integration-related costs as part of the Pringles acquisition as follows: $46 million recorded in SGA, $15 million recorded in COGS and $5 million in net sales. Transaction fees and other integration-related costs incurred through December 29, 2012 were as follows: $73 million recorded in SGA, $3 million recorded in COGS and $5 million in fees for a bridge financing facility which are recorded in OIE.

For the year ended December 28, 2013, Pringles contributed net revenues of $1,658 million and net earnings of $132 million, including the integration-related costs discussed above. Through December 29, 2012, Pringles contributed net revenues of $887 million and net earnings of $31 million, including the transaction fees and other integration-related costs discussed above. The unaudited pro forma combined historical results, as if Pringles had been acquired at the beginning of fiscal 2011 are estimated to be:

(millions, except per share data)	2012	2011
Net sales	$14,862	$14,722
Net income	$ 1,001	$ 954
Net income (loss) attributable to noncontrolling interests	—	(2)
Net income attributable to Kellogg Company	$ 1,001	$ 956
Net earnings per share	$ 2.78	$ 2.63

The pro forma results include transaction and bridge financing costs, interest expense on the debt issued to finance the acquisition, amortization of the definite lived intangible assets, and depreciation based on estimated fair value and useful lives. The pro forma results are not necessarily indicative of what actually would have occurred if the acquisition had been completed as of the beginning of 2011, nor are they necessarily indicative of future consolidated results.

The pro-forma disclosure is also to be included in the notes for an acquisition that occurs after the balance sheet date but prior to the issuance date of the financial statement. If the initial accounting for the acquisition is incomplete, those disclosures that could not be made and why they could not be made must be stated.

REFLECTION

- There are detailed disclosure requirements for the period in which an acquisition occurs.
- Disclosure includes pro forma amounts for revenue and earnings for the entire period and for prior periods shown in comparative statements.

7
OBJECTIVE

Apply the impairment test
to goodwill and adjust
goodwill when needed.

GOODWILL ACCOUNTING AFTER THE ACQUISITION

Publicly traded companies do not amortize goodwill. Instead they impairment test it each period and record an impairment loss when appropriate. This is not parallel to tax law in the U.S., which provides for the amortization of goodwill over a 15-year life. That difference will create an inter-period tax allocation procedure.

Effective December 14, 2014, non-public (privately held) companies can elect to amortize new or existing goodwill over a period not to exceed 10 years.[7] The amortized balance is still subject to impairment testing.

Five specific concerns need to be addressed to apply impairment testing.

1. Goodwill must be allocated to reporting units if the acquired company contains more than one reporting unit.
2. Methods for valuing the reporting unit must be established.
3. Impairment testing is normally done on an annual basis. There are, however, exceptions to annual testing and some cases where testing may be required between annual testing dates.
4. The procedure for determining if impairment has occurred must be established.
5. The procedure for determining the amount of the impairment loss, which is also the decrease in the goodwill amount recorded, must be established.

Allocating Goodwill to Reporting Units

In most cases, the company acquired will be made up of more than one reporting unit. For purposes of segment reporting, under FASB ASC 280-10-50-1,[8] a reporting unit is either the same level or one level lower than an operating segment. To be a reporting unit that is one level below an operating unit, both of the following criteria must be met:

◆ Segment managers measure and review performance at this level.
◆ The unit has separate financial information available and has economic characteristics that distinguish it from other units of the operating segment.

All assets and liabilities are to be allocated to the underlying reporting units. Goodwill is allocated to the reporting segments by subtracting the identifiable net assets of the unit from the estimated fair value of the entire reporting unit. The method of estimating the fair value of the reporting unit should be documented. In essence, an estimate must be made of the price that would have been paid for only the specific reporting unit.

Reporting Unit Valuation Procedures

The steps in the reporting unit measurement process will be illustrated with the following example of the acquisition of Lakeland Company, which is a purchase of a single operating unit.

A. Determine the valuation method and estimated fair value of the identifiable assets, goodwill, and all liabilities of the reporting unit.

At the time of acquisition, the valuations of Lakeland Company's identifiable assets, liabilities, and goodwill were as shown on page 31. [The asterisk (*) indicates numbers have been rounded for presentation purposes.]

---

7 FASB 350-20-35-62
8 FASB ASC 280-10-50-1, *Segment Reporting—Overall—Disclosure* (Norwalk, CT, 2010).

Assets	Comments	Valuation Method	Fair Value
Inventory available	Replacement cost	Market replacement cost for similar items	$ 45,000
Accounts receivable	Recorded amount is adjusted for estimated bad debts	Aging schedule used for valuation	28,000
Land	Per-acre value well established	Five acres at $10,000 per acre	50,000
Building	Most reliable measure is rent potential	Rent estimated at $20,000 per year for 20 years, discounted at 14% return for similar properties; present value of $132,463 reduced for $50,000 land value	80,000*
Equipment	Cost of replacement capacity can be estimated	Estimated purchase cost of equipment with similar capacity	50,000
Patent	Recorded by seller at only legal cost; has significant future value	Added profit made possible by patent is $11,600 per year for four years; discounted at risk adjusted rate for similar investments of 20% per year; PV equals $30,029	30,000*
Brand-name copyright	Not recorded by seller	Estimated sales value	40,000
Current liabilities	Recorded amounts are accurate	Recorded value	(5,000)
Bonds payable	Specified interest rate is above market rate	Discount at market interest rate	(21,000)
Net identifiable assets at fair value			$297,000
Price paid for reporting unit			360,000
Goodwill	Believed to exist based on projected future cash flows	Implied by price paid	$ 63,000

*Rounded to nearest thousands to reflect nature of estimate.

B. Measure the fair value of the reporting unit and document assumptions and models used to make the measurement. This measurement is made to:

- Serve as a test for the amount of goodwill recorded for the reporting unit.
- Establish the procedure to be used to value the reporting unit in later periods.

If the stock of the reporting unit is publicly traded, the market capitalization of the reporting unit may be indicative of its fair value, but it need not be the only measure considered. The price paid to acquire all of the shares or a controlling interest could exceed the product of the fair value per share times the number of shares outstanding. A common method used to estimate fair value is to determine the present value of the unit's future cash flows. The following is an example of that approach.

Assumptions:

1. The reporting unit will provide operating cash flows, net of tax, of $40,000 during the next reporting period.
2. Operating cash flows will increase at the rate of 10% per year for the next four reporting periods and then will remain steady for 15 more years.
3. Forecast cash flows will be adjusted for capital expenditures needed to maintain market position and productive capacity.
4. Cash flows defined as net of cash from operations less capital expenditures will be discounted at an after-tax discount rate of 12%. An annual rate of 12% is a reasonable risk-adjusted rate of return for investments of this type.
5. An estimate of salvage value (net of tax effect of gains or losses) of the assets at the end of 20 years will be used to approximate salvage value. This is a conservative assumption, since the unit may be operated after that period.

Schedule of net tax cash flows:

Year	Net of Tax Operating Flow*	Capital Expenditure	Salvage Value	Net Cash Flow
1	$40,000			$ 40,000
2	44,000			44,000
3	48,400			48,400
4	53,240			53,240
5	58,564	$(25,000)		33,564
6	58,564			58,564
7	58,564			58,564
8	58,564			58,564
9	58,564			58,564
10	58,564	(30,000)		28,564
11	58,564			58,564
12	58,564			58,564
13	58,564			58,564
14	58,564			58,564
15	58,564	(35,000)		23,564
16	58,564			58,564
17	58,564			58,564
18	58,564			58,564
19	58,564			58,564
20	58,564		$75,000	133,564

Net present value at 12% annual rate $376,173

*Reflects assumed 10% annual increase in years 2–5.

C. Compare fair value of reporting unit with amounts assigned to identifiable net assets plus goodwill.

Estimated fair value of reporting unit $376,173
Price paid for reporting unit................................. 360,000
Excess of fair value of reporting unit over net assets........... $16,173

An excess of the fair value of the reporting unit over the value of the net assets indicated that the price paid was reasonable and below a theoretical maximum purchase price. It requires no adjustment of assigned values. If, however, the fair value of the net assets, including goodwill, exceeds the fair value of the reporting unit, the model used to determine the fair value of the reporting unit should be reassessed. If the re-estimation of the values assigned to the net assets, including goodwill, and the reporting unit still indicates an excess of the value of the net assets, including goodwill, over the value of the reporting unit, goodwill is to be tested for impairment. This would likely result in an impairment loss being recorded on the goodwill at the time of the acquisition.

Impairment Procedures for Goodwill after Acquisition

The normal procedure is to perform impairment testing of goodwill on an annual basis. Impairment testing should also be done between annual tests if it is more likely than not that events or circumstances have occurred that could reduce the fair value of a reporting unit below its carrying value.

An entity has the option of assessing qualitative factors to determine if it is likely (greater than 50% probability) that the fair value of the reporting unit is less than its carrying value. In making that evaluation the company is to consider events and circumstances that cause the decline in value. Examples would be macroeconomic events, industry and market considerations, and cost factors. Qualitative testing is not required; an entity can make an annual election to bypass the qualitative assessment and proceed directly to the first step of the goodwill impairment test.

Step 1: Quantitative Impairment Test. **Goodwill is considered to be impaired if the implied fair value of the reporting unit is less than the *carrying value* of the reporting unit's net assets *(including* goodwill).** Remember, since the acquired net assets were recorded at their fair values as of the acquisition date, it is the subsequent carrying (book) value based on those amounts that is used for later periods of impairment testing.

Let us revisit the Lakeland Company example. Assume that the following new estimates were made at the end of the first year:

Estimated implied fair value of the reporting unit, based on analysis of
    projected cash flow (discounted at 12% annual rate) $320,000
Existing net book value (including values assigned on acquisition date) of the
    reporting unit (including goodwill)   345,000

Since the recorded net book value of the reporting unit exceeds its implied fair value, goodwill is considered to be impaired. If the estimated fair value exceeds the existing book value, there is no impairment, and there is no need to proceed to Step 2 to calculate a goodwill impairment loss.

Step2: Impairment Loss Calculation. If Step 1 indicates impairment, the impairment loss must be estimated. **The impairment loss for goodwill is the excess of the *implied fair value* of the reporting unit over the fair value of the reporting unit's identifiable net assets (*excluding* goodwill) on the impairment date.** These are the values that would be assigned to those accounts if the reporting unit were purchased on the date of impairment measurement.

For our example, the following calculation was made for the impairment loss:

Estimated implied fair value of reporting unit, based on cash flow analysis
    (discounted at a 12% annual rate) $320,000
Less: Fair value of net assets on the date of measurement, exclusive of
    goodwill   285,000
Implied fair value of goodwill . . . . $ 35,000
Existing recorded goodwill   63,000
Estimated impairment loss . . . . $ (28,000)

The following journal entry would be made:

Goodwill Impairment Loss.   28,000
Goodwill   28,000

The impairment loss will be shown as a separate line item within the operating section unless it is identified with a discontinued operation, in which case, it is part of the gain or loss on disposal. **Once goodwill is written down, it cannot be adjusted to a higher amount.**

Two important issues must be understood at this point.

1. Step 1: **qualitative impairment test** compares the implied fair value of the reporting unit, $320,000, to the unit's **book value (including goodwill), $345,000.** Step 2: **impairment loss calculation** compares the implied fair value of the reporting unit, $320,000, to the unit's **estimated fair values (excluding goodwill), $285,000,** on the impairment date.
2. While fair values of net assets are used to measure the impairment loss, they are not recorded. The existing book values on the impairment date remain in place (unless they are adjusted for their own impairment loss).
3. If a non-public company elects to amortize goodwill, Steps 1 and 2 still are applied to the remaining, unamortized goodwill balance.

Significant disclosure requirements for goodwill exist in any period in which goodwill changes. A note must accompany the balance sheet in any period that has a change in goodwill. The note would explain the goodwill acquired, the goodwill impairment losses, and the goodwill written off as part of a disposal of a reporting unit. It is further required that information be included that provides the details of any impairment loss recorded during the period. The information would include the reporting unit involved, the circumstances leading to the impairment, and the possibility of further adjustments.

REFLECTION

- Procedures must be established for estimating goodwill.
- Goodwill is subject to impairment testing.
- When impaired, the goodwill is reduced to a lower estimated value.

8

OBJECTIVE

Estimate the value of goodwill.

APPENDIX: ESTIMATING THE VALUE OF GOODWILL

An acquirer may attempt to forecast the future income of a target company in order to arrive at a logical purchase price. Goodwill is often, at least in part, a payment for above-normal expected future earnings. A forecast of future income may start by projecting recent years' incomes into the future. When this is done, it is important to factor out "one-time" occurrences that will not likely recur in the near future. Examples would include extraordinary items, discontinued operations, or any other unusual event. Expected future income is compared to "normal" income. Normal income is the product of the appropriate industry rate of return on assets times the fair value of the gross assets (no deduction for liabilities) of the acquired company. Gross assets include specifically identifiable intangible assets such as patents and copyrights but do not include existing goodwill. The following calculation of earnings in excess of normal might be made for the Johnson Company example on pages 16 and 17:

Expected average future income		$100,000
Less normal return on assets:		
Fair value of total identifiable assets	$846,000	
Industry normal rate of return	× 10%	
Normal return on assets		84,600
Expected annual earnings in excess of normal		$ 15,400

Several methods use the expected annual earnings in excess of normal to estimate goodwill. A common approach is to pay for a given number of years of excess earnings. For instance, Acquisitions, Inc., might offer to pay for four years of excess earnings, which would total $61,600 ($15,400 × 4 years). Alternatively, the excess earnings could be viewed as an annuity. The most optimistic purchaser might expect the excess earnings to continue forever. If so, the buyer might capitalize the excess earnings as a perpetuity at the normal industry rate of return according to the following formula:

$$\text{Goodwill} = \frac{\text{Annual Excess Earnings}}{\text{Industry Normal Rate of Return}}$$
$$= \frac{\$15,400}{0.10}$$
$$= \$154,000$$

Another estimation method views the factors that produce excess earnings to be of limited duration, such as 10 years, for example. This purchaser would calculate goodwill as follows:

Goodwill = Discounted present value of a $15,400-per-year annuity for 10 years at 10%

     = $15,400 × 10-year, 10% present value of annuity factor

     = $15,400 × 6.1446

     = $94,627

Other analysts view the normal industry earning rate to be appropriate only for identifiable assets and not goodwill. Thus, they might capitalize excess earnings at a higher rate of return to reflect the higher risk inherent in goodwill.

All calculations of goodwill are only estimates used to assist in the determination of the price to be paid for a company. For example, Acquisitions might add the $94,627 estimate of goodwill to the $705,000 fair value of Johnson's other net assets to arrive at a tentative maximum price of $799,627. However, estimates of goodwill may differ from actual negotiated goodwill. If the final agreed-upon price for Johnson's net assets was $790,000, the actual negotiated goodwill would be $85,000, which is the price paid less the fair value of the net assets acquired.

REFLECTION

- Goodwill estimates are based on an estimate of predicted income in excess of normal.
- Predicted excess income is typically discounted either as perpetuity or as a limited term annuity.

UNDERSTANDING THE ISSUES

1. Identify each of the following business combinations as being vertical-backward, vertical-forward, horizontal, product extension, market extension, or conglomerate:

   a. An inboard marine engine manufacturer is acquired by an outboard engine manufacturer.
   b. A cosmetics manufacturer acquires a drug store chain.
   c. A financial holding company acquires a mail order movie rental company.
   d. A computer manufacturer acquires a chip manufacturer.
   e. The Walt Disney Company acquires a broadcasting company.
   f. A California-based electric utility acquires a Colorado electric utility company.

2. Abrams Company is a sole proprietorship. The book value of its identifiable net assets is $400,000, and the fair value of the same net assets is $600,000. It is agreed that the business is worth $850,000. What advantage might there be for the seller if the company is exchanged for the common stock of another corporation as opposed to receiving cash? Consider both the immediate and future impact.

3. Major Corporation is acquiring Abrams Company by issuing its common stock in a nontaxable exchange. Major is issuing common stock with a fair value of $850,000 for net identifiable assets with book and fair values of $400,000 and $600,000, respectively. What values will Major assign to the identifiable assets, to goodwill, and to the deferred tax liability? Assume a 40% tax rate.

4. Panther Company is about to acquire a 100% interest in Snake Company. Snake has identifiable net assets with book and fair values of $300,000 and $500,000, respectively. As payment, Panther will issue common stock with a fair value of $750,000. How would the transaction be recorded if the acquisition is:

   a. An acquisition of net assets?
   b. An acquisition of Snake's common stock and Snake remains a separate legal entity?

5. Puncho Company is acquiring the net assets of Semos Company in exchange for common stock valued at $900,000. The Semos identifiable net assets have book and fair values of $400,000 and $800,000, respectively. Compare accounting for the acquisition (including assignment of the price paid) by Puncho with accounting for the sale by Semos.

6. Panther Company is acquiring the net assets of Sharon Company. The book and fair values of Sharon's accounts are as follows:

Accounts	Book	Fair
Current Assets	$100,000	$120,000
Land	50,000	80,000
Building and Equipment	300,000	400,000
Customer List	0	20,000
Liabilities	100,000	100,000

What values will be assigned to current assets, land, building and equipment, the customer list, liabilities, goodwill, and gain under each of the following acquisition price scenarios?

a. $800,000
b. $450,000

7. Pam Company acquires the net assets of Jam Company for an agreed-upon price of $900,000 on July 1, 2015. The value is tentatively assigned as follows:

Current assets	$ 100,000
Land...	50,000
Equipment.....................................	200,000 (5-year life)
Building	500,000 (20-year life)
Current liabilities	(150,000)
Goodwill	200,000

Values are subject to change during the measurement period. Depreciation is taken to the nearest month. The measurement period expires on July 1, 2016, at which time the fair values of the equipment and building as of the acquisition date are revised to $180,000 and $550,000, respectively.

At the end of 2016, what adjustments are needed for the financial statements for the period ending December 31, 2015 and 2016?

8. Harms acquires Blake on January 1, 2015, for $1,000,000. The amount of $800,000 is assigned to identifiable net assets. Goodwill is being impairment tested on December 31, 2019. There have not been any prior impairment adjustments. The following values apply on that date:

Estimated fair value of the Blake operating unit...........................	$1,200,000
Fair value of net identifiable assets (excluding goodwill)	1,120,000
Book value of net identifiable assets (including goodwill)	1,250,000

The book values include those resulting from assignment of fair value to accounts included in the January 1, 2015, acquisition.

Is goodwill impaired? If it is, what is the amount of the impairment adjustment?

9. What are the accounting ramifications of each of the three following situations involving the payment of contingent consideration in an acquisition?

a. P Company issues 100,000 shares of its $50 fair value ($1 par) common stock as payment to buy S Company on January 1, 2015. P agrees to pay $100,000 cash two years later if S income exceeds an income target. The target is exceeded.

b. P Company issues 100,000 shares of its $50 fair value ($1 par) common stock as payment to buy S Company on January 1, 2015. P agrees to issue 10,000 additional shares of its stock two years later if S income exceeds an income target. The target is exceeded.

c. P Company issues 100,000 shares of its $50 fair value ($1 par) common stock as payment to buy S Company on January 1, 2015. P agrees to issue 5,000 additional shares two years later if the fair value of P shares falls below $50 per share. Two years later, the stock has a fair value below $50, and added shares are issued to S.

10. P Company acquired the S Company for an agreed value of $900,000 and issues its common stock to make the deal. The fair value of the Company S net identifiable assets is $800,000. The issue costs of the stock used for payment is $50,000. If P Company was eligible to use IFRS for SME's and decided to do so, how would the recording of the transaction differ from U.S. GAAP?

EXERCISES

Exercise 1 *(LO 2, 3, 4)* **Asset versus stock acquisition.** Barstow Company is contemplating the acquisition of the net assets of Crown Company for $875,000 cash. To complete the transaction, acquisition costs are $15,000. The balance sheet of Crown Company on the purchase date is as follows:

Crown Company
Balance Sheet
December 31, 2015

Assets		Liabilities and Equity	
Current assets	$ 80,000	Liabilities	$100,000
Land	70,000	Common stock ($10 par)	100,000
Building	450,000	Paid-in capital in excess of par	150,000
Accumulated depreciation—building	(200,000)	Retained earnings	250,000
Equipment	300,000		
Accumulated depreciation—equipment	(100,000)		
Total assets	$ 600,000	Total liabilities and equity	$600,000

The following fair values have been obtained for Crown's identifiable assets and liabilities:

Current assets	$ 85,000
Land	90,000
Building	300,000
Equipment	275,000
Liabilities	102,000

1. Record the acquisition of the net assets of Crown Company on Barstow Company's books.
2. Record the sale of the net assets on the books of Crown Company.
3. Record the acquisition of 100% of the common stock of Crown Company on Barstow's books. Crown Company will remain a separate legal entity.

Exercise 2 *(LO 3, 4)* **Acquisition with goodwill.** Smith Company is acquired by Roan Corporation on July 1, 2015. Roan exchanges 60,000 shares of its $1 par stock, with a fair value of $18 per share, for the net assets of Smith Company.

Roan incurs the following costs as a result of this transaction:

Acquisition costs	$25,000
Stock registration and issuance costs	10,000
Total costs	$35,000

The balance sheet of Smyth Company, on the day of the acquisition, is as follows:

Smith Company
Balance Sheet
July 1, 2015

Assets			Liabilities and Equity		
Cash		$ 100,000	Current liabilities	$ 80,000	
Inventory		250,000	Bonds payable	500,000	$ 580,000
Property, plant, and equipment:			Stockholders' equity:		
Land	$200,000		Common stock	$200,000	
Buildings (net)	250,000		Paid-in capital in excess of par	100,000	
Equipment (net)	200,000	650,000	Retained earnings	120,000	420,000
Total assets		$1,000,000	Total liabilities and equity		$1,000,000

The appraised fair values as of July 1, 2015, is as follows:

Inventory	$270,000
Equipment	220,000
Land	180,000
Buildings	300,000
Current liabilities	80,000
Bonds payable	425,000

Record the acquisition of Smyth Company on the books of Radar Corporation.

Exercise 3 *(LO 3, 4)* **Acquisition with special valuations.** Pederson Company acquires the net assets of Shelby Company by issuing 100,000 of its $1 par value shares of common stock. The shares have a fair value of $20 each. Just prior to the acquisition, Shelby's balance sheet is as follows:

Shelby Company
Balance Sheet
January 1, 2015

Assets		Liabilities and Equity		
Accounts receivable	$100,000	Current liabilities	$ 80,000	
Inventory	210,000	Bonds payable	200,000	$280,000
Equipment (net)	100,000	Stockholders' equity:		
Land	200,000	Common stock ($1 par)	$ 10,000	
Building (net)	300,000	Retained earnings	620,000	630,000
Total assets	$910,000	Total liabilities and equity		$910,000

Fair values agree with book values except for the building, which is appraised at $450,000. The following additional information is available:

♦ The equipment will be sold for an estimated price of $200,000. A 10% commission will be paid to a broker.

♦ A major R&D project is underway. The accumulated costs are $56,000, and the estimated value of the work is $90,000.

♦ A warranty attaches to products sold in the past. The estimated future repair costs under the warranty are $40,000.

♦ Shelby has a customer list that has value. It is estimated that the list will provide additional income of $100,000 for three years. An intangible asset such as this is valued at a 20% rate of return.

Record the acquisition of Shelby Company on the books of Pederson Company. Provide calculations where needed.

Exercise 4 *(LO 3, 4)* **Bargain acquisition.** Norton Corporation agrees to acquire the net assets of Payco Corporation. Just prior to the acquisition, Payco's balance sheet is as follows:

Payco Corporation
Balance Sheet
January 1, 2015

Assets		Liabilities and Equity		
Accounts receivable	$200,000	Current liabilities	$ 80,000	
Inventory	270,000	Mortgage payable	250,000	$330,000
Equipment (net)	100,000	Stockholders' equity:		
		Common stock ($10 par)	$100,000	
		Retained earnings	140,000	240,000
Total assets	$570,000	Total liabilities and equity		$570,000

Fair values agree with book values except for the equipment, which has an estimated fair value of $40,000. Also, it has been determined that brand-name copyrights have an estimated value of $15,000. Norton Corporation pays $25,000 in acquisition costs to consummate the transaction.

Record the acquisition on the books of Norton Corporation assuming the cash paid to Payco Corporation is $160,000.

Suggestion: Use value analysis to guide your calculations and entries.

Exercise 5 *(LO 4)* **Measurement period.** Avery Company acquires the net assets of Iowa Company on July 1, 2015. The net assets acquired include plant assets that are provisionally estimated to have a fair value of $600,000 with a 10-year usable life and no salvage value. Depreciation is recorded based on months in service. The remaining unallocated amount of the price paid is $300,000, which is recorded as goodwill.

At the end of 2015, Avery prepares the following statements (includes Iowa Company for the last six months):

Balance Sheet

Current assets	$ 300,000	Current liabilities	$ 300,000
Equipment (net)	600,000	Bonds payable	500,000
Plant assets (net).	1,600,000	Common stock ($1 par).	50,000
Goodwill	300,000	Paid-in capital in excess of par . . .	1,300,000
		Retained earnings	650,000
Total assets.	$2,800,000	Total liabilities and equity	$2,800,000

Summary Income Statement

Sales revenue		$800,000
Cost of goods sold.		520,000
Gross profit		$280,000
Operating expenses	$150,000	
Depreciation expense	80,000	230,000
Net income		$ 50,000

In March 2016, the final estimated fair value of the acquired plant assets is $700,000 with no change in the estimate of useful life or salvage value.

1. Prepare any journal entries required in March 2016.
2. Prepare the revised balance sheet and income statement for 2015 that will be included in the 2016 comparative statements.

Exercise 6 *(LO 5)* **Deferred tax liability.** Your client, Lewison International, has informed you that it has reached an agreement with Herro Company to acquire all of Herro's assets. This transaction will be accomplished through the issue of Lewison's common stock.

After your examination of the financial statements and the acquisition agreement, you have discovered the following important facts.

The Lewison common stock issued has a fair value of $800,000. The fair value of Herro's assets, net of all liabilities, is $700,000. All asset book values equal their fair values except for one machine valued at $200,000. This machine was originally purchased two years ago by Herro for $180,000. This machine has been depreciated using the straight-line method with an assumed useful life of 10 years and no salvage value. The acquisition is to be considered a tax-free exchange for tax purposes.

Assuming a 30% tax rate, what amounts will be recorded for the machine, deferred tax liability, and goodwill?

Exercise 7 *(LO 5)* **Tax loss carryover.** Lakecraft Company has the following balance sheet on December 31, 2015, when it is acquired for $950,000 in cash by Argo Corporation:

Lakecraft Company
Balance Sheet
December 31, 2015

Assets		Liabilities and Equity		
Current assets	$100,000	Current liabilities		$ 60,000
Equipment (net)	200,000	Stockholders' equity:		
Building (net)	270,000	Common stock ($5 par)	$100,000	
		Retained earnings	410,000	510,000
Total assets	$570,000	Total liabilities and equity		$570,000

All assets have fair values equal to their book values. The combination is structured as a tax-free exchange. Lakecraft Company has a tax loss carryforward of $300,000, which it has not recorded. The balance of the $300,000 tax loss carryover is considered fully realizable. Argo is taxed at a rate of 30%.

Record the acquisition of Lakecraft Company by Argo Corporation.

Exercise 8 *(LO 4)* **Contingent consideration.** Grant Company purchased the net assets of Harding Company on January 1, 2015, and made the following entry to record the purchase:

Current Assets	100,000	
Equipment	160,000	
Land	50,000	
Buildings	300,000	
Goodwill	100,000	
Note Payable		50,000
Account to be determined		40,000
Common Stock ($1 par)		100,000
Paid-in Capital in Excess of Par		520,000

Provide the correct title for the $40,000 credit account above and make the required entry on January 1, 2017, for each of the following independent contingency agreements:

1. An additional cash payment would be made on January 1, 2017, equal to twice the amount by which average annual earnings of the Harding Division exceed $25,000 per year, prior to January 1, 2017. Net income was $50,000 in 2015 and $60,000 in 2016. Assume that the expected value of the agreement on the purchase date was $40,000. Assume that no adjustment was made at the end of 2015 or 2016.
2. Added shares would be issued on January 1, 2017, equal in value to twice the amount by which average annual earnings of the Harding Division exceed $25,000 per year, prior to January 1, 2017. Net income was $50,000 in 2015 and $60,000 in 2016. The market price of the shares on January 1, 2017, was $5. Assume that the expected value of the agreement on the purchase date was $40,000. The agreement is classified as an equity transaction.
3. Added shares or cash (at the option of the acquirer) would be issued on January 1, 2017, to compensate for any fall in the value of Grant common stock below $6 per share. The market price of the shares on January 1, 2017, was $5. Assume that the expected value of the agreement on the purchase date was $40,000 and that it is classified as a liability. Assume that no adjustment was made at the end of 2015 or 2016. Shares were issued on January 1, 2017.

Exercise 9 *(LO 7)* **Goodwill impairment.** Anton Company acquired the net assets of Hair Company on January 1, 2015, for $600,000. Using a business valuation model, the estimated value of Anton Company was $650,000 immediately after the acquisition. The fair value of Anton's net assets was $400,000.

1. What amount of goodwill was recorded by Anton Company when it acquired Hair Company?

2. Using the information on page 40, answer the questions posed in the following two independent situations:

   a. On December 31, 2016, there were indications that goodwill might have been impaired. At that time, the existing recorded book value of Anton Company's net assets, including goodwill, was $500,000. The fair value of the net assets, exclusive of goodwill, was estimated to be $340,000. The value of the business was estimated to be $520,000. Is goodwill impaired? If so, what adjustment is needed?

   b. On December 31, 2018, there were indications that goodwill might have been impaired. At that time, the existing recorded book value of Anton Company's net assets, including goodwill, was $450,000. The fair value of the net assets, exclusive of goodwill, was estimated to be $340,000. The value of the business was estimated to be $400,000. Is goodwill impaired? If so, what adjustment is needed?

APPENDIX EXERCISE

Exercise 1A-1 *(LO 9)* **Estimating goodwill.** Green Company is considering acquiring the assets of Gold Corporation by assuming Gold's liabilities and by making a cash payment. Gold Corporation has the following balance sheet on the date negotiations occur:

Gold Corporation
Balance Sheet
January 1, 2016

Assets		Liabilities and Equity	
Accounts receivable	$100,000	Total liabilities	$200,000
Inventory	100,000	Capital stock ($10 par)	100,000
Land.	100,000	Paid-in capital in excess of par	200,000
Building (net)	220,000	Retained earnings	300,000
Equipment (net)	280,000		
Total assets.	$800,000	Total liabilities and equity	$800,000

Appraisals indicate that the inventory is undervalued by $25,000, the building is undervalued by $80,000, and the equipment is overstated by $30,000. Past earnings have been considered above average and were as follows:

Year	Net Income
2011	$ 90,000
2012	110,000
2013	120,000
2014	140,000*
2015	130,000

*Includes a nonrecurring gain of $40,000.

It is assumed that the average operating income of the past five years will continue. In this industry, the average return on assets is 12% on the fair value of the total identifiable assets.

1. Prepare an estimate of goodwill based on each of the following assumptions:

   a. The purchasing company paid for five years of excess earnings.
   b. Excess earnings will continue indefinitely and are to be capitalized at the industry normal return.
   c. Excess earnings will continue for only five years and should be capitalized at a higher rate of 16%, which reflects the risk applicable to goodwill.

2. Determine the actual goodwill recorded if Green pays $690,000 cash for the net assets of Gold Corporation and assumes all existing liabilities.

PROBLEMS

Problem 1-1 *(LO 3, 4)* **Value analysis, alternative prices.** Born Corporation agrees to acquire the net assets of Wren Corporation on January 1, 2015. Wren has the following balance sheet on the date of acquisition:

Wren Corporation
Balance Sheet
January 1, 2015

Assets		Liabilities and Equity	
Accounts receivable	$ 79,000	Current liabilities	$125,000
Inventory	92,000	Bonds payable	100,000
Other current assets..........	55,000	Common stock...............	200,000
Equipment (net)	294,000	Paid-in capital in excess of par ...	50,000
Trademark.................	30,000	Retained earnings	75,000
Total assets..............	$550,000	Total liabilities and equity	$550,000

An appraiser determines that in-process R&D exists and has an estimated value of $20,000. The appraisal indicates that the following assets have fair values that differ from their book values:

	Fair Value
Inventory	$ 98,000
Equipment	340,000
Trademark.........................	30,000

Required ▶ ▶ ▶ ▶ ▶ Use value analysis to prepare the entry on the books of Born Corporation to acquire the net assets of Wren Corporation under each of the following purchase price scenarios:

1. Purchase price is $540,000.
2. Purchase price is $350,000.

Problem 1-2 *(LO 3)* **Purchase of two companies with goodwill.** Bar Corporation has been looking to expand its operations and has decided to acquire the assets of Vicker Company and Kendal Company. Bar will issue 30,000 shares of its $10 par common stock to acquire the net assets of Vicker Company and will issue 15,000 shares to acquire the net assets of Kendal Company.

Vicker and Kendal have the following balance sheets as of December 31, 2015:

Assets	Vicker	Kendal
Accounts receivable	$ 200,000	$ 80,000
Inventory	150,000	85,000
Property, plant, and equipment:		
Land...	150,000	50,000
Buildings	500,000	300,000
Accumulated depreciation................................	(150,000)	(110,000)
Total assets	$ 850,000	$ 405,000

Liabilities and Equity	Vicker	Kendal
Current liabilities	$160,000	$ 55,000
Bonds payable	100,000	100,000
Stockholders' equity:		
Common stock ($10 par)	300,000	100,000
Retained earnings	290,000	150,000
Total liabilities and equity	$850,000	$405,000

The following fair values are agreed upon by the firms:

Assets	Vicker	Kendal
Inventory	$190,000	$100,000
Land	300,000	80,000
Buildings	450,000	400,000
Bonds payable	90,000	95,000

Bar's stock is currently trading at $40 per share. Bar will incur $5,000 of acquisition costs in acquiring Vicker and $4,000 of acquisition costs in acquiring Kendal. Bar will also incur $15,000 of registration and issuance costs for the shares issued in both acquisitions.

Bar's stockholders' equity is as follows:

Common stock ($10 par)	$1,200,000
Paid-in capital in excess of par	800,000
Retained earnings	750,000

Record the acquisitions on the books of Bar Corporation. Value analysis is suggested to guide your work. ◄ ◄ ◄ ◄ ◄ **Required**

Problem 1-3 *(LO 3, 4, 6)* **Pro forma income after an acquisition.** Moon Company is contemplating the acquisition of Yount, Inc., on January 1, 2015. If Moon acquires Yount, it will pay $730,000 in cash to Yount and acquisition costs of $20,000.

The January 1, 2015, balance sheet of Yount, Inc., is anticipated to be as follows:

Yount, Inc.
Pro Forma Balance Sheet
January 1, 2015

Assets		Liabilities and Equity	
Cash equivalents	$100,000	Current liabilities	$ 30,000
Accounts receivable	120,000	Long-term liabilities	165,000
Inventory	50,000	Common stock ($10 par)	80,000
Depreciable fixed assets	200,000	Retained earnings	115,000
Accumulated depreciation	(80,000)		
Total assets	$390,000	Total liabilities and equity	$390,000

Fair values agree with book values except for the inventory and the depreciable fixed assets, which have fair values of $70,000 and $400,000, respectively.

Your projections of the combined operations for 2015 are as follows:

Combined sales	$200,000
Combined cost of goods sold, including Yount's beginning inventory, at book value,	
which will be sold in 2015	120,000
Other expenses not including depreciation of Yount assets	25,000

Depreciation on Yount fixed assets is straight-line using a 20-year life with no salvage value.

Required ▶ ▶ ▶ ▶ ▶
1. Prepare a value analysis for the acquisition and record the acquisition.
2. Prepare a pro forma income statement for the combined firm for 2015. Show supporting calculations for consolidated income. Ignore tax issues.

Problem 1-4 *(LO 3, 4)* **Alternate consideration, bargain.** Kiln Corporation is considering the acquisition of Williams Incorporated. Kiln has asked you, its accountant, to evaluate the various offers it might make to Williams Incorporated. The December 31, 2015, balance sheet of Williams is as follows:

Williams Incorporated
Balance Sheet
December 31, 2015

Assets			Liabilities and Equity			
Current assets:			Accounts payable			$ 40,000
Accounts receivable.	$ 50,000					
Inventory	300,000					
		$350,000	Stockholders' equity:			
Noncurrent assets:			Common stock	$ 40,000		
Land.	$ 20,000		Paid-in capital in excess of par . . .	110,000		
Building (net)	70,000	90,000	Retained earnings	250,000	400,000	
Total assets		$440,000	Total liabilities and equity			$440,000

The following fair values differ from existing book values:

Inventory	$250,000
Land.	40,000
Building	120,000

Required ▶ ▶ ▶ ▶ ▶ Record the acquisition entry for Kiln Corporation that would result under each of the alternative offers. Value analysis is suggested.

1. Kiln Corporation issues 20,000 of its $10 par common stock with a fair value of $25 per share for the net assets of Williams Incorporated.
2. Kiln Corporation pays $385,000 in cash.

Problem 1-5 *(LO 3, 4)* **Revaluation of assets.** Jack Company is a corporation that was organized on July 1, 2015. The June 30, 2020, balance sheet for Jack is as follows:

Assets

Investments		$ 400,500
Accounts receivable	$1,250,000	
Allowance for doubtful accounts	(300,000)	950,000
Inventory		1,500,000
Prepaid insurance		18,000
Land.		58,000
Machinery and equipment (net)		1,473,500
Goodwill		100,000
Total assets.		$4,500,000

Liabilities and Equity

Current liabilities	$1,475,000
Common stock ($10 par).	1,200,000
Retained earnings	1,825,000
Total liabilities and equity	$4,500,000

The experience of other companies over the last several years indicates that the machinery and equipment can be sold at 130% of its book value.

An analysis of the accounts receivable indicates that the realizable value is $925,000. An independent appraisal made in June 2020 values the land at $70,000. Using the lower-of-cost-or-market rule, inventory is to be restated at $1,200,000.

Calway Corporation plans to exchange 18,000 of its shares for the 120,000 Jack shares. During June 2020, the fair value of a share of Calway Corporation is $270. Acquisition costs are $12,000.

The stockholders' equity account balances of Calway Corporation as of June 30, 2015, are as follows:

Common stock ($10 par)...	$2,000,000
Paid-in capital in excess of par	580,000
Retained earnings	2,496,400
Total stockholders' equity	$5,076,400

Record the acquisition of Jack Company by Calway on July 1, 2020. Use value analysis to support the acquisition entries. ◄ ◄ ◄ ◄ ◄ **Required**

Problem 1-6 *(LO 3, 4)* **Cash purchase with goodwill.** Tweeden Corporation is contemplating the acquisition of the net assets of Sylvester Corporation in anticipation of expanding its operations. The balance sheet of Sylvester Corporation on December 31, 2015, is as follows:

Sylvester Corporation
Balance Sheet
December 31, 2015

Current assets:			**Current liabilities:**		
Notes receivable	$ 24,000		Accounts payable	$ 45,000	
Accounts receivable	56,000		Payroll and benefit-related liabilities	12,500	
Inventory	31,000				
Other current assets............	18,000		Debt maturing in one year........	10,000	
Total current assets...........		$129,000	Total current liabilities		$ 67,500
Investments		65,000			
Fixed assets:			**Other liabilities:**		
Land........................	$ 32,000		Long-term debt.................	$248,000	
Building	245,000		Payroll and benefit-related liabilities	156,000	
Equipment	387,000				
Total fixed assets		664,000	Total other liabilities...........		404,000
Intangibles:			**Stockholders' equity:**		
Goodwill	$ 45,000		Common stock.................	$100,000	
Patents......................	23,000		Paid-in capital in excess of par	250,000	
Trade names	10,000		Retained earnings	114,500	
Total intangibles		78,000	Total equity		464,500
Total assets		$936,000	Total liabilities and equity		$936,000

An appraiser for Tweeden determined the fair values of Sylvester's assets and liabilities to be as shown on next page.

Assets		Liabilities	
Notes receivable	$ 24,000	Accounts payable	$ 45,000
Accounts receivable	56,000	Payroll and benefit-related liabilities—current	12,500
Inventory	30,000		
Other current assets	15,000	Debt maturing in one year	10,000
Investments	63,000		
Land	55,000	Long-term debt	248,000
Building	275,000	Payroll and benefit-related liabilities—long-term	156,000
Equipment	426,000		
Goodwill	—		
Patents	20,000		
Trade names	15,000		

The agreed-upon purchase price is $580,000 in cash. Acquisition costs paid in cash total $20,000.

Required ▶ ▶ ▶ ▶ ▶ Using the above information, do value analysis and prepare the entry on the books of Tweeden Corporation to acquire the net assets of Sylvester Corporation on December 31, 2015.

Problem 1-7 *(LO 3, 4)* **Acquisition with contingent consideration.** Holt Corporation is contemplating the acquisition of Sambo Company's net assets on December 31, 2015. It is considering making an offer, which would include a cash payout of $225,000 along with giving 15,000 shares of its $2 par value common stock that is currently selling for $20 per share. Holt also agrees that it will pay an additional $50,000 on January 1, 2018, if the average net income of Sambo's business unit exceeds $80,000 for 2016 and 2017. The likelihood of reaching that target is estimated to be 60%. The balance sheet of Sambo Company is given below, along with estimated fair values of the net assets to be acquired.

Sambo Company
Balance Sheet
December 31, 2015

	Book Value	Fair Value		Book Value	Fair Value
Current assets:			**Current liabilities:**		
Notes receivable	$ 33,000	$ 33,000	Accounts payable	$ 63,000	$ 63,000
Inventory	80,000	80,000	Taxes payable	15,000	15,000
Prepaid expenses	15,000	15,000	Interest payable	3,000	3,000
Total current assets	$128,000	$128,000	Total current liabilities	$ 81,000	$ 81,000
Investments	$ 36,000	$ 55,000			
Fixed assets:			**Other liabilities:**		
Land	$ 15,000	$ 90,000	Bonds payable	$250,000	$250,000
Buildings	115,000	170,000	Discount on bonds payable	(18,000)	(30,000)
Equipment	256,000	250,000			
Vehicles	32,000	25,000			
Total fixed assets	$418,000	$535,000	Total other liabilities	$232,000	$220,000
Intangibles:			**Stockholders' equity:**		
Franchise	$ 56,000	$ 70,000	Common stock	$ 50,000	
			Paid-in capital in excess of par	200,000	
			Retained earnings	75,000	
			Total equity	$325,000	
Total assets	$638,000	$788,000	Total liabilities and equity	$638,000	

1. Do value analysis and prepare the entry on the books of Holt Corporation to record the ◀ ◀ ◀ ◀ ◀ **Required** acquisition of Sambo Company.
2. Assume that the net income of the Sambo business unit is $120,000 for 2016. As a result, the likelihood of paying the contingent consideration is believed to be 90%. What, if any, adjusting entry is required as of December 31, 2016?

Problem 1-8 *(LO 3, 4)* **Cash acquisition with a gain.** Heinrich Company, owned by Elennor and Al Heinrich, has been experiencing financial difficulty for the past several years. Both Elennor and Al have not been in good health and have decided to find a buyer. P&F International, after reviewing the financial statements for the previous three years, has decided to make an offer of $150,000 for the net assets of Heinrich Company on January 1, 2016. The balance sheet as of this date is as follows:

Heinrich Company
Balance Sheet
January 1, 2016

Current assets:			**Current liabilities:**		
Accounts receivable		$ 87,000	Accounts payable		$ 56,000
Inventory		36,000	Accrued liabilities		14,000
Other current assets		14,000			
Total current assets		$137,000	Total current liabilities		$ 70,000
Fixed assets:			**Other liabilities:**		
Equipment		$105,000	Notes payable		$ 30,000
Vehicles		69,000			
Total fixed assets		$174,000	Total liabilities		$100,000
Intangibles:			**Stockholders' equity:**		
Mailing lists		$ 4,000	Common stock		$ 60,000
			Paid-in capital in excess of par		100,000
			Retained earnings		55,000
			Total equity		$215,000
Total assets		$315,000	Total liabilities and equity		$315,000

In reviewing the above balance sheet, P&F's appraiser felt the liabilities were stated at their fair values. He placed the following fair values on the assets of the company.

Heinrich Company
Fair Values
January 1, 2016

Current assets:		
Accounts receivable		$ 90,000
Inventory		30,000
Other current assets		8,000
Total current assets		$128,000
Fixed assets:		
Equipment		$ 80,000
Vehicles		50,000
Total fixed assets		$130,000
Intangibles:		
Mailing list		$ 10,000
Total assets		$268,000

Required ▶ ▶ ▶ ▶ ▶ Using this information, do value analysis, and prepare the entry to record the acquisition of the net assets of Heinrich Company on the books of P&F International.

Problem 1-9 *(LO 6)* **Income statements after acquisition.** On July 1, 2015, Faber Enterprises acquired Ann's Tool Company. Prior to the merger of the two companies, each company calculated its income for the entire year ended December 31, 2015. (It may be assumed that all Ann amounts occurred evenly over the year.) These estimates are as follows:

Income Statement Accounts	Faber Enterprises		Ann's Tool Company	
Sales Revenue		$550,000		$140,000
Cost of Goods Sold		200,000		50,000
Gross Profit		$350,000		$ 90,000
Selling Expenses	$125,000		$30,000	
Administrative Expenses	150,000		45,000	
Depreciation Expense	13,800		7,500	
Amortization Expense	5,600		2,000	
Total Operating Expenses		294,400		84,500
Operating Income		$ 55,600		$ 5,500
Nonoperating Revenues and Expenses:				
Interest Expense				4,000
Interest Income		7,000		
Dividend Income		4,000		
Income Before Taxes		$ 66,600		$ 1,500
Provision for Income Taxes (30% rate). . . .		19,980		450
Net Income		$ 46,620		$ 1,050

An analysis of the merger agreement revealed that the purchase price exceeded the fair value of all assets by $40,000. The book and fair values of Ann's Tool Company on July 1, 2015, are given in the table below along with an estimate of the useful lives of each of these asset categories.

Asset Account	Book Value	Fair Value	Useful Life
Inventory	$30,000	$ 28,000	Sold August 2015
Land.	50,000	80,000	Unlimited
Buildings	75,000	125,000	25 years
Equipment	32,000	56,000	8 years
Truck	1,000	3,000	2 years
Patent.	12,000	18,000	6 years
Computer Software	0	10,000	2 years
Copyright	0	20,000	10 years

Management believes the company will be in a combined tax bracket of 30%. The company uses the straight-line method of computing depreciation and amortization and assigns a zero salvage value.

Required ▶ ▶ ▶ ▶ ▶ 1. Using the above information, prepare the Faber Enterprises income statement for the year ending December 31, 2015. Provide supporting calculations.
2. Prepare the required summarized disclosure of 2015 results if the acquisition occurs at the start of the year.

Problem 1-10 *(LO 3, 4, 6)* **Issue stock, goodwill, pro forma disclosure.**

Part A. Garman International wants to expand its operations and decides to acquire the net assets of Iris Company as of January 1, 2016. Garman issues 10,000 shares of its $5 par value common stock for the net assets of Iris. Garman's stock is selling for $27 per share. In addition,

Garman pays $10,000 in acquisition costs. A balance sheet for Iris Company as of December 31, 2015, is as follows:

Current assets:			**Current liabilities:**		
Accounts receivable		$ 15,000	Accounts payable		$ 22,000
Inventory		38,000	Interest payable		2,000
Prepaid expenses		12,000			
Total current assets		$ 65,000	Total current liabilities		$ 24,000
Investments		19,000			
Fixed assets:			**Other liabilities:**		
Land	$30,000		Long-term notes payable		40,000
Building	70,000				
Equipment	56,000				
Total fixed assets		156,000	Total liabilities		$ 64,000
Intangibles:			**Stockholders' equity:**		
Patent	$17,000		Common stock	$ 40,000	
Copyrights	22,000		Paid-in capital in excess of par	120,000	
Goodwill	8,000		Retained earnings	63,000	
Total intangibles		47,000	Total equity		223,000
Total assets		$287,000	Total liabilities and equity		$287,000

In reviewing Iris's balance sheet and in consulting with various appraisers, Garman has determined that the inventory is understated by $2,000, the land is understated by $10,000, the building is understated by $15,000, and the copyrights are understated by $4,000. Garman has also determined that the equipment is overstated by $6,000, and the patent is overstated by $5,000.

The investments have a fair value of $33,000 on December 31, 2015, and the amount of goodwill (if any) must be determined.

Part A1. Using the information above, do value analysis, and record the acquisition of Iris ◄ ◄ ◄ ◄ ◄ **Required**
Company on Garman International's books on January 1, 2016.

Part A2. Garman International wishes to estimate its pro forma disclosure of operations for 2016 resulting from acquisition of Iris. Pro forma disclosure includes revenue and net income. Projected income statements for 2016 are as follows:

Income Statement Accounts	Garman International	Iris Company
Sales Revenue	$(350,000)	$(125,000)
Cost of Goods Sold	147,000	55,000
Gross Profit	$(203,000)	$ (70,000)
Selling Expenses*	$ 100,000	$ 20,000
Administrative Expenses*	50,000	30,000
Depreciation Expense	12,500	8,600
Amortization Expense	1,000	3,900
Total Operating Expenses	$ 163,500	$ 62,500
Operating Income	$ (39,500)	$ (7,500)
Nonoperating Revenues and Expenses:		
Interest Expense		3,000
Investment Income	(12,000)	(4,500)
Income Before Taxes	$ (51,500)	$ (9,000)
Provision for Income Taxes (40% rate)	20,600	3,600
Net Income	$ (30,900)	$ (5,400)

*Does not include depreciation or amortization expense.

Garman International estimates that the following amount of depreciation and amortization should be taken on the revalued assets of Iris Company:

Building depreciation	$4,000
Equipment depreciation	5,000
Patent amortization	1,200
Copyright amortization	2,600

Required ▶ ▶ ▶ ▶ ▶ **Part B1.** Using the above information, prepare a pro forma income statement for Garman International combined with Iris Company for the year ended December 31, 2016. Schedule your calculations for revenue and net income.

Problem 1-11 *(LO 3, 4)* **Revaluation of leases** Sentry, Inc., acquires for $2,300,000 in cash, the net assets of New Equipment Company. The acquisition is made on December 31, 2015, at which time New Equipment has prepared the following balance sheet:

New Equipment Company
Balance Sheet
December 31, 2015

Assets		Liabilities and Equity	
Current assets	$ 100,000	Current liabilities	$ 150,000
Assets under operating leases	520,000	Obligation under capital lease of equipment	35,000
Net investment in direct financing (capital leases)	730,000	Common stock ($5 par)	100,000
		Paid-in capital in excess of par	400,000
Leased equipment under capital lease (net)	40,000	Retained earnings	955,000
Buildings (net)	200,000		
Land	50,000		
Total assets	$1,640,000	Total liabilities and equity	$1,640,000

The following information is available concerning the assets and liabilities of New Equipment:

a. Current assets and liabilities are stated fairly. No payments resulting from leases are included in current accounts, since all payments are due each December 31 and payment for 2015 has been made.

b. Assets under operating leases have an estimated value of $580,000. This figure includes consideration of remaining rents and the value of the assets at the end of the lease terms.

c. The net investment in direct financing leases represents receivables at their discounted present values. All leases except one are based on the current market interest rate of 12%. One equipment lease is included at an amount of $199,636. This lease includes five and of the year payments of $50,000 present valued at an 8% interest rate. This lease should be adjusted to its real fair value using a 12% annual interest rate.

d. The buildings and land have appraised fair values of $400,000 and $100,000, respectively.

e. The leased equipment under the capital lease pertains to a computer used by New Equipment. The obligation under the capital lease of equipment includes the present value of five remaining payments of $9,233 due at the end of each year and discounted at 10%. Title transfers to the lessee at the end of the lease term. The current interest rate for this type of transaction is 12%. The fair value of the equipment under the lease is $60,000.

f. New Equipment has expended $100,000 on R&D leading to new equipment applications. Sentry estimates the value of this work to be $200,000.

g. New Equipment has been named in a $200,000 lawsuit involving an accident by a lessee using its equipment. It is likely that New Equipment will be found liable in the amount of $50,000.

Required ▶ ▶ ▶ ▶ ▶ Record the acquisition of New Equipment Company by Sentry, Inc. Carefully support your entry. You may assume that the price will allow goodwill to be recorded.

Problem 1-12 *(LO 5)* **Tax-free exchange, tax loss carryover.** Hanson Company issues 10,000 shares of $10 par common stock for the net assets of Marcus Incorporated on December 31, 2016. The stock has a fair value of $65 per share. Acquisition costs are $10,000, and the cost of issuing the stock is $3,000. At the time of the purchase, Marcus had the following summarized balance sheet:

Assets		Liabilities and Equity	
Current assets	$150,000	Bonds payable	$200,000
Equipment (net)	200,000	Common stock ($10 par).	100,000
Land and buildings (net)	250,000	Retained earnings	300,000
Total assets.	$600,000	Total liabilities and equity . . .	$600,000

The only fair value differing from book value is equipment, which is worth $350,000. Marcus has $180,000 in operating losses in prior years. The previous asset values are also the tax basis of the assets, which will be the tax basis for Hanson, since the acquisition is a tax-free exchange. Hanson is confident that it will recover the entire tax loss carryforward applicable to the past losses of Marcus. The applicable tax rate is 30%.

Record the acquisition of the net assets of Marcus Incorporated by Hanson Company. You may ◄ ◄ ◄ ◄ ◄ **Required** assume the price paid will allow goodwill to be recorded. Use value analysis to support your solution.

Problem 1-13 *(LO 4, 6)* **Contingent consideration.** Duko Corporation is acquiring the net assets, exclusive of cash, of Weber Company as of January 1, 2015, at which time Weber Company's balance sheet is as follows:

Assets		
Current assets:		
Cash	$ 30,000	
Accounts receivable.	50,000	$ 80,000
Noncurrent assets:		
Investments in marketable securities	$120,000	
Land.	600,000	
Buildings (net)	450,000	
Equipment (net)	800,000	
Goodwill	100,000	2,070,000
Total assets		$2,150,000

Liabilities and Stockholders' Equity		
Current liabilities:		
Accounts payable	$ 150,000	
Income tax payable	190,000	$ 340,000
Equity:		
Common stock ($5 par)	$1,200,000	
Retained earnings	610,000	1,810,000
Total liabilities and equity		$2,150,000

Duko Corporation feels that the following fair values should be used for Weber's book values:

Cash (no change)	$ 30,000
Accounts receivable	60,000
Investment in marketable securities	150,000
Land.	450,000
Buildings (no change)	450,000
Equipment	600,000
Accounts payable	120,000
Income tax payable (no change).	190,000

Duko will issue 20,000 shares of its common stock with a $2 par value and a quoted fair value of $60 per share on January 1, 2015, to Weber Company to acquire the net assets. Duko also agrees that two years from now it will issue additional securities to compensate Weber shareholders for any decline in value below that on the date of issue. The estimated settlement amount is $20,000. This is considered to be an equity agreement (not a liability).

Required ▶ ▶ ▶ ▶ ▶
1. Record the acquisition on the books of Duko Corporation on January 1, 2015. Include support for calculations used to arrive at the values assigned to the assets and liabilities. Use value analysis to aid your solution.
2. Record settlement (if any) for contingent consideration on January 1, 2017, assuming that the quoted value of the Duko stock is $57.50. (Round shares to nearest whole share.)

APPENDIX PROBLEM

Problem 1A-1 *(LO 9)* **Estimate goodwill, record acquisition.** Caswell Company is contemplating the purchase of LaBelle Company as of January 1, 2016. LaBelle Company has provided the following current balance sheet:

Assets		Liabilities and Equity	
Cash and receivables	$ 150,000	Current liabilities	$120,000
Inventory	180,000	9% Bonds payable	300,000
Land.	50,000	Common stock ($5 par)	100,000
Building	600,000	Paid-in capital in excess of par .	200,000
Accumulated depreciation	(150,000)	Retained earnings	150,000
Goodwill	40,000		
Total assets.	$ 870,000	Total liabilities and equity . . .	$870,000

The following information exists relative to balance sheet accounts:

a. The inventory has a fair value of $200,000.
b. The land is appraised at $100,000 and the building at $600,000.
c. The 9% bonds payable have five years to maturity and pay annual interest each December 31. The current interest rate for similar bonds is 8% per year.
d. It is likely that there will be a payment for goodwill based on projected income in excess of the industry average, which is 10% on total assets. Caswell will project the average past five years' operating income and will pay for excess income based on an assumption of a 5-year life and a risk rate of return of 16%. The past five years' net incomes for LaBelle are as follows:

2011	$120,000
2012	140,000
2013	150,000
2014	200,000 (includes $40,000 extraordinary gain)
2015	180,000

Required ▶ ▶ ▶ ▶ ▶
1. Provide an estimate of fair value for the bonds and for goodwill.
2. Using the values derived in part (1), record the acquisition on the Caswell books.

CASES

Structured Example of Goodwill Impairment   *Case 1-1*

(Note: The use of a financial calculator or Excel is suggested for this case.)

Modern Company acquires the net assets of Frontier Company for $ 1,300,000 on January 1, 2015. A business valuation consultant arrives at the price and deems it to be a good value.

Part A. The following list of fair values is provided to you by the consultant:

Assets and Liabilities	Comments	Valuation Method	Fair Value
Cash equivalents	Seller's values are accepted.	Existing book value.	$ 80,000
Inventory	Replacement cost is available.	Market replacement cost for similar items is used.	150,000
Accounts receivable	Asset is adjusted for estimated bad debts.	Aging schedule is used for valuation.	180,000
Land	Per-acre value is well established.	Calculation is based on 20 acres at $10,000 per acre.	200,000
Building	Most reliable measure is rent potential.	Rent is estimated at $80,000 per year for 20 years, discounted at 14% return for similar properties. Present value is reduced for land value.	329,850
Equipment	Cost of replacement capacity can be estimated.	Estimated purchase cost of equipment with similar capacity is used.	220,000
Patent	Recorded by seller at only legal cost; has significant future value.	Added profit made possible by patent is $40,000 per year for four years. Discounted at risk-adjusted rate for similar investments of 20% per year.	103,550
Current liabilities	Recorded amounts are accurate.	Recorded value is used.	(120,000)
Mortgage payable	Specified interest rate is below market rate.	Discount the $50,000 annual payments for five years at annual market rate of 7%.	(205,010)
Net identifiable assets at fair value			$ 938,390
Price paid for reporting unit			1,300,000
Goodwill	Believed to exist based on reputation and customer list.	Implied by price paid.	$ 361,610

Using the information in the preceding table, confirm the accuracy of the present value calculations made for the building, patent, and mortgage payable.   ◀ ◀ ◀ ◀ ◀ **Required**

Part B. Frontier does not have publicly traded stock. You make an estimate of the value of the company based on the following assumptions that will later be included in the reporting unit valuation procedure:

a. Frontier will provide operating cash flows, net of tax, of $150,000 during the next fiscal year.
b. Operating cash flows will increase at the rate of 10% per year for the next four fiscal years and then will remain steady for 15 more years.
c. Cash flows, defined as net of cash from operations less capital expenditures, will be discounted at an after-tax discount rate of 12%. An annual rate of 12% is a reasonable risk-adjusted rate of return for investments of this type.
d. Added capital expenditures will be $100,000 in year 5, $120,000 in year 10, and $130,000 in year 15.
e. An estimate of salvage value (net of the tax effect of gains or losses) of the assets after 20 years is estimated to be $300,000. This is a conservative assumption since the unit may be operated after that period.

Required ▶ ▶ ▶ ▶ ▶

1. Prepare a schedule of net-of-tax cash flows for Frontier and discount them to present value.
2. Compare the estimated fair value of the reporting unit with amounts assigned to identifiable assets plus goodwill less liabilities.
3. Record the acquisition.

Part C. Revisit the information in Part A that illustrates the reporting unit valuation procedure.

Assume that by fiscal year-end, December 31, 2015, events occur that suggest goodwill could be impaired. You have the following information. These new estimates are made at the end of the first year:

Net book value of Frontier Company including goodwill	$1,300,000
Estimated implied fair value of the reporting unit, based on cash flow analysis discounted at a 12% annual rate.	1,200,000
Estimated fair value of identifiable net assets using methods excluding goodwill	1,020,000

Required ▶ ▶ ▶ ▶ ▶

Has goodwill been impaired? Perform the impairment testing procedure. If goodwill has been impaired, calculate the adjustment to goodwill and make the needed entry.

Case 1-2   *Disney Acquires Marvel Entertainment*

On December 31, 2009, The Walt Disney Company acquired all the capital stock of Marvel Entertainment Company. Marvel has created heroes such as Spiderman, the Hulk, and Iron Man.

Disney acquired 79.2 million shares of Marvel Entertainment's shares. Disney issued 59 million shares of Disney stock plus $30 for each share of Marvel Entertainment stock. Disney stock, which has a par value of $0.01 per share, had a market value of $32.25 per share. The estimated fair value of Marvel Entertainment accounts were as follows:

Cash and cash eqivalents	$ 105,000,000
Receivables	141,000,000
Capitalized film costs	269,000,000
Intangible assets	3,140,000,000
Accounts payable	(325,000,000)
Other liabilities*	(83,000,000)
Deferred income tax liability	(1,121,000,000)

* Other liabilities was actually a noncontrolling interest which is actually an equity interest that is discussed in Chapter 2.

Required ▶ ▶ ▶ ▶ ▶

1. Using the Federal Trade Commission's classification of merger types, how would you classify the acquisition?
2. Calculate the total price paid for Marvel Entertainment. Is there goodwill or a gain?
3. Record the acquisition.

Chapter 2

Consolidated Statements: Date of Acquisition

Learning Objectives

When you have completed this chapter, you should be able to

1. Differentiate among the accounting methods used for investments, based on the level of common stock ownership in another company.

2. State the criteria for presenting consolidated statements, and explain why disclosure of separate subsidiary financial information might be important.

3. Demonstrate the worksheet procedures needed to eliminate the investment account.

4. Demonstrate the worksheet procedures needed to consolidate parent and subsidiary accounts.

5. Apply value analysis to guide the adjustment process to reflect the price paid for the controlling interest.

6. Develop a determination and distribution of excess (D&D) schedule that will guide the worksheet procedures needed to consolidate a subsidiary.

7. Explain the impact of a noncontrolling interest on worksheet procedures and financial statement preparation.

8. Show the impact of preexisting goodwill on the consolidation process, and be able to include prior investments in the acquisition price.

9. Define push-down accounting, and explain when it may be used and its impact.

10. Demonstrate worksheet procedures for reverse acquisitions. (Appendix)

The preceding chapter dealt with business combinations that are accomplished as asset acquisitions. The net assets of an entire company are acquired and recorded directly on the books of the acquiring company. Consolidation of the two companies is automatic because all subsequent transactions are recorded on a single set of books.

A company will commonly acquire a large enough interest in another company's voting common stock to obtain control of operations. The company owning the controlling interest is termed the *parent*, while the controlled company is termed the *subsidiary*. Legally, the parent company has only an investment in the stock of the subsidiary and will only record an investment account in its accounting records. The subsidiary will continue to prepare its own financial statements. However, accounting principles require that when one company has effective control over another, a single set of *consolidated statements* must be prepared for the companies under common control. The consolidated statements present the financial statements of the parent and its subsidiaries as those of a single economic entity. Worksheets are prepared to merge the separate statements of the parent and its subsidiary(s) into a single set of consolidated statements.

This chapter is the first of several that will show how to combine the separate statements of a parent and its subsidiaries. The theory of *acquisition accounting*, developed in Chapter 1, is applied in the consolidation process. In fact, the consolidated statements of a parent and its 100%

owned subsidiary look exactly like they would have had the net assets been acquired. **This chapter contains only the procedures necessary to prepare consolidated statements on the day that the controlling investment is acquired.** The procedures for consolidating controlling investments in periods subsequent to the acquisition date will be developed in Chapter 3. The effect of operating activities between the parent and its subsidiaries, such as intercompany loans, merchandise sales, fixed asset sales, bonds, and leases, will be discussed in Chapters 4 and 5. Later chapters will deal with taxation issues and changes in the level of ownership.

1

Differentiate among the accounting methods used for investments, based on the level of common stock ownership in another company.

LEVELS OF INVESTMENT

The purchase of the voting common stock of another company receives different accounting treatments depending on the level of ownership and the amount of influence or control caused by the stock ownership. The ownership levels and accounting methods can be summarized as follows:

Level of Ownership	Initial Recording	Recording of Income
Passive—generally under 20% ownership.	At cost including brokers' fees.	Dividends as declared (except stock dividends).
Influential—generally 20% to 50% ownership.	At cost including brokers' fees.	Ownership share of income (or loss) is reported. Shown as investment income on financial statements. (Dividends declared are distributions of income already recorded; they reduce the investment account.)
Controlling—generally over 50% ownership.	At cost.	Ownership share of income (or loss). (Some adjustments are explained in later chapters.) Accomplished by consolidating the subsidiary income statement accounts with those of the parent in the consolidation process.

To illustrate the differences in reporting the income applicable to the common stock shares owned, consider the following example based on the reported income of the investor and investee (the company whose shares are owned by investor):

Account	Investor*	Investee
Sales	$500,000	$300,000
Less: Cost of goods sold.	250,000	180,000
Gross profit	$250,000	$120,000
Less: Selling and administrative expenses	100,000	80,000
Net income	$150,000	$ 40,000

*Does not include any income from investee.

Assume that the investee company paid $10,000 in cash dividends. The investor would prepare the following income statements, depending on the level of ownership:

Level of Ownership	10% Passive	30% Influential	80% Controlling
Sales	$ 500,000	$ 500,000	$ 800,000
Less: Cost of goods sold.	250,000	250,000	430,000
Gross profit	$ 250,000	$ 250,000	$ 370,000
Less: Selling and administrative expenses	100,000	100,000	180,000

(continued)

Level of Ownership	10% Passive	30% Influential	80% Controlling
Operating income	$ 150,000	$ 150,000	
Dividend income (10% × $10,000 dividends)	1,000		
Investment income (30% × $40,000 reported income)		12,000	
Net income	**$151,000**	**$162,000**	$ 190,000
Distribution of income:			
Noncontrolling interest (20% × $40,000 reported income)			$ 8,000
Controlling interest (100% of investor's $150,000 + 80% of investee's $40,000)			**$182,000**

With a 10% passive interest, the investor included only its share of the dividends declared by the investee as its income. With a 30% influential ownership interest, the investor reported 30% of the investee income as a separate source of income. With an 80% controlling interest, the investor (now termed the parent) merges the investee's (now a subsidiary) nominal accounts with its own amounts. Dividend and investment income no longer exist. A single set of financial statements replaces the separate statement of the entities. If the parent owned a 100% interest, net income would simply be reported as $190,000. Since this is only an 80% interest, the net income must be shown as distributed between the noncontrolling and controlling interests. The noncontrolling interest is the 20% of the subsidiary that is not owned by the parent. The controlling interest is the parent income plus 80% of the subsidiary income.

R E F L E C T I O N

- An influential investment (generally over 20% ownership) requires recording, as a single line-item amount, the investor's share of the investee's income as it is earned.

- A controlling investment (generally over 50% ownership) requires that subsidiary income statement accounts be combined with those of the parent company.

- The essence of consolidated reporting is the portrayal of the separate legal entities as a single economic entity.

FUNCTION OF CONSOLIDATED STATEMENTS

2

OBJECTIVE

State the criteria for presenting consolidated statements, and explain why disclosure of separate subsidiary financial information might be important.

Consolidated financial statements are designed to present the results of operations, cash flow, and the balance sheet of both the parent and its subsidiaries as if they were a single company. Generally, consolidated statements are the most informative to the stockholders of the controlling company. Yet, consolidated statements do have their shortcomings. The rights of the noncontrolling shareholders are limited to only the company they own, and, therefore, they get little value from consolidated statements. They really need the separate statements of the subsidiary. Similarly, creditors of the subsidiary need its separate statements because they may look only to the legal entity that is indebted to them for satisfaction of their claims. The parent's creditors should be content with the consolidated statements, since the investment in the subsidiary will produce cash flows that can be used to satisfy their claims.

Consolidated statements have been criticized for being too aggregated. Unprofitable subsidiaries may not be very obvious because, when consolidated, their performance is combined with that of other affiliates. However, this shortcoming is easily overcome. One option is to prepare separate statements of the subsidiary as supplements to the consolidated statements. The second option, which may be required, is to provide disclosure for major business segments. When subsidiaries are in businesses distinct from the parent, the definition of a segment may parallel that of a subsidiary.

Criteria for Consolidated Statements

Under U.S. GAAP, there are two models that determine when consolidation of financial statements is required. The most common model is based on control of a voting interest entity. That is an entity with common stock where the investor company owns over 50% of the voting common shares. That ownership interest is referred to as a "Controlling Interest." There are, however, exceptions where control may also exist with a lesser percentage of ownership such as when there is control via contract, lease, agreement with other shareholders, or by court decree.[1] The Securities and Exchange Commission (SEC) also requires consolidation where an affiliate is not majority-owned. The situations where this could apply are:

1. The company financed the affiliate directly or indirectly.
2. The company owns securities that upon exercise or conversion would create majority ownership.
3. The company will compensate the affiliate for incurred start-up losses.

The second FASB model applies to variable interest entities (VIE). The definition of a VIE is based on an entity meeting one of four requirements:

1. The possible investor and its related companies participate significantly in the design of the entity. The entity cannot be a joint venture or a franchisee.
2. The entity is designed such that almost all of its activities include or are for the benefit of the investor.
3. The investor and its related companies provide over 50% of the equity, subordinated debt, or other subordinated financial support of the entity. This test is based on the fair value of the entity.
4. The entity's activities are mainly financial in nature involving securitizations, asset-backed financing, or leasing benefiting the investor.

The unique consolidation procedures for VIEs are covered in an appendix to this chapter.

Consolidation may also be required when a not-for-profit (NFP) entity has a controlling interest in another NFP. Control can be based on ownership of a majority interest or if there are an economic interest and a majority voting interest. This topic is treated in Chapter 18.

REFLECTION

- The combining of the statements of a parent and its subsidiaries into consolidated statements is required when parent ownership exceeds 50% of the controlled firm's shares.

- Consolidation is required for any company that is controlled, even in cases where less than 51% of the company's shares is owned by the parent.

TECHNIQUES OF CONSOLIDATION

3

OBJECTIVE

Demonstrate the worksheet procedures needed to eliminate the investment account.

This chapter builds an understanding of the techniques used to consolidate the separate balance sheets of a parent and its subsidiary immediately subsequent to the acquisition. The consolidated balance sheet as of the acquisition date is discussed first. The impact of consolidations on operations after the acquisition date is discussed in Chapters 3 through 8.

Chapter 1 emphasized that there are two means of achieving control over the assets of another company. A company may directly acquire the assets of another company, or it may acquire a controlling interest in the other company's voting common stock. In an *asset acquisition,* the company

---

1 FASB 810-10-15-8.

whose assets were acquired is dissolved. The assets acquired are recorded directly on the books of the acquirer, and consolidation of balance sheet amounts is automatic. Where control is achieved through a *stock acquisition,* the acquired company (the subsidiary) remains as a separate legal entity with its own financial statements. While the initial accounting for the two types of acquisitions differs significantly, a 100% stock acquisition and an asset acquisition have the same effect of creating one larger single reporting entity and should produce the same consolidated balance sheet. There is, however, a difference if the stock acquisition is less than 100%. Then, there will be a noncontrolling interest in the consolidated balance sheet. This is not possible when the assets are purchased directly.

In the following discussion, the recording of an asset acquisition and a 100% stock acquisition are compared, and the balance sheets that result from each type of acquisition are studied. Then, the chapter deals with the accounting procedures needed when there is less than a 100% stock ownership and a noncontrolling equity interest exists.

Reviewing an Asset Acquisition

Illustration 2-1 demonstrates an asset acquisition of Company S by Company P for cash. Part A of the exhibit presents the balance sheets of the two companies just prior to the acquisition. Part B shows the entry to record Company P's payment of $500,000 in cash for the net assets of Company S. The book values of the assets and liabilities acquired are assumed to be representative of their fair values, and no goodwill is acknowledged. The assets and liabilities of Company S are added to those of Company P to produce the balance sheet for the combined company, shown in Part C. Since account balances are combined in recording the acquisition, **statements for the single combined reporting entity are produced automatically, and no consolidation process is needed**.

Illustration 2-1
Asset Acquisition

Part A. Balance sheets of Companies P and S prior to acquisition:

Company P Balance Sheet

Assets		Liabilities and Equity	
Cash	$ 800,000	Current liabilities	$ 150,000
Accounts receivable	300,000	Bonds payable	500,000
Inventory	100,000	Common stock............	100,000
Equipment (net)	150,000	Retained earnings	600,000
Total.................	$1,350,000	Total.................	$1,350,000

Company S Balance Sheet

Assets		Liabilities and Equity	
Accounts receivable	$200,000	Current liabilities	$100,000
Inventory	100,000	Common stock............	200,000
Equipment (net)	300,000	Retained earnings	300,000
Total.................	$600,000	Total.................	$600,000

Part B. Entry on Company P's books to record acquisition of the net assets of Company S by Company P:

Accounts Receivable	200,000	
Inventory	100,000	
Equipment	300,000	
Current Liabilities.................................		100,000
Cash		500,000

(continued)

Part C. Balance sheet of Company P (the combined company) subsequent to asset acquisition:

Company P Balance Sheet

Assets		Liabilities and Equity	
Cash	$ 300,000	Current liabilities	$ 250,000
Accounts receivable	500,000	Bonds payable	500,000
Inventory	200,000	Common stock.	100,000
Equipment (net)	450,000	Retained earnings	600,000
Total.	$1,450,000	Total.	$1,450,000

Consolidating a Stock Acquisition

In a stock acquisition, the acquiring company deals only with existing shareholders, not the company itself. Assuming the same facts as those used in Illustration 2-1, except that Company P will acquire all the outstanding stock of Company S from its shareholders for $500,000, Company P would make the following entry:

Investment in Subsidiary S	500,000	
Cash		500,000

This entry does not record the individual underlying assets and liabilities over which control is achieved. Instead, the acquisition is recorded in an investment account that represents the controlling interest in the net assets of the subsidiary. If no further action was taken, the investment in the subsidiary account would appear as a long-term investment on Company P's balance sheet. However, such a presentation is permitted only if consolidation were not required (i.e., when control does not exist).

Assuming consolidated statements are required (i.e., when control does exist), the balance sheet of the two companies must be combined into a single consolidated balance sheet. The consolidation process is separate from the existing accounting records of the companies and requires completion of a worksheet. No journal entries are actually made to the parent's or subsidiary's books, so the elimination process starts anew each year.

Worksheet 2-1: page 89
The first example of a consolidated worksheet, Worksheet 2-1, appears later in the chapter on page 89. (The icon in the margin indicates the location of the worksheet at the end of the chapter.) The first two columns of the worksheet include the trial balances (balance sheet only for this chapter) for Companies P and S. The trial balances and the consolidated balance sheet are presented in single columns to save space. Credit balances are shown in parentheses. Obviously, since there are no nominal accounts listed, the income statement accounts have already been closed to Retained Earnings.

The consolidated worksheet requires elimination of the investment account balance because the two companies will be treated as one. (How can a company have an investment in itself?) Similarly, the subsidiary's stockholders' equity accounts are eliminated because its assets and liabilities belong to the parent, not to outside equity owners. In general journal form, the elimination entry is as follows:

(EL)	Common Stock, Company S	200,000	
	Retained Earnings, Company S.	300,000	
	Investment in Company		500,000

Note that the key (EL) will be used in all future worksheets. Keys, once introduced, will be assigned to all similar items throughout the text. For quick reference, a listing of these keys is provided on the inside front cover of this text. The balances in the Consolidated Balance Sheet column (the last column) are exactly the same as in the balance sheet prepared for the preceding asset acquisition example—as they should be for a 100% stock acquisition.

REFLECTION

- Consolidation when a parent owns 100% of the subsidiary's voting common stock produces the same balance sheet that would result in an asset acquisition.

- Consolidated statements are derived from the individual statements of the parent and its subsidiaries.

ADJUSTMENT OF SUBSIDIARY ACCOUNTS

In the last example, the price paid for the investment in the subsidiary was equal to the net book value of the subsidiary (which means the price was also equal to the subsidiary's stockholders' equity). In most acquisitions, the price will exceed the book value of the subsidiary's net assets. Typically, fair values will exceed the recorded book values of assets. The price may also reflect unrecorded intangible assets, including goodwill. Let us revisit the last example and assume that instead of paying $500,000 cash, Company P paid $700,000 cash for all the common stock shares of Company S and made the following entry for the purchase:

Investment in Subsidiary S	700,000	
Cash		700,000

Use the same Company S balance sheet as in Illustration 2-1, with the following additional information on fair values:

Company S Book and Estimated Fair Values
December 31, 2015

Assets	Book Value	Fair Value	Liabilities and Equity	Book Value	Fair Value
Accounts receivable	$ 200,000	$ 200,000	Current liabilities	$100,000	$ 100,000
Inventory	100,000	120,000			
Equipment (net)	300,000	400,000	**Market value of net assets**		
			(assets − liabilities)		**$620,000**
Total assets	**$600,000**	**$720,000**			

If this were an asset acquisition, the identifiable assets and liabilities would be recorded at fair value and goodwill at $80,000. This is the price paid of $700,000 minus the $620,000 ($720,000 total assets − $100,000 total liabilities) fair value of net assets. Adding fair values to Company P's accounts, the new balance sheet would appear as follows:

Company P
Consolidated Balance Sheet
December 31, 2015

Assets		Liabilities and Equity	
Current assets:		Current liabilities	$250,000
Cash	$100,000	Bonds payable	500,000
Accounts receivable.	500,000	Total liabilities	$ 750,000
Inventory	220,000		
Total current assets.		$ 820,000	

(continued)

Assets		Liabilities and Equity	
Long-term assets:		**Stockholders' equity:**	
Equipment (net)	$550,000	Common stock	$100,000
Goodwill	80,000	Retained earnings	600,000
Total long-term assets ...	630,000	Total equity	700,000
Total assets	$1,450,000	Total liabilities and equity ...	$1,450,000

Worksheet 2-2: page 90

As before, the consolidated worksheet should produce a consolidated balance sheet that looks exactly the same as the preceding balance sheet for an asset acquisition. Worksheet 2-2, on page 90, shows how this is accomplished.

◆ The (EL) entry is the same as before: $500,000 of subsidiary equity is eliminated against the investment account.

◆ Entry **(D)** distributes the remaining cost of $200,000 to the acquired assets to bring them from book to fair value and to record goodwill of $80,000.

In general journal entry form, the elimination entries are as follows:

(EL)	Common Stock, Company S	200,000	
	Retained Earnings, Company S	300,000	
	Investment in Company S		500,000
(D1)	Inventory (to increase from $100,000 to $120,000)	20,000	
(D2)	Equipment (to increase from $300,000 to $400,000)	100,000	
(D3)	Goodwill ($700,000 price minus $620,000 fair value		
	assets)	80,000	
(D)	Investment in Company S ($700,000 price minus		
	$500,000 book value eliminated above)		200,000

The Consolidated Balance Sheet column of Worksheet 2-2 includes the subsidiary accounts at full fair value and reflects the $80,000 of goodwill included in the purchase price. The formal balance sheet for Company P, based on the worksheet, would be exactly the same as shown above for the asset acquisition.

Acquisition of a subsidiary at a price in excess of the fair values of the subsidiary equity is as simple as the case just presented, especially where there are a limited number of assets to adjust to fair value. For more involved acquisitions, where there are many accounts to adjust and/or the price paid is less than the fair value of the net assets, a more complete analysis is needed. We will now proceed to develop these tools.

Analysis of Complicated Purchases—100% Interest

5

OBJECTIVE

Apply value analysis to guide the adjustment process to reflect the price paid for the controlling interest.

The previous examples assumed the purchase of the subsidiary for cash. However, most acquisitions are accomplished by the parent issuing common stock (or, less often, preferred stock) in exchange for the subsidiary common shares being acquired. This avoids the depletion of cash and, if other criteria are met, allows the subsidiary shareholders to have a tax-free exchange. In most cases, the shares are issued by a publicly traded parent company that provides a readily determinable market price for the shares issued. The investment in the subsidiary is then recorded at the fair value of the shares issued. Less frequently, a nonpublicly traded parent may issue shares to subsidiary shareholders. In these cases, the fair values are determined for the net assets of the subsidiary company, and the total estimated fair value of the subsidiary company is recorded as the cost of the investment.

In order to illustrate the complete procedures used to record the investment in and the consolidation of a subsidiary, we will consider the acquisition of a 100% interest in Sample Company. The book and fair values of the net assets of Sample Company on December 31, 2015, when Parental, Inc., acquired 100% of its shares, were as follows:

Assets	Book Value	Market Value	Liabilities and Equity	Book Value	Market Value
Accounts receivable	$ 20,000	$ 20,000	Current liabilities	$ 40,000	$ 40,000
Inventory	50,000	55,000	Bonds payable	100,000	100,000
Land....................	40,000	70,000	**Total liabilities**...............	**$140,000**	**$140,000**
Buildings	200,000	250,000			
Accumulated depreciation ..	(50,000)		Stockholders' equity:		
Equipment	60,000	60,000	Common stock ($1 par).............	$ 10,000	
Accumulated depreciation ..	(20,000)		Paid-in capital in excess of par	90,000	
Copyright		50,000	Retained earnings	60,000	
			Total equity	**$160,000**	
Total assets	$300,000	$505,000	**Net assets**....................	**$160,000**	**$365,000**

Assume that Parental, Inc., issued 20,000 shares of its $1 par value common stock for 100% (10,000 shares) of the outstanding shares of Sample Company. The fair value of a share of Parental, Inc., stock is $25. Parental also pays $25,000 in accounting and legal fees to accomplish the purchase. Parental would make the following entry to record the purchase:

Investment in Sample Company (20,000 shares issued × $25 fair value) ...	500,000	
Common Stock ($1 par value) (20,000 shares × $1 par)............		20,000
Paid-In Capital in Excess of Par ($500,000 − $20,000 par value)		480,000

Parental would record the costs of the acquisition as follows:

Acquisition Expense (closed to Retained Earnings since only balance sheets are being examined)..	25,000	
Cash...		25,000

A value analysis schedule has been designed to compare the fair value of the company acquired with the fair value of the net assets. In this case, the fair value of the company is based on the value of the shares exchanged by Parental, Inc. The schedule includes a column for a noncontrolling interest (NCI) for later cases when the parent does not acquire a 100% interest.

Value Analysis Schedule	Company Implied Fair Value	Parent Price (100%)	NCI Value (0%)
Company fair value..................................	$ 500,000	$ 500,000	N/A
Fair value of net assets excluding goodwill	365,000	365,000	
Goodwill......................................	**$135,000**	**$135,000**	
Gain on acquisition................................	N/A	N/A	

Notice the following features of the value analysis:

◆ In this case, the company fair value exceeds the fair value of the net assets. This means that all subsidiary accounts will be adjusted to fair value, and goodwill of $135,000 will be shown on the consolidated balance sheet.

◆ If the company fair value was less than the fair value of the net assets, all of the subsidiary accounts would still be adjusted to fair value and a gain on the acquisition would be recorded.

REFLECTION

• The value analysis schedule determines if there will be goodwill or a gain as a result of consolidating the subsidiary with the parent.

DETERMINATION AND DISTRIBUTION OF EXCESS SCHEDULE

The *determination and distribution of excess (D&D) schedule* is used to compare the company fair value with the recorded book value of the subsidiary. It also schedules the adjustments that will be made to all subsidiary accounts in the consolidated worksheet process. The D&D schedule below is for a 100% interest, but is built to accommodate an NCI in later examples.

Determination and Distribution of Excess Schedule

	Company Implied Fair Value	Parent Price (100%)	NCI Value (0%)
Fair value of subsidiary	$ 500,000	$500,000	N/A
Less book value of interest acquired:			
Common stock ($1 par)	$ 10,000		
Paid-in capital in excess of par	90,000		
Retained earnings	60,000		
Total stockholders' equity	$ 160,000	$160,000	
Interest acquired		100%	
Book value		$160,000	
Excess of fair value over book value	**$340,000** ←	$340,000	

Adjustment of identifiable accounts:

	Adjustment	**Worksheet Key**
Inventory ($55,000 fair − $50,000 book value)	$ 5,000	**debit D1**
Land ($70,000 fair − $40,000 book value)	30,000	**debit D2**
Buildings ($250,000 fair − $150,000 net book value)	100,000	**debit D3**
Equipment ($60,000 fair − $40,000 net book value) .	20,000	**debit D4**
Copyright ($50,000 fair − $0 book value)	50,000	**debit D5**
Goodwill	**135,000**	**debit D6**
Total	**$340,000** ←	

Note the following features of the above D&D schedule:

♦ Since this is a 100% interest, the parent price and the implied value of the subsidiary are equal.

♦ The total adjustment that will have to be made to subsidiary net assets on the worksheet is $340,000.

♦ The schedule shows the adjustments to each subsidiary account. Recall that in Chapter 1, we recorded the entire value of the subsidiary accounts in the acquisition entry. Now the subsidiary assets are already listed on the worksheet at book value, and they only need to be adjusted to fair value.

Worksheet 2-3: page 91

The D&D schedule provides complete guidance for the worksheet eliminations. Study Worksheet 2-3 on page 91 and note the following:

♦ Elimination (EL) eliminated the subsidiary equity purchased (100% in this example) against the investment account as follows:

(EL)	Common Stock ($1 par)—Sample	10,000	
	Paid-In Capital in Excess of Par—Sample	90,000	
	Retained Earnings—Sample	60,000	
	Investment in Sample Company		160,000

◆ The (D) series eliminations distribute the $340,000 excess to the appropriate accounts, as indicated by the D&D schedule. A valuable check is to be sure that the investment account is now eliminated. If it has not been eliminated, there has been an error in the balances entered into the Balance Sheet columns of the worksheet. Worksheet eliminations are as follows:

(D1)	Inventory	5,000	
(D2)	Land	30,000	
(D3)	Buildings	100,000	
(D4)	Equipment	20,000	
(D5)	Copyright	50,000	
(D6)	Goodwill	135,000	
(D)	Investment in Sample Company [remaining excess after (EL)]		340,000
Dr. = Cr.	Check Totals	340,000	340,000

The amounts that will appear on the consolidated balance sheet are shown in the final column of Worksheet 2-3. Notice that we have consolidated 100% of the fair values of subsidiary accounts with the existing book values of parent company accounts.

Formal Balance Sheet

The formal consolidated balance sheet resulting from the 100% purchase of Sample Company, in exchange for 20,000 Parental shares, has been taken from the Consolidated Balance Sheet column of Worksheet 2-3.

Parental, Inc.
Consolidated Balance Sheet
December 31, 2015

Assets			Liabilities and Equity		
Current assets:			Current liabilities	$120,000	
Cash	$ 84,000		Bonds payable	300,000	
Accounts receivable	92,000		Total liabilities		$ 420,000
Inventory	135,000				
Total current assets		$ 311,000			
Long-term assets:			Stockholders' equity:		
Land	$ 170,000		Common stock ($1 par)	$ 40,000	
Buildings	800,000		Paid-in capital in excess of par	680,000	
Accumulated			Retained earnings	456,000	
depreciation	(130,000)				
Equipment	320,000		Total controlling equity		1,176,000
Accumulated					
depreciation	(60,000)				
Copyright (net)	50,000				
Goodwill (net)	135,000				
Total long-term assets		1,285,000			
Total assets		$1,596,000	Total liabilities and equity		$1,596,000

Bargain Purchase

A bargain purchase refers to an acquisition at a price that is less than the fair value of the subsidiary net identifiable assets. Let us change the prior example to assume that Parental, Inc., issued only 12,000 shares of its stock. The entry to record the purchase would be as shown on next page.

Investment in Sample Company (12,000 shares issued × $25 fair value) . .	300,000	
Common Stock ($1 par value) (12,000 shares × $1 par).		12,000
Paid-In Capital in Excess of Par ($300,000 − $12,000 par value)		288,000

The entry to record the costs of the acquisition would be as follows:

Acquisition Expense (closed to Retained Earnings since only balance sheets are being examined)	25,000	
Cash		25,000

The value analysis schedule would compare the price paid with the fair value of the subsidiary net identifiable assets as follows:

Value Analysis Schedule	Company Implied Fair Value	Parent Price (100%)	NCI Value (0%)
Company fair value.	$ 300,000	$ 300,000	N/A
Fair value of net assets excluding goodwill . .	365,000	365,000	
Goodwill	N/A	N/A	
Gain on acquisition	**$(65,000)**	**$(65,000)**	

The D&D schedule would be as follows for the $300,000 price:

Determination and Distribution of Excess Schedule

	Company Implied Fair Value	Parent Price (100%)	NCI Value (0%)
Fair value of subsidiary	$ 300,000	$300,000	N/A
Less book value of interest acquired:			
Common stock ($1 par)	$ 10,000		
Paid-in capital in excess of par	90,000		
Retained earnings	60,000		
Total equity	$ 160,000	$160,000	
Interest acquired		100%	
Book value.		$160,000	
Excess of fair value over book value	**$140,000**	$140,000	

Adjustment of identifiable accounts:

	Adjustment	Worksheet Key
Inventory ($55,000 fair − $50,000 book value)	$ 5,000	**debit D1**
Land ($70,000 fair − $40,000 book value).	30,000	**debit D2**
Buildings ($250,000 fair − $150,000 net book value)	100,000	**debit D3**
Equipment ($60,000 fair − $40,000 net book value)	20,000	**debit D4**
Copyright ($50,000 fair − $0 book value).	50,000	**debit D5**
Gain on acquisition	**(65,000)**	**credit D7**
Total	**$140,000**	

Note the following features of the above D&D schedule:

◆ All identifiable net assets are still adjusted to full fair value even though it was a bargain purchase.

◆ A gain will be distributed to the parent on the worksheet.

The D&D schedule provides complete guidance for the worksheet eliminations. Study Worksheet 2-4 on page 92 and note the following:

Worksheet 2-4: page 92

◆ Elimination (EL) eliminated the subsidiary equity purchased (100% in this example) against the investment account as follows:

(EL)	Common Stock ($1 par)—Sample	10,000	
	Paid-In Capital in Excess of Par—Sample	90,000	
	Retained Earnings—Sample	60,000	
	Investment in Sample Company		160,000

◆ The (D) series eliminations distribute the $100,000 excess to the appropriate accounts, as indicated by the D&D schedule. Worksheet eliminations are as follows:

(D1)	Inventory	5,000	
(D2)	Land	30,000	
(D3)	Buildings	100,000	
(D4)	Equipment	20,000	
(D5)	Copyright	50,000	
(D7)	**Retained Earnings—Parental***		**65,000**
(D)	Investment in Sample Company [remaining excess after (EL)]		140,000
Dr. = Cr.	Check Totals	205,000	205,000

*Since only a balance sheet is being prepared, the gain on the acquisition is closed directly to Parental Retained Earnings.

The amounts that will appear on the consolidated balance sheet are shown in the final column of Worksheet 2-4. Notice that 100% of the fair values of subsidiary accounts has been consolidated with the existing book values of parent company accounts.

There could be an unusual situation where the price paid by the parent is less than the book value of the subsidiary net assets. For example, if the price paid by the parent was only $150,000, the value analysis schedule would be as follows:

Value Analysis Schedule	Company Implied Fair Value	Parent Price (100%)	NCI Value (0%)
Company fair value....................	$ 150,000	$ 150,000	N/A
Fair value of net assets excluding goodwill . .	365,000	365,000	
Goodwill	N/A	N/A	
Gain on acquisition	**$(215,000)**	**$(215,000)**	

The D&D schedule would be as follows for the $150,000 price:

Determination and Distribution of Excess Schedule

	Company Implied Fair Value	Parent Price (100%)	NCI Value (0%)
Fair value of subsidiary	$ 150,000	$150,000	N/A
Less book value of interest acquired:			
Common stock ($1 par).................	$ 10,000		
Paid-in capital in excess of par	90,000		
Retained earnings	60,000		
Total equity.........................	$ 160,000	$160,000	
Interest acquired		100%	
Book value...........................		$160,000	
Excess of fair value over book value	$ (10,000)	$ (10,000)	

Adjustment of identifiable accounts:

	Adjustment		Worksheet Key
Inventory ($55,000 fair − $50,000 book value)	$ 5,000		**debit D1**
Land ($70,000 fair − $40,000 book value)...	30,000		**debit D2**
Buildings ($250,000 fair − $150,000 book value)	100,000		**debit D3**
Equipment ($60,000 fair − $40,000 book value)	20,000		**debit D4**
Copyright ($50,000 fair − $0 book value)....	50,000		**debit D5**
Gain on acquisition*	**(215,000)**		**credit D7**
Total	**$ (10,000)**		

*Agrees with total (company) gain in the value analysis schedule.

The eliminations on the worksheet would be as follows:

◆ Elimination (EL) eliminated the subsidiary equity purchased (100% in this example) against the investment account as follows:

(EL)	Common Stock ($1 par)—Sample	10,000	
	Paid-In Capital in Excess of Par—Sample	90,000	
	Retained Earnings—Sample	60,000	
	Investment in Sample Company.....................		160,000

◆ The (D) series eliminations distribute the $10,000 negative excess to the appropriate accounts, as indicated by the D&D schedule. Worksheet eliminations are as follows:

(D1)	Inventory	5,000	
(D2)	Land	30,000	
(D3)	Buildings	100,000	
(D4)	Equipment	20,000	
(D5)	Copyright	50,000	
(D7)	Retained Earnings—Parental*		215,000
(D)	Investment in Sample Company [remaining excess after **(EL)**]	10,000	
Dr. = Cr.	Check Totals	215,000	215,000

*Since only a balance sheet is being prepared, the gain on the acquisition is closed directly to Parental Retained Earnings.

A worksheet, in this case, would debit the investment account $10,000 to cure the distribution of adjustments to subsidiary accounts that exceed the amount available for distribution.

REFLECTION

• The D&D schedule compares the price paid for the investment in the subsidiary with subsidiary book values and schedules the adjustments to be made on the worksheet.

• The worksheet adjusts the subsidiary accounts to fair values and adds them to the parent accounts to arrive at a consolidated balance sheet.

CONSOLIDATING WITH A NONCONTROLLING INTEREST

7

OBJECTIVE

Explain the impact of a noncontrolling interest on worksheet procedures and financial statement preparation.

Consolidation of financial statements is required whenever the parent company controls a subsidiary. In other words, a parent company could consolidate far less than a 100% ownership interest. If a parent company owns 80% of the common stock of a company, the remaining 20% interest is noncontrolling interest. Several important ramifications may arise when less than 100% interest is consolidated.

◆ The parent's investment account is eliminated against only its ownership percentage of the underlying subsidiary equity accounts.[2] The NCI is shown on the consolidated balance sheet in total and is not broken into par, paid-in capital in excess of par, and retained earnings. The NCI must be shown as a component of stockholders' equity. In the past, the NCI has also been displayed on the consolidated balance sheet as a liability, or in some cases has appeared between the liability and equity sections of the balance sheet. These alternatives are no longer allowed.

◆ The entire amount of every subsidiary nominal (income statement) account is merged with the nominal accounts of the parent to calculate consolidated income. *The noncontrolling interest is allocated its percentage ownership times the reported income of the subsidiary only.* The precise methods and display of this interest are discussed in Chapter 3. In the past, this share of income has often been treated as an other expense in the consolidated income statement. FASB ASC 810-10-65-1 requires that it not be shown as an expense but, rather, as a distribution of consolidated income.

◆ Subsidiary accounts are adjusted to full fair value regardless of the controlling interest percentage. Prior to 2009, subsidiary accounts would only be adjusted to the controlling interest percentage ownership interest. For example, assume that the parent owns an 80% interest in the subsidiary. Further assume that the book value of equipment is $100,000 and

2 FASB ASC 810-10-65-1.

that its fair value is $150,000. Past practice would have been to adjust the asset by $40,000 (80% ownership interest × $50,000 fair value-book value difference). The new requirement is that the asset will be adjusted for the full $50,000 difference no matter what size the controlling interest is.

Analysis of Complicated Purchase with a Noncontrolling Interest

We will illustrate consolidation procedures using the 80% acquisition of Sample Company by Parental, Inc. Presented below are the balance sheet amounts and the fair values of the assets and liabilities of Sample Company as of December 31, 2015 (same as prior example on page 63).

Assets	Book Value	Market Value	Liabilities and Equity	Book Value	Market Value
Accounts receivable	$ 20,000	$ 20,000	Current liabilities	$ 40,000	$ 40,000
Inventory	50,000	55,000	Bonds payable	100,000	100,000
Land.	40,000	70,000	**Total liabilities**.	**$140,000**	**$140,000**
Buildings	200,000	250,000			
Accumulated depreciation	(50,000)		Stockholders' equity:		
Equipment	60,000	60,000	Common stock ($1 par).	$ 10,000	
Accumulated depreciation	(20,000)		Paid-in capital in excess of par	90,000	
Copyright		50,000	Retained earnings	60,000	
			Total equity	$ 160,000	
Total assets	**$300,000**	**$505,000**	**Net assets**.	**$160,000**	**$365,000**

Assume that Parental, Inc., issued 16,000 shares of its $1 par value common stock for 80% (8,000 shares) of the outstanding shares of Sample Company. The fair value of a share of Parental, Inc., stock is $25. Parental also pays $25,000 in accounting and legal fees to accomplish the purchase. Parental would make the following entry to record the purchase:

Investment in Sample Company (16,000 shares issued × $25 fair value)	400,000	
Common Stock ($1 par value) (16,000 shares × $1 par).		16,000
Paid-In Capital in Excess of Par ($400,000 − $16,000 par value)		384,000

Parental would record the costs of the acquisition as follows:

Acquisition Expense (closed to Retained Earnings since only balance sheets are being examined)	25,000	
Cash		25,000

The following value analysis would be prepared for the 80% interest:

Value Analysis Schedule	Company Implied Fair Value	Parent Price (80%)	NCI Value (20%)
Company fair value.	$ 500,000	$ 400,000	$100,000
Fair value of net assets excluding goodwill . .	365,000	292,000	73,000
Goodwill.	**$135,000**	**$108,000**	**$ 27,000**
Gain on acquisition	N/A	N/A	

Several assumptions went into the above calculation.

◆ Company fair value—It is assumed that if the parent would pay $400,000 for an 80% interest, then the entire subsidiary company is worth $500,000 ($400,000/80%). We will refer to this as the "implied value" of the subsidiary company. Assuming this to be true, the NCI is worth 20% of the total subsidiary company value (20% × $500,000 = $100,000).

This approach assumes that the price the parent would pay is directly proportional to the size of the interest purchased. We will later study the situation where this presumption is defeated. **Unless otherwise stated, exercises and problems in this text will assume the value of the NCI is "implied" by the price the parent pays for the controlling interest.**

◆ Fair value of net assets excluding goodwill ($365,000)—The fair values of the subsidiary accounts are from the comparison of book and fair values. All identifiable assets and all liabilities will be adjusted to 100% of fair value regardless of the size of the controlling interest purchased.

◆ Goodwill—The total goodwill is the excess of the "company fair value" over the fair value of the subsidiary net assets. It is proportionately allocated to the controlling interest and NCI.

Determination and Distribution of Excess Schedule

The D&D schedule that follows revalues the entire entity, including the NCI.

Determination and Distribution of Excess Schedule

	Company Implied Fair Value	Parent Price (80%)	NCI Value (20%)
Fair value of subsidiary	$ 500,000	$400,000	$100,000
Less book value of interest acquired:			
Common stock ($1 par)	$ 10,000		
Paid-in capital in excess of par	90,000		
Retained earnings	60,000		
Total equity.	$ 160,000	$160,000	$160,000
Interest acquired		80%	20%
Book value.		$128,000	$ 32,000
Excess of fair value over book value	**$340,000**	$272,000	$ 68,000

Adjustment of identifiable accounts:

	Adjustment		Worksheet Key
Inventory ($55,000 fair − $50,000 book value)	$ 5,000		**debit D1**
Land ($70,000 fair − $40,000 book value).	30,000		**debit D2**
Buildings ($250,000 fair − $150,000 net book value)	100,000		**debit D3**
Equipment ($60,000 fair − $40,000 net book value) .	20,000		**debit D4**
Copyright ($50,000 fair − $0 book value).	50,000		**debit D5**
Goodwill ($500,000 fair − $365,000 book value) .	**135,000***		**debit D6**
Total.	**$340,000**		

*Agrees with total (company) goodwill in the value analysis schedule.

Note the following features of a D&D schedule for a less than 100% parent ownership interest:

◆ The "fair value of subsidiary" line contains the implied value of the entire company, the parent price paid, and the implied value of the NCI from the above value analysis schedule.

◆ The total stockholders' equity of the subsidiary (equal to the net assets of the subsidiary at book value) is allocated 80/20 to the controlling interest and the NCI.

◆ The excess of fair value over book value is shown for the company, the controlling interest, and the NCI. This line means that the entire adjustment of subsidiary net assets will be $340,000. The controlling interest paid $272,000 more than the underlying book value of subsidiary net assets. This is the excess that will appear on the worksheet when the parent's 80% share of subsidiary stockholders' equity is eliminated against the investment account.

Finally, the NCI share of the increase to fair value is $68,000.

♦ All subsidiary assets and liabilities will be increased to 100% of fair value, just as would be the case for a 100% purchase.

Worksheet 2-5: page 93

The D&D schedule provides complete guidance for the worksheet eliminations. Study Worksheet 2-5 on page 93 and note the following:

♦ Elimination (EL) eliminated the subsidiary equity purchased (80% in this example) against the investment account as follows:

(EL)	Common Stock ($1 par)—Sample	8,000	
	Paid-In Capital in Excess of Par—Sample	72,000	
	Retained Earnings—Sample	48,000	
	Investment in Sample Company....................		128,000

♦ The (D) series eliminations distribute the excess applicable to the controlling interest plus the increase in the NCI [labeled (NCI)] to the appropriate accounts, as indicated by the D&D schedule. The adjustment of the NCI is carried to subsidiary retained earnings. Recall, however, that only the total NCI will appear on the consolidated balance sheet. Worksheet eliminations are as follows:

(D1)	Inventory	5,000	
(D2)	Land..	30,000	
(D3)	Buildings	100,000	
(D4)	Equipment	20,000	
(D5)	Copyright	50,000	
(D6)	Goodwill	135,000	
(D)	Investment in Sample Company [remaining excess after (EL)]...................................		272,000
(NCI)	Retained Earnings Sample (NCI share of fair market adjustment).................................		68,000
Dr. = Cr.	Check Totals	340,000	340,000

Worksheet 2-5 has an additional column, the NCI column. The components of the NCI are summed and presented as a single amount in this balance sheet column. Notice that 100% of the fair values of subsidiary accounts has been consolidated with the existing book values of parent company accounts. The amounts that will appear on the consolidated balance sheet are shown in the final column of Worksheet 2-5. The Balance Sheet columns of the worksheet will show the components of controlling equity (par, paid-in capital in excess of par, and retained earnings) and the total NCI.

Formal Balance Sheet

The formal consolidated balance sheet resulting from the 80% purchase of Sample Company, in exchange for 16,000 Parental shares, has been taken from the Consolidated Balance Sheet column of Worksheet 2-5. Recall, this is the date of acquisition. Chapter 3 will explain the impact of subsequent period activities on the consolidated financial statements.

Parental, Inc.
Consolidated Balance Sheet
December 31, 2015

Assets			Liabilities and Equity		
Current assets:			Current liabilities	$120,000	
Cash	$ 84,000		Bonds payable	300,000	
Accounts receivable.	92,000		Total liabilities		$ 420,000
Inventory	135,000				
Total current assets		$ 311,000	Stockholders' equity:		
Long-term assets:			Common stock ($1 par)	$ 36,000	
Land.	$ 170,000		Paid-in capital in excess of par. .	584,000	
Buildings	800,000		Retained earnings	456,000	
Accumulated depreciation. . .	(130,000)		Total controlling equity		1,076,000
Equipment	320,000		**Noncontrolling interest**		**100,000**
Accumulated depreciation. . .	(60,000)		Total equity.		$1,176,000
Copyright.	50,000				
Goodwill	135,000				
Total long-term assets		1,285,000			
Total assets		$1,596,000	Total liabilities and equity		$ 1,596,000

Adjustment of Goodwill Applicable to NCI

The NCI goodwill value can be reduced below its implied value if there is evidence that the implied value exceeds the real fair value of the NCI's share of goodwill. This could occur when a parent pays a premium to achieve control, which is not dependent on the size of the ownership interest.

The NCI share of goodwill could be reduced to zero, but the NCI share of the fair value of net tangible assets is never reduced. **The total NCI can never be less than the NCI percentage of the fair value of the net assets** (in this case, it cannot be less than 20% × $365,000 = $73,000).

If the fair value of the NCI was estimated to be $90,000 ($10,000 less than the value implied by parent purchase price), the value analysis would be modified as follows (changes are boldfaced):

Value Analysis Schedule	Company Implied Fair Value	Parent Price (80%)	NCI Value (20%)
Company fair value.	**$490,000**	$400,000	**$90,000**
Fair value of net assets excluding goodwill	365,000	292,000	73,000
Goodwill.	**$125,000**	$108,000	**$17,000**
Gain on acquisition	N/A	N/A	

Several assumptions went into the above calculation.

◆ Company fair value—This is now the sum of the price paid by the parent plus the newly estimated fair value of the NCI.

◆ Fair value of net assets excluding goodwill—The fair values of the subsidiary accounts are from the comparison of book and fair values. These values are never less than fair value.

◆ Goodwill—The total goodwill is the excess of the "company fair value" over the fair value of the subsidiary net assets.

The revised D&D schedule with changes (from the previous example) in boldfaced type would be as shown on next page.

Determination and Distribution of Excess Schedule

	Company Implied Fair Value	Parent Price (80%)	NCI Value (20%)
Fair value of subsidiary	$ 490,000	$400,000	**$ 90,000**
Less book value of interest acquired:			
Common stock ($1 par).	$ 10,000		
Paid-in capital in excess of par	90,000		
Retained earnings	60,000		
Total equity.	$ 160,000	$160,000	$ 160,000
Interest acquired		80%	20%
Book value.		$128,000	$ 32,000
Excess of fair value over book value	**$330,000**	$272,000	**$ 58,000**

Adjustment of identifiable accounts:

	Adjustment	Worksheet Key
Inventory ($55,000 fair − $50,000 book value)	$ 5,000	**debit D1**
Land ($70,000 fair − $40,000 book value).	30,000	**debit D2**
Buildings ($250,000 fair − $150,000 book value) . . .	100,000	**debit D3**
Equipment ($60,000 fair − $40,000 book value)	20,000	**debit D4**
Copyright ($50,000 fair − $0 book value).	50,000	**debit D5**
Goodwill ($490,000 fair − $365,000 book value) .	**125,000***	**debit D6**
Total	**$330,000**	

*Agrees with total (company) goodwill in the value analysis schedule.

If goodwill becomes impaired in a future period, the impairment charge would be allocated to the controlling interest and the NCI based on the percentage of total goodwill each equity interest received on the D&D schedule. In the original example, where goodwill on the NCI was assumed to be proportional to that recorded on the controlling interest, the impairment charge would be allocated 80/20 to the controlling interest and NCI. In the above example, where goodwill was not proportional, a new percentage would be developed as follows:

	Value	Percentage of Total
Goodwill applicable to parent from value analysis schedule	$108,000	86.4%
Goodwill applicable to NCI from value analysis schedule	17,000	13.6%
Total goodwill	$125,000	

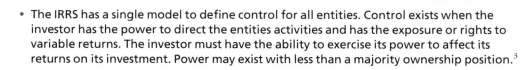

IASB PERSPECTIVES

- The IRRS has a single model to define control for all entities. Control exists when the investor has the power to direct the entities activities and has the exposure or rights to variable returns. The investor must have the ability to exercise its power to affect its returns on its investment. Power may exist with less than a majority ownership position.[3]

IASB *standards*

No Goodwill on the Noncontrolling Interest

Currently, International Accounting Standards provide a choice in accounting for the noncontrolling interest. The NCI can be recorded at fair value, which would result in goodwill applicable to

3 IFRS 10, *Consolidated Financial Statements.*

the NCI, as demonstrated above. The other choice is to record the NCI at the NCI percentage of the fair value of the net identifiable assets only, with no goodwill on the NCI. Under the non-NCI goodwill model, the preceding example would be modified to appear as shown below.[4]

If the fair value of the NCI is estimated to be $73,000 (20% × $365,000 fair value of subsidiary company net identifiable assets), the value analysis would be modified as follows (changes are boldfaced):

Value Analysis Schedule	Company Implied Fair Value	Parent Price (80%)	NCI Value (20%)
Company fair value.	**$473,000**	$400,000	**$73,000**
Fair value of net assets excluding goodwill . .	365,000	292,000	73,000
Goodwill.	**$108,000**	$108,000	$ 0
Gain on acquisition	N/A	N/A	

Several assumptions went into the calculation on page 74.

◆ Company fair value—This is now the sum of the price paid by the parent plus the NCI share of net identifiable assets.

◆ Fair value of net assets excluding goodwill—The fair values of the subsidiary accounts are from the comparison of book and fair values. These values are never less than fair value.

◆ Goodwill—The only goodwill recorded is that applicable to the controlling interest.

The revised D&D schedule with changes (from the previous example) in boldfaced type would be as follows:

Determination and Distribution of Excess Schedule

	Company Implied Fair Value	Parent Price (80%)	NCI Value (20%)	
Fair value of subsidiary	$ 473,000	$400,000	**$ 73,000**	
Less book value of interest acquired:				
Common stock ($1 par)	$ 10,000			
Paid-in capital in excess of par	90,000			
Retained earnings	60,000			
Total equity.	$ 160,000	$160,000	$160,000	
Interest acquired		80%	20%	
Book value.		$128,000	$ 32,000	
Excess of fair value over book value	**$313,000**	$272,000	**$ 41,000**	

Adjustment of identifiable accounts:

	Adjustment	Worksheet Key
Inventory ($55,000 fair − $50,000 book value)	$ 5,000	**debit D1**
Land ($70,000 fair − $40,000 book value).	30,000	**debit D2**
Buildings ($250,000 fair − $150,000 book value) . .	100,000	**debit D3**
Equipment ($60,000 fair − $40,000 book value) . . .	20,000	**debit D4**
Copyright ($50,000 fair − $0 book value).	50,000	**debit D5**
Goodwill ($473,000 fair − $365,000 book value)	**108,000***	**debit D6**
Total	**$313,000**	

*Agrees with total (company) goodwill in the value analysis schedule.

If goodwill becomes impaired in a future period, the impairment charge would apply only to the controlling interest.

---

4 IFRS 3, *Business Combinations* (International Accounting Standards Board, January 2008), para. 19.

Gain on Purchase of Subsidiary

Let us now study the same example, except that the price paid by the parent will be low enough to result in a gain. Assume that Parental, Inc., issued 10,000 shares of its $1 par value common stock for 80% of the outstanding shares of Sample Company. The fair value of a share of Parental, Inc., stock is $25. Parental also pays $25,000 in accounting and legal fees to complete the purchase. Parental would make the following journal entry to record the purchase:

Investment in Sample Company (10,000 shares issued × $25 fair value) . .	250,000	
Common Stock ($1 par value) (10,000 shares × $1 par)		10,000
Paid-In Capital in Excess of Par ($250,000 − $10,000 par value) . . .		240,000

Parental would record the costs of the acquisition as follows:

Acquisition Expense (closed to Retained Earnings since only balance sheets are being examined)	25,000	
Cash.		25,000

Refer back to the prior comparison of book and fair values for the subsidiary. The following value analysis would be prepared for the 80% interest:

Value Analysis Schedule	Company Implied Fair Value	Parent Price (80%)	NCI Value (20%)
Company fair value.	$ 323,000	$ 250,000	$73,000
Fair value of net assets excluding goodwill . .	365,000	292,000	73,000
Goodwill	N/A	N/A	
Gain on acquisition	**$(42,000)**	**$(42,000)**	

Several assumptions went into the above calculation.

◆ Company fair value—It is assumed that if the parent would pay $250,000 for an 80% interest, then the entire subsidiary company is worth $312,500 ($250,000/80%). We will refer to this as the "implied value" of the subsidiary company. Assuming this to be true, the NCI is worth 20% of the total subsidiary company value (20% × $312,500 = $62,500). The NCI value, however, can never be less than its share of net identifiable assets ($73,000). Thus, the NCI share of company value is raised to $73,000 (replacing the $62,500).

◆ Fair value of net assets excluding goodwill—The fair values of the subsidiary accounts are from the comparison of book and fair values.

◆ Goodwill—There can be no goodwill when the price paid is less than the fair value of the parent's share of the fair value of net identifiable assets.

◆ Gain on acquisition—The only gain recognized is that applicable to the controlling interest.

The following D&D would be prepared:

	Company Implied Fair Value	Parent Price (80%)	NCI Value (20%)	
Determination and Distribution of Excess Schedule				
Fair value of subsidiary	$ 323,000	$250,000	$ 73,000	
Less book value of interest acquired:				
Common stock ($1 par)	$ 10,000			
Paid-in capital in excess of par	90,000			
Retained earnings	60,000			
Total equity.	$ 160,000	$160,000	$160,000	
Interest acquired		80%	20%	
Book value.		$128,000	$ 32,000	
Excess of fair value over book value	**$163,000**	$122,000	$ 41,000	

Adjustment of identifiable accounts:

	Adjustment	Worksheet Key
Inventory ($55,000 fair − $50,000 book value)	$ 5,000	**debit D1**
Land ($70,000 fair − $40,000 book value).	30,000	**debit D2**
Buildings ($250,000 fair − $150,000 book value) . .	100,000	**debit D3**
Equipment ($60,000 fair − $40,000 book value) . . .	20,000	**debit D4**
Copyright ($50,000 fair − $0 book value).	50,000	**debit D5**
Gain (only applies to controlling interest). . . .	**(42,000)**	**credit D7**
Total	**$163,000**	

Worksheet 2-6 on page 94 is the consolidated worksheet for the $250,000 price. The D&D schedule provides complete guidance for the worksheet eliminations.

Worksheet 2-6: page 94

◆ Elimination (EL) eliminated the subsidiary equity purchased (80% in this example) against the investment account as follows:

(EL)	Common Stock ($1 par)	8,000	
	Paid-In Capital in Excess of Par	72,000	
	Retained Earnings	48,000	
	Investment in Sample Company.		128,000

◆ The (D) series eliminations distribute the excess applicable to the controlling interest plus the increase in the NCI [labeled (NCI)] to the appropriate accounts as indicated by the D&D schedule. Worksheet eliminations are as follows:

(D1)	Inventory	5,000	
(D2)	Land.	30,000	
(D3)	Buildings	100,000	
(D4)	Equipment	20,000	
(D5)	Copyright	50,000	
(D7)	Gain on Purchase of Subsidiary (since we are dealing only with a balance sheet, this would be credited to Controlling Retained Earnings)		42,000
(D)	Investment in Sample Company [remaining excess after (EL)]		122,000
(NCI)	Retained Earnings—Sample (NCI share of fair market adjustment)		41,000
Dr. = Cr.	*Check Totals*	*205,000*	*205,000*

Valuation Schedule Strategy

Here are steps to valuation that will always work if prepared in the order shown below.

Step 1: Enter ownership percentages in C2 and D2. Then enter fair value of net assets of acquired company in B4, and multiply by ownership percentages to fill C4 and D4.

	A	B	C	D
		Company Implied Fair Value	Parent Price	NCI Value
1.	Value Analysis Schedule			
2.	Ownership percentages		80%	20%
3.	Company fair value			
4.	Fair value of net assets excluding goodwill	**365,000**	**292,000**	**73,000**
5.	Goodwill			
6.	Gain on bargain acquisition			

Step 2: Enter the price paid by the parent in C3. Then, enter value of NCI in D3. Normally, this is proportionate to price paid by parent. It can be a separate value, but never less than D4. This would happen when the parent pays a control premium. B3 is sum of C3 and D3.

	A	B	C	D
1.	Value Analysis Schedule	Company Implied Fair Value	Parent Price	NCI Value
2.	Ownership percentages		80%	20%
3.	Company fair value	**525,000**	**420,000**	**105,000**
4.	Fair value of net assets excluding goodwill	365,000	292,000	73,000
5.	Goodwill			
6.	Gain on bargain acquisition			

Step 3: Compare company fair value (B3) with fair value of net assets, excluding goodwill (B4). If B3 is greater than B4, follow Step 3A (Goodwill). If B3 is less than B4, follow Step 3B (Gain).

Step 3A (Goodwill): Calculate goodwill for B5–D5 by subtracting line 4 from line 3 in columns B–D.

	A	B	C	D
1.	Value Analysis Schedule	Company Implied Fair Value	Parent Price	NCI Value
2.	Ownership percentages		80%	20%
3.	Company fair value	525,000	420,000	105,000
4.	Fair value of net assets excluding goodwill	365,000	292,000	73,000
5.	Goodwill	**160,000**	**128,000**	**32,000**
6.	Gain on bargain acquisition			

Step 3B (Gain): Enter the new values for line 3. The NCI value cannot be less than D4 and normally will be equal to D4. (An exception where it exceeds D4 follows.) B4 is the sum of C4 and D4. Calculate and enter C6. It is C4 minus C3. No other cells are filled.

	A	B	C	D
1.	Value Analysis Schedule	Company Implied Fair Value	Parent Price	NCI Value
2.	Ownership percentages		80%	20%
3.	Company fair value	**323,000**	**250,000**	**73,000**
4.	Fair value of net assets excluding goodwill	365,000	292,000	73,000
5.	Goodwill			
6.	Gain on bargain acquisition		**(42,000)**	

Step 3B (Gain) Exception for NCI: This exception is for a situation where the NCI value exceeds its share of fair value of net assets, excluding goodwill.

Enter new Value for D3. Then calculate and enter values for C6 and D6. B6 is sum of C6 and D6.

	A	B	C	D
1.	Value Analysis Schedule	Company Implied Fair Value	Parent Price	NCI Value
2.	Ownership percentages		80%	20%
3.	Company fair value	**340,000**	**250,000**	**90,000**
4.	Fair value of net assets excluding goodwill	365,000	292,000	73,000
5.	Goodwill			
6.	Gain on bargain acquisition	**(25,000)**	**(42,000)**	**17,000**

The entry to distribute the excess on the worksheet would be as follows:

Investment in Subsidiary	42,000	
NCI		17,000
Gain on Acquisition of Subsidiary		25,000

Parent Exchanges Noncash Assets for Controlling Interest

The parent must bring to fair value any assets, other than cash, that it exchanges for the controlling interest. If those assets are retained and used by the subsidiary company, the gain must be eliminated in the consolidation process.

Assets transferred would be retained by the subsidiary when either:

1. The assets are transferred to the former shareholders of the subsidiary company and the shareholders sell the assets to the subsidiary company, or
2. The assets are transferred directly to the subsidiary company in exchange for newly issued shares or treasury shares.

The gain would be deferred using the procedures demonstrated in Chapter 4 for the parent sale of a fixed asset to the subsidiary.

REFLECTION

- A less than 100% interest requires that value analysis be applied to the entire subsidiary.
- Subsidiary accounts are adjusted to full fair value regardless of the controlling percentage ownership.
- The noncontrolling interest shares in all asset and liability fair value adjustments.
- The noncontrolling interest does not share a gain on the acquisition (when applicable).
- The noncontrolling share of subsidiary equity appears as a single line-item amount within the equity section of the balance sheet.

PREEXISTING GOODWILL

8

OBJECTIVE

Show the impact of preexisting goodwill on the consolidation process, and be able to include prior investments in the acquisition price.

If a subsidiary is purchased and it has goodwill on its books, that goodwill is ignored in the value analysis. The only complication caused by existing goodwill is that the D&D schedule will adjust existing goodwill, rather than only recording new goodwill. Let us return to the example involving the 80% acquisition of Sample Company on page 63 and change only two facts: assume Sample has goodwill of $40,000 and its retained earnings is $40,000 greater. The revised book and fair values would be as follows:

Assets	Book Value	Market Value	Liabilities and Equity	Book Value	Market Value
Accounts receivable	$ 20,000	$ 20,000	Current liabilities	$ 40,000	$ 40,000
Inventory	50,000	55,000	Bonds payable	100,000	100,000
Land	40,000	70,000	**Total liabilities**	**$140,000**	**$140,000**
Buildings	200,000	250,000	**Stockholders' equity:**		
Accumulated depreciation	(50,000)		Common stock ($1 par)	$ 10,000	
Equipment	60,000	60,000	Paid-in capital in excess of par...	90,000	
Accumulated depreciation	(20,000)		Retained earnings	100,000	
Copyright		50,000	Total equity	$ 200,000	
Goodwill	40,000		Total liabilities and equity	**$340,000**	
Total assets	**$340,000**	**$505,000**	**Net assets**		**$365,000**

Assume that Parental, Inc., issued 16,000 shares of its $1 par value common stock for 80% (8,000 shares) of the outstanding shares of Sample Company. The fair value of a share of Parental, Inc., stock is $25. Parental also pays $25,000 in accounting and legal fees to accomplish the purchase. Parental would make the following entry to record the purchase:

Investment in Sample Company (16,000 shares issued × $25 fair value)	400,000	
Common Stock ($1 par value) (16,000 shares × $1 par)		16,000
Paid-In Capital in Excess of Par ($400,000 − $16,000 par value)		384,000

Parental would record the costs of the acquisition as follows:

Acquisition Expense (closed to Retained Earnings since only balance sheets are being examined)	25,000	
Cash.		25,000

The value analysis schedule is unchanged. The fair value of the Sample Company net assets does not include goodwill.

Value Analysis Schedule	Company Implied Fair Value	Parent Price (80%)	NCI Value (20%)
Company fair value.	$ 500,000	$ 400,000	$100,000
Fair value of net assets excluding goodwill	365,000	292,000	73,000
Goodwill.	**$135,000**	**$108,000**	**$ 27,000**
Gain on acquisition			

The D&D schedule differs from the earlier one only to the extent that:

◆ The Sample Company retained earnings is $40,000 greater.
◆ The implied goodwill of $135,000 is compared to existing goodwill of $40,000.

Determination and Distribution of Excess Schedule

	Company Implied Fair Value	Parent Price (80%)	NCI Value (20%)
Fair value of subsidiary	$ 500,000	$400,000	$100,000
Less book value of interest acquired:			
Common stock ($1 par)	$ 10,000		
Paid-in capital in excess of par	90,000		
Retained earnings	**100,000**		
Total equity.	$ 200,000	$200,000	$200,000
Interest acquired		80%	20%
Book value.		$160,000	$ 40,000
Excess of fair value over book value	**$300,000**	$240,000	$ 60,000

Adjustment of identifiable accounts:

	Adjustment	Worksheet Key
Inventory ($55,000 fair − $50,000 book value)	$ 5,000	**debit D1**
Land ($70,000 fair − $40,000 book value).	30,000	**debit D2**
Buildings ($250,000 fair − $150,000 net book value)	100,000	**debit D3**
Equipment ($60,000 fair − $40,000 net book value) .	20,000	**debit D4**
Copyright ($50,000 fair − $0 book value).	50,000	**debit D5**
Goodwill ($135,000 fair − $40,000 book value) . .	**95,000**	**debit D6**
Total	**$300,000**	

The D&D schedule provides complete guidance for the worksheet eliminations. Changes from Worksheet 2-5 are in boldface. Study Worksheet 2-7 on page 95 and note the following:

Worksheet 2-7: page 95

◆ Elimination (EL) eliminated the subsidiary equity purchased (80% in this example) against the investment account as follows:

(EL)	Common Stock ($1 par)—Sample	8,000	
	Paid-In Capital in Excess of Par—Sample	72,000	
	Retained Earnings—Sample	**80,000**	
	Investment in Sample Company....................		160,000

◆ The (D) series eliminations distribute the excess applicable to the controlling interest plus the increase in the NCI [labeled (NCI)] to the appropriate accounts, as indicated by the D&D schedule. The adjustment of the NCI is carried to subsidiary retained earnings.

(D1)	Inventory	5,000	
(D2)	Land...	30,000	
(D3)	Buildings	100,000	
(D4)	Equipment	20,000	
(D5)	Copyright	50,000	
(D6)	Goodwill **($135,000 — $40,000 book value)**	**95,000**	
(D)	Investment in Sample Company [remaining excess after (EL)] ...		240,000
(NCI)	Retained Earnings Sample (NCI share of fair market adjustment)		60,000
Dr. = Cr.	Check Totals	300,000	300,000

The Consolidated Balance Sheet column of Worksheet 2-7 is the same as those for Worksheet 2-5 and the resulting balance sheet (as shown on page 73 is unchanged).

R E F L E C T I O N

- Where the acquired firm already has goodwill on its books, the D&D adjusts from the recorded goodwill to the goodwill calculated in the valuation schedule.

OWNERSHIP OF A PRIOR NONCONTROLLING INTEREST

The acquirer may already own a noncontrolling investment (less than 50%) interest in a company. It may then decide to buy additional shares of common stock to achieve a controlling interest. The previously owned shares are adjusted to fair value and a gain or loss is recorded on the investment. The fair value of the shares is then added to the price paid for the new shares. The prior plus new interest is treated as one price paid for a controlling interest. Normally, the fair value of the previously owned shares is based on the price paid for the controlling interest.

For example, assume Company P owns a 10% interest (10,000 shares) in Company S that Company P purchased at a prior date for $20 per share. At a later date, Company P purchases another 50,000 shares (50% interest) for $30 per share.

The 10,000 previously purchased shares would be adjusted to fair value as follows:

Investment in Company S shares (10,000 shares × $10 increase)	100,000	
Unrealized Gain on Revaluation of Investments		100,000

This entry would increase the carrying value of the 10,000 previously owned shares to $300,000. The acquisition price for the controlling 60% interest would be calculated as follows:

Fair value of previously owned 10% interest	$ 300,000
Acquisition of 50,000 shares at $30	1,500,000
Total acquisition cost	$1,800,000

Assuming cash is paid for the 50,000 shares, the acquisition entry would be as follows:

Investment in Subsidiary Company S	1,800,000	
Cash (50,000 shares at $30)		1,500,000
Investment in Company S (10,000 shares × $30)		300,000

Value analysis and the D&D schedule would be constructed for a single 60% interest with an acquisition price of $1,800,000.

Two observations that should be made about the prior investment that is rolled into the total acquisition cost are as follows:

1. The above investment was a passive investment and was not an influential investment accounted for under the equity method. Most likely, it would have been an "Available for Sale" investment. It would have been adjusted to fair value on prior balance sheet dates with the adjustment going to "Other Comprehensive Income" (OCI). That portion of the portfolio and OCI adjustment attributable to this investment would be included in future portfolio valuations. It is unlikely, but possible, that the investment could have been a "Trading Investment." In that case, prior portfolio adjustments were recorded as unrealized gains or losses and were included in net income. The above investment would no longer be included in the future portfolio adjustments.

2. The previously owned interest may be large enough to be accounted for under the equity method (typically greater than a 20% interest). If that is the case, the investment will be carried at equity-adjusted cost. It will be adjusted to fair value on the date of the later acquisition that creates control.

REFLECTION

- Any previously owned interest in the acquiree is adjusted to fair value based on the price paid for the later interest that creates control.

9
OBJECTIVE

Define push-down accounting, and explain when it may be used and its impact.

PUSH-DOWN ACCOUNTING

Thus far, it has been assumed that the subsidiary's statements are unaffected by the parent's purchase of a controlling interest in the subsidiary. None of the subsidiary's accounts is adjusted on the subsidiary's books. In all preceding examples, adjustments to reflect fair value are made only on the consolidated worksheet. This is the most common but not the only accepted method.

Some accountants object to the inconsistency of using book values in the subsidiary's separate statements while using fair value-adjusted values when the same accounts are included in the consolidated statements. They would advocate *push-down accounting*, whereby the subsidiary's accounts are adjusted to reflect the fair value adjustments. In accordance with the new basis of accounting, retained earnings are eliminated, and the balance (as adjusted for fair value adjustments) is added to paid-in capital. It is argued that the purchase of a controlling interest gives rise to a new basis of accountability for the interest traded, and the subsidiary accounts should reflect those values.

If the push-down method were applied to the example of a 100% purchase for $500,000 on page 63, the following entry would be made by the subsidiary on its books:

Inventory	5,000	
Land	30,000	
Buildings	100,000	
Equipment	20,000	
Copyright	50,000	
Goodwill	135,000	
Paid-In Capital in Excess of Par		340,000

This entry would raise the subsidiary equity to $500,000. The $500,000 investment account would be eliminated against the $500,000 subsidiary equity with no excess remaining. All accounts are adjusted to full fair value, even if there is a noncontrolling interest. The SEC staff has adopted a policy of requiring push-down accounting, in some cases, for the separately published statements of a subsidiary. The existence of any significant noncontrolling interests (usually above 5%) and/or significant publicly held debt or preferred stock generally eliminates the need to use push-down accounting. **Note that the consolidated statements are unaffected by this issue.** The only difference is in the placement of the adjustments from the determination and distribution of excess schedule. The conventional approach, which is used in this text, makes the adjustments on the consolidated worksheet. The push-down method makes the same adjustments directly on the books of the subsidiary. Under the push-down method, the adjustments are already made when consolidation procedures are applied. Since all accounts are adjusted to reflect fair values, the investment account is eliminated against subsidiary equity with no excess. The difference in methods affects only the presentation on the subsidiary's separate statements.

IASB PERSPECTIVES

- IFRS does not allow "push-down" accounting to be used.

IASB *standards*

REFLECTION

- Push-down accounting revalues subsidiary accounts directly on the books of the subsidiary based on adjustments indicated in the D&D schedule.

- Since assets are revalued before the consolidation process starts, no distribution of excess (to adjust accounts) is required on the consolidated worksheet.

APPENDIX: REVERSE ACQUISITION

A reverse acquisition occurs when a usually larger firm, that is not publicly traded, wishes to acquire a controlling interest in a usually smaller company, which does not have publicly traded common stock. The "reverse" nature of the transaction concerns the common shares used in the exchange. So far, we have assumed that the potential controlling company issues its common stock shares to make the acquisition. In a "reverse acquisition," the shares of the "to be" acquired publicly traded company are used for the exchange. The intent is to end up with a consolidated company that has easily tradable stock.

10

OBJECTIVE

Demonstrate worksheet procedures for reverse acquisitions.

The following example is taken from FASB ASC 805-40-55-4 to allow the reader additional information on the process. Prior to the acquisition, assume that Private Company (the acquirer) and Public Company (the acquiree) have the following balance sheets:

Private Company (the acquirer, but the company receiving public shares)
Balance Sheet
December 31, 2015

Assets		Liabilities and Equity	
Current assets	$ 700	Long-term liabilities	$1,700
Fixed assets	3,000	Common stock (60 shares) ($1 par) . .	60
		Paid-in capital in excess of par	540
		Retained earnings	1,400
Total assets.	$3,700	Total liabilities and equity	$3,700

Public Company (the acquiree, but the company issuing public shares)
Balance Sheet
December 31, 2015

Assets	Book Value	Fair Value	Liabilities and Equity	Book Value	Fair Value
Current assets	$ 500	$ 500	Long-term liabilities	$ 700	$700
Fixed assets	1,300	1,500	Common stock (100 shares)		
			($1 par)	100	
			Paid-in capital in excess of		
			par	200	
			Retained earnings	800	
Total assets.	$1,800	$2,000	Total liabilities and equity	$1,800	

Public Company will issue 150 new shares to Private Company shareholders in exchange for their 60 outstanding shares of Private Company. Assuming that the fair value of a Public Company share is $16, the transaction would be recorded by Public Company as follows:

Investment in Private Company (150 shares × $16)	2,400	
Common Stock ($1 par) (150 shares × $1 par)		150
Paid-In Capital in Excess of Par ($2,400 – $150 par)		2,250

The following diagram depicts the change in ownership:

December 31, 2015

Prior to Exchange

Private Company	**Public Company**
60 shares outstanding	100 shares outstanding

After Exchange

Private Company	**Public Company**
60 shares outstanding	250 shares outstanding Investment in Private Company, $2,400

After the exchange, all of the shares of Private Company are owned by Public Company. In most cases, Public Company will distribute Public Company shares to the former Private Company shareholders. However, the 150 shares of Public Company are owned by the former Private Company shareholders. The former Private Company shareholders now own 60% of the 250 total Public Company shares. They, collectively, now have control of Public Company.

Since control of Public Company has been transferred, the company is considered to have been sold. Thus, it is the Public Company assets and liabilities that must be adjusted to fair value. Since the fair value per share of Public Company is $16, it is assumed that Public Company was worth $1,600 (100 shares × $16) prior to the transfer.

Because the shareholders of Private Company are the controlling interest, Private Company cannot revalue its assets to fair value. The controlled company is Public Company; thus, it is the company that must have its net assets adjusted to fair value. This means that value analysis is only applied to Public Company.

The following value analysis would be prepared for Public Company. The fair value analysis would apply to only those assets present just prior to the acquisition. The fair value of Public Company at the time of the acquisition can be calculated as $1,600 (100 shares × $16 market value).

The value analysis schedule for Public Company would be as follows:

Value Analysis Schedule	Company Implied Fair Value	Parent Price (100%)	NCI Value
Company fair value	$1,600	$1,600	
Fair value of assets excluding goodwill ($1,100 net book value + $200 adjustment to fixed assets)	1,300	1,300	
Goodwill	**$ 300**	**$ 300**	
Gain on acquisition	N/A	N/A	

The determination and distribution of excess schedule would be prepared as follows:

Determination and Distribution of Excess Schedule	Company Implied Fair Value	Parent Price (100%)	NCI Value
Fair value of subsidiary	$1,600	$1,600	
Less book value of interest acquired:			
Common stock ($1 par)	$ 100		
Paid-in capital in excess of par	200		
Retained earnings	800		
Total equity	$1,100	$1,100	
Interest acquired		100%	
Book value		$1,100	
Excess of fair value over book value	$ 500	$ 500	

Adjustment of identifiable accounts:		
Fixed assets	$ 200
Goodwill	**300**
Total	**$ 500**

Worksheet 2A-1 on page 96 includes the consolidation procedures that may be used for the acquisition on the acquisition date. The first step is to eliminate the investment account against the increase in Public Company equity *recorded at the time of the acquisition* as follows:

Worksheet 2A-1: page 96

(EL)	Common Stock ($1 par)—Public Company (150 shares × $1)	150	
	Paid-In Capital in Excess of Par—Public Company (150 shares × $15)	2,250	
	Investment in Private Company		2,400

The assets of Public Company are then adjusted to fair value on the acquisition date, using the information from the above determination and distribution of excess schedule. The total adjustment is credited to Public Company retained earnings.

(D1)	Fixed Assets...	200	
(D2)	Goodwill...	300	
(D)	Retained Earnings—Public Company..............................		500

Then, the Private Company par and paid-in capital in excess of par amounts are transferred to the par and paid-in value of the public shares. The retained earnings of the acquired, Public Company, are also transferred to the paid-in capital in excess of par account of Public Company as follows:

(Trans)	**Common Stock ($1 par)—Private Company**	**60**	
	Paid-In Capital in Excess of Par—Private Company...	**540**	
	Retained Earnings—Public Company (as adjusted by "D")..	**1,300**	
	Common Stock ($1 par)—Public Company (150 shares × $1)....................................		**150**
	Paid-In Capital in Excess of Par—Public Company ($1,900 – $150)		**1,750**

The consolidation steps can be summarized as follows:

(EL) Remove the investment account and the additions to paid-in capital that occurred on the purchase date.

(D) Bring the acquired company's assets and liabilities to fair value on the acquisition date.

(Trans) Assign all remaining equity account values, except the controlling interest share of retained earnings, to paid-in capital accounts of the publicly traded company. The only retained earnings that can emerge from the combination are that of the controlling interest.

The following balance sheet results:

Public Company and Subsidiary Private Company
Balance Sheet
December 31, 2015

Assets		Liabilities and Equity	
Current assets	$1,200	Long-term liabilities	$2,400
Fixed assets	4,500	Equity:	
Goodwill	300	Common stock ($1 par)............	$ 250
		Paid-in capital in excess of par	1,950
		Retained earnings	1,400
		Total controlling interest..........	$3,600
Total assets	$6,000	Total liabilities and equity	$6,000

There are alternative procedures that could be used on the worksheet, but the end result is that the controlling equity can only include the retained earnings of the acquiring company. In this case, that is the original $1,400 attributable to Private Company. The total paid-in capital can be confirmed as follows:

Total equity of acquired Public Company ($100 + $200 + $800)	$1,100
Adjustment of Public Company to fair value	500
Total paid-in capital of Private Company ($60 + $540)	600
Total paid-in capital of consolidated Public Company	$2,200

Reverse Acquisition with Noncontrolling Interest

A portion of the acquiring company shareholders may choose not to exchange their shares for the company being acquired. Let us change the prior example to assume that only 80% or 48 Private Company shares participate in the exchange. The 20% or 12 Private Company shares become a noncontrolling interest in Private Company.

Public Company will issue 120 new shares to the Private Company shareholders in exchange for their 48 outstanding shares of Private Company. Assuming that the fair value of a Public Company share is $16, the transaction would be recorded by Public Company as follows:

Investment in Private Company (120 shares × $16)	1,920	
Common Stock ($1 par) (120 shares × $1 par)		120
Paid-In Capital in Excess of Par ($1,920 – $120 par)		1,800

The following diagram depicts the change in ownership:

December 31, 2015

Prior to Exchange

Private Company	**Public Company**
60 shares outstanding	100 shares outstanding

After Exchange

Private Company	**Public Company**
60 shares outstanding	220 shares outstanding Investment in Private Company, $1,920

After the exchange, 80% of the shares of Private Company are owned by Public Company. However, the 120 shares of Public Company are owned by former Private Company shareholders. The former Private Company shareholders now own 54.5% of the 220 total Public Company shares. They, collectively, now have control of Public Company.

Since the control of Public Company has been transferred, the company is considered to have been sold. Thus, it is the Public Company assets and liabilities that must be adjusted to fair value. Since the fair value per share of Public Company is $16, it is assumed that Public Company was worth $1,600 (100 shares × $16) prior to the transfer.

There is no change in the value analysis or the determination and distribution of excess schedule. Since the noncontrolling interest is applicable to Private Company, it does not share in the revaluation.

Worksheet 2A-2 on page 97 includes the consolidation procedures that may be used for the acquisition on the acquisition date. The first step is to eliminate the investment account against the increase in Public Company equity *recorded at the time of the acquisition* as follows: **Worksheet 2A-2:** page 97

(EL)	Common Stock ($1 par)—Public Company (120 shares × $1)	120	
	Paid-In Capital in Excess of Par—Public Company (120 shares × $15) .	1,800	
	Investment in Public Company		1,920

The assets of Public Company are then adjusted to fair value on the acquisition date, using the information from the above determination and distribution of excess schedule. The total adjustment is credited to Public Company retained earnings.

(D1)	Fixed Assets...................................	200	
(D2)	Goodwill....................................	300	
(D)	Retained Earnings—Public Company		500

Then, the Private Company par and paid-in capital in excess of par amounts are transferred to the par and paid-in value of the public shares. The retained earnings of the acquired, Public Company, are also transferred to the paid-in capital in excess of par account of Public Company as follows:

(Trans)	**Common Stock ($1 par)—Private Company**		
	($60 × 80%).....................................	**48**	
	Paid-In Capital in Excess of Par—Private Company		
	($540 × 80%)	**432**	
	Retained Earnings—Public Company (as adjusted		
	by "D")..	**1,300**	
	Common Stock ($1 par)—Public Company (120		
	shares × $1)....................................		**120**
	Paid-In Capital in Excess of Par—Public Company		
	($1,780 – $120)		**1,660**

The following balance sheet results:

Public Company and Subsidiary Private Company
Balance Sheet
December 31, 2015

Assets		Liabilities and Equity	
Current assets	$1,200	Long-term liabilities	$2,400
Fixed assets	4,500	Equity:	
Goodwill	300	Common stock ($1 par).............	$ 220
		Paid-in capital in excess of par	1,860
		Retained earnings	1,120
		Total controlling interest...........	$3,200
		Noncontrolling interest	400
		Total equity	$3,600
Total assets	$6,000	Total liabilities and equity	$6,000

There are alternative procedures that could be used on the worksheet, but the end result is that the controlling equity can only include the retained earnings of the acquiring company. In this case, that is $1,120 (80% × $1,400) attributable to the Private Company controlling interest. The total paid-in capital can be confirmed as follows:

Public Company equity ($100 + $200 + $800)	$1,100
Fair value adjustment	500
80% of Private Company paid-in capital (80% × $600)	480
Total paid-in capital in excess of par, Public Company	$2,080

Worksheet 2-1

100% Interest; Price Equals Book Value
Company P and Subsidiary Company S
Worksheet for Consolidated Balance Sheet
December 31, 2015

Worksheet 2-1 (see page 60)

		Trial Balance		Eliminations & Adjustments		Consolidated Balance Sheet	
		Company P	Company S	Dr.	Cr.		
1	Cash	300,000				300,000	1
2	Accounts Receivable	300,000	200,000			500,000	2
3	Inventory	100,000	100,000			200,000	3
4	Investment in Company S	500,000			(EL) 500,000		4
5							5
6	Equipment (net)	150,000	300,000			450,000	6
7	Goodwill						7
8	Current Liabilities	(150,000)	(100,000)			(250,000)	8
9	Bonds Payable	(500,000)				(500,000)	9
10	Common Stock—Company S		(200,000)	(EL) 200,000			10
11	Retained Earnings—Company S		(300,000)	(EL) 300,000			11
12	Common Stock—Company P	(100,000)				(100,000)	12
13	Retained Earnings—Company P	(600,000)				(600,000)	13
14	Totals	0	0	500,000	500,000	0	14

Eliminations and Adjustments:

(EL) Eliminate the investment in the subsidiary against the subsidiary equity accounts.

Worksheet 2-2

100% Interest; Price Exceeds Book Value
Company P and Subsidiary Company S
Worksheet for Consolidated Balance Sheet
December 31, 2015

Worksheet 2-2 (see page 62)

| | Trial Balance | | Eliminations & Adjustments | | Consolidated | |
	Company P	Company S	Dr.	Cr.	Balance Sheet	
Cash	100,000				100,000	1
Accounts Receivable	300,000	200,000			500,000	2
Inventory	100,000	100,000	(D1) 20,000		220,000	3
Investment in Company S	700,000			(EL) 500,000		4
				(D) 200,000		5
Equipment (net)	150,000	300,000	(D2) 100,000		550,000	6
Goodwill			(D3) 80,000		80,000	7
Current Liabilities	(150,000)	(100,000)			(250,000)	8
Bonds Payable	(500,000)				(500,000)	9
Common Stock—Company S		(200,000)	(EL) 200,000			10
Retained Earnings—Company S		(300,000)	(EL) 300,000			11
Common Stock—Company P	(100,000)				(100,000)	12
Retained Earnings—Company P	(600,000)				(600,000)	13
Totals	0	0	700,000	700,000	0	14

Eliminations and Adjustments:

(EL) Eliminate the investment in the subsidiary against the subsidiary equity accounts.
(D) Distribute $200,000 excess of cost over book value as follows:
(D1) Inventory, $20,000.
(D2) Equipment, $100,000.
(D3) Goodwill, $80,000.

Worksheet 2-3

100% Interest; Price Exceeds Market Value of Identifiable Net Assets

Parental, Inc. and Subsidiary Sample Company
Worksheet for Consolidated Balance Sheet
December 31, 2015

Worksheet 2-3 (see page 64)

(Credit balance amounts are in parentheses.)	Balance Sheet Parental	Balance Sheet Sample	Eliminations & Adjustments Dr.	Eliminations & Adjustments Cr.	Consolidated Balance Sheet	
Cash	84,000				84,000	1
Accounts Receivable	72,000	20,000			92,000	2
Inventory	80,000	50,000	(D1) 5,000		135,000	3
Land	100,000	40,000	(D2) 30,000		170,000	4
Investment in Sample Company	500,000			(EL) 160,000		5
				(D) 340,000		6
Buildings	500,000	200,000	(D3) 100,000		800,000	7
Accumulated Depreciation	(80,000)	(50,000)			(130,000)	8
Equipment	240,000	60,000	(D4) 20,000		320,000	9
Accumulated Depreciation	(40,000)	(20,000)			(60,000)	10
Copyright			(D5) 50,000		50,000	11
Goodwill			(D6) 135,000		135,000	12
Current Liabilities	(80,000)	(40,000)			(120,000)	14
Bonds Payable	(200,000)	(100,000)			(300,000)	13
Common Stock—Sample		(10,000)	(EL) 10,000			14
Paid-In Capital in Excess of Par—Sample		(90,000)	(EL) 90,000			15
Retained Earnings—Sample		(60,000)	(EL) 60,000			16
Common Stock—Parental	(40,000)				(40,000)	17
Paid-In Capital in Excess of Par—Parental	(680,000)				(680,000)	18
Retained Earnings—Parental	(456,000)				(456,000)	19
Totals	0	0	500,000	500,000	0	20

Eliminations and Adjustments:

(EL) Eliminate 100% subsidiary equity against investment account.
(D)   Distribute remaining excess in investment account plus NCI adjustment to:
(D1) Inventory.
(D2) Land.
(D3) Buildings (recorded cost is increased without removing accumulated depreciation). The alternative is to debit Accumulated Depreciation for $50,000 and Buildings for $50,000. This would also restate the net asset at fair value.

(D4) Equipment (recorded cost is increased without removing accumulated depreciation). The alternative is to debit Accumulated Depreciation for $20,000. This would also restate the net asset at fair value.
(D5) Copyright.
(D6) Goodwill.

Worksheet 2-4

100% Interest; Price Exceeds Fair Value of Net Identifiable Assets

Parental, Inc. and Subsidiary Sample Company
Worksheet for Consolidated Balance Sheet
December 31, 2015

Worksheet 2-4 (see page 67)

(Credit balance amounts are in parentheses.)	Balance Sheet		Eliminations & Adjustments		Consolidated Balance Sheet	
	Parental	Sample	Dr.	Cr.		
Cash	84,000				84,000	1
Accounts Receivable	72,000	20,000			92,000	2
Inventory	80,000	50,000	(D1) 5,000		135,000	3
Land	100,000	40,000	(D2) 30,000		170,000	4
Investment in Sample Company	300,000			(EL) 160,000		5
				(D) 140,000		6
Buildings	500,000	200,000	(D3) 100,000		800,000	7
Accumulated Depreciation	(80,000)	(50,000)			(130,000)	8
Equipment	240,000	60,000	(D4) 20,000		320,000	9
Accumulated Depreciation	(40,000)	(20,000)			(60,000)	10
Copyright			(D5) 50,000		50,000	11
Goodwill						12
Current Liabilities	(80,000)	(40,000)			(120,000)	13
Bonds Payable	(200,000)	(100,000)			(300,000)	14
Common Stock—Sample		(10,000)	(EL) 10,000			15
Paid-In Capital in Excess of Par—Sample		(90,000)	(EL) 90,000			16
Retained Earnings—Sample		(60,000)	(EL) 60,000			17
Common Stock—Parental	(32,000)				(32,000)	18
Paid-In Capital in Excess of Par—Parental	(488,000)				(488,000)	19
Retained Earnings—Parental	(456,000)			(D7) 65,000	(521,000)	20
Totals	0	0	365,000	365,000	0	21

Eliminations and Adjustments:

(EL) Eliminate 100% subsidiary equity against investment account.
(D) Distribute remaining excess in investment account plus NCI adjustment to:
(D1) Inventory.
(D2) Land.
(D3) Buildings (recorded cost is increased without removing accumulated depreciation).
 The alternative is to debit Accumulated Depreciation for $50,000 and Buildings for $50,000. This would also restate the net asset at fair value.

(D4) Equipment (recorded cost is increased without removing accumulated depreciation).
 The alternative is to debit Accumulated Depreciation for $20,000. This would also restate the net asset at fair value.
(D5) Copyright.
(D7) Gain on acquisition (close to Parental's Retained Earnings since balance sheet only worksheet)

Worksheet 2-5

80% Interest; Price Exceeds Fair Value of Net Identifiable Assets

Parental, Inc. and Subsidiary Sample Company
Worksheet for Consolidated Balance Sheet
December 31, 2015

Worksheet 2-5 (see page 72)

	(Credit balance amounts are in parentheses.)	Balance Sheet — Parental	Balance Sheet — Sample	Eliminations & Adjustments — Dr.	Eliminations & Adjustments — Cr.	NCI	Consolidated Balance Sheet	
1	Cash	84,000					84,000	1
2	Accounts Receivable	72,000	20,000				92,000	2
3	Inventory	80,000	50,000	(D1) 5,000			135,000	3
4	Land	100,000	40,000	(D2) 30,000			170,000	4
5	Investment in Sample Company	400,000			(EL) 128,000			5
6					(D) 272,000			6
7	Buildings	500,000	200,000	(D3) 100,000			800,000	7
8	Accumulated Depreciation	(80,000)	(50,000)				(130,000)	8
9	Equipment	240,000	60,000	(D4) 20,000			320,000	9
10	Accumulated Depreciation	(40,000)	(20,000)				(60,000)	10
11	Copyright			(D5) 50,000			50,000	11
12	Goodwill			(D6) 135,000			135,000	12
13	Current Liabilities	(80,000)	(40,000)				(120,000)	13
14	Bonds Payable	(200,000)	(100,000)				(300,000)	14
15	Common Stock—Sample		(10,000)	(EL) 8,000		(2,000)		15
16	Paid-In Capital in Excess of Par—Sample		(90,000)	(EL) 72,000		(18,000)		16
17	Retained Earnings—Sample		(60,000)	(EL) 48,000	(NCI) 68,000	(80,000)		17
18	Common Stock—Parental	(36,000)					(36,000)	18
19	Paid-In Capital in Excess of Par—Parental	(584,000)					(584,000)	19
20	Retained Earnings—Parental	(456,000)					(456,000)	20
21	Totals	0	0	468,000	468,000			21
22	NCI					(100,000)	(100,000)	22
23	Totals						0	23

Eliminations and Adjustments:

(EL) Eliminate **80%** subsidiary equity against investment account.
(NCI) **Adjust NCI to fair value (credit to Sample's Retained Earnings).**
(D) **Distribute remaining excess in investment account plus NCI adjustment to:**
(D1) Inventory.
(D2) Land.
(D3) Buildings (recorded cost is increased without removing accumulated depreciation). The alternative is to debit Accumulated Depreciation for $50,000 and Buildings for $50,000. This would also restate the net asset at fair value.
(D4) Equipment (recorded cost is increased without removing accumulated depreciation). The alternative is to debit Accumulated Depreciation for $20,000. This would also restate the net asset at fair value.
(D5) Copyright.
(D6) Goodwill.

Worksheet 2-6

80% Interest; Price Is Less Than Fair Value of Net Identifiable Assets

Parental, Inc. and Subsidiary Sample Company
Worksheet for Consolidated Balance Sheet
December 31, 2015

Worksheet 2-6 (see page 77)

	(Credit balance amounts are in parentheses.)	Balance Sheet Parental	Balance Sheet Sample	Elim. & Adj. Dr.		Elim. & Adj. Cr.		NCI	Consolidated Balance Sheet	
1	Cash	254,000							254,000	1
2	Accounts Receivable	72,000	20,000						92,000	2
3	Inventory	80,000	50,000	(D1)	5,000				135,000	3
4	Land	100,000	40,000	(D2)	30,000				170,000	4
5	Investment in Sample Company	250,000				(EL)	128,000			5
6						(D)	122,000			6
7	Buildings	500,000	200,000	(D3)	100,000				800,000	7
8	Accumulated Depreciation	(80,000)	(50,000)						(130,000)	8
9	Equipment	240,000	60,000	(D4)	20,000				320,000	9
10	Accumulated Depreciation	(40,000)	(20,000)						(60,000)	10
11	Copyright			(D5)	50,000				50,000	11
12	Goodwill									12
13	Current Liabilities	(80,000)	(40,000)						(120,000)	13
14	Bonds Payable	(200,000)	(100,000)						(300,000)	14
15	Common Stock—Sample		(10,000)	(EL)	8,000			(2,000)		15
16	Paid-In Capital in Excess of Par—Sample		(90,000)	(EL)	72,000			(18,000)		16
17	Retained Earnings—Sample		(60,000)	(EL)	48,000	(NCI)	41,000	(53,000)		17
18	Common Stock—Parental	(36,800)							(36,800)	18
19	Paid-In Capital in Excess of Par—Parental	(603,200)							(603,200)	19
20	Retained Earnings—Parental	(456,000)				(D7)	42,000		(498,000)	20
21	Totals	0	0		333,000		333,000			21
22	NCI							(73,000)	(73,000)	22
23	Totals		0						0	23

Eliminations and Adjustments:

(EL) Eliminate 80% subsidiary equity against investment account.
(NCI) Adjust NCI to fair value (credit to Sample's Retained Earnings).
(D) Distribute remaining excess in investment account plus NCI adjustment to:
(D1) Inventory.
(D2) Land.
(D3) Buildings (recorded cost is increased without removing accumulated depreciation). The alternative is to debit Accumulated Depreciation for $50,000 and Buildings for $50,000. This would also restate the net asset at fair value.

(D4) Equipment (recorded cost is increased without removing accumulated depreciation). The alternative is to debit Accumulated Depreciation for $20,000. This would also restate the net asset at fair value.
(D5) Copyright.
(D7) Gain on acquisition (close to Parental's Retained Earnings since balance-sheet-only worksheet).

Worksheet 2-7

80% Interest; Price Exceeds Fair Value of Net Identifiable Assets

Preexisting Goodwill

Parental, Inc. and Subsidiary Sample Company
Worksheet for Consolidated Balance Sheet
December 31, 2015

Worksheet 2-7 (see page 81)

	(Credit balance amounts are in parentheses.)	Balance Sheet		Eliminations & Adjustments		NCI	Consolidated Balance Sheet	
		Parental	Sample	Dr.	Cr.			
1	Cash	84,000					84,000	1
2	Accounts Receivable	72,000	20,000				92,000	2
3	Inventory	80,000	50,000	(D1) 5,000			135,000	3
4	Land	100,000	40,000	(D2) 30,000			170,000	4
5	Investment in Sample Company	400,000			(EL) 160,000			5
6					(D) 240,000			6
7	Buildings	500,000	200,000	(D3) 100,000			800,000	7
8	Accumulated Depreciation	(80,000)	(50,000)				(130,000)	8
9	Equipment	240,000	60,000	(D4) 20,000			320,000	9
10	Accumulated Depreciation	(40,000)	(20,000)				(60,000)	10
11	Copyright			(D5) 50,000			50,000	11
12	Goodwill		40,000	(D6) 95,000			135,000	12
13	Current Liabilities	(80,000)	(40,000)				(120,000)	13
14	Bonds Payable	(200,000)	(100,000)				(300,000)	14
15	Common Stock—Sample		(10,000)	(EL) 8,000		(2,000)		15
16	Paid-In Capital in Excess of Par—Sample		(90,000)	(EL) 72,000		(18,000)		16
17	Retained Earnings—Sample		(100,000)	(EL) 80,000	NCI 60,000	(80,000)		17
18	Common Stock—Parental	(36,000)					(36,000)	18
19	Paid-In Capital in Excess of Par—Parental	(584,000)					(584,000)	19
20	Retained Earnings—Parental	(456,000)					(456,000)	20
21	Totals	0	0	460,000	460,000			21
22	NCI					(100,000)	(100,000)	22
23	Totals					0	0	23

Eliminations and Adjustments:

(EL) Eliminate 80% subsidiary equity against investment account.
(NCI) Adjust NCI to fair value (credit to Sample's Retained Earnings).
(D) Distribute remaining excess in investment account plus NCI adjustment to:
(D1) Inventory.
(D2) Land.
(D3) Building (recorded cost is increased without removing accumulated depreciation). The alternative is to debit Accumulated Depreciation for $50,000 and Buildings for $50,000. This would also restate the net asset at fair value.

(D4) Equipment (recorded cost is increased without removing accumulated depreciation). The alternative is to debit Accumulated Depreciation for $20,000. This would also restate the net asset at fair value.
(D5) Copyright.
(D6) **Goodwill.**

Worksheet 2A-1

Reverse Acquisition
Public Company and Subsidiary Private Company
Worksheet for Consolidated Balance Sheet
December 31, 2015

Worksheet 2A-1 (see page 85)

(Credits are in parentheses.)	Balance Sheet		Eliminations & Adjustments		NCI	Consolidated Balance Sheet	
	Private	Public	Dr.	Cr.			
1 Current Assets	700	500				1,200	1
2 Investment in Private Company		2,400		(EL) 2,400			2
3							3
4 Fixed Assets	3,000	1,300	(D1) 200			4,500	4
5 Goodwill			(D2) 300			300	5
6 Long-Term Liabilities	(1,700)	(700)				(2,400)	6
7 Common Stock—Private	(60)		(Trans) 60				7
8 Paid-In Capital in Excess of Par—Private	(540)		(Trans) 540				8
9 Retained Earnings—Private	(1,400)					(1,400)	9
10 Common Stock—Public (100 + 150)		(250)	(EL) 150	(Trans) 150		(250)	10
11 Paid-In Capital in Excess of Par—Public (200 + 2,250)		(2,450)	(EL) 2,250	(Trans) 1,750		(1,950)	11
12 Retained Earnings—Public		(800)	(Trans) 1,300	(D) 500			12
13 Totals	0	0	4,800	4,800		0	13
14 NCI					0	0	14
15 Totals					0	0	15

Eliminations and Adjustments:

(EL)   Eliminate investment account and entries to Public equity made to record the acquisition.
(D)   Distribute fair market value adjustment to Public Company retained earnings as of the acquisition date.
(D1)   Increase fixed assets from $1,300 to $1,500.
(D2)   Record goodwill.
(Trans) Transfer Private paid-in equity and Public retained earnings into value assigned to newly issued Public shares.

Worksheet 2A-2

Reverse Acquisition with Noncontrolling Interest in the Private Company
Public Company and Subsidiary Private Company
Worksheet for Consolidated Balance Sheet
December 31, 2015

Worksheet 2A-2 (see page 87)

(Credits are in parentheses.)	Balance Sheet		Eliminations & Adjustments		NCI	Consolidated Balance Sheet	
	Private	Public	Dr.	Cr.			
Current Assets	700	500				1,200	1
Investment in Private Company		1,920		(EL) 1,920			2
							3
Fixed Assets	3,000	1,300	(D1) 200			4,500	4
Goodwill			(D2) 300			300	5
Long-Term Liabilities	(1,700)	(700)				(2,400)	6
Common Stock—Private	(60)		(Trans) 48		(12)		7
Paid-In Capital in Excess of Par—Private	(540)		(Trans) 432		(108)		8
Retained Earnings—Private	(1,400)				(280)	(1,120)	9
Common Stock—Public (100 + 120)		(220)	(EL) 120	(Trans) 120		(220)	10
Paid-In Capital in Excess of Par—Public (200 + 1,800)		(2,000)	(EL) 1,800	(Trans) 1,660		(1,860)	11
Retained Earnings—Public		(800)	(Trans) 1,300	(D) 500			12
Totals	0	0	4,200	4,200		0	13
NCI					(400)	(400)	14
Totals						0	15

Eliminations and Adjustments:

(EL) Eliminate investment account and entries to Public equity made to record the acquisition.
(D) Distribute fair market value adjustment to Public Company retained earnings as of the acquisition date.
(D1) Increase fixed assets from $1,300 to $1,500.
(D2) Record goodwill.
(Trans) Roll Private paid-in equity and Public retained earnings into value assigned to newly issued Public shares.

UNDERSTANDING THE ISSUES

1. Jacobson Company is considering an investment in the common stock of Biltrite Company. What are the accounting issues surrounding the recording of income in future periods if Jacobson purchases:

   a. 15% of Biltrite's outstanding shares.
   b. 40% of Biltrite's outstanding shares.
   c. 100% of Biltrite's outstanding shares.
   d. 80% of Biltrite's outstanding shares.

2. What does the elimination process accomplish?

3. Paulos Company purchases a controlling interest in Sanjoy Company. Sanjoy had identifiable net assets with a book value of $500,000 and a fair value of $800,000. It was agreed that the total fair value of Sanjoy's common stock was $1,200,000. Use value analysis schedules to determine what adjustments will be made to Sanjoy's accounts and what new accounts and amounts will be recorded if:

   a. Paulos purchases 100% of Sanjoy's common stock for $1,200,000.
   b. Paulos purchases 80% of Sanjoy's common stock for $960,000.

4. Pillow Company is purchasing a 100% interest in the common stock of Sleep Company. Sleep's balance sheet amounts at book and fair values are as follows:

Account	Book Value	Fair Value
Current Assets	$ 200,000	$ 250,000
Fixed Assets	350,000	800,000
Liabilities	(200,000)	(200,000)

   Use valuation analysis schedules to determine what adjustments to recorded values of Sleep Company's accounts will be made in the consolidation process (including the creation of new accounts), if the price paid for the 100% is:
   a. $1,000,000.
   b. $500,000.

5. Pillow Company is purchasing an 80% interest in the common stock of Sleep Company. Sleep's balance sheet amounts at book and fair values are as follows:

Account	Book Value	Fair Value
Current Assets	$ 200,000	$ 250,000
Fixed Assets	350,000	800,000
Liabilities	(200,000)	(200,000)

   Use valuation analysis schedules to determine what adjustments to recorded values of Sleep Company's accounts will be made in the consolidation process (including the creation of new accounts), if the price paid for the 80% is:

   a. $800,000.
   b. $600,000.

6. Pillow Company is purchasing an 80% interest in the common stock of Sleep Company for $800,000. Sleep's balance sheet amounts at book and fair value are as follows:

Account	Book Value	Fair Value
Current Assets	$ 200,000	$ 250,000
Fixed Assets	350,000	800,000
Liabilities	(200,000)	(200,000)

Use a valuation analysis schedule to determine what will be the amount of the non-controlling interest in the consolidated balance sheet and how will it be displayed in the consolidated balance sheet.

EXERCISES

Exercise 1 *(LO 1)* **Investment recording methods.** Santos Corporation is considering investing in Fenco Corporation, but is unsure about what level of ownership should be undertaken. Santos and Fenco have the following reported incomes:

	Santos	Fenco
Sales	$700,000	$450,000
Cost of goods sold.	300,000	300,000
Gross profit	$400,000	$150,000
Selling and administrative expenses . . .	120,000	80,000
Net income	$280,000	$ 70,000

Fenco paid $15,000 in cash dividends to its investors. Prepare a pro forma income statement for Santos Corporation that compares income under 10%, 30%, and 80% ownership levels.

Exercise 2 *(LO 3)* **Asset compared to stock purchase.** Glass Company is thinking about acquiring Plastic Company. Glass Company is considering two methods of accomplishing control and is wondering how the accounting treatment will differ under each method. Glass Company has estimated that the fair values of Plastic's net assets are equal to their book values, except for the equipment, which is understated by $20,000.

The following balance sheets have been prepared on the date of acquisition:

Assets	Glass	Plastic
Cash	$540,000	$ 20,000
Accounts receivable	50,000	70,000
Inventory	50,000	100,000
Property, plant, and equipment (net) . . .	230,000	270,000
Total assets.	$870,000	$460,000

Liabilities and Equity		
Current liabilities	$140,000	$ 80,000
Bonds payable	250,000	100,000
Stockholders' equity:		
Common stock ($100 par).	200,000	150,000
Retained earnings	280,000	130,000
Total liabilities and equity	$870,000	$460,000

1. Assume Glass Company purchased the net assets directly from Plastic Company for $530,000.

   a. Prepare the entry that Glass Company would make to record the purchase.
   b. Prepare the balance sheet for Glass Company immediately following the purchase.

2. Assume that 100% of the outstanding stock of Plastic Company is purchased from the former stockholders for a total of $530,000.

   a. Prepare the entry that Glass Company would make to record the purchase.
   b. State how the investment would appear on Glass's unconsolidated balance sheet prepared immediately after the purchase.
   c. Indicate how the consolidated balance sheet would appear.

Exercise 3 *(LO 5)* **Simple value analysis.** Flom Company is considering the cash purchase of 100% of the outstanding stock of Vargas Company. The terms are not set, and alternative prices are being considered for negotiation. The balance sheet of Vargas Company shows the following values:

Assets		Liabilities and Equity	
Cash equivalents	$ 60,000	Current liabilities	$ 60,000
Inventory	120,000	Common stock ($5 par)	100,000
Land.	100,000	Paid-in capital in excess of par . . .	150,000
Building (net)	200,000	Retained earnings	170,000
Total assets.	$480,000	Total liabilities and equity	$480,000

Appraisals reveal that the inventory has a fair value of $160,000 and that the land and building have fair values of $120,000 and $300,000, respectively.

1. Above what price will goodwill be recorded?
2. Below what price will a gain be recorded?

 Exercise 4 *(LO 5, 6)* **Recording purchase with goodwill.** Woolco, Inc., purchased all the outstanding stock of Paint, Inc., for $980,000. Woolco also paid $10,000 in direct acquisition costs. Just before the investment, the two companies had the following balance sheets:

Assets	Woolco, Inc.	Paint, Inc.
Accounts receivable	$ 900,000	$ 500,000
Inventory	600,000	200,000
Depreciable fixed assets (net)	1,500,000	600,000
Total assets.	$3,000,000	$1,300,000

Liabilities and Equity		
Current liabilities	$ 950,000	$ 400,000
Bonds payable	500,000	200,000
Common stock ($10 par).	400,000	300,000
Paid-in capital in excess of par	500,000	380,000
Retained earnings	650,000	20,000
Total liabilities and equity	$3,000,000	$1,300,000

Appraisals for the assets of Paint, Inc., indicate that fair values differ from recorded book values for the inventory and for the depreciable fixed assets, which have fair values of $250,000 and $750,000, respectively.

1. Prepare the entries to record the purchase of the Paint, Inc., common stock and payment of acquisition costs.
2. Prepare the value analysis and the determination and distribution of excess schedule for the investment in Paint, Inc.
3. Prepare the elimination entries that would be made on a consolidated worksheet.

Exercise 5 *(LO 5, 6)* **Purchase with a gain.** Libra Company is purchasing 100% of the outstanding stock of Genall Company for $700,000. Genall has the following balance sheet on the date of acquisition:

Assets		Liabilities and Equity	
Accounts receivable	$ 300,000	Current liabilities	$ 250,000
Inventory	200,000	Bonds payable	200,000
Property, plant, and equipment		Common stock ($5 par).........	200,000
(net)......................	500,000		
		Paid-in capital in excess of par ...	300,000
Computer software	125,000	Retained earnings	175,000
Total assets.................	$1,125,000	Total liabilities and equity	$1,125,000

Appraisals indicate that the following fair values for the assets and liabilities should be acknowledged:

Accounts receivable	$300,000
Inventory	215,000
Property, plant, and equipment.......	700,000
Computer software	130,000
Current liabilities	250,000
Bonds payable	210,000

1. Prepare the value analysis schedule and the determination and distribution of excess schedule.
2. Prepare the elimination entries that would be made on a consolidated worksheet prepared on the date of purchase.

Exercise 6 *(LO 5, 6, 7)* **80% purchase, alternative values for goodwill.** Quail Company purchases 80% of the common stock of Commo Company for $800,000. At the time of the purchase, Commo has the following balance sheet:

Assets		Liabilities and Equity	
Cash equivalents	$ 120,000	Current liabilities	$ 200,000
Inventory	200,000	Bonds payable	400,000
Land........................	100,000	Common stock ($5 par).........	100,000
Building (net)	450,000	Paid-in capital in excess of par ...	150,000
Equipment (net)	230,000	Retained earnings	250,000
Total assets.................	$1,100,000	Total liabilities and equity	$1,100,000

The fair values of assets are as follows:

Cash equivalents	$120,000
Inventory	250,000
Land...........................	200,000
Building	650,000
Equipment	200,000

1. Prepare the value analysis schedule and the determination and distribution of excess schedule under three alternatives for valuing the NCI:

   a. The value of the NCI is implied by the price paid by the parent for the controlling interest.
   b. The market value of the shares held by the NCI is $45 per share.
   c. The international accounting option, which does not allow goodwill to be recorded as part of the NCI, is used.

2. Prepare the elimination entries that would be made on a consolidated worksheet prepared on the date of purchase under the three alternatives for valuing the NCI:

   a. The value of the NCI is implied by the price paid by the parent for the controlling interest.
   b. The market value of the shares held by the NCI is $45 per share.
   c. The international accounting option, which does not allow goodwill to be recorded as part of the NCI, is used.

Exercise 7 *(LO 5, 6, 7, 8)* **80% purchase with a gain and preexisting goodwill.** Venus Company purchases 8,000 shares of Sundown Company for $64 per share. Just prior to the purchase, Sundown Company has the following balance sheet:

Assets		Liabilities and Equity	
Cash	$ 20,000	Current liabilities	$250,000
Inventory	280,000	Common stock ($5 par)...........	50,000
Property, plant, and equipment (net) .	400,000	Paid-in capital in excess of par	130,000
Goodwill	100,000	Retained earnings	370,000
Total assets..................	$800,000	Total liabilities and equity	$800,000

Venus Company believes that the inventory has a fair value of $400,000 and that the property plant, and equipment is worth $500,000.

1. Prepare the value analysis schedule and the determination and distribution of excess schedule.
2. Prepare the elimination entries that would be made on a consolidated worksheet prepared on the date of acquisition.

Exercise 8 *(LO 1, 5, 6, 7, 8)* **Prior investment, control with later acquisition.** Barns Corporation purchased a 10% interest in Delta Company on January 1, 2015, as an available-for-sale investment for a price of $42,000.

On January 1, 2020, Barns Corporation purchased 7,000 additional shares of Delta Company from existing shareholders for $350,000. This purchase raised Barns's interest to 80%. Delta Company had the following balance sheet just prior to Barns's second purchase:

Assets		Liabilities and Equity	
Current assets	$165,000	Liabilities	$ 65,000
Buildings (net)	140,000	Common stock ($10 par).........	100,000
Equipment (net)	100,000	Retained earnings	240,000
Total assets..................	$405,000	Total liabilities and equity	$405,000

At the time of the second purchase, Barns determined that Delta's equipment was understated by $50,000 and had a 5-year remaining life. All other book values approximated fair values. Any remaining excess was attributed to goodwill.

1. Prepare the value analysis and the determination and distribution of excess schedule for the 2020 purchase.
2. Record the investment made by Barns on January 1, 2020, and any required adjustment of the prior 10% interest.

Exercise 9 *(LO 9)* **Push-down accounting.** On January 1, 2021, Knight Corporation purchases all the outstanding shares of Craig Company for $950,000. It has been decided that Craig Company will use push-down accounting principles to account for this transaction. The current balance sheet is stated at historical cost.

The following balance sheet is prepared for Craig Company on January 1, 2021:

Assets			Liabilities and Equity		
Current assets:			Current liabilities		$ 90,000
Cash	$ 80,000		Long-term liabilities:		
Accounts receivable...........	260,000		Bonds payable...............	$300,000	
			Deferred taxes	50,000	350,000
Prepaid expenses.............	20,000	$ 360,000	Stockholders' equity:		
Property, plant, and equipment:			Common stock ($10 par)........	$300,000	
Land.......................	$200,000		Retained earnings	420,000	720,000
Building (net)	600,000	800,000			
Total assets..................		$1,160,000	Total liabilities and equity		$1,160,000

Knight Corporation receives the following appraisals for Craig Company's assets and liabilities:

Cash	$ 80,000
Accounts receivable	260,000
Prepaid expenses	20,000
Land.	250,000
Building (net)	700,000
Current liabilities	90,000
Bonds payable	280,000
Deferred tax liability	40,000

1. Record the investment.
2. Prepare the value analysis schedule and the determination and distribution of excess schedule.
3. Record the adjustments on the books of Craig Company.
4. Prepare the entries that would be made on the consolidated worksheet to eliminate the investment.

APPENDIX EXERCISE

Exercise 2A-1 *(LO 10)* **Reverse acquisition.** Small Company acquired a controlling interest in Big Company. Private Company had the following balance sheet on the acquisition date:

Small Company (the acquirer)
Balance Sheet
December 31, 2015

Assets		Liabilities and Equity	
Current assets	$1,000	Long-term liabilities	$2,000
Fixed assets	5,000	Common stock ($1 par) (100 shares)	100
		Paid-in capital in excess of par	900
		Retained earnings	3,000
Total assets.	$6,000	Total liabilities and equity	$6,000

Big Company had the following book and fair values on the acquisition date:

Assets	Book Value	Fair Value	Liabilities and Equity	Book Value	Fair Value
Current assets	$1,000	$1,000	Long-term liabilities	$1,000	$1,000
Fixed assets	2,000	3,000	Common stock ($1 par)		
			(200 shares)	200	
			Paid-in capital in excess		
			of par.	800	
			Retained earnings	1,000	
			Total liabilities and		
Total assets.	$3,000	$4,000	equity.	$3,000	

The shareholders of Small Company requested 300 Big Company shares in exchange for all of their 100 shares. This was an exchange ratio of 3 to 1. The fair value of a share of Big Company was $25.

Prepare an appropriate value analysis and a determination and distribution of excess schedule.

PROBLEMS

Problem 2-1 *(LO 3, 4, 5, 6)* **100% purchase, goodwill, consolidated balance sheet.** On July 1, 2016, Roland Company exchanged 18,000 of its $45 fair value ($1 par value) shares for all the outstanding shares of Downes Company. Roland paid acquisition costs of $40,000. The two companies had the following balance sheets on July 1, 2016:

Assets	Roland	Downes
Other current assets...............	$ 50,000	$ 70,000
Inventory	120,000	60,000
Land...........................	100,000	40,000
Building (net)	300,000	120,000
Equipment (net)	430,000	110,000
Total assets....................	$1,000,000	$400,000

Liabilities and Equity		
Current liabilities	$ 180,000	$ 60,000
Common stock ($1 par).............	40,000	20,000
Paid-in capital in excess of par	360,000	180,000
Retained earnings	420,000	140,000
Total liabilities and equity	$1,000,000	$400,000

The following fair values applied to Downes's assets:

Other current assets...........	$ 70,000
Inventory	80,000
Land.......................	90,000
Building	150,000
Equipment	100,000

Required ▶ ▶ ▶ ▶ ▶
1. Record the investment in Downes Company and any other entry necessitated by the purchase.
2. Prepare the value analysis and the determination and distribution of excess schedule.
3. Prepare a consolidated balance sheet for July 1, 2016, immediately subsequent to the purchase.

Problem 2-2 *(LO 3, 4, 5, 6, 7)* **80% purchase, goodwill, consolidated balance sheet.** Using the data given in Problem 2-1, assume that Roland Company exchanged 14,000 of its $45 fair value ($1 par value) shares for 16,000 of the outstanding shares of Downes Company.

Required ▶ ▶ ▶ ▶ ▶
1. Record the investment in Downes Company and any other purchase-related entry.
2. Prepare the value analysis schedule and the determination and distribution of excess schedule.
3. Prepare a consolidated balance sheet for July 1, 2016, immediately subsequent to the purchase.

Problem 2-3 *(LO 3, 4, 5, 6)* **100% purchase, bargain, elimination entries only.** On March 1, 2015, Carlson Enterprises purchases a 100% interest in Entro Corporation for $400,000. Entro Corporation has the following balance sheet on February 28, 2015:

Entro Corporation
Balance Sheet
February 28, 2015

Assets			Liabilities and Equity		
Accounts receivable	$ 60,000		Current liabilities	$ 50,000	
Inventory	80,000		Bonds payable	100,000	

(continued)

Assets		Liabilities and Equity	
Land...........................	40,000	Common stock ($5 par).........	50,000
Buildings	300,000	Paid-in capital in excess of par ...	250,000
Accumulated depreciation—building ..	(120,000)	Retained earnings	70,000
Equipment	220,000		
Accumulated depreciation—equipment	(60,000)		
Total assets....................	$ 520,000	Total liabilities and equity	$520,000

Carlson Enterprises receives an independent appraisal on the fair values of Entro Corporation's assets and liabilities. The controller has reviewed the following figures and accepts them as reasonable:

Accounts receivable	$ 60,000
Inventory	100,000
Land........................	40,500
Building	202,500
Equipment	162,000
Current liabilities	50,000
Bonds payable	95,000

1. Record the investment in Entro Corporation.
2. Prepare the value analysis and the determination and distribution of excess schedule.
3. Prepare the elimination entries that would be made on a consolidated worksheet prepared on the date of acquisition.

 **Required**

Problem 2-4 *(LO 3, 4, 5, 6, 7)* **80% purchase, bargain, elimination entries only.** On March 1, 2015, Penson Enterprises purchases an 80% interest in Express Corporation for $320,000 cash. Express Corporation has the following balance sheet on February 28, 2015:

Express Corporation
Balance Sheet
February 28, 2015

Assets		Liabilities and Equity	
Accounts receivable .... $	60,000	Current liabilities .... $	50,000
Inventory	80,000	Bonds payable	100,000
Land..........................	40,000	Common stock ($10 par)............	50,000
Buildings	300,000	Paid-in capital in excess of par	250,000
Accumulated depreciation—buildings .	(120,000)	Retained earnings	70,000
Equipment	220,000		
Accumulated depreciation—equipment	(60,000)		
Total assets.................... $	520,000	Total liabilities and equity	$520,000

Penson Enterprises receives an independent appraisal on the fair values of Express Corporation's assets and liabilities. The controller has reviewed the following figures and accepts them as reasonable:

Accounts receivable	$ 60,000
Inventory	100,000
Land........................	50,000
Buildings	200,000
Equipment	162,000
Current liabilities	50,000
Bonds payable	95,000

Required ▶ ▶ ▶ ▶ ▶
1. Record the investment in Express Corporation.
2. Prepare the value analysis schedule and the determination and distribution of excess schedule.
3. Prepare the elimination entries that would be made on a consolidated worksheet prepared on the date of acquisition.

Problem 2-5 *(LO 5, 6, 9)* **100% purchase, goodwill, push-down accounting.** On March 1, 2015, Collier Enterprises purchases a 100% interest in Robby Corporation for $480,000 cash. Robby Corporation applies push-down accounting principles to account for this acquisition.

Robby Corporation has the following balance sheet on February 28, 2015:

Robby Corporation
Balance Sheet
February 28, 2015

Assets		Liabilities and Equity	
Accounts receivable	$ 60,000	Current liabilities	$ 50,000
Inventory	80,000	Bonds payable	100,000
Land	40,000	Common stock ($5)	50,000
Buildings	300,000	Paid-in capital in excess of par	250,000
Accumulated depreciation—buildings	(120,000)	Retained earnings	70,000
Equipment	220,000		
Accumulated depreciation—equipment	(60,000)		
Total assets	$ 520,000	Total liabilities and equity	$520,000

Collier Enterprises receives an independent appraisal on the fair values of Robby Corporation's assets and liabilities. The controller has reviewed the following figures and accepts them as reasonable:

Accounts receivable	$ 60,000
Inventory	100,000
Land	55,000
Buildings	200,000
Equipment	150,000
Current liabilities	50,000
Bonds payable	98,000

Required ▶ ▶ ▶ ▶ ▶
1. Record the investment in Robby Corporation.
2. Prepare the value analysis schedule and the determination and distribution of excess schedule.
3. Give Robby Corporation's adjusting entry.

Problem 2-6 *(LO 3, 4, 5, 6)* **100% purchase, goodwill, worksheet.** On December 31, 2015, Aron Company purchases 100% of the common stock of Shield Company for $450,000 cash. On this date, any excess of cost over book value is attributed to accounts with fair values that differ from book values. These accounts of Shield Company have the following fair values:

Cash	$ 40,000
Accounts receivable	30,000
Inventory	140,000
Land	45,000
Buildings and equipment	225,000
Copyrights	25,000
Current liabilities	65,000
Bonds payable	105,000

The following comparative balance sheets are prepared for the two companies immediately after the purchase:

	Aron	Shield
Cash	$ 185,000	$ 40,000
Accounts receivable	70,000	30,000
Inventory	130,000	120,000
Investment in Shield Company	450,000	
Land........................	50,000	35,000
Buildings and equipment...........	350,000	230,000
Accumulated depreciation	(100,000)	(50,000)
Copyrights.....................	40,000	10,000
Total assets....................	$1,175,000	$415,000
Current liabilities	$ 192,000	$ 65,000
Bonds payable		100,000
Common stock ($10 par)—Aron......	100,000	
Common stock ($5 par)—Shield......		50,000
Paid-in capital in excess of par	250,000	70,000
Retained earnings	633,000	130,000
Total liabilities and equity	$1,175,000	$415,000

1. Prepare the value analysis schedule and the determination and distribution of excess schedule for the investment in Shield Company. ◀ ◀ ◀ ◀ ◀ **Required**
2. Complete a consolidated worksheet for Aron Company and its subsidiary Shield Company as of December 31, 2015.

Problem 2-7 *(LO 3, 4, 5, 6, 7)* **80% purchase, goodwill, worksheet.** Using the data given in Problem 2-6, assume that Aron Company purchases 80% of the common stock of Shield Company for $320,000 cash.

The following comparative balance sheets are prepared for the two companies immediately after the purchase:

	Aron	Shield
Cash	$ 315,000	$ 40,000
Accounts receivable	70,000	30,000
Inventory	130,000	120,000
Investment in Shield Company	320,000	
Land........................	50,000	35,000
Buildings and equipment...........	350,000	230,000
Accumulated depreciation	(100,000)	(50,000)
Copyrights.....................	40,000	10,000
Total assets....................	$1,175,000	$415,000
Current liabilities	$ 192,000	$ 65,000
Bonds payable		100,000
Common stock ($10 par)—Aron......	100,000	
Common stock ($5 par)—Shield......		50,000
Paid-in capital in excess of par	250,000	70,000
Retained earnings	633,000	130,000
Total liabilities and equity	$1,175,000	$415,000

1. Prepare the value analysis and the determination and distribution of excess schedule for the investment in Shield Company. ◀ ◀ ◀ ◀ ◀ **Required**
2. Complete a consolidated worksheet for Aron Company and its subsidiary Shield Company as of December 31, 2015.

Use the following information for Problems 2-8 through 2-11:

In an attempt to expand its operations, Palto Company acquires Saleen Company on January 1, 2015. Palto pays cash in exchange for the common stock of Saleen. On the date of acquisition, Saleen has the following balance sheet:

Saleen Company
Balance Sheet
January 1, 2015

Assets		Liabilities and Equity	
Accounts receivable	$ 20,000	Current liabilities	$ 40,000
Inventory	50,000	Bonds payable	100,000
Land	40,000	Common stock ($1 par)	10,000
Buildings	200,000	Paid-in capital in excess of par	90,000
Accumulated depreciation	(50,000)	Retained earnings	60,000
Equipment	60,000		
Accumulated depreciation	(20,000)		
Total assets	$300,000	Total liabilities and equity	$300,000

An appraisal provides the following fair values for assets:

Accounts receivable	$ 20,000
Inventory	60,000
Land	80,000
Buildings	320,000
Equipment	60,000
Copyright	50,000

Problem 2-8 *(LO 3, 4, 5, 6)* **100% purchase, goodwill, worksheet.** Use the preceding information for Palto's purchase of Saleen common stock. Assume Palto purchases 100% of the Saleen common stock for $500,000 cash. Palto has the following balance sheet immediately after the purchase:

Palto Company
Balance Sheet
January 1, 2015

Assets		Liabilities and Equity	
Cash	$ 61,000	Current liabilities	$ 80,000
Accounts receivable	65,000	Bonds payable	200,000
Inventory	80,000	Common stock ($1 par)	20,000
Investment in Saleen	500,000	Paid-in capital in excess of par	180,000
Land	100,000	Retained earnings	546,000
Buildings	250,000		
Accumulated depreciation	(80,000)		
Equipment	90,000		
Accumulated depreciation	(40,000)		
Total assets	**$1,026,00**	**Total liabilities and equity**	**$1,026,00**

Required ▶ ▶ ▶ ▶ ▶

1. Prepare the value analysis schedule and the determination and distribution of excess schedule for the investment in Saleen.
2. Complete a consolidated worksheet for Palto Company and its subsidiary Saleen Company as of January 1, 2015.

Problem 2-9 *(LO 3, 4, 5, 6, 7)* **100% purchase, bargain, worksheet.** Use the preceding information for Palto's purchase of Saleen common stock. Assume Palto purchases 100% of the Saleen common stock for $400,000 cash. Palto has the following balance sheet immediately after the purchase:

Palto Company
Balance Sheet
January 1, 2015

Assets		Liabilities and Equity	
Cash	$ 161,000	Current liabilities	$ 80,000
Accounts receivable	65,000	Bonds payable ($1 par)	200,000
Inventory	80,000	Common stock................	20,000
Investment in Saleen	400,000	Paid-in capital in excess of par ..	180,000
Land......................	100,000	Retained earnings	546,000
Buildings	250,000		
Accumulated depreciation	(80,000)		
Equipment	90,000		
Accumulated depreciation	(40,000)		
Total assets...............	$1,026,000	Total liabilities and equity	$1,026,000

◄ ◄ ◄ ◄ ◄ **Required**

1. Prepare the value analysis schedule and the determination and distribution of excess schedule for the investment in Saleen.
2. Complete a consolidated worksheet for Palto Company and its subsidiary Saleen Company as of January 1, 2015.

Problem 2-10 *(LO 3, 4, 5, 6, 7)* **80% purchase, goodwill, worksheet.** Use the preceding information for Palto's purchase of Saleen common stock. Assume Palto purchases 80% of the Saleen common stock for $400,000 cash. The shares of the noncontrolling interest have a fair value of $46 each. Palto has the following balance sheet immediately after the purchase:

Palto Company
Balance Sheet
January 1, 2015

Assets		Liabilities and Equity	
Cash	$ 161,000	Current liabilities	$ 80,000
Accounts receivable	65,000	Bonds payable	200,000
Inventory	80,000	Common stock ($1 par)........	20,000
Investment in Saleen	400,000	Paid-in capital in excess of par ...	180,000
Land......................	100,000	Retained earnings	546,000
Buildings	250,000		
Accumulated depreciation	(80,000)		
Equipment	90,000		
Accumulated depreciation	(40,000)		
Total assets...............	$1,026,000	Total liabilities and equity	$1,026,000

◄ ◄ ◄ ◄ ◄ **Required**

1. Prepare the value analysis schedule and the determination and distribution of excess schedule for the investment in Saleen.
2. Complete a consolidated worksheet for Palto Company and its subsidiary Saleen Company as of January 1, 2015.

Problem 2-11 *(LO 3, 4, 5, 6, 7)* **80% purchase, bargain, purchase, worksheet.** Use the preceding information for Palto's purchase of Saleen common stock. Assume Palto purchases 80% of the Saleen common stock for $300,000 cash. Palto has the following balance sheet immediately after the purchase:

Palto Company
Balance Sheet
January 1, 2015

Assets		Liabilities and Equity	
Cash	$ 261,000	Current liabilities	$ 80,000
Accounts receivable	65,000	Bonds payable	200,000
Inventory	80,000	Common stock ($1 par)	20,000
Investment in Saleen	300,000	Paid-in capital in excess of par	180,000
Land	100,000	Retained earnings	546,000
Buildings	250,000		
Accumulated depreciation	(80,000)		
Equipment	90,000		
Accumulated depreciation	(40,000)		
Total assets	$1,026,000	Total liabilities and equity	$1,026,000

Required ▶ ▶ ▶ ▶ ▶

1. Prepare the value analysis and the determination and distribution of excess schedule for the investment in Saleen.
2. Complete a consolidated worksheet for Palto Company and its subsidiary Saleen Company as of January 1, 2015.

Use the following information for Problems 2-12 through 2-15:

Purnell Corporation acquires Sentinel Corporation on December 31, 2015. Sentinel has the following balance sheet on the date of acquisition:

Sentinel Corporation
Balance Sheet
December 31, 2015

Assets		Liabilities and Equity	
Accounts receivable	$ 50,000	Current liabilities	$ 90,000
Inventory	120,000	Bonds payable	200,000
Land	100,000	Common stock ($1 par)	10,000
Buildings	300,000	Paid-in capital in excess of par	190,000
Accumulated depreciation	(100,000)	Retained earnings	140,000
Equipment	140,000		
Accumulated depreciation	(50,000)		
Patent	10,000		
Goodwill	60,000		
Total assets	$ 630,000	Total liabilities and equity	$630,000

An appraisal is performed to determine whether the book values of Sentinel's net assets reflect their fair values. The appraiser also determines that intangible assets exist, although they are not recorded. The following fair values for assets and liabilities are agreed upon:

Accounts receivable	$ 50,000
Inventory	100,000
Land.......................	200,000
Buildings	400,000
Equipment	200,000
Patent.....................	150,000
Computer software	50,000
Current liabilities	90,000
Bonds payable	210,000

Problem 2-12 *(LO 3, 4, 5, 6, 8)* **100% purchase, goodwill, several adjustments, worksheet.** Use the preceding information for Purnell's purchase of Sentinel common stock. Assume Purnell exchanges 22,000 shares of its own stock for 100% of the common stock of Sentinel. The stock has a market value of $50 per share and a par value of $1. Purnell has the following trial balance immediately after the purchase:

Purnell Corporation
Trial Balance
December 31, 2015

Cash	20.000
Accounts Receivable	300,000
Inventory	410,000
Investment in Sentinel	1,100,000
Land..	800,000
Buildings	2,800,000
Accumulated Depreciation	(500,000)
Equipment	600,000
Accumulated Depreciation	(230,000)
Current Liabilities................................	(150,000)
Bonds Payable..................................	(300,000)
Common Stock ($1 par)	(95,000)
Paid-In Capital in Excess of Par	(3,655,000)
Retained Earnings	(1,100,000)
Total.....................................	0

1. Prepare the value analysis schedule and the determination and distribution of excess schedule for the investment in Sentinel.   ◄ ◄ ◄ ◄ ◄ **Required**
2. Complete a consolidated worksheet for Purnell Corporation and its subsidiary Sentinel Corporation as of December 31, 2015.

Problem 2-13 *(LO 3, 4, 5, 6, 8)* **100% purchase, bargain, several adjustments, worksheet.** Use the preceding information for Purnell's purchase of Sentinel common stock. Assume Purnell exchanges 16,000 shares of its own stock for 100% of the common stock of Sentinel. The stock has a market value of $50 per share and a par value of $1. Purnell has the following trial balance immediately after the purchase, as shown on next page.

Purnell Corporation
Trial Balance
December 31, 2015

Cash	20,000
Accounts Receivable	300,000
Inventory	410,000
Investment in Sentinel	800,000
Land	800,000
Buildings	2,800,000
Accumulated Depreciation	(500,000)
Equipment	600,000
Accumulated Depreciation	(230,000)
Current Liabilities	(150,000)
Bonds Payable	(300,000)
Common Stock ($1 par)	(89,000)
Paid-In Capital in Excess of Par	(3,361,000)
Retained Earnings	(1,100,000)
Total	0

Required ▶ ▶ ▶ ▶ ▶

1. Prepare the value analysis schedule and the determination and distribution of excess schedule for the investment in Sentinel.
2. Complete a consolidated worksheet for Purnell Corporation and its subsidiary Sentinel Corporation as of December 31, 2015.

Problem 2-14 *(LO 3, 4, 5, 6, 7, 8)* **80% purchase, goodwill, several adjustments, worksheet.** Use the preceding information for Purnell's purchase of Sentinel common stock. Assume Purnell exchanges 19,000 shares of its own stock for 80% of the common stock of Sentinel. The stock has a market value of $50 per share and a par value of $1. Purnell has the following trial balance immediately after the purchase:

Purnell Corporation
Trial Balance
December 31, 2015

Cash	20,000
Accounts Receivable	300,000
Inventory	410,000
Investment in Sentinel	950,000
Land	800,000
Buildings	2,800,000
Accumulated Depreciation	(500,000)
Equipment	600,000
Accumulated Depreciation	(230,000)
Current Liabilities	(150,000)
Bonds Payable	(300,000)
Common Stock ($1 par)	(92,000)
Paid-In Capital in Excess of Par	(3,508,000)
Retained Earnings	(1,100,000)
Total	0

Required ▶ ▶ ▶ ▶ ▶

1. Prepare the value analysis schedule and the determination and distribution of excess schedule for the investment in Sentinel.
2. Complete a consolidated worksheet for Purnell Corporation and its subsidiary Sentinel Corporation as of December 31, 2015.

Problem 2-15 *(LO 3, 4, 5, 6, 7, 8)* **80% purchase, bargain, several adjustments, worksheet.** Use the preceding information for Purnell's purchase of Sentinel common stock. Assume Purnell exchanges 10,000 shares of its own stock for 80% of the common stock of Sentinel. The stock has a market value of $50 per share and a par value of $1. Purnell has the following trial balance immediately after the purchase:

Purnell Corporation
Trial Balance
December 31, 2015

Cash	20,000
Accounts Receivable	300,000
Inventory	410,000
Investment in Sentinel	500,000
Land	800,000
Buildings	2,800,000
Accumulated Depreciation	(500,000)
Equipment	600,000
Accumulated Depreciation	(230,000)
Current Liabilities	(150,000)
Bonds Payable	(300,000)
Common Stock ($1 par)	(83,000)
Paid-In Capital in Excess of Par	(3,067,000)
Retained Earnings	(1,100,000)
Total	0

1. Prepare the value analysis schedule and the determination and distribution of excess schedule for the investment in Sentinel.
2. Complete a consolidated worksheet for Purnell Corporation and its subsidiary Sentinel Corporation as of December 31, 2015.

◄ ◄ ◄ ◄ ◄ **Required**

APPENDIX PROBLEM

Problem 2A-1 *(LO 10)* **Reverse acquisition** On January 1, 2016, the shareholders of Unknown Company request 6,000 Famous shares in exchange for all of their 5,000 shares. This is an exchange ratio of 1.2 to 1. The fair value of a share of Famous Company is $60. The acquisition occurs when the two companies have the following balance sheets:

Unknown Company (the acquirer)
Balance Sheet
December 31, 2015

Assets		Liabilities and Equity	
Current assets	$ 10,000	Long-term liabilities	$ 5,000
Building (net)	150,000	Common stock ($1 par) (5,000 shares)	5,000
Equipment (net)	100,000	Paid-in capital in excess of par	115,000
		Retained earnings	135,000
Total assets	$260,000	Total liabilities and equity	$260,000

Famous Company (the acquiree)
Balance Sheet
December 31, 2015

Assets	Book Value	Fair Value	Liabilities and Equity	Book Value	Fair Value
Current assets	$ 5,000	$ 5,000	Long-term liabilities	$ 10,000	$10,000
Building (net)	100,000	200,000	Common stock ($1 par)		
			(4,000 shares)	4,000	
Equipment (net)	20,000	40,000	Paid-in capital in excess of par	96,000	
			Retained earnings	15,000	
Total assets.	$125,000	$245,000	Total liabilities and equity . . .	$125,000	

Required ▶ ▶ ▶ ▶ ▶

1. Prepare an appropriate value analysis and a determination and distribution of excess schedule.
2. Complete a consolidated worksheet for Unknown Company and its subsidiary, Famous Company, as of January 1, 2016.

CASES

Case 2-1

Consolidating a Bargain Purchase

Your client, Great Value Hardware Stores, has come to you for assistance in evaluating an opportunity to purchase a controlling interest in a hardware store in a neighboring city. The store under consideration is a closely held family corporation. Owners of 60% of the shares are willing to sell you the 60% interest, 30,000 common stock shares in exchange for 7,500 of Great Value shares, which have a fair value of $40 each and a par value of $10 each.

Your client sees this as a good opportunity to enter a new market. The controller of Great Value knows, however, that all is not well with the store being considered. The store, Al's Hardware, has not kept pace with the market and has been losing money. It also has a major lawsuit against it stemming from alleged faulty electrical components it supplied that caused a fire. The store is not insured for the loss. Legal counsel advises that the store will likely pay $300,000 in damages.

The following balance sheet was provided by Al's Hardware as of December 31, 2015:

Assets		Liabilities and Equity	
Cash	$ 180,000	Current liabilities	$ 425,000
Accounts receivable	460,000	8% Mortgage payable	600,000
Inventory	730,000	Common stock ($5 par).	250,000
Land.	120,000	Paid-in capital in excess of par	750,000
Building	630,000	Retained earnings	(80,000)
Accumulated depreciation—building . .	(400,000)		
Equipment	135,000		
Accumulated depreciation—equipment	(85,000)		
Goodwill	175,000		
Total assets.	$1,945,000	Total liabilities and equity . .	$1,945,000

Your analysis raises substantial concerns about the values shown. You have gathered the following information:

1. Aging of the accounts receivable reveals a net realizable value of $350,000.
2. The inventory has many obsolete items; the fair value is $600,000.
3. Appraisals for long-lived assets are as follows:

Land.	$100,000
Building	300,000
Equipment	100,000

4. The goodwill resulted from the purchase of another hardware store that has since been consolidated into the existing location. The goodwill was attributed to customer loyalty.
5. Liabilities are fairly stated except that there should be a provision for the estimated loss on the lawsuit.

On the basis of your research, you are convinced that the statements of Al's Hardware are not representative and need major restatement. Your client is not interested in being associated with statements that are not accurate.

Your client asks you to make recommendations on two concerns:

1. Does the price asked seem to be a real bargain? Consider the fair value of the entire equity of Al's Hardware; then decide if the price is reasonable for a 60% interest.
2. If the deal were completed, what accounting methods would you recommend either on the books of Al's Hardware or in the consolidation process? Al's Hardware would remain a separate legal entity with a substantial noncontrolling interest.

Chapter 3

Consolidated Statements: Subsequent to Acquisition

Learning Objectives

When you have completed this chapter, you should be able to

1. Show how an investment in a subsidiary account is maintained under the simple equity, sophisticated equity, and cost methods.

2. Complete a consolidated worksheet using the simple equity method for the parent's investment account.

3. Complete a consolidated worksheet using the cost method for the parent's investment account.

4. Describe the special worksheet procedures that are used for an investment maintained under the sophisticated equity method (investment account is adjusted for amortizations of excess resulting from purchase).

5. Distribute and amortize multiple adjustments resulting from the difference between the price paid for an investment in a subsidiary and the subsidiary equity eliminated.

6. Demonstrate the worksheet procedures used for investments purchased during the financial reporting period.

7. Demonstrate an understanding of when goodwill impairment loss exists and how it is calculated.

8. Consolidate a subsidiary using vertical worksheet format. (Appendix A)

9. Explain the impact of tax-related complications arising on the purchase date. (Appendix B)

This chapter's mission is to teach the procedures needed to prepare consolidated income statements, retained earnings statements, and balance sheets in periods subsequent to the acquisition of a subsidiary. There are several worksheet models to master. This variety is caused primarily by the alternative methods available to a parent for maintaining its investment in a subsidiary account. **Accounting principles do not address the method used by a parent to record its investment in a subsidiary that is to be consolidated. The method used is of no concern to standard setters since the investment account is always eliminated when consolidating.** Thus, the method chosen to record the investment usually is based on convenience.

In the preceding chapter, worksheet procedures included asset and liability adjustments to reflect fair values on the date of the purchase. This chapter discusses the subsequent depreciation and amortization of these asset and liability revaluations in conjunction with its analysis of worksheet procedures for preparing consolidated financial statements. Appendix A, page 143, explains the vertical worksheet as an alternative approach to the horizontal worksheet, which is primarily used in this text chapter for developing consolidated statements.

This chapter does not deal with the income tax issues of the consolidated company except to the extent that they are reflected in the original acquisition price. Appendix B, page 144, considers tax issues that arise as part of the original purchase. These include recording procedures for deferred tax liabilities arising in a tax-free exchange and tax loss carryovers. A full discussion of tax issues in consolidations is included in Chapter 6.

1

OBJECTIVE

Show how an investment in a subsidiary account is maintained under the simple equity, sophisticated equity, and cost methods.

ACCOUNTING FOR THE INVESTMENT IN A SUBSIDIARY

A parent may choose one of two basic methods when accounting for its investment in a subsidiary: the equity method or the cost method. The equity method records as income an ownership percentage of the reported income of the subsidiary, whether or not it was received by the parent. The cost method treats the investment in the subsidiary like a passive investment by recording income only when dividends are declared by the subsidiary.

Equity Method

The equity method records as income the parent's ownership interest percentage multiplied by the subsidiary reported net income. The income is added to the parent's investment account. In a like manner, the parent records its share of a subsidiary loss and lowers its investment account for its share of the loss. Dividends received from the subsidiary are viewed as a conversion of a portion of the investment account into cash; thus, dividends reduce the investment account balance. The investment account at any point in time can be summarized as follows:

Investment in Subsidiary (equity method)

Original cost
plus: Ownership interest × Reported income of
        subsidiary since acquisition
	less: Ownership interest × Reported losses of
	        subsidiary since acquisition
	less: Ownership interest × Dividends declared by
	        subsidiary since acquisition

equals: Equity-adjusted balance	

The real advantage of using the *simple equity method* when consolidating is that every dollar of change in the stockholders' equity of the subsidiary is recorded on a pro rata basis in the investment account. This method expedites the elimination of the investment account in the consolidated worksheets in future periods. It is favored in this text because of its simplicity.

For some unconsolidated investments, the *sophisticated equity method* is required. Under this method, a company's investment is adjusted for amortizations of excess shown on the determination and distribution of excess schedule. For example, assume that the price paid for an investment in a subsidiary exceeded underlying book value and that the determination and distribution of excess schedule attributed the entire excess to a building. Just as a building will decrease in value and should be depreciated, so should that portion of the price paid for the investment attributed to the building also be amortized. If the estimated life of the building is 10 years, then the portion of the investment price attributed to the building should be amortized over 10 years. This would be accomplished by reducing the investment income each year by the amortization, which means that the income posted to the investment account each year is also less by the amount of the amortization.

The sophisticated equity method is required for influential investments (normally 20% to 50% interests) and for those rare subsidiaries that are not consolidated. Its use for these types of investments is fully discussed in the Special Appendix. The sophisticated equity method also is used by some parent companies to maintain the investment in a subsidiary that is to be consolidated. This better reflects the investment account in the parent-only statements, but such statements may not be used as the primary statements for external reporting purposes. Parent-only statements may be used only as supplemental statements when the criteria for consolidated statements are met. The use of this method for investments to be consolidated makes recording the investment income and the elimination of the investment account more difficult than under the simple equity method.

Cost Method

When the *cost method* is used, the investment in subsidiary account is retained at its original cost-of-acquisition balance. No adjustments are made to the account for income as it is earned by the subsidiary. Income on the investment is limited to dividends received from the subsidiary. The cost method is acceptable for subsidiaries that are to be consolidated because, in the consolidation process, the investment account is eliminated entirely.

The cost method is the most common method used in practice by parent companies. It is simple to use during the accounting period and avoids the risk of incorrect adjustments. Typically, the correct income of the subsidiary is not known until after the end of the accounting period. Awaiting its determination would delay the parent company's closing procedures. This text will follow a procedure of converting cost method investments to the simple equity method as part of the worksheet investment elimination procedures.

Example of the Equity and Cost Methods

The simple equity, sophisticated equity, and cost methods will be illustrated by an example covering two years. This example, which will become the foundation for several consolidated worksheets in this chapter, is based on the following facts:

1. The following D&D schedule was prepared on the January 1, 2015, date of purchase. It is assumed that the value of the NCI is proportionate to the price paid by Company P for the controlling interest. This schedule is similar to that of the preceding chapter but is modified to indicate the period over which adjustments to the subsidiary book values will be amortized. This expanded format will be used in preparing all future worksheets.

2. Income during 2015 was $25,000 for Company S; dividends declared by Company S at the end of 2015 totaled $10,000.

3. During 2016, Company S had a loss of $12,000 and declared dividends of $5,000.

4. The balance in Company S's retained earnings account on December 31, 2016, is $73,000.

Company P and Subsidiary Company S
Determination and Distribution of Excess Schedule

	Company Implied Fair Value	Parent Price (90%)	NCI Value (10%)
Fair value of subsidiary	$150,000	$135,000	$ 15,000
Less book value of interest acquired:			
Common stock ($10 par).	$ 50,000		
Retained earnings	70,000		
Total stockholders' equity.	$120,000	$120,000	$120,000
Interest acquired		90%	10%
Book value.		$108,000	$ 12,000
Excess of fair value over book value	**$ 30,000**	$ 27,000	$ 3,000

Adjustment of identifiable accounts:

	Adjustment	Amortization per Year	Life	Worksheet Key
Patent ($150,000 fair – $120,000 book value)	**$ 30,000**	$ 3,000	10	**debit D**

Event		Entries on Parent Company's Books—Simple Equity Method		
2015				
Jan. 1	Purchase of stock	Investment in Company S	135,000	
		Cash..................................		135,000
Dec. 31	Subsidiary income of $25,000 reported to parent	Investment in Company S	22,500	
		Subsidiary Income		22,500
31	Dividends of $10,000 declared by subsidiary	Dividends Receivable	9,000	
		Investment in Company S................		9,000
		Investment Balance, Dec. 31, 2015		**$148,500**
2016				
Dec. 31	Subsidiary loss of $12,000 reported to parent	Loss on Subsidiary Operations	10,800	
		Investment in Company S................		10,800
31	Dividends of $5,000 declared by subsidiary	Dividends Receivable	4,500	
		Investment in Company S................		4,500
		Investment Balance, Dec. 31, 2016		**$133,200**

The journal entries and resulting investment account balances shown above and on page 121 record this information on the books of Company P using the simple equity, cost, and sophisticated equity methods. Note that the only difference between the sophisticated and simple equity methods is that the former records 90% of the subsidiary's reported income of $25,000. The sophisticated equity method records 90% of the subsidiary's income of $25,000 less the amortization adjustment of $3,000. Thus, the sophisticated equity share of income the first year is 90% of $22,000, or $19,800.

REFLECTION

- The simple equity method records investment income (loss) equal to the parent ownership interest multiplied by the reported subsidiary income (loss).

- The sophisticated equity method records investment income (loss) equal to the parent ownership interest multiplied by the reported subsidiary income (loss) and deducts amortizations of excess allocable to the controlling interest.

- The cost method records only dividends as received.

2

OBJECTIVE

Complete a consolidated worksheet using the simple equity method for the parent's investment account.

ELIMINATION PROCEDURES

Worksheet procedures necessary to prepare consolidated income statements, retained earnings statements, and balance sheets are examined in the following section. **Recall that the consolidation process is performed independently each year since the worksheet eliminations of previous years are never recorded by the parent or subsidiary.**

Entries on Parent Company's Books—Sophisticated Equity Method		Entries on Parent Company's Books—Cost Method	
Investment in Company S 135,000		Investment in Company S 135,000	
Cash.	135,000	Cash.	135,000
Investment in Company S[a]........ 19,800		No entry.	
Subsidiary Income	19,800		
Dividends Receivable 9,000		Dividends Receivable 9,000	
Investment in Company S.......	9,000	Subsidiary (Dividend) Income	9,000
Investment Balance,		**Investment Balance,**	
Dec. 31, 2015.	**$145,800**	**Dec. 31, 2015**	**$135,000**
Loss on Subsidiary Operations 13,500		No entry.	
Investment in Company S[b]......	13,500		
Dividends Receivable 4,500		Dividends Receivable 4,500	
Investment in Company S.......	4,500	Subsidiary (Dividend) Income	4,500
Investment Balance,		**Investment Balance,**	
Dec. 31, 2016.	**$127,800**	**Dec. 31, 2016.**	**$135,000**

[a]Parent's share of subsidiary income = 90% × ($25,000 – $3,000 amortization adjustment).
[b]Parent's share of subsidiary loss = 90% × (–$12,000 – $3,000 amortization adjustment).

The illustrations that follow are based on the facts concerning the investment in Company S, as detailed in the previous example. The procedures for consolidating an investment maintained under the simple equity method will be discussed first, followed by an explanation of how procedures would differ under the cost and sophisticated equity methods. (See the inside front cover for a complete listing of the elimination codes used in this text.)

Effect of Simple Equity Method on Consolidation

Examine Worksheet 3-1 on pages 150 and 151, noting that the worksheet trial balances for Company P and Company S are preclosing trial balances and, thus, include the income statement accounts of both companies. Look at Company P's trial balance and note that Investment in Company S is now at the equity-adjusted cost at the end of the year. The balance reflects the following information:

Worksheet 3-1: page 150

Cost	$135,000
Plus equity income (90% × $25,000 Company S income).	22,500
Less dividends received (90% × $10,000 dividends paid by Company S)	(9,000)
Balance	$148,500

If we are going to eliminate the subsidiary equity against the investment account and get the correct excess, **the investment account and subsidiary equity must be at the same point in time.** Right now, the investment account is adjusted through the end of the year, and the subsidiary retained earnings is still at its January 1 balance. Eliminating (reversing) the entries that affected the investment balance during the current year creates date alignment. First, the entry for (CY1) [for Current Year entry #1] eliminates the subsidiary income recorded against the investment account as follows:

Eliminate current-year investment income for **date alignment**:

(CY1)	Subsidiary Income (Company P account)	22,500	
	Investment in Company S.		22,500

This elimination also removes the subsidiary income account. This is appropriate because we will, instead, be including the income statement accounts of the subsidiary. The intercompany dividends paid by the subsidiary to the parent will be eliminated next as follows with entry (CY2):

Eliminate intercompany dividends:

(CY2)   Investment in Company S   9,000
        Dividends Declared (Company S account)   9,000

After this entry, only subsidiary dividends paid to the noncontrolling shareholders will remain. These are dividends paid to the "outside world" and, as such, belong in the consolidated statements.

Once you have created date alignment, it is appropriate to eliminate 90% of the subsidiary equity against the investment account with entry (EL) [for Elimination entry]. This entry is the same as described in Chapter 2.

(EL)   Eliminate 90% subsidiary equity against investment
        account:
    Common Stock ($10 par)—Company S (90% eliminated)   45,000
    Retained Earnings, January 1, 2015—Company S
        (90% eliminated)   63,000
        Investment in Company S.......................   108,000

The excess ($135,000 balance after eliminating current-year entries – $108,000 = $27,000) should always agree with that indicated by the D&D schedule. The next procedure is to distribute the excess and adjust the NCI with entry (D) [for Distribute entry] and (NCI) [to adjust the NCI] as indicated by the D&D schedule as follows:

(D)/(NCI)   Distribute excess investment account balance to accounts
        to be adjusted:
    Patent.......................................   30,000
        Investment in Company S (remaining balance)   27,000
        NCI (use the subsidiary's retained earnings account) ..   3,000

The D&D schedule indicates that the life of the patent was 10 years. It must now be amortized for the first year with entry (A) [for Amortization entry]:

(A)   Amortize excess for current year:
    Patent Amortization Expense ($30,000/10 years)   3,000
        Patent.......................................   3,000

Patent amortization expense should be maintained in a separate account, so that it will be available for the income statement as a separate item.

The Consolidated Income Statement column follows the Eliminations & Adjustments columns. The adjusted income statement accounts of the constituent companies are used to calculate the *consolidated net income* of $62,000. This income is distributed to the controlling interest and NCI. Note that the NCI receives 10% of the $22,000 adjusted net income of the subsidiary, or $2,200. The controlling interest receives the balance of the consolidated net income, or $59,800.

The distribution of income is handled best by using *income distribution schedules (IDS)*, which appear at the end of Worksheet 3-1. The subsidiary IDS is a "T account" that begins with the reported net income of the subsidiary. This income is termed *internally generated net income*, which connotes the income of only the company being analyzed without consideration of income derived from other members of the affiliated group. **All amortizations of excess resulting from the consolidations process are adjusted to the subsidiary's IDS.** Since the NCI shares in the original asset adjustments, it is also adjusted for the amortizations. Subsidiary adjusted net income is calculated after adjustment for the amortizations of excess. In Worksheet 3-1, the subsidiary adjusted net income is multiplied by the noncontrolling ownership percentage to calculate the NCI share of income. A similar T account is used for the parent IDS. The parent's share of subsidiary net income is added to the internally generated net income of the parent. The balance in the parent T account is the controlling share of the consolidated net income. **The IDS is a valuable self-check procedure since the sum of the income distributions should equal the consolidated net income on the worksheet.**

The NCI column of the worksheet summarizes the total ownership interest of noncontrolling stockholders on the balance sheet date. The noneliminated portion of subsidiary common stock at par, additional paid-in capital in excess of par, retained earnings (including the NCI adjustment), the NCI share of income, and dividends declared are extended to this column. The total of this column is then extended to the Consolidated Balance Sheet column as the noncontrolling interest. The formal balance sheet will show only the total NCI and will not provide information on the components of this balance.

The Controlling Retained Earnings column produces the controlling retained earnings balance on the balance sheet date. The beginning parent retained earnings balance, as adjusted by eliminations and adjustments (in later worksheets), is extended to this column. Dividends declared by the parent are also extended to this column. The controlling share of consolidated income is extended to this column to produce the ending balance. The balance is extended to the balance sheet column as the retained earnings of the consolidated company.

The Consolidated Balance Sheet column includes the consolidated asset and liability balances. The capital accounts balances of the parent are extended as the consolidated capital accounts balances. As mentioned above, the aggregate balances of the NCI and the Controlling Retained Earnings columns are also extended to the Consolidated Balance Sheet column.

Separate debit and credit columns may be used for the consolidated balance sheet. This arrangement may minimize errors and aid analysis. Single columns are not advocated but are used to facilitate the inclusion of lengthy worksheets in a summarized fashion.

The information for the following formal statements is taken directly from Worksheet 3-1:

Company P
Consolidated Income Statement
For Year Ended December 31, 2015

Revenue.	$ 175,000
Expenses	(110,000)
Patent amortization expense	(3,000)
Consolidated net income.	$ 62,000
Distributed to:	
Noncontrolling interest	$ 2,200
Controlling interest.	$ 59,800

Company P
Consolidated Retained Earnings Statement
For Year Ended December 31, 2015

	Noncontrolling	Controlling
Retained earnings, January 1, 2015.	$10,000	$123,000
Consolidated net income.	2,200	59,800
Dividends declared	(1,000)	
Retained earnings, December 31, 2015.	$11,200*	$182,800

*This does not appear as a separate item on the worksheet.

(continued)

Company P
Consolidated Balance Sheet
December 31, 2015

Assets		Stockholders' Equity		
Net tangible assets	$372,000	Controlling interest:		
Patent.................	27,000	Common stock..........	$200,000	
		Retained earnings	182,800	$382,800
		Noncontrolling interest		16,200
Total assets	$399,000	Total stockholders' equity ...		$399,000

You should notice several features of the consolidated statements.

◆ Consolidated net income is the total income earned by the consolidated entity. The consolidated net income is then distributed to the noncontrolling interest (NCI) and the controlling interest.

◆ The retained earnings statement includes Noncontrolling and Controlling Interest columns. The Noncontrolling Interest column includes the dividends declared to noncontrolling shareholders.

◆ The consolidated balance sheet shows the NCI as a subdivision of stockholders' equity as discussed in Chapter 2. The NCI is shown only as a total and is not itemized.

Exhibit 3-1 is taken from the 2013 financial statements of Pfizer Inc. for a real-world example of disclosure for the NCI. Look at the lower portion of the consolidated income statement, and you will see the highlighted allocation of income to the noncontrolling interest. Look at the lower area of the equity section of the consolidated balance sheet, and you will see the highlighted noncontrolling interest in equity.

Exhibit 3-1
Pfizer, Inc. and Subsidiaries
Consolidated Statements of Income and Balance Sheets

Consolidated Balance Sheets
Pfizer Inc. and Subsidiary Companies

(Millions, Except Preferred Stock Issued and per Common Share Data)	As of December 31,	
	2013	2012
Assets		
Cash and cash equivalents	$ 2,183	$ 10,081
Short-term investments..................................	30,225	22,318
Accounts receivable, less allowance for doubtful accounts:		
2013—$478; 2012—$324...........................	9,357	10,675
Inventories......................................	6,166	6,076
Current deferred tax assets and other current tax assets	4,624	6,170
Other current assets....................................	3,613	3,567
Assets of discontinued operations and other assets held for sale..	76	5,944
Total current assets..................................	56,244	64,831
Long-term investments	16,406	14,149
Property, plant and equipment, less accumulated depreciation ..	12,397	13,213
Goodwill..	42,519	43,661
Identifiable intangible assets, less accumulated amortization....	39,385	45,146
Noncurrent deferred tax assets and other noncurrent tax assets ..	1,554	1,565
Other noncurrent assets.................................	3,596	3,233
Total assets..	$172,101	$185,798

(Millions, Except Preferred Stock Issued and per Common Share Data)	As of December 31, 2013	2012
Liabilities and Equity		
Short-term borrowings, including current portion of long-term debt: 2013—$2,060; 2012—$2,449	$ 6,027	$ 6,424
Accounts payable	3,234	2,921
Dividends payable	1,663	1,733
Income taxes payable	678	979
Accrued compensation and related items	1,792	1,875
Other current liabilities	9,951	13,812
Liabilities of discontinued operations	21	1,442
Total current liabilities	23,366	29,186
Long-term debt	30,462	31,036
Pension benefit obligations, net	4,635	7,782
Postretirement benefit obligations, net	2,668	3,491
Noncurrent deferred tax liabilities	25,590	21,193
Other taxes payable	3,993	6,581
Other noncurrent liabilities	4,767	4,851
Total liabilities	95,481	104,120
Commitments and Contingencies		
Preferred stock, no par value, at stated value; 27 shares authorized; issued: 2013—829; 2012—967	33	39
Common stock, $0.05 par value; 12,000 shares authorized; issued: 2013—9,051; 2012—8,956	453	448
Additional paid-in capital	77,283	72,608
Treasury stock, shares at cost: 2013—2,652; 2012—1,680	(67,923)	(40,122)
Retained earnings	69,732	54,240
Accumulated other comprehensive loss	(3,271)	(5,953)
Total Pfizer Inc. shareholders' equity	76,307	81,260
Equity attributable to noncontrolling interests	313	418
Total equity	76,620	81,678
Total liabilities and equity	$172,101	$185,798

See Notes to Consolidated Financial Statements, which are an integral part of these statements.

Consolidated Statements of Income
Pfizer Inc. and Subsidiary Companies

(Millions, Except per Common Share Data)	Year Ended December 31, 2013	2012	2011
Revenues	$51,584	$54,657	$61,035
Costs and expenses:			
Cost of sales[a]	9,586	9,821	12,500
Selling, informational and administrative expenses[a]	14,355	15,171	17,581
Research and development expenses[a]	6,678	7,482	8,681
Amortization of intangible assets	4,599	5,109	5,465
Restructuring charges and certain acquisition-related costs	1,182	1,810	2,841
Other (income)/deductions—net	(532)	4,022	2,486
Income from continuing operations before provision for taxes on income	15,716	11,242	11,481
Provision for taxes on income	4,306	2,221	3,621
Income from continuing operations	11,410	9,021	7,860

(continued)

(Millions, Except per Common Share Data)	Year Ended December 31,		
	2013	2012	2011
Discontinued operations:			
Income from discontinued operations—net of tax	**308**	794	885
Gain on disposal of discontinued operations—net of tax . .	**10,354**	4,783	1,304
Discontinued operations—net of tax	**10,662**	5,577	2,189
Net income before allocation to noncontrolling interests	**22,072**	14,598	10,049
Less: Net income attributable to noncontrolling interests . .	**69**	28	40
Net income attributable to Pfizer Inc.	**$22,003**	$14,570	$10,009
Earnings per common share—basic:			
Income from continuing operations attributable to Pfizer Inc. common shareholders	**$ 1.67**	$ 1.21	$ 1.00
Discontinued operations—net of tax	**1.56**	0.75	0.28
Net income attributable to Pfizer Inc. common shareholders	**$ 3.23**	$ 1.96	$ 1.28
Earnings per common share—diluted:			
Income from continuing operations attributable to Pfizer Inc. common shareholders	**$ 1.65**	$ 1.20	$ 0.99
Discontinued operations—net of tax	**1.54**	0.74	0.28
Net income attributable to Pfizer Inc. common shareholders	**$ 3.19**	$ 1.94	$ 1.27
Weighted-average shares—basic.	**6,813**	7,442	7,817
Weighted-average shares—diluted	**6,895**	7,508	7,870
Cash dividends paid per common share	**$ 0.96**	$ 0.88	$ 0.80

[a]Exclusive of amortization of intangible assets, except as disclosed in *Note 1K. Basis of Presentation and Significant Accounting Policies: Amortization of Intangible Assets, Depreciation and Certain Long-Lived Assets.*

See Notes to Consolidated Financial Statements, which are an integral part of these statements.

Now consider consolidation procedures for 2016 as they would apply to Companies P and S under the simple equity method. This will provide added practice in preparing worksheets and will emphasize that, at the end of each year, consolidation procedures are applied to the separate statements of the constituent firms. In essence, **each year's consolidation procedures begin as if there had never been a previous consolidation.** However, reference to past worksheets is commonly used to save time.

Worksheet 3-2: page 152 The separate trial balances of Companies P and S are displayed in the first two columns of Worksheet 3-2, pages 152 and 153. The investment in subsidiary account includes the simple equity-adjusted investment balance as calculated on page 120. Note that the balances in the retained earnings accounts of Companies P and S are for January 1, 2016, because these are the preclosing trial balances. The beginning retained earnings amounts are calculated as follows:

Company P:	January 1, 2015, balance.	$123,000
	Net income, 2015 (including Company P's share of subsidiary income under simple equity method)	62,500*
	Balance, January 1, 2016	$185,500

*Company P's own 2015 net income ($100,000 revenue – $60,000 expenses) + Company P's share of Company S 2015, $25,000 net income ($25,000 × 90%) = $40,000 + $22,500 = $62,500.

Company S:	January 1, 2015, balance.	$ 70,000
	Net income, 2015.	25,000
	Dividends declared	(10,000)
	Balance, January 1, 2016.	$ 85,000

As before, entry (CY1) eliminates the subsidiary income recorded by the parent, and entry (CY2) eliminates the intercompany dividends. Neither subsidiary income nor dividends declared by the subsidiary to the parent should remain in the consolidated statements. In journal form, the entries are as follows:

Create date alignment and eliminate current-year
 subsidiary income:

(CY1) Investment in Company S 10,800
   Subsidiary Loss 10,800
(CY2) Investment in Company S 4,500
   Dividends Declared (Company S account) 4,500

At this point, the investment account balance is returned to $148,500 ($133,200 on the trial balance + $10,800 loss + $4,500 dividends), which is the balance on January 1, 2016. Date alignment now exists, and elimination of the investment account may proceed. Entry (EL) eliminates 90% of the subsidiary equity accounts against the investment account. Entry (EL) differs in amount from the prior year's (2015) entry only because Company S's retained earnings balance has changed. Always eliminate the subsidiary's equity balances as they appear on the worksheet, not in the original D&D schedule. In journal form, entry (EL) is as follows:

Eliminate investment account at beginning-of-year balance:

(EL) Common Stock—Company S (90%) 45,000
  Retained Earnings, January 1, 2016—Company S (90%) .. 76,500
   Investment in Company S.......................... 121,500

Entries (D) and (NCI) are exactly the same as they were on the 2015 worksheet. We are always adjusting the subsidiary accounts as of the acquisition date. It will be necessary to make this same entry every year until the markup caused by the purchase is fully amortized or the asset is sold. In entry form, entry (D)/(NCI) is as follows:

Distribute excess of cost (patent):

(D)/(NCI) Patent... 30,000
  Investment in Company S.......................... 27,000
  NCI (Retained Earnings—Company S) 3,000

Finally, entry (A) includes $3,000 per year amortization of the patent for 2015 and 2016. The expense for 2015 is charged to Company P retained earnings and the NCI in the 90%/10% ratio. The charge is made to both interests because the asset adjustment was made to both interests. In journal form, the entry is as follows:

Amortize patent for current and prior year:

(A) Retained Earnings, January 1, 2016—Company P 2,700
  NCI (Retained Earnings—Company S) 300
  Patent Amortization Expense (for current year) 3,000
   Patent.. 6,000

Note that the 2017 worksheet will include three total years of amortization, since **the entries made in prior periods' worksheets have not been recorded in either the parent's or subsidiary's books.** Even in later years, when the patent is past its 10-year life, it will be necessary to use a revised entry (D), which would adjust all prior years' amortizations to the patent as follows:

Retained Earnings—Company P (10 years × $2,700)................. 27,000
NCI 3,000
 Investment in Company S (the excess) 30,000

Note that the original D&D schedule prepared on the date of acquisition becomes the foundation for all subsequent worksheets. Once prepared, the schedule is used without modification.

REFLECTION

- Date alignment is needed before an investment can be eliminated.

- For an equity method investment, date alignment means removing current-year entries to return to the beginning-of-year investment balance.

- All amortizations of excess resulting from the consolidations process are adjusted to the subsidiary's IDS.

- Many distributions of excess must be followed by amortizations that cover the current and prior years.

- The consolidated net income derived on a worksheet is allocated to the controlling and noncontrolling interests using an income distribution schedule.

- Each year's consolidation procedures begin as if there had never been a previous consolidation.

3

OBJECTIVE

Complete a consolidated worksheet using the cost method for the parent's investment account.

Worksheet 3-3: page 154

Effect of Cost Method on Consolidation

Recall that parent companies often may choose to record their investments in a subsidiary under the cost method, whereby the investments are maintained at their original costs. Income from the investments is recorded only when dividends are declared by the subsidiary. The use of the cost method means that the investment account does not reflect changes in subsidiary equity. Rather than develop a new set of procedures for the elimination of an investment under the cost method, **the cost method investment will be converted to its simple equity balance at the beginning of the period** to create date alignment. Then, the elimination procedures developed earlier can be applied.

Worksheet 3-3, pages 154 and 155, is a consolidated financial statements worksheet for Companies P and S for the first year of combined operations. The worksheet is based on the entries made under the cost method, as shown on page 121. Company P's Trial Balance column in Worksheet 3-3 reveals that the investment in the subsidiary account at year-end is still stated at the original $135,000 cost, and the income recorded by the parent as a result of subsidiary ownership is limited to $9,000, or 90% of the dividends declared by the subsidiary. **When the cost method is used, the account title *Dividend Income* may be used in place of *Subsidiary Income*.**

There is no need for an equity conversion at the end of the first year. Date alignment is automatic; the investment in Company S account and the subsidiary retained earnings are both as of January 1, 2015. There is no entry (CY1) under the cost method; only entry (CY2) is needed to eliminate intercompany dividends. All remaining eliminations are the same as for 2015 under the equity method. In journal form, the complete set of entries for 2015 is as follows:

Eliminate current-year dividends:

(CY2) Subsidiary (or Dividend) Income 9,000
    Dividends Declared (Company S account) 9,000

Eliminate investment account at beginning-of-year balance:

(EL) Common Stock—Company S 45,000
    Retained Earnings, January 1, 2015—Company S 63,000
    Investment in Company S 108,000

Distribute excess of cost (patent):

(D)/(NCI) Patent 30,000
    Investment in Company S 27,000
    NCI (use Retained Earnings—Company S) 3,000

Amortize patent for current year:

(A)   Patent Amortization Expense.   3,000

        Patent.   3,000

The last four columns of Worksheet 3-3 are exactly the same as those for Worksheet 3-1, resulting in the same consolidated statements.

For periods after 2015 (first year of consolidation), date alignment will not exist, and an equity conversion entry will be needed. Worksheet 3-4 on pages 156 and 157 is such an example. The worksheet is for 2016 and parallels Worksheet 3-2 except that the cost method is in use. The balance in the investment account is still the original cost of $135,000. The retained earnings of the subsidiary is, however, at its January 1, 2016, balance of $85,000. Note that the parent's January 1, 2016, retained earnings balance is $172,000, which is $13,500 less than in Worksheet 3-2 because it does not include the 2015 undistributed subsidiary income of $13,500 ($22,500 income less $9,000 dividends received). In order to get date alignment, an equity conversion entry, (CV), is made to convert the investment account to its January 1, 2016, simple equity balance. This conversion entry is always calculated as follows:

Worksheet 3-4: page 156

Parent's % × (Subsidiary retained earnings at the beginning of the current year
  −Subsidiary retained earnings on the date of purchase) = Equity conversion adjustment

For example:

	Date	Amount
Retained earnings—Company S (start of current year)	Jan. 1, 2016	$85,000
Retained earnings (date of purchase)	Jan. 1, 2015	70,000
Change in subsidiary retained earnings		$15,000
Parent ownership interest.		× 90%
Equity conversion adjustment (parent share of change)		$13,500

Based on this calculation, the conversion entry on Worksheet 3-4 is as follows in journal entry form:

Convert investment to simple equity method as of
    January 1, 2016:

(CV)   Investment in Company S   13,500

        Retained Earnings, January 1, 2016—Company P.   13,500

With date alignment created, remaining eliminations parallel Worksheet 3-2 except that there is no entry (CY1) for current-year equity income. Entry (CY2) is still used to eliminate intercompany dividends. In journal form, the remaining entries for Worksheet 3-4 are as follows:

Eliminate current-year dividends:

(CY2)   Subsidiary (or Dividend) Income   4,500

        Dividends Declared (Company S account)   4,500

Eliminate investment account at beginning-of-year balance:

(EL)   Common Stock—Company S   45,000

        Retained Earnings, January 1, 2016—Company S   76,500

        Investment in Company S.   121,500

Distribute excess of cost (patent):

(D)/(NCI)   Patent.   30,000

        Investment in Company S.   27,000

        NCI (Retained Earnings—Company S)   3,000

Amortize patent for current and prior years:

(A)	Retained Earnings, January 1, 2016—Company P	2,700	
	NCI (Retained Earnings—Company S)	300	
	Patent Amortization Expense.	3,000	
	Patent.		6,000

The last four columns of Worksheet 3-4 are exactly the same as those for Worksheet 3-2, as are the consolidated financial statements for 2016.

The simplicity of this technique of converting from the cost to the simple equity method should be appreciated. At any future date, in order to convert to the simple equity method, it is necessary only to compare the balance of the subsidiary retained earnings account on the worksheet trial balance with the balance of that account on the original date of acquisition (included in the D&D schedule). Specific reference to income earned and dividends paid by the subsidiary in each intervening year is unnecessary. The only complications occur when stock dividends have been issued by the subsidiary or when the subsidiary has issued or retired stock. These complications are examined in Chapter 8.

R E F L E C T I O N

- For a cost method investment, date alignment means converting the investment account to its equity-adjusted balance at the start of the year. (No adjustment is needed the first year.)

- Once converted, all other investment eliminations are the same as for the equity method.

4

OBJECTIVE

Describe the special worksheet procedures that are used for an investment maintained under the sophisticated equity method (investment account is adjusted for amortizations of excess resulting from purchase).

EFFECT OF SOPHISTICATED EQUITY METHOD ON CONSOLIDATION

In some cases, a parent may desire to prepare its own separate statements as a supplement to the consolidated statements. In this situation, the investment in the subsidiary must be shown on the parent's separate statements at the sophisticated equity balance. This requirement may lead the parent to maintain its subsidiary investment account under the sophisticated equity method. Two ramifications occur when such an investment is consolidated. **First, the current year's equity adjustment is net of excess amortizations; second, the investment account contains only the remaining unamortized excess applicable to the investment.**

The use of the sophisticated equity method complicates the elimination of the investment account in that the worksheet distribution and amortization of the excess procedures are altered. However, there is no impact on the other consolidation procedures. To illustrate, the information given in Worksheet 3-2 will be used as the basis for an example covering 2016. The trial balance of Company P will show the following changes as a result of using the sophisticated equity method:

1. The Investment in Company S will be carried at $132,300 ($137,700 simple equity balance less parent's share of two years' amortization of excess at $2,700 per year).

2. The January 1, 2016, balance for Company P Retained Earnings will be $187,300 ($190,000 under simple equity less parent's share of one year's amortization of excess of $2,700).

3. The subsidiary loss account of the parent will have a balance of $13,500 ($10,800 share of the subsidiary loss plus $2,700 amortization of excess).

Based on these changes, a partial worksheet under the sophisticated equity method follows:

Company P and Subsidiary Company S
Partial Worksheet for Consolidated Financial Statements
For Year Ended December 31, 2016

(Credit balance amounts are in parentheses.)	Trial Balance		Eliminations & Adjustments			
	Company P	Company S	Dr.		Cr.	
Investment in Company S	132,300		(CY1)	13,500	(EL)	126,000
			(CY2)	4,500	(D)	24,300
Patent			(D)	27,000	(A)	3,000
Retained Earnings, January 1, 2016—Company P	(187,300)					
Common Stock ($10 par)—Company S		(50,000)	(EL)	45,000		
Retained Earnings, January 1, 2016—Company S		(90,000)	(EL)	81,000	(NCI)	2,700
Revenue	(100,000)	(50,000)				
Expenses	80,000	62,000				
Patent Amortization			(A)	3,000		
Subsidiary Loss	13,500				(CY1)	13,500
Dividends Declared		5,000			(CY2)	4,500

Eliminations and Adjustments:

(CY1)   Eliminate the current-year entries made in the investment account to record the subsidiary loss. The loss account now includes the $2,700 excess amortization.

(CY2)   Eliminate intercompany dividends.

(EL)   Using the balances at the beginning of the year, eliminate 90% of the Company S equity balance against the remaining investment account.

(D)/(NCI)   Distribute the remaining unamortized excess applicable to the controlling interest on January 1, 2015 ($27,000 on purchase date less $2,700 amortization), to the patent account. Adjust the NCI for the remaining excess attributable to its 10% share ($3,000 – $300 amortization for 2015). The total adjustment to the patent account is $27,000 (the remaining balance at the start of the year).

(A)   Amortize the patent for the current year only; prior-year amortization has been recorded in the parent's investment account and has been reflected in the NCI adjustment.

The sophisticated equity method essentially is a modification of simple equity procedures. The major difference in the consolidation procedures under the two methods is that, subsequent to the acquisition, the original excess calculated on the determination and distribution of excess schedule does not appear when the sophisticated equity method is used. Only the remaining unamortized excess appears. Since the investment account is eliminated in the consolidation process, the added complexities of the sophisticated method are not justified for most companies and seldom are applied to consolidated subsidiaries.

REFLECTION

- The investment account is already adjusted for amortizations of excess resulting from the D&D schedule.

- Only the remaining unamortized excess remains in the investment account, and only the unamortized balance is distributed to appropriate accounts.

- Comparison of worksheet methods (shown on page 132):

	Simple Equity	Sophisticated Equity	Cost
Investment balance	Cost + parent % of sub (income – dividends)	Cost + parent % of sub (income – dividends – amortization of excess)	Cost
Adjustment needed to eliminate	None	None	Convert to simple equity as of start of year (first year not needed)
Elimination entry	Eliminate beginning-of-year balance	Eliminate beginning-of-year balance	Eliminate beginning-of-year balance
Excess distribution	Original amount from D&D	Remaining **unamortized** balance from D&D	Original amount from D&D
Amortizations of excess	Prior years to retained earnings; current year to nominal accounts	**Only** current year to nominal accounts	Prior years to retained earnings; current year to nominal accounts

5

OBJECTIVE

Distribute and amortize multiple adjustments resulting from the difference between the price paid for an investment in a subsidiary and the subsidiary equity eliminated.

DETERMINATION OF THE METHOD BEING USED

Before you attempt to prepare a consolidated worksheet, you need to know which of the three methods is being used by the parent to record its investment in the subsidiary. You cannot begin to eliminate the intercompany investment until that is determined. The most efficient approach is as follows:

1. Test for the use of the cost method. If the cost method is used:
   a. The investment account will be at the *original cost* shown on the determination and distribution of excess schedule.
   b. The parent will have recorded as its share of subsidiary income its *ownership interest times the dividends declared* by the subsidiary. In most cases, this income will be called "subsidiary dividend income," but some may call it "subsidiary income" or "dividend income." Therefore, do not rely on the title of the account.

2. If the method used is not cost, check for the use of simple equity as follows:
   a. The investment account will *not be at the original cost.*
   b. The parent will have recorded as subsidiary income its *ownership percentage times the reported net income of the subsidiary.*

3. If the method used is neither cost nor simple equity, it must be the sophisticated equity method. Confirm that it is by noting that:
   a. The investment account will *not be at the original cost.*
   b. The parent will have recorded as subsidiary income its ownership percentage times the reported net income of the subsidiary *minus the amortizations of excess for the current period.*

COMPLICATED PURCHASE, SEVERAL DISTRIBUTIONS OF EXCESS

In Worksheets 3-1 through 3-4, it was assumed that the entire excess of cost over book value was attributable to a patent. In reality, the excess will seldom apply to a single asset. The following example illustrates a more complicated purchase.

Worksheet 3-5: page 158

Worksheet 3-5 on pages 158 to 159 is an example of the first year of an 80% purchase with goodwill. The following table shows book and fair values of Carlos Company on the date of purchase:

Carlos Company Book and Estimated Fair Values
December 31, 2015

	Book Value	Market Value	Life		Book Value	Market Value	Life
Assets				**Liabilities**			
Inventory	$ 75,000	$ 80,000	1	Current liabilities	$ 50,000	$ 50,000	1
Land.	150,000	200,000	—	Bonds payable	200,000	186,760	4
Buildings	600,000	500,000	20	Total liabilities	$250,000	$236,760	
Accumulated depreciation	(300,000)			Stockholders' equity:			
Equipment	150,000	80,000	5	Common stock.	$100,000		
Accumulated depreciation	(50,000)			Paid-in capital in excess of par . .	150,000		
Patent.	125,000	150,000	10	Retained earnings	250,000		
				Total equity	$500,000		
Total assets.	$ 750,000	$1,010,000		Net assets	$500,000	$773,240	

The parent company, Paulos, paid $720,000 for an 80% interest in Carlos Company on January 1, 2015. It is assumed that the fair value of the NCI is proportionate to the price paid by Paulos for the controlling interest. The following value analysis schedule was prepared:

Value Analysis Schedule	Company Implied Fair Value	Parent Price (80%)	NCI Value (20%)
Company implied fair value	$ 900,000	$ 720,000	$180,000
Fair value of net assets excluding goodwill	773,240	618,592	154,648
Goodwill	**$126,760**	**$101,408**	**$ 25,352**

Based on the above information, the following D&D schedule is prepared:

Determination and Distribution of Excess Schedule

	Company Implied Fair Value	Parent Price (80%)	NCI Value (20%)
Fair value of subsidiary	$ 900,000	$720,000	$180,000
Less book value of interest acquired:			
Common stock ($10 par).	$ 100,000		
Paid-in capital in excess of par	150,000		
Retained earnings	250,000		
Total equity.	$ 500,000	$500,000	$500,000
Interest acquired		80%	20%
Book value.		$400,000	$100,000
Excess of fair value over book value	**$400,000**	$320,000	$ 80,000

(continued)

Adjustment of identifiable accounts:

	Adjustment	Amortization per Year	Life	Worksheet Key
Inventory ($80,000 – $75,000)	$ 5,000		1	**debit D1**
Land ($200,000 – $150,000)	50,000			**debit D2**
Buildings ($500,000 – $300,000 net book value). . . .	200,000	$ 10,000	20	**debit D3**
Equipment ($80,000 – $100,000 net book value). . . .	(20,000)	(4,000)	5	**credit D4**
Patent ($150,000 – $125,000)	25,000	2,500	10	**debit D5**
Discount on bonds payable ($200,000 – $186,760) .	13,240	3,310	4	**debit D6**
Goodwill.	**126,760**			**debit D7**
Total	**$400,000**			

Eliminations for 2015, in journal entry form, are as follows:

Eliminate subsidiary income recorded by the parent company:

(CY1)	Subsidiary Income	48,000	
	Investment in Carlos		48,000

Eliminate dividends paid by Carlos to Paulos:

(CY2)	Investment in Carlos	16,000	
	Dividends Declared by Carlos		16,000

Eliminate 80% of Carlos equity against investment in Carlos:

(EL)	Common Stock—Carlos	80,000	
	Paid-In Capital in Excess of Par—Carlos	120,000	
	Retained Earnings, January 1, 2015—Carlos	200,000	
	Investment in Carlos		400,000

Distribute excess of cost over book value:

(D1)	Cost of Goods Sold (inventory)	5,000	
(D2)	Land	50,000	
(D3)	Buildings	200,000	
(D4)	Equipment		20,000
(D5)	Patent	25,000	
(D6)	Discount on Bonds Payable	13,240	
(D7)	Goodwill	126,760	
(D)	Investment in Carlos (noneliminated excess)		320,000
(NCI)	Retained Earnings—Carlos (to adjust NCI to fair value)		80,000

Amortize excess for current year as shown on schedule with
  following entry:

(A3)	Depreciation Expense—Buildings	10,000	
(A3)	Accumulated Depreciation—Buildings		10,000
(A4)	Accumulated Depreciation—Equipment	4,000	
(A4)	Depreciation Expense—Equipment		4,000
(A5)	Other Expenses (patent amortization)	2,500	
(A5)	Patent		2,500
(A6)	Interest Expense	3,310	
(A6)	Discount on Bonds Payable		3,310

A summary of depreciation and amortization adjustments is as follows:

Account Adjustments to Be Amortized	Life	Annual Amount	Current Year	Prior Years	Total	Key
Inventory	1	$ 5,000	$ 5,000	—	$ 5,000	(D1)
Subject to annual amortization:						
Buildings	20	$10,000	$10,000	—	$10,000	(A3)
Equipment	5	(4,000)	(4,000)	—	(4,000)	(A4)
Patent.	10	2,500	2,500	—	2,500	(A5)
Bonds payable	4	3,310	3,310	—	3,310	(A6)
Total amortizations		$11,810	$11,810	—	$11,810	
Controlling retained earnings adjustment.					—	
NCI retained earnings adjustment.					—	

Note also in Worksheet 3-5 that the subsidiary IDS schedule picks up the entire adjustment of the cost of goods sold and all current-year amortizations. This means in the end that the NCI will absorb 20% of all adjustments, and the remaining 80% will go to the controlling interest. This is automatic because the adjusted subsidiary income is distributed 20%/80%.

Worksheet 3-6 on pages 162 and 163 is based on the same example, but is prepared as of December 31, 2016, the end of the second year.   **Worksheet 3-6: page 162**

Eliminations in journal entry form are as follows:

	Eliminate subsidiary income recorded by the parent company:		
(CY1)	Subsidiary Income.	80,000	
	Investment in Carlos.		80,000
	Eliminate dividends paid by Carlos to Paulos:		
(CY2)	Investment in Carlos.	16,000	
	Dividends Declared by Carlos.		16,000
	Eliminate 80% of Carlos equity against investment in Carlos:		
(EL)	Common Stock—Carlos	80,000	
	Paid-In Capital in Excess of Par—Carlos	120,000	
	Retained Earnings, January 1, 2016—Carlos	232,000	
	Investment in Carlos.		432,000
	Distribute excess of cost over book value:		
(D1)	Retained Earnings, January 1, 2016—Paulos		
	(80% of $5,000 prior-year inventory amount)	4,000	
(D1)	Retained Earnings, January 1, 2016—Carlos		
	(20% of $5,000 prior-year inventory amount)	1,000	
(D2)	Land.	50,000	
(D3)	Buildings	200,000	
(D4)	Equipment		20,000
(D5)	Patent.	25,000	
(D6)	Discount on Bonds Payable	13,240	
(D7)	Goodwill	126,760	
(D)	Investment in Carlos (noneliminated excess)		320,000
(NCI)	Retained Earnings—Carlos (to adjust NCI to fair value)		80,000

(continued)

Amortize excess for current year as shown on schedule with following entry:

(A3)	Depreciation Expense—Buildings........................	10,000	
(A3)	Accumulated Depreciation—Buildings		20,000
(A4)	Accumulated Depreciation—Equipment..................	8,000	
(A4)	Depreciation Expense—Equipment....................		4,000
(A5)	Other Expenses (patent amortization)...................	2,500	
(A5)	Patent..		5,000
(A6)	Interest Expense.....................................	3,310	
(A6)	Discount on Bonds Payable		6,620
(A3–A6)	Retained Earnings, January 1, 2016—Paulos	9,448	
(A3–A6)	Retained Earnings, January 1, 2016—Carlos	2,362	

A summary of depreciation and amortization adjustments is as follows:

Account Adjustments to Be Amortized	Life	Annual Amount	Current Year	Prior Years	Total	Key
Inventory	1	$ 5,000	$ —	$ 5,000	$ 5,000	(D1)
Subject to annual amortization:						
Buildings	20	$10,000	$10,000	$10,000	$20,000	(A3)
Equipment	5	(4,000)	(4,000)	(4,000)	(8,000)	(A4)
Patent....................	10	2,500	2,500	2,500	5,000	(A5)
Bonds payable	4	3,310	3,310	3,310	6,620	(A6)
Total amortizations		$11,810	$11,810	$11,810	$23,620	
Controlling retained earnings adjustment...............					$ 9,448*	(A3–A6)
NCI retained earnings adjustment...............					2,362**	(A3–A6)

*$11,810 × 80% = $9,448
**$11,810 × 20% = $2,362

Take note of the following issues in Worksheet 3-6:

◆ The adjustment of the inventory, at the time of the purchase on January 1, 2015, now goes to parent and NCI retained earnings, since it is a correction of the 2015 cost of goods sold.

◆ The amortizations of excess for prior periods and the inventory adjustment are carried to controlling (80%) and NCI (20%) retained earnings. Since the NCI shared in the fair value adjustments as of the purchase date, it must share in current- and prior-year amortizations.

◆ The controlling and NCI retained earnings balances are adjusted for the above amortizations of excess before they are extended to the Controlling Retained Earnings and NCI columns.

If a worksheet were prepared for December 31, 2017, the prior years' amortizations of excess would cover two prior years as follows:

Account Adjustments to Be Amortized	Life	Annual Amount	Current Year	Prior Years	Total	Key
Inventory	1	$ 5,000	$ —	$ 5,000	$ 5,000	(D1)
Subject to amortization:						
Buildings	20	$10,000	$10,000	$20,000	$ 30,000	(A3)
Equipment	5	(4,000)	(4,000)	(8,000)	(12,000)	(A4)

Account Adjustments to Be Amortized	Life	Annual Amount	Current Year	Prior Years	Total	Key
Patent.	10	2,500	2,500	5,000	7,500	(A5)
Bonds payable	4	3,310	3,310	6,620	9,930	(A6)
Total amortizations		$11,810	$11,810	$23,620	$ 35,430	
Controlling retained earnings adjustment . . .				$18,896*		(A3–A6)
NCI RE adjustment.				4,724**		(A3–A6)

*$23,620 × 80% = $18,896
**$23,620 × 20% = $4,724

Worksheet 3-6 would be the source document for the formal consolidated statements included in Exhibit 3-2.

Exhibit 3-2
Consolidated Financial Statements for Paulos Company

Paulos Company
Consolidated Income Statement
Period Ending December 31, 2016

Sales revenue		$700,000
Less cost of goods sold.		320,000
Gross profit		$380,000
Less operating expenses:		
Depreciation expense (building $65,000 + equipment $36,000)	$101,000	
Other operating expenses (with patent amortization $2,500).	125,500	226,500
Operating income.		$153,500
Interest expense.		15,310*
Consolidated net income.		$138,190
Distributed to noncontrolling interest		$ 17,638
Distributed to controlling interest		$120,552

* Rounded down from $15,313 to tie to worksheet income

Paulos Company
Consolidated Retained Earnings Statement
Period Ending December 31, 2016

	Controlling Retained Earnings	Noncontrolling Interest
Balance, January 1, 2016.	$714,552	$134,638
Net income	120,552	17,638
Dividends paid		(4,000)
Balance, December 31, 2016	$835,104	$148,276

(continued)

Paulos Company
Consolidated Balance Sheet
December 31, 2016

Assets			Liabilities and Equity		
Current assets:			Current liabilities	$ 190,000	
Cash	$ 452,000		Bonds payable		
			(6%, due December 31, 2018) .	200,000	
Inventory	330,000		Discount on bonds payable.	(6,620)	
Total current assets.		$ 782,000	Total liabilities		$ 383,380
Long-term assets:					
Land.	$ 400,000				
Buildings	1,600,000				
Accumulated depreciation.	(470,000)		Stockholders' equity:		
Equipment	530,000		Common stock.	$1,500,000	
			Retained earnings	835,104	
Accumulated depreciation.	(172,000)		Controlling interest.	$2,335,104	
Patent (net)	120,000		Noncontrolling interest		198,276
Goodwill	126,760				
Total long-term assets		2,134,760	Total equity.		$2,533,380
Total assets		$2,916,760	Total liabilities and equity		$2,916,760

REFLECTION

- There may be many asset (and possibly liability) adjustments resulting from the D&D schedule. Each adjustment is distributed as a part of the elimination procedure.

- Most distribution adjustments will require amortization, each over the appropriate life. The amortizations should be keyed to the distribution entry.

6

OBJECTIVE

Demonstrate the worksheet procedures used for investments purchased during the financial reporting period.

INTRAPERIOD PURCHASE UNDER THE SIMPLE EQUITY METHOD

The accountant will be required to apply special procedures when consolidating a controlling investment in common stock that is acquired during the fiscal year. The D&D schedule must be based on the subsidiary stockholders' equity on the interim purchase date, including the subsidiary retained earnings balance on that date. Also, the consolidated income of the consolidated company, as derived on the worksheet, is to include only subsidiary income earned subsequent to the acquisition date.

Assume that Company S has the following trial balance on July 1, 2015, the date of an 80% acquisition by Company P:

Current Assets	68,000	
Equipment	80,000	
Accumulated Depreciation		30,000
Liabilities		10,000

Common Stock ($10 par)		50,000
Retained Earnings, January 1, 2015.		45,000
Dividends Declared.	5,000	
Sales		90,000
Cost of Goods Sold	60,000	
Expenses	12,000	
Total.	225,000	225,000

If Company P requires Company S to close its nominal accounts as of July 1, Company S would increase its retained earnings account by $13,000 with the following entries:

Sales	90,000	
Cost of Goods Sold		60,000
Expenses		12,000
Retained Earnings		18,000
Retained Earnings	5,000	
Dividends Declared		5,000

Assume Company P pays $106,400 for its 80% interest in Company S. Assume also that all assets have fair values equal to book value and that any excess is attributed to goodwill. It is assumed that the value of the NCI is proportional to the price paid by the parent for the controlling interest. The value analysis would be as follows:

Value Analysis Schedule	Company Implied Fair Value	Parent Price (80%)	NCI Value (20%)
Company fair value.	$133,000	$106,400	$26,600
Fair value of net assets excluding goodwill	108,000*	86,400	21,600
Goodwill.	**$25,000**	$ 20,000	$ 5,000

*Common stock $50,000 + retained earnings ($45,000 + $18,000 − $5,000) = $108,000

Based on the above information, the following D&D schedule is prepared:

Determination and Distribution of Excess Schedule

	Company Implied Fair Value	Parent Price (80%)	NCI Value (20%)
Fair value of subsidiary	$133,000	$106,400	$ 26,600
Less book value of interest acquired:			
Common stock ($10 par).	$ 50,000		
Retained earnings	58,000		
Total equity.	$108,000	$108,000	$108,000
Interest acquired		80%	20%
Book value.		$ 86,400	$ 21,600
Excess of fair value over book value	**$25,000**	$ 20,000	$ 5,000

Adjustment of identifiable accounts:

	Adjustment		Worksheet Key
Goodwill	**$ 25,000**		**debit D1**

Worksheet 3-7: page 166

Proceeding to the end of the year, assume that the operations of Company S for the last six months result in a net income of $20,000 and dividends of $5,000 are declared by Company S on December 31. Worksheet 3-7, pages 166 to 167, includes Company S nominal accounts for only the second 6-month period since the nominal accounts were closed on July 1. Company S Retained Earnings shows the July 1, 2015, balance. The trial balance of Company P includes operations for the entire year. The subsidiary income listed by Company P includes 80% of the subsidiary's $20,000 second six months' income. Company P's investment account balance shows the following:

Original cost	$106,400
80% of subsidiary's second six months' income of $20,000	16,000
80% of $5,000 dividends declared by subsidiary on December 31	(4,000)
Investment balance, December 31, 2015	$118,400

In conformance with acquisition theory, the Consolidated Income Statement column of Worksheet 3-7 includes only subsidiary income earned after the acquisition date. Likewise, only subsidiary income earned after the purchase date is distributed to the NCI and controlling interest. Income earned and dividends declared prior to the purchase date by Company S are reflected in its July 1, 2015, retained earnings balance, of which the NCI is granted its share. The notes to the statements would have to disclose what the income of the consolidated company would have been had the purchase occurred at the start of the year.

INTRAPERIOD PURCHASE UNDER THE COST METHOD

There are only two variations of the procedures discussed in the preceding section if the cost method is used by the parent company to record its investment in the subsidiary:

1. During the year of acquisition, the parent would record as income only its share of dividends declared by the subsidiary. Thus, eliminating entries would be confined to the intercompany dividends.
2. For years after the purchase, the cost-to-equity conversion adjustment would be based on the change in the subsidiary retained earnings balance from the intraperiod purchase date to the beginning of the year for which the worksheet is being prepared.

DISCLOSURE FOR AN INTRAPERIOD PURCHASE

A company's consolidated income statement can only include subsidiary account amounts starting on the acquisition date. Page 28 of Chapter 1 included Note 2 from Kellogg's 2013 annual report. Kellogg's 2013 income statement included the results of Pringles only for the period after May 31, 2012 (the date Pringles was acquired). It is, however, required that the footnotes to the financial statements show what income would have been had the subsidiary (acquired during the year) been consolidated for the entire reporting period. Refer back to Note 2 from Kellogg's 2013 annual report. The second financial display is the pro forma disclosure that shows what income would have been had Pringles been consolidated for all of 2012. In a like manner, since the 2011 income statement is included in the 2013 annual report, there must be pro forma disclosure of what income would have been had Pringles been consolidated for all of the 2011 fiscal year. In summary:

◆ When a subsidiary is purchased during the year, the current year must include disclosure of what income would have been for the year if the subsidiary had been consolidated for the entire period.

◆ For each period for which prior income statements are included in the annual report, there must be disclosure of what consolidated income would have been had the subsidiary been consolidated in those prior periods.

R E F L E C T I O N

- Purchases during the year require the D&D schedule to be based on the subsidiary equity on the "during the year" purchase date.

- The parent's share of subsidiary income that was earned prior to the purchase date was earned by stockholders that are not members of the consolidated company. The accounts of the acquired company are included in the consolidated income statement starting on the date of the acquisition.

- Disclosure is required as to what income would have been had the acquisition occurred on the first day of the earliest year included in the comparative income statements.

SUMMARY: WORKSHEET TECHNIQUE

At this point, it is wise to review the overall mechanical procedures used to prepare a consolidated worksheet. It will help you to have this set of procedures at your side for the first few worksheets you do. Later, the process will become automatic. The following procedures are designed to provide for both efficiency and correctness:

1. When recopying the trial balances, always sum them and make sure they balance before proceeding with the eliminations. At this point, you want to be sure that there are no errors in transporting figures to the worksheet. An amazing number of students' consolidated balance sheets are out of balance because their trial balances did not balance from the start.

2. Carefully key all eliminations to aid future reference. You may want to insert a symbol, a little "p" for parent or a little "s" for subsidiary, to identify each worksheet adjustment entry that affects consolidated net income. Such an identification will make it easier to locate the adjustments that must be posted later to the income distribution schedules. Recall that any adjustment to income must be assigned to one of the company's income distribution schedules. (In this chapter, all adjustments are to the subsidiary IDS schedule.) This second step will become particularly important in the next two chapters where there will be many adjustments to income that will go to either the controlling or the NCI IDS schedule.

3. Sum the eliminations to be sure that they balance before you begin to extend the account totals.

4. Now that the eliminations are completed, cross foot account totals and then extend them to the appropriate worksheet column. Extend each account in the order that it appears on the trial balance. Do not select just the accounts needed for a particular statement. For example, do not work only on the income statement. This can lead to errors. There may be some accounts that you will forget to extend, and you may not be aware of the errors until your Consolidated Balance Sheet column total fails to equal zero. Extending each account in order assures that none will be overlooked and allows careful consideration of the appropriate destination of each account balance.

5. Calculate consolidated net income.

6. Prepare income distribution schedules. Verify that the sum of the distributions equals the consolidated net income on the worksheet. Distribute the NCI in income to the NCI column and distribute the controlling interest in income to the Controlling Retained Earnings column.

7. Sum the NCI column and extend that total to the Consolidated Balance Sheet column. Sum the Controlling Retained Earnings column and extend that total to the Consolidated Balance Sheet column as well.

8. Verify that the Consolidated Balance Sheet column total equals zero (or that the totals are equal if two columns are used).

7

OBJECTIVE

Demonstrate an understanding of when goodwill impairment loss exists and how it is calculated.

GOODWILL IMPAIRMENT LOSSES

When circumstances indicate that the goodwill may have become impaired (see Chapter 1), the remaining goodwill will be estimated. If the resulting estimate is less than the book value of the goodwill, a *goodwill impairment loss* is recorded. The impairment loss is reported in the consolidated income statement for the period in which it occurs. It is presented on a before-tax basis as part of continuing operations and may appear under the caption "other gains and losses."

The parent company could handle the impairment loss in using one of two methods:

1. The parent could record its share of the impairment loss on its books and credit the investment in subsidiary account. This would automatically reduce the excess available for distribution, including the amount available for goodwill. This would mean that the impairment loss on the controlling interest would already exist before consolidation procedures start. The NCI share of the loss would be recorded on the worksheet. The summed loss would automatically be extended to the Consolidated Income Statement column. Since the parent already recorded its share of the loss, the NCI share would be a bottom line deduction from the NCI share of consolidated income on the subsidiary IDS schedule.

2. The impairment loss could be recorded only on the consolidated worksheet. This would adjust consolidated net income and produce a correct balance sheet. The only complication affects consolidated worksheets in periods subsequent to the impairment. The investment account, resulting goodwill, and the controlling retained earnings would be overstated. Thus, on the worksheet, an adjustment reducing the goodwill account, the controlling retained earnings, and the NCI would be needed.

Recall from Chapter 1, that small and medium-sized entities (SMEs) may elect to use IASB accounting standards for SMEs. Under these standards, goodwill is amortized rather than being subject to impairment procedures. Unless the company can defend a different life, the presumed life is 10 years.

The procedure used in this text will be to follow the first method (shown above) and directly adjust the investment account on the parent's books. This approach would mean the price used in the D&D schedule would be reduced by the amount of the impairment.

The impairment test is based on adjusted subsidiary balance sheet amounts. The impairment procedures are based on the subsidiary values as adjusted for distributions of excess. The impairment test must use the sophisticated equity investment balance (simple equity balance less amortizations of excess to date). For example, suppose Company P purchased an 80% interest in Company S in 2016 and the price resulted in total subsidiary goodwill of $165,000. On a future balance sheet date, say December 31, 2018, the following information would apply to Company S:

Subsidiary book value based on acquisition date, amortized balances on December 31, 2018	$1,000,000
Estimated fair value of Company S	900,000
Estimated fair value of net identifiable assets	850,000

Determining if goodwill has been impaired would be calculated as shown here.

Subsidiary (adjusted for acquisition values) book value on December 31, 2018	$1,000,000
Estimated fair value of subsidiary	900,000

Because the investment amount exceeds the fair value, goodwill is impaired, and a loss must be calculated.

The impairment loss would be calculated as follows:

Estimated fair value of Company S	$ 900,000
Estimated fair value of net identifiable assets	850,000
Estimated goodwill	$ 50,000
Existing goodwill	165,000
Goodwill impairment loss	$(115,000)

The impairment entry on Company P's books would be as follows:

Goodwill Impairment Loss (80% × $115,000).   92,000
    Investment in Company S.   92,000

The remaining $23,000 impairment loss applicable to the NCI would be entered on the conso-
lidated worksheet. The above example assumes that original goodwill was allocated 80%/20% on
the acquisition date based on the assumption that the value of the NCI was proportionate to the
price paid for the controlling interest. If that were not the case and the NCI share was less than 20%
of the total goodwill, the allocation percentage used in the above example would be adjusted.

IASB PERSPECTIVES

IASB *standards*

- Recall that including goodwill on the noncontrolling interest is optional under IFRS. If no
  goodwill was recorded applicable to the noncontrolling interest, then impairment
  testing and adjustment would only apply to the controlling interest share of goodwill.

REFLECTION

- When the fair value of a subsidiary is less than its consolidated balance sheet equity, any
  goodwill arising from the acquisition is impaired, and a related loss must be recognized.

APPENDIX A: THE VERTICAL WORKSHEET

This chapter has used the horizontal format for its worksheet examples. Columns for eliminations and adjustments, consolidated income, NCI, controlling retained earnings, and the balance sheet are arranged horizontally in adjacent columns. This format makes it convenient to
extend account balances from one column to the next. This is the format that you used for trial
balance working papers in introductory and intermediate accounting. It is also the most common worksheet format used in practice. The horizontal format will be used in all nonappendix
worksheets in subsequent chapters and in all worksheet problems unless otherwise stated.

    The alternative format is the vertical format. Rather than beginning the worksheet with the trial
balances of the parent and the subsidiary, this format begins with the completed income statements,
statements of retained earnings, and the balance sheets of the parent and subsidiary. This method,
which is seldom used in practice and harder to master, commonly has been used on the CPA Exam.

    The vertical format is used in Worksheet 3-8 on pages 168 and 169. This worksheet is based
on the same facts used for Worksheet 3-6 (an equity method example for the second year of a
purchase with a complicated distribution of excess cost). Worksheet 3-8 is based on the determination and distribution of excess schedule shown on page 133.

    Note that the original separate statements are stacked vertically upon each other. Be sure to
follow the carrydown procedure as it is applied to the separate statements. The net income from
the income statement is carried down to the retained earnings statement. Then, the ending
retained earnings balance is carried down to the balance sheet. Later, this same carrydown procedure is applied to the consolidated statements.

    Understand that there are no differences in the elimination and adjustment procedures as a
result of this alternative format. Compare the elimination entries to those in Worksheet 3-6.
Even though there is no change in the eliminations, there are two areas of caution. First, the
order in which the accounts appear is reversed; that is, nominal accounts precede balance sheet

8

OBJECTIVE

Consolidate a subsidiary
using vertical worksheet
format.

Worksheet 3-8: page 168

accounts. This difference in order will require care in making eliminations. Second, the eliminations to retained earnings must be made against the January 1 beginning balances, not the December 31 ending balances. The ending retained earnings balances are never adjusted but are derived after all eliminations have been made.

The complicated aspect of the vertical worksheet is the carrydown procedure used to create the retained earnings statement and the balance sheet. Arrows are used in Worksheet 3-8 to emphasize the carrydown procedure. Note that the net income line in the retained earnings statement and the retained earnings lines on the balance sheet are never available to receive eliminations. These balances are always carried down. The net income balances are derived from the same income distribution schedules used in Worksheet 3-6.

REFLECTION

- On vertical worksheets for consolidations subsequent to acquisition, the income statement accounts appear at the top, followed by the retained earnings statement accounts, and then the balance sheet accounts appear in the bottom section.

- Net income is carried down to the retained earnings section.

- Ending retained earnings is then carried down to the balance sheet section.

9

OBJECTIVE

Explain the impact of tax-related complications arising on the purchase date.

APPENDIX B: TAX-RELATED ADJUSTMENTS

Recall from Chapter 1 that a deferred tax liability results when the fair value of an asset may not be used in future depreciation calculations for tax purposes. (This occurs when the acquisition is a *tax-free exchange* to the seller.) In this situation, future depreciation charges for tax purposes must be based on the book value of the asset, and a liability should be acknowledged in the determination and distribution of excess schedule by creating a deferred tax liability account. Consider the following determination and distribution of excess schedule for a subsidiary that has a building with a book value for tax purposes of $120,000 and a fair value of $200,000. Assuming a tax rate of 30%, there is a deferred tax liability of $24,000 ($80,000 excess of fair value over tax basis × 30%).

As is true in all determination and distribution of excess schedules, any remaining unallocated value becomes goodwill. In the following example, the remaining unallocated value on the determination and distribution of excess schedule is $44,000.

Determination and Distribution of Excess Schedule

	Company Implied Fair Value	Parent Price (100%)	NCI Value
Fair value of subsidiary	$ 600,000	$600,000	N/A
Less book value of interest acquired:			
Common stock ($10 par)......................	$ 100,000		
Retained earnings	400,000		
Total equity.................................	$ 500,000	$500,000	
Interest acquired		100%	
Book value......................................		$500,000	
Excess of fair value over book value	**$100,000**	$100,000	

Adjustment of identifiable accounts:

	Adjustment	Amortization per Year	Life	Worksheet Key
Building ($200,000 − $120,000)	$ 80,000	$4,000	20	**debit D1**
Deferred tax liability (building), 30% × $80,000	(24,000)	(1,200)	20	**credit D2**
Goodwill (balance)	**44,000**			**debit D3**
Total	**$100,000**			

The worksheet entry to distribute the excess of cost over book value would be as follows:

Building (to fair value)	80,000	
Goodwill (balance of excess)	44,000	
Deferred Tax Liability		24,000
Investment in Subsidiary S (excess cost after elimination of subsidiary equity)		100,000

Worksheet eliminations will be simpler if each deferred tax liability is recorded below the asset to which it relates. It is possible that inventory could have a fair value in excess of its book value used for tax purposes. This, too, would require the recognition of a deferred tax liability.

A second tax complication arises when the subsidiary has tax loss carryovers. To the extent that the tax loss carryovers are not recorded or are reduced by a valuation allowance by the subsidiary on its balance sheet, the carryovers may be an asset to be considered in the determination and distribution of excess schedule. When a tax-free exchange occurs during the accounting period, a portion of the tax loss carryover may be used during that period.[1] The amount that may be used is the acquiring company's tax liability for the year times the percentage of the year that the companies were under common control. If, for example, the acquiring company's tax liability was $100,000 and the acquisition occurred on April 1, 3/4 of $100,000, or $75,000, of the tax loss carryover could be utilized. The current portion of the tax loss carryover is recorded as *Current Deferred Tax Asset*. Any remaining carryover is carried forward and recorded as a noncurrent asset using the account, *Noncurrent Deferred Tax Asset*. If it is probable that the deferred tax expense will not be fully realized, a contra-valuation allowance is provided.

Let us consider the example of a subsidiary that has the following tax loss carryovers on the date of purchase:

Tax loss carryover to be used in current period	$100,000
Tax loss carryover to be used in future periods	200,000

Assume that the parent has anticipated future tax liabilities against which the tax loss carryovers may be offset and has a 30% tax rate. The value analysis would be prepared as follows:

Value Analysis Schedule	Company Implied Fair Value	Parent Price (80%)	NCI Value (20%)
Company fair value	$1,118,750	$895,000	$223,750
Fair value of net assets excluding goodwill	987,500	790,000	197,500
Goodwill	**$ 131,250**	$105,000	$ 26,250

---

1 Section 381(c) (1) (B) of the Federal Tax Code.

Based on the information shown on page 145, the following D&D schedule is prepared:

Determination and Distribution of Excess Schedule

	Company Implied Fair Value	Parent Price (80%)	NCI Value (20%)
Fair value of subsidiary	$1,118,750	$895,000	$223,750
Less book value of interest acquired:			
Common stock ($10 par).	$ 300,000		
Retained earnings	597,500		
Total equity.	$ 897,500	$897,500	$897,500
Interest acquired		80%	20%
Book value.		$718,000	$179,500
Excess of fair value over book value	$ 221,250	$177,000	$ 44,250

Adjustment of identifiable accounts:

	Adjustment	Amortization per Year	Life	Worksheet Key
Current deferred tax asset ($100,000 × 30%).	$ 30,000		1	**debit D1**
Noncurrent deferred tax asset ($200,000 × 30%). . . .	60,000			**debit D2**
Goodwill ($1,118,750 fair – $987,500 book				
value)	**131,250**			**debit D3**
Total	**$221,250**			

Comprehensive Example.. Both of the preceding tax issues will complicate the consolidated worksheet. Our example will consider the distribution of the tax adjustments on the worksheet and the resulting amortization adjustments needed to calculate consolidated net income. We will consider a nontaxable exchange with fixed asset and goodwill adjustments in addition to a tax loss carryover.

Assume that Paro Company acquired an 80% interest in Sunstran Corporation on January 1, 2015. Paro expects to utilize $100,000 of tax loss carryovers in the current period and $250,000 in future periods.[2] A building, which has a 20-year remaining life, is understated by $200,000. The following value analysis was prepared:

Value Analysis Schedule	Company Implied Fair Value	Parent Price (80%)	NCI Value (20%)
Company fair value.	$1,237,500	$990,000	$247,500
Fair value of net assets excluding goodwill	1,045,000	836,000	209,000
Goodwill.	**$ 192,500**	$154,000	$ 38,500

---

2 Considers tax limitations and assumes full realizability of tax loss carryovers.

Based on the information shown on page 146, the following D&D schedule is prepared:

Determination and Distribution of Excess Schedule

	Company Implied Fair Value	Parent Price (80%)	NCI Value (20%)
Fair value of subsidiary	$1,237,500	$ 990,000	$247,500
Less book value of interest acquired:			
Common stock ($10 par).	$ 100,000		
Paid-in capital in excess of par	300,000		
Retained earnings	400,000		
Total equity.	$ 800,000	$ 800,000	$800,000
Interest acquired		80%	20%
Book value.		$ 640,000	$160,000
Excess of fair value over book value	**$ 437,500**	$ 350,000	$ 87,500

Adjustment of identifiable accounts:

	Adjustment	Amortization per Year	Life	Worksheet Key
Current deferred tax asset ($100,000 × 30% tax rate)	$ 30,000		1	**debit D1**
Noncurrent deferred tax asset ($250,000 × 30%). . . .	75,000			**debit D2**
Building	200,000	$ 10,000	20	**debit D3**
Deferred tax liability ($200,000 × 30% tax rate).	(60,000)	(3,000)	20	**credit D3t**
Goodwill.	**192,500**			**debit D4**
Total.	**$ 437,500**			

Worksheet 3-9, pages 170 to 171, is the consolidated worksheet for Paro Company and it subsidiary, Sunstran Corporation, at the end of 2015. Unlike previous worksheets, the nominal accounts of both firms include a 30% provision for tax on internally generated net income. (Paro does not include a tax on subsidiary income recorded.). The calculation of the tax liabilities for affiliated firms is discussed further in Chapter 6. Paro's internally generated income before tax is $800,000. The 30% tax provision would be $240,000. Only $210,000 is currently payable. The parent company is aware of the $30,000 reduction of the tax liability made possible by the current portion of the DTA included in the IDS schedule. On its separate statements, the parent company records the $30,000 as a temporary deferred tax liability (DTL). The parent's tax entry was:

Worksheet 3-9: page 170

Provision for Tax ($800,000 × 30%)	240,000	
Current Tax Liability.		210,000
Deferred Tax Liability.		30,000

The procedures to eliminate the investment account are the same as for previous examples using the equity method. In journal entry form, the eliminations are as follows:

(CY1) Eliminate subsidiary income recorded by parent company:		
Subsidiary Income.	84,000	
Investment in Sunstran		84,000
(CY2) Eliminate dividends paid by Sunstran to Paro:		
Investment in Sunstran	16,000	
Dividends Declared (by Sunstran)		16,000

(EL)   Eliminate 80% of Sunstran equity against Investment in Sunstran:

Common Stock—Sunstran.................................	80,000	
Paid-In Capital in Excess of Par—Sunstran	240,000	
Retained Earnings—Sunstran	320,000	
Investment in Sunstran		640,000

Distribute excess of cost over book value and adjustment to NCI:

(D1) Deferred Tax Liability (consumption of current DTA)	30,000	
(D2) Noncurrent Deferred Tax Asset	75,000	
(D3) Building	200,000	
(D3t) Deferred Tax Liability (applicable to building).................		60,000
(D4) Goodwill	192,500	
(D) Investment in Sunstran (noneliminated excess)		350,000
(NCI) Retained Earnings—Sunstran		87,500

Amortize excess for current year as shown on the following schedule:

(A3) Expenses (for depreciation)................................	10,000	
Accumulated Depreciation—Building		10,000
(A3t) Deferred Tax Liability....................................	3,000	
Provision for Tax		3,000

Amortizations of excess are made for the current year using the following schedule:

Account Adjustments to Be Amortized	Life	Amount Annual	Current Year	Prior Years	Total	Key
Building	20	$10,000	$10,000		$10,000	(A3)
Deferred tax liability (building)	20	(3,000)	(3,000)		(3,000)	(A3t)
Total (excluding inventory)		$ 7,000	$ 7,000		$ 7,000	

Notice that entry (D1) distributes $30,000 to the parent's deferred tax liability account and eliminates the temporary tax liability recorded by the parent. Entry (D2) records the noncurrent portion of the tax loss carryforward as a deferred tax asset. Entry (D3) increases the building by $200,000, and entry (D3t) records the deferred tax liability applicable to the building adjustment. Entry (D4) records goodwill of $192,500.

As a result of the increase in the value of the building, entry (A3) increases the depreciation for the building by $10,000. Given the 30% tax rate, entry (A3t) reduces the provision for tax account by $3,000 as a result of the depreciation adjustment. *This entry is not a reduction in the current taxes payable.* Instead, it is a reduction in the deferred tax liability recorded as part of the distribution of excess [entry (D3)]. Remember that the deferred tax liability reflects the loss of future tax deductions caused by the difference between the building's higher fair value and its lower book value on the date of the purchase. Thus, the net result of the entry is to record the tax provision as if the deductions were allowable (for tax purposes) without changing the tax payable for the current period. There is no amortization of the noncurrent deferred tax asset since it is not used in the current period. **All amortizations of excess and all tax adjustments are carried to the subsidiary's income distribution schedule.** This is again the case since both interests share in the allocation of the excess and, thus, share in its amortization.

REFLECTION

- One of the assets that may be included in the purchase is a tax loss carryover. It should be separated into its current and noncurrent components.

- When assets are part of a tax-free exchange, they must be accompanied by a deferred tax liability equal to the value of the forfeited tax deduction.

Worksheet 3-1

Simple Equity Method
Company P and Subsidiary Company S
Worksheet for Consolidated Financial Statements
For Year Ended December 31, 2015

	(Credit balance amounts are in parentheses.)	Trial Balance	
		Company P	Company S
1	Investment in Company S	148,500	
2			
3			
4	**Patent**		
5	Other Assets (net of liabilities)	237,000	135,000
6	Common Stock ($10 par)—Company P	(200,000)	
7	Retained Earnings, January 1, 2015—Company P	(123,000)	
8	Common Stock ($10 par)—Company S		(50,000)
9	Retained Earnings, January 1, 2015—Company S		(70,000)
10	Revenue	(100,000)	(75,000)
11	**Expenses**	60,000	50,000
12	**Patent Amortization Expense**		
13	**Subsidiary Income**	(22,500)	
14	**Dividends Declared**		10,000
15		0	0
16	**Consolidated Net Income**		
17	**To NCI (see distribution schedule)**		
18	**Balance to Controlling Interest (see distribution schedule)**		
19	Total NCI		
20	Retained Earnings, Controlling Interest, December 31, 2015		
21			

Eliminations and Adjustments:

(CY1)   Eliminate subsidiary income against the investment account.

(CY2)   Eliminate dividends paid by subsidiary to parent. After (CY1) and (CY2), the investment account and subsidiary retained earnings are at a common point in time. Then, elimination of the investment account can proceed.

(EL)   Eliminate the pro rata share of Company S equity balances *at the beginning of the year* against the investment account. The elimination of the parent's share of subsidiary stockholders' equity leaves only the noncontrolling interest in each element of the equity.

(D)/(NCI)   Distribute the $27,000 excess cost and $3,000 NCI adjustment as required by the D&D schedule on page 119. In this example, Patent is recorded for $30,000.

(A)   Amortize the resulting patents over the 10-year period. The current portion is $3,000 per year ($30,000/10 years).

Worksheet 3-1 (see page 121)

Eliminations & Adjustments				Consolidated Income Statement	NCI	Controlling Retained Earnings	Consolidated Balance Sheet	
Dr.		**Cr.**						
(CY2)	**9,000**	**(CY1)**	**22,500**					1
		(EL)	108,000					2
		(D)	27,000					3
(D)	30,000	**(A)**	**3,000**				27,000	4
							372,000	5
							(200,000)	6
						(123,000)		7
(EL)	45,000				(5,000)			8
(EL)	63,000	(NCI)	3,000		(10,000)			9
				(175,000)				10
				110,000				11
(A)	**3,000**			3,000				12
(CY1)	**22,500**							13
		(CY2)	**9,000**		1,000			14
	172,500		172,500					15
				(62,000)				16
				2,200	(2,200)			17
				59,800		(59,800)		18
					(16,200)		(16,200)	19
						(182,800)	(182,800)	20
							0	21

Subsidiary Company S Income Distribution

Patent amortization ....(A)	**$3,000**	Internally generated net income	$25,000
		Adjusted net income	$22,000
		NCI share	× 10%
		NCI	$ 2,200

Parent Company P Income Distribution

	Internally generated net income	$40,000
	90% × Company S adjusted income of $22,000......................	19,800
	Controlling interest	$59,800

Worksheet 3-2

Simple Equity Method, Second Year
Company P and Subsidiary Company S
Worksheet for Consolidated Financial Statements
For Year Ended December 31, 2016

	(Credit balance amounts are in parentheses.)	Trial Balance	
		Company P	Company S
1	**Investment in Company S**	133,200	
2			
3	**Patent**		
4	Other Assets (net of liabilities)	261,500	118,000
5	Common Stock ($10 par)—Company P	(200,000)	
6	**Retained Earnings, January 1, 2016—Company P**	(185,500)	
7	Common Stock ($10 par)—Company S		(50,000)
8	Retained Earnings, January 1, 2016—Company S		(85,000)
9			
10	Revenue	(100,000)	(50,000)
11	Expenses	80,000	62,000
12	**Patent Amortization**		
13	**Subsidiary Loss**	10,800	
14	**Dividends Declared**		5,000
15		0	0
16	**Consolidated Net Income**		
17	**To NCI (see distribution schedule)**		
18	**Balance to Controlling Interest (see distribution schedule)**		
19	Total NCI		
20	Retained Earnings, Controlling Interest, December 31, 2016		
21			

Eliminations and Adjustments:

(CY1)   Eliminate controlling share of subsidiary loss.

(CY2)   Eliminate dividends paid by subsidiary to parent. The investment account is now returned to its January 1, 2016 balance so that elimination may proceed.

(EL)   Using balances at the beginning of the year, eliminate 90% of the Company S equity balances against the remaining investment account.

(D)/(NCI)   Distribute the $30,000 excess cost as indicated by the D&D schedule that was prepared on the date of acquisition. The amount is the $27,000 investment excess and the $3,000 NCI adjustment.

(A)   Amortize the patent over the selected 10-year period. It is necessary to record the amortization for current and past periods, because asset adjustments resulting from the consolidation process do not appear on the separate statements of the constituent companies. Thus, entry (A) reduces Patent by $6,000 for the 2015 and 2016 amortizations. The amount for the current year is expensed, while the cumulative amortization for prior years ($3,000) is deducted from the beginning controlling ($2,700) and noncontrolling ($300) retained earnings accounts. The NCI shares in the adjustments because the NCI was adjusted for the original asset adjustment.

Worksheet 3-4 (see page 129)

Eliminations & Adjustments Dr.		Eliminations & Adjustments Cr.		Consolidated Income Statement	NCI	Controlling Retained Earnings	Consolidated Balance Sheet	
(CV)	13,500	(EL)	121,500					1
		(D)	27,000					2
(D)	30,000	(A)	6,000				24,000	3
							379,500	4
							(200,000)	5
(A)	2,700	(CV)	13,500			(182,800)		6
(EL)	45,000				(5,000)			7
(EL)	76,500	(NCI)	3,000		(11,200)			8
(A)	300							9
				(150,000)				10
				142,000				11
(A)	3,000			3,000				12
(CY2)	4,500							13
		(CY2)	4,500		500			14
	175,500		175,500					15
				(5,000)				16
				(1,500)	1,500			17
				6,500		(6,500)		18
					(14,200)		(14,200)	19
						(189,300)	(189,300)	20
							0	21

Subsidiary Company S Income Distribution

Internally generated loss	$ 12,000
Patent amortization . . . . (A)	3,000
Adjusted loss	$ 15,000
NCI share . . . . ×	10%
NCI	$ 1,500

Parent Company P Income Distribution

90% × Company S adjusted loss of $15,000 . . . . $13,500	Internally generated net income	$20,000
	Controlling interest	$ 6,500

Worksheet 3-5

Simple Equity Method, First Year
Paulos Company and Subsidiary Carlos Company
Worksheet for Consolidated Financial Statements
For the Year Ended December 31, 2015

	(Credit balance amounts are in parentheses.)	Trial Balance	
		Paulos	Carlos
1	Cash	80,000	50,000
2	Inventory	226,000	62,500
3	Land	200,000	150,000
4	Investment in Carlos	752,000	
5			
6			
7			
8	Buildings	800,000	600,000
9	Accumulated Depreciation	(80,000)	(315,000)
10	Equipment	400,000	150,000
11	Accumulated Depreciation	(50,000)	(70,000)
12	Patent (net)		112,500
13			
14	Goodwill		
15	Current Liabilities	(100,000)	
16	Bonds Payable		(200,000)
17	Discount (Premium)		
18			
19	Common Stock—Carlos		(100,000)
20	Paid-In Capital in Excess of Par—Carlos		(150,000)
21	Retained Earnings, January 1, 2015—Carlos		(250,000)
22			
23	Common Stock—Paulos	(1,500,000)	
24	Retained Earnings, January 1, 2015—Paulos	(600,000)	
25			
26	Sales	(350,000)	(200,000)
27	Cost of Goods Sold	150,000	80,000
28	Depreciation Expense—Buildings	40,000	15,000
29	Depreciation Expense—Equipment	20,000	20,000
30	Other Expenses	60,000	13,000
31	Interest Expense		12,000
32	Subsidiary Income	(48,000)	
33	Dividends Declared—Carlos		20,000
34	Totals	0	0
35	Consolidated Net Income		
36	NCI Share		
37	Controlling Share		
38	Total NCI		
39	Retained Earnings, Controlling Interest, December 31, 2015		
40	Totals		

Worksheet 3-5 (see page 132)

Eliminations & Adjustments				Consolidated Income Statement	NCI	Controlling Retained Earnings	Consolidated Balance Sheet	
Dr.		Cr.						
							130,000	1
							288,500	2
(D2)	50,000						400,000	3
		(CY1)	48,000					4
(CY2)	16,000							5
		(EL)	400,000					6
		(D)	320,000					7
(D3)	200,000						1,600,000	8
		(A3)	10,000				(405,000)	9
		(D4)	20,000				530,000	10
(A4)	4,000						(116,000)	11
(D5)	25,000						135,000	12
		(A5)	2,500					13
(D7)	126,760						126,760	14
							(100,000)	15
							(200,000)	16
(D6)	13,240							17
		(A6)	3,310				9,930	18
(EL)	80,000				(20,000)			19
(EL)	120,000				(30,000)			20
(EL)	200,000				(130,000)			21
		(NCI)	80,000					22
							(1,500,000)	23
								24
						(600,000)		25
				(550,000)				26
(D1)	5,000			235,000				27
(A3)	10,000			65,000				28
		(A4)	4,000	36,000				29
(A5)	2,500			75,500				30
(A6)	3,310			15,310				31
(CY1)	48,000							32
		(CY2)	16,000		4,000			33
903,810		903,810						34
				(123,190)				35
				8,638	(8,638)			36
				114,552		(114,552)		37
					(184,638)		(184,638)	38
						(714,552)	(714,552)	39
							0	40

Eliminations and Adjustments:

(CY1)	Eliminate subsidiary income against the investment account
(CY2)	Eliminate dividends paid by subsidiary to parent. After (CY1) and (CY2), the investment account and the subsidiary retained earnings are at the January 1 balances. Then, the investment account can be eliminated.
(EL)	Eliminate the controlling share of subsidiary equity balance (as of January 1) against the investment account.
	The elimination of the controlling share of subsidiary equity leaves only the NCI portion of each subsidiary equity account.
(D)/(NCI)	Distribute the $400,000 fair value excess (Paulos share = $320,000; NCI share = $80,000) as follows:
(D1)	Inventory is assumed to have been sold, adjust cost of goods sold.
(D2)	Land.
(D3)	Buildings
(D4)	Equipment.
(D5)	Patent.
(D6)	Discount on Bonds Payable.
(D7)	Goodwill.
(A)	Amortize distributions as follows:

Account Adjustments to Be Amortized	Life	Annual Amount	Current Year	Prior Years	Total	Key
Inventory	1	$ 5,000	$ 5,000	—	$ 5,000	(D1)
Subject to amortization:						
Buildings	20	$10,000	$10,000	—	$10,000	(A3)
Equipment	5	(4,000)	(4,000)	—	(4,000)	(A4)
Patent.	10	2,500	2,500	—	2,500	(A5)
Bonds payable	4	3,310	3,310	—	3,310	(A6)
Total amortizations		$11,810	$11,810	—	$11,810	
Controlling retained earnings adjustment .			N/A*			
NCI retained earnings adjustment.			N/A*			

*There is no retained earnings adjustment for the parent or for the NCI because this is the first year of the amortization of excess.

Subsidiary Carlos Company Income Distribution

Adjustment to cost of goods sold . . . . (D1)	$ 5,000	Internally generated net income	$ 60,000
Current-year amortizations of excess . . . . (A3–A6)	11,810		
		Adjusted income	$ 43,190
		NCI share	× 20%
		NCI	$ 8,638

Parent Paulos Company Income Distribution

		Internally generated net income	$ 80,000
		Controlling share of subsidiary (80% × $43,190)	34,552
		Controlling interest	$114,552

Worksheet 3-6

Simple Equity Method, Second Year
Paulos Company and Subsidiary Carlos Company
Worksheet for Consolidated Financial Statements
For Year Ended December 31, 2016

| | (Credit balance amounts are in parentheses.) | Trial Balance | |
		Paulos	Carlos
1	Cash	292,000	160,000
2	Inventory	210,000	120,000
3	Land	200,000	150,000
4	Investment in Carlos	816,000	
5			
6			
7			
8	Buildings	800,000	600,000
9	Accumulated Depreciation	(120,000)	(330,000)
10	Equipment	400,000	150,000
11	Accumulated Depreciation	(90,000)	(90,000)
12	Patent (net)		100,000
13			
14	Goodwill		
15	Current Liabilities	(150,000)	(40,000)
16	Bonds Payable		(200,000)
17	Discount (Premium)		
18			
19	Common Stock—Carlos		(100,000)
20	Paid-In Capital in Excess of Par—Carlos		(150,000)
21	Retained Earnings, January 1, 2016—Carlos		(290,000)
22			
23			
24			
25	Common Stock—Paulos	(1,500,000)	
26	Retained Earnings, January 1, 2016—Paulos	(728,000)	
27			
28			
29			
30	Sales	(400,000)	(300,000)
31	Cost of Goods Sold	200,000	120,000
32	Depreciation Expense—Buildings	40,000	15,000
33	Depreciation Expense—Equipment	20,000	20,000
34	Other Expenses	90,000	33,000
35	Interest Expense		12,000
36	Subsidiary Income	(80,000)	
37	Dividends Declared—Carlos		20,000
38	Totals	0	0
39	Consolidated Net Income		
40	NCI Share		
41	Controlling Share		
42	Total NCI		
43	Retained Earnings, Controlling Interest, December 31, 2016		
44	Totals		

Worksheet 3-6 (see page 135)

Eliminations & Adjustments				Consolidated Income Statement	NCI	Controlling Retained Earnings	Consolidated Balance Sheet	
Dr.		Cr.						
							452,000	1
							330,000	2
(D2)	50,000						400,000	3
		(CY1)	80,000					4
(CY2)	16,000							5
		(EL)	432,000					6
		(D)	320,000					7
(D3)	200,000						1,600,000	8
		(A3)	20,000				(470,000)	9
		(D4)	20,000				530,000	10
(A4)	8,000						(172,000)	11
(D5)	25,000						120,000	12
		(A5)	5,000					13
(D7)	126,760						126,760	14
							(190,000)	15
							(200,000)	16
(D6)	13,240							17
		(A6)	6,620				6,620	18
(EL)	80,000				(20,000)			19
(EL)	120,000				(30,000)			20
(EL)	232,000				(134,638)			21
		(NCI)	80,000					22
(D1)	1,000							23
(A3–A6)	2,362							24
							(1,500,000)	25
								26
(D1)	4,000							27
(A3–A6)	9,448							28
						(714,552)		29
				(700,000)				30
				320,000				31
(A3)	10,000			65,000				32
		(A4)	4,000	36,000				33
(A5)	2,500			125,500				34
(A6)	3,310			15,310				35
(CY1)	80,000							36
		(CY2)	16,000		4,000			37
	983,620		983,620					38
				(138,190)				39
				17,638	(17,638)			40
				120,552		(120,552)		41
					(198,276)		(198,276)	42
						(835,104)	(835,104)	43
							0	44

Eliminations and Adjustments:

(CY1)   Eliminate subsidiary income against the investment account.

(CY2)   Eliminate dividends paid by subsidiary to parent. After (CY1) and (CY2), the investment account and the subsidiary retained earnings are at the January 1 balances. Then, the investment account can be eliminated.

(EL)   Eliminate the controlling share of subsidiary equity balance (as of January 1) against the investment account. The elimination of the controlling share of subsidiary equity leaves only the NCI portion of each subsidiary equity account.

(D)   Distribute the $400,000 fair value excess as follows:

    (D1)   Prior-year inventory is sold, distribute 80%/20% to controlling interest and NCI (subsidiary) retained earnings.

    (D2)   Land.

    (D3)   Buildings.

    (D4)   Equipment.

    (D5)   Patent.

    (D6)   Discount on Bonds Payable.

    (D7)   Goodwill.

(A)   Amortize distributions as follows:

Account Adjustments to Be Amortized	Life	Annual Amount	Current Year	Prior Years	Total	Key
Inventory	1	$ 5,000	$ —	$ 5,000	$ 5,000	(D1)
Subject to amortization:						
Buildings	20	$10,000	$10,000	$10,000	$20,000	(A3)
Equipment	5	(4,000)	(4,000)	(4,000)	(8,000)	(A4)
Patent	10	2,500	2,500	2,500	5,000	(A5)
Bonds payable	4	3,310	3,310	3,310	6,620	(A6)
Total amortizations		$11,810	$11,810	$11,810	$23,620	
Controlling retained earnings adjustment (80% × $11,810)				$ 9,448		(A3–A6)
NCI retained earnings adjustment (20% × $11,810)				2,362		(A3–A6)

Subsidiary Carlos Company Income Distribution

Current-year amortizations of excess .... (A3–A6)	$11,810	Internally generated net income..............	$100,000
		Adjusted income	$ 88,190
		NCI share...............................	× 20%
		NCI	$ 17,638

Parent Paulos Company Income Distribution

	Internally generated net income..............	$ 50,000
	Controlling share of subsidiary (80% × $88,190)	70,552
	Controlling interest........................	$120,552

Worksheet 3-7

Intraperiod Purchase; Subsidiary Books Closed on Purchase Date
Company P and Subsidiary Company S
Worksheet for Consolidated Financial Statements
For Year Ended December 31, 2015

	(Credit balance amounts are in parentheses.)	Trial Balance	
		Company P	Company S
1	Current Assets	187,600	87,500
2	**Investment in Company S**	118,400	
3			
4			
5	Goodwill		
6	Equipment	400,000	80,000
7	Accumulated Depreciation	(200,000)	(32,500)
8	Liabilities	(60,000)	(12,000)
9	Common Stock—Company P	(250,000)	
10	Retained Earnings, **January 1, 2015—Company P**	(100,000)	
11	Common Stock—Company S		(50,000)
12	Retained Earnings, **July 1, 2015—Company S**		(58,000)
13	Sales	(500,000)	(92,000)
14	Cost of Goods Sold	350,000	60,000
15	Expenses	70,000	12,000
16	**Subsidiary Income**	(16,000)	
17	Dividends Declared		5,000
18			
19		0	0
20			
21	Consolidated Net Income		
22	To NCI (see distribution schedule)		
23	Balance to Controlling Interest (see distribution schedule)		
24	Total NCI		
25	Retained Earnings, Controlling Interest, December 31, 2015		
26			

Eliminations and Adjustments:

(CY1)   Eliminate the entries made in the investment in Company S account and in the subsidiary income account to record the parent's 80% controlling interest in the subsidiary's second *six months' income.*

(CY2)   Eliminate intercompany dividends. This restores the investment account to its balance as of the **July 1, 2015**, investment date.

(EL)   Eliminate 80% of the subsidiary's **July 1, 2015**, equity balances against the *balance* of the investment account.

(D)   Distribute the excess of cost over book value of $20,000 to Goodwill in accordance with the D&D schedule.

Worksheet 3-7 (see page 140)

Eliminations & Adjustments		Consolidated	NCI	Controlling	Consolidated	
Dr.	Cr.	Income Statement		Retained Earnings	Balance Sheet	
					275,100	1
(CY2) 4,000	(CY1) 16,000					2
	(EL) 86,400					3
	(D) 20,000					4
(D) 25,000					25,000	5
					480,000	6
					(232,500)	7
					(72,000)	8
					(250,000)	9
				(100,000)		10
(EL) 40,000			(10,000)			11
(EL) 46,400	(NCI) 5,000		(16,600)			12
		(592,000)				13
		410,000				14
		82,000				15
(CY1) 16,000						16
	(CY2) 4,000		1,000			17
						18
131,400	131,400					19
						20
		(100,000)				21
		4,000	(4,000)			22
		96,000		(96,000)		23
			(29,600)		(29,600)	24
				(196,000)	(196,000)	25
					0	26

Subsidiary Company S Income Distribution

Internally generated net income **(last six months)**	**$20,000**
Adjusted income	$ 20,000
NCI share	× 20%
NCI	$ 4,000

Parent Company P Income Distribution

Internally generated net income	$ 80,000
80% × Company S adjusted income of $20,000 **(last six months)**.	**16,000**
Controlling interest	$ 96,000

Worksheet 3-8

Vertical Format, Simple Equity Method
Paulos Company and Subsidiary Carlos Company
Worksheet for Consolidated Financial Statements
For Year Ended December 31, 2016

Worksheet 3-8 (see page 143)

#		Financial Statements Paulos	Carlos	Eliminations & Adjustments Dr.	Cr.	NCI	Nonconsolidated Balance Sheet
1	**Income Statement**						
2	Sales	(400,000)	(300,000)				(700,000)
3	Cost of Goods Sold	200,000	120,000				320,000
4	Depreciation Expense—Buildings	40,000	15,000	(A3) 10,000			65,000
5	Depreciation Expense—Equipment	20,000	20,000		(A4) 4,000		36,000
6	Other Expenses	90,000	33,000	(A5) 2,500			125,500
7	Interest Expense	20,000	12,000	(A6) 3,310			15,310
8	Subsidiary Income	(80,000)		(CY1) 80,000			
9	Net Income	(130,000)	(100,000)				
10	Consolidated Net Income						(138,190)
11	Noncontrolling Interest (see distribution schedule)					(17,638)	
12	Controlling Interest (see distribution schedule WS 3-6)						(120,552)
13	**Retained Earnings Statement**						
14	Retained Earnings, January 1, 2016—Paulos	(728,000)		(D1) 4,000			
15				(A3–A6) 9,448			
16	Retained Earnings, January 1, 2016—Carlos		(290,000)	(EL) 232,000	(NCI) 80,000	(134,638)	(714,552)
17				(D1) 1,000			
18				(A3–A6) 2,362			
19							
20	Net Income (carrydown)	(130,000)	(100,000)			(17,638)	(120,552)
21	Dividends Declared		20,000		(CY2) 16,000	4,000	
22	Retained Earnings, December 31, 2016	(858,000)	(370,000)				
23	Noncontrolling Interest in Retained Earnings, December 31, 2016					(148,276)	
24	Controlling Interest in Retained Earnings, December 31, 2016						(835,104)

	Balance Sheet			Eliminations & Adjustments Dr.	Eliminations & Adjustments Cr.	NCI	Controlling/Consolidated
25	**Balance Sheet**						
26	Cash	292,000	160,000				452,000
27	Inventory	210,000	120,000				330,000
28	Land	200,000	150,000	(D2) 50,000			400,000
29	Buildings	800,000	600,000	(D3) 200,000			1,600,000
30	Accumulated Depreciation—Buildings	(120,000)	(330,000)		(A3) 20,000		(470,000)
31	Equipment	400,000	150,000		(D4) 20,000		530,000
32	Accumulated Depreciation—Equipment	(90,000)	(90,000)	(A4) 8,000			(172,000)
33	Investment in Carlos Company	816,000		(CY2) 16,000	(CY1) 80,000		
34					(EL) 432,000		
35					(D) 320,000		
36	Patent		100,000	(D5) 25,000	(A5) 5,000		120,000
37	Goodwill			(D7) 126,760			126,760
38	Current Liabilities	(150,000)	(40,000)				(190,000)
39	Bonds Payable		(200,000)				(200,000)
40	Discount (Premium)			(D6) 13,240	(A6) 6,620		6,620
41	Common Stock—Paulos	(1,500,000)					(1,500,000)
42	Common Stock—Carlos		(100,000)	(EL) 80,000		(20,000)	
43	Paid-In Capital in Excess of Par—Carlos		(150,000)	(EL) 120,000		(30,000)	
44	Retained Earnings (carrydown)	(858,000)	(370,000)				
45	Retained Earnings, Controlling Interest, December 31, 2016						(835,104)
46	Retained Earnings, NCI, December 31, 2016					(148,276)	
47	Total NCI					(198,276)	(198,276)
48	Total	0	0	983,620	983,620		0

Worksheet 3-9

Equity Method, Tax Issues
Paro Company and Subsidiary Sunstran Corporation
Worksheet for Consolidated Financial Statements
For Year Ended December 31, 2015

	(Credit balance amounts are in parentheses.)	Trial Balance	
		Paro	Sunstran
1	Cash	330,000	30,000
2	Accounts Receivable (net)	354,000	95,000
3	Inventory	540,000	100,000
4	Land	100,000	30,000
5	Building	1,300,000	950,000
6	Accumulated Depreciation—Building	(400,000)	(300,000)
7	**Noncurrent Deferred Tax Asset**		
8	Investment in Sunstran Corporation	1,058,000	
9			
10			
11	Goodwill		
12	Current Liabilities	(248,000)	(20,000)
13	**Deferred Tax Liability**	(30,000)	
14			
15	Common Stock—Paro	(510,000)	
16	Retained Earnings, January 1, 2015, Paro	(1,950,000)	
17			
18	Common Stock—Sunstran		(100,000)
19	Paid-In Capital in Excess of Par—Sunstran		(300,000)
20	Retained Earnings, January 1, 2015—Sunstran		(400,000)
21			
22	Sales	(3,400,000)	(900,000)
23	Cost of Goods Sold	2,070,000	600,000
24	Expenses	530,000	150,000
25			
26	Subsidiary Income	(84,000)	
27	Provision for Tax	240,000	45,000
28			
29	Dividends Declared	100,000	20,000
30		0	0
31	Consolidated Net Income		
32	To NCI (see distribution schedule)		
33	Balance to Controlling Interest (see distribution schedule)		
34	Total NCI		
35	Retained Earnings, Controlling Interest, December 31, 2015		
36			

Worksheet 3-9 (see page 147)

Eliminations & Adjustments			Consolidated Income Statement	NCI	Controlling Retained Earnings	Consolidated Balance Sheet	
Dr.		Cr.					
						360,000	1
						449,000	2
						640,000	3
						130,000	4
(D3)	200,000					2,450,000	5
		(A3)	10,000				(710,000)	6
(D2)	75,000						75,000	7
(CY2)	16,000	(CY1)	84,000					8
		(EL)	640,000					9
		(D)	350,000					10
(D4)	192,500						192,500	11
						(268,000)	12
(D1)						(57,000)	13
(A3t)	3,000	(D3t)	60,000					14
						(510,000)	15
					(1,950,000)		16
							17
(EL)	80,000				(20,000)			18
(EL)	240,000				(60,000)			19
(EL)	320,000	(NCI)	87,500		(167,500)			20
							21
				(4,300,000)				22
				2,670,000				23
(A3)	10,000			690,000				24
							25
(CY1)	84,000							26
		(A3t)	3,000	282,000				27
							28
		(CY2)	16,000		4,000	100,000		29
	1,250,500		1,250,500					30
				(658,000)				31
				13,600	(13,600)			32
				644,400		(644,400)		33
					(257,100)		(257,100)	34
						(2,494,400)	(2,494,400)	35
							0	36

Eliminations and Adjustments:

(CY1)	Eliminate the parent's share of subsidiary income.
(CY2)	Eliminate the current-year intercompany dividends. The investment account is adjusted now to its January 1, 2015, balance so that it may be eliminated.
(EL)	Eliminate the 80% ownership portion of the subsidiary equity accounts against the investment. A $350,000 excess cost remains.
(D)/(NCI)	Distribute the $350,000 excess cost and $87,500 NCI adjustment as follows, in accordance with the determination and distribution of excess schedule:
(D1)	Record the current portion of tax loss carryover used this period.
(D2)	Record the noncurrent portion of the tax loss carryover.
(D3)	Increase the building by $200,000.
(D3t)	Record the deferred tax liability related to the building increase.
(D4)	Record the goodwill.
(A3)	Record the annual increase in building depreciation; $200,000 net increase in the building divided by its 20-year life equals $10,000.
(A3t)	Reduce the provision for tax account by 30% of the increase in depreciation expense ($3,000).

Subsidiary Sunstran Corporation Income Distribution

Building depreciation	(A3)	$10,000	Internally generated net income	$	105,000
Current tax carryover	**(D1)**	**30,000**	**Decrease in tax provision (A3t)**		**3,000**
			Adjusted income	$	68,000
			NCI share	×	20%
			NCI	$	**13,600**

Parent Paro Company Income Distribution

Internally generated net income	$	590,000
80% × Sunstran Corporation adjusted income of $68,000		54,400
Controlling interest		**$644,400**

UNDERSTANDING THE ISSUES

1. A parent company paid $500,000 for a 100% interest in a subsidiary. At the end of the first year, the subsidiary reported net income of $40,000 and paid $5,000 in dividends. The price paid reflected understated equipment of $70,000, which will be amortized over 10 years. What would be the subsidiary income reported on the parent's unconsolidated income statement, and what would the parent's investment balance be at the end of the first year under each of these methods?

   a. The simple equity method
   b. The sophisticated equity method
   c. The cost method

2. What is meant by date alignment? Does it exist on the consolidated worksheet under the following methods, and if not, how is it created prior to elimination of the investment account under each of these methods?

   a. The simple equity method
   b. The sophisticated equity method
   c. The cost method

3. What is the noncontrolling share of consolidated net income? Does it reflect adjustments based on fair values at the purchase date? How has it been displayed in income statements in the past, and how should it be displayed?

4. A parent company acquired an 80% interest in a subsidiary on July 1, 2015. The subsidiary closed its books on that date. The subsidiary reported net income of $60,000 for 2015, earned evenly during the year. The parent's net income, exclusive of any income of the subsidiary, was $140,000. The fair value of the subsidiary exceeded book value by $100,000. The entire difference was attributed to a patent with a 10-year life.

   a. What is consolidated net income for 2015?
   b. What is the noncontrolling share of net income for 2015?

5. A parent company acquired an 80% interest in a subsidiary on January 1, 2015, at a price high enough to result in goodwill. Included in the assets of the subsidiary are inventory with a book value of $50,000 and a fair value of $55,000 and equipment with a book value of $100,000 and a fair value of $160,000. The equipment has a 5-year remaining life. What impact would the inventory and equipment, acquired in the acquisition, have on consolidated net income in 2015 and 2016?

6. You are working on a consolidated trial balance of a parent and an 80% owned subsidiary. What components will enter into the total noncontrolling interest, and how will it be displayed in the consolidated balance sheet?

7. It seems as if consolidated net income is always less than the sum of the parent's and subsidiary's separately calculated net incomes. Is it possible that the consolidated net income of the two affiliated companies could actually exceed the sum of their individual net incomes?

EXERCISES

Exercise 1 *(LO 1)* **Compare alternative methods for recording income.** Cardinal Company acquires an 80% interest in Huron Company common stock for $420,000 cash on January 1, 2015. At that time, Huron Company has the following balance sheet:

Assets		Liabilities and Equity	
Current assets	$ 60,000	Accounts payable	$ 60,000
Land......................	100,000	Common stock ($5 par)..........	50,000
Equipment	350,000	Paid-in capital in excess of par	100,000
Accumulated depreciation	(150,000)	Retained earnings	150,000
Total assets...............	$ 360,000	Total liabilities and equity	$360,000

Appraisals indicate that accounts are fairly stated except for the equipment, which has a fair value of $240,000 and a remaining life of five years. Any remaining excess is goodwill.

Huron Company experiences the following changes in retained earnings during 2015 and 2016:

Retained earnings, January 1, 2015............................		$150,000
Net income, 2015......................................	$ 50,000	
Dividends paid in 2015.................................	(10,000)	40,000
Balance, December 31, 2015		$190,000
Net income, 2016......................................	$ 45,000	
Dividends paid in 2016.................................	(10,000)	35,000
Balance, December 31, 2016		$225,000

Prepare a determination and distribution of excess schedule for the investment in Huron Company (a value analysis is not needed). Prepare journal entries that Cardinal Company would make on its books to record income earned and/or dividends received on its investment in Huron Company during 2015 and 2016 under the following methods: simple equity, sophisticated equity, and cost.

 Exercise 2 *(LO 1)* **Alternative investment models, more complex D&D.** Mast Corporation acquires a 75% interest in the common stock of Shaw Company on January 1, 2014, for $462,500 cash. Shaw has the following balance sheet on that date:

Assets		Liabilities and Equity	
Current assets	$ 80,000	Current liabilities	$ 50,000
Inventory	40,000	Common stock ($5 par)..........	50,000
Land......................	100,000	Paid-in capital in excess of par	150,000
Buildings and equipment (net) ..	200,000	Retained earnings	200,000
Patent.....................	30,000		
Total assets...............	$450,000	Total liabilities and equity	$450,000

Appraisals indicate that the book values for inventory, buildings and equipment, and patent are below fair values. The inventory has a fair value of $50,000 and is sold during 2014. The buildings and equipment have an appraised fair value of $300,000 and a remaining life of 20 years. The patent, which has a 10-year life, has an estimated fair value of $50,000. Any remaining excess is goodwill.

Shaw Company reports the following income earned and dividends paid during 2014 and 2015:

Retained earnings, January 1, 2014............................		$200,000
Net income, 2014......................................	$ 70,000	
Dividends paid in 2014.................................	(20,000)	50,000
Balance, December 31, 2014		$250,000
Net income, 2015......................................	$ 48,000	
Dividends paid in 2015.................................	(20,000)	28,000
Balance, December 31, 2015		$278,000

Prepare a determination and distribution of excess schedule (a value analysis is not needed) for the investment in Shaw Company and determine the balance in Investment in Shaw Company on Mast Corporation's books as of December 31, 2015, under the following methods that could be used by the parent, Mast Corporation: simple equity, sophisticated equity, and cost.

Exercise 3 *(LO 2)* **Equity method, first year, eliminations, statements.** Parker Company acquires an 80% interest in Sargent Company for $300,000 in cash on January 1, 2015, when Sargent Company has the following balance sheet:

Assets		Liabilities and Equity	
Current assets	$100,000	Current liabilities	$ 50,000
Depreciable fixed assets (net) . .	200,000	Common stock ($10 par)	100,000
		Retained earnings	150,000
Total assets	$300,000	Total liabilities and equity	$300,000

The excess of the price paid over book value is attributable to the fixed assets, which have a fair value of $250,000, and to goodwill. The fixed assets have a 10-year remaining life. Parker Company uses the simple equity method to record its investment in Sargent Company.

The following trial balances of the two companies are prepared on December 31, 2015:

	Parker	Sargent
Current Assets	10,000	130,000
Depreciable Fixed Assets	400,000	200,000
Accumulated Depreciation	(106,000)	(20,000)
Investment in Sargent Company	316,000	
Current Liabilities	(60,000)	(40,000)
Common Stock ($10 par)	(300,000)	(100,000)
Retained Earnings, January 1, 2015	(200,000)	(150,000)
Sales	(150,000)	(100,000)
Expenses	110,000	75,000
Subsidiary Income	(20,000)	
Dividends Declared		5,000
Totals	0	0

1. Prepare a determination and distribution of excess schedule (a value analysis is not needed) for the investment.
2. Prepare all the eliminations and adjustments that would be made on the 2015 consolidated worksheet.
3. Prepare the 2015 consolidated income statement and its related income distribution schedules.
4. Prepare the 2015 statement of retained earnings.
5. Prepare the 2015 consolidated balance sheet.

Exercise 4 *(LO 2)* **Equity method, second year, eliminations, income statement.** The trial balances of Parker and Sargent companies of Exercise 3 for December 31, 2016, are presented as follows:

	Parker	Sargent
Current Assets	102,000	115,000
Depreciable Fixed Assets	400,000	200,000
Accumulated Depreciation	(130,000)	(40,000)
Investment in Sargent Company	320,000	
Current Liabilities	(80,000)	
Common Stock ($10 par)	(300,000)	(100,000)

(continued)

	Parker	Sargent
Retained Earnings, January 1, 2016.	(260,000)	(170,000)
Sales	(200,000)	(100,000)
Expenses	160,000	85,000
Subsidiary Income.	(12,000)	
Dividends Declared.		10,000
Totals	0	0

Parker Company continues to use the simple equity method.

1. Prepare all the eliminations and adjustments that would be made on the 2016 consolidated worksheet.
2. Prepare the 2016 consolidated income statement and its related income distribution schedules.

 Exercise 5 *(LO 4)* **Sophisticated equity method, first year, eliminations, statements.** *(Note: Read carefully, as this is not the same as Exercise 3.)* Parker Company acquires an 80% interest in Sargent Company for $300,000 on January 1, 2015, when Sargent Company has the following balance sheet:

Assets		Liabilities and Equity	
Current assets	$100,000	Current liabilities	$ 50,000
Depreciable fixed assets	200,000	Common stock ($10 par).	100,000
		Retained earnings	150,000
Total assets.	$300,000	Total liabilities and equity	$300,000

The excess of the price paid over book value is attributable to the fixed assets, which have a fair value of $250,000, and to goodwill. The fixed assets have a 10-year remaining life. Parker uses the sophisticated equity method to record the investment in Sargent Company.

The following trial balances of the two companies are prepared on December 31, 2015:

	Parker	Sargent
Current Assets	10,000	130,000
Depreciable Fixed Assets	400,000	200,000
Accumulated Depreciation	(106,000)	(20,000)
Investment in Sargent Company	312,000	
Current Liabilities.	(60,000)	(40,000)
Common Stock ($10 par)	(300,000)	(100,000)
Retained Earnings, January 1, 2015.	(200,000)	(150,000)
Sales	(150,000)	(100,000)
Expenses	110,000	75,000
Subsidiary Income (from Sargent Company).	(16,000)	
Dividends Declared.		5,000
Totals	0	0

1. If you did not solve Exercise 3, prepare a determination and distribution of excess schedule for the investment (a value analysis is not needed).
2. Prepare all the eliminations and adjustments that would be made on the 2015 consolidated worksheet.
3. If you did not solve Exercise 3, prepare the 2015 consolidated income statement and its related income distribution schedule.

4. If you did not solve Exercise 3, prepare the 2015 statement of retained earnings.
5. If you did not solve Exercise 3, prepare the 2015 consolidated balance sheet.

Exercise 6 *(LO 4)* **Sophisticated equity method, second year, eliminations, income statement.** The trial balances of Parker and Sargent companies of Exercise 5 for December 31, 2016, are presented as follows:

	Parker	Sargent
Current Assets	102,000	115,000
Depreciable Fixed Assets	400,000	200,000
Accumulated Depreciation	(130,000)	(40,000)
Investment in Sargent Company	312,000	
Current Liabilities.	(80,000)	
Common Stock ($10 par)	(300,000)	(100,000)
Retained Earnings, January 1, 2016.	(256,000)	(170,000)
Sales	(200,000)	(100,000)
Expenses	160,000	85,000
Subsidiary Income (from Sargent Company).	(8,000)	
Dividends Declared.		10,000
Totals	0	0

Parker Company continues to use the sophisticated equity method.

1. Prepare all the eliminations and adjustments that would be made on the 2016 consolidated worksheet.
2. If you did not solve Exercise 4, prepare the 2016 consolidated income statement and its related income distribution schedules.

Exercise 7 *(LO 3)* **Cost method, first year, eliminations, statements.** *(Note: Read carefully, as this is not the same as Exercise 3 or 5.)* Parker Company acquires an 80% interest in Sargent Company for $300,000 in cash on January 1, 2015, when Sargent Company has the following balance sheet:

Assets		Liabilities and Equity	
Current assets	$100,000	Current liabilities	$ 50,000
Depreciable fixed assets	200,000	Common stock ($10 par).	100,000
		Retained earnings	150,000
Total assets.	$300,000	Total liabilities and equity	$300,000

The excess of the price paid over book value is attributable to the fixed assets, which have a fair value of $250,000, and to goodwill. The fixed assets have a 10-year remaining life. Parker Company uses the cost method to record its investment in Sargent Company.

The following trial balances of the two companies are prepared on December 31, 2015:

	Parker	Sargent
Current Assets	10,000	130,000
Depreciable Fixed Assets	400,000	200,000
Accumulated Depreciation	(106,000)	(20,000)
Investment in Sargent Company	300,000	
Current Liabilities.	(60,000)	(40,000)
Common Stock ($10 par)	(300,000)	(100,000)

(continued)

	Parker	Sargent
Retained Earnings, January 1, 2016.	(200,000)	(150,000)
Sales	(150,000)	(100,000)
Expenses	110,000	75,000
Dividend Income (from Sargent Company)	(4,000)	
Dividends Declared.		5,000
Totals	0	0

1. If you did not solve Exercise 3 or 5, prepare a determination and distribution of excess schedule for the investment (a value analysis is not needed).
2. Prepare all the eliminations and adjustments that would be made on the 2015 consolidated worksheet.
3. If you did not solve Exercise 3 or 5, prepare the 2015 consolidated income statement and its related income distribution schedules.
4. If you did not solve Exercise 3 or 5, prepare the 2015 statement of retained earnings.
5. If you did not solve Exercise 3 or 5, prepare the 2015 consolidated balance sheet.

Exercise 8 *(LO 3)* **Cost method, second year, eliminations, income statement.** The trial balances of Parker and Sargent companies of Exercise 7 for December 31, 2016, are presented as follows:

	Parker	Sargent
Current Assets	102,000	115,000
Depreciable Fixed Assets	400,000	200,000
Accumulated Depreciation	(130,000)	(40,000)
Investment in Sargent Company	300,000	
Current Liabilities.	(80,000)	
Common Stock ($10 par)	(300,000)	(100,000)
Retained Earnings, January 1, 2016.	(244,000)	(170,000)
Sales	(200,000)	(100,000)
Expenses	160,000	85,000
Dividend Income (from Sargent Company)	(8,000)	
Dividends Declared.		10,000
Totals	0	0

Parker Company continues to use the cost method.

1. Prepare all the eliminations and adjustments that would be made on the 2016 consolidated worksheet.
2. If you did not solve Exercise 4 or 6, prepare the 2016 consolidated income statement and its related income distribution schedules.

Exercise 9 *(LO 5)* **Amortization procedures, several years.** Whitney Company acquires an 80% interest in Masters Company common stock on January 1, 2015. Appraisals of Masters' assets and liabilities are performed, and Whitney ends up paying an amount that is greater than the fair value of Masters' net assets and reflects a premium to achieve control. The fair value of the NCI is $235,000. The following partial determination and distribution of excess schedule is created on January 1, 2015, to assist in putting together the consolidated financial statements:

Determination and Distribution of Excess Schedule

	Company Implied Fair Value	Parent Price (80%)	NCI Value (20%)
Fair value of subsidiary	$1,335,000	$1,100,000	$235,000
Less book value of interest acquired:			
Common stock	$ 100,000		
Paid-in capital in excess of par	150,000		
Retained earnings	350,000		
Total equity.	$ 600,000	$ 600,000	$600,000
Interest acquired		80%	20%
Book value.		$ 480,000	$120,000
Excess of fair value over book value	**$ 735,000**	$ 620,000	$115,000

Adjustment of identifiable accounts:

	Adjustment	Amortization per Year	Life	Worksheet Key
Inventory	$ 6,250			
Investments	15,000		3	
Land.	50,000			
Buildings	250,000		20	
Equipment	172,500		5	
Patent.	22,500		10	
Trademark	20,000		10	
Discount on bonds payable.	12,500		5	
Goodwill.	**186,250**			
Total	**$ 735,000**			

Prepare amortization schedules for the years 2015, 2016, 2017, and 2018.

Exercise 10 *(LO 6)* **Acquisition during the year, elimination entries, income statement.** Kraus Company has the following balance sheet on July 1, 2016:

Assets		Liabilities and Equity	
Current assets	$200,000	Current liabilities	$100,000
Equipment (net)	300,000	Common stock ($10 par).	100,000
		Retained earnings	300,000
Total assets.	$500,000	Total liabilities and equity	$500,000

On July 1, 2016, Neiman Company purchases 80% of the outstanding common stock of Kraus Company for $310,000. Any excess of book value over cost is attributed to the equipment, which has an estimated 5-year life. Kraus Company closes its books before the acquisition on July 1.

On December 31, 2016, Neiman Company and Kraus Company prepare the following trial balances:

	Neiman	Kraus (July 1–Dec. 31)
Current Assets	220,000	220,000
Equipment	500,000	300,000
Accumulated Depreciation—Equipment	(140,000)	(20,000)
Investment in Kraus Company	310,000	

(continued)

	Neiman	Kraus (July 1–Dec. 31)
Current Liabilities.	(200,000)	(70,000)
Common Stock ($10 par)	(200,000)	(100,000)
Retained Earnings, July 1, 2016	(430,000)	(300,000)
Sales	(300,000)	(100,000)
Cost of Goods Sold	180,000	45,000
General Expenses	60,000	25,000
Totals	0	0

1. Prepare a determination and distribution of excess schedule for the investment (a value analysis is not needed).
2. Prepare all the eliminations and adjustments that would be made on the December 31, 2016, consolidated worksheet.
3. Prepare the 2016 consolidated income statement and its related income distribution schedules.

Exercise 11 *(LO 7)* **Impairment loss.** Albers Company acquires an 80% interest in Barker Company on January 1, 2015, for $850,000. The following determination and distribution of excess schedule is prepared at the time of purchase:

Determination and Distribution of Excess Schedule

	Company Implied Fair Value	Parent Price (80%)	NCI Value (20%)
Fair value of subsidiary	$1,062,500	$850,000	$212,500
Less book value of interest acquired:			
Total equity.	$ 600,000	$600,000	$600,000
Interest acquired		80%	20%
Book value.		$480,000	$120,000
Excess of fair value over book value	**$ 462,500**	$370,000	$ 92,500

Adjustment of identifiable accounts:

	Adjustment	Amortization per Year	Life	Worksheet Key
Buildings	$ 200,000	$ 10,000	20	**debit D1**
Goodwill.	**262,500**			**debit D2**
Total	**$ 462,500**			

Albers uses the simple equity method for its investment in Barker. As of December 31, 2019, Barker has earned $200,000 since it was purchased by Albers. Barker pays no dividends during 2015–2019.

On December 31, 2019, the following values are available:

Fair value of Barker's identifiable net assets (100%)	$ 900,000
Estimated fair value of Barker Company (net of liabilities)	1,000,000

Determine if goodwill is impaired. If not, explain your reasoning. If so, calculate the loss on impairment.

APPENDIX EXERCISES

Exercise 3B-1 *(LO 9)* **D&D for nontaxable exchange.** Rainman Corporation is considering the acquisition of Largo Company through the acquisition of Largo's common stock. Rainman Corporation will issue 20,000 shares of its $5 par common stock, with a fair value of $25 per share, in exchange for all 10,000 outstanding shares of Largo Company's voting common stock.

The acquisition meets the criteria for a tax-free exchange as to the seller. Because of this, Rainman Corporation will be limited for future tax returns to the book value of the depreciable assets. Rainman Corporation falls into the 30% tax bracket.

The appraisal of the assets of Largo Company shows that the inventory has a fair value of $120,000, and the depreciable fixed assets have a fair value of $270,000 and a 10-year life. Any remaining excess is attributed to goodwill. Largo Company has the following balance sheet just before the acquisition:

Largo Company
Balance Sheet
December 31, 2015

Assets		Liabilities and Equity		
Cash	$ 40,000	Current liabilities		$ 70,000
Accounts receivable	150,000	Bonds payable		100,000
Inventory	100,000	Stockholders' equity:		
Depreciable fixed assets (net)	210,000	Common stock ($10 par)...	$100,000	
		Retained earnings	230,000	330,000
Total assets	$500,000	Total liabilities and equity		$500,000

1. Record the acquisition of Largo Company by Rainman Corporation.
2. Prepare a value analysis and a determination and distribution of excess schedule.
3. Prepare the elimination entries that would be made on the consolidated worksheet on the date of acquisition.

Exercise 3B-2 *(LO 9)* **D&D and income statement for nontaxable exchange.** Lucy Company issues securities with a fair value of $468,000 for a 90% interest in Diamond Company on January 1, 2015, at which time Diamond Company has the following balance sheet:

Assets		Liabilities and Equity	
Accounts receivable	$ 50,000	Current liabilities	$ 70,000
Inventory	80,000	Common stock ($5 par)..........	100,000
Land......................	20,000	Paid-in capital in excess of par	130,000
Building (net)	200,000	Retained earnings	50,000
Total assets..............	$350,000	Total liabilities and equity	$350,000

It is believed that the inventory and the building are undervalued by $20,000 and $50,000, respectively. The building has a 10-year remaining life; the inventory on hand on January 1, 2015, is sold during the year. The deferred tax liability associated with the asset revaluations is to be reflected in the consolidated statements. Each company has an income tax rate of 30%. Any remaining excess is goodwill.

The separate income statements of the two companies prepared for 2015 are as follows:

	Lucy	Diamond
Sales	$ 400,000	$150,000
Cost of goods sold..	(200,000)	(90,000)
Gross profit	$ 200,000	$ 60,000

(continued)

	Lucy	Diamond
General expenses	(50,000)	(25,000)
Depreciation expense	(60,000)	(15,000)
Operating income	$ 90,000	$ 20,000
Subsidiary income (90% × $14,000 subsidiary net income)	12,600	
Net income before income tax	$ 102,600	$ 20,000
Provision for tax (does not include tax on subsidiary income)	(27,000)	(6,000)
Net income	$ 75,600	$ 14,000

1. Prepare a value analysis and a determination and distribution of excess schedule for the investment.
2. Prepare the 2015 consolidated income statement and its related income distribution schedules.

Exercise 3B-3 *(LO 9)* **D&D for nontaxable exchange with tax loss carryforward.**
Palto issues 20,000 of its $5 par value common stock shares, with a fair value of $35 each, for a 100% interest in Sword Company on January 1, 2015. The balance sheet of Sword Company on that date is as follows:

Assets		Liabilities and Equity	
Current assets	$100,000	Current liabilities	$ 50,000
Buildings and equipment (net) . .	300,000	Common stock ($5 par)	250,000
		Retained earnings	100,000
Total assets.	$400,000	Total liabilities and equity	$400,000

On the purchase date, the buildings and equipment are understated $50,000 and have a remaining life of 10 years. Sword has tax loss carryovers of $200,000. They are believed to be fully realizable at a tax rate of 30%. $40,000 of the tax loss carryovers will be utilized in 2015. The purchase is a tax-free exchange. The tax rate applicable to all transactions is 30%. Any remaining excess is attributed to goodwill.

Prepare a value analysis and a determination and distribution of excess schedule for this investment.

PROBLEMS

Problem 3-1 *(LO 1)* **Alternative investment account methods, effect on eliminations.** On January 1, 2015, Port Company acquires 8,000 shares of Solvo Company by issuing 10,000 of its common stock shares with a par value of $10 per share and a fair value of $70 per share. The price paid reflects a control premium. The market value of the shares owned by the NCI is $80 per share. At the time of the purchase, Solvo has the following balance sheet:

Assets		Liabilities and Equity	
Current assets	$100,000	Current liabilities	$ 80,000
Investments	150,000	Bonds payable	250,000
Land.	120,000	Common stock ($10 par).	100,000
Building (net)	350,000	Paid-in capital in excess of par	200,000
Equipment (net)	160,000	Retained earnings	250,000
Total assets.	$880,000	Total liabilities and equity	$880,000

Appraisals indicate that book values are representative of fair values with the exception of the land and building. The land has a fair value of $180,000, and the building is appraised at

$450,000. The building has an estimated remaining life of 20 years. Any remaining excess is goodwill.

The following summary of Solvo's retained earnings applies to 2015 and 2016:

Balance, January 1, 2015...................	$250,000
Net income for 2015....................	60,000
Dividends paid in 2015..................	(10,000)
Balance, December 31, 2015	$300,000
Net income for 2016....................	50,000
Dividends paid in 2016..................	(10,000)
Balance, December 31, 2016	$340,000

◀ ◀ ◀ ◀ ◀ **Required**

1. Prepare a value analysis and a determination and distribution of excess schedule for the investment in Solvo Company. As a part of the schedule, indicate annual amortization of excess adjustments.
2. For 2015 and 2016, prepare the entries that Port would make concerning its investment in Solvo under the simple equity, sophisticated equity, and cost methods You may want to set up a worksheet with side-by-side columns for each method so that you can easily compare the entries.
3. For 2015 and 2016, prepare the worksheet elimination that would be made on a consolidated worksheet under the simple equity, sophisticated equity, and cost methods. You may want to set up a worksheet with side-by-side columns for each method so that you can easily compare the entries.

Problem 3-2 *(LO 2)* **Simple equity method adjustments, consolidated worksheet.** On January 1, 2015, Paro Company purchases 80% of the common stock of Solar Company for $320,000. Solar has common stock, other paid-in capital in excess of par, and retained earnings of $50,000, $100,000, and $150,000, respectively. Net income and dividends for two years for Solar are as follows:

	2015	2016
Net income	$60,000	$90,000
Dividends......................	20,000	30,000

On January 1, 2015, the only undervalued tangible assets of Solar are inventory and the building. Inventory, for which FIFO is used, is worth $10,000 more than cost. The inventory is sold in 2015. The building, which is worth $30,000 more than book value, has a remaining life of 10 years, and straight-line depreciation is used. The remaining excess of cost over book value is attributed to goodwill.

1. Using this information and the information in the following trial balances on December 31, 2016, prepare a value analysis and a determination and distribution of excess schedule:

◀ ◀ ◀ ◀ ◀ **Required**

	Paro Company	Solar Company
Inventory, December 31	100,000	50,000
Other Current Assets	136,000	180,000
Investment in Solar Company	400,000	
Land...	50,000	50,000
Buildings and Equipment......................................	350,000	320,000
Accumulated Depreciation	(100,000)	(60,000)
Goodwill..		
Other Intangibles...	20,000	
Current Liabilities...	(120,000)	(40,000)

(continued)

	Paro Company	Solar Company
Bonds Payable.		(100,000)
Other Long-Term Liabilities	(200,000)	
Common Stock—Paro Company	(200,000)	
Other Paid-In Capital in Excess of Par—Paro Company	(100,000)	
Retained Earnings—Paro Company	(214,000)	
Common Stock—Solar Company		(50,000)
Other Paid-In Capital in Excess of Par—Solar Company.		(100,000)
Retained Earnings—Solar Company.		(190,000)
Net Sales.	(520,000)	(450,000)
Cost of Goods Sold	300,000	260,000
Operating Expenses	120,000	100,000
Subsidiary Income.	(72,000)	
Dividends Declared—Paro Company	50,000	
Dividends Declared—Solar Company		30,000
Totals	0	0

2. Complete a worksheet for consolidated financial statements for 2016. Include columns for eliminations and adjustments, consolidated income, NCI, controlling retained earnings, and consolidated balance sheet.

Problem 3-3 *(LO 4)* **Sophisticated equity method adjustments, consolidated worksheet.** (This is the same as Problem 3-2, except that the sophisticated equity method is used.) On January 1, 2015, Paro Company purchases 80% of the common stock of Solar Company for $320,000. On this date, Solar has common stock, other paid-in capital in excess of par, and retained earnings of $50,000, $100,000, and $150,000, respectively. Net income and dividends for two years for Solar Company are as follows:

	2015	2016
Net income	$60,000	$90,000
Dividends.	20,000	30,000

On January 1, 2015, the only undervalued tangible assets of Solar are inventory and the building. Inventory, for which FIFO is used, is worth $10,000 more than cost. The inventory is sold in 2015. The building, which is worth $30,000 more than book value, has a remaining life of 10 years, and straight-line depreciation is used. The remaining excess of cost over book value is attributable to goodwill.

The trial balances for Paro and Solar are as follows:

	Paro Company	Solar Company
Inventory, December 31	100,000	50,000
Other Current Assets	136,000	180,000
Investment in Solar Company	Note 1	
Land.	50,000	50,000
Buildings and Equipment.	350,000	320,000
Accumulated Depreciation	(100,000)	(60,000)
Goodwill		
Other Intangibles.	20,000	
Current Liabilities.	(120,000)	(40,000)
Bonds Payable.		(100,000)
Other Long-Term Liabilities	(200,000)	

	Paro Company	Solar Company
Common Stock—Paro Company	(200,000)	
Other Paid-In Capital in Excess of Par—Paro Company	(100,000)	
Retained Earnings—Paro Company	(203,600)	
Common Stock—Solar Company		(50,000)
Other Paid-In Capital in Excess of Par—Solar Company.............		(100,000)
Retained Earnings—Solar Company...........................		(190,000)
Net Sales......................................	(520,000)	(450,000)
Cost of Goods Sold	300,000	260,000
Operating Expenses	120,000	100,000
Subsidiary Income...................................	Note 1	
Dividends Declared—Paro Company	50,000	
Dividends Declared—Solar Company		30,000

Note 1: To be calculated.

◄ ◄ ◄ ◄ ◄ **Required**

1. Prepare a value analysis and a determination and distribution of excess schedule.
2. Paro Company carries the investment in Solar Company under the sophisticated equity method. In general journal form, record the entries that would be made to apply the equity method in 2015 and 2016.
3. Compute the balance that should appear in Investment in Solar Company and in Subsidiary Income on December 31, 2016 (the second year). Fill in these amounts on Paro Company's trial balance for 2016.
4. Complete a worksheet for consolidated financial statements for 2016. Include columns for eliminations and adjustments, consolidated income, NCI, controlling retained earnings, and consolidated balance sheet.

Problem 3-4 *(LO 3)* **Cost method, consolidated statements.** The trial balances of Charles Company and its subsidiary, Lehto, Inc., are as follows on December 31, 2017:

	Charles	Lehto
Current Assets	590,000	130,000
Depreciable Fixed Assets	1,805,000	440,000
Accumulated Depreciation	(405,000)	(70,000)
Investment in Lehto, Inc.................................	400,000	
Liabilities	(900,000)	(225,000)
Common Stock ($1 par)	(220,000)	
Common Stock ($5 par)		(50,000)
Paid-In Capital in Excess of Par	(1,040,000)	(15,000)
Retained Earnings, January 1, 2017........................	(230,000)	(170,000)
Revenues	(460,000)	(210,000)
Expenses	450,000	170,000
Dividends Declared......................................	10,000	
Totals	0	0

On January 1, 2015, Charles Company exchanges 20,000 shares of its common stock, with a fair value of $20 per share, for all the outstanding stock of Lehto, Inc. Fixed assets with a 10-year life are understated by $50,000. Any excess of cost over book value is attributed to goodwill. The stockholders' equity of Lehto, Inc., on the purchase date is as follows:

Common stock ($5 par).......................	$ 50,000
Paid-in capital in excess of par	15,000
Retained earnings	135,000
Total equity	$200,000

Required ▶ ▶ ▶ ▶ ▶
1. Prepare a determination and distribution of excess schedule for the investment. (A value analysis schedule is not needed.)
2. Prepare the 2017 consolidated statements, including the income statement, retained earnings statement, and balance sheet. (A worksheet is not required.)

Problem 3-5 *(LO 3)* **Cost method, worksheet, statements.** Bell Corporation purchases all of the outstanding stock of Stockdon Corporation for $220,000 in cash on January 1, 2017. On the purchase date, Stockdon Corporation has the following condensed balance sheet:

Assets		Liabilities and Equity	
Cash	$ 60,000	Liabilities	$150,000
Inventory	40,000	Common stock ($10 par).........	100,000
Land.....................	120,000	Paid-in capital in excess of par	50,000
Building (net)	180,000	Retained earnings	100,000
Total assets..............	$400,000	Total liabilities and equity	$400,000

Any excess of book value over cost is attributable to the building, which is currently overstated on Stockdon's books. All other assets and liabilities have book values equal to fair values. The building has an estimated 10-year life with no salvage value.

The trial balances of the two companies on December 31, 2017, appear as follows:

	Bell	Stockdon
Cash	180,000	143,000
Inventory	60,000	30,000
Land..	120,000	120,000
Building (net)	600,000	162,000
Investment in Stockdon Corporation	220,000	
Accounts Payable	(405,000)	(210,000)
Common Stock ($3 par)	(300,000)	
Common Stock ($10 par)		(100,000)
Paid-In Capital in Excess of Par	(180,000)	(50,000)
Retained Earnings, January 1, 2017........................	(255,000)	(100,000)
Sales	(210,000)	(40,000)
Cost of Goods Sold	120,000	35,000
Other Expenses	45,000	10,000
Dividends Declared...................................	5,000	
Totals	0	0

Required ▶ ▶ ▶ ▶ ▶
1. Prepare a determination and distribution of excess schedule for the investment. (A value analysis is not needed.)
2. Prepare the 2017 consolidated worksheet. Include columns for the eliminations and adjustments, the consolidated income statement, the controlling retained earnings, and the consolidated balance sheet.
3. Prepare the 2017 consolidated statements, including the income statement, retained earnings statement, and balance sheet.

Problem 3-6 *(LO 2)* **Equity method, 80% interest, worksheet, statements.** Sandin Company prepares the following balance sheet on January 1, 2015:

Assets		Liabilities and Equity	
Current assets	$ 50,000	Liabilities	$140,000
Land.....................	75,000	Common stock ($10 par).........	100,000
Buildings	350,000	Paid-in capital in excess of par	120,000

Assets		Liabilities and Equity	
Accumulated depreciation— buildings	(140,000)	Retained earnings (deficit)	(25,000)
Total assets	$ 335,000	Total liabilities and equity	$335,000

On this date, Prescott Company purchases 8,000 shares of Sandin Company's outstanding stock for a total price of $270,000. Also on this date, the buildings are understated by $40,000 and have a 10-year remaining life. Any remaining discrepancy between the price paid and book value is attributed to goodwill. Since the purchase, Prescott Company has used the simple equity method to record the investment and its related income.

Prescott Company and Sandin Company prepare the following separate trial balances on December 31, 2016:

	Prescott	Sandin
Current Assets	180,000	115,000
Land	150,000	75,000
Buildings	590,000	350,000
Accumulated Depreciation—Buildings	(265,000)	(182,000)
Investment in Sandin Company	294,000	
Liabilities	(175,000)	(133,000)
Common Stock ($10 par)	(200,000)	(100,000)
Paid-In Capital in Excess of Par		(120,000)
Retained Earnings, January 1, 2016	(503,000)	15,000
Sales	(360,000)	(120,000)
Cost of Goods Sold	179,000	50,000
Expenses	120,000	45,000
Subsidiary Income	(20,000)	
Dividends Declared	10,000	5,000
Totals	0	0

1. Prepare a value analysis and a determination and distribution of excess schedule for the investment.   ◀ ◀ ◀ ◀ ◀ **Required**
2. Prepare the 2016 consolidated worksheet. Include columns for the eliminations and adjustments, the consolidated income statement, the NCI, the controlling retained earnings, and the consolidated balance sheet. Prepare supporting income distribution schedules.
3. Prepare the 2016 consolidated statements including the income statement, retained earnings statement, and the balance sheet.

Problem 3-7 *(LO 6)* **Intraperiod purchase, 80% interest, worksheet, statements.** Jeter Corporation purchases 80% of the outstanding stock of Super Company for $275,000 on July 1, 2015. Super Company has the following stockholders' equity on July 1, 2015:

Common stock ($5 par)	$150,000
Retained earnings, July 1, 2015	50,000
Total equity	$200,000

The fair values of Super's assets and liabilities agree with the book values, except for the equipment and the building. The equipment is undervalued by $10,000 and is thought to have a 5-year life; the building is undervalued by $50,000 and is thought to have a 20-year life. The remaining excess of cost over book value is attributable to goodwill. Jeter Corporation uses the simple equity method to record its investments.

Since the purchase date, both firms have operated separately, and no intercompany transactions have occurred. Super Company closes its books on the date of acquisition.

The separate trial balances of the firms on December 31, 2015, are as follows:

	Jeter Corporation	Super Company
Cash	296,600	91,000
Land	160,000	90,000
Building	225,000	135,000
Accumulated Depreciation—Building	(100,000)	(50,000)
Equipment	450,000	150,000
Accumulated Depreciation—Equipment	(115,000)	(60,000)
Investment in Super Company	284,600	
Liabilities	(480,000)	(150,000)
Common Stock ($100 par)	(400,000)	
Common Stock ($5 par)		(150,000)
Paid-In Capital in Excess of Par	(40,000)	
Retained Earnings, January 1, 2015	(251,600)	
Retained Earnings, July 1, 2015		(50,000)
Sales	(460,000)	(60,000)
Cost of Goods Sold	220,000	30,000
Other Expenses	210,000	24,000
Subsidiary Income	(9,600)	
Dividends Declared	10,000	
Totals	0	0

Required ▶ ▶ ▶ ▶ ▶

1. Prepare a value analysis and a determination and distribution of excess schedule for the investment.
2. Prepare the 2015 consolidated worksheet. Include columns for the eliminations and adjustments, the consolidated income statement, the NCI, the controlling retained earnings, and the consolidated balance sheet. Prepare supporting income distribution schedules as well.
3. Prepare the 2015 consolidated statements, including the income statement, retained earnings statement, and balance sheet.

Problem 3-8 *(LO 3, 5)* **Cost method, 80% interest, worksheet, several adjustments.** Detner International purchases 80% of the outstanding stock of Hardy Company for $1,600,000 on January 1, 2015. At the purchase date, the inventory, equipment, and patents of Hardy Company have fair values of $10,000, $50,000, and $100,000, respectively, in excess of their book values. The other assets and liabilities of Hardy Company have book values equal to their fair values. The inventory is sold during the month following the purchase. The two companies agree that the equipment has a remaining life of eight years and the patents 10 years. On the purchase date, the owners' equity of Hardy Company is as follows:

Common stock ($10 stated value)	$1,000,000
Additional paid-in capital in excess of par	300,000
Retained earnings	400,000
Total equity	$1,700,000

During 2015 and 2016, Hardy Company has income and pays dividends as follows:

	Income	Dividends
2015	$ 90,000	$30,000
2016	150,000	30,000

The trial balances of the two companies as of December 31, 2017, shown on page 189.

	Detner International	Hardy Company
Current Assets	632,000	505,000
Equipment (net)	1,320,000	940,000
Patents	100,000	35,000
Other Assets	1,620,000	730,000
Investment in Hardy	1,600,000	
Accounts Payable	(658,000)	(205,000)
Common Stock ($5 par)	(2,000,000)	
Common Stock ($10 par)		(1,000,000)
Additional Paid-In Capital in Excess of Par	(1,200,000)	(300,000)
Retained Earnings, January 1, 2017.	(1,255,000)	(580,000)
Sales	(905,000)	(425,000)
Cost of Goods Sold	470,000	170,000
Other Expenses	250,000	100,000
Dividend Income	(24,000)	
Dividends Declared	50,000	30,000
Totals	0	0

The remaining excess of cost over book value is attributable to goodwill.

1. Prepare the original value analysis and a determination and distribution of excess schedule ◄ ◄ ◄ ◄ ◄ **Required** for the investment.
2. Prepare the consolidated worksheet for December 31, 2017. Include columns for the eliminations and adjustments, the consolidated income statement, the controlling retained earnings, and the consolidated balance sheet.

Use the following information for Problems 3-9 through 3-13:

Paulcraft Corporation builds large powerboats. On January 1, 2015, Paulcraft acquires Switzer Corporation, a company that manufactures smaller power boats. Paulcraft pays cash in exchange for Switzer common stock. Switzer has the following balance sheet on January 1, 2015:

Switzer Corporation
Balance Sheet
January 1, 2015

Assets		Liabilities and Equity	
Accounts receivable	$ 82,000	Current liabilities	$ 90,000
Inventory	40,000	Bonds payable	100,000
Land.	60,000	Common stock ($1 par)	10,000
Buildings	200,000	Paid-in capital in excess of par . . .	90,000
Accumulated depreciation . . .	(50,000)	Retained earnings	112,000
Equipment	100,000		
Accumulated depreciation . . .	(30,000)		
Total assets.	$402,000	Total liabilities and equity	$402,000

Appraisal values for identifiable assets and liabilities are as follows:

Accounts receivable	$ 82,000
Inventory (sold during 2015).	38,000
Land.	150,000
Buildings (20-year life)	280,000

(continued)

Equipment (5-year life)	100,000
Current liabilities	90,000
Bonds payable (5-year life)	96,000

Any remaining excess is attributed to goodwill.

Problem 3-9 *(LO 2, 5)* **100%, equity method worksheet, several adjustments, third year, bargain.** Refer to the preceding information for Paulcraft's acquisition of Switzer's common stock. Assume that Paulcraft pays $420,000 for 100% of Switzer common stock. Paulcraft uses the simple equity method to account for its investment in Switzer. Paulcraft and Switzer have the following trial balances on December 31, 2017:

	Paulcraft	Switzer
Cash	160,000	110,000
Accounts Receivable	90,000	55,000
Inventory	120,000	86,000
Land.	100,000	60,000
Investment in Switzer	515,000	
Buildings	800,000	250,000
Accumulated Depreciation	(220,000)	(80,000)
Equipment	150,000	100,000
Accumulated Depreciation	(90,000)	(72,000)
Current Liabilities.	(60,000)	(102,000)
Bonds Payable.		(100,000)
Common Stock	(100,000)	(10,000)
Paid-In Capital in Excess of Par	(900,000)	(90,000)
Retained Earnings, January 1, 2017.	(385,000)	(182,000)
Sales	(800,000)	(350,000)
Cost of Goods Sold	450,000	210,000
Depreciation Expense—Buildings.	30,000	15,000
Depreciation Expense—Equipment.	15,000	14,000
Other Expenses	140,000	68,000
Interest Expense.		8,000
Subsidiary Income.	(35,000)	
Dividends Declared.	20,000	10,000
Totals	0	0

Required ▶ ▶ ▶ ▶ ▶

1. Prepare a value analysis and a determination and distribution of excess schedule for the investment in Switzer.
2. Complete a consolidated worksheet for Paulcraft Corporation and its subsidiary Switzer Corporation as of December 31, 2017. Prepare supporting amortization and income distribution schedules.

Problem 3-10 *(LO 3, 5)* **100%, cost method worksheet, several adjustments, third year.** Refer to the preceding information for Paulcraft's acquisition of Switzer's common stock. Assume that Paulcraft pays $480,000 for 100% of Switzer common stock. Paulcraft uses the cost method to account for its investment in Switzer. Paulcraft and Switzer have the following trial balances on December 31, 2017 as shown on page 191.

	Paulcraft	Switzer
Cash	100,000	110,000
Accounts Receivable	90,000	55,000
Inventory	120,000	86,000
Land.	100,000	60,000
Investment in Switzer	480,000	
Buildings	800,000	250,000
Accumulated Depreciation	(220,000)	(80,000)
Equipment	150,000	100,000
Accumulated Depreciation	(90,000)	(72,000)
Current Liabilities.	(60,000)	(102,000)
Bonds Payable.		(100,000)
Common Stock	(100,000)	(10,000)
Paid-In Capital in Excess of Par	(900,000)	(90,000)
Retained Earnings, January 1, 2017.	(315,000)	(182,000)
Sales	(800,000)	(350,000)
Cost of Goods Sold	450,000	210,000
Depreciation Expense—Buildings.	30,000	15,000
Depreciation Expense—Equipment.	15,000	14,000
Other Expenses	140,000	68,000
Interest Expense.		8,000
Dividend Income	(10,000)	
Dividends Declared.	20,000	10,000
Totals	0	0

1. Prepare a value analysis and a determination and distribution of excess schedule for the ◀ ◀ ◀ ◀ ◀ **Required**
   investment in Switzer.
2. Complete a consolidated worksheet for Paulcraft Corporation and its subsidiary Switzer
   Corporation as of December 31, 2017. Prepare supporting amortization and income distribution schedules.

Problem 3-11 *(LO 3, 5)* **80%, equity method worksheet, several adjustments, third year.** Refer to the preceding common information for Paulcraft's acquisition of Switzer's common stock. Assume that Paulcraft pays $440,000 for 80% of Switzer common stock. Paulcraft uses the simple equity method to account for its investment in Switzer. Paulcraft and Switzer have the following trial balances on December 31, 2017:

	Paulcraft	Switzer
Cash	138,000	110,000
Accounts Receivable	90,000	55,000
Inventory	120,000	86,000
Land.	100,000	60,000
Investment in Switzer	516,000	
Buildings	800,000	250,000
Accumulated Depreciation	(220,000)	(80,000)
Equipment	150,000	100,000
Accumulated Depreciation	(90,000)	(72,000)
Current Liabilities.	(60,000)	(102,000)
Bonds Payable.		(100,000)
Common Stock	(100,000)	(10,000)
Paid-In Capital in Excess of Par	(900,000)	(90,000)
Retained Earnings, January 1, 2017.	(371,000)	(182,000)
Sales	(800,000)	(350,000)

(continued)

	Paulcraft	Switzer
Cost of Goods Sold	450,000	210,000
Depreciation Expense—Buildings	30,000	15,000
Depreciation Expense—Equipment	15,000	14,000
Other Expenses	140,000	68,000
Interest Expense		8,000
Subsidiary Income	(28,000)	
Dividends Declared	20,000	10,000
Totals	0	0

Required ▶ ▶ ▶ ▶ ▶

1. Prepare a value analysis and a determination and distribution of excess schedule for the investment in Switzer.
2. Complete a consolidated worksheet for Paulcraft Corporation and its subsidiary Switzer Corporation as of December 31, 2017. Prepare supporting amortization and income distribution schedules.

Problem 3-12 *(LO 3, 5)* **80%, cost method worksheet, several adjustments, first year.** Refer to the preceding information for Paulcraft's acquisition of Switzer's common stock. Assume that Paulcraft pays $400,000 for 80% of Switzer common stock. Paulcraft uses the cost method to account for its investment in Switzer. Paulcraft and Switzer have the following trial balances on December 31, 2015:

	Paulcraft	Switzer
Cash	178,000	81,000
Accounts Receivable	80,000	35,000
Inventory	90,000	52,000
Land	100,000	60,000
Investment in Switzer	400,000	
Buildings	800,000	200,000
Accumulated Depreciation	(200,000)	(60,000)
Equipment	150,000	100,000
Accumulated Depreciation	(75,000)	(44,000)
Current Liabilities	(50,000)	(88,000)
Bonds Payable		(100,000)
Common Stock	(100,000)	(10,000)
Paid-In Capital in Excess of Par	(900,000)	(90,000)
Retained Earnings, January 1, 2015	(300,000)	(112,000)
Sales	(750,000)	(300,000)
Cost of Goods Sold	400,000	180,000
Depreciation Expense—Buildings	30,000	10,000
Depreciation Expense—Equipment	15,000	14,000
Other Expenses	120,000	54,000
Interest Expense		8,000
Dividend Income	(8,000)	
Dividends Declared	20,000	10,000
Totals	0	0

Required ▶ ▶ ▶ ▶ ▶

1. Prepare a value analysis and a determination and distribution of excess schedule for the investment in Switzer.
2. Complete a consolidated worksheet for Paulcraft Corporation and its subsidiary Switzer Corporation as of December 31, 2015. Prepare supporting amortization and income distribution schedules.

Problem 3-13 *(LO 3, 5)* **70%, cost method worksheet, several adjustments, third year.** Refer to the preceding information for Paulcraft's acquisition of Switzer's common stock. Assume that Paulcraft pays $420,000 for 70% of Switzer common stock. Paulcraft uses the cost method to account for its investment in Switzer. Paulcraft and Switzer have the following trial balances on December 31, 2017:

	Paulcraft	Switzer
Cash	157,000	110,000
Accounts Receivable	90,000	55,000
Inventory	120,000	86,000
Land.	100,000	60,000
Investment in Switzer	420,000	
Buildings	800,000	250,000
Accumulated Depreciation	(220,000)	(80,000)
Equipment	150,000	100,000
Accumulated Depreciation	(90,000)	(72,000)
Current Liabilities.	(60,000)	(102,000)
Bonds Payable.		(100,000)
Common Stock	(100,000)	(10,000)
Paid-In Capital in Excess of Par	(900,000)	(90,000)
Retained Earnings, January 1, 2017.	(315,000)	(182,000)
Sales	(800,000)	(350,000)
Cost of Goods Sold	450,000	210,000
Depreciation Expense—Buildings.	30,000	15,000
Depreciation Expense—Equipment.	15,000	14,000
Other Expenses	140,000	68,000
Interest Expense.		8,000
Dividend Income	(7,000)	
Dividends Declared.	20,000	10,000
Totals	0	0

1. Prepare a value analysis and a determination and distribution of excess schedule for the ◄ ◄ ◄ ◄ ◄ **Required**
   investment in Switzer.
2. Complete a consolidated worksheet for Paulcraft Corporation and its subsidiary Switzer
   Corporation as of December 31, 2017. Prepare supporting amortization and income distribution schedules.

Use the following information for Problems 3-14 through 3-18:
Fast Cool Company and Fast Air Company are both manufacturers of air conditioning
equipment. On January 1, 2015, Fast Cool acquires the common stock of Fast Air by
exchanging its own $1 par, $20 fair value common stock. On the date of acquisition, Fast
Air has the following balance sheet:

Fast Air Company
Balance Sheet
January 1, 2015

Assets		Liabilities and Equity	
Accounts receivable	$ 40,000	Current liabilities	$ 30,000
Inventory	60,000	Mortgage payable	200,000
Land.	50,000	Common stock ($1 par).	100,000
Buildings	400,000	Paid-in capital in excess of par . . .	200,000
Accumulated depreciation . . .	(50,000)	Retained earnings	180,000
Equipment	150,000		
Accumulated depreciation . . .	(30,000)		
Patent (net).	40,000		
Goodwill	50,000		
Total assets.	$710,000	Total liabilities and equity	$710,000

(continued)

Fast Cool requests that an appraisal be done to determine whether the book value of Fast Air's net assets reflect their fair values. The appraiser determines that several intangible assets exist, although they are unrecorded. If the intangible assets do not have an observable market, the appraiser estimates their value. The appraiser determines the following fair values and estimates:

Accounts receivable	$ 40,000
Inventory (sold during 2015)	65,000
Land	100,000
Buildings (20-year life)	500,000
Equipment (5-year life)	100,000
Patent (5-year life)	50,000
Current liabilities	30,000
Mortgage payable (5-year life)	205,000
Favorable purchase contract (2-year life)	10,000

Any remaining excess is attributed to goodwill.

Problem 3-14 *(LO 2, 5)* **100%, complicated excess, equity method, first year.** Refer to the preceding information for Fast Cool's acquisition of Fast Air's common stock. Assume Fast Cool issues 40,000 shares of its $20 fair value common stock for 100% of Fast Air's common stock. Fast Cool uses the simple equity method to account for its investment in Fast Air. Fast Cool and Fast Air have the following trial balances on December 31, 2015:

	Fast Cool	Fast Air
Cash	147,000	37,000
Accounts Receivable	70,000	100,000
Inventory	150,000	60,000
Land	60,000	50,000
Investment in Fast Air	837,500	
Buildings	1,200,000	400,000
Accumulated Depreciation	(176,000)	(67,500)
Equipment	140,000	150,000
Accumulated Depreciation	(68,000)	(54,000)
Patent (net)		32,000
Goodwill		50,000
Current Liabilities	(80,000)	(40,000)
Mortgage Payable		(200,000)
Common Stock	(100,000)	(100,000)
Paid-In Capital in Excess of Par	(1,500,000)	(200,000)
Retained Earnings, January 1, 2015	(400,000)	(180,000)
Sales	(700,000)	(400,000)
Cost of Goods Sold	380,000	210,000
Depreciation Expense—Buildings	10,000	17,500
Depreciation Expense—Equipment	7,000	24,000
Other Expenses	50,000	85,000
Interest Expense		16,000
Subsidiary Income	(47,500)	
Dividends Declared	20,000	10,000
Totals	0	0

1. Prepare a value analysis and a determination and distribution of excess schedule for the ◄ ◄ ◄ ◄ ◄ **Required** investment in Fast Air.
2. Complete a consolidated worksheet for Fast Cool Company and its subsidiary Fast Air Company as of December 31, 2015. Prepare supporting amortization and income distribution schedules.

Problem 3-15 *(LO 2, 5)* **100%, complicated excess, equity method, second year.** Refer to the preceding information for Fast Cool's acquisition of Fast Air's common stock. Assume Fast Cool issues 40,000 shares of its $20 fair value common stock for 100% of Fast Air's common stock. Fast Cool uses the simple equity method to account for its investment in Fast Air. Fast Cool and Fast Air have the following trial balances on December 31, 2016:

	Fast Cool	Fast Air
Cash	396,000	99,000
Accounts Receivable	200,000	120,000
Inventory	120,000	95,000
Land	60,000	50,000
Investment in Fast Air	895,000	
Buildings	1,200,000	400,000
Accumulated Depreciation	(200,000)	(85,000)
Equipment	140,000	150,000
Accumulated Depreciation	(80,000)	(78,000)
Patent (net)		24,000
Goodwill		50,000
Current Liabilities	(150,000)	(50,000)
Mortgage Payable		(200,000)
Common Stock	(100,000)	(100,000)
Paid-In Capital in Excess of Par	(1,500,000)	(200,000)
Retained Earnings, January 1, 2016	(680,500)	(217,500)
Sales	(700,000)	(500,000)
Cost of Goods Sold	380,000	260,000
Depreciation Expense—Buildings	10,000	17,500
Depreciation Expense—Equipment	7,000	24,000
Other Expenses	50,000	115,000
Interest Expense		16,000
Subsidiary Income	(67,500)	
Dividends Declared	20,000	10,000
Totals	0	0

1. Prepare a value analysis and a determination and distribution of excess schedule for the ◄ ◄ ◄ ◄ ◄ **Required** investment in Fast Air.
2. Complete a consolidated worksheet for Fast Cool Company and its subsidiary Fast Air Company as of December 31, 2016. Prepare supporting amortization and income distribution schedules.

Problem 3-16 *(LO 2, 5)* **100% bargain, complicated equity method, second year.** Refer to the preceding information for Fast Cool's acquisition of Fast Air's common stock. Assume Fast Cool issues 25,000 shares of its $20 fair value common stock for 100% of Fast Air's common stock. Fast Cool uses the simple equity method to account for its investment in Fast Air. Fast Cool and Fast Air have the following trial balances on December 31, 2016, shown on page 196.

	Fast Cool	Fast Air
Cash	396,000	99,000
Accounts Receivable	200,000	120,000
Inventory	120,000	95,000
Land	60,000	50,000
Investment in Fast Air	595,000	
Buildings	1,200,000	400,000
Accumulated Depreciation	(200,000)	(85,000)
Equipment	140,000	150,000
Accumulated Depreciation	(80,000)	(78,000)
Patent (net)		24,000
Goodwill		50,000
Current Liabilities	(150,000)	(50,000)
Mortgage Payable		(200,000)
Common Stock	(85,000)	(100,000)
Paid-In Capital in Excess of Par	(1,215,000)	(200,000)
Retained Earnings, January 1, 2016	(680,500)	(217,500)
Sales	(700,000)	(500,000)
Cost of Goods Sold	380,000	260,000
Depreciation Expense—Buildings	10,000	17,500
Depreciation Expense—Equipment	7,000	24,000
Other Expenses	50,000	115,000
Interest Expense		16,000
Subsidiary Income	(67,500)	
Dividends Declared	20,000	10,000
Totals	0	0

Required ▶ ▶ ▶ ▶ ▶

1. Prepare a value analysis and a determination and distribution of excess schedule for the investment in Fast Air.
2. Complete a consolidated worksheet for Fast Cool Company and its subsidiary Fast Air Company as of December 31, 2016. Prepare supporting amortization and income distribution schedules.

Problem 3-17 *(LO 2, 5)* **80%, first year, equity method, complicated excess.** Refer to the preceding information for Fast Cool's acquisition of Fast Air's common stock. Assume Fast Cool issues 35,000 shares of its $20 fair value common stock for 80% of Fast Air's common stock. Fast Cool uses the simple equity method to account for its investment in Fast Air. Fast Cool and Fast Air have the following trial balances on December 31, 2015:

	Fast Cool	Fast Air
Cash	145,000	37,000
Accounts Receivable	70,000	100,000
Inventory	150,000	60,000
Land	60,000	50,000
Investment in Fast Air	730,000	
Buildings	1,200,000	400,000
Accumulated Depreciation	(176,000)	(67,500)
Equipment	140,000	150,000
Accumulated Depreciation	(68,000)	(54,000)
Patent (net)		32,000
Goodwill		50,000
Current Liabilities	(80,000)	(40,000)
Mortgage Payable		(200,000)

	Fast Cool	Fast Air
Common Stock	(95,000)	(100,000)
Paid-In Capital in Excess of Par	(1,405,000)	(200,000)
Retained Earnings, January 1, 2015	(400,000)	(180,000)
Sales	(700,000)	(400,000)
Cost of Goods Sold	380,000	210,000
Depreciation Expense—Buildings	10,000	17,500
Depreciation Expense—Equipment	7,000	24,000
Other Expenses	50,000	85,000
Interest Expense		16,000
Subsidiary Income	(38,000)	
Dividends Declared	20,000	10,000
Totals	0	0

1. Prepare a value analysis and a determination and distribution of excess schedule for the ◀ ◀ ◀ ◀ ◀ **Required**
investment in Fast Air.
2. Complete a consolidated worksheet for Fast Cool Company and its subsidiary Fast Air
Company as of December 31, 2015. Prepare supporting amortization and income distribution schedules.

Problem 3-18 *(LO 2, 5)* **80%, second year, equity method, complicated excess.**
Refer to the preceding information for Fast Cool's acquisition of Fast Air's common stock.
Assume Fast Cool issues 35,000 shares of its $20 fair value common stock for 80% of Fast Air's
common stock. Fast Cool uses the simple equity method to account for its investment in Fast
Air. Fast Cool and Fast Air have the following trial balances on December 31, 2016:

	Fast Cool	Fast Air
Cash	392,000	99,000
Accounts Receivable	200,000	120,000
Inventory	120,000	95,000
Land	60,000	50,000
Investment in Fast Air	776,000	
Buildings	1,200,000	400,000
Accumulated Depreciation	(200,000)	(85,000)
Equipment	140,000	150,000
Accumulated Depreciation	(80,000)	(78,000)
Patent (net)		24,000
Goodwill		50,000
Current Liabilities	(150,000)	(50,000)
Mortgage Payable		(200,000)
Common Stock	(95,000)	(100,000)
Paid-In Capital in Excess of Par	(1,405,000)	(200,000)
Retained Earnings, January 1, 2016	(671,000)	(217,500)
Sales	(700,000)	(500,000)
Cost of Goods Sold	380,000	260,000
Depreciation Expense—Buildings	10,000	17,500
Depreciation Expense—Equipment	7,000	24,000
Other Expenses	50,000	115,000
Interest Expense		16,000
Subsidiary Income	(54,000)	
Dividends Declared	20,000	10,000
Totals	0	0

Required ▶ ▶ ▶ ▶ ▶

1. Prepare a value analysis and a determination and distribution of excess schedule for the investment in Fast Air.
2. Complete a consolidated worksheet for Fast Cool Company and its subsidiary Fast Air Company as of December 31, 2016. Prepare supporting amortization and income distribution schedules.

APPENDIX PROBLEMS

Problem 3A-1 *(LO 2, 8)* **Simple equity method adjustments, vertical consolidated worksheet.** (Same as Problem 3-2 except vertical format worksheet is used.) On January 1, 2015, Paro Company purchases 80% of the common stock of Solar Company for $320,000. On this date, Solar has common stock, other paid-in capital in excess of par, and retained earnings of $50,000, $100,000, and $150,000, respectively. Net income and dividends for two years for Solar Company are as follows:

	2015	2016
Net income	$60,000	$90,000
Dividends.	20,000	30,000

On January 1, 2015, the only undervalued tangible assets of Solar are inventory and the building. Inventory, for which FIFO is used, is worth $10,000 more than cost. The inventory is sold in 2015. The building, which is worth $30,000 more than book value, has a remaining life of 10 years, and straight-line depreciation is used. The remaining excess of cost over book value is attributable to goodwill.

Required ▶ ▶ ▶ ▶ ▶

1. Using this information or the information in the following statements for the year ended December 31, 2016, prepare a determination and distribution of excess schedule.
2. Complete the vertical worksheet for consolidated financial statements for 2016.

Statement—Accounts	Paro Company	Solar Company
Income Statement:		
Net Sales	(520,000)	(450,000)
Cost of Goods Sold	300,000	260,000
Operating Expenses	120,000	100,000
Subsidiary Income	(72,000)	
Noncontrolling Interest in Income		
Net Income.	(172,000)	(90,000)
Retained Earnings Statement:		
Balance, January 1, 2016—Paro Company.	(214,000)	
Balance, January 1, 2016—Solar Company		(190,000)
Net Income (from above).	(172,000)	(90,000)
Dividends Declared—Paro Company	50,000	
Dividends Declared—Solar Company		30,000
Balance, December 31, 2016.	(336,000)	(250,000)
Consolidated Balance Sheet:		
Inventory, December 31, 2016.	100,000	50,000
Other Current Assets	136,000	180,000
Investment in Solar Company	400,000	
Land.	50,000	50,000

Statement—Accounts	Paro Company	Solar Company
Building and Equipment.	350,000	320,000
Accumulated Depreciation	(100,000)	(60,000)
Goodwill		
Other Intangibles.	20,000	
Current Liabilities	(120,000)	(40,000)
Bonds Payable.		(100,000)
Other Long-Term Liabilities.	(200,000)	
Common Stock—Paro Company.	(200,000)	
Other Paid-In Capital in Excess of Par—Paro Company	(100,000)	
Common Stock—Solar Company		(50,000)
Other Paid-In Capital in Excess of Par—Solar Company.		(100,000)
Retained Earnings, December 31, 2016 (from above)	(336,000)	(250,000)
Totals	0	0

Problem 3A-2 *(LO 2, 6, 8)* **Equity method, later period, vertical worksheet, several excess adjustments.** Baker Enterprises purchases an 80% interest in Kohlenberg International for $850,000 on January 1, 2015. The estimated fair value of the NCI is $190,000. On the purchase date, Kohlenberg International has the following stockholders' equity:

Common stock ($10 par).	$150,000
Paid-in capital in excess of par	200,000
Retained earnings	400,000
	$750,000

Also on the purchase date, it is determined that Kohlenberg International's assets are understated as follows:

Equipment, 10-year remaining life	$80,000
Land.	20,000
Building, 20-year remaining life	60,000

The remaining excess of cost over book value is attributed to goodwill. The following summarized statements of Baker Enterprises and Kohlenberg International are for the year ended December 31, 2017:

	Baker Enterprises	Kohlenberg International
Income Statements:		
Sales	(650,000)	(320,000)
Cost of Goods Sold	260,000	240,000
Operating Expenses	170,000	70,000
Depreciation Expense	65,000	30,000
Subsidiary (Income)/Loss	16,000	
Net (Income)/Loss	(139,000)	20,000
Retained Earnings:		
Retained Earnings, January 1, 2017—Baker	(625,000)	
Retained Earnings, January 1, 2017—Kohlenberg		(460,000)

(continued)

	Baker Enterprises	Kohlenberg International
Net (Income)/Loss	(139,000)	20,000
Dividends Declared		10,000
Retained Earnings, December 31, 2017	(764,000)	(430,000)
Balance Sheets:		
Cash	288,000	170,000
Inventory	135,000	400,000
Land	145,000	150,000
Building	900,000	500,000
Accumulated Depreciation—Building	(345,000)	(360,000)
Equipment	350,000	250,000
Accumulated Depreciation—Equipment	(135,000)	(90,000)
Investment in Kohlenberg International	874,000	
Liabilities	(248,000)	(40,000)
Bonds Payable		(200,000)
Common Stock—Baker	(1,200,000)	
Common Stock—Kohlenberg		(150,000)
Paid-In Capital in Excess of Par		(200,000)
Retained Earnings, December 31, 2017	(764,000)	(430,000)
Balance	0	0

Required ▶ ▶ ▶ ▶ ▶ Using the vertical format, prepare a consolidated worksheet for December 31, 2017. Precede the worksheet with a value analysis and a determination and distribution of excess schedule. Include income distribution schedules to allocate the consolidated net income to the noncontrolling and controlling interests.

Suggestion: Remember that all adjustments to retained earnings are to beginning retained earnings, and it is the beginning balance of the subsidiary retained earnings account that is subject to elimination. Carefully follow the "carrydown" procedure to calculate the ending retained earnings balances.

Problem 3A-3 *(LO 5, 8)* **Cost method, later period, vertical worksheets.** Harvard Company purchases a 90% interest in Bart Company for $720,000 on January 1, 2015. The investment is accounted for under the cost method. At the time of the purchase, a building owned by Bart is understated by $180,000; it has a 20-year remaining life on the purchase date. The remaining excess is attributed to goodwill. The stockholders' equity of Bart Company on the purchase date is as follows:

Common stock ($10 par)	$350,000
Retained earnings	200,000
Total equity	$550,000

The following summarized statements are for the year ended December 31, 2016. (Credit balance amounts are in parentheses.)

	Harvard	Bart
Income Statements:		
Sales	(580,000)	(280,000)
Cost of Goods Sold	285,000	155,000
Operating Expenses	140,000	55,000
Depreciation Expense	72,000	30,000
Dividend Income	(9,000)	
Net Income	(92,000)	(40,000)

	Harvard	Bart
Retained Earnings Statements:		
Retained Earnings, January 1, 2016—Harvard	(484,000)	
Retained Earnings, January 1, 2016—Bart.		(320,000)
Net Income	(92,000)	(40,000)
Dividends Declared	20,000	10,000
Retained Earnings, December 31, 2016.	(556,000)	(350,000)
Balance Sheets:		
Cash	330,000	170,000
Inventory	260,000	340,000
Land.	99,000	150,000
Building	800,000	500,000
Accumulated Depreciation—Building	(380,000)	(360,000)
Equipment	340,000	250,000
Accumulated Depreciation—Equipment	(190,000)	(90,000)
Investment in Bart Company	720,000	
Current Liabilities.	(123,000)	(60,000)
Bonds Payable.		(200,000)
Common Stock—Harvard	(800,000)	
Paid-In Capital in Excess of Par—Harvard.	(500,000)	
Common Stock—Bart		(350,000)
Retained Earnings, December 31, 2016.	(556,000)	(350,000)
Balance	0	0

Using the vertical format, prepare a consolidated worksheet for December 31, 2016. Precede ◄ ◄ ◄ ◄ ◄ **Required**
the worksheet with a value analysis and a determination and distribution of excess schedule.
Include income distribution schedules to allocate the consolidated net income to the noncontrolling and controlling interests.

Suggestion: Remember that all adjustments to retained earnings are to beginning retained earnings, and it is the beginning balance of the subsidiary retained earnings account that is subject to elimination. One of the adjustments to the parent retained earnings account is the cost-to-equity conversion entry. Be sure to follow the carrydown procedure to calculate the ending retained earnings balances.

Problem 3B-1 *(LO 9)* **D&D only, nontaxable exchange, tax loss carryover.** On
December 31, 2015, Bryant Company exchanges 10,000 of its $10 par value shares for a 90%
interest in Jones Company. The purchase is recorded at the $72 per-share fair value of Bryant
shares. Jones Company has the following balance sheet on the date of the purchase:

Assets		Liabilities and Equity	
Cash	$ 100,000	Current liabilities	$ 130,000
Accounts receivable	200,000	Deferred rental income	120,000
Inventory	150,000	Bonds payable	250,000
Investment in marketable		Common stock ($10 par).	100,000
securities	150,000		
Depreciable fixed assets	400,000	Paid-in capital in excess of par	150,000
		Retained earnings	250,000
Total assets.	$1,000,000	Total liabilities and equity	$1,000,000

It is determined that the following fair values differ from book values for the assets of Jones Company:

Inventory	$200,000
Depreciable fixed assets (net)	500,000 (20-year life)
Investment in marketable securities	170,000

The purchase is a tax-free exchange to the seller, which means Bryant Company will use the book value of Jones's assets for tax purposes. Jones Company has $200,000 of tax loss carryovers. Bryant will be able to utilize $40,000 of the losses to offset taxes to be paid in 2016. The balance of the tax loss carryover will not be used within a year but is considered fully realizable in the future. The tax rate for both firms is 30%.

Required ▶ ▶ ▶ ▶ ▶ Record the investment and prepare a value analysis schedule and a determination and distribution of excess schedule.

Suggestion: Asset adjustments should be accompanied by the appropriate deferred tax liability.

Problem 3B-2 *(LO 2, 9)* **Worksheet for nontaxable exchange.** On December 31, 2016, immediately after Todd Company's acquisition of 80% of Keller Company, their balance sheets are as follows:

	Todd	Keller
Cash	$ 1,200,000	$ 50,000
Accounts receivable	2,400,000	300,000
Inventory	11,200,000	1,500,000
Prepayments	422,000	47,000
Depreciable fixed assets	18,978,000	2,100,000
Investment in Keller Company	2,240,000	
Total assets	$36,440,000	$3,997,000
Payables	$ 7,200,000	$1,750,000
Accruals	1,615,000	400,000
Common stock ($100 par)	1,000,000	1,000,000
Paid-in capital in excess of par	8,900,000	
Retained earnings	17,725,000	847,000
Total liabilities and equity	$36,440,000	$3,997,000

An appraisal on December 31, 2016, which is considered carefully and approved by the boards of directors of both companies, places a total replacement value, less depreciation, of $2,800,000 on Keller's depreciable fixed assets. The remaining depreciable life is 20 years.

Todd Company offers to purchase all the assets of Keller Company, subject to its liabilities, as of December 31, 2016, for $2,500,000. Some of the stockholders of Keller Company object to the price because it does not include enough consideration for goodwill. 20% of the shareholders elect not to sell their shares. A counterproposal is made to 80% of the shareholders and an agreement is reached. In exchange for its own shares, Todd acquires 8,000 shares of the common stock of Keller at the agreed-upon $280 per share. The price includes a control premium. The shares held by the NCI are estimated to have a fair value of $250 each. The purchase is structured as a tax-free exchange to the seller; thus, Todd will use the book value of the assets for future tax purposes. The tax rate for both companies is 30%.

Required ▶ ▶ ▶ ▶ ▶ Prepare a consolidated worksheet and a consolidated balance sheet as of December 31, 2016. Include a value analysis and a determination and distribution schedule.

(AICPA adapted)

Problem 3B-3 *(LO 2, 9)* **Worksheet for nontaxable exchange with tax loss carryover.** The trial balances of Campton Corporation and Dorn Corporation as of December 31, 2015, are as shown on page 203.

	Campton Corporation	Dorn Corporation
Current Assets	150,000	100,000
Land.	400,000	100,000
Building and Equipment (net).	900,000	240,000
Investment in Dorn Corporation.	642,600	
Current Tax Liability.	(3,000)	(12,000)
Other Current Liabilities.	(130,000)	(100,000)
Common Stock ($5 par)	(500,000)	
Common Stock ($50 par)		(200,000)
Paid-In Capital in Excess of Par	(750,000)	
Retained Earnings, January 1, 2015.	(650,000)	(100,000)
Sales	(309,000)	(170,000)
Subsidiary Income.	(12,600)	
Cost of Goods Sold	170,000	80,000
Expenses	89,000	50,000
Provision for Tax	3,000*	12,000
Totals	0	0

*$15,000 tax liability ($50,000 income × 30%) – $12,000 tax loss carryover ($40,000 × 30%)

On January 1, 2015, Campton purchases 90% of the outstanding stock of Dorn Corporation for $630,000. The acquisition is a tax-free exchange for the seller. At the purchase date, Dorn's equipment is undervalued by $100,000 and has a remaining life of 10 years. All other assets have book values that approximate their fair values. Dorn Corporation has a tax loss carryover of $200,000, of which $50,000 is utilizable in 2015 and the balance in future periods. The tax loss carryover is expected to be fully utilized. Any remaining excess is considered to be goodwill. A tax rate of 30% applies to both companies.

◄ ◄ ◄ ◄ ◄ **Required**

1. Prepare a value analysis and a determination and distribution of excess schedule for the investment.
2. Prepare the 2015 consolidated worksheet. Include columns for the eliminations and adjustments, the consolidated income statement, the NCI, the controlling retained earnings, and the consolidated balance sheet. Prepare supporting income distribution schedules as well.
3. Prepare the 2015 consolidated statements, including the income statement, retained earnings statement, and balance sheet.

Suggestion: A deferred tax liability results from the increase in the fair value of the equipment. As the added depreciation is recognized on the equipment, the deferred tax liability becomes payable. Note that income distribution schedules record net-of-tax income. Therefore, be sure that any adjustments to the income distribution schedules consider tax where appropriate.

Chapter 4

Intercompany Transactions: Merchandise, Plant Assets, and Notes

C H A P T E R

Learning Objectives

When you have completed this chapter, you should be able to

1. **Explain why transactions between members of a consolidated firm should not be reflected in the consolidated financial statements.**

2. **Defer intercompany profits on merchandise sales when appropriate and eliminate the double counting of sales between affiliates.**

3. **Defer profits on intercompany sales of long-term assets and realize the profits over the period of use and/or at the time of sale to a firm outside the consolidated group.**

4. **Eliminate intercompany loans and notes.**

5. **Discuss the complications intercompany profits create for the use of the sophisticated equity method.**

6. **Apply intercompany profit eliminations on a vertical worksheet. (Appendix)**

The elimination of the parent's investment in a subsidiary is only the start of the procedures that are necessary to consolidate a parent and a subsidiary. It is common for affiliated companies to transact business with one another. The more integrated the affiliates are with respect to operations, the more common intercompany transactions become. This chapter considers the most often encountered types of intercompany transactions. These include intercompany sales of merchandise and fixed assets as well as loans between members of the consolidated group.

Transactions between the separate legal and accounting entities must be recorded on each affiliate's books. The consolidation process starts with the assumption that these transactions are recorded properly on the separate books of the parent and the subsidiary. However, consolidated statements are those that portray the parent and its subsidiary as a single economic entity. There should not be any intercompany transactions found in these consolidated statements. Only the effect of those transactions between the consolidated company and the companies outside the consolidated company should appear in the consolidated statements. Intercompany transactions must be eliminated as part of the consolidation process. For each type of intercompany transaction, sound reasoning will be developed to support the worksheet procedures. The guiding principle shall come from answering this question: **From the standpoint of a single consolidated company, what accounts and amounts should remain in the financial statements?**

The worksheet eliminations for intercompany transactions are the same no matter what method is used by the parent to maintain its investment in the subsidiary account. The examples in this chapter assume the use of the simple equity method. This is done because any investment that is maintained under the cost method is converted to the simple equity method on the consolidation worksheet. The impact of intercompany transactions on the investment account under the sophisticated equity method is considered later in this chapter. Note, however, that even where the sophisticated equity method is used, there is no change in the procedures for the individual intercompany transactions.

INTERCOMPANY MERCHANDISE SALES

It is common to find that the goods sold by one member of an affiliated group have been purchased from another member of the group. One company may produce component parts that are assembled by its affiliate that sells the final product. In other cases, the product may be produced entirely by one member company and sold on a wholesale basis to another member company that is responsible for selling and servicing the product to the final users. Merchandise sales represent the most common type of intercompany transaction and must be understood as a basic feature of consolidated reporting.

Sales between affiliated companies will be recorded in the normal manner on the books of the separate companies. Remember that each company is a separate legal entity maintaining its own accounting records. Thus, sales to and purchases from an affiliated company are recorded as if they were transactions made with a company outside the consolidated group, and the separate financial statements of the affiliated companies will include these purchase and sale transactions. However, when the statements of the affiliates are consolidated, such sales become transfers of goods within the consolidated entity. Since these sales do not involve parties outside the consolidated group, they cannot be acknowledged in consolidated statements.

Following are the procedures for consolidating affiliated companies engaged in intercompany merchandise sales:

1. The intercompany sale must be eliminated to avoid double counting. To understand this requirement, assume that Company P sells merchandise costing $1,000 to a subsidiary Company S, for $1,200. Company S, in turn, sells the merchandise to an outside party for $1,500. If no elimination is made, the consolidated income statement would show the following with respect to the two transactions:

Sales	$2,700	($1,500 outside sale + $1,200 sale to Company S)
Less cost of goods sold.	2,200	($1,000 cost to Company P + $1,200 purchase by Company S)
Gross profit	$ 500	(18.5% gross profit rate)

While the gross profit is correct, sales and the cost of goods sold are inflated because they are included twice. As a result, the gross profit percentage is understated, since the $500 gross profit appears to relate to $2,700 of sales rather than to the outside sale of $1,500. The intercompany sale must be eliminated from the consolidated statements. All that should remain on the consolidated income statement with respect to the two transactions is as follows:

Sales	$1,500	(only the final sale to the outside party)
Less cost of goods sold.	1,000	(only the purchase from the outside party)
Gross profit	$ 500	(33.3% gross profit rate)

When the goods sold between the affiliated companies are manufactured by the selling affiliate, the consolidated cost of goods sold includes only those costs that can be inventoried, such as labor, materials, and overhead, and may not include any profit.

The intercompany sale, though eliminated, does have an effect on the distribution of consolidated net income to the controlling interest and NCI. This is true because the reported net income of the subsidiary reflects the intercompany sales price, and the subsidiary's separate income statement becomes the base from which the noncontrolling share of income is calculated. In effect, the intercompany transfer price becomes an agreement as to how a portion of consolidated net income will be divided. For example, if Company S is an 80%-owned subsidiary, the NCI will receive 20% of the $300 ($1,500 − $1,200) profit made on the final sale by Company S, or $60. If the intercompany transfer price is increased from $1,200 to $1,300 and the final sales price remains at $1,500, Company S would earn only $200, and the NCI would receive 20% of $200, or $40.

2. Often, intercompany sales will be made on credit. Thus, intercompany trade balances will appear in the separate accounts of the affiliated companies. From a consolidated viewpoint, intercompany receivables and payables represent internal agreements to transfer funds. As such, **this internal debt should not appear on consolidated statements and must be eliminated.** Only debt transactions with entities *outside* the consolidated group should appear on the consolidated balance sheet.

3. **No profit on intercompany sales may be recognized until the profit is realized by a sale to an *outside* party.** This means that any profit contained in the ending inventory of intercompany goods must be eliminated and its recognition deferred until the period in which the goods are sold to outsiders. In the first example above, assume that the sale by Company P to Company S was made on December 30, 2015, and that Company S did not sell the goods until March 2016. From a consolidated viewpoint, there can be no profit recognized until the outside sale occurs in March of 2016. At that time, consolidation theory will acknowledge a $500 profit, of which $200 will be distributed to Company P and $300 will be distributed to Company S as part of the 2016 consolidated net income. However, until that time, the $200 profit on the intercompany sale recorded by Company P must be deferred. In addition, not only must the $1,200 intercompany sale be eliminated, but the inventory on December 31, 2015, must be reduced by $200 (the amount of the intercompany profit) to its $1,000 cost to the consolidated companies.

Care must be taken in calculating the profit applicable to intercompany inventory. It is most convenient when the gross profit rate is provided so that it can be multiplied by the inventory value to arrive at the intercompany profit. In some instances, however, the profit on sales may be stated as a percentage of cost. For example, one might be told that the cost of units is "marked up" 25% to arrive at the intercompany sales price. If the inventory sales price is $1,000, it cannot be multiplied by 25% to calculate the intercompany profit because the 25% applies to the *cost* and not the sales price at which the inventory is stated. Instead, the gross profit rate, which is a percentage of sales price, should be calculated. The easiest method of accomplishing this is to pick the theoretical cost of $1 and mark it up by 25% (the given percentage of cost) to $1.25 and ask: "What is the gross profit percentage?" In this example, it is $0.25 ÷ $1.25, or 20%. From this point, the $1,000 inventory value can be multiplied by 20% to arrive at the intercompany profit of $200.

The worksheet procedures to eliminate the effects of intercompany inventory sales are discussed in the next four sections as follows:

1. There are no intercompany goods in the beginning or ending inventories.

2. Intercompany goods remain in the ending inventory. A perpetual inventory is maintained.

3. There are intercompany goods in the ending inventory, and there were intercompany goods in the beginning inventory. A perpetual inventory is maintained. This is the most common situation.

4. Instead of the perpetual inventory method assumed in sections 1-3 above, the companies use the periodic inventory method. There are intercompany goods in the ending inventory, and there were intercompany goods in the beginning inventory.

No Intercompany Goods in Purchasing Company's Inventories

In the simplest case, which is illustrated in Worksheet 4-1, pages 226 and 227, all goods sold between the affiliates have been sold, in turn, to outside parties by the end of the accounting period. Worksheet 4-1 is based on the following assumptions:

Worksheet 4-1: page 226

1. Company S is an 80%-owned subsidiary of Company P. On January 1, 2015, Company P purchased its interest in Company S at a price equal to its pro rata share of Company S's book value. Company P uses the equity method to record the investment.

2. Companies P and S had the following separate income statements for 2015:

	Company P	Company S
Sales	$700,000	$500,000
Less cost of goods sold	510,000	350,000
Gross profit	$190,000	$150,000
Other expenses	(90,000)	(75,000)
Subsidiary income	60,000	
Net income	$160,000	$ 75,000

Note that under the equity method, Company P's income includes 80% of the reported income of Company S.

3. During the year, Company S sold goods that cost $80,000 to Company P for $100,000 (a 20% gross profit). Company P then sold all of the goods purchased from Company S to outside parties for $150,000. Company P had not paid $25,000 of the invoices received from Company S for the goods. (Note that it is assumed in this and Worksheets 4-2 and 4-3 that a **perpetual** inventory system is used.) Consider the journal entries made by each affiliate:

Company S

Accounts Receivable (from Company P)	100,000	
Sales (to Company P)		100,000
Cost of Goods Sold (to Company P)	80,000	
Inventory		80,000
Cash	75,000	
Accounts Receivable (from Company P)		75,000

Company P

Inventory	100,000	
Accounts Payable (to Company S)		100,000
Accounts Receivable (from outside parties)	150,000	
Sales (to outside parties)		150,000
Cost of Goods Sold (to outside parties)	100,000	
Inventory		100,000
Accounts Payable (to Company S)	75,000	
Cash		75,000

The elimination entries for Worksheet 4-1 in journal entry form are as follows:

(CY1)	Eliminate current-year equity income:		
	Subsidiary Income	60,000	
	Investment in Company S		60,000
(EL)	Eliminate 80% of subsidiary equity against investment in subsidiary account:		
	Common Stock ($10 par)—Company S	80,000	
	Retained Earnings, January 1, 2015—Company S	56,000	
	Investment in Company S		136,000
(IS)	Eliminate intercompany merchandise sales:		
	Sales	100,000	
	Cost of Goods Sold		100,000

(IA)   Eliminate intercompany unpaid trade balances at year-end:

Accounts Payable	25,000	
Accounts Receivable		25,000

Entry (IS) is a simplified summary entry that can be further analyzed with the following entry:

Sales (to Company P)	100,000	
Cost of Goods Sold (by Company S to Company P— the intercompany sale)		80,000
Cost of Goods Sold (by Company P to outside parties— the profit recorded by Company S)		20,000

The preceding expanded entry removes the cost of goods sold with respect to the intercompany sale and removes the intercompany profit from the sales made by the parent to outside parties. Note that the parent recorded the cost of the goods sold to outside parties at $100,000, which contains $20,000 of Company S's profit. As shown in the expanded (IS) entry above, the true cost of the goods to the consolidated company is $80,000 ($100,000 less the 20% internal gross profit).

Entry (IA) eliminates the intercompany receivables/payables still remaining unpaid at the end of the year. Income distribution schedules are used in Worksheet 4-1 to distribute the $175,000 of consolidated net income to the noncontrolling and controlling interests. It should be noted that all of the above procedures remain unchanged if the parent is the seller of the intercompany goods.

Intercompany Goods in Purchasing Company's Ending Inventory

Let us now change the example in Worksheet 4-1 to assume that Company P did not resell $40,000 of the total of $100,000 of goods it purchased from Company S. This means that $40,000 of goods purchased from Company S remain in Company P's ending inventory. As shown below, Company S (the intercompany seller) will have the same entries as presented on page 208, and Company P will have the following revised entries:

2

OBJECTIVE

Defer intercompany profits on merchandise sales when appropriate and eliminate the double counting of sales between affiliates.

Company S

Accounts Receivable (from Company P)	100,000	
Sales (to Company P)		100,000
Cost of Goods Sold (to Company P)	80,000	
Inventory		80,000
Cash	75,000	
Accounts Receivable (from Company P)		75,000

Company P

Inventory	100,000	
Accounts Payable (to Company S)		100,000
Accounts Receivable (from outside parties)	90,000	
Sales (to outside parties)		90,000
Cost of Goods Sold (to outside parties)	60,000	
Inventory		60,000
Accounts Payable (to Company S)	75,000	
Cash		75,000

Let us now consider what has happened to the $100,000 of goods sold to Company P by Company S, shown on next page.

$80,000 is the original cost of the goods sold by Company S that should be removed from the consolidated cost of goods sold since it is derived from the intercompany sale and not the outside sale.

$12,000 is the intercompany profit included in the goods sold by Company P to outside parties. The cost of these sales should be reduced by $12,000 (20% × $60,000) to arrive at the true cost of the goods to the consolidated company.

$8,000 is the intercompany profit remaining in the Company P ending inventory. This inventory, now at $40,000, should be reduced by $8,000 (20% × $40,000) to $32,000. Another way to view this is that 60% of the original intercompany goods (60% × $100,000 = $60,000) has been sold to outside parties. Thus, only the profit on these sales (20% × $60,000 = $12,000) has been realized.

If we follow the above analysis to the letter, we would make the following elimination in entry form:

Sales (by Company S to Company P)	100,000	
Cost of Goods Sold (by Company S)		80,000
Cost of Goods Sold (by Company P)		12,000
Inventory, December 31, 2015 (held by Company P).		8,000

Worksheet 4-2: page 228

In practice, this entry is cumbersome in that it requires an analysis of the destiny of all intercompany sales. The approach used in Worksheet 4-2, pages 228 and 229, is simplified first to eliminate the intercompany sales under the assumption that all goods have been resold, and then to adjust for those goods still remaining in the inventory. This method simplifies worksheet procedures, including the distribution of combined net income. In journal form, the simplified entries are:

(CY1)	Eliminate current-year equity income:		
	Subsidiary Income	60,000	
	Investment in Company S.		60,000
(EL)	Eliminate 80% of subsidiary equity against investment in subsidiary account:		
	Common Stock ($10 par)—Company S	80,000	
	Retained Earnings, January 1, 2015—Company S	56,000	
	Investment in Company S.		136,000
(IS)	Eliminate intercompany merchandise sales:		
	Sales	100,000	
	Cost of Goods Sold		100,000
(EI)	Eliminate intercompany profit in ending inventory:		
	Cost of Goods Sold	8,000	
	Inventory, December 31, 2015.		8,000
(IA)	Eliminate intercompany unpaid trade balance at year-end:		
	Accounts Payable	25,000	
	Accounts Receivable		25,000

The $8,000 adjustment is viewed as the unrealized intercompany inventory profit that may not be realized until a later period when the goods are sold to outside parties.

The unrealized intercompany profit is subtracted from the *seller's* income distribution schedule. In the income distribution schedules for Worksheet 4-2, the unrealized profit of $8,000 is deducted from the subsidiary's internally generated net income of $75,000. The adjusted net income of $67,000 is apportioned, with $13,400 (20%) distributed to the noncontrolling interest and $53,600 (80%) distributed to the controlling interest.

There is no change in worksheet elimination procedures if the parent is the seller and the subsidiary has intercompany goods in its ending inventory. Only the distribution of combined net income changes. To illustrate, assume the parent, Company P, is the seller of the intercompany goods. The income distribution schedules would be prepared as shown on next page.

Subsidiary Company S Income Distribution

	Internally generated net income	$ 75,000
	Adjusted income	$ 75,000
	NCI share	× 20%
	NCI	$ 15,000

Parent Company P Income Distribution

Unrealized profit in ending	Internally generated net income	$100,000
inventory.......................... **(EI)** **$8,000**	80% × Company S adjusted income of	
	$75,000	60,000
	Controlling interest	$152,000

Intercompany Goods in Purchasing Company's Beginning and Ending Inventories

When intercompany goods are included in the purchaser's beginning inventory, the inventory value includes the profit made by the seller. The intercompany seller of the goods has included in the prior period such sales in its separate income statement as though the transactions were consummated. Thus, the beginning retained earnings balance of the seller also includes the profit on these goods. While this profit is reflected on the separate books of the affiliates, it should not be recognized when a consolidated view is taken. Remember: **Profit must not be recognized on a consolidated statement until it is realized in the subsequent period through the sale of goods to an outside party.** Therefore, in the consolidating process, the beginning inventory of intercompany goods must be reduced to its cost to the consolidated company. Likewise, the retained earnings of the consolidated entity must be reduced by deleting the profit that was recorded in prior periods on intercompany goods contained in the buyer's beginning inventory.

To illustrate, using the example of Company P and Company S from Worksheet 4-3 on pages 230 and 231, assume the two companies have the following individual income data for **2016**:

Worksheet 4-3: page 230

	Company P	Company S
Sales	$ 800,000	$ 600,000
Less cost of goods sold........................	610,000	440,000
Gross profit	$ 190,000	$ 160,000
Other expenses	(120,000)	(100,000)
Subsidiary income...........................	48,000	
Net income	$ 118,000	$ 60,000

Assume the following additional facts:

1. Company P's 2016 beginning inventory includes $40,000 of the goods purchased from Company S in **2015**. The gross profit rate on the internal sale was 20%.
2. Company S sold $120,000 of goods to Company P during **2016**.
3. Company S recorded a 20% gross profit on these sales.
4. At the end of **2016**, Company P still owed $60,000 to Company S for the purchases.
5. Company P also had $30,000 of the intercompany purchases in its **2016** ending inventory.

Worksheet 4-3 contains the **2016** year-end trial balances of Company P and Company S. The elimination entries in journal entry form are as follows:

(CY1)	Eliminate current-year equity income:		
	Subsidiary Income.................................	48,000	
	Investment in Company S...........................		48,000

(continued)

(EL)	Eliminate subsidiary equity against investment in subsidiary account:		
	Common Stock ($10 par)—Company S	80,000	
	Retained Earnings, January 1, 2016—Company S	116,000	
	Investment in Company S.		196,000
(BI)	Eliminate intercompany profit in beginning inventory and reduce current-year cost of goods sold:		
	Retained Earnings, January 1, 2016—Company P	6,400	
	Retained Earnings, January 1, 2016—Company S	1,600	
	Cost of Goods Sold		8,000
(IS)	Eliminate intercompany merchandise sales:		
	Sales	120,000	
	Cost of Goods Sold		120,000
(EI)	Eliminate intercompany profit in ending inventory:		
	Cost of Goods Sold	6,000	
	Inventory, December 31, 2016.		6,000
(IA)	Eliminate intercompany unpaid trade balance at year-end:		
	Accounts Payable	60,000	
	Accounts Receivable		60,000

Entry (BI) adjusts for the intercompany profit contained in the beginning inventory. At the start of 2016, Company P included $40,000 of goods purchased from Company S in its beginning inventory. During 2016, the inventory was debited to Cost of Goods Sold at $40,000. The cost of goods sold must now be reduced to cost by removing the $8,000 intercompany profit. The intercompany profit also was included in last year's income by the subsidiary. That income was closed to Retained Earnings. Thus, the beginning retained earnings of Company S are overstated by $8,000. That $8,000 is divided between the noncontrolling and controlling interests in retained earnings. Subsidiary retained earnings have been 80% eliminated, and only the 20% noncontrolling interest remains. The other 80% of beginning retained earnings is included in Company P's retained earnings through the use of the equity method.

Note that once the controlling share of subsidiary retained earnings is eliminated, there is a transformation of what was **subsidiary** retained earnings into what now is **NCI** in retained earnings. Entries (IS), (EI), and (IA) eliminate the intercompany sales, ending inventory, and trade accounts in the same manner as was done in Worksheet 4-2. After all eliminations and adjustments are made, the consolidated net income of $132,000 is distributed as shown in the income distribution schedules. **The adjustments for intercompany inventory profits are reflected in the *selling company's schedule.***

It might appear that the intercompany goods in the beginning inventory are always assumed to be sold in the current period, since the deferred profit of the previous period is realized during the current period as reflected by the seller's income distribution schedule. That assumption need not be made, however. Even if part of the beginning inventory is unsold at year-end, it still would be a part of the $30,000 ending inventory, on which $6,000 of profit is deferred. Note that the use of the LIFO method for inventories could cause a given period's inventory profit to be deferred indefinitely. Unless otherwise stated, the examples and problems of this text will assume a FIFO flow.

Worksheet 4-3 assumed the intercompany merchandise sales were made by the subsidiary. Procedures would differ as follows if the sales were made by the parent:

1. The beginning inventory profit would be subtracted entirely from the beginning controlling retained earnings since only the parent recorded the profit.
2. The adjustments for the beginning and ending inventory profits would be included in the parent income distribution schedule and not in the subsidiary schedule.

Eliminations for Periodic Inventories

In Worksheets 4-1 through 4-3, the cost of goods sold was included in the trial balances, since both the parent and the subsidiary used a perpetual inventory system. However, in Worksheet 4-4 on pages 232 and 233, a periodic inventory system is used. In this illustration, which is based on the same facts as Worksheet 4-3, the following differences in worksheet procedures result from the use of a periodic inventory system:

Worksheet 4-4: page 232

1. The 2016 beginning inventories of $70,000 and $40,000, rather than the ending inventories, appear as assets in the trial balances. The beginning inventories less the intercompany profit in Company P's beginning inventory are extended to the Consolidated Income Statement column as a debit.

2. The purchases accounts, rather than the cost of goods sold, appear in the trial balances and, after adjustment, are extended to the Consolidated Income Statement column.

3. Entry (BI) credits the January 1 inventory to eliminate the intercompany profit.

4. Entry (IS) credits the purchases account, which is still open under the periodic method, and makes the usual debit to the sales account.

5. The ending inventories of both Company P and Company S are entered in each company's trial balances as both a debit (the ending inventory balance sheet amount) and a credit (the adjustment to the cost of goods sold). These inventories are recorded at the price paid for them, which, for intercompany goods, includes the intercompany sales profit. Entry (EI) removes the $6,000 intercompany profit applicable to the ending inventory. The balance sheet inventory is reduced to $104,000. The $104,000 credit balance is extended to the Consolidated Income Statement column.

The elimination entries in journal entry form are as follows:

(CY1)	Eliminate current-year equity income:		
	Subsidiary Income.	48,000	
	Investment in Company S.		48,000
(EL)	Eliminate subsidiary equity against investment in subsidiary account:		
	Common Stock ($10 par), Company S.	80,000	
	Retained Earnings, January 1, 2016—Company S	116,000	
	Investment in Company S.		196,000
(BI)	Eliminate intercompany profit in beginning inventory and reduce current-year cost of goods sold:		
	Retained Earnings, January 1, 2016—Company P	6,400	
	Retained Earnings, January 1, 2016—Company S	1,600	
	Inventory, January 1, 2016		8,000
(IS)	Eliminate intercompany merchandise sales:		
	Sales	120,000	
	Purchases.		120,000
(EI)	Eliminate intercompany profit in ending inventory:		
	Cost of Goods Sold	6,000	
	Inventory, December 31, 2016.		6,000
(IA)	Eliminate intercompany unpaid trade balance at year-end:		
	Accounts Payable	60,000	
	Accounts Receivable		60,000

Effect of Lower-of-Cost-or-Market Method on Inventory Profit

Intercompany inventory in the hands of the purchaser may have been written down by the purchaser to a market value below its intercompany transfer cost. Assume that, for $50,000, Company S purchased goods that cost its parent company $40,000. Assume further that Company S has all the goods in its ending inventory but has written them down to $42,000, the lower market value at the end of the period. As a result of this markdown, the inventory needs to be reduced by only another $2,000 to reflect its cost to the consolidated company ($40,000). The only remaining issue is how to defer the $2,000 inventory profit in the income distribution schedules. As before, such profit is deferred by entering it as a debit on the intercompany seller's schedule. In the subsequent period, the profit will be realized by the seller.

It may seem strange that the $8,000 of profit written off is realized, in effect, by the seller, since it is not deducted in the seller's distribution schedule. This procedure is proper, however, since the loss recognized by the buyer is offset. Had the inventory been written down to $40,000 or less, there would be no need to defer the offsetting profit in the consolidated worksheet or in the income distribution schedules.

Losses on Intercompany Sales

Assume a parent sells goods to a subsidiary for $5,000 and the goods cost the parent $6,000. If the market value of the goods is $5,000 or less, the loss may be recognized in the consolidated income statement, even if the goods remain in the subsidiary's ending inventory. Such a loss can be recognized under the lower-of-cost-or-market principle that applies to inventory. However, if the intercompany sales price is below market value, the part of the loss that results from the price being below market value cannot be recognized until the subsidiary sells the goods to an outside party. Elimination procedures would be similar, but opposite in direction, to those used for unrealized gains.

REFLECTION

- Merchandise sales between affiliated companies are eliminated; only the purchase and sale to the "outside world" should remain in the statements.

- The profit must be removed from beginning inventory by reducing cost of goods sold and retained earnings.

- The profit must be removed from ending inventory both by reducing inventory and by increasing cost of goods sold. The deduction of inventory from the goods available for sale is too great prior to this adjustment.

- Unpaid intercompany trade payables/receivables resulting from intercompany merchandise sales are eliminated.

3

OBJECTIVE

Defer profits on intercompany sales of long-term assets and realize the profits over the period of use and/or at the time of sale to a firm outside the consolidated group.

INTERCOMPANY PLANT ASSET SALES

Any plant asset may be sold between members of an affiliated group, and such a sale may result in a gain for the seller. The buyer will record the asset at a price that includes the gain, and when the sale involves a depreciable asset, the buyer will base future depreciation charges on the price paid. While these recordings are proper for the companies as separate entities, they must not be reflected in the consolidated statements. Consolidation theory views the sale as an *internal transfer of assets*. There is no basis for recognizing a gain at the time of the internal transfer. A gain on the sale of a nondepreciable asset cannot be reflected in the consolidated statements until the asset is resold to the outside world. However, the recognition of a gain on the sale of a depreciable asset does not have to wait until resale occurs. Instead, the intercompany gain is amortized over the depreciable life of the asset. The buyer's normal intent is to use the asset, not to resell it. Since the asset is overstated by the amount of the intercompany gain, subsequent depreciation is overstated as well. The consolidation process reduces depreciation in future years so that depreciation charges in the consolidated statements reflect the book value of the asset to the consolidated company on the date of the sale. While the gain is deferred in the year of sale, it is realized later through the increased combined net income resulting from the reduction in depreciation expense in subsequent periods. The decrease in depreciation expense for each and every period is equal to the difference between the depreciation based on the intercompany sales price and the depreciation based on the book value of the asset on the sale date.

Intercompany Sale of a Nondepreciable Asset

One member of an affiliated group may sell land to another affiliate and record a gain. For consolidating purposes, there has been no sale; thus, there is no cause to recognize a gain. Since the asset is not depreciable, the entire gain must be deferred until the land is sold to an outside party. This deferment may become permanent if there is no intent to sell at a later date. For example, assume that in 2015, Company S (80% owned) sells land to its parent company, Company P. The sale price is $30,000, and the original cost of the land to Company S was $20,000. Consolidation theory would rule that, until Company P sells the land to an outside party, recognition of the $10,000 profit must be deferred. Elimination (LA) eliminates the intercompany gain in the year of sale.

	Partial Trial Balance		Eliminations & Adjustments	
	Company P	Company S	Dr.	Cr.
Land	30,000			(LA) 10,000
Gain on Sale of Land		(10,000)	(LA) 10,000	

As usual, the selling company's income distribution schedule would reflect the deferment of the gain.

In subsequent years, assuming the land is not sold by Company P, the gain must be removed from the consolidated retained earnings. Since the sale was made by Company S, which is an 80%-owned subsidiary of Company P, the controlling interest must absorb 80% of the deferment, while the noncontrolling interest must absorb 20%. For example, the adjustments in 2016 would be as follows:

	Partial Trial Balance		Eliminations & Adjustments	
	Company P	Company S	Dr.	Cr.
Land	30,000			(LA) 10,000
Retained Earnings, January 1, 2016—Company P	(100,000)*		(LA) 8,000	
Retained Earnings, January 1, 2016—Company S		(20,000)*	(LA) 2,000	

*Arbitrary balance.

Now, assume Company P sells the land in 2017 to an outside party for $45,000, recording a gain of $15,000. When this sale occurs, the $10,000 intercompany gain also is realized. The following elimination would remove the previously unrealized gain from the consolidated retained earnings and would add it to the gain already recorded by Company P. The retained earnings adjustment is allocated 80% to the controlling interest and 20% to the noncontrolling interest, since the original sale was made by the subsidiary.

	Partial Trial Balance		Eliminations & Adjustments	
	Company P	Company S	Dr.	Cr.
Gain on Sale of Land	(15,000)			**(LA) 10,000**
Retained Earnings, January 1, 2017—Company P	(120,000)*		**(LA) 8,000**	
Retained Earnings, January 1, 2017—Company S		(17,000)*	**(LA) 2,000**	

*Arbitrary balance.

The income distribution schedule would add the $10,000 gain to the 2017 internally generated net income of Company S. At this point, it should be clear that the gain on the intercompany sale was deferred, not eliminated. The original gain of $10,000 eventually is credited to the subsidiary. Thus, the gain does affect the noncontrolling share of consolidated net income at a future date. Any sale of a nondepreciable asset should be viewed as an agreement between the controlling and noncontrolling interests regarding the future distribution of consolidated net income.

When a parent sells a nondepreciable asset to a subsidiary, the worksheet procedures are the same, except for these areas:

1. The deferment of the gain in the year of the intercompany sale and the recognition of the gain in the year of the sale of the asset to an outside party flow through only the parent company income distribution schedule.
2. In the years subsequent to the intercompany sale through the year the land is sold to an external company, the related adjustment is made exclusively through the controlling retained earnings.

Intercompany Sale of a Depreciable Asset

Turning to the case where a depreciable plant asset is sold between affiliates, the following example illustrates the worksheet procedures necessary for the **deferment of a gain on the sale *over the asset's useful life.*** Assume that the parent, Company P, sells a machine to a subsidiary, Company S, for $30,000 on January 1, 2015. Originally, the machine cost $32,000. Accumulated depreciation as of January 1, 2015, is $12,000. Therefore, the book value of the machine is $20,000, and the reported gain on the sale is $10,000. Further assume that Company S (*the buyer*) believes the asset has a 5-year remaining life; thus, it records straight-line depreciation of $6,000 ($30,000 cost ÷ 5 years) annually.

The eliminations defer the gain over the 5-year life of the asset by reducing annual depreciation charges. For consolidated reporting purposes, depreciation is based on the asset's $20,000 book value to the consolidated company. Worksheet 4-5 on pages 234 and 235, is based on the following additional facts:

Worksheet 4-5: page 234

1. Company P owns an 80% investment in Company S. The amount paid for the investment was equal to the book value of Company S's underlying equity. The simple equity method is used by Company P to record its investment.
2. There were no beginning or ending inventories, and the companies had the following separate income statements for 2015:

	Company P	Company S
Sales	$ 200,000	$100,000
Cost of goods sold	(150,000)	(59,000)
Gross profit	$ 50,000	$ 41,000
Depreciation expense	(30,000)	(16,000)
Gain on sale of machine	10,000	
Subsidiary income (80%)	20,000	
Net income	$ 50,000	$ 25,000

The elimination entries in journal entry form are:

(CY1)   Eliminate current-year equity income:
        Subsidiary Income.   20,000
           Investment in Company S.   20,000

(EL)   Eliminate subsidiary equity against investment in
        subsidiary account:
        Common Stock ($10 par)—Company S   40,000
        Retained Earnings, January 1, 2015—Company S   60,000
           Investment in Company S.   100,000

(F1)   Eliminate intercompany gain on machine sale and reduce
        machine to cost:
        Gain on Sale of Machinery   10,000
           Machinery   10,000

(F2)   Reduce machinery depreciation to amount based on book value:
        Accumulated Depreciation—Machinery.   2,000
           Depreciation Expense   2,000

Entry (F1) eliminates the $10,000 intercompany gain and restates the asset at its book value of $20,000 on the date of the intercompany sale.

Entry (F2) reduces the depreciation expense for the year by the difference between depreciation based on:

1. The book value [($32,000 − $12,000 = $20,000 depreciable base) ÷ 5 years = $4,000] and
2. The intercompany sales price ($30,000 depreciable base ÷ 5 years = $6,000).

The allocation of consolidated net income of $47,000 is shown in the income distribution schedules. Note that Company S (the buyer in this example) must absorb depreciation based on the agreed-upon sales price, and it is the controlling interest that realizes the benefit of the reduced depreciation as the asset is used. Also, note that the realizable profit for Company P (the seller) in any year is the depreciation absorbed by the buyer minus the depreciation for consolidated purposes ($6,000 − $4,000). If the sale had been made by Company S, the profit deferment and recognition entries would flow through the Company S income distribution schedule.

Worksheets for periods subsequent to the sale of the machine must correct the current-year nominal accounts and remove the unrealized profit in the beginning consolidated retained earnings. Worksheet 4-6 on pages 236 and 237, portrays a consolidated worksheet for 2016, based on the following separate income statements of Company P and Company S:

Worksheet 4-6: page 236

	Company P	Company S
Sales	$ 250,000	$120,000
Cost of goods sold.	(180,000)	(80,000)
Gross profit	$ 70,000	$ 40,000
Depreciation expense	(20,000)	(16,000)
Subsidiary income (80%)	19,200	
Net income	$ 69,200	$ 24,000

The elimination entries in journal entry form are as follows:

(CY1)   Eliminate current-year equity income:
        Subsidiary Income.   19,200
           Investment in Company S.   19,200

(EL)   Eliminate subsidiary equity against investment in
        subsidiary account:
        Common Stock ($10 par)—Company S   40,000
        Retained Earnings, January 1, 2016—Company S   80,000
           Investment in Company S.   120,000

(continued)

(F1)   Eliminate remaining intercompany gain on machine sale, reduce machine to cost, and adjust accumulated depreciation as of January 1, 2016:

Retained Earnings, January 1, 2016—Company P	8,000	
Accumulated Depreciation—Machinery.	2,000	
Machinery		10,000

(F2)   Reduce current-year machinery depreciation to amount based on book value:

Accumulated Depreciation—Machinery.	2,000	
Depreciation Expense		2,000

Entry (F1) in this worksheet corrects the asset's net book value, accumulated depreciation, and retained earnings as of the beginning of the year. Since the sale was by the parent, only the controlling interest in beginning retained earnings is adjusted. Had the sale been by the subsidiary, the adjustment would have been split 20%/80% to the noncontrolling and controlling interests, respectively, in beginning retained earnings.

Entry (F2) corrects the depreciation expense, and the accumulated depreciation accounts for the current year. The resulting consolidated net income of $76,000 is distributed as shown in the income distribution schedules that follow Worksheet 4-6. During each year, Company S must absorb the larger depreciation expense that resulted from its purchase of the asset. Company P has the right to realize $2,000 more of the original deferred profit.

It may occur that an asset purchased from an affiliate is sold before it is fully depreciated. To illustrate this possibility, assume that Company S of the previous example sells the asset to a third party for $14,000 at the end of the second year. Since Company S's asset cost is $30,000, with $12,000 of accumulated depreciation, the loss recorded by Company S is $4,000 ($14,000 − $18,000 net book value). However, on a consolidated basis, the $4,000 loss becomes a $2,000 gain, determined as follows:

	On Books of Company S		For Consolidated Entity	
Selling price of machine sold by Company S		$14,000		$14,000
Less book value at end of second year following sale to Company S:				
Cost of machine	$ 30,000		$20,000*	
Accumulated depreciation	(12,000)	18,000	(8,000)	12,000
Gain (loss)		$ (4,000)		$ 2,000

*($32,000 − $12,000) = the net book value on January 1, 2015, the date of intercompany sale.

Worksheet 4-7: page 238

Worksheet 4-7 on pages 238 and 239, is a revision of the previous worksheet so that Company S's subsequent sale of the depreciable asset at the end of the second year is included. The elimination entries in journal entry form are as follows:

(CY1)   Eliminate current-year equity income:

Subsidiary Income.	16,000	
Investment in Company S.		16,000

(EL)   Eliminate subsidiary equity against investment in subsidiary account:

Common Stock ($10 par)—Company S	40,000	
Retained Earnings, January 1, 2016—Company S	80,000	
Investment in Company S.		120,000

(F3)   Eliminate remaining machinery gain on January 1, 2016,
       and adjust recorded loss on sale to reflect book value at
       the time of sale:

Retained Earnings, January 1, 2016—Company P	8,000	
Depreciation Expense		2,000
Loss on Sale of Machine (as recorded by Company S)		4,000
Gain on Sale of Machine (on consolidated basis)		2,000

Entry (F3) removes the $8,000 remaining intercompany profit ($10,000 original gain − $2,000 realized in 2015) on the asset sale from controlling retained earnings, adjusts current depreciation by $2,000, and converts the $4,000 loss on the sale recorded by the subsidiary into a $2,000 gain on the consolidated statements.

However, a loss on an intercompany sale of plant assets does not have to be deferred if the loss could have been recorded in the absence of a sale. Where there has been an impairment in the value of a fixed asset, it may be written down to a lower market value. Where, however, the asset is sold to an affiliated company at a price below fair market value, the loss is to be deferred in the same manner as an intercompany gain. The loss would be deferred over the depreciation life of the asset. If the asset were sold to a nonaffiliated company, the remaining deferred loss would be recognized at the time of the sale.

INTERCOMPANY DEBT

Typically, a parent company is larger than any one of its subsidiaries and can secure funds under more favorable terms. Because of this, a parent company often will advance cash to a subsidiary. The parent may accept a note from the subsidiary as security for the loan, or the parent may discount a note that the subsidiary received from a customer. In most cases, the parent will charge a competitive interest rate for the funds advanced to the subsidiary.

In the examples that follow, the more common situation in which the parent is the lender is assumed. If the subsidiary were the lender, the theory and practice would be identical, with the only differences being the books on which the applicable accounts appear and the procedure for the distribution of combined net income.

Assume that on July 1, 2015, an 80%-owned subsidiary, Company S, borrows $10,000 from its parent, Company P, signing a 1-year, 8% note, with interest payable on the due date. This intercompany loan will cause the following accounts and their balances to appear on the December 31, 2015, trial balances of the separate affiliated companies:

4

OBJECTIVE

Eliminate intercompany
loans and notes.

Parent Company P		Subsidiary Company S	
Notes Receivable.	10,000	Notes Payable	(10,000)
Interest Income.	(400)	Interest Expense.	400
Interest Receivable.	400	Interest Payable	(400)

While this information is required on the books of the separate companies, it should not appear on the consolidated statements. The procedures needed to eliminate this intercompany note and its related interest amounts are demonstrated in Worksheet 4-8, pages 240 and 241. The elimination entries in journal entry form are as follows:

Worksheet 4-8: page 240

(CY1)   Eliminate current-year equity income:

Subsidiary Income.	8,000	
Investment in Company S.		8,000

(EL)   Eliminate subsidiary equity against investment in
       subsidiary account:

Common Stock ($10 par)—Company S	40,000	
Retained Earnings, January 1, 2015—Company S	80,000	
Investment in Company S.		120,000

(LN1)	Eliminate intercompany note and accrued interest:		
	Note Payable to Company P	10,000	
	Accrued Interest Payable	400	
	Note Receivable from Company S		10,000
	Accrued Interest Receivable		400
(LN2)	Eliminate intercompany interest income and expense:		
	Interest Income	400	
	Interest Expense		400

Entry (LN1) eliminates the intercompany receivable and payable for the note and the accrued interest on the note. Entry (LN2) eliminates the intercompany interest income and expense amounts. In this worksheet, it is assumed that the intercompany note is the only note recorded. However, sometimes an intercompany note and its related interest expense, revenue, and accruals are commingled with notes to outside parties. Before the trial balances are entered on the worksheet and before consolidation is attempted, intercompany interest expense and revenue must be accrued properly on the books of the parent and subsidiary.

There might be a temptation to increase the noncontrolling share of consolidated net income by $400 as a result of eliminating the interest expense on the intercompany note, but it is not correct to do so. Even though the interest does not appear on the consolidated income statement, it is a legitimate expense for Company S as a separate entity and a legitimate revenue for Company P as a separate entity. In essence, Company S has agreed to transfer $400 to Company P for interest during 2015, and the NCI must respect this agreement when calculating its share of consolidated net income. Thus, the basis for calculating the noncontrolling share is the net income of Company S as a separate entity. The NCI receives 20% of this $10,000 net income, which is net of the $400 of intercompany interest expense.

A parent receiving a note from a subsidiary subsequently may discount the note at a nonaffiliated financial institution in order to receive immediate cash. This results in a note receivable discounted being recorded by the parent. From a consolidated viewpoint, there is a note payable to outside parties. Consolidation procedures should eliminate the internal note receivable against the note receivable discounted. This elimination will result in the note, now payable to an outside party, being extended to the consolidated balance sheet. Intercompany interest accrued prior to the discounting is eliminated. Interest paid by the subsidiary subsequent to the discounting is paid to the outside party and is not eliminated. The net interest expense or revenue on the discounting of the note is a transaction between the parent and the outside party and, thus, is not eliminated. When consolidated statements are prepared, however, it is desirable to net the interest expense on the note recorded by the maker subsequent to the discounting of the note against the net interest expense or revenue on the discounting transaction.

REFLECTION

- Intercompany debt balances, including accrued interest receivable/payable, are eliminated.

- Intercompany interest expense/revenue is also eliminated. These amounts are equal; thus, there is no effect on consolidated net income.

5

O B J E C T I V E

Discuss the complications intercompany profits create for the use of the sophisticated equity method.

SOPHISTICATED EQUITY METHOD: INTERCOMPANY TRANSACTIONS

Chapter 3 demonstrated the use of the sophisticated equity method for the parent's recording of its investment in a subsidiary. Recall that one major difference between the simple and sophisticated equity methods was that the latter records subsidiary income net of amortizations of excess. In contrast, the simple equity method ignores amortizations and records as income for the parent the subsidiary reported income multiplied by the parent's percentage of ownership. Some companies using the sophisticated equity method will proceed to the next level of complexity. Instead of adjusting for their share of the income reported by the subsidiary (as under the simple equity method), they will adjust for their share of subsidiary income after it is adjusted for intercompany profits. This means that, before the parent can make an equity adjustment for income of the subsidiary, it must prepare an income distribution schedule for the subsidiary company. **The adjusted net income derived in the income distribution schedule will become the income to which the parent ownership percentage is applied to arrive at equity income.**

The added complexity of the sophisticated equity method is unwarranted when statements are to be consolidated, since the subsidiary income and the investment in subsidiary accounts are eliminated entirely. However, this procedure must be used in the rare case when a subsidiary is not to be consolidated or when parent-only statements are to be prepared as a supplement to the consolidated statements.

Unrealized Profits of the Current Period

The case of intercompany profits generated only during the current period will be considered first. Although the same procedure applies to all types of subsidiary-generated unrealized intercompany profits and losses of the current period, the impact of the sophisticated equity method will be demonstrated assuming only the existence of inventory profits.

The following example is based on the information presented in Worksheet 4-2, but this time the parent is using the sophisticated equity method. Because of this fact, the parent has to prepare a subsidiary income distribution schedule before it can record its share of subsidiary income. This schedule is shown below. Note that, instead of recording **on its books** a subsidiary income of $60,000, the parent would have recorded $53,600.

Equity Income: Subsidiary Company S

Unrealized profit in ending inventory	$8,000	Internally generated net income	$ 75,000
		Adjusted income	$ 67,000
		Controlling share	× 80%
		Controlling interest	**$ 53,600***

*This is the same amount that is shown in the parent's income distribution schedule for Worksheet 4-2.

The only elimination procedure in this example that differs from Worksheet 4-2 is entry (CY1), which eliminates the entry made by the parent to record its share of the subsidiary current-period income. There is no impact on the other worksheet procedures, and the balance of Worksheet 4-2 would be unchanged. A portion of the revised worksheet is shown on page 222.

Unrealized Profits of Current and Prior Periods

The effect of the sophisticated equity method when there are intercompany profits from current and prior periods is demonstrated in the following example, which is based on the information given in Worksheet 4-3. The subsidiary income reported by the parent in 2016 under the sophisticated equity method is calculated as follows:

Equity Income: Parent Company P

Unrealized profit in ending inventory	$6,000	Internally generated net income	$ 60,000
		Realized profit in beginning inventory.	8,000
		Adjusted income	$ 62,000
		Controlling share	× 80%
		Controlling interest	**$ 49,600**

The elimination procedures illustrated in the following partial worksheets are applicable to all types of subsidiary-generated intercompany profits and losses of prior and current periods. The differences in the parent's trial balance are explained in the notes that follow the partial worksheet on page 223.

Company P and Subsidiary Company S
Partial Worksheet
For Year Ended December 31, **2015**

(Credit balance amounts are in parentheses.)		Partial Trial Balance		Eliminations & Adjustments			
		Company P	Company S	Dr.		Cr.	
Accounts Receivable		110,000	150,000			(IA)	25,000
Inventory, December 31, 2015		70,000	40,000			(EI)	8,000
Investment in Company S	(b)	**189,600**				**(CY1)**	**53,600**
						(EL)	136,000
Other Assets		314,000	155,000				
Accounts Payable		(80,000)	(100,000)	(IA)	25,000		
Common Stock ($10 par)—Company P		(200,000)					
Retained Earnings, January 1, 2015—Company P		(250,000)					
Common Stock ($10 par)—Company S			(100,000)	(EL)	80,000		
Retained Earnings, January 1, 2015—Company S			(70,000)	(EL)	56,000		
Sales		(700,000)	(500,000)	(IS)	100,000		
Cost of Goods Sold		510,000	350,000	(EI)	8,000	(IS)	100,000
Expenses		90,000	75,000				
Subsidiary Income	(a)	**(53,600)**		**(CY1)**	**53,600**		
		0	0		322.600		322.600

Notes to Trial Balance:

(a) See the previously prepared income distribution schedule.
(b) $136,000 beginning-of-year balance + $53,600 sophisticated equity method income.

Eliminations and Adjustments:

(CY1) Eliminate the entry recording the parent's share (80%) of the subsidiary net income under the sophisticated equity method.
(EL, IS, EI, and IA) Same as Worksheet 4-2.

Company P and Subsidiary Company S
Partial Worksheet
For Year Ended December 31, **2016**

(Credit balance amounts are in parentheses.)		Partial Trial Balance		Eliminations & Adjustments			
		Company P	Company S	Dr.		Cr.	
Accounts Receivable		160,000	170,000			(IA)	60,000
Inventory, December 31, 2016		60,000	50,000			(EI)	6,000
Investment in Company S	(c) 239,200					(CY1)	49,600
						(EL)	189,600
Other Assets		354,000	165,000				
Accounts Payable		(90,000)	(80,000)	(IA)	60,000		
Common Stock ($10 par)—Company P		(200,000)					
Retained Earnings, January 1, 2016—Company P	(b) (403,600)						
Common Stock ($10 par)—Company S			(100,000)	**(EL)**	**80,000**		
Retained Earnings, January 1, 2016—Company S			(145,000)	**(Adj)**	**8,000**		
				(EL)	**109,600**		
Sales		(800,000)	(600,000)	(IS)	120,000		
Cost of Goods Sold		610,000	440,000	(EI)	6,000	**(Adj)**	**8,000**
						(IS)	120,000
Expenses		120,000	100,000				
Subsidiary Income	(a) **(49,600)**			**(CY1)**	**49,600**		
		0	0		433,200		433,200

Notes to Trial Balance:

(a) See the previously prepared income distribution schedule.
(b) $410,000 simple equity balance − (80% × $8,000 subsidiary beginning inventory profit).
(c) $136,000 original balance + $53,600 sophisticated equity method income for 2015 + $49,600 sophisticated equity method income for 2016.

Eliminations and Adjustments:

(Adj) Eliminate the $8,000 beginning inventory profit from the cost of goods sold and the subsidiary beginning retained earnings accounts. This entry replaces entry (BI) of Worksheet 4-3.
(CY1) Eliminate the entry recording the parent's share (80%) of the subsidiary net income under the sophisticated equity method.
(EL) Eliminate 80% of the subsidiary equity balances against the investment account. The elimination of retained earnings is 80% of the adjusted balance of $137,000 ($145,000 − $8,000).

(IS, EI, and IA) Same as Worksheet 4-3.

When the sophisticated equity method is used, the worksheet elimination of the parent's investment account against the stockholders' equity of the subsidiary is more complicated because there is an inconsistency between the parent's accounts and those of the subsidiary. In the 2016 partial worksheet illustrated, the parent's investment and retained earnings accounts do not reflect the $8,000 beginning inventory profit recorded by the subsidiary. The intercompany profit was removed in the prior period before the parent's share of the subsidiary's net income was recorded. The subsidiary's trial balance does include the $8,000 beginning inventory profit in the January 1 retained earnings balance, and the parent's beginning inventory, now in the cost of goods sold, does include the profit. The inconsistency is removed on the worksheet by making an adjustment, coded "Adj," that removes the intercompany profit from the subsidiary's beginning retained earnings and the parent's beginning inventory. This entry replaces entry (BI) in Worksheet 4-3.

Entry (CY1) of the partial worksheet removes the subsidiary income as recorded by the parent. Entry (EL) reflects the adjustment of the subsidiary's retained earnings. The remaining entries and worksheet procedures are identical to those in Worksheet 4-3.

R E F L E C T I O N

- When used properly, the sophisticated equity method should record annual subsidiary income net of all intercompany profits.

- The parent's beginning retained earnings will not include prior periods' intercompany profits, but the subsidiary's beginning retained earnings does when the subsidiary is the seller. The subsidiary's beginning retained earnings must be adjusted for these profits prior to its elimination.

6
OBJECTIVE

Apply intercompany profit eliminations on a vertical worksheet.

Worksheet 4-9: page 242

APPENDIX: INTERCOMPANY PROFIT ELIMINATIONS ON THE VERTICAL WORKSHEET

In keeping with the overall worksheet format approach of this text, all previous examples in this chapter have been presented using the horizontal worksheet style. Worksheet 4-9, page 242 and 243, provides the reader an opportunity to study the vertical worksheet when intercompany merchandise and plant asset transactions are involved. This worksheet is based on the following facts:

1. Company P acquired an 80% interest in Company S on January 1, 2015. At that time, the following determination and distribution of excess schedule was prepared:

Determination and Distribution of Excess Schedule

	Company Implied Fair Value	Parent Price (80%)	NCI Value (20%)
Fair value of subsidiary	$625,000	$500,000	$125,000
Less book value interest acquired:			
Common stock ($5 par)	$200,000		
Retained Earnings	350,000		
Total equity.	$550,000	$550,000	$550,000
Interest acquired		80%	20%
Book value.		$440,000	$110,000
Excess of fair value over book value	**$ 75,000**	$ 60,000	$ 15,000

Adjustment of identifiable accounts:

	Adjustment	Worksheet Key
Goodwill	$ 75,000	debit D1

2. Company P accounts for the investment under the simple equity method.

3. Company S sells merchandise to Company P to yield a gross profit of 20%. Sales totaled $150,000 during 2016. There were $40,000 of such goods in Company P's beginning inventory and $50,000 of such goods in Company P's ending inventory. As of December 31, 2016, Company P had not paid the $20,000 owed for the purchases.

4. On July 1, 2015, Company P sold a new machine that cost $20,000 to Company S for $25,000. At that time, both companies believed that the machine had a 5-year remaining life; both companies use straight-line depreciation.

5. Company S declared and paid $20,000 in dividends during 2016.

Notice that the eliminations in Worksheet 4-9 are identical to those required for the horizontal format. Also, when working with the vertical format, keep in mind the cautions that are stated in Chapter 3: (a) the nominal accounts are presented above the balance sheet accounts, and (b) the eliminations are made only to the beginning retained earnings accounts. The carry-down procedures for the vertical worksheet are the same as those presented in Chapter 3.

REFLECTION

- On a vertical worksheet, the eliminating and adjusting entries are the same as those on a trial balance worksheet.

Worksheet 4-1

Intercompany Sales; No Intercompany Goods in Inventories
Company P and Subsidiary Company S
Worksheet for Consolidated Financial Statements
For Year Ended December 31, **2015**

	(Credit balance amounts are in parentheses.)	Trial Balance	
		Company P	Company S
1	**Accounts Receivable**	110,000	150,000
2	Inventory, December 31, 2015	70,000	40,000
3	Investment in Company S	196,000	
4			
5	Other Assets	314,000	155,000
6	**Accounts Payable**	(80,000)	(100,000)
7	Common Stock ($10 par)—Company P	(200,000)	
8	Retained Earnings, January 1, 2015—Company P	(250,000)	
9	Common Stock ($10 par)—Company S		(100,000)
10	Retained Earnings, January 1, 2015—Company S		(70,000)
11	**Sales**	(700,000)	(500,000)
12	**Cost of Goods Sold**	510,000	350,000
13	Expenses	90,000	75,000
14	Subsidiary Income	(60,000)	
15		0	0
16	Consolidated Net Income		
17	To NCI (see distribution schedule)		
18	Balance to Controlling Interest (see distribution schedule)		
19	Total NCI		
20	Retained Earnings, Controlling Interest, December 31, 2015		
21			

Eliminations and Adjustments:

(CY1)   Eliminate the entry recording the parent's share of subsidiary net income.

(EL)   Eliminate against the investment in Company S account the pro rata portion of the subsidiary equity balances (80%) owned by the parent. To simplify the elimination, there is no discrepancy between the cost and book values of the investment in this example. Also, note that the worksheet process is expedited by always eliminating the intercompany investment first.

(IS)   Eliminate $100,000 intercompany sales to avoid double counting. Now only Company S's original purchase from third parties and Company P's final sale to third parties remain in the consolidated income statement.

(IA)   Eliminate the $25,000 intercompany trade balances resulting from the intercompany sale.

Worksheet 4-1 (see page 207)

| Eliminations & Adjustments | | Consolidated Income Statement | NCI | Controlling Retained Earnings | Consolidated Balance Sheet | |
Dr.	Cr.					
	(IA) 25,000				235,000	1
					110,000	2
	(CY1) 60,000					3
	(EL) 136,000					4
					469,000	5
(IA) 25,000					(155,000)	6
					(200,000)	7
				(250,000)		8
(EL) 80,000			(20,000)			9
(EL) 56,000			(14,000)			10
(IS) 100,000		(1,100,000)				11
	(IS) 100,000	760,000				12
		165,000				13
(CY1) 60,000						14
321,000	321,000					15
		(175,000)				16
		15,000	(15,000)			17
		160,000		(160,000)		18
			(49,000)		(49,000)	19
				(410,000)	(410,000)	20
					0	21

Subsidiary Company S Income Distribution

Internally generated net income	$ 75,000
Adjusted income	$ 75,000
NCI share	× 20%
NCI	$ 15,000

Parent Company P Income Distribution

Internally generated net income	$100,000
80% × Company S adjusted income of $75,000. . . .	60,000
Controlling interest	$160,000

Worksheet 4-2

Intercompany Goods in Ending Inventory
Company P and Subsidiary Company S
Worksheet for Consolidated Financial Statements
For Year Ended December 31, **2015**

	(Credit balance amounts are in parentheses.)	Trial Balance	
		Company P	Company S
1	Accounts Receivable	110,000	150,000
2	**Inventory, December 31, 2015**	**70,000**	**40,000**
3	Investment in Company S	196,000	
4			
5	Other Assets	314,000	155,000
6	Accounts Payable	(80,000)	(100,000)
7	Common Stock ($10 par)—Company P	(200,000)	
8	Retained Earnings, January 1, 2015—Company P	(250,000)	
9	Common Stock ($10 par)—Company S		(100,000)
10	Retained Earnings, January 1, 2015—Company S		(70,000)
11	Sales	(700,000)	(500,000)
12	**Cost of Goods Sold**	**510,000**	**350,000**
13	Expenses	90,000	75,000
14	Subsidiary Income	(60,000)	
15		0	0
16	Consolidated Net Income		
17	To NCI (see distribution schedule)		
18	Balance to Controlling Interest (see distribution schedule)		
19	Total NCI		
20	Retained Earnings, Controlling Interest, December 31, 2015		
21			

Eliminations and Adjustments:

(CY1) Eliminate the entry recording the parent's share of subsidiary net income.
(EL)   Eliminate 80% of the subsidiary equity balances against the investment in Company S account. There is no excess of cost or
       book value in this example.
(IS)   Eliminate the intercompany sale of $100,000.
(EI)   Eliminate intercompany profit in ending inventory, 20% × $40,000.
(IA)   Eliminate the intercompany trade balances.

Worksheet 4-2 (see page 210)

Eliminations & Adjustments				Consolidated Income Statement	NCI	Controlling Retained Earnings	Consolidated Balance Sheet	
Dr.		Cr.						
		(IA)	25,000				235,000	1
		(EI)	**8,000**				102,000	2
		(CY1)	60,000					3
		(EL)	136,000					4
							469,000	5
(IA)	25,000						(155,000)	6
							(200,000)	7
						(250,000)		8
(EL)	80,000				(20,000)			9
(EL)	56,000				(14,000)			10
(IS)	100,000			(1,100,000)				11
(EI)	**8,000**	(IS)	100,000	768,000				12
				165,000				13
(CY1)	60,000							14
	329,000		329,000					15
				(167,000)				16
				13,400	(13,400)			17
				153,600		(153,600)		18
					(47,400)		(47,400)	19
						(403,600)	(403,600)	20
							0	21

Subsidiary Company S Income Distribution

Unrealized profit in ending inventory . . . . **(EI)** **$8,000**	Internally generated net income	$ 75,000
	Adjusted income	$ 67,000
	NCI share	× 20%
	NCI	$ 13,400

Parent Company P Income Distribution

Internally generated net income	$ 100,000
80% × Company S adjusted income of $67,000.	53,600
Controlling interest	$ 153,600

Worksheet 4-3

Intercompany Goods in Beginning and Ending Inventories
Company P and Subsidiary Company S
Worksheet for Consolidated Financial Statements
For Year Ended December 31, **2016**

	(Credit balance amounts are in parentheses.)	Trial Balance	
		Company P	Company S
1	Accounts Receivable	160,000	170,000
2	**Inventory, December 31, 2016**	**60,000**	**50,000**
3	Investment in Company S	244,000	
4			
5	Other Assets	354,000	165,000
6	Accounts Payable	(90,000)	(80,000)
7	Common Stock ($10 par)—Company P	(200,000)	
8	**Retained Earnings, January 1, 2016—Company P**	**(410,000)**	
9	Common Stock ($10 par)—Company S		(100,000)
10	**Retained Earnings, January 1, 2016—Company S**		**(145,000)**
11			
12	Sales	(800,000)	(600,000)
13	**Cost of Goods Sold**	**610,000**	**440,000**
14			
15	Expenses	120,000	100,000
16	Subsidiary Income	(48,000)	
17		0	0
18	Consolidated Net Income		
19	To NCI (see distribution schedule)		
20	Balance to Controlling Interest (see distribution schedule)		
21	Total NCI		
22	Retained Earnings, Controlling Interest, December 31, 2016		
23			

Eliminations and Adjustments:

(CY1)   Eliminate the entry recording the parent's share of subsidiary net income.
(EL)   Eliminate 80% of the subsidiary equity balances against the investment in Company S account. There is no excess of cost or book value in this example.
(BI)   Eliminate the intercompany profit of $8,000 (20% × $40,000) in the beginning inventory by reducing both the cost of goods sold and the beginning retained earnings accounts. 20% of the decrease in retained earnings is shared by the noncontrolling interest, since, in this case, the *selling company was the subsidiary*. If the parent had been the seller, only the controlling interest in retained earnings would be decreased. It should be noted that the $8,000 profit is shifted from 2015 to 2016, since, as a result of the entry, the 2016 consolidated cost of goods sold balance is reduced by $8,000. This procedure emphasizes the concept that intercompany inventory profit is not eliminated but only deferred until inventory is sold to an outsider.
(IS)   Eliminate $120,000 intercompany sales to avoid double counting.
(EI)   Eliminate the intercompany profit of $6,000 (20% × $30,000) recorded by Company S for the intercompany goods contained in Company P's ending inventory, and increase the cost of goods sold balance by this same amount.
(IA)   Eliminate the intercompany trade balances.

Worksheet 4-3 (see page 211)

Eliminations & Adjustments				Consolidated Income Statement	NCI	Controlling Retained Earnings	Consolidated Balance Sheet	
Dr.		Cr.						
		(IA)	60,000				270,000	1
		(EI)	**6,000**				104,000	2
		(CY1)	48,000					3
		(EL)	196,000					4
							519,000	5
(IA)	60,000						(110,000)	6
							(200,000)	7
(BI)	**6,400**					(403,600)		8
(EL)	80,000				(20,000)			9
(EL)	116,000							10
(BI)	**1,600**				(27,400)			11
(IS)	120,000			(1,280,000)				12
(EI)	**6,000**	**(BI)**	**8,000**					13
		(IS)	120,000	928,000				14
				220,000				15
(CY1)	48,000							16
	438,000		438,000					17
				(132,000)				18
				12,400	(12,400)			19
				119,600		(119,600)		20
					(59,800)		(59,800)	21
						(523,200)	(523,200)	22
							0	23

Subsidiary Company S Income Distribution

Unrealized profit in ending inventory, 20% × $30,000 .... **(EI)** **$6,000**	Internally generated net income	$ 60,000
	Realized profit in beginning inventory, 20% × $40,000 .... **(BI)**	**8,000**
	Adjusted income	$ 62,000
	NCI share	× 20%
	NCI	$ 12,400

Parent Company P Income Distribution

	Internally generated net income	$ 70,000
	80% × Company S adjusted income of $62,000......	49,600
	Controlling interest	$119,600

Worksheet 4-4

Intercompany Goods in Beginning and Ending Inventories; Periodic Inventory
Company P and Subsidiary Company S
Worksheet for Consolidated Financial Statements
For Year Ended December 31, **2016**

	(Credit balance amounts are in parentheses.)	Trial Balance	
		Company P	Company S
1	Accounts Receivable	160,000	170,000
2	**Inventory, January 1, 2016**	**70,000**	**40,000**
3	Investment in Company S	244,000	
4			
5	Other Assets	354,000	165,000
6	Accounts Payable	(90,000)	(80,000)
7	Common Stock ($10 par)—Company P	(200,000)	
8	**Retained Earnings, January 1, 2016—Company P**	**(410,000)**	
9	Common Stock ($10 par)—Company S		(100,000)
10	**Retained Earnings, January 1, 2016—Company S**		**(145,000)**
11			
12	Sales	(800,000)	(600,000)
13	**Purchases**	**600,000**	**450,000**
14	**Inventory, December 31, 2016**	**60,000**	**50,000**
15	**Cost of Goods Sold**	**(60,000)**	**(50,000)**
16	Expenses	120,000	100,000
17	Subsidiary Income	(48,000)	
18		0	0
19	Consolidated Net Income		
20	To NCI (see distribution schedule)		
21	Balance to Controlling Interest (see distribution schedule)		
22	Total NCI		
23	Retained Earnings, Controlling Interest, December 31, 2016		
24			

Eliminations and Adjustments:

(CY1) Eliminate the entry recording the parent's share of subsidiary net income.
(EL) Eliminate 80% of the subsidiary equity balances against the investment in Company S account. There is no excess of cost or book value in this example.
(BI) Eliminate the intercompany profit of $8,000 (20% × $40,000) in the beginning inventory by reducing both the cost of goods sold and the beginning retained earnings accounts. 20% of the decrease in retained earnings is shared by the noncontrolling interest, since, in this case, the *selling company was the subsidiary*. If the parent had been the seller, only the controlling interest in retained earnings would be decreased. It should be noted that the $8,000 profit is shifted from 2015 to 2016, since, as a result of the entry, the 2016 consolidated cost of goods sold balance is reduced by $8,000. This procedure emphasizes the concept that intercompany inventory profit is not eliminated but only deferred until inventory is sold to an outsider.
(IS) Eliminate $120,000 intercompany sales to avoid double counting.
(EI) Enter the combined ending inventories of Company P and Company S, $60,000 and $50,000, respectively, less the intercompany profit of $6,000 (20% × $30,000) recorded by Company S for the intercompany goods contained in Company P's ending inventory.
(IA) Eliminate the intercompany trade balances.

Worksheet 4-4 (see page 213)

Eliminations & Adjustments				Consolidated Income Statement	NCI	Controlling Retained Earnings	Consolidated Balance Sheet	
Dr.		Cr.						
		(IA)	60,000				270,000	1
		(BI)	**8,000**	102,000				2
		(CY1)	48,000					3
		(EL)	196,000					4
							519,000	5
(IA)	60,000						(110,000)	6
							(200,000)	7
(BI)	**6,400**					(403,600)		8
(EL)	80,000				(20,000)			9
(EL)	116,000							10
(BI)	**1,600**				(27,400)			11
(IS)	**120,000**			(1,280,000)				12
		(IS)	120,000	930,000				13
		(EI)	6,000				104,000	14
(EI)	6,000			(104,000)				15
				220,000				16
(CY1)	48,000							17
	438,000		438,000					18
				(132,000)				19
				12,400	(12,400)			20
				119,600		(119,600)		21
					(59,800)		(59,800)	22
						(523,200)	(523,200)	23
							0	24

Subsidiary Company S Income Distribution

	Internally generated net income	$ 60,000
Unrealized profit in ending inventory, 20% × $30,000 . . . .**(EI)** **$6,000**	**Realized profit in beginning inventory, 20% × $40,000** . . . . **(BI)**	**8,000**
	Adjusted income	$ 62,000
	NCI share	× 20%
	NCI	$ 12,400

Parent Company P Income Distribution

	Internally generated net income	$ 70,000
	80% × Company S adjusted income of $62,000	49,600
	Controlling interest	$119,600

Worksheet 4-5

Intercompany Sale of Depreciable Asset
Company P and Subsidiary Company S
Worksheet for Consolidated Financial Statements
For Year Ended December 31, **2015**

| | (Credit balance amounts are in parentheses.) | Trial Balance | |
		Company P	Company S
1	Current Assets	15,000	20,000
2	**Machinery**	50,000	(a) **230,000**
3	**Accumulated Depreciation—Machinery**	(25,000)	(b) **(100,000)**
4	Investment in Company S	120,000	
5			
6	Common Stock ($10 par)—Company P	(100,000)	
7	Retained Earnings, January 1, 2015—Company P	(10,000)	
8	Common Stock ($10 par)—Company S		(50,000)
9	Retained Earnings, January 1, 2015—Company S		(75,000)
10	Sales	(200,000)	(100,000)
11	Cost of Goods Sold	150,000	59,000
12	**Depreciation Expense**	30,000	(b) **16,000**
13	**Gain on Sale of Machine**	**(10,000)**	
14	Subsidiary Income	(20,000)	
15		0	0
16	Consolidated Net Income		
17	To NCI (see distribution schedule)		
18	Balance to Controlling Interest (see distribution schedule)		
19	Total NCI		
20	Retained Earnings, Controlling Interest, December 31, 2015		
21			

Notes to Trial Balance:

(a) Includes machine purchased for $30,000 from Company P on January 1, 2015.
(b) Includes $6,000 depreciation on machine purchased from Company P on January 1, 2015.

Eliminations and Adjustments:

(CY1) Eliminate the entry recording the parent's share of subsidiary net income for the current year.
(EL) Eliminate 80% of the subsidiary equity balances against the investment account. There is no excess to be distributed.
(F1) Eliminate the $10,000 gain on the intercompany sale of the machine, and reduce machine to book value.
(F2) Reduce the depreciation expense and accumulated depreciation accounts to reflect the depreciation ($4,000 per year) based on the consolidated book value of the machine, rather than the depreciation ($6,000 per year) based on the sales price.

Worksheet 4-5 (see page 216)

Eliminations & Adjustments				Consolidated Income Statement	NCI	Controlling Retained Earnings	Consolidated Balance Sheet	
Dr.		Cr.						
							35,000	1
		(F1)	10,000				270,000	2
(F2)	2,000						(123,000)	3
		(CY1)	20,000					4
		(EL)	100,000					5
							(100,000)	6
						(10,000)		7
(EL)	40,000				(10,000)			8
(EL)	60,000				(15,000)			9
				(300,000)				10
				209,000				11
		(F2)	2,000	44,000				12
(F1)	10,000							13
(CY1)	20,000							14
	132,000		132,000					15
				(47,000)				16
				5,000	(5,000)			17
				42,000		(42,000)		18
					(30,000)		(30,000)	19
						(52,000)	(52,000)	20
							0	21

Subsidiary Company S Income Distribution

Internally generated net income	$ 25,000
Adjusted income	$ 25,000
NCI share	× 20%
NCI	$ 5,000

Parent Company P Income Distribution

Unrealized gain on sale		Internally generated net income	
of machine . . . . **(F1) $10,000**		(including sale of machine)	$30,000
		80% × Company S adjusted income of $25,000	20,000
		Gain realized through use of	
		machine sold to subsidiary . . . . **(F2) 2,000**	
		Controlling interest	$42,000

Worksheet 4-6

Intercompany Sale of Depreciable Asset
Company P and Subsidiary Company S
Worksheet for Consolidated Financial Statements
For Year Ended December 31, **2016**

	(Credit balance amounts are in parentheses.)	Trial Balance Company P	Trial Balance Company S
1	Current Assets	85,000	60,000
2	**Machinery**	50,000	(a) 230,000
3	**Accumulated Depreciation—Machinery**	(45,000)	(b) (116,000)
4			
5	Investment in Company S	139,200	
6			
7	Common Stock ($10 par)—Company P	(100,000)	
8	**Retained Earnings, January 1, 2016—Company P**	**(60,000)**	
9	Common Stock ($10 par)—Company S		(50,000)
10	Retained Earnings, January 1, 2016—Company S		(100,000)
11	Sales	(250,000)	(120,000)
12	**Cost of Goods Sold**	180,000	80,000
13	**Depreciation Expense**	20,000	(c) 16,000
14	Subsidiary Income	(19,200)	
15		0	0
16	Consolidated Net Income		
17	To NCI (see distribution schedule)		
18	Balance to Controlling Interest (see distribution schedule)		
19	Total NCI		
20	Retained Earnings, Controlling Interest, December 31, 2016		
21			

Notes to Trial Balance:

(a) Includes machine purchased for $30,000 from Company P on January 1, 2015.
(b) Includes $12,000 accumulated depreciation ($6,000 per year) on machine purchased from Company P on January 1, 2015.
(c) Includes $6,000 depreciation on machine purchased from Company P on January 1, 2015.

Eliminations and Adjustments:

(CY1) Eliminate the entry recording the parent's share of subsidiary net income for the current year.
(EL) Eliminate 80% of the subsidiary equity balances against the investment account. There is no excess to be distributed.
(F1) Eliminate the gain on the intercompany sale as it is reflected in beginning retained earnings on the parent's trial balance. Since the sale was made by the *parent*, Company P, the entire unrealized gain at the beginning of the year (now $8,000) is removed from the controlling retained earnings beginning balance. If the sale had been made by the subsidiary, the adjustment of beginning retained earnings would be split 80% to the controlling interest and 20% to the noncontrolling interest.
(F2) Reduce the depreciation expense and accumulated depreciation accounts by $2,000 to reflect the depreciation based on the consolidated book value of the asset on the date of sale. This entry will bring the accumulated depreciation account to its correct consolidated year-end balance.

Worksheet 4-6 (see page 217)

Eliminations & Adjustments				Consolidated Income Statement	NCI	Controlling Retained Earnings	Consolidated Balance Sheet	
Dr.		Cr.						
							145,000	1
		(F1)	10,000				270,000	2
(F1)	2,000						(157,000)	3
(F2)	2,000							4
		(CY1)	19,200					5
		(EL)	120,000					6
							(100,000)	7
(F1)	8,000					(52,000)		8
(EL)	40,000				(10,000)			9
(EL)	80,000				(20,000)			10
				(370,000)				11
				260,000				12
		(F2)	2,000	34,000				13
(CY1)	19,200							14
	151,200		151,200					15
				(76,000)				16
				4,800	(4,800)			17
				71,200		(71,200)		18
					(34,800)		(34,800)	19
						(123,200)	(123,200)	20
							0	21

Subsidiary Company S Income Distribution

Internally generated net income	$ 24,000
Adjusted income	$ 24,000
NCI share	× 20%
NCI	$ 4,800

Parent Company P Income Distribution

Internally generated net income	$50,000
80% of Company S adjusted income of $24,000	19,200
Gain realized through use of machine sold to subsidiary . . . . **(F2)**	**2,000**
Controlling interest	$71,200

Worksheet 4-7

Intercompany Sale of a Depreciable Asset; Subsequent Sale of Asset to an Outside Party
Company P and Subsidiary Company S
Worksheet for Consolidated Financial Statements
For Year Ended December 31, **2016**

	(Credit balance amounts are in parentheses.)	Trial Balance	
		Company P	Company S
1	Current Assets	85,000	74,000
2	Machinery	50,000	200,000
3	Accumulated Depreciation—Machinery	(45,000)	(104,000)
4	Investment in Company S	136,000	
5			
6	Common Stock ($10 par)—Company P	(100,000)	
7	**Retained Earnings, January 1, 2016—Company P**	**(60,000)**	
8	Common Stock ($10 par)—Company S		(50,000)
9	Retained Earnings, January 1, 2016—Company S		(100,000)
10	Sales	(250,000)	(120,000)
11	Cost of Goods Sold	180,000	80,000
12	**Depreciation Expense**	20,000	**16,000**
13	**Loss on Sale of Machine**		**4,000**
14	Subsidiary Income	(16,000)	
15	**Gain on Sale of Machine**		
16		0	0
17	Consolidated Net Income		
18	To NCI (see distribution schedule)		
19	Balance to Controlling Interest (see distribution schedule)		
20	Total NCI		
21	Retained Earnings, Controlling Interest, December 31, 2016		
22			

Eliminations and Adjustments:

(CY1) Eliminate the entry recording the parent's share of subsidiary net income for the current year.
(EL) Eliminate 80% of the subsidiary equity balances against the investment account. There is no excess to be distributed.
(F3) Eliminate the gain on the intercompany sale as it is reflected in the parent's beginning retained earnings account, adjust the current year's depreciation expense, and revise the recording of the sale of the equipment to an outside party to reflect the net book value of the asset to the consolidated company.

Worksheet 4-7 (see page 218)

Eliminations & Adjustments				Consolidated Income Statement	NCI	Controlling Retained Earnings	Consolidated Balance Sheet	
Dr.		Cr.						
							159,000	1
							250,000	2
							(149,000)	3
		(CY1)	16,000					4
		(EL)	120,000					5
							(100,000)	6
(F3)	8,000					(52,000)		7
(EL)	40,000				(10,000)			8
(EL)	80,000				(20,000)			9
				(370,000)				10
				260,000				11
		(F3)	2,000	34,000				12
		(F3)	4,000					13
(CY1)	16,000							14
		(F3)	2,000	(2,000)				15
	144,000		144,000					16
				(78,000)				17
				4,000	(4,000)			18
				74,000		(74,000)		19
					(34,000)		(34,000)	20
						(126,000)	(126,000)	21
							0	22

Subsidiary Company S Income Distribution

Internally generated net income	$ 20,000
Adjusted income	$ 20,000
NCI share	× 20%
NCI	$ 4,000

Parent Company P Income Distribution

Internally generated net income		$ 50,000
80% × Company S adjusted income of $20,000		16,000
Gain realized on sale of machine	**(F3)**	**8,000***
Controlling interest		$ 74,000

*$10,000 original gain − $2,000 realized in 2015.

Worksheet 4-8

Intercompany Notes
Company P and Subsidiary Company S
Worksheet for Consolidated Financial Statements
For Year Ended December 31, **2015**

	(Credit balance amounts are in parentheses.)	Trial Balance	
		Company P	Company S
1	Cash	35,000	20,400
2	**Note Receivable from Company S**	10,000	
3	**Interest Receivable**	400	
4	Property, Plant, and Equipment (net)	140,000	150,000
5	Investment in Company S	128,000	
6			
7	**Note Payable to Company P**		(10,000)
8	**Interest Payable**		(400)
9	Common Stock—Company P	(100,000)	
10	Retained Earnings, January 1, 2015—Company P	(200,000)	
11	Common Stock—Company S		(50,000)
12	Retained Earnings, January 1, 2015—Company S		(100,000)
13	Sales	(120,000)	(50,000)
14	**Interest Income**	(400)	
15	Subsidiary Income	(8,000)	
16	Cost of Goods Sold	75,000	20,000
17	Other Expenses	40,000	19,600
18	**Interest Expense**		400
19		0	0
20	Consolidated Net Income		
21	To NCI (see distribution schedule)		
22	Balance to Controlling Interest (see distribution schedule)		
23	Total NCI		
24	Retained Earnings, Controlling Interest, December 31, 2015		
25			

Eliminations and Adjustments:

(CY1) Eliminate the parent's share (80%) of subsidiary net income.
(EL)   Eliminate the controlling portion (80%) of the Company S January 1, 2015, stockholders' equity against the investment in Company S account. No excess results.
(LN1) Eliminate the intercompany note and accrued interest applicable to the note. This entry removes the *internal note* from the consolidated balance sheet.
(LN2) Eliminate the intercompany interest expense and revenue. Since an equal amount of expense and revenue is eliminated, there is no change in the combined net income as a result of this entry.

Worksheet 4-8 (see page 219)

Eliminations & Adjustments				Consolidated Income Statement	NCI	Controlling Retained Earnings	Consolidated Balance Sheet	
Dr.		Cr.						
							55,400	1
		(LN1)	10,000					2
		(LN1)	400					3
							290,000	4
		(CY1)	8,000					5
		(EL)	120,000					6
(LN1)	10,000							7
(LN1)	400							8
							(100,000)	9
						(200,000)		10
(EL)	40,000				(10,000)			11
(EL)	80,000				(20,000)			12
				(170,000)				13
(LN2)	400							14
(CY1)	8,000							15
				95,000				16
				59,600				17
		(LN2)	400					18
	138,800		138,800					19
				(15,400)				20
				2,000	(2,000)			21
				13,400		(13,400)		22
					(32,000)		(32,000)	23
						(213,400)	(213,400)	24
							0	25

Subsidiary Company S Income Distribution

Internally generated net income	$ 10,000
Adjusted income	$ 10,000
NCI share	× 20%
NCI	$ 2,000

Parent Company P Income Distribution

Internally generated net income	$ 5,400
80% × Company S adjusted income of $10,000.	8,000
Controlling interest	$ 13,400

Worksheet 4-9

Vertical Worksheet Alternative
Company P and Subsidiary Company S
Worksheet for Consolidated Financial Statements
For Year Ended December 31, **2016**

Worksheet 4-9 (see page 224)

#	(Credit balance amounts are in parentheses.)	Trial Balance — Company P	Trial Balance — Company S	Elim. & Adj. Dr.	Elim. & Adj. Cr.	NCI	Consolidated
1	**Income Statement**						
2	Sales	(600,000)	(530,000)	(IS) 150,000			(980,000)
3	Cost of Goods Sold	400,000	280,000	(EI) 10,000	(IS) 150,000		532,000
4					(BI) 8,000		
5	Depreciation Expense	40,000	50,000		(F2) 1,000		89,000
6	Other Expenses	60,000	70,000				130,000
7	Subsidiary Income	(104,000)		(CY1) 104,000			
8	**Net Income**	(204,000)	(130,000)				(229,000)
9	NCI (see distribution schedule)					(25,600)	
10	Controlling Interest (see distribution schedule)						(203,400)
11							
12	**Retained Earnings Statement**						
13	Retained Earnings, January 1, 2016—Company P	(600,000)					
14				(BI) 6,400			
15				(F1) 4,500			
16	Retained Earnings, January 1, 2016—Company S		(400,000)	(EL) 320,000	(NCI) 15,000	(93,400)	(589,100)
17				(BI) 1,600			
18	**Net Income (carrydown)**	(204,000)	(130,000)			(25,600)	(203,400)
19	Dividends Declared		20,000		(CY2) 16,000	4,000	
20	**Retained Earnings, December 31, 2016**	(804,000)	(510,000)				
21	NCI, Retained Earnings, December 31, 2016					115,000	
22	Controlling Interest, Retained Earnings, December 31, 2016						(792,500)
23							
24	**Balance Sheet**						
25	Inventory	300,000	250,000		(EI) 10,000		540,000
26	Accounts Receivable	120,000	180,000		(IA) 20,000		280,000
27	Plant Assets	236,000	400,000		(F1) 5,000		631,000
28	Accumulated Depreciation	(100,000)	(60,000)	(F1) 500 / (F2) 1,000			(158,500)
29							
30	Investment in Company S	628,000		(CY2) 16,000	(CY1) 104,000 / (EL) 480,000 / (D1) 60,000		
31							
32							
33	Goodwill			(D1) 75,000			75,000
34	Current Liabilities	(80,000)	(60,000)	(IA) 20,000			(120,000)
35	Common Stock ($5 par)—Company S		(200,000)	(EL) 160,000		(40,000)	
36	Common Stock ($10 par)—Company P	(300,000)					(300,000)
37	**Retained Earnings (carrydown)**	(804,000)	(510,000)				
38	Retained Earnings, Controlling Interest, December 31, 2016						(792,500)
39	Retained Earnings, NCI, December 31, 2016					(115,000)	
40	Total NCI					(155,000)	(155,000)
41	Totals	0	0	869,000	869,000		0

Eliminations and Adjustments:

(CY1)	Eliminate the current-year entries recording the parent's share (80%) of subsidiary net income.
(CY2)	Eliminate intercompany dividends.
(EL)	Eliminate the pro rata portion of the subsidiary equity balances owned by the parent (80%) against the balance of the investment account.
(D1)/(NCI)	Distribute the excess to the goodwill account according to the determination and distribution of excess schedule.
(IS)	Eliminate the intercompany sales made during 2016.
(BI)	Eliminate the intercompany profit in the beginning inventory, 20% multiplied by $40,000. Since it was a subsidiary sale, the profit is shared 20% by the NCI.
(EI)	Eliminate the intercompany profit (20%) applicable to the $50,000 of intercompany goods in the ending inventory.
(IA)	Eliminate the intercompany trade balances.
(F1)	Eliminate the intercompany gain remaining on January 1, 2016, applicable to the sale of the machine by Company P ($5,000 original gain less one-half-year's gain of $500).
(F2)	Reduce the depreciation expense and accumulated depreciation accounts ($1,000 for the current year) in order to reflect depreciation based on the original cost.

Subsidiary Company S Income Distribution

Unrealized profit in ending inventory (20% × $50,000) .... (EI)	$10,000	Internally generated net income	$ 130,000
		Realized profit in beginning inventory (20% × $40,000) .... (BI)	8,000
		Adjusted income	$ 128,000
		NCI share	× 20%
		NCI	$ 25,600

Parent Company P Income Distribution

	Internally generated net income	$ 100,000
	Gain realized on sale of machine .... (F2)	1,000
	80% × Company S adjusted income of $128,000	102,400
	Controlling interest	$203,400

UNDERSTANDING THE ISSUES

1. During 2015, Company P sold $50,000 of goods to subsidiary Company S at a profit of $12,000. One-fourth of the goods remain unsold at year-end. If no adjustments were made on the consolidated worksheet, what errors would there be on the consolidated income statement and balance sheet?

2. During 2015, Company P sold $50,000 of goods to subsidiary Company S at a profit of $12,000. One-fourth of the goods remain unsold at year-end. What specific adjustments are needed on the consolidated worksheet to deal with these issues?

3. Company S is 80% owned by Company P. Near the end of 2015, Company S sold merchandise with a cost of $6,000 to Company P for $7,000. Company P sold the merchandise to a nonaffiliated firm in 2016 for $10,000. How much total profit should be recorded on the consolidated income statements in 2015 and 2016? How much profit should be awarded to the controlling and noncontrolling interests in 2015 and 2016?

4. Subsidiary Company S is 80% owned by Company P. Company S sold a machine with a book value of $100,000 to Company P for $150,000. The asset has a 5-year life and is depreciated under the straight-line method. The president of Company S thinks it has scored a $50,000 immediate profit for the noncontrolling interest. Explain how much profit the noncontrolling interest will realize and when it will be awarded.

5. On January 1, 2015, Company P sold a machine to its 70%-owned subsidiary, Company S, for $60,000. The book value of the machine was $50,000. The machine was depreciated using the straight-line method over five years. On December 31, 2017, Company S sold the machine to a nonaffiliated firm for $35,000. On the consolidated statements, how much gain or loss on the intercompany machine sale should be recognized in 2015, 2016, and 2017?

6. Company S is an 80%-owned subsidiary of Company P. Company S needed to borrow $500,000 on January 1, 2015. The best interest rate it could secure was 10% annual. Company P has a better credit rating and decided to borrow the funds needed from a bank at 8% annual and then loaned the money to Company S at 9.5% annual.

   a. Is Company S better off as a result of borrowing the funds from Company P?
   b. What are the interest revenue and expense amounts recorded by Company P and Company S during 2016?
   c. How much interest expense and/or interest revenue should appear on the 2015 consolidated income statement?

EXERCISES

Exercise 1 *(LO 1, 2)* **Gross profit: separate firms versus consolidated.** Sorel is an 80%-owned subsidiary of Pattern Company. The two affiliates had the following separate income statements for 2015 and 2016.

	Sorel Company		Pattern Company	
	2015	2016	2015	2016
Sales revenue	$250,000	$350,000	$500,000	$540,000
Cost of goods sold	150,000	210,000	310,000	360,000
Gross profit	$100,000	$140,000	$190,000	$180,000
Expenses	45,000	66,000	120,000	125,000
Net income	$ 55,000	$ 74,000	$ 70,000	$ 55,000

Sorel sells at the same gross profit percentage to all customers. During 2015, Sorel sold goods to Pattern for the first time in the amount of $120,000. $30,000 of these sales remained in Pattern's ending inventory. During 2016, sales to Pattern by Sorel were $150,000, of which $25,000 sales were still in Pattern's December 31, 2016, inventory.

Prepare consolidated income statements including the distribution of income to the controlling and noncontrolling interests for 2015 and 2016.

Exercise 2 *(LO 2)* **Inventory profits with lower-of-cost-or-market adjustment.** Hide Corporation is a wholly owned subsidiary of Seek Company. During 2015, Hide sold all of its production to Seek Company for $400,000, a price that includes a 25% gross profit. 2015 was the first year that such intercompany sales were made. By year-end, Seek sold, for $416,000, 80% of the goods it had purchased. The balance of the intercompany goods, $80,000, remained in the ending inventory and was adjusted to a lower fair value of $70,000. The adjustment was a charge to the cost of goods sold.

1. Determine the gross profit on sales recorded by both companies.
2. Determine the gross profit to be shown on the consolidated income statement.

Exercise 3 *(LO 2)* **Distribution of income with inventory profits.** Norco Company is an 80%-owned subsidiary of Victory Corporation. The separate income statements of the two companies for 2016 are as follows:

	Victory Corporation	Norco Company
Sales	$ 220,000	$ 150,000
Cost of goods sold	(150,000)	(112,500)
Gross profit	$ 70,000	$ 37,500
Other expenses	(40,000)	(15,000)
Other income	5,000	
Operating income	$ 35,000	$ 22,500
Subsidiary income	14,400	
Net income	$ 49,400	$ 22,500

The following facts apply to 2016:

a. Norco Company sold $90,000 of goods to Victory Corporation. The gross profits on sales to Victory and to unrelated companies are equal and have not changed from the previous years.
b. Victory Corporation held $20,000 of the goods purchased from Norco Company in its beginning inventory and $30,000 of such goods in ending inventory.
c. Victory Corporation billed Norco Company $5,000 for computer services. The charge was expensed by Norco Company and treated as other income by Victory Corporation.

Prepare the consolidated income statement for 2016, including the distribution of the consolidated net income to the controlling and noncontrolling interests. The supporting income distribution schedules should be prepared as well.

Exercise 4 *(LO 3)* **Machinery sale.** On January 1, 2016, Jungle Company sold a machine to Safari Company for $30,000. The machine had an original cost of $24,000, and accumulated depreciation on the asset was $9,000 at the time of the sale. The machine has a 5-year remaining life and will be depreciated on a straight-line basis with no salvage value. Safari Company is an 80%-owned subsidiary of Jungle Company.

1. Explain the adjustments that would have to be made to arrive at consolidated net income for the years 2016 through 2020 as a result of this sale.

2. Prepare the elimination that would be required on the December 31, 2016, consolidated worksheet as a result of this sale.
3. Prepare the entry for the December 31, 2017, worksheet as a result of this sale.

Exercise 5 *(LO 3)* **Land and building profit.** Wavemasters Inc., owns an 80% interest in Sayner Development Company. In a prior period, Sayner Development purchased a parcel of land for $50,000. During 2015, it constructed a building on the land at a cost of $500,000. The land and building were sold to Wavemasters at the very end of 2015 for $750,000, of which $100,000 was for the land. It is estimated that the building has a 20-year life with no salvage value.

1. Prepare all worksheet eliminations that would be made on the 2015 consolidated worksheet as a result of the real estate sale.
2. Prepare all worksheet eliminations that would be made on the 2017 consolidated worksheet as a result of the 2015 real estate sale.

Exercise 6 *(LO 3)* **Resale of intercompany asset.** Hilton Corporation sold a press to its 80%-owned subsidiary, Agri Fab Inc., for $5,000 on January 1, 2016. The press originally was purchased by Hilton on January 1, 2015, for $20,000, and $6,000 of depreciation for 2015 had been recorded. The fair value of the press on January 1, 2016, was $10,000. Agri Fab proceeded to depreciate the press on a straight-line basis, using a 5-year life and no salvage value. On December 31, 2017, Agri Fab, having no further need for the machine, sold it for $2,000 and recorded a loss on the sale.

Explain the adjustments that would have to be made to the separate income statements of the two companies to arrive at the consolidated income statements for 2016 and 2017.

Exercise 7 *(LO 3)* **Fixed asset sales by parent and subsidiary.** The separate income statements of Danner Company and its 90%-owned subsidiary, Link Company, for the year ended December 31, 2016, are as follows:

	Danner Company	Link Company
Sales	$ 650,000	$ 280,000
Cost of goods sold	(400,000)	(190,000)
Gross profit	$ 250,000	$ 90,000
Other expenses	(180,000)	(70,000)
Other income	20,000	
Operating income	$ 90,000	$ 20,000
Subsidiary income	18,000	
Net income	$ 108,000	$ 20,000

The following additional facts apply:

a. On January 1, 2015, Link Company purchased a building, with a book value of $100,000 and an estimated 20-year life, from Danner Company for $150,000. The building was being depreciated on a straight-line basis with no salvage value.
b. On January 1, 2016, Link Company sold a machine with a cost of $40,000 to Danner Company for $60,000. The machine had an expected life of five years and is being depreciated on a straight-line basis with no salvage value. Link Company is a dealer for the machine.

Prepare a worksheet that shows income statements of Danner and Link with a column for eliminations. Be sure to include the distribution of income to the controlling and non-controlling interest.

Exercise 8 *(LO 2, 3)* **Merchandise and fixed asset sale.** Peninsula Company owns an 80% controlling interest in Sandbar Company. Sandbar regularly sells merchandise to Peninsula, which then sells to outside parties. The gross profit on all such sales is 40%. On January 1, 2015, Peninsula sells land and a building to Sandbar. Tax assessments divide the value of the parcel 20% to land and 75% to structures. Pertinent information for the companies is summarized as follows:

	Peninsula	Sandbar
Internally generated net income, 2015	$520,000	$250,000
Internally generated net income, 2016	340,000	235,000
Intercompany merchandise sales, 2015		100,000
Intercompany merchandise sales, 2016		120,000
Intercompany inventory, December 31, 2015	15,000	
Intercompany inventory, December 31, 2016	20,000	
Cost of real estate sold on January 1, 2015	600,000	
Sale price for real estate on January 1, 2015	800,000	
Depreciable life of building		20 years

Prepare income distribution schedules for 2015 and 2016 for Peninsula and Sandbar as they would be prepared to distribute income to the noncontrolling and controlling interests in support of consolidated worksheets.

Exercise 9 *(LO 5)* **Intercompany note.** Saratoga Company owns 80% of the outstanding common stock of Windsor Company. On May 1, 2017, Windsor Company arranges a 1-year, $50,000 loan from Saratoga Company. The loan agreement specifies that interest will accrue at the rate of 6% per annum and that all interest will be paid on the maturity date of the loan. The financial reporting period ends on December 31, 2017, and the note originating from the loan remains outstanding.

1. Prepare the entries that both companies would have made on their separate books, including the accrual of interest.
2. Prepare the eliminations, in entry form, that will be made on a consolidated worksheet prepared as of December 31, 2017.

Exercise 10 *(LO 5)* **Intercompany note discounted.** Assume the same facts as in Exercise 11, but in addition, assume that Saratoga is itself in need of cash. It discounts the note received from Windsor at First Bank on July 1, 2017, at a discount rate of 8% per annum.

1. Prepare the entries that both companies would have made on their separate books, including interest accruals.
2. Prepare the eliminations, in entry form, that will be made on a consolidated worksheet prepared as of December 31, 2017.

PROBLEMS

Problem 4-1 *(LO 2)* **100%, equity, ending inventory.** On January 1, 2015, 100% of the outstanding stock of Solo Company was purchased by Plato Corporation for $3,300,000. At that time, the book value of Solo's net assets equaled $3,000,000. The excess was attributable to equipment with a 10-year life.

The following trial balances of Plato Corporation and Solo Company were prepared on December 31, 2015:

	Plato Corporation	Solo Company
Cash	735,000	370,000
Accounts Receivable	400,000	365,000
Inventory	600,000	275,000

(continued)

	Plato Corporation	Solo Company
Property, Plato, and Equipment (net)	4,000,000	2,300,000
Investment in Solo Company	3,510,000	
Accounts Payable	(35,000)	(100,000)
Common Stock ($10 par)	(1,000,000)	(400,000)
Paid-In Capital in Excess of Par	(1,500,000)	(200,000)
Retained Earnings, January 1, 2015.	(5,500,000)	(2,400,000)
Sales	(12,000,000)	(1,000,000)
Cost of Goods Sold	7,000,000	750,000
Other Expenses	4,000,000	40,000
Subsidiary Income.	(210,000)	
Totals	0	0

Throughout 2015, sales to Plato Corporation made up 30% of Solo's revenue and produced a 25% gross profit rate. At year-end, Plato Corporation had sold $250,000 of the goods purchased from Solo Company and still owed Solo $30,000. None of the Solo products were in Plato's January 1, 2015, beginning inventory.

Required ▶ ▶ ▶ ▶ ▶

Prepare the worksheet necessary to produce the consolidated income statement and balance sheet of Plato Corporation and its subsidiary for the year ended December 31, 2015. Include the determination and distribution of excess schedule.

Problem 4-2 *(LO 2)* **80%, cost, beginning and ending inventory.** On April 1, 2015, Benton Corporation purchased 80% of the outstanding stock of Crandel Company for $425,000. A condensed balance sheet of Crandel Company at the purchase date is shown below.

Assets		Liabilities and Equity	
Current assets	$180,000	Liabilities	$100,000
Long-lived assets (net)	320,000	Common stock.	200,000
		Paid-in capital in excess of par	100,000
		Retained earnings	100,000
Total assets.	$500,000	Total liabilities and equity	$500,000

All book values approximated fair values on the purchase date. Any excess cost was attributed to goodwill.

The following information was gathered pertaining to the first two years of operation since Benton's purchase of Crandel Company stock:

a. Intercompany merchandise sales were summarized as follows:

Date	Transaction	Sales	Gross Profit	Merchandise Remaining in Purchaser's Ending Inventory
April 1, 2015 to	Benton to Crandel	$40,000	20%	$9,000
March 31, 2016	Crandel to Benton	20,000	25	4,000
April 1, 2016 to	Benton to Crandel	32,000	20	6,000
March 31, 2017	Crandel to Benton	30,000	25	3,000

b. On March 31, 2017, Benton owed Crandel $10,000, and Crandel owed Benton $5,000 as a result of the intercompany sales.

c. Benton paid $25,000 in cash dividends on March 20, 2016 and 2017. Crandel paid its first cash dividend on March 10, 2017, giving each share of outstanding common stock a $0.15 cash dividend.

d. The trial balances of the two companies as of March 31, 2017, follow:

	Benton Corporation	Crandel Company
Cash	191,200	44,300
Accounts Receivable (net)	290,000	97,000
Inventory	310,000	80,000
Investment in Crandel Company	450,000	
Land	1,081,000	150,000
Building and Equipment	1,850,000	400,000
Accumulated Depreciation	(940,000)	(210,000)
Goodwill	60,000	
Accounts Payable	(242,200)	(106,300)
Bonds Payable	(400,000)	
Common Stock ($0.50 par)	(250,000)	
Common Stock ($1 par)		(200,000)
Paid-In Capital in Excess of Par	(1,250,000)	(100,000)
Retained Earnings, April 1, 2016	(1,105,000)	(140,000)
Sales	(880,000)	(630,000)
Dividend Income (from Crandel Company)	(24,000)	
Cost of Goods Sold	704,000	504,000
Other Expenses	130,000	81,000
Dividends Declared	25,000	30,000
Totals	0	0

◄ ◄ ◄ ◄ ◄ Required

1. Prepare the worksheet necessary to produce the consolidated financial statements of Benton Corporation and its subsidiary for the year ended March 31, 2017. Include the value analysis and a determination and distribution of excess schedule and the income distribution schedules.
2. Prepare the formal consolidated income statement for the fiscal year ending March 31, 2017.

Use the following information for Problems 4-3 and 4-4:

On January 1, 2015, Packard Corporation acquired 70% of the common stock of Stude Corporation for $400,000. On this date, Stude had the following balance sheet:

Stude Corporation
Balance Sheet
January 1, 2015

Assets		Liabilities and Equity	
Accounts receivable	$ 60,000	Accounts payable	$ 40,000
Inventory	40,000	Bonds payable	100,000
Land	60,000	Common stock ($1 par)	10,000
Buildings	200,000	Paid-in capital in excess of par	90,000
Accumulated depreciation	(50,000)	Retained earnings	112,000
Equipment	72,000		
Accumulated depreciation	(30,000)		
Total assets	$352,000	Total liabilities and equity	$352,000

Buildings, which have a 20-year life, were understated by $150,000. Equipment, which has a 5-year life, was understated by $60,000. The 3,000 NCI shares had a fair

(continued)

value of $50 each. Any remaining excess was considered to be goodwill. Packard used the simple equity method to account for its investment in Stude.

Packard and Stude had the following trial balances on December 31, 2016:

	Packard Corporation	Stude Corporation
Cash	66,000	132,000
Accounts Receivable	90,000	45,000
Inventory	120,000	56,000
Land	100,000	60,000
Investment in Stude	428,000	
Buildings	800,000	200,000
Accumulated Depreciation	(220,000)	(65,000)
Equipment	150,000	72,000
Accumulated Depreciation	(90,000)	(46,000)
Accounts Payable	(60,000)	(102,000)
Bonds Payable		(100,000)
Common Stock	(100,000)	(10,000)
Paid-In Capital in Excess of Par	(800,000)	(90,000)
Retained Earnings, January 1, 2016	(325,000)	(142,000)
Sales	(800,000)	(350,000)
Cost of Goods Sold	450,000	208,500
Depreciation Expense—Buildings	30,000	7,500
Depreciation Expense—Equipment	15,000	8,000
Other Expenses	140,000	98,000
Interest Expense		8,000
Subsidiary Income	(14,000)	
Dividends Declared	20,000	10,000
Totals	0	0

Problem 4-3 *(LO 2)* **70%, equity, beginning and ending inventory, subsidiary seller.** Refer to the preceding facts for Packard's acquisition of Stude common stock. On January 1, 2016, Packard held merchandise acquired from Stude for $10,000. This beginning inventory had an applicable gross profit of 25%. During 2016, Stude sold $40,000 worth of merchandise to Packard. Packard held $6,000 of this merchandise at December 31, 2016. This ending inventory had an applicable gross profit of 30%. Packard owed Stude $11,000 on December 31 as a result of these intercompany sales.

Required ▶ ▶ ▶ ▶ ▶
1. Prepare a value analysis and a determination and distribution of excess schedule for the investment in Stude.
2. Complete a consolidated worksheet for Packard Corporation and its subsidiary Stude Corporation as of December 31, 2016. Prepare supporting amortization and income distribution schedules.

Problem 4-4 *(LO 2)* **70%, equity, beginning and ending inventory, parent and subsidiary seller.** Refer to the preceding facts for Packard's acquisition of Stude common stock. On January 1, 2016, Packard held merchandise acquired from Stude for $10,000. This beginning inventory had an applicable gross profit of 25%. During 2016, Stude sold $40,000 worth of merchandise to Packard. Packard held $6,000 of this merchandise at December 31, 2016. This ending inventory had an applicable gross profit of 30%. Packard owed Stude $11,000 on December 31 as a result of this intercompany sale.

On January 1, 2016, Stude held merchandise acquired from Packard for $20,000. This beginning inventory had an applicable gross profit of 40%. During 2016, Packard sold $60,000 worth of merchandise to Stude. Stude held $30,000 of this merchandise at December 31, 2016. This ending inventory had an applicable gross profit of 35%. Stude owed Packard $23,000 on December 31 as a result of this intercompany sale.

1. Prepare a value analysis and a determination and distribution of excess schedule for the   ◀ ◀ ◀ ◀ ◀ **Required**
   investment in Stude.
2. Complete a consolidated worksheet for Packard Corporation and its subsidiary Stude Corporation as of December 31, 2016. Prepare supporting amortization and income distribution schedules.

Problem 4-5 *(LO 2)* **80%, equity, beginning and ending inventory, write-down, note.** On January 1, 2015, Silvio Corporation exchanged on a 1-for-3 basis common stock it held in its treasury for 80% of the outstanding stock of Jenko Company. Silvio Corporation common stock had a market price of $40 per share on the exchange date. On the date of the acquisition, the stockholders' equity section of Jenko Company was as follows:

Common stock ($5 par).........................	$ 450,000
Paid-in capital in excess of par	180,000
Retained earnings	370,000
Total.....................................	$1,000,000

Also on that date, Jenko Company's book values approximated fair values, except for the land, which was undervalued by $75,000. The remaining excess was attributable to goodwill. Information regarding intercompany transactions for 2017 follows:

a. Silvio Corporation sold merchandise to Jenko Company, realizing a 30% gross profit. Sales during 2017 were $140,000. Jenko had $25,000 of the 2016 purchases in its beginning inventory for 2017 and $35,000 of the 2017 purchases in its ending inventory for 2017. Jenko wrote down to $28,000 the merchandise purchased from Silvio Corporation and remaining in its 2017 ending inventory.
b. Jenko signed a 12%, 4-month, $10,000 note to Silvio in order to cover the remaining balance of its payables on November 1, 2017. No new merchandise was purchased after this date.

The trial balances of Silvio Corporation and Jenko Company as of December 31, 2017, were as follows:

	Silvio Corporation	Jenko Company
Cash	140,000	205,200
Accounts Receivable	285,000	110,000
Interest Receivable.............................	1,500	
Notes Receivable..............................	50,000	
Inventory	470,000	160,000
Land..	350,000	300,000
Depreciable Fixed Assets	1,110,000	810,000
Accumulated Depreciation	(500,000)	(200,000)
Intangibles...................................	60,000	
Investment in Jenko Company	1,128,000	
Accounts Payable	(611,500)	(165,000)
Note Payable.................................		(10,000)
Interest Payable		(200)
Common Stock ($1 par)	(400,000)	
Common Stock ($5 par)		(450,000)

(continued)

	Silvio Corporation	Jenko Company
Paid-In Capital in Excess of Par	(1,235,000)	(180,000)
Retained Earnings, January 1, 2017	(958,500)	(470,000)
Treasury Stock (at cost)	315,000	
Sales	(1,020,000)	(500,000)
Interest Income	(1,500)	
Subsidiary Income	(88,000)	
Cost of Goods Sold	705,000	300,000
Other Expenses	200,000	90,000
Totals	0	0

Required ▶ ▶ ▶ ▶ ▶   Prepare the worksheet necessary to produce the consolidated financial statements of Silvio Corporation and its subsidiary for the year ended December 31, 2017. Include the value analysis and determination and distribution of excess schedule and the income distribution schedules.

Problem 4-6 *(LO 3)* **80%, equity, fixed asset sales by subsidiary and parent.** On September 1, 2015, Parcel Corporation purchased 80% of the outstanding common stock of Sack Corporation for $152,000. On that date, Sack's net book values equaled fair values, and there was no excess of cost or book value resulting from the purchase. Parcel has been maintaining its investment under the simple equity method.

Over the next three years, the intercompany transactions between the companies were as follows:

a. On September 1, 2015, Sack sold its 4-year-old delivery truck to Parcel for $14,000 in cash. At that time, Sack had depreciated the truck, which had cost $15,000, to its $5,000 salvage value. Parcel estimated on the date of the sale that the asset had a remaining useful life of three years and no salvage value.

b. On September 1, 2016, Parcel sold equipment to Sack for $103,000. Parcel originally paid $80,000 for the equipment and planned to depreciate it over 20 years, assuming no salvage value. However, Parcel had the property for only 10 years and carried it at a net book value of $40,000 on the sale date. Sack will use the equipment for 10 years, at which time Sack expects no salvage value.

Both companies use straight-line depreciation for all assets.

Trial balances of Parcel Corporation and Sack Corporation as of the August 31, 2017, year-end were as shown below.

	Parcel Corporation	Sack Corporation
Cash	120,000	50,000
Accounts Receivable (net)	115,000	18,000
Notes Receivable		10,000
Inventory, August 31, 2017	175,000	34,000
Investment in Sack Corporation	217,440	
Plant and Equipment	990,700	295,000
Accumulated Depreciation	(170,000)	(85,000)
Other Assets	28,000	
Accounts Payable	(80,000)	(50,200)
Notes Payable	(25,000)	
Bonds Payable (12%)	(300,000)	
Common Stock ($10 par)	(290,000)	(70,000)
Paid-In Capital in Excess of Par	(110,000)	(62,000)

	Parcel Corporation	Sack Corporation
Retained Earnings, September 1, 2016	(498,850)	(118,000)
Sales	(920,000)	(240,000)
Cost of Goods Sold	598,000	132,000
Selling and General Expenses.	108,000	80,000
Subsidiary Income.	(23,040)	
Interest Income.		(800)
Interest Expense.	37,750	
Gain on Sale of Equipment	(63,000)	
Dividends Declared.	90,000	7,000
Totals	0	0

Prepare the worksheet necessary to produce the consolidated financial statements of Parcel ◄ ◄ ◄ ◄ ◄ **Required**
Corporation and its subsidiary for the year ended August 31, 2017. Include the income distribution schedules.

Use the following information for Problems 4-7 and 4-8:

On January 1, 2015, Panther Company acquired Sandin Company. Panther paid $60 per share for 80% of Sandin's common stock. The price paid by Panther reflected a control premium. The NCI shares were estimated to have a market value of $55 per share. On the date of acquisition, Sandin had the following balance sheet:

Sandin Company
Balance Sheet
January 1, 2015

Assets		Liabilities and Equity	
Accounts receivable	$ 60,000	Accounts payable	$ 40,000
Inventory	40,000	Bonds payable	100,000
Land.	60,000	Common stock ($1 par).	10,000
Buildings	200,000	Paid-in capital in excess of par . . .	90,000
Accumulated depreciation	(50,000)	Retained earnings	112,000
Equipment	72,000		
Accumulated depreciation	(30,000)		
Total assets.	$352,000	Total liabilities and equity	$352,000

Buildings, which have a 20-year life, were understated by $120,000. Equipment, which has a 5-year life, was understated by $40,000. Any remaining excess was considered goodwill. Panther used the simple equity method to account for its investment in Sandin.

Panther and Sandin had the following trial balances on December 31, 2016:

	Panther Company	Sandin Company
Cash	24,000	132,000
Accounts Receivable	90,000	45,000
Inventory	120,000	56,000
Land.	100,000	60,000
Investment in Sandin	512,000	
Buildings	800,000	200,000
Accumulated Depreciation	(220,000)	(65,000)
Equipment	150,000	72,000

(continued)

	Panther Company	Sandin Company
Accumulated Depreciation	(90,000)	(46,000)
Accounts Payable	(60,000)	(102,000)
Bonds Payable.		(100,000)
Common Stock	(100,000)	(10,000)
Paid-In Capital in Excess of Par	(800,000)	(90,000)
Retained Earnings, January 1, 2016.	(365,000)	(142,000)
Sales	(800,000)	(350,000)
Cost of Goods Sold	450,000	208,500
Depreciation Expense—Buildings.	30,000	7,500
Depreciation Expense—Equipment.	15,000	8,000
Other Expenses	160,000	98,000
Interest Expense.		8,000
Gain on Sale of Fixed Assets	(20,000)	
Subsidiary Income.	(16,000)	
Dividends Declared	20,000	10,000
Totals	0	0

Problem 4-7 *(LO 3)* **80%, equity, several excess distributions, fixed asset sale.** Refer to the preceding facts for Panther's acquisition of Sandin common stock. On January 1, 2016, Panther held merchandise sold to it from Sandin for $12,000. This beginning inventory had an applicable gross profit of 25%. During 2016, Sandin sold merchandise to Panther for $75,000. On December 31, 2016, Panther held $18,000 of this merchandise in its inventory. This ending inventory had an applicable gross profit of 30%. Panther owed Sandin $20,000 on December 31 as a result of this intercompany sale.

On January 1, 2016, Panther sold equipment with a book value of $35,000 to Sandin for $50,000. Panther also sold some fixed assets to nonaffiliates. During 2016, the equipment was used by Sandin. Depreciation is computed over a 5-year life, using the straight-line method.

Required ▶ ▶ ▶ ▶ ▶
1. Prepare a value analysis and a determination and distribution of excess schedule for the investment in Sandin.
2. Complete a consolidated worksheet for Panther Company and its subsidiary Sandin Company as of December 31, 2016. Prepare supporting amortization and income distribution schedules.

Problem 4-8 *(LO 3)* **80%, equity, several excess distributions, fixed asset sale by parent and subsidiary.** Refer to the preceding facts for Panther's acquisition of Sandin common stock. On January 1, 2016, Sandin held merchandise sold to it from Panther for $20,000. During 2016, Panther sold merchandise to Sandin for $100,000. On December 31, 2016, Sandin held $25,000 of this merchandise in its inventory. Panther has a gross profit of 30%. Sandin owed Panther $15,000 on December 31 as a result of this intercompany sale.

On January 1, 2015, Sandin sold equipment to Panther at a profit of $24,000. Panther also sold some fixed assets to nonaffiliates. Depreciation is computed over a 6-year life, using the straight-line method.

Required ▶ ▶ ▶ ▶ ▶
1. Prepare a value analysis and a determination and distribution of excess schedule for the investment in Sandin.
2. Complete a consolidated worksheet for Panther Company and its subsidiary Sandin Company as of December 31, 2016. Prepare supporting amortization and income distribution schedules.

Problem 4-9 *(LO 2, 5)* **90%, cost, merchandise, note payable.** The December 31, 2016, trial balances of Pettie Corporation and its 90%-owned subsidiary Sunco Corporation are as follows:

	Pettie Corporation	Sunco Corporation
Cash	15,000	45,500
Accounts and Other Current Receivables	410,900	170,000
Inventory	920,000	739,400
Property, Plant, and Equipment (net)	1,000,000	400,000
Investment in Sunco Corporation.	1,260,000	
Accounts Payable and Other Current Liabilities	(140,000)	(305,900)
Common Stock ($10 par)	(500,000)	
Common Stock ($10 par)		(200,000)
Retained Earnings, January 1, 2016.	(2,800,000)	(650,000)
Dividends Declared.		1,000
Sales	(2,000,000)	(650,000)
Dividend Income	(900)	
Interest Expense.		5,000
Interest Income.	(5,000)	
Cost of Goods Sold	1,500,000	400,000
Other Expenses	340,000	45,000
Totals	0	0

Pettie's investment in Sunco was purchased for $1,260,000 in cash on January 1, 2015, and was accounted for by the cost method. On January 1, 2015, Sunco had the following equity balances:

Common stock.	$200,000
Retained earnings	600,000
Total equity	$800,000

Pettie's excess of cost over book value on Sunco's investment has been identified as goodwill.

Sunco borrowed $100,000 from Pettie on June 30, 2016, with the note maturing on June 30, 2017, at 10% interest. Correct accruals have been recorded by both companies.

During 2016, Pettie sold merchandise to Sunco at an aggregate invoice price of $300,000, which included a profit of $75,000. As of December 31, 2016, Sunco had not paid Pettie for $90,000 of these purchases, and 10% of the total merchandise purchased from Pettie still remained in Sunco's inventory.

Sunco declared a $1,000 cash dividend in December 2016 payable in January 2017.

◀ ◀ ◀ ◀ ◀ **Required** Prepare the worksheet required to produce the consolidated statements of Pettie Corporation and its subsidiary, Sunco Corporation, for the year ended December 31, 2016. Include the valuation analysis, the determination and distribution of excess schedule, and the income distribution schedules.

(AICPA adapted)

Problem 4-10 *(LO 2, 3)* **80%, equity, excess distributions, merchandise, equipment sales.** On January 1, 2015, Peanut Company acquired 80% of the common stock of Salt Company for $200,000. On this date, Salt had total owners' equity of $200,000 (including retained earnings of $100,000). During 2015 and 2016, Peanut appropriately accounted for its investment in Salt using the simple equity method.

Any excess of cost over book value is attributable to inventory (worth $12,500 more than cost), to equipment (worth $25,000 more than book value), and to goodwill. FIFO is used for inventories. The equipment has a remaining life of four years, and straight-line depreciation is used. On January 1, 2016, Peanut held merchandise acquired from Salt for $20,000. During 2016, Salt sold merchandise to Peanut for $40,000, $10,000 of which was still held by Peanut on December 31, 2016. Salt's usual gross profit is 50%.

On January 1, 2015, Peanut sold equipment to Salt at a gain of $15,000. Depreciation is being computed using the straight-line method, a 5-year life, and no salvage value.

The following trial balances were prepared for the Peanut and Salt companies for December 31, 2016:

	Peanut Company	Salt Company
Inventory, December 31	130,000	50,000
Other Current Assets	241,000	235,000
Investment in Salt Company	308,000	
Other Long-Term Investments	20,000	
Land	140,000	80,000
Buildings and Equipment	375,000	200,000
Accumulated Depreciation	(120,000)	(30,000)
Other Intangible Assets		20,000
Current Liabilities	(150,000)	(70,000)
Bonds Payable		(100,000)
Other Long-Term Liabilities	(200,000)	(50,000)
Common Stock	(200,000)	(50,000)
Paid-In Capital in Excess of Par	(100,000)	(50,000)
Retained Earnings, January 1, 2016	(320,000)	(150,000)
Sales	(600,000)	(315,000)
Cost of Goods Sold	350,000	150,000
Operating Expenses	150,000	60,000
Subsidiary Income	(84,000)	
Dividends Declared	60,000	20,000
Totals	0	0

Required ▶ ▶ ▶ ▶ ▶

Complete the worksheet for consolidated financial statements for the year ended December 31, 2016. Include the necessary determination and distribution of excess schedule and income distribution schedules.

Problem 4-11 *(LO 2, 3)* **80%, cost, excess distributions, merchandise, equipment sales.** (This is the same as Problem 4-10 except for use of the cost method.) On January 1, 2015, Peanut Company acquired 80% of the common stock of Salt Company for $200,000. On this date, Salt had total owners' equity of $200,000 (including retained earnings of $100,000). During 2015 and 2016, Peanut accounted for its investment in Salt using the cost method.

Any excess of cost over book value is attributable to inventory (worth $12,500 more than cost), to equipment (worth $25,000 more than book value), and to goodwill. FIFO is used for inventories. The equipment has a remaining life of four years, and straight-line depreciation is used.

On January 1, 2016, Peanut held merchandise acquired from Salt for $20,000. During 2016, Salt sold merchandise to Peanut for $40,000, $10,000 of which was still held by Peanut on December 31, 2016. Salt's usual gross profit is 50%.

On January 1, 2015, Peanut sold equipment to Salt at a gain of $15,000. Depreciation is being computed using the straight-line method, a 5-year life, and no salvage value.

The following trial balances were prepared for the Peanut and Salt companies for December 31, 2016:

	Peanut Company	Salt Company
Inventory, December 31	130,000	50,000
Other Current Assets	241,000	235,000
Investment in Salt Company	200,000	
Other Long-Term Investments	20,000	
Land	140,000	80,000
Buildings and Equipment	375,000	200,000
Accumulated Depreciation	(120,000)	(30,000)
Other Intangible Assets		20,000
Current Liabilities	(150,000)	(70,000)
Bonds Payable		(100,000)
Other Long-Term Liabilities	(200,000)	(50,000)
Common Stock	(200,000)	(50,000)
Paid-In Capital in Excess of Par	(100,000)	(50,000)
Retained Earnings, January 1, 2016	(280,000)	(150,000)
Sales	(600,000)	(315,000)
Cost of Goods Sold	350,000	150,000
Operating Expenses	150,000	60,000
Dividend Income	(16,000)	
Dividends Declared	60,000	20,000
Totals	0	0

Required ◀ ◀ ◀ ◀ ◀ Complete the worksheet for consolidated financial statements for the year ended December 31, 2016. Include any necessary determination and distribution of excess schedule and income distribution schedules.

Problem 4-12 *(LO 2, 3, 6)* **80%, sophisticated equity, several excess distributions, merchandise, equipment sales.** (This is the same as Problem 4-10 except for use of the sophisticated equity method.) On January 1, 2015, Peanut Company acquired 80% of the common stock of Salt Company for $200,000. On this date, Salt had total owners' equity of $200,000. During 2015 and 2016, Peanut appropriately accounted for its investment in Salt using the sophisticated equity method.

Any excess of cost over book value is attributable to inventory (worth $12,500 more than cost), to equipment (worth $25,000 more than book value), and to goodwill. FIFO is used for inventories. The equipment has a remaining life of four years, and straight-line depreciation is used.

On January 1, 2016, Peanut held merchandise acquired from Salt for $20,000. During 2016, Salt sold merchandise to Peanut for $40,000, $10,000 of which was still held by Peanut on December 31, 2016. Salt's usual gross profit is 50%.

On January 1, 2015, Peanut sold equipment to Salt at a gain of $15,000. Depreciation is being computed using the straight-line method, a 5-year life, and no salvage value.

The following trial balances were prepared for the Peanut and Salt companies for December 31, 2016:

	Peanut Company	Salt Company
Inventory, December 31	130,000	50,000
Other Current Assets	241,000	235,000
Investment in Salt Company	284,000	
Other Long-Term Investments	20,000	
Land	140,000	80,000

(continued)

	Peanut Company	Salt Company
Buildings and Equipment.	375,000	200,000
Accumulated Depreciation	(120,000)	(30,000)
Other Intangible Assets		20,000
Current Liabilities.	(150,000)	(70,000)
Bonds Payable.		(100,000)
Other Long-Term Liabilities	(200,000)	(50,000)
Common Stock	(200,000)	(50,000)
Paid-In Capital in Excess of Par	(100,000)	(50,000)
Retained Earnings, January 1, 2016.	(297,000)	(150,000)
Sales	(600,000)	(315,000)
Cost of Goods Sold	350,000	150,000
Operating Expenses	150,000	60,000
Subsidiary Income.	(83,000)	
Dividends Declared.	60,000	20,000
Totals	0	0

Required ▶ ▶ ▶ ▶ ▶   Complete the worksheet for consolidated financial statements for the year ended December 31, 2016. Include any necessary determination and distribution of excess schedule and income distribution schedules.

Use the following information for Problems 4-13 and 4-14:

On January 1, 2015, Purple Company acquired Salmon Company. Purple paid $300,000 for 80% of Salmon's common stock. On the date of acquisition, Salmon had the following balance sheet:

Salmon Company
Balance Sheet
January 1, 2015

Assets		Liabilities and Equity	
Accounts receivable	$ 50,000	Accounts payable	$ 60,000
Inventory	60,000	Bonds payable	200,000
Land.	100,000	Common stock ($1 par).	10,000
Buildings	150,000	Paid-in capital in excess of par . . .	90,000
Accumulated depreciation	(50,000)	Retained earnings	60,000
Equipment	100,000		
Accumulated depreciation	(30,000)		
Goodwill	40,000		
Total assets.	$420,000	Total liabilities and equity	$420,000

Buildings, which have a 20-year life, are understated by $100,000. Equipment, which has a 5-year life, is understated by $50,000. Any remaining excess is goodwill. Purple uses the simple equity method to account for its investment in Salmon.

Problem 4-13 *(LO 2, 3)* **80%, equity, several excess distributions, inventory, fixed assets, parent and subsidiary sales.** Refer to the preceding facts for Purple's acquisition of Salmon common stock. On January 1, 2016, Salmon held merchandise sold to it by Purple for $14,000. This beginning inventory had an applicable gross profit of 40%. During 2016, Purple sold merchandise to Salmon for $60,000. On December 31, 2016, Salmon held $12,000 of this merchandise in its inventory. This ending inventory had an applicable gross profit of 35%. Salmon owed Purple $8,000 on December 31 as a result of this intercompany sale.

Purple held $12,000 worth of merchandise in its beginning inventory from sales from Salmon. This beginning inventory had an applicable gross profit of 25%. During 2016, Salmon sold merchandise to Purple for $30,000. Purple held $16,000 of this inventory at the end of the year. This ending inventory had an applicable gross profit of 30%. Purple owed Salmon $6,000 on December 31 as a result of this intercompany sale.

On January 1, 2015, Purple sold equipment to Salmon at a profit of $40,000. Depreciation on this equipment is computed over an 8-year life using the straight-line method.

On January 1, 2016, Salmon sold equipment with a book value of $30,000 to Purple for $54,000. This equipment has a 6-year life and is depreciated using the straight-line method.

Purple and Salmon had the following trial balances on December 31, 2016:

	Purple Company	Salmon Company
Cash	92,400	57,500
Accounts Receivable	130,000	36,000
Inventory	105,000	76,000
Land	100,000	100,000
Investment in Salmon Company	381,200	
Buildings	800,000	150,000
Accumulated Depreciation	(250,000)	(60,000)
Equipment	210,000	220,000
Accumulated Depreciation	(115,000)	(80,000)
Goodwill		40,000
Accounts Payable	(70,000)	(78,000)
Bonds Payable		(200,000)
Common Stock	(100,000)	(10,000)
Paid-In Capital in Excess of Par	(800,000)	(90,000)
Retained Earnings, January 1, 2016	(325,000)	(142,000)
Sales	(800,000)	(350,000)
Cost of Goods Sold	450,000	208,500
Depreciation Expense—Buildings	30,000	5,000
Depreciation Expense—Equipment	25,000	23,000
Other Expenses	140,000	92,000
Interest Expense		16,000
Gain on Sale of Fixed Asset		(24,000)
Subsidiary Income	(23,600)	
Dividends Declared	20,000	10,000
Totals	0	0

1. Prepare a value analysis and a determination and distribution of excess schedule for the investment in Salmon. ◄ ◄ ◄ ◄ ◄ **Required**

2. Complete a consolidated worksheet for Purple Company and its subsidiary Salmon Company as of December 31, 2016. Prepare supporting amortization and income distribution schedules.

Problem 4-14 *(LO 2, 3)* **80%, equity, several excess distributions, inventory, fixed assets, parent and subsidiary sales.** Refer to the preceding facts for Purple's acquisition of Salmon common stock. On January 1, 2017, Salmon held merchandise sold to it from Purple for $12,000. This beginning inventory had an applicable gross profit of 35%. During 2017, Purple sold merchandise to Salmon for $55,000. On December 31, 2017, Salmon held $10,000 of this merchandise in its inventory. This ending inventory had an applicable gross profit of 40%. Salmon owed Purple $7,500 on December 31 as a result of this intercompany sale.

Purple held $16,000 worth of merchandise in its January 1, 2017, inventory from sales from Salmon. This beginning inventory had an applicable gross profit of 30%. During 2017, Salmon sold merchandise to Purple for $35,000. Purple held $20,000 of this inventory at the end of the year. This ending inventory had an applicable gross profit of 35%. Purple owed Salmon $5,000 on December 31 as a result of this intercompany sale.

On January 1, 2015, Purple sold equipment to Salmon at a profit of $40,000. Depreciation on this equipment is computed over an 8-year life using the straight-line method.

On January 1, 2016, Salmon sold equipment with a book value of $30,000 to Purple for $54,000. This equipment has a 6-year life and is depreciated using the straight-line method. Purple and Salmon had the following trial balances on December 31, 2017:

	Purple Company	Salmon Company
Cash	195,400	53,500
Accounts Receivable	140,000	53,000
Inventory	140,000	81,000
Land	100,000	60,000
Investment in Salmon Company	443,600	
Buildings	800,000	150,000
Accumulated Depreciation	(280,000)	(65,000)
Equipment	150,000	220,000
Accumulated Depreciation	(115,000)	(103,000)
Goodwill		40,000
Accounts Payable	(25,000)	(50,000)
Bonds Payable		(100,000)
Common Stock	(100,000)	(10,000)
Paid-In Capital in Excess of Par	(800,000)	(90,000)
Retained Earnings, January 1, 2017	(510,000)	(169,500)
Sales	(850,000)	(500,000)
Cost of Goods Sold	480,000	290,000
Depreciation Expense—Buildings	30,000	5,000
Depreciation Expense—Equipment	15,000	23,000
Other Expenses	210,000	94,000
Interest Expense		8,000
Subsidiary Income	(64,000)	
Dividends Declared	40,000	10,000
Totals	0	0

Required ▶ ▶ ▶ ▶ ▶

1. Prepare a value analysis and a determination and distribution of excess schedule for the investment in Salmon.
2. Complete a consolidated worksheet for Purple Company and its subsidiary Salmon Company as of December 31, 2017. Prepare supporting amortization and income distribution schedules.

APPENDIX PROBLEMS

Problem 4A-1 *(LO 2, 3, 7)* **Vertical worksheet, 100%, cost, fixed asset and merchandise sales.** Arther Corporation acquired all of the outstanding $10 par voting common stock of Trent Inc., on January 1, 2016, in exchange for 50,000 shares of its $10 par voting common stock. On December 31, 2015, the common stock of Arther had a closing market price of $15 per share on a national stock exchange. The retained earnings balance of Trent Inc., was $156,000 on the date of the acquisition. Both companies continued to operate as separate business entities maintaining separate accounting records with years ending December 31.

On December 31, 2018, after year-end adjustments but before the nominal accounts were closed, the companies had the following condensed statements:

	Arther Corporation	Trent, Inc.
Income Statement:		
Sales	$(1,900,000)	$(1,500,000)
Dividend Income (from Trent, Inc.)	(40,000)	
Cost of Goods Sold	1,180,000	870,000
Operating Expenses (includes depreciation)	550,000	440,000
Net Income.	$ (210,000)	$ (190,000)
Retained Earnings:		
Retained Earnings, January 1, 2018.	$ (250,000)	$ (206,000)
Net Income	(210,000)	(190,000)
Dividends Paid.		40,000
Balance, December 31, 2018.	$ (460,000)	$ (356,000)
Balance Sheet:		
Cash	$ 285,000	$ 150,000
Accounts Receivable (net)	430,000	350,000
Inventories	530,000	410,000
Land, Building, and Equipment	660,000	680,000
Accumulated Depreciation	(185,000)	(210,000)
Investment in Trent Inc., (at cost)	750,000	
Accounts Payable and Accrued Expenses	(670,000)	(544,000)
Common Stock ($10 par)	(1,200,000)	(400,000)
Additional Paid-In Capital in Excess of Par	(140,000)	(80,000)
Retained Earnings, December 31, 2018.	(460,000)	(356,000)
Totals	$ 0	$ 0

Additional information is as follows:

a. There have been no changes in the common stock and additional paid-in capital in excess of par accounts since the one necessitated in 2016 by Arther's acquisition of Trent, Inc.

b. At the acquisition date, the market value of Trent's machinery exceeded book value by $54,000. This excess is being amortized over the asset's estimated average remaining life of six years. The fair value of Trent's other assets and liabilities were equal to book value. Any remaining excess is goodwill.

c. On July 1, 2016, Arther sold a warehouse facility to Trent for $129,000 in cash. At the date of sale, Arther's book values were $33,000 for the land and $66,000 for the building. Trent allocated the $129,000 purchase price to the land for $43,000 and to the building for $86,000. Trent is depreciating the building over its estimated 5-year remaining useful life by the straight-line method with no salvage value.

d. During 2018, Arther purchased merchandise from Trent at an aggregate invoice price of $180,000, which included a 100% markup on Trent's cost. On December 31, 2018, Arther owed Trent $75,000 on these purchases, and $36,000 of the merchandise purchased remained in Arther's inventory.

Complete the vertical worksheet necessary to prepare the consolidated income statement ◄ ◄ ◄ ◄ ◄ **Required** and retained earnings statement for the year ended December 31, 2018, and a consolidated balance sheet as of December 31, 2018, for Arther Corporation and its subsidiary. Formal consolidated statements and journal entries are not required. Include the determination and distribution of excess schedule and the income distribution schedules.

(AICPA adapted)

Problem 4A-2 *(LO 2, 3, 7)* **Vertical worksheet, 80%, cost, several excess distributions, merchandise, equipment sales.** (This is similar to Problem 4-10; it uses the simple equity method and vertical worksheet format.) On January 1, 2015, Peanut Company acquired 80% of the common stock of Salt Company for $200,000. On this date, Salt had total owners' equity of $200,000, which included retained earnings of $100,000. During 2015 and 2016, Peanut accounted for its investment in Salt using the simple equity method.

Any excess of cost over book value is attributable to inventory (worth $12,500 more than cost), to equipment (worth $25,000 more than book value), and to goodwill. FIFO is used for inventories. The equipment has a remaining life of four years, and straight-line depreciation is used. Any remaining excess is attributed to goodwill.

On January 1, 2016, Peanut held merchandise acquired from Salt for $20,000. During 2016, Salt sold merchandise to Peanut for $40,000, $10,000 of which was still held by Peanut on December 31, 2016. Salt's usual gross profit is 50%.

On January 1, 2015, Peanut sold equipment to Salt at a gain of $15,000. Depreciation is being computed using the straight-line method, a 5-year life, and no salvage value.

The following condensed statements were prepared for the Peanut and Salt companies for December 31, 2016.

	Peanut Company	Salt Company
Income Statement:		
Net Sales	$ (600,000)	$(315,000)
Cost of Goods Sold	350,000	150,000
Operating Expenses	150,000	60,000
Subsidiary Income	(84,000)	
Net Income	$ (184,000)	$(105,000)
Retained Earnings Statement:		
Balance, January 1, 2016	$ (320,000)	$(150,000)
Net Income (from above)	(184,000)	(105,000)
Dividends Declared	60,000	20,000
Balance, December 31, 2016	$ (444,000)	$(235,000)
Consolidated Balance Sheet:		
Inventory, December 31	$ 130,000	$ 50,000
Other Current Assets	241,000	235,000
Investment in Salt Company	308,000	
Other Long-Term Investments	20,000	
Land	140,000	80,000
Building and Equipment	375,000	200,000
Accumulated Depreciation	(120,000)	(30,000)
Other Intangible Assets		20,000
Current Liabilities	(150,000)	(70,000)
Bonds Payable		(100,000)
Other Long-Term Liabilities	(200,000)	(50,000)
Common Stock	(200,000)	(50,000)
Paid-In Capital in Excess of Par	(100,000)	(50,000)
Retained Earnings, December 31, 2016	(444,000)	(235,000)
Totals	$ 0	$ 0

Required ▶ ▶ ▶ ▶ ▶   Complete the worksheet for consolidated financial statements for the year ended December 31, 2016. Include any necessary determination and distribution of excess schedule and income distribution schedules.

CASES

The Noncontrolling Interest's Concern
with Intercompany Transactions

Case 4-1

Henderson Window Company was a privately held corporation until January 1, 2015. On January 1, 2015, Cool Glass Company acquired a 70% interest in Henderson at a price well in excess of book value. There were some minor differences between book and fair values, but the bulk of the excess was attributed to goodwill.

Harvey Henderson did not sell his shares to Cool Glass as a part of the January 1, 2015, Cool Glass purchase. He wanted to remain a Henderson shareholder since he felt Henderson was a more profitable and stable company than was Cool Glass. Harvey remains an employee of Henderson Window, working in an accounting capacity.

Harvey is concerned about some accounting issues that he feels are detrimental to his ownership interest. Harvey told you that Henderson always bought most of its glass from Cool Glass. He never felt the prices charged for the glass were unreasonable. Since the purchase of Henderson by Cool Glass, he feels the price charged to Henderson by Cool Glass has risen dramatically and that it is out of step with what would be paid to other glass suppliers.

The second concern is the sale of a large Henderson warehouse to Cool Glass for less than what Harvey would consider to be the market value. Harvey agrees that the sale is reasonable since the new just-in-time order system has made the space unnecessary. He just feels the sale price is below market.

Harvey did make his concerns known to the president of Cool Glass. The president made several points. First, she said that the price charged for the glass was a little high, but Harvey should consider its high quality. She went on to say that the transfer price washes out in the annual report, and it has no impact on reported net income of the corporation. She also stated that the warehouse sale was at a low price, but there was a reason. It was a good year, and a large gain wasn't needed. She would rather have lower depreciation in future years. Her last point was: "We paid a big price for Henderson. We are stuck with a big investment in goodwill, and our stockholders expect a return on that investment. We should get some benefits from it!"

Write a memo to Harvey Henderson suggesting how he might respond to the president's comments. ◄ ◄ ◄ ◄ ◄ **Required**

Chapter 5

Intercompany Transactions: Bonds and Leases

C H A P T E R

Learning Objectives

When you have completed this chapter, you should be able to

1. Explain the alternatives a parent company has if it wishes to acquire outstanding subsidiary bonds from outside owners.

2. Follow the procedures used to retire intercompany bonds on a consolidated worksheet.

3. Explain why a parent company would lease assets to the subsidiary.

4. Show how to eliminate intercompany operating lease transactions from the consolidated statements.

5. Eliminate intercompany capital leases on the consolidated worksheet.

6. Demonstrate an understanding of the process used to defer intercompany profits on sales-type leases.

7. Explain the complications caused by unguaranteed residual values with intercompany leases. (Appendix)

This chapter focuses on intercompany transactions that create a long-term debtor-creditor relationship between the members of a consolidated group. The usual impetus for these transactions is the parent's ability to borrow larger amounts of capital at more favorable terms than would be available to the subsidiary. In addition, the parent company may desire to manage all capital needs of the consolidated company for better control of all capital sources. Intercompany leasing with the parent as the lessor also may be motivated by centralized asset management and credit control.

Intercompany bond holdings will be analyzed first. Here, one member of the consolidated group, usually the subsidiary, has issued bonds that appear on its balance sheet as long-term liabilities. Another member, typically the parent company, may purchase the bonds and list them on its balance sheet as an investment. However, when consolidated statements are prepared, the intercompany purchase should be viewed as a retirement of the bonds. Only bonds that involve nonaffiliated companies may appear in the consolidated statements.

Consideration of intercompany leasing of assets will follow the bond coverage. In this case, one member of the consolidated group purchases the asset and leases it to another member. While the leasing transaction is recorded as such on the separate books of the affiliates, the lease has no substance from a consolidated viewpoint. Only a lease that involves a nonaffiliated company may appear in the consolidated statements.

INTERCOMPANY INVESTMENT IN BONDS

To secure long-term funds, one member of a consolidated group may sell its bonds directly to another member of the group. Clearly, such a transaction results in intercompany debt that must be eliminated from the consolidated statements. On the worksheet, the investment in bonds recorded by one company must be eliminated against the bonds payable of the other. In addition, the applicable interest expense recorded by one affiliate must be eliminated against

1

O B J E C T I V E

Explain the alternatives a parent company has if it wishes to acquire outstanding subsidiary bonds from outside owners.

the applicable interest revenue recorded by the other affiliate. Interest accruals recorded on the books of the separate companies must be eliminated as well.

There are situations where one affiliate (usually the subsidiary) has outstanding bonds that have been purchased by parties that are not members of the affiliated group, and a decision is made by another affiliate (usually the parent) to purchase these bonds. The simplest way to acquire subsidiary bonds from outsiders is for the parent to loan money to the subsidiary so that the subsidiary can retire the bonds. From an accounting standpoint, this transaction is easy to record. The former debt is retired and a new, long-term intercompany debt originates. The only procedures required on future consolidated worksheets involve the elimination of the resulting intercompany debt.

A more complicated method is to have the parent purchase the subsidiary bonds from the outside parties and to hold them as an investment. This method creates an investment in subsidiary bonds. Each affiliate continues to accrue and record interest on the bonds. While the intercompany bonds are treated as a liability on the subsidiary books and as an investment on the parent's books, from a consolidated viewpoint the bonds have been retired and the debt to outside parties has been liquidated. The purchase of intercompany bonds has the following ramifications when consolidating:

1. Consolidated statements prepared for the period in which the bonds are purchased must portray the intercompany purchase as a retirement of the bonds. It is possible, but unlikely, that the bonds will be purchased at book value. There usually will be a gain or loss on retirement; this gain or loss is recognized on the consolidated income statement.
2. For all periods during which the intercompany investment exists, the intercompany bonds, interest accruals, and interest expense/revenue must be eliminated since the bonds no longer exist from a consolidated viewpoint.

The complexity of the elimination procedures depends on whether the bonds originally were issued at face value or at a premium or discount. Additionally, one must exercise extra care in the application of elimination procedures when only a portion of the outstanding subsidiary bonds is purchased by the parent company.

Bonds Originally Issued at Face Value

2

OBJECTIVE

Follow the procedures used to retire intercompany bonds on a consolidated worksheet.

When bonds are issued at face value by a subsidiary to outside parties, contract (nominal) interest agrees with the effective, or market, interest, and no amortizations of issuance premiums or discounts need to be recorded. However, subsequent to the issuance, the market rate of interest most likely will deviate from the contract rate. Thus, while there is no original issuance premium or discount, there will be what could be termed an *investment premium* or *discount* resulting from the intercompany purchase of the bonds.

To illustrate the procedures required for intercompany bonds originally issued at face value, assume a subsidiary, Company S, issued 5-year, 8% bonds at a face value of $100,000 to outside parties on January 1, 2015. Interest is paid on January 1 for the preceding year. On January 2, 2017, the parent, Company P, purchased the bonds from the outside parties for $103,600.

Company S will continue to list the $100,000 bonded debt and to record interest expense of $8,000 during 2017, 2018, and 2019. However, Company P will record a bond investment of $103,600 and will amortize $1,200 per year, for the remaining life of the bond, by reducing the investment account and adjusting interest revenue. Though the interest method of amortization is preferable, the straight-line method is permitted if results are not materially different. This initial example and most others in this chapter use the straight-line method in order to simplify analysis. A summary example is used to demonstrate the interest method of amortization.

Although the investment and liability accounts continue to exist on the separate books of the affiliated companies, retirement has occurred from a consolidated viewpoint. Debt with a book value of $100,000 was retired by a payment of $103,600, and there is a $3,600 loss on retirement. If a consolidated worksheet is prepared on the day the bonds are purchased, Bonds Payable would be eliminated against Investment in Company S Bonds, and a *loss on retirement* would be reported on the consolidated income statement. The following abbreviated worksheet prepared as of January 2, 2017, displays the procedures used to retire the bonds as part of the elimination process:

	Partial Trial Balance		Eliminations & Adjustments	
	Company P	Company S	Dr.	Cr.
Investment in Company S Bonds	103,600			(B) 103,600
Bonds Payable		(100,000)	(B) 100,000	
Loss on Bond Retirement			(B) 3,600	

This partial worksheet, prepared on January 2, 2017, is only hypothetical since, in reality, there will be no consolidated worksheet prepared until December 31, 2017, the end of the period. During 2017, Companies P and S will record the transactions for interest as follows:

Company P			Company S		
Interest Receivable...............	8,000		Interest Expense.............	8,000	
Investment in Company S Bonds ...		1,200	Interest Payable		8,000
Interest Income................		6,800	To record interest expense.		
To record interest revenue, net of $1,200 per-year premium amortization.					

These entries will be reflected in the trial balances of the December 31, 2017, consolidated worksheet, shown in Worksheet 5-1 on pages 284 and 285. Note that Investment in Company S Bonds reflects the premium amortization since the balance is $102,400 ($103,600 original cost − $1,200 amortization). In this worksheet, it is assumed that Investment in Company S Stock reflects a 90% interest purchased at a price equal to the book value of the underlying equity, and the simple equity method is used by Company P to record the investment in stock.

Worksheet 5-1: page 284

Entries (CY1) and (EL) eliminate the intercompany stock investment. Entry (B1) eliminates the intercompany bonds at their year-end balances and the intercompany interest expense and revenue recorded during the year. In journal entry form, elimination entries are as follows:

(CY1) Eliminate current-year equity income:
Subsidiary Income.................................... 10,800
Investment in Company S Stock......................... 10,800

(EL) Eliminate 90% of subsidiary equity:
Common Stock ($10 par)—Company S.................... 72,000
Retained Earnings, January 1, 2017—Company S 18,000
Investment in Company S Stock......................... 90,000

(B1) Eliminate intercompany bonds and interest expense:
Bonds Payable.. 100,000
Investment in Company S Bonds 102,400
Interest Income...................................... 6,800
Interest Expense..................................... 8,000
Loss on Bond Retirement 3,600

(B2) Eliminate intercompany accrued interest:
Interest Payable..................................... 8,000
Interest Receivable.................................... 8,000

The amount of the gain or loss is the sum of the difference between the remaining book value of the investment on bonds compared to the debt and the difference between interest expense and debt. For this example:

Investment in Bonds Balance, December 31, 2017	$102,400	
Bonds Payable, December 31, 2017	100,000	$2,400
Interest Expense, 2017	$ 8,000	
Interest Revenue, 2017	6,800	1,200
Loss, January 2, 2017		$3,600

As a result of the elimination entries, the consolidated income statement will include the retirement loss but will exclude intercompany interest payments and accruals. The consolidated balance sheet will not list the intercompany bonds payable or investment in bonds accounts.

The only remaining problem is the distribution of consolidated net income to the controlling and noncontrolling interests. The income distribution schedule shows Company S absorbing all of the retirement loss. It is most common to view the purchasing affiliate as a mere agent of the issuing affiliate. Therefore, it is the issuer, not the purchaser, who must bear the entire gain or loss on retirement. Even though the debt is retired from a consolidated viewpoint, it still exists internally. Company P has a right to collect the interest as part of its share of Company S's operations. Based on the value of the debt on January 2, 2017, the interest expense/revenue is $6,800. The interest expense of $8,000 recorded by Company S must be corrected to reflect the internal interest expense of $6,800. The income distribution schedule increases the income of Company S to reflect the adjustment ($1,200) to interest expense. It should be noted that the retirement loss borne by Company S will entirely offset the adjustments to interest expense by the time the bonds mature. If the parent, Company P, had issued the bonds to outside parties and if the subsidiary, Company S, later had purchased them, the only change would be that the income distribution schedule of Company P would absorb the loss on retirement and the interest adjustment.

Worksheet 5-2: page 286
The worksheet procedures that would be needed at the end of 2018 are shown in Worksheet 5-2 on pages 286 and 287. The interest revenue and expense have been recorded on the books of the separate companies. The investment in Company S bonds account on the parent's books reflects its book value at the end of 2018.

The eliminations in journal entry form are as follows:

(CY1)	Eliminate current-year equity income:		
	Subsidiary Income	19,800	
	Investment in Company S Stock		19,800
(EL)	Eliminate 90% of subsidiary equity:		
	Common Stock ($10 par)—Company S	72,000	
	Retained Earnings, January 1, 2018—Company S	28,800	
	Investment in Company S Stock		100,800
(B1)	Eliminate intercompany bonds and interest expense:		
	Bonds Payable	100,000	
	Investment in Company S Bonds		101,200
	Interest Income	6,800	
	Interest Expense		8,000
	Retained Earnings, January 1, 2018—Company P	2,160	
	Retained Earnings, January 1, 2018—Company S	240	
(B2)	Eliminate intercompany accrued interest:		
	Interest Payable	8,000	
	Interest Receivable		8,000

Entry (B1) eliminates the intercompany bonds at their year-end balances and the intercompany interest expense and revenue. Recall that the original retirement loss was $3,600 when the bonds had three years to maturity. By the start of the second period, 2018, $1,200 of that loss was already amortized on the separate books of the affiliates. The loss remaining is $2,400 [which is verified in the explanation to entry (B1) in Worksheet 5-2]. This remaining loss is debited to Retained Earnings since the retirement occurred in a prior period. The adjustment is allocated to noncontrolling and controlling beginning retained earnings since the bonds were issued by the subsidiary.

The 2018 consolidated income statement will not include intercompany interest expense or revenue. The income distribution schedules for Worksheet 5-2 reflect the fact that the debt still existed internally during the period. However, the interest expense recorded by Company S is reduced to reflect the interest cost based on the January 2, 2017, purchase price.

If Company S was the purchaser and Company P the issuer of the bonds, Worksheet 5-2 would differ as follows:

1. The January 1, 2018, retained earnings adjustment would be absorbed completely by the controlling retained earnings, since the parent company would be the issuer absorbing the loss.
2. The income distribution schedule of the parent would contain the interest adjustment.

Bonds Not Originally Issued at Face Value

The principles of eliminating intercompany investments in bonds are not altered by the existence of a premium or discount stemming from original issuance. The numerical calculations just become more complex. To illustrate, assume Company S issued $100,000 of 5-year, 8% bonds on January 1, 2015. The market interest rate approximated 9%, and, as a result, the bonds sold at a discount of $3,890. Interest is paid each December 31. On each interest payment date, the discount is amortized $778 ($3,890 ÷ 5 years) by decreasing the discount and increasing interest expense. On December 31, 2017, the balance of the discount is $1,556 [$3,890 − (3 × $778 annual amortization)].

The parent, Company P, purchased the bonds for $103,600 on December 31, 2017, after interest had been paid. The parent will amortize $1,800 of the investment each subsequent December 31, reducing the parent's interest income to $6,200 ($8,000 cash − $1,800 amortization) for 2018 and 2019.

The following abbreviated December 31, 2017 (date of purchase), worksheet lists the investment in Company S bonds account, the bonds payable account, and the remaining issuance discount. Eliminating the $103,600 price paid for the bonds by Company P against the book value of $98,444 ($100,000 − $1,556) creates a loss on retirement of $5,156, which is carried to consolidated net income. Worksheet procedures may be aided by linking the bonds payable and the related discount or premium on the worksheet. This is done on our worksheets by circling the amounts in the trial balance and in the eliminations.

	Partial Trial Balance		Eliminations & Adjustments	
	Company P	Company S	Dr.	Cr.
Investment in Company S Bonds	103,600			**(B) 103,600**
Bonds Payable (8%)		(100,000)	**(B) 100,000**	
Discount on Bonds Payable		1,556		**(B)** 1,556
Loss on Bond Retirement			**(B)** 5,156	
Interest Expense		8,778*		

*$8,000 cash + $778 straight-line amortization.

Interest expense on the books of Company S is extended to the consolidated income statement, since this interest was incurred as a result of transactions with outside parties. There would be no interest adjustment for 2017, since the bonds were not purchased by the parent until December 31, 2017. The income distribution schedules accompanying the worksheet would assess the retirement loss against the issuer, Company S.

Worksheet 5-3: page 288

The implications of these intercompany bonds on the 2018 consolidated worksheet are reflected in Worksheet 5-3 on pages 288 and 289. Assume Company P acquired a 90% interest in the common stock of Company S at a price equal to the book value of the underlying equity. The simple equity method is used by the parent to record the investment in the stock of Company S. The trial balances include the following items:

1. The investment in Company S bonds at its amortized December 31, 2018, balance of $101,800 ($103,600 − $1,800 amortization);
2. The interest revenue (adjusted for amortization) of $6,200 on the books of Company P;
3. The discount on bonds account at its amortized December 31, 2018, balance of $778; and
4. The interest expense (adjusted for discount amortization) of $8,778 ($8,000 cash + $778 amortization) on the books of Company S.
5. There is no accrued interest receivable/payable since interest was paid on December 31, 2018.

The eliminations in journal entry form are as follows:

(CY1)	Eliminate current-year equity income:		
	Subsidiary Income.	8,874	
	Investment in Company S Stock		8,874
(EL)	Eliminate 90% of subsidiary equity:		
	Common Stock ($10 par)—Company S	36,000	
	Retained Earnings, January 1, 2018—Company S	99,000	
	Investment in Company S Stock		135,000
(B)	Eliminate intercompany bonds and interest expense:		
	Bonds Payable.	100,000	
	Discount on Bonds		778
	Investment in Company S Bonds		101,800
	Interest Income.	6,200	
	Interest Expense		8,778
	Retained Earnings, January 1, 2018—Company P	4,640	
	Retained Earnings, January 1, 2018—Company S	516	

Entry (B) eliminates the investment in bonds against the bonds payable and the applicable remaining discount. Entry (B) also eliminates interest expense and revenue. Be sure to understand the calculation of the adjustment to beginning retained earnings that is explained in the entry (B) information. The loss at the start of the year is the sum of the loss remaining at year-end and the loss amortized on the books of the separate affiliates during the year.

Again, the consolidated income statement does not include intercompany interest. However, the Company S income distribution schedule does reflect the adjustment of Company S's interest expense. The original $8,778 interest expense has been replaced by a $6,200 expense, based on the purchase price paid by Company P. The smaller interest expense compensates the subsidiary for the retirement loss absorbed in a previous period.

Purchase of Only a Portion of the Bonds

The preceding examples assume that the parent company purchases all of the outstanding bonds of the subsidiary. In such cases, all of the bonds are retired on the worksheet. There may be cases, however, where the parent purchases only a portion of the subsidiary's outstanding bonds. Suppose, for example, that the parent purchased 80% of the subsidiary's outstanding bonds. Only the 80% interest in the bonds would be eliminated on the consolidated worksheet, and only the interest expense and revenue applicable to 80% of the bonds would be eliminated on the worksheet. **The 20% interest in the subsidiary bonds owned by persons outside the control group remains as a valid debt of the consolidated company and should not be**

eliminated. It is a common error for students to eliminate the 80% interest in intercompany bonds owned by a parent against 100% of the bonds issued by the subsidiary. Such a mistake improperly eliminates valid debt and greatly miscalculates the gain or loss on retirement. It also should be noted that the interest paid to persons outside the control group should remain a part of the consolidated statements. Only the interest paid to the affiliated company is to be eliminated.

Interest Method of Amortization

The procedures used to eliminate intercompany bonds are not altered by the interest method of amortization; only the dollar values change. To illustrate the calculations, assume that Company S issued $100,000 of 5-year, 8% bonds on January 1, 2015. The market interest rate on that date was 9%, so the bonds sold at a discount of $3,890. Interest on the bonds is paid each December 31. The discount amortization for the term of the bonds follows:

Year	Debt Balance, January 1	Effective Interest	Nominal Interest	Discount Amortization
2015	$96,110	$8,650 (0.09 × $96,110)	$8,000	$ 650
2016	96,760 ($96,110 + $650)	8,708 (0.09 × $96,760)	8,000	708
2017	97,468 ($96,760 + $708)	8,772 (0.09 × $97,468)	8,000	772
2018	98,240 ($97,468 + $772)	8,842 (0.09 × $98,240)	8,000	842
2019	99,082 ($98,240 + $842)	8,918* (0.09 × $99,082)	8,000	918
*Adjusted for rounding.				$3,890

On December 31, 2017, after interest had been paid, the bonds were purchased by parent Company P at a price to yield 6%. Based on present value computations, $103,667 was paid for the bonds. The premium on the bonds would be amortized by Company P as follows:

Year	Investment Balance, January 1	Effective Interest	Nominal Interest	Premium Amortization
2018	$103,667	$6,220 (0.06 × $103,667)	$8,000	$1,780
2019	101,887 ($103,667 − $1,780)	6,113 (0.06 × $101,887)	8,000	1,887
				$3,667

The following abbreviated December 31, 2017 (date of purchase) worksheet lists the investment in Company S bonds account, the bonds payable account, and the remaining issuance discount. Eliminating the $103,667 price paid by Company P against the book value of $98,240 ($100,000 − $1,760) creates a loss on retirement of $5,427 that is carried to consolidated net income.

	Partial Trial Balance		Eliminations & Adjustments			
	Company P	Company S	Dr.		Cr.	
Investment in Company S Bonds	103,667				(B)	103,667
Bonds Payable, 8%		(100,000)	(B)	100,000		
Discount on Bonds Payable		1,760			(B)	1,760
Loss on Bond Retirement			(B)	5,427		
Interest Expense		8,772*				

*See preceding discount amortization schedule for issuer.

Worksheet 5-4: page 290   The differences in the 2018 consolidated worksheet caused by the interest method of amortization are shown in Worksheet 5-4 on pages 290 and 291. Note particularly the change in the Company S income distribution schedule. The original 9% interest, totaling $8,842, has been replaced by the $6,220 of interest calculated using the 6% rate.

The eliminations in journal entry form are as follows:

(CY1)   Eliminate current-year equity income:
      Subsidiary Income. 8,820
        Investment in Company S Stock 8,820

(EL)   Eliminate 90% of subsidiary equity:
      Common Stock ($10 par)—Company S 36,000
      Retained Earnings, January 1, 2018—Company S 99,180
        Investment in Company S Stock 135,180

(B)   Eliminate intercompany bonds and interest expense:
      Bonds Payable. 100,000
        Discount on Bonds 918
        Investment in Company S Bonds 101,887
      Interest Income. 6,220
        Interest Expense 8,842
      Retained Earnings, January 1, 2018—Company P 4,884
      Retained Earnings, January 1, 2018—Company S 543

REFLECTION

- The parent can effectively retire subsidiary bonds by lending money to the subsidiary and letting the subsidiary purchase the bonds from existing owners or by simply buying the bonds from existing owners.

- When the parent buys subsidiary bonds, the bonds cease to exist from a consolidated viewpoint. They are retired on the consolidated worksheet by elimination.

- When the intercompany bonds are eliminated, there will be a difference between the amortized cost and the price paid; this creates a gain or loss on retirement.

- In periods subsequent to the intercompany purchase, the bonds must continue to be eliminated, and retained earnings is adjusted for the remaining retirement gain or loss that has not already been amortized.

- Intercompany interest expense/revenue and accrued interest receivable/payable are also eliminated.

INTERCOMPANY LEASES

Intercompany leases have become one of the most frequently encountered types of transactions between affiliated companies. It is particularly common for parent companies with substantial financial resources to acquire major assets and to lease the assets to their subsidiaries. This action may occur because the financially stronger parent may be able to both purchase and finance assets on more favorable terms. Also, the parent company may desire close control over plant assets and may prefer centralized ownership and management of assets. Leasing becomes a mechanism through which the parent can convey the use of centrally owned assets to subsidiaries. Some companies achieve centralized asset management by forming separate leasing subsidiaries whose major function is to lease assets to affiliated companies. When such subsidiaries exist, they are consolidated automatically with the parent regardless of the ownership percentage of the parent.[1]

3

OBJECTIVE

Explain why a parent company would lease assets to the subsidiary.

Operating Leases

Consolidation procedures for intercompany leases depend on the original recording of the lease by the separate companies. When an operating lease exists, the lessor has recorded the purchase of the asset and depreciates it. The lessor records rent revenue, while the lessee records rent expense. In such cases, it is necessary in the consolidation process to eliminate the intercompany rent expense/revenue and any related rent receivable/payable. The lessor's asset and related accumulated depreciation should be reclassified as a normal productive asset rather than as property under an operating lease. As an example, assume the parent, Company P, has both productive equipment used in its own operations and equipment that is under operating lease to a subsidiary, Company S. The following partial worksheet may be used to analyze required consolidation procedures:

4

OBJECTIVE

Show how to eliminate intercompany operating lease transactions from the consolidated statements.

	Partial Trial Balance		Eliminations & Adjustments	
	Company P	Company S	Dr.	Cr.
Equipment	800,000			
Accumulated Depreciation—Equipment	(300,000)			
Rent Receivable	1,200			(OL2) 1,200
Rent Payable		(1,200)	(OL2) 1,200	
Rent Income	(14,400)		(OL1) 14,400	
Rent Expense		14,400		(OL1) 14,400
Depreciation Expense	50,000			

Eliminations and Adjustments:

(OL1) Eliminate intercompany rent expense and revenue of $1,200 per month.
(OL2) Eliminate one month's accrued rent.

No adjustments are made in the income distribution schedules as a result of operating leases. The eliminations made on the worksheet do not change the amount of income or the distribution of income between the noncontrolling and controlling interests.

---

1 FASB 840-10-45-10, *Leases—Overall—Other Presentation Matters* (Norwalk CT, 2010).

Capitalized Leases

5

O B J E C T I V E

Eliminate intercompany
capital leases on the
consolidated worksheet.

Consolidation procedures become more complicated when the lease is recorded as a capital lease by the lessee and as a direct-financing or sales-type lease by the lessor. The lessee records both an asset and intercompany long-term debt. Generally, the criteria for determining when a lease is a capital lease are the same for affiliated companies as for independent companies. However, when the terms of the lease are significantly affected by the fact that the lessee and lessor are affiliates, the usual criteria for classification of leases do not apply. Lease terms could be considered "significantly affected" when they could not reasonably be expected to occur between independent companies.[2] For example, a parent might lease to its subsidiary at a rent far below the market rate, or a parent might rent a highly specialized machine to its subsidiary on a month-to-month basis. Typically, such specialized machinery would be leased only on a long-term lease promising a full recovery of cost to the lessor, since there would be no use for the machine by other lessees if it were returned to the lessor. The month-to-month lease is possible only because the parent's control of the subsidiary assures a continued flow of rent payments. When, in the accountant's judgment, the terms of the lease are affected significantly by the parent-subsidiary relationship, the normal criteria are not used and the transaction is recorded so as to reflect its true economic substance.[3] Usually, in these circumstances, the lessee is viewed as having purchased the asset using funds borrowed from the lessor.

Consolidation Procedures for Direct-Financing Leases. A direct-financing lease is viewed as a unique type of asset transfer by the lessor, who accepts a long-term receivable from the lessee as consideration for the asset received by the lessee. There is no profit or loss to the lessor on the transfer, only future interest revenue as payments become due.

Prior to studying consolidated worksheet procedures, we will analyze the entries made by the affiliated lessee and lessor. In its simplest form, a direct-financing lease is recorded by the lessee as an asset and as debt. The lessor records the lease as a receivable from the lessee. If all payments to be received by the lessor will come from or are guaranteed by the original lessee, the present value of the net receivable recorded by the lessor will equal the present value of the payable recorded by the lessee, and the interest rates used to amortize the debt will be equal.

To illustrate, assume Company S is an 80%-owned subsidiary of Company P. On January 1, 2015, Company P purchased a machine for $5,851 and leased it to Company S. The terms of the direct-financing lease provide for rental payments of $2,000 per year at the beginning of each period and allow the lessee to exercise an option to purchase the machine for $1,000 at the end of 2017. The $1,000 purchase option is considered a bargain purchase option that will be exercised and is included in the minimum lease payments. The implicit interest rate (which equates all payments, including the bargain purchase option, to the lessor's purchase cost) is 16%. The lessee will depreciate the capitalized cost of the machine over five years, using the straight-line method. The lessee may use a 5-year life, despite the 3-year lease term, because it is assumed that the bargain purchase option will be exercised and that the asset will be used for five years.

The amortization of the debt at the implicit 16% interest rate is as follows:

Date	Payment	Interest at 16% on Previous Balance	Reduction of Principal	Principal Balance
January 1, 2015 . . .	$2,000		$2,000	$3,851*
January 1, 2016 . . .	2,000	$ 616	1,384	2,467
January 1, 2017 . . .	2,000	395	1,605	862
December 31, 2017	1,000	138	862	
Total	$7,000	$1,149	$5,851	

*Purchase price of $5,851 − $2,000 initial payment.

---

2 FASB 840-10-25-6, *Leases—Overall—Recognition* (Norwalk, CT, 2010).
3 *Ibid.*

The journal entries for the separate companies would be as follows for the first two years:

Date	Company S (Lessee)			Company P (Lessor)		
2015						
Jan. 1	Assets Under Capital Lease	5,851		Minimum Lease Payments Receivable . .	5,000	
	Obligations Under Capital Lease . .		3,851	Cash	2,000	
	Cash		2,000	Unearned Interest Income		1,149
				Accounts Payable (for asset)		5,851
Dec. 31	Interest Expense (at 16%)	616		Unearned Interest Income	616	
	Interest Payable		616	Interest Income (at 16%)		616
	Depreciation Expense					
	($1/5 \times \$5,851$)	1,170				
	Accumulated Depreciation—Assets					
	Under Capital Lease.		1,170			
2016						
Jan. 1	Obligations Under Capital Lease	1,384		Cash	2,000	
	Interest Payable	616		Minimum Lease Payments		
	Cash		2,000	Receivable		2,000
Dec. 31	Interest Expense (at 16%)	395		Unearned Interest Income	395	
	Interest Payable		395	Interest Income (at 16%)		395
	Depreciation Expense	1,170				
	Accumulated Depreciation—Assets					
	Under Capital Lease.		1,170			

At the end of each period, consolidation procedures would be needed to eliminate the inter-company transactions. In substance, there appears on the separate records of the affiliates an intercompany transfer of a plant asset with resulting intercompany debt. The intercompany debt, related interest expense/revenue, and interest accruals must be eliminated. Also, it is necessary to reclassify the assets under capital leases as productive assets owned by the consolidated group. The adjusted partial worksheets (pages 276 and 277) illustrate consolidation procedures at the end of 2015 and 2016.

A review of the worksheet eliminations and adjustments reveals that **consolidated net income is not changed because equal amounts of interest expense and revenue were eliminated.** Therefore, no adjustments are required in the income distribution schedules.

Some capital leases will designate a portion of the annual rent as being applicable to executory costs, such as property taxes or maintenance, incurred by the lessor. Such payments for executory costs are not included in the obligation of the lessee or the minimum lease payments receivable recorded by the lessor. Instead, such payments are recorded as rent expense and revenue in each period. In the consolidation process, that portion of rent applicable to executory costs is eliminated like any other charge for intercompany services.

Partial Worksheet
Direct Financing Lease For Year Ended December 31, 2015

	Trial Balance		Eliminations & Adjustments			
	Company P	Company S	Dr.		Cr.	
Assets Under Capital Lease		5,851			(CL3)	5,851
Accumulated Depreciation—Assets						
Under Capital Lease		(1,170)	(CL3)	1,170		
Property, Plant, and Equipment	200,000	120,000	(CL3)	5,851		
Accumulated Depreciation—Property,						
Plant, and Equipment	(80,000)	(50,000)			(CL3)	1,170
Obligations Under Capital Lease		(3,851)	**(CL2)**	**3,851**		
Interest Payable		(616)	**(CL2)**	**616**		
Minimum Lease Payments Receivable	5,000				**(CL2)**	**5,000**
Unearned Interest Income	(533)		**(CL2)**	**533***		
Interest Expense		616			(CL1)	616
Interest Income	(616)		(CL1)	616		

Eliminations and Adjustments:

(CL1)   Eliminate intercompany interest expense/revenue of $616.

(CL2)   Eliminate the intercompany debt recorded by the lessee (obligation under capital lease $3,851 plus accrued interest payable $616) against the net intercompany receivable of the lessor (minimum lease payments receivable $5,000 less unearned interest income $533).

(CL3)   Reclassify the asset under capital lease and its related accumulated depreciation as a productive asset owned by the consolidated company.

*From the amortization table on page 274; $533 = $395 + $138

The preceding example has a bargain purchase option. This means that all payments to be received by the lessor would come from the original lessee. Equality of payments for both parties to a lease between affiliates is the most common case. However, there may be intercompany leases where there is an unguaranteed residual value for the lessor. This means that a portion of the total payments to be received by the lessor will come from parties outside the control group. Therefore, the stream of payments to be received by the lessor exceeds the stream of payments to be paid by the lessee. This complicates the consolidation process. (The appendix to this chapter illustrates a revised version of the preceding example that deals with an unequal stream of payments.)

Consolidation Procedures for Sales-Type Leases. Under a sales-type lease, a lessor records a sales profit or loss at the inception of the lease. The sales profit or loss is the difference between the fair value of the asset at the inception of the lease and the cost of an asset purchased (or the net book value of an asset previously used by the seller) for the lessor. Consolidation procedures do not allow recognition of this intercompany profit or loss at the inception of the lease. This is exactly the same as the procedure for the deferral of gains and losses on fixed asset sales in Chapter 4. Instead, the profit or loss is deferred and then amortized over the lessee's period of usage. This period will be the lease term unless there is a bargain purchase or bargain renewal option, in which case the asset's useful life would be used.

6

OBJECTIVE

Demonstrate an understanding of the process used to defer intercompany profits on sales-type leases.

Partial Worksheet
Direct Financing Lease For Year Ended December 31, 2016

	Trial Balance		Eliminations & Adjustments			
	Company P	Company S	Dr.		Cr.	
Assets Under Capital Lease		5,851			(CL3)	5,851
Accumulated Depreciation—Assets						
Under Capital Lease		(2,340)	(CL3)	2,340		
Property, Plant, and Equipment	200,000	120,000	(CL3)	5,851		
Accumulated Depreciation—Property,						
Plant, and Equipment	(100,000)	(60,000)			(CL3)	2,340
Obligations Under Capital Lease		(2,467)	(CL2)	2,467		
Interest Payable		(395)	(CL2)	395		
Minimum Lease Payments Receivable	3,000				(CL2)	3,000
Unearned Interest Income	(138)		(CL2)	138		
Interest Expense		395			(CL1)	395
Interest Income	(395)		(CL1)	395		

Eliminations and Adjustments:

(CL1)   Eliminate intercompany interest expense/revenue of $395.

(CL2)   Eliminate intercompany debt and net receivable.

(CL3)   Reclassify the asset under the capital lease and its related accumulated depreciation as a productive asset owned by the consolidated company.

To illustrate, assume that in the previous example the asset leased to Company S had a cost to Company P of $4,951. Company P would have recorded the following entry at the inception of the sales-type lease:

Minimum Lease Payments Receivable	5,000	
Cash	2,000	
Unearned Interest Income		1,149
Asset (cost of asset leased)		4,951
Sales Profit on Leases		900

This entry differs from that of the previous example only to the extent of recording the gain and transferring an existing asset. None of the lessor's subsequent entries recording the earning of interest and the payment of the receivable would change. The lessee's entries are unaffected by the existence of the sales profit.

Consolidation procedures for a sales-type lease, however, do require added steps to those already illustrated. The sales profit is similar to a profit on the sale of a plant asset. The $900 profit in this example must be deferred over the 3-year lease term. Thus, the asset and its related depreciation accounts must be adjusted to reflect the original sales profit.

The following added adjustments on the 2015 partial consolidated worksheet (page 276) would be needed for the original $900 sales profit:

(F1)	Sales Profit on Leases	900	
	Property, Plant, and Equipment		900
	To reduce cost of asset for gain on sales-type lease.		

(F2)	Accumulated Depreciation—Property, Plant, and Equipment........	300	
	Depreciation Expense		300
	To reduce depreciation expense at the rate of $300 per year.		

The income distribution schedule of the parent (lessor) would reflect the deferral of the original $900 profit in the year of the sale and would recognize $300 per year during the asset's life.

For the 2016 partial consolidated worksheet (page 277), the following added adjustments would be required if a sales-type lease were involved:

(F1)	Retained Earnings—Controlling Interest	600	
	Accumulated Depreciation—Property, Plant, and Equipment.............	300	
	Property, Plant, and Equipment		900
	To adjust the remaining sales profit at the beginning of the period.		
(F2)	Accumulated Depreciation—Property, Plant, and Equipment.............	300	
	Depreciation Expense		300
	To reduce depreciation expense at the rate of $300 per year.		

REFLECTION

- Intercompany leases provide the opportunity for the parent company to control the assets used by a subsidiary.

- Intercompany operating leases are the most common type of lease and are easy to eliminate. Intercompany rent expense/revenue is eliminated with no effect on consolidated income. The leased assets should also be reclassified as productive, rather than leased assets.

- An intercompany capital lease creates an intercompany receivable/payable that must be eliminated along with the resulting intercompany interest expense/revenue and the intercompany accrued interest, all of which must be eliminated. The asset under the capital lease must also be reclassified as a productive asset.

- An intercompany sales-type lease requires all of the same elimination procedures of a capital lease. In addition, the intercompany sales profit must be eliminated and deferred over the life of the asset in the same manner as was a profit on fixed assets in Chapter 4.

INTERCOMPANY TRANSACTIONS PRIOR TO BUSINESS COMBINATION

It is possible that the companies involved in a business combination may have had dealings with each other prior to the acquisition of one company by another. Under acquisition accounting procedures, profits made prior to the acquisition are allowed to stand and require no adjustment. However, debt and lease instruments between the parties change their nature on the acquisition date. Amounts that were due between separate entities now become intercompany debt or leases, and they must be eliminated. Consider the following examples:

1. Trade receivables/payables of the former independent companies become intercompany trade debt on the acquisition date. If still existing on the balance sheet date, they are eliminated. Only interest expense/revenue applicable to the period after the acquisition is eliminated.

2. Bonds of one of the affiliates that are owned by another affiliate were valid when the firms were not affiliated. Once the acquisition occurs, the bonds become intercompany bonds and are eliminated on the consolidated worksheet. Interest expense/revenue prior to the acquisition stands, but interest expense/revenue applicable to the period after the acquisition is eliminated.

3. Operating leases may have existed between the affiliated companies prior to the acquisition. Once the purchase occurs, rent expense/revenue for periods after the acquisition becomes intercompany and must be eliminated.

4. If there were capitalized leases between the companies prior to the acquisition date, the capital lease amounts remaining in each company's accounts must be eliminated after the acquisition date. The interest expense/revenue for periods after the acquisition is also eliminated.

All of the above eliminations of amounts that become intercompany, after the acquisition occurs, do not affect income or balance sheet amounts for periods prior to the acquisition. No restatement of prior-period statements is required.

REFLECTION

- When an acquisition occurs, prior sales between the two entities are not eliminated on the consolidated worksheet.

- Debt and lease instruments between the parties change their nature on the acquisition date and become intercompany relationships that must be eliminated when consolidating.

APPENDIX: INTERCOMPANY LEASES WITH UNGUARANTEED RESIDUAL VALUE

7

OBJECTIVE

Explain the complications caused by unguaranteed residual values with intercompany leases.

The intercompany lease may contain an unguaranteed residual value. This means that the original intercompany lessee will supply only a portion of the total cash flow to be received by the lessor. At the end of the original lease term, the lessor may lease the asset again or sell it. In either case, there is no obligation on the part of the lessee to renew the lease or to purchase the asset. Since the original lessee is contractually bound to provide only a portion of the payments to be received by the lessor, the lessee will record as its lease obligation only the present value of the minimum lease payments for which it is obligated. The lessee must calculate the present value of the minimum lease payments using its incremental borrowing rate, unless the lessee knows the lessor's implicit rate (and the implicit rate is lower). Since it is an intercompany lease, the interest rate used would normally be the implicit rate of the lessor. As part of the consolidation process, if any other rate is used, the present value of the payments would be adjusted to reflect the implicit lessor rate.

The lessor records the gross investment in the lease, which is the sum of the minimum lease payments receivable and the unguaranteed residual value. Unearned interest income is recorded as a contra account at an amount that reduces the gross investment to the market value of the asset at the inception of the lease. Unearned interest is amortized using the implicit rate of the lessor. The implicit rate of the lessor thus equates the present value of all payments expected, including the unguaranteed residual value, to the market value of the asset.

The recording methods used by the lessee and lessor for leases with an unguaranteed residual value present a complication to the consolidation process. The amount of the asset under the capital lease recorded by the lessee will be less than the asset's market value, since the present value of the lease payments recorded by the lessee will not include the asset's unguaranteed residual value. To understand this complication, the previous example may be used with one change. Instead of the $1,000 bargain purchase option that was included in the set of minimum lease payments, assume there is a $1,000 unguaranteed residual value. Since the residual value is not guaranteed, it is not part of the minimum lease payments. The revised facts are as follows:

1. Cost of asset to lessor: $5,851.
2. Lease terms: Three annual payments of $2,000, due at the start of each year. Unguaranteed residual value of $1,000 to lessor at the end of 2017.
3. Lessor implicit rate: 16% equates the three $2,000 payments plus the unguaranteed residual value to $5,851.
4. Lessee interest rate: 16% (lessor implicit rate) which, when applied only to the lease payments, results in a present value of $5,210.
5. Depreciation: Straight-line over the 3-year lease term, since the contractual use of the asset is for three years.
6. Amortization tables:

Lessor

Date	Payment	Interest at 16% on Previous Balance	Reduction of Principal	Principal Balance
January 1, 2015 . . .	$2,000		$2,000	$3,851*
January 1, 2016 . . .	2,000	$ 616	1,384	2,467
January 1, 2017 . . .	2,000	395	1,605	862
December 31, 2017	1,000	138	862	
Total.	$7,000	$1,149	$5,851	

*Purchase price of $5,851 − $2,000 initial payment.

Lessee (16%)

Date	Payment	Interest at 16% on Previous Balance	Reduction of Principal	Principal Balance
January 1, 2015 . . .	$2,000		$2,000	$3,210*
January 1, 2016 . . .	2,000	$514	1,486	1,724
January 1, 2017 . . .	2,000	276	1,724	
Total.	$6,000	$790	$5,210	

*Present value of $5,210 − $2,000 initial payment.

The journal entries for the separate companies would be as shown on page 281 for the first two years.

Date	Company S (Lessee)			Company P (Lessor)		
2015						
Jan. 1	Assets Under Capital Lease	5,210		Minimum Lease Payments Receivable . .	4,000	
	Cash		2,000	Unguaranteed Residual Value.	1,000	
	Obligations Under Capital Lease . .		3,210	Cash	2,000	
				Unearned Interest Income		1,149
				Accounts Payable (for asset)		5,851
Dec. 31	Interest Expense (at 16%)	514		Unearned Interest Income	616	
	Interest Payable		514	Interest Income (at 16%)		616
	Depreciation Expense					
	(⅓ × $5,210)	1,737				
	Accumulated Depreciation—Assets					
	Under Capital Lease.		1,737			
2016						
Jan. 1	Obligations Under Capital Lease	1,486		Cash	2,000	
	Interest Payable	514		Minimum Lease Payments		
	Cash		2,000	Receivable		2,000
Dec. 31	Interest Expense (at 16%)	276		Unearned Interest Income	395	
	Interest Payable		276	Interest Income (at 16%)		395
	Depreciation Expense	1,737				
	Accumulated Depreciation—Assets					
	Under Capital Lease.		1,737			

A comparison of the lessor and lessee's amortization tables shows the following difference between the lessee's interest expense and the lessor's interest income each period:

Year Ending December 31	16% Lessor Implicit Interest	16% Lessee Interest	Difference
2015	$ 616	$514	$102
2016	395	276	119
2017	138		138
Total	$1,149	$790	$359

The difference is the interest on the unguaranteed residual value, which is recorded only by the lessor. This can be demonstrated as follows:

Date	16% Implicit Interest	Present Value of Unguaranteed Residual Value
January 1, 2015		$ 641*
December 31, 2015 . .	$102	743
December 31, 2016 . .	119	862
December 31, 2017 . .	138	1,000

*$5,851 − $5,210.

In the consolidation process, the intercompany debt and all interest applicable to the lease are eliminated. Even the interest income recorded on the unguaranteed residual value is eliminated, since it is a ramification of a lease that, from a consolidated viewpoint, does not exist. The asset recorded by the lessee and the unguaranteed residual value recorded by the lessor are eliminated and replaced by a productive asset recorded by the consolidated company.

Worksheet 5-5: page 292   Worksheet 5-5, page 292 and 293, contains the detailed steps for the elimination of the intercompany lease at the end of 2015. In this worksheet, it is assumed that the interest in the 80%-owned subsidiary was purchased at its book value.

The eliminations in journal entry form are as follows:

(CY1)	Eliminate current-year equity income:		
	Subsidiary Income.....................................	15,634	
	Investment in Company S.............................		15,634
(EL)	Eliminate 80% of subsidiary equity:		
	Common Stock ($10 par)—Company S....................	32,000	
	Retained Earnings, January 1, 2015—Company S	40,000	
	Investment in Company S.............................		72,000
(CL1)	Eliminate intercompany interest and restore unearned interest on unguaranteed residual:		
	Interest Income......................................	616	
	Interest Expense.....................................		514
	Unearned Interest Income		102
(CL2)	Eliminate intercompany debt, unguaranteed residual value and restate asset as owned asset:		
	Property, Plant, and Equipment.........................	5,851	
	Asset Under Capital Lease.............................		5,210
	Unearned Interest Income	635	
	Minimum Lease Payments Receivable		4,000
	Unguaranteed Residual Value..........................		1,000
	Obligation Under Capital Lease	3,210	
	Interest Payable	514	
(CL3)	Adjust and reclassify depreciation:		
	Accumulated Depreciation—Asset Under Capital Lease	1,737*	
	Accumulated Depreciation—Property, Plant, and Equipment..		1,617**
	Depreciation Expense		120

*$5,210/3 years = $1,737
**($5,851 cost − $1,000 residual)/3 = $1,617

Entry (CL1) eliminates the $616 of interest income against the $514 of interest expense. The $102 disparity reflects the interest applicable to the unguaranteed residual value and is returned to unearned interest income. Entry (CL2) eliminates the intercompany debt applicable to the lease. The $359 disparity reflects the interest applicable to the unguaranteed residual value over the life of the lease. This amount is used to reduce the unguaranteed residual value to its original present value of $641. The $641, combined with the $5,210 asset under capital lease, is eliminated and replaced by an owned asset and recorded at the $5,851 original cost to the consolidated company. Entry (CL3) adjusts the depreciation to reflect the cost and the residual value of the asset to the consolidated company. The accumulated depreciation also is reclassified as that applicable to an owned asset.

In Worksheet 5-6 on pages 296 and 297, the consolidation procedures for the second year of the lease term are illustrated.

Worksheet 5-6: page 296

REFLECTION

- An unguaranteed residual value causes the present value of the lease for the lessor to exceed that of the lessee. The interest applicable to the unguaranteed residual value is allowed to remain in the consolidated statements, since it will come from the outside world.

- All remaining procedures parallel those used for ordinary capital leases.

Worksheet 5-1

Intercompany Investment in Bonds, Year of Acquisition; Straight-Line Method of Amortization
Company P and Subsidiary Company S
Worksheet for Consolidated Balance Sheet
For Year Ended December 31, 2017

	(Credit balance amounts are in parentheses.)	Trial Balance	
		Company P	Company S
1	Other Assets	56,400	220,000
2	**Interest Receivable**	**8,000**	
3	Investment in Company S Stock (90%)	100,800	
4			
5	**Investment in Company S Bonds (100%)**	**102,400**	
6	**Interest Payable**		**(8,000)**
7	**Bonds Payable (8%)**		**(100,000)**
8	Common Stock ($10 par)—Company P	(100,000)	
9	Retained Earnings, January 1, 2017—Company P	(120,000)	
10	Common Stock ($10 par)—Company S		(80,000)
11	Retained Earnings, January 1, 2017—Company S		(20,000)
12	Operating Revenue	(100,000)	(80,000)
13	Operating Expense	70,000	60,000
14	**Interest Income**	**(6,800)**	
15	**Interest Expense**		**8,000**
16	Subsidiary Income	(10,800)	
17	**Loss on Bond Retirement**		
18		0	0
19	Consolidated Net Income		
20	To NCI (see distribution schedule)		
21	Balance to Controlling Interest (see distribution schedule)		
22	Total NCI		
23	Retained Earnings, Controlling Interest, December 31, 2017		
24			

Eliminations and Adjustments:

(CY1)   Eliminate the entry recording the parent's share of subsidiary net income for the current year. This entry returns the investment in Company S stock account to its January 1, 2017, balance to aid the elimination process.

(EL)   Eliminate 90% of the subsidiary equity balances of January 1, 2017, against the investment in stock account. No excess results.

(B1)   Eliminate intercompany interest revenue and expense. Eliminate the balance of the investment in bonds against the bonds payable. Note that the investment in bonds is at its year-end amortized balance. The loss on retirement at the date the bonds were purchased is calculated as follows:

Loss remaining at year-end:

Investment in bonds at December 31, 2017	$102,400	
Less: Carrying value of bonds at December 31, 2017	100,000	$2,400
Loss amortized during year:		
Interest expense eliminated	$ 8,000	
Less: Interest revenue eliminated	6,800	1,200
Loss at January 2, 2017		$3,600

(B2)   Eliminate intercompany interest payable and receivable.

Worksheet 5-1 (see page 267)

Eliminations & Adjustments Dr.	Eliminations & Adjustments Cr.	Consolidated Income Statement	NCI	Controlling Retained Earnings	Consolidated Balance Sheet	
					276,400	1
	(B2) 8,000					2
	(CY1) 10,800					3
	(EL) 90,000					4
	(B1) 102,400					5
(B2) 8,000						6
(B1) 100,000						7
					(100,000)	8
				(120,000)		9
(EL) 72,000			(8,000)			10
(EL) 18,000			(2,000)			11
		(180,000)				12
		130,000				13
(B1) 6,800						14
	(B1) 8,000					15
(CY1) 10,800						16
(B1) 3,600		3,600				17
219,200	219,200					18
		(46,400)				19
		960	(960)			20
		45,440		(45,440)		21
			(10,960)		(10,960)	22
				(165,440)	(165,440)	23
					0	24

Subsidiary Company S Income Distribution

Loss on bond retirement . . . .(B1)	**$3,600**	Internally generated net income, **including**	
		interest expense	**$12,000**
		Interest adjustment ($3,600 ÷ 3) . . . . . . (B1)	**1,200**
		Adjusted income	$ 9,600
		NCI share	× 10%
		NCI	$ 960

Parent Company P Income Distribution

Internally generated net income, **including**	
interest revenue.	**$36,800**
90% × Company S adjusted income of $9,600	8,640
Controlling interest	$ 45,440

Worksheet 5-2

Intercompany Investment in Bonds, Year Subsequent to Acquisition; Straight-Line Method of Amortization
Company P and Subsidiary Company S
Worksheet for Consolidated Financial Statements
For Year Ended December 31, 2018

	(Credit balance amounts are in parentheses.)	Trial Balance	
		Company P	Company S
1	Other Assets	94,400	242,000
2	Interest Receivable	8,000	
3	Investment in Company S Stock (90%)	120,600	
4			
5	**Investment in Company S Bonds (100%)**	**101,200**	
6	Interest Payable		(8,000)
7	**Bonds Payable (8%)**		**(100,000)**
8	Common Stock ($10 par)—Company P	(100,000)	
9	**Retained Earnings, January 1, 2018—Company P**	**(167,600)**	
10	Common Stock ($10 par)—Company S		(80,000)
11	**Retained Earnings, January 1, 2018—Company S**		**(32,000)**
12			
13	Operating Revenue	(130,000)	(100,000)
14	Operating Expense	100,000	70,000
15	Subsidiary Income	(19,800)	
16	**Interest Expense**		**8,000**
17	**Interest Income**	**(6,800)**	
18		0	0
19	Consolidated Net Income		
20	To NCI (see distribution schedule)		
21	Balance to Controlling Interest (see distribution schedule)		
22	Total NCI		
23	Retained Earnings, Controlling Interest, December 31, 2018		
24			

Eliminations and Adjustments:

(CY1) Eliminate the entry recording the parent's share of subsidiary net income for the current year.
(EL) Eliminate 90% of the subsidiary equity balances of January 1, 2018, against the investment in stock account. There is no excess to be distributed.
(B1) Eliminate intercompany interest revenue and expense. Eliminate the balance of the investment in bonds against the bonds payable. Note that the investment in bonds is at its year-end amortized balance. The remaining unamortized loss on retirement at the start of the year is calculated as follows:

Loss remaining at year-end:

Investment in bonds at December 31, 2018	$101,200	
Less: Carrying value of bonds at December 31, 2018	100,000	$1,200

Loss amortized during year:

Interest expense eliminated	$ 8,000	
Less: Interest revenue eliminated	6,800	1,200
Remaining loss at January 1, 2018		$2,400

The remaining unamortized loss of $2,400 on January 1, 2018, is allocated 90% to the controlling retained earnings and 10% to the noncontrolling retained earnings since the bonds were issued by the subsidiary.
(B2) Eliminate intercompany interest payable and receivable.

Worksheet 5-2 (see page 268)

Eliminations & Adjustments				Consolidated Income Statement	NCI	Controlling Retained Earnings	Consolidated Balance Sheet	
Dr.		Cr.						
							336,400	1
		(B2)	8,000					2
		(CY1)	19,800					3
		(EL)	100,800					4
		(B1)	**101,200**					5
(B2)	8,000							6
(B1)	**100,000**							7
							(100,000)	8
(B1)	**2,160**					(165,440)		9
(EL)	72,000				(8,000)			10
(EL)	28,800				(2,960)			11
(B1)	**240**							12
				(230,000)				13
				170,000				14
(CY1)	19,800							15
		(B1)	**8,000**					16
(B1)	**6,800**							17
	237,800		237,800					18
				(60,000)				19
				2,320	(2,320)			20
				57,680		(57,680)		21
					(13,280)		(13,280)	22
						(223,120)	(223,120)	23
							0	24

Subsidiary Company S Income Distribution

Internally generated net income, including interest expense		$22,000
Interest adjustment ($3,600 ÷ 3) . . . . **(B1)**		1,200
Adjusted income		$23,200
NCI share		× 10%
NCI		$ 2,320

Parent Company P Income Distribution

Internally generated net income, including interest revenue		$36,800
90% × Company S adjusted income of $23,200. . .		20,880
Controlling interest		$57,680

Worksheet 5-3

Intercompany Bonds, Subsequent Period; Straight-Line Method of Amortization
Company P and Subsidiary Company S
Worksheet for Consolidated Financial Statements
For Year Ended December 31, 2018

	(Credit balance amounts are in parentheses.)	Trial Balance	
		Company P	Company S
1	Other Assets	59,400	259,082
2	Investment in Company S Stock	143,874	
3			
4	**Investment in Company S Bonds**	101,800	
5	**Bonds Payable**		(100,000)
6	**Discount on Bonds**		778
7	Common Stock—Company P	(100,000)	
8	**Retained Earnings, January 1, 2018—Company P**	(160,000)	
9	Common Stock—Company S		(40,000)
10	**Retained Earnings, January 1, 2018—Company S**		(110,000)
11			
12	Sales	(80,000)	(50,000)
13	**Interest Income**	(6,200)	
14	Cost of Goods Sold	50,000	31,362
15	**Interest Expense**		8,778
16	Subsidiary Income	(8,874)	
17		0	0
18	Consolidated Net Income		
19	To NCI (see distribution schedule)		
20	Balance to Controlling Interest (see distribution schedule)		
21	Total NCI		
22	Retained Earnings, Controlling Interest, December 31, 2018		
23			

Eliminations and Adjustments:

(CY1) Eliminate the entry recording the parent's share of subsidiary net income for the current year.
(EL) Eliminate 90% of the January 1, 2018, subsidiary equity balances against the January 1, 2018, investment in Company S stock balance. No excess results.
(B) Eliminate intercompany interest revenue and expense. Eliminate the balance of the investment in bonds against the bonds payable. Note that the investment in bonds and the discount on bonds are at their year-end amortized balances. The remaining unamortized loss on retirement at the start of the year is calculated as follows:

Loss remaining at year-end:			
Investment in bonds at December 31, 2018		$101,800	
Less: Bonds payable at December 31, 2018	$100,000		
Discount on bonds at December 31, 2018	(778)	99,222	$2,578
Loss amortized during year:			
Interest expense eliminated		$ 8,778	
Less: Interest revenue eliminated		6,200	2,578
Remaining loss at January 1, 2018			$5,156

Since from the consolidated viewpoint the bonds were retired in the prior year and since the bonds were issued by the subsidiary, the remaining unamortized loss of $5,156 on January 1, 2018, is allocated 90% to the controlling retained earnings and 10% to the noncontrolling retained earnings.

Worksheet 5-3 (see page 270)

| Eliminations & Adjustments | | Consolidated Income Statement | NCI | Controlling Retained Earnings | Consolidated Balance Sheet | |
Dr.	Cr.					
					318,482	1
	(CY1) 8,874					2
	(EL) 135,000					3
	(B) 101,800					4
(B) 100,000						5
	(B) 778					6
					(100,000)	7
(B) 4,640				(155,360)		8
(EL) 36,000			(4,000)			9
(EL) 99,000			(10,484)			10
(B) 516						11
		(130,000)				12
(B) 6,200						13
		81,362				14
	(B) 8,778					15
(CY1) 8,874						16
255,230	255,230					17
		(48,638)				18
		1,244	(1,244)			19
		47,394		(47,394)		20
			(15,728)		(15,728)	21
				(202,754)	(202,754)	22
					0	23

Subsidiary Company S Income Distribution

Internally generated net income, including interest expense.....................	$ 9,860
Interest adjustment ($8,778 − $6,200)... (B)	**2,578**
Adjusted income	$12,438
NCI share	× 10%
NCI	$ 1,244

Parent Company P Income Distribution

Internally generated net income, including interest revenue	$36,200
90% × Company S adjusted income of $12,438....	11,194
Controlling interest	$47,394

Worksheet 5-4

Intercompany Bonds; Interest Method of Amortization
Company P and Subsidiary Company S
Worksheet for Consolidated Financial Statements
For Year Ended December 31, 2018

	(Credit balance amounts are in parentheses.)	Trial Balance	
		Company P	Company S
1	Other Assets	59,333	259,082
2	Investment in Company S Stock	144,000	
3			
4	**Investment in Company S Bonds**	**101,887**	
5	**Bonds Payable**		**(100,000)**
6	**Discount on Bonds**		**918**
7	Common Stock—Company P	(100,000)	
8	**Retained Earnings, January 1, 2018—Company P**	**(160,180)**	
9	Common Stock—Company S		(40,000)
10	**Retained Earnings, January 1, 2018—Company S**		**(110,200)**
11			
12	Sales	(80,000)	(50,000)
13	**Interest Income**	**(6,220)**	
14	Cost of Goods Sold	50,000	31,358
15	**Interest Expense**		**8,842**
16			
17	Subsidiary Income	(8,820)	
18		0	0
19	Consolidated Net Income		
20	To NCI (see distribution schedule)		
21	Balance to Controlling Interest (see distribution schedule)		
22	Total NCI		
23	Retained Earnings, Controlling Interest, December 31, 2018		
24			

Eliminations and Adjustments:

(CY1) Eliminate the entry recording the parent's share of subsidiary net income for the current year.
(EL) Eliminate 90% of the January 1, 2018, subsidiary equity balances against the January 1, 2018, investment in Company S stock balance. No excess results.
(B) Eliminate intercompany interest revenue and expense. Eliminate the balance of the investment in bonds against the bonds payable. Note that the investment in bonds and the discount on bonds are at their year-end amortized balances. The remaining unamortized loss on retirement at the start of the year is calculated as follows:

Loss remaining at year-end:			
Investment in bonds at December 31, 2018		$101,887	
Less: Bonds payable at December 31, 2018	$100,000		
Discount on bonds at December 31, 2018	(918)	99,082	$2,805
Loss amortized during year:			
Interest expense eliminated		$ 8,842	
Less: Interest revenue eliminated		6,220	2,622
Remaining loss at January 1, 2018			$5,427

Since from the consolidated viewpoint the bonds were retired in the prior year and since the bonds were issued by the subsidiary, the remaining unamortized loss of $5,427 on January 1, 2018, is allocated 90% to the controlling retained earnings and 10% to the noncontrolling retained earnings.

Worksheet 5-4 (see page 272)

Eliminations & Adjustments		Consolidated Income Statement	NCI	Controlling Retained Earnings	Consolidated Balance Sheet	
Dr.	**Cr.**					
					318,415	1
	(CY1) 8,820					2
	(EL) 135,180					3
	(B) 101,887					4
(B) 100,000						5
	(B) 918					6
					(100,000)	7
(B) 4,884				(155,296)		8
(EL) 36,000			(4,000)			9
(EL) 99,180			(10,477)			10
(B) 543						11
		(130,000)				12
(B) 6,220						13
		81,358				14
	(B) 8,842					15
						16
(CY1) 8,820						17
255,647	255,647					18
		(48,642)				19
		1,242	(1,242)			20
		47,400		(47,400)		21
			(15,719)		(15,719)	22
				(202,696)	(202,696)	23
					0	24

Subsidiary Company S Income Distribution

Internally generated net income, including interest expense....................	$ 9,800
Interest adjustment ($8,842 − $6,220) .... **(B)**	2,622
Adjusted income	$ 12,422
NCI share	× 10%
NCI	$ 1,242

Parent Company P Income Distribution

Internally generated net income, including interest revenue	$36,220
90% × Company S adjusted income of $12,422...	11,180
Controlling interest	$47,400

Worksheet 5-5

Intercompany Capital Lease with Unguaranteed Residual Value
Company P and Subsidiary Company S
Worksheet for Consolidated Financial Statements
For Year Ended December 31, 2015

	(Credit balance amounts are in parentheses.)	Trial Balance	
		Company P	Company S
1	Accounts Receivable	30,149	44,793
2	**Minimum Lease Payments Receivable**	**4,000**	
3	**Unguaranteed Residual Value**	**1,000**	
4	**Unearned Interest Income**	**(533)**	
5	**Assets Under Capital Lease**		**5,210**
6	**Accumulated Depreciation—Assets Under Capital Lease**		**(1,737)**
7	**Property, Plant, and Equipment**	200,000	120,000
8	**Accumulated Depreciation—Property, Plant, and Equipment**	(80,000)	(50,000)
9	Investment in Company S	87,634	
10			
11	Accounts Payable	(21,000)	(5,000)
12	**Obligations Under Capital Lease**		**(3,210)**
13	**Interest Payable**		**(514)**
14	Common Stock ($10 par)—Company P	(50,000)	
15	Retained Earnings, January 1, 2015—Company P	(120,000)	
16	Common Stock ($5 par)—Company S		(40,000)
17	Retained Earnings, January 1, 2015—Company S		(50,000)
18	Sales	(120,000)	(70,000)
19	**Interest Income**	**(616)**	
20	Subsidiary Income	(15,634)	
21	Operating Expense	65,000	38,207
22	**Interest Expense**		**514**
23	**Depreciation Expense**	20,000	11,737
24		0	0
25	Consolidated Net Income		
26	To NCI (see distribution schedule)		
27	Balance to Controlling Interest (see distribution schedule)		
28	Total NCI		
29	Retained Earnings, Controlling Interest, December 31, 2015		
30			

Worksheet 5-5 (see page 282)

Eliminations & Adjustments		Consolidated Income Statement	NCI	Controlling Retained Earnings	Consolidated Balance Sheet	
Dr.	Cr.					
					74,942	1
	(CL2) 4,000					2
	(CL2) 1,000					3
(CL2) 635	(CL1) 102					4
	(CL2) 5,210					5
(CL3) 1,737						6
(CL2) 5,851					325,851	7
	(CL3) 1,617				(131,617)	8
	(CY1) 15,634					9
	(EL) 72,000					10
					(26,000)	11
(CL2) 3,210						12
(CL2) 514						13
					(50,000)	14
				(120,000)		15
(EL) 32,000			(8,000)			16
(EL) 40,000			(10,000)			17
		(190,000)				18
(CL1) 616						19
(CY1) 15,634						20
		103,207				21
	(CL1) 514					22
	(CL3) 120	31,617				23
100,197	100,197					24
		(55,176)				25
		3,908	(3,908)			26
		51,268		(51,268)		27
			(21,908)		(21,908)	28
				(171,268)	(171,268)	29
					0	30

Eliminations and Adjustments:

(CY1) Eliminate the parent company's entry recording its share of Company S net income. This step returns the investment account to its January 1, 2015, balance to aid the elimination process.

(EL) Eliminate 80% of the January 1, 2015, Company S equity balances against the investment in Company S balance.

(CL1) Eliminate the interest income recorded by the lessor, $616, and the interest expense recorded by the lessee, $514. The $102 disparity reflects the interest recorded on the unguaranteed residual value. This amount is returned to the unearned interest income.

(CL2) Eliminate the intercompany debt and the unguaranteed residual value. Eliminate the asset under capital lease and record the owned asset. The amounts are reconciled as follows:

Disparity in recorded debt:

Lessor balance, **$4,000 − $635** unearned interest income	$ 3,365
Lessee balance, **$3,210 + $514** accrued interest	3,724
Interest applicable to unguaranteed residual value	$ (359)
Unguaranteed residual value	**1,000**
Net original present value of unguaranteed residual value	$ 641
Asset under capital lease	**5,210**
Owned asset at original cost	$ 5,851

(CL3) Reclassify accumulated depreciation and adjust the depreciation expense to acknowledge cost of asset. The adjustment to depreciation expense is determined as follows:

Capitalized cost by lessee		$5,210
Depreciable cost:		
Cost	$5,851	
Less residual (salvage) value	1,000	4,851
Decrease in depreciable cost		$ 359
Adjustment to depreciation expense ($359 ÷ 3-year lease term)		**$ 120**

Subsidiary Company S Income Distribution

Internally generated net income, **including interest income on lease**	$19,542
Adjusted income	$19,542
NCI share	× 20%
NCI	$ 3,908

Parent Company P Income Distribution

Net interest eliminated. . . . . **(CL1)**	**$102**	Internally generated net income, **including interest income on lease**	$35,616
		80% × Company S adjusted income of $19,542. . .	15,634
		Decrease in depreciation . . . . **(CL3)**	**120**
		Controlling interest	$51,268

Worksheet 5-6

Intercompany Capital Lease with Unguaranteed Residual Value, Subsequent Period
Company P and Subsidiary Company S
Worksheet for Consolidated Financial Statements
For Year Ended December 31, 2016

	(Credit balance amounts are in parentheses.)	Trial Balance	
		Company P	Company S
1	Accounts Receivable	102,149	82,925
2	**Minimum Lease Payments Receivable**	**2,000**	
3	**Unguaranteed Residual Value**	**1,000**	
4	**Unearned Interest Income**	**(138)**	
5			
6	**Assets Under Capital Lease**		**5,210**
7	**Accumulated Depreciation—Assets Under Capital Lease**		**(3,474)**
8	**Property, Plant, and Equipment**	200,000	120,000
9	**Accumulated Depreciation—Property, Plant, and Equipment**	(100,000)	(60,000)
10	Investment in Company S	102,129	
11			
12	Accounts Payable	(41,000)	(15,000)
13	**Obligations Under Capital Lease**		**(1,724)**
14	**Interest Payable**		**(276)**
15	Common Stock ($10 par)—Company P	(50,000)	
16	**Retained Earnings, January 1, 2016—Company P**	**(171,250)**	
17	Common Stock ($5 par)—Company S		(40,000)
18	Retained Earnings, January 1, 2016—Company S		(69,542)
19	Sales	(150,000)	(80,000)
20	**Interest Income**	**(395)**	
21	Subsidiary Income	(14,495)	
22	Operating Expense	100,000	49,868
23	**Interest Expense**		**276**
24	**Depreciation Expense**	20,000	11,737
25		0	0
26	Consolidated Net Income		
27	To NCI (see distribution schedule)		
28	Balance to Controlling Interest (see distribution schedule)		
29	Total NCI		
30	Retained Earnings, Controlling Interest, December 31, 2016		
31			

Worksheet 5-6 (see page 283)

Eliminations & Adjustments Dr.		Eliminations & Adjustments Cr.		Consolidated Income Statement	NCI	Controlling Retained Earnings	Consolidated Balance Sheet	
							185,074	1
		(CL2)	2,000					2
		(CL2)	1,000					3
(CL2)	359	(CL1a)	119					4
		(CL1b)	102					5
		(CL2)	5,210					6
(CL3)	3,474							7
(CL2)	5,851						325,851	8
		(CL3)	3,234				(163,234)	9
		(CY1)	14,495					10
		(EL)	87,634					11
							(56,000)	12
(CL2)	1,724							13
(CL2)	276							14
							(50,000)	15
(CL1b)	102	(CL3)	120			(171,268)		16
(EL)	32,000				(8,000)			17
(EL)	55,634				(13,908)			18
				(230,000)				19
(CL1a)	395							20
(CY1)	14,495							21
				149,868				22
		(CL1a)	276					23
		(CL3)	120	31,617				24
	114,310		114,310					25
				(48,515)				26
				3,624	(3,624)			27
				44,891		(44,891)		28
					(25,532)		(25,532)	29
						(216,159)	(216,159)	30
							0	31

Eliminations and Adjustments:

(CY1) Eliminate the parent company's entry recording its share of Company S net income.

(EL)   Eliminate 80% of the January 1, 2016, Company S equity balances against the investment in Company S balance.

(CL1a) Eliminate the interest income recorded by the lessor, $395, and the interest expense recorded by the lessee, $276. The $119 disparity reflects the interest recorded on the unguaranteed residual value. This amount is returned to the unearned interest income.

(CL1b) Adjust the unearned income and the parent's retained earnings for the $102 interest recorded in 2015 on the unguaranteed residual value.

(CL2) Eliminate the intercompany debt and the unguaranteed residual value. Eliminate the asset under capital lease and record the owned asset. The amounts are reconciled as follows:

Disparity in recorded debt:	
Lessor balance, **$2,000 − $359** unearned interest income.	$ 1,641
Lessee balance, **$1,724 + $276** accrued interest	2,000
Interest applicable to unguaranteed residual value	$ (359)
Unguaranteed residual value	**1,000**
Net original present value of unguaranteed residual value	$ 641
Asset under capital lease	**5,210**
Owned asset at original cost	$ 5,851

(CL3) Reclassify $3,474 depreciation and reduce it to depreciation based on cost ($3,234). This includes reducing current depreciation expense by $120 and prior year for $120 (credit to retained earning, contolling interest). The adjustment to the depreciation expense and the retained earnings is determined as follows:

Capitalized cost by lessee		$5,210
Depreciable cost:		
Cost	$5,851	
Less residual (salvage) value	1,000	4,851
Decrease in depreciable cost		$ 359
Adjustment to depreciation expense and retained earnings ($359 ÷ 3-year lease term)		**$ 120**

Subsidiary Company S Income Distribution

	Internally generated net income, **including interest on lease**.	$ 18,119
	Adjusted income	$ 18,119
	NCI share	× 20%
	NCI	$ 3,624

Parent Company P Income Distribution

Net interest eliminated. . . . . **(CL1a)** **$119**		Internally generated net income, **including interest income on lease**	$30,395
		80% × Company S adjusted income of $18,119	14,495
		Decrease in depreciation . . . . **(CL3)**	**120**
		Controlling interest	$44,891

UNDERSTANDING THE ISSUES

1. Subsidiary Company S has $1,000,000 of bonds outstanding. The bonds have 10 years to maturity and pay interest at 8% annually. The parent has an average annual borrowing cost of 6% and wishes to reduce the interest cost of the consolidated company. What methods could be used to maintain the subsidiary as the debtor?

2. Subsidiary Company S has $1,000,000 of bonds outstanding at 8% annual interest. The bonds have 10 years to maturity. If the parent, Company P, is able to purchase the bonds at a price that reflects 6% annual interest, what effect will the purchase have on consolidated income in the current and future years? What would the effects be if the purchase price reflected a 9% annual interest rate? Your response need not be quantified.

3. Subsidiary Company S has $1,000,000 of bonds outstanding at 8% annual interest. The bonds have 10 years to maturity. If the parent, Company P, is able to purchase the bonds at a price that reflects 6% annual interest, how will the noncontrolling interest be affected in the current and future years? Your response need not be quantified.

4. Company P purchased $100,000 of subsidiary Company S's bonds for $96,000 on January 1, 2015, when the bonds had five years to maturity. The bonds had been issued at face value and pay interest at 8% annually. What will the impact of this transaction be on consolidated net income for the current and future four years? Assuming a 20% noncontrolling interest, how will the NCI be affected in the current and next four years? Quantify your response.

5. Your friend is a noncontrolling interest shareholder in a large company. He knows that the subsidiary company leases most of its assets from the parent company under operating leases. He further believes that the lease rates are in excess of market rates. He made his concern known to the parent company management. Their response was: "Don't worry about it; it washes out in the consolidation process and ends up having no effect on income." Your friend wants to know if this is true and if he was wrong to be concerned.

6. A parent company may want to shift profits to the controlling interest and may use intercompany capital leases to accomplish that end. Is there an opportunity to do that with both direct financing and sales-type leases? What are the differences between the two types of leases with respect to income shifting?

7. A parent company is a producer of production equipment, some of which is acquired and used by the parent's subsidiary companies. The parent offers a discount to the subsidiaries but still earns a significant profit on the sales of equipment to a subsidiary. Is there any difference in the consolidated company's ability to recognize the profit on these sales if, instead of selling equipment to the subsidiaries, the equipment is leased to them under capital leases? Are there any other profit opportunities for the controlling interest in leasing as opposed to selling equipment to the subsidiaries?

EXERCISES

Exercise 1 *(LO 1)* **Options to lower interest cost.** Model Engineering is a large corporation with the ability to obtain financing by selling its bonds at favorable rates. Currently, it pays 5% interest on its 10-year bond issues. In the past year, Model acquired an 80% interest in Mercer Industries. Mercer Industries has $1,000,000 of bonds outstanding that mature in six years. Interest is paid annually at a stated rate of 8%. The bonds were issued at face value.

Interest rates have come down, but Mercer Industries can still expect to pay 5% to 6.5% interest on a long-term issue. Mercer Industries is a smaller company with a lower credit rating than Model.

Model would like to reduce interest costs on the Mercer Industries debt. The company has asked your advice on whether it should purchase the bonds or loan Mercer Industries the money to retire its own debt. Compare the options with a focus on the impact on consolidated statements.

Exercise 2 *(LO 1)* **Effect of intercompany bonds on income.** Darcy Company is an 80%-owned subsidiary of Kraco Industries. Darcy Company issued 10-year, 8% bonds in the amount of $1,000,000 on January 1, 2015. The bonds were issued at face value, and interest is payable each January 1. On January, 1, 2017, Kraco Industries purchased all of the Darcy bonds for $975,000. Kraco will amortize the discount on a straight-line basis. For the years ending (a) December 31, 2017, and (b) December 31, 2018, determine the effects of this transaction:

1. On consolidated net income.
2. On the distribution of income to the controlling and noncontrolling interests.

Exercise 3 *(LO 2)* **Bond eliminations, straight-line.** Cardinal Company is an 80%-owned subsidiary of Dove Corporation. Cardinal Company issued $100,000 of 8%, 10-year bonds for $96,000 on January 1, 2011. Annual interest is paid on January 1. Dove Corporation purchased the bonds on January 1, 2015, for $101,500. Both companies use the straight-line method to amortize the premium/discount on the bonds.

1. Prepare the eliminations and adjustments that would be made on the December 31, 2015, consolidated worksheet as a result of this purchase.
2. Prepare the eliminations and adjustments that would be made on the December 31, 2016, consolidated worksheet.

Exercise 4 *(LO 2)* **Bond eliminations, effective interest.** On January 1, 2014, Dunbar Corporation, an 85%-owned subsidiary of Garfield Industries, received $48,055 for $50,000 of 8%, 5-year bonds it issued when the market rate was 9%. When Garfield Industries purchased these bonds for $47,513 on January 2, 2016, the market rate was 10%. Given the following effective interest amortization schedules for both companies, calculate the gain or loss on retirement and the interest adjustments to the issuer's income distribution schedules over the remaining term of the bonds.

Dunbar (issuer):

Date	Effective Interest (9%)	Nominal Interest (8%)	Discount Amortization	Balance
1/1/14				$48,055
1/1/15	$4,325	$4,000	$325	48,380
1/1/16	4,354	4,000	354	48,734
1/1/17	4,386	4,000	386	49,120
1/1/18	4,421	4,000	421	49,541
1/1/19	4,459	4,000	459	50,000

Garfield (purchaser):

Date	Effective Interest (10%)	Nominal Interest (8%)	Discount Amortization	Balance
1/2/16				$47,513
1/1/17	$4,751	$4,000	$751	48,264
1/1/18	4,826	4,000	826	49,090
1/1/19	4,909	4,000	909	50,000*

*Adjusted for rounding.

Exercise 5 *(LO 2)* **Bond eliminations, partial purchase.** Carlton Company is an 80%-owned subsidiary of Mirage Company. On January 1, 2015, Carlton sold $100,000 of 10-year, 7% bonds for $101,000. Interest is paid annually on January 1. The market rate for this type of bond was 9% on January 2, 2017, when Mirage purchased 60% of the Carlton bonds for $53,600. Discounts may be amortized on a straight-line basis.

1. Prepare the eliminations and adjustments required for this bond purchase on the December 31, 2017, consolidated worksheet.
2. Prepare the eliminations and adjustments required on the December 31, 2018, consolidated worksheet.

Exercise 6 *(LO 2)* **Bond calculations, effective interest.** Linco Industries is a 90%-owned subsidiary of Sharp Incorporated. On January 1, 2015, Linco issued $100,000 of 10-year, 6% bonds for $86,580, to yield 8% interest. Interest is paid annually on January 1. The effective interest method is used to amortize the premium. Sharp purchased the bonds for $84,901 on January 2, 2018, when the market rate of interest was 9%. On the purchase date, the remaining discount on the bonds was $10,413. Linco's 2018 net income was $500,000.

1. Prepare the eliminations and adjustments required for this purchase on the December 31, 2018, consolidated worksheet. Amortization schedules will be needed to January 1, 2019.
2. Prepare the 2018 income distribution schedule for the NCI.

Exercise 7 *(LO 4)* **Operating lease, entries, and eliminations.** Grande Machinery Company purchased, for cash, a $60,000 custom machine on January 1, 2015. The machine has an estimated 5-year life and will be straight-line depreciated with no salvage value. The machine was then leased to Sunshine Engineering Company, an 80%-owned subsidiary, under a 5-year operating lease for $15,000 per year, payable each January.

1. Record the 2015 entries for the purchase of the machine and the lease to Sunshine Engineering Company on the books of Grande Machinery Company.
2. Record the 2015 entries for the transaction on the books of Sunshine Engineering Company.
3. Provide the elimination entries that would be made on the 2015 consolidated worksheet.

Exercise 8 *(LO 5)* **Direct-financing lease eliminations.** On January 1, 2015, Traylor Company, an 80%-owned subsidiary of Parker Electronics, Inc., signed a 4-year direct-financing lease with its parent for the rental of electronic equipment. The lease agreement requires a $12,000 payment on January 1 of each year, and title transfers to Traylor on January 1, 2019. The equipment originally cost $40,822 and had an estimated remaining life of five years at the start of the lease term. The lessor's implicit interest rate is 12%. The lessee also used the 12% rate to record the transaction.

1. Prepare a lease payment amortization schedule for the life of the lease.
2. Prepare the eliminations and adjustments required for this lease on the December 31, 2015, consolidated worksheet.
3. Prepare the eliminations and adjustments for the December 31, 2016, consolidated worksheet.

Exercise 9 *(LO 6)* **Sales-type lease eliminations.** The Auto Clinic is a wholly owned subsidiary of Fast-Check Equipment Company. Fast-Check Equipment sells and leases 4-wheel alignment machines. The usual selling price of each machine is $35,000; it has a cost to Fast-Check Equipment of $25,000. On January 1, 2015, Fast-Check Equipment leased such a machine to Auto Clinic. The lease provided for payments of $9,096 at the start of each year for five years. The payments include $1,000 per year for maintenance to be provided by the seller. There is a bargain purchase price of $2,000 at the end of the fifth year. The implicit interest rate in the lease is 10% per year. The equipment is being depreciated over eight years.

The amortization schedule for the lease prepared by Fast-Check Equipment is as follows:

Date	Payment	Interest at 10% on Previous Balance	Reduction of Principal	Principal Balance
				$35,000
1/1/15	$ 8,096		$ 8,096	26,904
1/1/16	8,096	$2,690	5,406	21,498
1/1/17	8,096	2,150	5,946	15,552
1/1/18	8,096	1,555	6,541	9,011
1/1/19	8,096	901	7,195	1,816
12/31/19	2,000	184*	1,816	0
Totals	$42,480	$7,480	$35,000	

*Adjusted for rounding.

Prepare the eliminations and adjustments, in entry form, that would be required on a consolidated worksheet prepared on December 31, 2015.

PROBLEMS

Problem 5-1 *(LO 2)* **Eliminations, equity, 100%, bonds with straight-line.** Since its 100% acquisition of Dancer Corporation stock on December 31, 2012, Jones Corporation has maintained its investment under the equity method. However, due to Dancer's earning potential, the price included a $40,000 payment for goodwill. At the time of the purchase, the fair value of Dancer's assets equaled their book value.

On January 2, 2014, Dancer Corporation issued 10-year, 7% bonds at a face value of $50,000. The bonds pay interest each December 31. On January 2, 2016, Jones Corporation purchased all of Dancer Corporation's outstanding bonds for $48,000. The discount is amortized on a straight-line basis. They have been included in Jones's long-term investment in bonds account. Below are the trial balances of both companies on December 31, 2016.

	Jones Corporation	Dancer Corporation
Cash	70,500	67,500
Accounts Receivable	450,000	75,000
Inventory	200,000	65,000
Investment in Bonds	48,250	
Plant and Equipment (net)	2,420,000	196,000
Investment in Dancer Corporation	350,000	
Accounts Payable	(275,000)	(18,000)
Bonds Payable (7%)		(50,000)
Common Stock ($10 par)—Jones	(1,000,000)	
Paid-In Capital in Excess of Par—Jones	(750,000)	
Retained Earnings, January 1, 2016—Jones	(730,000)	
Common Stock ($10 par)—Dancer		(100,000)
Paid-In Capital in Excess of Par—Dancer		(130,000)
Retained Earnings, January 1, 2016—Dancer		(80,000)
Sales	(2,500,000)	(540,000)
Cost of Goods Sold	1,000,000	405,000
Other Expenses	720,000	106,000
Interest Income	(3,750)	
Interest Expense	0	3,500
Totals	0	0

1. Prepare the worksheet entries needed to eliminate the intercompany debt on ◀ ◀ ◀ ◀ ◀ **Required** December 31, 2016.
2. Prepare a consolidated income statement for the year ended December 31, 2016.

   Note: No worksheet is required.

Problem 5-2 *(LO 2)* **Cost method, 90%, straight-line bonds.** On January 1, 2015, Parker Company acquired 90% of the common stock of Stride Company for $351,000. On this date, Stride had common stock, other paid-in capital in excess of par, and retained earnings of $100,000, $40,000, and $210,000, respectively. The excess of cost over book value is due to goodwill. In both 2015 and 2016, Parker accounted for the investment in Stride using the cost method.

On January 1, 2015, Stride sold $100,000 par value of 10-year, 8% bonds for $94,000. The bonds pay interest semiannually on January 1 and July 1 of each year. On December 31, 2015, Parker purchased all of Stride's bonds for $98,200. The bonds are still held on December 31, 2016. Both companies correctly recorded all entries relative to bonds and interest, using straight-line amortization for premium or discount.

The trial balances of Parker Company and its subsidiary were as follows on December 31, 2016:

	Parker Company	Stride Company
Interest Receivable.	4,000	
Other Current Assets	246,400	315,200
Investment in Stride Company	351,000	
Investment in Stride Bonds	98,400	
Land.	80,000	60,000
Buildings and Equipment.	400,000	280,000
Accumulated Depreciation	(120,000)	(60,000)
Interest Payable		(4,000)
Other Current Liabilities.	(98,000)	(56,000)
Bonds Payable (8%)		(100,000)
Discount on Bonds Payable		4,800
Other Long-Term Liabilities	(200,000)	
Common Stock—Parker Company	(100,000)	
Other Paid-In Capital in Excess of Par—Parker Company	(200,000)	
Retained Earnings—Parker Company.	(365,000)	
Common Stock—Stride Company		(100,000)
Other Paid-In Capital in Excess of Par—Stride Company		(40,000)
Retained Earnings—Stride Company		(260,000)
Net Sales.	(640,000)	(350,000)
Cost of Goods Sold	360,000	200,000
Operating Expenses	168,400	71,400
Interest Expense.		8,600
Interest Income.	(8,200)	
Dividend Income	(27,000)	
Dividends Declared.	50,000	30,000
Totals	0	0

Prepare the worksheet necessary to produce the consolidated financial statements of Parker and ◀ ◀ ◀ ◀ ◀ **Required** its subsidiary Stride for the year ended December 31, 2016. Round all computations to the nearest dollar.

Problem 5-3 *(LO 2)* **80%, cost method, straight-line bonds, fixed asset sale.** On ◀ January 1, 2013, Appliance Outlets had the following balances in its stockholders' equity accounts: Common Stock ($10 par), $800,000; Paid-In Capital in Excess of Par, $625,000; and Retained Earnings, $450,000. General Appliances acquired 64,000 shares of Appliance

Outlets' common stock for $1,700,000 on that date. Any excess of cost over book value was attributed to goodwill.

Appliance Outlets issued $500,000 of 8-year, 11% bonds on December 31, 2012. The bonds sold for $476,000. General Appliances purchased one-half of these bonds in the market on January 1, 2015, for $256,000. Both companies use the straight-line method of amortization of premiums and discounts.

On July 1, 2016, General Appliances sold to Appliance Outlets an old building with a book value of $167,500, remaining life of 10 years, and $30,000 salvage value, for $195,000. The building is being depreciated on a straight-line basis. Appliance Outlets paid $20,000 in cash and signed a mortgage note with its parent for the balance. Interest, at 11% of the unpaid balance, and principal payments are due annually beginning July 1, 2017. (For convenience, the mortgage balances are not divided into current and long-term portions.)

The trial balances of the two companies at December 31, 2016, were as follows:

	General Appliances	Appliance Outlets
Cash	404,486	72,625
Accounts Receivable (net)	752,500	105,000
Interest Receivable	9,625	
Inventory	1,950,000	900,000
Investment in Appliance Outlets	1,700,000	
Investment in 11% Bonds	254,000	
Investment in Mortgage	175,000	
Property, Plant, and Equipment	9,000,000	2,950,000
Accumulated Depreciation	(1,695,000)	(940,000)
Accounts Payable	(670,000)	(80,000)
Interest Payable	(18,333)	(9,625)
Bonds Payable (11%)	(2,000,000)	(500,000)
Discount on Bonds Payable	10,470	12,000
Mortgage Payable		(175,000)
Common Stock ($5 par)	(3,200,000)	
Common Stock ($10 par)		(800,000)
Paid-In Capital in Excess of Par	(4,550,000)	(625,000)
Retained Earnings, January 1, 2016	(1,011,123)	(770,000)
Sales	(9,800,000)	(3,000,000)
Gain on Sale of Building	(27,500)	
Interest Income	(36,125)	
Dividend Income	(48,000)	
Cost of Goods Sold	4,940,000	1,700,000
Depreciation Expense	717,000	95,950
Interest Expense	223,000	67,544
Other Expenses	2,600,000	936,506
Dividends Declared	320,000	60,000
Totals	0	0

Required ▶ ▶ ▶ ▶ ▶ Prepare the worksheet necessary to produce the consolidated financial statements of General Appliances and its subsidiary for the year ended December 31, 2016. Include the determination and distribution of excess and income distribution schedules.

Use the following information for Problems 5-4 and 5-5:

On January 1, 2014, Pontiac Company acquired an 80% interest in the common stock of Stark Company for $400,000. Stark had the following balance sheet on the date of acquisition:

Stark Company
Balance Sheet
January 1, 2014

Assets		Liabilities and Equity	
Accounts receivable	$ 40,000	Accounts payable	$ 42,297
Inventory	20,000	Bonds payable	100,000
Land....................	35,000	Discount on bonds payable...	(2,297)
Buildings	250,000	Common stock ($10 par).....	10,000
Accumulated depreciation ...	(50,000)	Paid-in capital in excess of par	90,000
Equipment	120,000	Retained earnings	115,000
Accumulated depreciation ...	(60,000)		
Total assets..............	$355,000	Total liabilities and equity ..	$355,000

Buildings (20-year life) are undervalued by $80,000. Equipment (5-year life) is undervalued by $50,000. Any remaining excess is considered to be goodwill.

Stark issued $100,000 of 8%, 10-year bonds for $96,719 on January 1, 2011. Annual interest is paid on December 31. Pontiac purchased the bonds on January 1, 2015, for $104,770. Both companies use the straight-line method to amortize the premium/discount on the bonds. Pontiac and Stark used the following bond amortization schedules:

	Stark				Pontiac		
Period	Cash	Interest	Balance	Period	Cash	Interest	Balance
1/2011			$ 96,719	1/2011			
1/2012	$8,000	$8,328	97,047	1/2012			
1/2013	8,000	8,328	97,375	1/2013			
1/2014	8,000	8,328	97,703	1/2014			
1/2015	8,000	8,328	98,031	1/2015			$104,770
1/2016	8,000	8,328	98,359	1/2016	$8,000	$7,205	103,975
1/2017	8,000	8,328	98,687	1/2017	8,000	7,205	103,180
1/2018	8,000	8,328	99,015	1/2018	8,000	7,205	102,385
1/2019	8,000	8,328	99,343	1/2019	8,000	7,205	101,590
1/2020	8,000	8,328	99,671	1/2020	8,000	7,205	100,795
1/2021	8,000	8,328	100,000*	1/2021	8,000	7,205	100,000

*Adjusted for rounding.

Problem 5-4 *(LO 2)* **80%, equity, straight-line bonds purchased this year, inventory profits.** Refer to the preceding facts for Pontiac's acquisition of 80% of Starks common stock and the bond transactions. Pontiac uses the simple equity method to account for its investment in Stark. On January 1, 2015, Stack held merchandise acquired from Pontiac for $15,000. During 2015, Pontiac sold $50,000 worth of merchandise to Stark. Stark held $20,000 of this merchandise at December 31, 2015. Stark owed Pontiac $10,000 on December 31 as a result of these intercompany sales. Pontiac has a gross profit rate of 30%. Pontiac and Stark had the trial balances on December 31, 2015, shown on next page.

	Pontiac Company	Stark Company
Cash	17,870	32,031
Accounts Receivable	90,000	60,000
Inventory	100,000	30,000
Land.....	150,000	45,000
Investment in Stark.....	435,738	
Investment in Stark Bonds	103,975	
Buildings	500,000	250,000
Accumulated Depreciation	(300,000)	(70,000)
Equipment	200,000	120,000
Accumulated Depreciation	(100,000)	(84,000)
Accounts Payable	(55,000)	(25,000)
Bonds Payable.....		(100,000)
Discount on Bonds Payable		1,641
Common Stock	(100,000)	(10,000)
Paid-In Capital in Excess of Par	(600,000)	(90,000)
Retained Earnings, January 1, 2015.....	(400,000)	(145,000)
Sales	(600,000)	(220,000)
Cost of Goods Sold	410,000	120,000
Depreciation Expense—Buildings.....	30,000	10,000
Depreciation Expense—Equipment.....	15,000	12,000
Other Expenses	109,360	45,000
Interest Revenue.....	(7,205)	
Interest Expense.....		8,328
Subsidiary Income.....	(19,738)	
Dividends Declared.....	20,000	10,000
Totals	0	0

Required ▶ ▶ ▶ ▶ ▶ Prepare the worksheet necessary to produce the consolidated financial statements for Pontiac Company and its subsidiary Stark Company for the year ended December 31, 2015. Include the determination and distribution of excess and income distribution schedules.

Problem 5-5 *(LO 2)* **80%, equity, straight-line bonds purchased last year, inventory profits.** Refer to the preceding facts for Pontiac's acquisition of 80% of Stark's common stock and the bond transactions. Pontiac uses the simple equity method to account for its investment in Stark. On January 1, 2016, Stark held merchandise acquired from Pontiac for $20,000. During 2016, Pontiac sold $60,000 worth of merchandise to Stark. Stark held $25,000 of this merchandise at December 31, 2016. Stark owed Pontiac $12,000 on December 31 as a result of these intercompany sales. Pontiac has a gross profit rate of 30%. Pontiac and Stark had the following trial balances on December 31, 2016:

	Pontiac Company	Stark Company
Cash	49,150	61,031
Accounts Receivable	110,000	60,000
Inventory	120,000	45,000
Land.....	150,000	45,000
Investment in Stark.....	453,075	
Investment in Stark Bonds	103,180	
Buildings	500,000	250,000
Accumulated Depreciation	(330,000)	(80,000)
Equipment	200,000	120,000
Accumulated Depreciation	(115,000)	(96,000)
Accounts Payable	(35,000)	(25,000)
Bonds Payable.....		(100,000)
Discount on Bonds Payable.....		1,313
Common Stock	(100,000)	(10,000)

	Pontiac Company	Stark Company
Paid-In Capital in Excess of Par	(600,000)	(90,000)
Retained Earnings, January 1, 2016.	(442,223)	(159,672)
Sales	(700,000)	(230,000)
Cost of Goods Sold	480,000	125,000
Depreciation Expense—Buildings.	30,000	10,000
Depreciation Expense—Equipment.	15,000	12,000
Other Expenses	124,360	43,000
Interest Revenue.	(7,205)	
Interest Expense.		8,328
Subsidiary Income.	(25,337)	
Dividends Declared.	20,000	10,000
Totals	0	0

Prepare the worksheet necessary to produce the consolidated financial statements for Pontiac ◄ ◄ ◄ ◄ ◄ **Required**
Company and its subsidiary Stark Company for the year ended December 31, 2016. Include
the determination and distribution of excess and income distribution schedules.

Use the following information for Problems 5-6 and 5-7:

On January 1, 2014, Postman Company acquired Spartan Company. Postman paid
$400,000 for 80% of Spartan's common stock. On the date of acquisition, Spartan had
the following balance sheet:

Spartan Company
Balance Sheet
January 1, 2014

Assets		Liabilities and Equity	
Accounts receivable	$ 90,000	Accounts payable	$ 17,352
Inventory	50,000	Bonds payable	100,000
Land.	60,000	Premium on bonds payable. . .	2,648
Buildings	100,000	Common stock ($1 par).	10,000
Accumulated depreciation . . .	(30,000)	Paid-in capital in excess of par	90,000
Equipment	80,000	Retained earnings	100,000
Accumulated depreciation . . .	(30,000)		
Total assets.	$320,000	Total liabilities and equity . .	$320,000

Buildings, which have a 20-year life, are undervalued by $130,000. Equipment,
which has a 5-year life, is undervalued by $50,000. Any remaining excess is considered to
be goodwill.

Spartan issued $100,000 of 8%, 10-year bonds for $103,432 on January 1, 2011,
when the market rate was 7.5%. Annual interest is paid on December 31. Postman purchased the bonds for $95,514 on January 1, 2015, when the market rate was 9%. Both
companies use the effective interest method to amortize the premium/discount on the
bonds. Postman and Spartan prepared the following bond amortization schedules:

	Spartan			Postman			
Period	Cash	Interest	Balance	Period	Cash	Interest	Balance
1/2011			$103,432	1/2011			
1/2012	$8,000	$7,757	103,189	1/2012			
1/2013	8,000	7,739	102,928	1/2013			
1/2014	8,000	7,720	102,648	1/2014			

(continued)

	Spartan				Postman		
Period	Cash	Interest	Balance	Period	Cash	Interest	Balance
1/2015	8,000	7,699	102,347	1/2015			$ 95,514
1/2016	8,000	7,676	102,023	1/2016	$8,000	$8,596	96,110
1/2017	8,000	7,652	101,675	1/2017	8,000	8,650	96,760
1/2018	8,000	7,626	101,301	1/2018	8,000	8,708	97,468
1/2019	8,000	7,598	100,899	1/2019	8,000	8,772	98,240
1/2020	8,000	7,567	100,466	1/2020	8,000	8,842	99,082
1/2021	8,000	7,534*	100,000	1/2021	8,000	8,918*	100,000

*Adjusted for rounding.

Problem 5-6 *(LO 2)* **80%, equity, effective interest bonds purchased this year, inventory profits.** Refer to the preceding facts for Postman's acquisition of 80% of Spartan's common stock and the bond transactions. Postman uses the simple equity method to account for its investment in Spartan. On January 1, 2015, Postman held merchandise acquired from Spartan for $9,000. During 2015, Spartan sold $20,000 worth of merchandise to Postman. Postman held $12,000 of this merchandise at December 31, 2015. Postman owed Spartan $7,000 on December 31 as a result of these intercompany sales. Spartan has a gross profit rate of 25%.

Postman and Spartan had the following trial balances on December 31, 2015:

	Postman	Spartan
Cash	144,486	99,347
Accounts Receivable	90,000	60,000
Inventory	120,000	55,000
Land	200,000	60,000
Investment in Spartan	429,859	
Investment in Spartan Bonds	96,110	
Buildings	600,000	100,000
Accumulated Depreciation	(310,000)	(40,000)
Equipment	150,000	80,000
Accumulated Depreciation	(90,000)	(50,000)
Accounts Payable	(55,000)	(25,000)
Bonds Payable		(100,000)
Discount on Bonds Payable		(2,023)
Common Stock	(100,000)	(10,000)
Paid-In Capital in Excess of Par	(800,000)	(90,000)
Retained Earnings, January 1, 2015	(300,000)	(120,000)
Sales	(850,000)	(320,000)
Cost of Goods Sold	500,000	200,000
Depreciation Expense—Buildings	30,000	5,000
Depreciation Expense—Equipment	15,000	10,000
Other Expenses	140,000	70,000
Interest Revenue	(8,596)	
Interest Expense		7,676
Subsidiary Income	(21,859)	
Dividends Declared	20,000	10,000
Totals	0	0

Required ▶ ▶ ▶ ▶ ▶ Prepare the worksheet necessary to produce the consolidated financial statements for Postman Company and its subsidiary Spartan Company for the year ended December 31, 2015. Include the determination and distribution of excess and income distribution schedules.

Problem 5-7 *(LO 2)* **80%, equity, effective interest bonds purchased last year, inventory profits.** Refer to the preceding facts for Postman's acquisition of 80% of Spartan's common stock and the bond transactions. Postman uses the simple equity method to account for its investment in Spartan. On January 1, 2016, Postman held merchandise acquired from Spartan for $12,000. During 2016, Spartan sold $25,000 worth of merchandise to Postman. Postman held $10,000 of this merchandise at December 31, 2016. Postman owed Spartan $6,000 on December 31 as a result of these intercompany sales. Spartan has a gross profit rate of 25%.

Postman and Spartan had the following trial balances on December 31, 2016:

	Postman	Spartan
Cash	290,486	99,347
Accounts Receivable	120,000	91,000
Inventory	140,000	55,000
Land	200,000	60,000
Investment in Spartan	435,737	
Investment in Spartan Bonds	96,760	
Buildings	600,000	100,000
Accumulated Depreciation	(340,000)	(45,000)
Equipment	150,000	80,000
Accumulated Depreciation	(105,000)	(60,000)
Accounts Payable	(40,000)	(34,000)
Bonds Payable		(100,000)
Premium on Bonds Payable		(1,675)
Common Stock	(100,000)	(10,000)
Paid-In Capital in Excess of Par	(800,000)	(90,000)
Retained Earnings, January 1, 2016	(475,455)	(137,324)
Sales	(900,000)	(350,000)
Cost of Goods Sold	530,000	230,000
Depreciation Expense—Buildings	30,000	5,000
Depreciation Expense—Equipment	15,000	10,000
Other Expenses	155,000	80,000
Interest Revenue	(8,650)	
Interest Expense		7,652
Subsidiary Income	(13,878)	
Dividends Declared	20,000	10,000
Totals	0	0

Prepare the worksheet necessary to produce the consolidated financial statements for Postman ◄ ◄ ◄ ◄ ◄ **Required** Company and its subsidiary Spartan Company for the year ended December 31, 2016. Include the determination and distribution of excess and income distribution schedules.

Problem 5-8 *(LO 2)* **CPA Objective, equipment, merchandise, bonds.** The problem below is an example of a question of the CPA "Other Objective Format" type as it was applied to the consolidations area. A mark-sensing answer sheet was used on the exam. You may just supply the answer, which should be accompanied by calculations where appropriate.

Presented below are selected amounts from the separate unconsolidated financial statements of Pero Corporation and its 90%-owned subsidiary Sean Company at December 31, 2016. Additional information follows:

	Pero Corporation	Sean Company
Selected income statement amounts:		
Sales	$ 710,000	$ 530,000
Cost of goods sold	490,000	370,000
Gain on the sale of equipment		21,000
Earnings from investment in subsidiary (equity)	63,000	
Other expenses	48,000	75,000
Interest expense		16,000
Depreciation	25,000	20,000
Selected balance sheet amounts:		
Cash	30,000	18,000
Inventories	229,000	150,000
Equipment	440,000	360,000
Accumulated depreciation	(200,000)	(120,000)
Investment in Sean (equity balance)	211,000	
Investment in bonds	(100,000)	
Discount on bonds	(9,000)	
Bonds payable		(200,000)
Discount on bonds payable		3,000
Common stock	100,000)	(10,000)
Additional paid-in capital in excess of par	(250,000)	(40,000)
Retained earnings	(402,000)	(140,000)
Selected statement of retained earnings amounts:		
Beginning balance, December 31, 2015	272,000	100,000
Net income	210,000	70,000
Dividends paid	80,000	30,000

Additional information is as follows:

1. On January 2, 2016, Pero purchased 90% of Sean's 100,000 outstanding common stock for cash of $175,000. On that date, Sean's stockholders' equity equaled $150,000, and the fair values of Sean's assets and liabilities equaled their carrying amounts. Any remaining excess is considered to be goodwill.
2. On September 4, 2016, Sean paid cash dividends of $30,000.
3. On December 31, 2016, Pero recorded its equity in Sean's earnings.

Required ▶ ▶ ▶ ▶ ▶

1. Items (a) through (c) on page 311 represent transactions between Pero and Sean during 2016. Determine the dollar amount effect of the consolidating adjustment on 2016 consolidated net income. Ignore income tax considerations.

Items to be answered:

    a. On January 3, 2016, Sean sold equipment with an original cost of $30,000 and a carrying value of $21,000 to Pero for $36,000. The equipment had a remaining life of three years and was depreciated using the straight-line method by both companies.

    b. During 2016, Sean sold merchandise to Pero for $60,000, which included a profit of $20,000. At December 31, 2016, half of this merchandise remained in Pero's inventory.

    c. On December 31, 2016, Pero paid $94,000 to purchase 50% of the outstanding bonds issued by Sean. The bonds mature on December 31, 2022, and were originally issued at a discount. The bonds pay interest annually on December 31, and the interest was paid to the prior investor immediately before Pero's purchase of the bonds.

2. Items (a) through (l) below refer to accounts that may or may not be included in Pero's consolidated financial statements. The list on the right refers to the various possibilities of those amounts to be reported in Pero's consolidated financial statements for the year ended December 31, 2016. Consider all transactions stated above in determining your answer. Ignore income tax considerations.

Items to be answered:
a. Cash
b. Equipment
c. Investment in subsidiary
d. Bonds payable
e. NCI
f. Common stock
g. Beginning retained earnings
h. Dividends paid
i. Gain on retirement of bonds
j. Cost of goods sold
k. Interest expense
l. Depreciation expense

Responses to be selected:
1. Sum of amounts on Pero's and Sean's separate unconsolidated financial statements.
2. Less than the sum of amounts on Pero's and Sean's separate unconsolidated financial statements, but not the same as the amount on either.
3. Same as amount for Pero only.
4. Same as amount for Sean only.
5. Eliminated entirely in consolidation.
6. Shown in consolidated financial statements but not in separate unconsolidated financial statements.
7. Neither in consolidated nor in separate unconsolidated financial statements.

(AICPA adapted)

Problem 5-9 *(LO 2)* **90%, cost, machine, merchandise, effective interest bonds.**
Princess Company acquired a 90% interest in Sundown Company on January 1, 2011, for $675,000. Any excess of cost over book value was due to goodwill.
    Capital balances of Sundown Company on January 1, 2011, were as follows:

Common stock ($10 par)	$200,000
Paid-in capital in excess of par	100,000
Retained earnings	300,000
Total equity	$600,000

    Sundown Company sold a machine to Princess for $30,000 on January 1, 2014. It cost Sundown $20,000 to build the machine, which had a 5-year remaining life on the date of the sale and is subject to straight-line depreciation.

    Princess purchased one-half of the outstanding 9% bonds of Sundown for $89,186 (to yield 12%) on December 31, 2015. The bonds were sold originally by Sundown to yield 10% to outside parties. The discount on the entire set of bonds was $7,582 on December 31, 2015. The effective interest method of amortization is used.

    During 2016, Princess Company sold merchandise to Sundown for $50,000. Princess recorded a 30% gross profit on the sales price. $20,000 of the merchandise purchased from Princess remains unsold at the end of the year.

The trial balances of Princess and its subsidiary, Sundown, are as follows on December 31, 2016:

	Princess Company	Sundown Company
Inventory	25,000	80,000
Equipment	371,190	1,522,413
Accumulated Depreciation	(200,000)	(600,000)
Investment in Sundown Stock	675,000	
Investment in Sundown Bonds	90,888	
Bonds Payable (9%)		(200,000)
Discount on Bonds Payable		6,345
Common Stock ($10 par)	(200,000)	(200,000)
Paid-In Capital in Excess of Par	(300,000)	(100,000)
Retained Earnings, January 1, 2016	(401,376)	(500,000)
Sales	(300,000)	(260,000)
Cost of Goods Sold	100,000	72,000
Interest Income	(10,702)	
Other Expenses	150,000	160,000
Interest Expense		19,242
Totals	0	0

Required ▶ ▶ ▶ ▶ ▶ Prepare the worksheet necessary to produce the consolidated financial statements of Princess Company and its subsidiary for the year ended December 31, 2016. Include the determination and distribution of excess and income distribution schedules.

Problem 5-10 *(LO 4)* **100%, cost, operating lease.** Sym Corporation, a wholly owned subsidiary of Paratec Corporation, leased equipment from its parent company on August 1, 2016. The terms of the agreement clearly do not require the lease to be accounted for as a capital lease. Both entities are accounting for the lease as an operating lease. The lease payment is $12,000 per year, paid in advance each August 1.

Paratec purchased its investment in Sym on December 31, 2011, when Sym had a retained earnings balance of $150,000. Paratec is accounting for its investment in Sym under the cost method. Included in the original purchase price was a $50,000 premium attributable to Sym's history of exceptional earnings.

The December 31, 2018, trial balances of Paratec and its subsidiary are presented below.

	Paratec Corporation	Sym Corporation
Cash	190,000	40,000
Accounts Receivable (net)	738,350	142,000
Inventory	500,000	75,000
Prepaid Rent on Equipment		7,000
Investment in Bonds	250,000	65,000
Investment in Sym Corporation	400,000	
Land	250,000	85,000
Plant and Equipment	1,950,000	295,000
Accumulated Depreciation—Plant and Equipment	(250,000)	(60,000)
Equipment Under Operating Lease	120,000	
Accumulated Depreciation—Assets Under Operating Lease	(36,000)	
Accounts Payable	(385,000)	(52,000)
Deferred Rent Revenue	(7,000)	
Common Stock (no par)	(2,000,000)	(200,000)
Retained Earnings, January 1, 2018	(1,076,350)	(310,000)

	Paratec Corporation	Sym Corporation
Sales	(4,720,000)	(500,000)
Rent Income	(12,000)	
Cost of Goods Sold	3,068,000	300,000
Rent Expense		12,000
Other Expenses	725,000	101,000
Dividends Declared	295,000	
Totals	0	0

Prepare the worksheet necessary to produce the consolidated income statement and balance ◀ ◀ ◀ ◀ ◀ **Required**
sheet of Paratec Corporation and its subsidiary for the year ended December 31, 2018.

Use the following information for Problems 5-11 through 5-14:

On January 1, 2015 Press Company acquired Simon Company. Press paid $450,000 for
80% of Simon's common stock. On the date of acquisition, Simon had the following
balance sheet:

Simon Company
Balance Sheet
January 1, 2015

Assets		Liabilities and Equity	
Accounts receivable	$ 40,000	Accounts payable	$ 80,000
Inventory	60,000	Common stock ($1 par)	10,000
Land.....................	100,000	Paid-in capital in excess of par ...	190,000
Buildings	400,000	Retained earnings	190,000
Accumulated depreciation ...	(200,000)		
Equipment	100,000		
Accumulated depreciation ...	(30,000)		
Total assets..............	$ 470,000	Total liabilities and equity	$470,000

Buildings, which have a 20-year life, are undervalued by $100,000. Any excess cost is
considered to be goodwill.

Problem 5-11 *(LO 5)* **80%, equity, financing lease, merchandise.** Refer to the preceding facts for Press's acquisition of Simon common stock. Press uses the simple equity method to account for its investment in Simon. On January 1, 2016, Press held merchandise acquired from Simon for $10,000. During 2016, Simon sold $40,000 worth of merchandise to Press. Press held $12,000 of this merchandise at December 31, 2016. Press owed Simon $6,000 on December 31 as a result of this intercompany sale. Simon has a gross profit rate of 25%.

On January 1, 2016, Simon signed a 5-year lease with Press for the rental of equipment, which has a 5-year life. Payments of $23,363 are due each January 1, and there is a guaranteed residual value of $10,000 at the end of the five years. The market value of the equipment at the inception of the lease was $100,000. Press has a 12% implicit rate on the lease. The following amortization table was prepared for the lease.

Period	Payment	Interest	Principal	Balance
Jan. 1, 2016	$23,363		$(23,363)	$76,637
Jan. 1, 2017	23,363	$9,196	(14,167)	62,470
Jan. 1, 2018	23,363	7,496	(15,867)	46,603
Jan. 1, 2019	23,363	5,592	(17,771)	28,832
Jan. 1, 2020	23,363	3,460	(19,903)	8,929
Jan. 1, 2021	10,000	1,071	(8,929)	0

(continued)

Press and Simon had the following trial balances on December 31, 2016:

	Press Company	Simon Company
Cash	72,363	73,637
Accounts Receivable	72,000	45,000
Inventory	120,000	56,000
Land	100,000	100,000
Investment in Simon	506,643	
Minimum Lease Payments Receivable	103,452	
Unearned Interest	(17,619)	
Buildings	800,000	400,000
Accumulated Depreciation	(220,000)	(220,000)
Equipment	150,000	100,000
Accumulated Depreciation	(90,000)	(50,000)
Equipment—Capital Lease		100,000
Accumulated Depreciation—Capital Lease		(18,000)
Accounts Payable	(60,000)	(40,000)
Obligation Under Capital Lease		(76,637)
Accrued Interest—Capital Lease		(9,196)
Common Stock	(100,000)	(10,000)
Paid-In Capital in Excess of Par	(800,000)	(190,000)
Retained Earnings, January 1, 2016	(450,000)	(230,000)
Sales	(800,000)	(400,000)
Cost of Goods Sold	450,000	240,000
Depreciation Expense—Buildings	30,000	10,000
Depreciation Expense—Equipment	15,000	28,000
Other Expenses	140,000	72,000
Interest Expense		9,196
Interest Revenue	(9,196)	
Subsidiary Income	(32,643)	
Dividends Declared	20,000	10,000
Totals	0	0

Required ▶ ▶ ▶ ▶ ▶ Prepare the worksheet necessary to produce the consolidated financial statements for Press Company and its subsidiary Simon Company for the year ended December 31, 2016. Include the determination and distribution of excess and income distribution schedules.

Problem 5-12 *(LO 5)* **80%, equity, financing lease, merchandise, later year.** Refer to the preceding facts for Press's acquisition of Simon common stock. Press uses the simple equity method to account for its investment in Simon. On January 1, 2017, Press held merchandise acquired from Simon for $12,000. During 2017, Simon sold $35,000 worth of merchandise to Press. Press held $8,000 of this merchandise at December 31, 2017. Press owed Simon $7,000 on December 31 as a result of this intercompany sale. Simon has a gross profit rate of 25%.

On January 1, 2016, Simon signed a 5-year lease with Press for the rental of equipment, which has a 5-year life. Payments of $23,363 are due each January 1, and there is a guaranteed residual value of $10,000 at the end of the five years. The market value of the equipment at the inception of the lease was $100,000. Press has a 12% implicit rate on the lease. The following amortization table was prepared for the lease:

Period	Payment	Interest	Principal	Balance
Jan. 1, 2016	$23,363		$(23,363)	$76,637
Jan. 1, 2017	23,363	$9,196	(14,167)	62,470
Jan. 1, 2018	23,363	7,496	(15,867)	46,603

Period	Payment	Interest	Principal	Balance
Jan. 1, 2019	23,363	5,592	(17,771)	28,832
Jan. 1, 2020	23,363	3,460	(19,903)	8,929
Jan. 1, 2021	10,000	1,071	(8,929)	0

Press and Simon had the following trial balances on December 31, 2017:

	Press Company	Simon Company
Cash	140,000	78,274
Accounts Receivable	87,000	55,000
Inventory	170,000	66,000
Land	168,726	100,000
Investment in Simon	516,646	
Minimum Lease Payments Receivable	80,089	
Unearned Interest	(10,123)	
Buildings	800,000	400,000
Accumulated Depreciation	(250,000)	(230,000)
Equipment	150,000	100,000
Accumulated Depreciation	(105,000)	(60,000)
Equipment—Capital Lease		100,000
Accumulated Depreciation—Capital Lease		(36,000)
Accounts Payable	(60,000)	(30,000)
Obligation Under Capital Lease		(62,470)
Accrued Interest—Capital Lease		(7,496)
Common Stock	(100,000)	(10,000)
Paid-In Capital in Excess of Par	(800,000)	(190,000)
Retained Earnings, January 1, 2017	(636,839)	(260,804)
Sales	(900,000)	(450,000)
Cost of Goods Sold	550,000	290,000
Depreciation Expense—Buildings	30,000	10,000
Depreciation Expense—Equipment	15,000	28,000
Other Expenses	160,000	92,000
Interest Expense		7,496
Interest Revenue	(7,496)	
Subsidiary Income	(18,003)	
Dividends Declared	20,000	10,000
Totals	0	0

Prepare the worksheet necessary to produce the consolidated financial statements for Press Company and its subsidiary Simon Company for the year ended December 31, 2017. Include the determination and distribution of excess and income distribution schedules. ◄ ◄ ◄ ◄ ◄ **Required**

Problem 5-13 *(LO 5, 6)* **80%, equity, sales-type lease, merchandise.** Refer to the preceding facts for Press's acquisition of Simon common stock. Press uses the simple equity method to account for its investment in Simon. On January 1, 2016, Press held merchandise acquired from Simon for $10,000. During 2016, Simon sold $40,000 worth of merchandise to Press. Press held $12,000 of this merchandise at December 31, 2016. Press owed Simon $6,000 on December 31 as a result of this intercompany sale. Simon has a gross profit rate of 25%.

On January 1, 2016, Simon signed a 5-year lease with Press for the rental of equipment, which has a 5-year life. Payments of $23,363 are due each January 1, and there is a guaranteed residual value of $10,000 at the end of the five years. The market value of the equipment at the inception of the lease was $100,000. The cost of the equipment to Press was $85,000. Press has a 12% implicit rate on the lease. The amortization table shown on next page was prepared for the lease.

Period	Payment	Interest	Principal	Balance
Jan. 1, 2016	$23,363		$(23,363)	$76,637
Jan. 1, 2017	23,363	$9,196	(14,167)	62,470
Jan. 1, 2018	23,363	7,496	(15,867)	46,603
Jan. 1, 2019	23,363	5,592	(17,771)	28,832
Jan. 1, 2020	23,363	3,460	(19,903)	8,929
Jan. 1, 2021	10,000	1,071	(8,929)	0

Press and Simon had the following trial balances on December 31, 2016:

	Press Company	Simon Company
Cash	72,363	73,637
Accounts Receivable	72,000	45,000
Inventory	120,000	56,000
Land	100,000	100,000
Investment in Simon	506,643	
Minimum Lease Payments Receivable	103,452	
Unearned Interest	(17,619)	
Buildings	800,000	400,000
Accumulated Depreciation	(220,000)	(220,000)
Equipment	150,000	100,000
Accumulated Depreciation	(90,000)	(50,000)
Equipment—Capital Lease		100,000
Accumulated Depreciation—Capital Lease		(18,000)
Accounts Payable	(60,000)	(40,000)
Obligation Under Capital Lease		(76,637)
Accrued Interest—Capital Lease		(9,196)
Common Stock	(100,000)	(10,000)
Paid-In Capital in Excess of Par	(800,000)	(190,000)
Retained Earnings, January 1, 2016	(450,000)	(230,000)
Sales	(800,000)	(400,000)
Cost of Goods Sold	465,000	240,000
Depreciation Expense—Buildings	30,000	10,000
Depreciation Expense—Equipment	15,000	28,000
Other Expenses	140,000	72,000
Interest Expense		9,196
Interest Revenue	(9,196)	
Gain on Fixed Asset Sale	(15,000)	
Subsidiary Income	(32,643)	
Dividends Declared	20,000	10,000
Totals	0	0

Required ▶ ▶ ▶ ▶ ▶ Prepare the worksheet necessary to produce the consolidated financial statements for Press Company and its subsidiary Simon Company for the year ended December 31, 2016. Include the determination and distribution of excess and income distribution schedules.

Problem 5-14 *(LO 5, 6)* **80%, equity, sales-type lease, merchandise, later year.** Refer to the preceding facts for Press's acquisition of Simon common stock. Press uses the simple equity method to account for its investment in Simon. On January 1, 2017, Press held merchandise acquired from Simon for $12,000. During 2017, Simon sold merchandise to Press for $35,000. Press held $8,000 of this merchandise at December 31, 2017. Press owed Simon $7,000 on December 31 as a result of this intercompany sale. Simon has a gross profit rate of 25%.

On January 1, 2016, Simon signed a 5-year lease with Press for the rental of equipment, which has a 5-year life. Payments of $23,363 are due each January 1, and there is a guaranteed residual value of $10,000 at the end of the five years. The market value of the equipment at the inception of the lease was $100,000. The cost of the equipment to Press was $85,000. Press has a 12% implicit rate on the lease. The following amortization table was prepared for the lease:

Period	Payment	Interest	Principal	Balance
Jan. 1, 2016	$23,363		$(23,363)	$76,637
Jan. 1, 2017	23,363	$9,196	(14,167)	62,470
Jan. 1, 2018	23,363	7,496	(15,867)	46,603
Jan. 1, 2019	23,363	5,592	(17,771)	28,832
Jan. 1, 2020	23,363	3,460	(19,903)	8,929
Jan. 1, 2021	10,000	1,071	(8,929)	0

Press and Simon had the following trial balances on December 31, 2017:

	Press Company	Simon Company
Cash	140,000	78,274
Accounts Receivable	87,000	55,000
Inventory	170,000	66,000
Land	168,726	100,000
Investment in Simon	516,646	
Minimum Lease Payments Receivable	80,089	
Unearned Interest	(10,123)	
Buildings	800,000	400,000
Accumulated Depreciation	(250,000)	(230,000)
Equipment	150,000	100,000
Accumulated Depreciation	(105,000)	(60,000)
Equipment—Capital Lease		100,000
Accumulated Depreciation—Capital Lease		(36,000)
Accounts Payable	(60,000)	(30,000)
Obligation Under Capital Lease		(62,470)
Accrued Interest—Capital Lease		(7,496)
Common Stock	(100,000)	(10,000)
Paid-In Capital in Excess of Par	(800,000)	(190,000)
Retained Earnings, January 1, 2017	(636,839)	(260,804)
Sales	(900,000)	(450,000)
Cost of Goods Sold	550,000	290,000
Depreciation Expense—Buildings	30,000	10,000
Depreciation Expense—Equipment	15,000	28,000
Other Expenses	160,000	92,000
Interest Expense		7,496
Interest Revenue	(7,496)	
Subsidiary Income	(18,003)	
Dividends Declared	20,000	10,000
Totals	0	0

Prepare the worksheet necessary to produce the consolidated financial statements for Press Company and its subsidiary Simon Company for the year ended December 31, 2017. Include the determination and distribution of excess and income distribution schedules.  **◄ ◄ ◄ ◄ ◄ Required**

Problem 5-15 *(LO 5, 6)* **80%, cost, financing and sales-type leases.** Plessor Industries acquired 80% of the outstanding common stock of Slammer Company on January 1, 2015, for $320,000. On that date, Slammer's book values approximated fair values, and the balance of its retained earnings account was $80,000. Any excess was attributed to goodwill. Slammer's net income was $20,000 for 2015 and $30,000 for 2016. No dividends were paid in either year.

On January 1, 2016, Slammer signed a 5-year lease with Plessor for the rental of a small factory building with a 10-year life. Payments of $25,000 are due at the beginning of each year on January 1, and Slammer is expected to exercise the $5,000 bargain purchase option at the end of the fifth year. The fair value of the factory was $103,770 at the start of the lease term. Plessor's implicit rate on the lease is 12%.

A second lease agreement, for the rental of production equipment with an 8-year life, was signed by Slammer on January 1, 2017. The terms of this 4-year lease require a payment of $15,000 at the beginning of each year on January 1. The present value of the lease payments at Plessor's 12% implicit rate was equal to the fair value of the equipment, $52,298, when the lease was signed. The cost of the equipment to Plessor was $45,000, and there is a $2,000 bargain purchase option. Eight-year, straight-line depreciation is being used, with no salvage value.

The following trial balances were prepared by the separate companies at December 31, 2017:

	Plessor Industries	Slammer Company
Cash	60,000	40,745
Accounts Receivable	97,778	76,000
Inventory	140,000	120,000
Minimum Lease Payments Receivable	127,000	
Unearned Interest Income	(14,417)	
Investment in Slammer Company	320,000	
Assets Under Capital Lease		156,068
Accumulated Depreciation—Assets Under Capital Lease		(27,291)
Property, Plant, and Equipment	1,900,000	310,000
Accumulated Depreciation—Property, Plant, and Equipment	(1,077,000)	(72,000)
Accounts Payable (includes accrued interest payable)	(148,000)	(45,065)
Obligations Under Capital Lease		(100,520)
Common Stock ($10 par)	(700,000)	(300,000)
Paid-In Capital in Excess of Par	(325,000)	
Retained Earnings, January 1, 2017	(295,000)	(130,000)
Sales	(1,400,000)	(600,000)
Sales Profit on Leases	(7,298)	
Interest Income	(12,063)	
Cost of Goods Sold	780,000	380,000
Interest Expense		12,063
Other Expenses	510,000	165,000
Dividend Income	(12,000)	
Dividends Declared	56,000	15,000
Totals	0	0

Required ▶ ▶ ▶ ▶ ▶ Prepare the worksheet necessary to produce the consolidated financial statements of Plessor Industries and its subsidiary for the year ended December 31, 2017. Include the determination and distribution of excess and income distribution schedules.

Problem 5-16 *(LO 4, 5, 6)* **80%, cost, operating, sales-type and financing leases.** Patter Inc. acquired an 80% interest in Swing Company for $480,000 on January 1, 2011, when Swing had the following stockholders' equity:

Common stock ($10 par)	$100,000
Additional paid-in capital in excess of par	300,000
Retained earnings	100,000
Total equity	$500,000

Any excess was attributed to goodwill.

The trial balances of Patter, Inc., and Swing Company were prepared on December 31, 2015, as follows:

	Patter, Inc.	Swing Company
Cash	91,013	26,050
Inventory	70,000	20,000
Property, Plant, and Equipment	320,000	50,000
Accumulated Depreciation—Property, Plant, and Equipment	(70,000)	(20,000)
Assets Under Capital Lease	40,676	
Accumulated Depreciation—Assets Under Capital Lease	(10,796)	
Assets Under Operating Lease		420,000
Accumulated Depreciation—Assets Under Operating Lease		(80,000)
Minimum Lease Payments Receivable		412,000
Unearned Interest Income on Leases		(4,000)
Investment in Swing Company	480,000	
Accounts Payable	(130,000)	(180,000)
Obligations Under Capital Lease	(24,560)	
Interest Payable	(4,440)	
Common Stock ($10 par)	(200,000)	(100,000)
Paid-In Capital in Excess of Par	(300,000)	(300,000)
Retained Earnings, January 1, 2015	(278,333)	(226,610)
Sales	(300,000)	(130,000)
Rent Income		(34,000)
Interest Income—Capital Lease		(4,440)
Depreciation Expense	41,000	23,000
Interest Expense	4,440	
Selling and General Expense	70,000	38,000
Cost of Goods Sold	190,000	90,000
Rent Expense	11,000	
Totals	0	0

The following intercompany leases have been written by Swing since the acquisition:

1. On January 1, 2013, Swing purchased for $140,000 land and a building, which it leased to Patter, Inc., under a 5-year operating lease. Payments of $11,000 per year are required at the beginning of each year. The $120,000 building cost is being depreciated over 20 years on a straight-line basis.
2. On January 1, 2014, Swing purchased a machine for $14,000 and leased it to Patter, Inc. The 4-year lease qualifies as a capital lease. The rentals are $5,000 per year, payable at the beginning of each year. There is a bargain purchase option whereby Patter will purchase the machine at the end of four years for $2,000.

   The fair value of the machine was $17,560 at the start of the lease term. The lease payments, including the purchase option, yield an implicit rate of 15% to the lessor. Patter is depreciating the machine over seven years on a straight-line basis with no salvage value.
3. January 1, 2015, Swing purchased a truck for $23,116 and leased it to Patter, Inc., under a 3-year capital lease. Payments of $8,000 per year are required at the beginning of each year. There is a bargain purchase agreement for $5,000. Patter, Inc., is depreciating the truck over four years, straight-line, with no salvage value. The lease has a lessor implicit rate of 20%.
4. Patter, Inc., has accrued interest in 2015 on its capital lease obligations. Swing has recognized earned interest for the year on its capital leases.

Prepare the worksheet necessary to produce the consolidated financial statements of Patter, Inc., and its subsidiary for the year ended December 31, 2015. Include the determination and distribution of excess and income distribution schedules.   ◀ ◀ ◀ ◀ ◀ **Required**

APPENDIX PROBLEMS

Problem 5A-1 *(LO 7)* **80%, equity, financing leases with unguaranteed residual value, fixed asset profit.** Steven Truck Company has been an 80%-owned subsidiary of Paulz Heavy Equipment since January 1, 2013, when Paulz acquired 128,000 shares of Steven common stock for $832,000, an amount equal to the book value of Steven's net assets at that date. Steven's net income and dividends paid since acquisition are as follows:

Year	Net Income	Dividends
2013	$ 70,000	$25,000
2014	75,600	25,000
2015	81,650	30,000
Totals	$227,250	$80,000

On January 1, 2015, Paulz leased a truck from Steven. The 3-year financing-type lease provides for payments of $10,000 each January 1 (including present value of unguaranteed residual value of $4,763). On January 1, 2015, the present value of the truck at Steven's 8% implicit rate, including the unguaranteed residual value of $6,000 at the end of the third year, was $32,596. Paulz has used the 8% implicit rate to record the lease. The truck is being depreciated over three years on a straight-line basis.

On January 1, 2016, Steven signed a 4-year financing-type lease with Paulz for the rental of specialized production machinery with an 8-year life. There is a $7,000 purchase option at the end of the fourth year. The lease agreement requires lease payments of $30,000 each January 1 plus $1,500 for maintenance of the equipment. It also calls for contingent payments equal to 10% of Steven's cost savings through the use of this equipment, as reflected in any increase in net income (excluding gains or losses on sale of assets) above the previous growth rate of Steven's net income. The present value of the equipment on January 1, 2016, at Paulz's 10% implicit rate was $109,388.

On October 1, 2016, Steven sold Paulz a warehouse having a 20-year remaining life, a book value of $135,000, and an estimated salvage value of $20,000. Paulz paid $195,000 for the building, which is being depreciated on a straight-line basis.

The trial balances were prepared by the separate companies on December 31, 2016, as follows:

	Paulz Heavy Equipment	Steven Truck Company
Cash	90,485	123,307
Accounts Receivable (net)	228,000	120,000
Inventory	200,000	140,000
Minimum Lease Payments Receivable	97,000	10,000
Unguaranteed Residual Value		6,000
Unearned Interest Income	(9,673)	(444)
Assets Under Capital Lease	27,833	109,388
Accumulated Depreciation—Assets Under Capital Lease	(18,556)	(13,674)
Property, Plant, and Equipment	2,075,000	1,145,000
Accumulated Depreciation—Property, Plant, and Equipment	(713,000)	(160,000)
Investment in Steven Truck Company	1,045,800	
Accounts Payable	(100,000)	(85,000)
Interest Payable	(740)	(7,939)
Obligations Under Capital Lease	(9,260)	(79,388)
Common Stock ($5 par)	(1,800,000)	(800,000)
Retained Earnings, January 1, 2016	(864,834)	(387,250)
Sales	(3,200,000)	(1,400,000)
Gain on Sale of Assets		(60,000)
Interest Income	(7,939)	(1,152)

	Paulz Heavy Equipment	Steven Truck Company
Rent Income	(2,182)	
Cost of Goods Sold	1,882,000	770,000
Interest Expense	740	7,939
Depreciation Expense	135,000	45,000
Other Expenses	924,326	483,213
Subsidiary Income	(124,000)	
Dividends Declared	144,000	35,000
Totals	0	0

Prepare the worksheet necessary to produce the consolidated financial statements of Paulz ◀ ◀ ◀ ◀ ◀ **Required**
Heavy Equipment and its subsidiary for the year ended December 31, 2016. Include income
distribution schedules.

Problem 5A-2 *(LO 7)* **Eliminations only, sales-type lease with unguaranteed residual value.** Penn Company leased a production machine to its 80%-owned subsidiary, Smith
Company. The lease agreement, dated January 1, 2015, requires Smith to pay $18,000 each
January 1 for three years. There is an unguaranteed residual value of $5,000. The machine cost
$50,098. The present value of the machine at Penn's 16% implicit interest rate was $50,098 on
January 1, 2015. Smith also uses the 16% lessor implicit rate to record the lease. The machine
is being depreciated over three years on a straight-line basis with a $5,000 salvage value. Lease
payment amortization schedules are as follows:

Penn

Date	Payment	Interest at 16% on Previous Balance	Reduction of Principal	Principal Balance
Jan. 1, 2015				$50,098
Jan. 1, 2015	$18,000		$18,000	32,098
Jan. 1, 2016	18,000	$5,136	12,864	19,234
Jan. 1, 2017	18,000	3,077	14,923	4,311
Jan. 1, 2018	5,000	689	4,311	
Totals	$59,000	$8,902	$50,098	

Smith

Date	Payment	Interest at 16% on Previous Balance	Reduction of Principal	Principal Balance
Jan. 1, 2015				$46,894
Jan. 1, 2015	$18,000		$18,000	28,894
Jan. 1, 2016	18,000	$4,623	13,377	15,517
Jan. 1, 2017	18,000	2,483	15,517	
Totals	$54,000	$7,106	$46,894	

1. Prepare the eliminations and adjustments required for this lease on the December 31, 2015, ◀ ◀ ◀ ◀ ◀ **Required**
   consolidated worksheet.
2. Prepare the eliminations and adjustments for the December 31, 2016, consolidated
   worksheet.

CASES

Case 5-1 — *Methods of Eliminating Subsidiary Debt*

Power Pro, Inc., is a large manufacturer of marine engines. In recent years, Power Pro, like other engine manufacturers, has purchased a controlling interest in independent boat builders. The intent of the acquisitions is to control the engine choice of the boat builder. By including the outboard engine in the boat package, it is not necessary to sell to and finance many small dealers.

Power Pro purchased an 80% interest in Swift-Craft during the last year. Swift-Crafts are built in California and are sold only in western states. Power Pro wants to build the boats in the Midwest as well, so as to expand sales without paying major shipping costs from the West. A new plant will cost $1,000,000 to build and another $1,500,000 to equip for production.

Currently, Swift-Craft has $800,000 in long-term debt. It has 11% annual interest bonds outstanding in the hands of local investors. Current investors have no interest in lending any more funds. The interest rate Swift-Craft pays is high due to its size and credit rating.

Power Pro has ready access to the bond market and borrows at 7.5% annual interest. Power Pro also has expertise in constructing and equipping new facilities since it has built many new plants. Power Pro also has a sophisticated fixed asset accounting system. Power Pro would prefer to build the new plant and turn it over to Swift-Craft when it is complete. It is considering either selling the building to Swift-Craft and taking back the mortgage or leasing the asset to Swift-Craft under a long-term capital lease.

Power Pro would like you to cover the options it has in using its borrowing ability and asset management experience in assisting Swift-Craft. There is a concern as to existing debt and with respect to funds needed to finance the new plant. Your discussion should consider the impact of alternatives on the consolidation process and on NCI shareholders.

Case 5-2 — *Impact of Alternative Methods to Retire Subsidiary Debt*

Magna Company is the parent company that owns an 80% interest in Metros Company. The interest was purchased at book value, and the simple equity method is used to record the ownership interest. The trial balances of the two companies on December 31, 2016, were as follows:

	Magna Company	Metros Company
Cash	258,000	100,000
Other Current Assets	50,000	200,000
Investment in Metros	316,000	
Plant and Equipment	800,000	500,000
Accumulated Depreciation	(300,000)	(200,000)
Current Liabilities	(40,000)	(5,000)
Bonds Payable		(200,000)
Common Stock (par)	(300,000)	(100,000)
Retained Earnings	(746,000)	(285,000)
Sales	(150,000)	(170,000)
Cost of Goods Sold	90,000	130,000
Expenses	30,000	10,000
Interest Expense		20,000
Subsidiary Income	(8,000)	
Totals	0	0

As of December 31, 2016, Magna Company was considering acquiring the $200,000 of Metros's 10% bonds from the current owner. Based on a 12% current interest rate for bonds of this risk, the purchase price of the bonds would be $185,000. There are two possible options as follows:

a. Magna could lend $185,000 to Metros at 8% annual interest. Metros would then use the funds to retire the bonds.
b. Magna could buy the bonds and hold them as an investment and enjoy the high interest rate.

1. Prepare a pro forma consolidated income statement and balance sheet for 2016 assuming ◄ ◄ ◄ ◄ ◄ **Required**
   option (a) is used.
2. Indicate how your solution to part (1) would change if the second option were used.

Alternative Ways to Transfer Asset to Subsidiary   *Case 5-3*

Pannier Company is the parent company that owns an 80% interest in Jodestar Company. The interest was acquired at book value, and the simple equity method is used to record the ownership interest. The trial balances of the two companies on December 31, 2016, were as follows:

	Pannier Company	Jodestar Company
Cash	258,000	100,000
Inventory	150,000	40,000
Other Current Assets	50,000	160,000
Investment in Jodestar	316,000	
Plant and Equipment	650,000	500,000
Accumulated Depreciation	(300,000)	(200,000)
Current Liabilities.................................	(40,000)	(5,000)
Long-Term Debt		(200,000)
Common Stock (par)	(300,000)	(100,000)
Retained Earnings	(746,000)	(285,000)
Sales	(150,000)	(170,000)
Cost of Goods Sold	90,000	130,000
Expenses	30,000	10,000
Interest Expense..................................		20,000
Subsidiary Income.................................	(8,000)	
Totals	0	0

As the year ended, Pannier was planning to transfer a major piece of equipment to Jodestar. The equipment was just purchased by Pannier and is included in its inventory account. The equipment cost Pannier $100,000 and would be transferred to Jodestar for $125,000. There are two options as follows:

a. Sell the equipment to Jodestar for $125,000 and finance it with a 5-year, 10% interest installment note.
b. Lease the equipment to Jodestar on a 5-year lease requiring payments of $29,977 in advance.

1. Make the journal entries for both companies if the intercompany sale was consummated on ◄ ◄ ◄ ◄ ◄ **Required**
   December 31.
2. Prepare a consolidated income statement and balance sheet for the company for 2016. (*Note:* The effect of the equipment sale is not included in the trial balance.)
3. Make the journal entries for both companies if the intercompany lease was executed on December 31.
4. If the lease were used, how would the consolidated statements differ from those in part (2)?

Chapter 6

Cash Flow, EPS, and Taxation

CHAPTER

Learning Objectives

When you have completed this chapter, you should be able to

1. **Demonstrate an understanding of the effect of a business combination on cash flow in and subsequent to the period of the purchase.**

2. **Compute earnings per share for a consolidated firm.**

3. **Calculate and prepare a consolidated worksheet where the consolidated firm is an "affiliated group" and pays a single consolidated tax.**

4. **Prepare a consolidated worksheet where the parent and subsidiary are separately taxed by employing tax allocation procedures.**

We begin with the procedures necessary to prepare a consolidated statement of cash flows. Fortunately, this requires only minor changes in the procedures used in your prior accounting courses. Also, only minor adjustments of typical earnings per share procedures are needed for consolidated companies. The final consolidation issue is taxation of the consolidated company. Prior worksheets are now enhanced to include the provision for tax. This is quite simple when the affiliated companies are taxed as a single entity. Procedures are a bit more involved when the individual companies are taxed separately.

CONSOLIDATED STATEMENT OF CASH FLOWS

FASB ASC 230-10 requires that a statement of cash flows accompany a company's published income statement and balance sheet. The process of preparing a consolidated statement of cash flows is similar to that which is used for a single company, a topic covered in depth in intermediate accounting texts. Since the analysis of changes in cash of a consolidated entity begins with consolidated balance sheets, intercompany transactions will have been eliminated and, thus, will not cause any complications. However, because of the parent-subsidiary relationship, some situations require special consideration. These situations are discussed in the following paragraphs.

Cash Acquisition of Controlling Interest

The cash acquisition of a controlling interest in a company is considered an *investing activity* and would appear as a cash outflow in the cash flows from investing activities section of the statement of cash flows. It also is necessary to explain the total increase in consolidated assets and the addition of the NCI to the consolidated balance sheet. This is a result of the requirement that the statement of cash flows disclose investing and *financing activities* that affect the company's financial position even though they do not impact cash.

To illustrate the disclosure required, consider an example of a cash acquisition of an 80% interest in Company S. Assume Company S had the balance sheet shown on page 326 on January 1, 2015, when Company P acquired an 80% interest for $540,000 in cash.

1

OBJECTIVE

Demonstrate an understanding of the effect of a business combination on cash flow in and subsequent to the period of the purchase.

Assets		Liabilities and Equity	
Cash and cash equivalents	$ 50,000	Long-term liabilities	$150,000
Inventory	60,000	Common stock ($10 par).	200,000
Equipment (net)	190,000	Retained earnings	350,000
Building (net)	400,000		
Total assets.	$700,000	Total liabilities and equity	$700,000

Assume the fair values of the equipment and building are $250,000 and $425,000, respectively, and any remaining excess of cost is attributed to goodwill. The estimated remaining life of the equipment is five years and of the building is 10 years.

The following value analysis schedule and D&D schedule were prepared:

Value Analysis Schedule	Company Implied Fair Value	Parent Price (80%)	NCI Value (20%)
Company fair value.	$675,000	$540,000	$135,000
Fair value of net assets excluding goodwill	635,000	508,000	127,000
Goodwill.	**$ 40,000**	**$ 32,000**	**$ 8,000**

Based on the above information, the following D&D schedule is prepared:

Determination and Distribution of Excess Schedule

	Company Implied Fair Value	Parent Price (80%)	NCI Value (20%)
Fair value of subsidiary	$ 675,000	$540,000	$135,000
Less book value of interest acquired:			
Common stock.	$ 200,000		
Retained earnings	350,000		
Total stockholders' equity.	$ 550,000	$550,000	$550,000
Interest acquired		80%	20%
Book value.		$440,000	$110,000
Excess of fair value over book value	**$125,000**	$100,000	$ 25,000

Adjustment of identifiable accounts:

	Adjustment	Life	Amortization per Year	Worksheet Key
Equipment ($250,000 − $190,000)	$ 60,000	5	$ 12,000	**debit D1**
Building ($425,000 − $400,000).	25,000	10	2,500	**debit D2**
Goodwill ($675,000 − $635,000)	**40,000**			**debit D3**
Total.	**$125,000**			

The effect of the purchase on the balance sheet accounts of the consolidated company for 2015 would be as follows:

	Debit	Credit
Cash ($540,000 paid − $50,000 subsidiary cash)		490,000
Inventory	60,000	
Equipment ($190,000 book value + $60,000 excess)	250,000	

	Debit	Credit
Building ($400,000 book value + $25,000 excess)	425,000	
Goodwill	40,000	
Long-term liabilities		150,000
Noncontrolling interest (20% × $550,000 subsidiary equity plus $25,000		
NCI adjustment)		135,000
Totals	775,000	775,000

The disclosure of the purchase on the statement of cash flows would be summarized as follows:

Under the heading "Cash flows from investing activities:"

Payment for purchase of Company S, net of cash acquired .... $(490,000)

In the supplemental schedule of noncash financing and investing activity:

Company P acquired 80% of the common stock of Company S for $540,000. In conjunction with the acquisition, liabilities were assumed and an NCI was created as follows:

Adjusted value of assets acquired ($700,000 book value + $125,000 excess)	$825,000
Cash paid for common stock	540,000
Balance (noncash)	$285,000
Liabilities assumed	$150,000
Noncontrolling interest	$135,000

Noncash Acquisition of Controlling Interest

Suppose that instead of paying cash for its controlling interest, Company P issued 10,000 shares of its $10 par stock for the controlling interest in Company S. Further assume the shares had a market value of $54 each. Since the acquisition price is the same ($540,000), the determination and distribution of excess schedule would not change. The analysis of balance sheet account changes would be as follows:

	Debit	Credit
Cash ($50,000 subsidiary cash received)	50,000	
Inventory	60,000	
Equipment ($190,000 book value + $60,000 excess)	250,000	
Building ($400,000 book value + $25,000 excess)	425,000	
Goodwill	40,000	
Long-term liabilities		150,000
Noncontrolling interest (20% × $550,000 subsidiary equity plus $25,000 NCI		
adjustment)		135,000
Common stock ($10 par)—Company P		100,000
Paid-in capital in excess of par—Company P		440,000
Totals	825,000	825,000

The disclosure of the purchase on the statement of cash flows would be summarized as follows:

Under the heading "Cash flows from investing activities:"

Cash acquired in purchase of Company S $50,000

In the supplemental schedule of noncash financing and investing activity:

Company P acquired 80% of the common stock of Company S in exchange for 10,000 shares of Company P common stock valued at $540,000. In conjunction with the acquisition, liabilities were assumed and a noncontrolling interest was created as follows:

Adjusted value of assets acquired ($700,000 book value + $125,000 excess)	$825,000
Common stock issued	$540,000
Liabilities assumed.	$150,000
Noncontrolling interest	$135,000

Adjustments Resulting from Business Combinations

A business combination will have ramifications on the statements of cash flows prepared in subsequent periods. An acquisition may create amortizations of excess deductions (noncash items) that need to be adjusted. In addition, there may be changes resulting from additional purchases of subsidiary shares and/or dividend payments by the subsidiary. Intercompany bonds and nonconsolidated investments also need to be considered for their impact.

Amortization of Excesses. Income statements prepared for periods including or following an acquisition of another company will include depreciation based on the fair values assigned to the assets on the acquisition date. Using the facts of the preceding examples, the following adjustments would appear on the cash flows statement for 2015:

Cash from operating activities:	
Consolidated net income.	$XXX,XXX
Add amortizations resulting from business combination:	
Depreciation on equipment [($190,000 book + $60,000 adj.) ÷ 5 years]	50,000
Depreciation on building [($400,000 book + $25,000 adj.) ÷ 10 years].	42,500

In addition, cash from operating activities would include adjustments for depreciation of book value recorded by the parent company.

Purchase of Additional Subsidiary Shares. The purchase of additional shares directly from the subsidiary results in no added cash flowing into the consolidated company. The transfer of cash within the consolidated company would not appear in the consolidated statement of cash flows. However, the purchase of additional shares from the noncontrolling interest does result in an outflow of cash. From a consolidated viewpoint, it is the equivalent of purchasing treasury shares. Thus, it would be listed under *financing activities.*

Subsidiary Dividends. Dividends paid by the subsidiary to the parent are a transfer of cash within the consolidated entity and thus would not appear in the consolidated statement of cash flows. However, dividends paid by the subsidiary to noncontrolling shareholders represent a flow of cash to parties outside the consolidated group and would appear as an outflow under the cash flows from financing activities heading of the consolidated statement of cash flows.

Purchase of Intercompany Bonds. The purchase of intercompany bonds from parties outside the consolidated company is a cash flow from a member of the consolidated group to parties outside the consolidated entity. The purchase of intercompany bonds is viewed as a retirement of the bonds on the consolidated worksheet (discussed in Chapter 5). The consolidated statement of cash flows also treats the purchase of the bonds as a retirement of the consolidated company's debt and includes the cash outflow under cash flows from financing activities. Since the process of constructing a cash flows statement starts with the consolidated income statement and balance sheet, intercompany interest payments and amortizations of premiums and/or discounts already are eliminated and will not enter into the analysis of consolidated cash flows. Only cash interest payments to bondholders outside the consolidated entity are important to the analysis and should be included in cash flows from *operating* activities.

Preparation of Consolidated Statement of Cash Flows

A complete example of the process of preparing a consolidated statement of cash flows is presented in this section. Assume Company P originally acquired an 80% interest in Company S on January 1, 2015. In addition, Company P purchased a 20% interest in Company E on January 2, 2016, and accounted for the investment under the sophisticated equity method. The following determination and distribution of excess schedules were prepared for each investment:

Determination and Distribution of Excess Schedule Investment in Company S

	Company Implied Fair Value	Parent Price (80%)	NCI Value (20%)
Fair value of subsidiary	$ 456,250	$365,000	$ 91,250
Less book value of interest acquired:			
Common stock ($5 par)	$ 50,000		
Paid-in capital in excess of par	150,000		
Retained earnings	100,000		
Total stockholders' equity	$ 300,000	$300,000	$300,000
Interest acquired		80%	20%
Book value		$240,000	$ 60,000
Excess of fair value over book value	**$156,250**	$125,000	$ 31,250

Adjustment of identifiable accounts:

	Adjustment	Life	Amortization per Year	Worksheet Key
Equipment	$ 31,250	5	$ 6,250	**debit D1**
Goodwill	**125,000**			**debit D2**
Total	**$156,250**			

The 20% investment is considered to be only an "influential investment." The price paid is compared to the interest purchased. There is no revaluation of the remaining 80% interest which was not acquired. The schedule is prepared as follows:

Determination and Distribution of Excess Schedule for Investment in Company E:

Price paid for investment in Company E		$255,000
Less interest acquired:		
Common stock	$ 500,000	
Retained earnings	750,000	
Total equity	$1,250,000	
Interest acquired	× 20%	250,000
Equipment (10-year life)		$ 5,000

Since this investment is not consolidated, there will be no recording of the increased value of the equipment. This information is used only to amortize the excess cost in future income statements. Because of this, there are no debits or credits accompanying the distribution of the excess. The following consolidated statements were prepared for Company P and its subsidiary, Company S, for 2017:

Company P and Subsidiary Company S
Consolidated Income Statement
For Year Ended December 31, 2017

Sales		$ 900,000
Less cost of goods sold.		525,000
Gross profit		$ 375,000
Less expenses:		
General and administrative.	$150,500	
Depreciation	**71,250***	**221,750**
Operating income.		$ 153,250
Investment income (equity method).		**15,500****
Consolidated net income.		$ 168,750
Distributed to:		
NCI		9,950
Controlling interest.		$ 158,800

*Includes $6,250 of depreciation resulting from the excess of the subsidiary equipment's fair value over book value on January 1, 2015, the date on which the 80% interest was acquired.

**20% of Company E net income of $80,000 less $500 amortization of equipment. (Dividends received were $2,000.)

Company P and Subsidiary Company S
Consolidated Retained Earnings Statement
For Year Ended December 31, 2017

	NCI	Controlling
Retained earnings, January 1, 2017.	$60,750	$440,000
Add distribution of consolidated net income	9,950	158,800
Less dividends declared.	(4,000)	(50,000)
Balance, December 31, 2017	$66,700	$548,800

Company P and Subsidiary Company S
Consolidated Balance Sheet
December 31, 2016 and 2017

Assets	2017	2016
Cash and cash equivalents	$ 179,000	$ 160,000
Inventory	210,000	180,000
Accounts receivable	154,000	120,000
Property, plant, and equipment.	1,336,250	1,256,250
Accumulated depreciation	(373,750)	(302,500)
Goodwill	125,000	125,000
Investment in Company E (20%)	333,500	320,000
Total assets.	$1,964,000	$1,858,750

Liabilities and Stockholders' Equity		
Accounts payable	$ 156,500	$ 166,000
Bonds payable	300,000	300,000
Noncontrolling interest	106,700	100,750
Controlling interest:		
Common stock (par).	200,000	200,000
Paid-in capital in excess of par	652,000	652,000
Retained earnings	548,800	440,000
Total liabilities and stockholders' equity	$1,964,000	$1,858,750

The following additional facts are available to aid in the preparation of a consolidated statement of cash flows:

1. Company P purchased a new piece of equipment during 2017 for $80,000.
2. In 2017, Company P declared and paid $50,000 in dividends and Company S declared and paid $20,000 in dividends.

Illustration 6-1 is a worksheet approach to calculating a statement of cash flows under the *indirect method.* Explanations 1 through 6 use changes in balance sheet accounts to analyze cash from operations. This information is taken from the income statement and is implied from changes in current assets and current liabilities. Explanation 7 reflects the only investing activity in this example. Explanations 8 and 9 show the financing activities. The worksheet provides the information needed to develop the statement of cash flows that follows Illustration 6-1.

If the *direct method* of disclosing cash from operating activities is used, the cash flows from the operating activities section of the statement of cash flows would be prepared as follows:

Cash flows from operating activities:	
Cash from customers ($900,000 sales − $34,000 increase in accounts receivable) . .	$ 866,000
Cash from investments (dividends received)	2,000
Cash to suppliers ($525,000 cost of goods sold + $30,000 inventory increase +	
$9,500 decrease in accounts payable).	(564,500)
Cash for general and administrative expenses	(150,500)
Net cash provided by operating activities	$ 153,000

Illustration 6-1
Company P and Subsidiary Company S
Worksheet for Analysis of Cash: Indirect Approach
For Year Ended December 31, 2017

	Account Change			Explanations			
	Debit	Credit		Debit		Credit	Balance
Inventory	30,000		(4)	30,000			0
Accounts receivable	34,000		(3)	34,000			0
Property, plant, and equipment.........	80,000		(7)	80,000			0
Accumulated depreciation		71,250			(2)	71,250	0
Goodwill	0						0
Investment in Company E (20%)	13,500		(6)	13,500			0
Accounts payable	9,500		(5)	9,500			0
Bonds payable							0
Noncontrolling interest		5,950	(9)	4,000	(1)	9,950	0
Controlling interest:							
Common stock (par)...............							0
Paid-in capital in excess of par							0
Retained earnings		108,800	(8)	50,000	(1)	158,800	0
	167,000	186,000		221,000		240,000	
Net change in cash	19,000	0		19,000		0	
Cash from Operations:							
Consolidated net income..............			(1)	168,750			
Depreciation expense			(2)	71,250			
Increase in accounts receivable.........					(3)	34,000	
Increase in inventory					(4)	30,000	
Decrease in accounts payable					(5)	9,500	
Equity income in excess of dividends.					(6)	13,500	
Net cash provided by operating activities .				153,000			
Cash from Investing:							
Purchase of equipment					(7)	80,000	
Net cash used in investing activities						80,000	
Cash from Financing:							
Dividend payment to controlling interest . .					(8)	50,000	
Dividend payment to noncontrolling							
interest..........................					(9)	4,000	
Net cash used in financing activities						54,000	
Net cash provided...................				19,000			

Company P and Subsidiary Company S
Consolidated Statement of Cash Flows
For Year Ended December 31, 2017

Cash flows from operating activities:		
Consolidated net income................................		$168,750
Adjustments to reconcile net income to net cash:		
Depreciation expense	$ 71,250	
Increase in accounts receivable......................	(34,000)	
Increase in inventory	(30,000)	

Decrease in accounts payable........................	(9,500)	
Equity income from Company E in excess of dividends Received	(13,500)	
Total adjustments		(15,750)
Net cash provided by operating activities		$153,000
Cash flows from investing activities:		
Purchase of equipment.............................		(80,000)
Cash flows from financing activities:		
Dividend payment to controlling interest	$(50,000)	
Dividend payment to noncontrolling interest	(4,000)	
Net cash used in financing activities		(54,000)
Net increase in cash and cash equivalents		$ 19,000
Cash and cash equivalents at beginning of year..............		160,000
Cash and cash equivalents at year-end		$179,000

REFLECTION

- The starting point for cash operations is consolidated net income, which includes the income attributed to the NCI.

- Subsequent to the period of acquisition, the only impact of consolidations on cash flow is the added amortization and depreciation caused by the acquisition.

- An acquisition of a subsidiary for cash is in the "investing" section of the cash flow statement. The cash outflow is net of the subsidiary's cash at acquisition.

- An acquisition of a subsidiary by issuing securities is a noncash investing/financing activity that must be disclosed in the notes to the cash flow statement. Any subsidiary cash received in the acquisition is a positive cash flow under "investing."

- The parent purchase of subsidiary bonds is treated as a retirement and is a financing activity.

- The parent purchase of additional shares of subsidiary stock is viewed as a treasury stock transaction and is considered a financing activity.

CONSOLIDATED EARNINGS PER SHARE

2

OBJECTIVE

Compute earnings per share for a consolidated firm.

The computation of *consolidated earnings per share (EPS)* remains virtually the same as that for single entities. For the purpose of this discussion, all calculations will be made only on an annual basis. *Basic earnings per share (BEPS)* is calculated as follows for the subsidiary and the consolidated firm:

Subsidiary BEPS = [Adjusted Subsidiary Net Income (as prepared on the income distribution schedule – Preferred Stock Dividends]/Subsidiary Weighted Average Common Shares Outstanding

$$\text{Consolidated BEPS} = \frac{\begin{pmatrix}\text{Parent Adjusted Internally Generated Net Income}\end{pmatrix} - \begin{pmatrix}\text{Parent Preferred Stock Dividends}\end{pmatrix} + \begin{pmatrix}\text{Parent-Owned Subsidiary Common Shares} \times \text{Subsidiary BEPS}\end{pmatrix} + \begin{pmatrix}\text{Parent-Owned Subsidiary Preferred Shares} \times \text{Subsidiary Preferred Dividends per Share}\end{pmatrix}}{\text{Weighted Average Parent Company Common Shares Outstanding}}$$

To illustrate the computation of consolidated BEPS, assume the following data concerning the subsidiary:

Net income (adjusted for intercompany profits) $22,000
Preferred stock cash dividend . . . . $ 2,000
Common stock shares outstanding   5,000

$$\text{Subsidiary BEPS} = \frac{\$22,000 - \overset{(1)}{\$2,000}}{5,000} = \$4.00$$

(1) Dividend on nonconvertible preferred stock, none of which is owned by the parent.

Now, assume the parent owns 80% of the subsidiary and has an adjusted internally generated net income of $40,000 and 10,000 shares of common stock outstanding.

$$\text{Consolidated BEPS} = \frac{\$40,000 + \overset{(1)}{\$16,000}}{10,000} = \$5.60$$

(1) Subsidiary common shares owned by parent (80% × 5,000).   4,000
Parent's interest in subsidiary income (4,000 shares × $4.00 subsidiary BEPS) $16,000

The calculation of *diluted earnings per share (DEPS)* is not complicated when applied to the consolidated company, provided that the subsidiary company has no dilutive securities. As long as no such securities exist, the controlling interest's share of consolidated net income is divided by the number of outstanding parent company shares. The numerator and denominator adjustments caused by parent company dilutive securities can be considered in the normal manner.

When the subsidiary has dilutive securities, the calculation of consolidated DEPS becomes a 2-stage process. First, the DEPS of the subsidiary must be calculated. Then, the consolidated DEPS is calculated using as a component of the calculation the adjusted DEPS of the subsidiary. This 2-stage process handles subsidiary dilutive securities which require the possible issuance of subsidiary company shares. A further complication occurs when the subsidiary has outstanding dilutive options, warrants, and/or convertible securities which may require the issuance of parent company shares.

First, consider the calculation of consolidated DEPS when the subsidiary has outstanding dilutive securities which may require the issuance of subsidiary company shares only. The EPS model for a single entity is modified in two ways:

1. Only the parent's adjusted internally generated net income, the parent's income adjusters, and the parent's share adjusters enter the formula directly.
2. The parent's share of the subsidiary's income is entered indirectly by multiplying the number of equivalent subsidiary shares owned by the parent by the subsidiary DEPS.

The basic model for computing consolidated DEPS in this situation is as follows:

$$\text{Consolidated DEPS} = \frac{\begin{pmatrix}\text{Parent's Adjusted Internally Generated Net Income}\end{pmatrix} + \begin{pmatrix}\text{Parent's DEPS Income Adjustments}\end{pmatrix} + \begin{pmatrix}\text{Parent-Owned Equivalent Shares} \times \text{Subsidiary DEPS}\end{pmatrix}}{\begin{pmatrix}\text{Parent's Common Shares Outstanding}\end{pmatrix} + \begin{pmatrix}\text{Parent's DEPS Share Adjustments}\end{pmatrix}}$$

The parent's adjusted internally generated net income includes adjustments for unrealized profits (on sales to the subsidiary) recorded during the current period and for realization of profits deferred from previous periods. **This would be all of the adjustments that appear on the parent's income distribution schedule, except for the inclusion of the parent's share of**

subsidiary income. Likewise, the income used to compute the subsidiary DEPS must be adjusted for intercompany transactions and amortizations of excess (as shown in the subsidiary income distribution schedule). To illustrate the computation of consolidated DEPS, assume the following data concerning the subsidiary:

Net income (adjusted for intercompany profits)	$22,000
Preferred stock cash dividend	$ 2,000
Interest paid on convertible bonds	$ 3,000
Common stock shares outstanding	5,000
Warrants to purchase one share of common stock	1,000
Warrants held by parent	500
Convertible bonds outstanding (convertible into 10 shares of common stock)	200
Convertible bonds held by parent	180

$$\frac{\text{Subsidiary}}{\text{DEPS}} = \frac{\overset{(1)}{\$22,000} - \$2,000 + \overset{(2)}{\$3,000}}{\underset{(3)}{5,000} + 2,000 + \underset{(4)}{500}} = \$3.07$$

(1) Dividend on nonconvertible preferred stock, none of which is owned by the parent.
(2) Income adjustment for convertible bonds, which are dilutive.
(3) Share adjustment associated with convertible debentures, 200 bonds × 10 shares per bond.
(4) Share adjustment (treasury stock method) associated with the warrants. It is assumed that, using the average fair value of the stock, 500 shares could be purchased with the proceeds of the sale and that 500 additional new shares would be issued.

Assume the parent owns 80% of the subsidiary and has an adjusted internally generated net income of $40,000 and 10,000 shares of common stock outstanding. Also assume the parent has dilutive bonds outstanding that are convertible into 3,000 shares of common stock and the interest paid on these bonds was $5,000. The consolidated DEPS would be computed as follows:

$$\frac{\text{Consolidated}}{\text{DEPS}} = \frac{\overset{(1)}{\$40,000} + \$5,000 + \overset{(2)}{\$18,574}}{10,000 + \underset{(3)}{3,000}} = \$4.89$$

(1) Income adjustment from interest on parent company convertible bonds, which are dilutive.

(2)
Subsidiary common shares owned by parent (80% × 5,000)	4,000
Parent-owned equivalent shares applicable to convertible bonds (180 × 10 shares)*	1,800
Parent-owned equivalent shares applicable to warrants (50% × 500)**	250
Total parent-owned equivalent shares	6,050
Parent's interest in subsidiary income (6,050 shares × $3.07 subsidiary DEPS)	$18,574

(3) Shares assumed to be issued in exchange for parent company convertible bonds (a common stock equivalent).

*Parent owns 180 (or 90%) of 200 subsidiary bonds.
**Parent owns 500 (or 50%) of 1,000 subsidiary warrants.

If the dilutive subsidiary securities enable the holder to acquire common stock of the parent, these securities are not included in the computation of subsidiary DEPS. However, these securities must be included in the parent's share adjustment in computing consolidated DEPS. The basic model by which to compute consolidated DEPS in this situation is as shown on page 336.

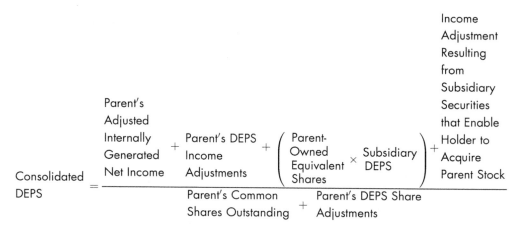

To illustrate, assume the following facts for a parent owning 90% of the outstanding subsidiary shares:

Parent internally adjusted net income	$20,000
Parent company common stock shares outstanding	10,000
Parent company dilutive convertible bonds:	
Interest expense	$ 1,000
Shares to be issued in conversion	2,000
Subsidiary adjusted net income	$ 7,000
Subsidiary common stock shares outstanding	4,000
Subsidiary preferred stock convertible into parent common stock:	
Dividend requirement	$ 1,200
Number of preferred shares	1,000
Number of parent company common shares required	2,000
Subsidiary common stock warrants to acquire 100 parent shares	100

The first step is to calculate the subsidiary's DEPS as follows:

$$\frac{\text{Subsidiary}}{\text{DEPS}} = \frac{\$7,000 - \$1,200 \text{ preferred dividends}}{4,000 \text{ outstanding common shares}} = \$1.45$$

Note that the subsidiary convertible preferred stock and stock warrants are not satisfied with subsidiary shares and, thus, are not considered converted for the purpose of calculating subsidiary DEPS. The consolidated DEPS would be computed as follows:

$$\frac{\text{Consolidated}}{\text{DEPS}} = \frac{\overset{(1)}{\$20,000 + \$1,000} + \overset{(2)}{[3,600 \times \$1.45]} + \overset{(3)}{\$1,080}}{\underset{(4)}{10,000 + (2,000 + 2,000 + 50)}} = \$1.94$$

(1) $1,000 income adjustment associated with the parent company convertible security.

(2) The parent's share of subsidiary DEPS. Again, since the subsidiary's preferred stock and warrants are not convertible into subsidiary shares, the total parent-owned equivalent shares is 90% × 4,000.

(3) Income adjustment representing the dividend on subsidiary preferred shares that would not be paid if the shares were converted into common stock of the parent. Note that 90% of the $1,200 dividend adjustment is added back to the controlling share of income

(4) The parent's share adjustment consisting of 2,000 shares traceable to the parent company convertible security; 2,000 shares traceable to the subsidiary preferred stock that is convertible into parent common stock; and 50 incremental shares traceable to the subsidiary warrants to acquire parent common stock. It is assumed that 50 of the 100 shares required to satisfy the warrants can be purchased with the proceeds of the exercise and 50 new shares must be issued.

Special analysis is required in computing consolidated BEPS and DEPS when an acquisition occurs during a reporting period. In that case, only subsidiary income since the acquisition date is included, and the number of subsidiary shares is weighted for the partial period.

REFLECTION

- Prior to calculating consolidated EPS, the subsidiary's EPS (including dilution adjustments that add more subsidiary shares) is calculated.

- The parent's numerator for EPS includes its own internally generated net income plus its share of subsidiary EPS.

- The parent also adjusts its numerator and denominator for dilative parent company securities and subsidiary securities that are satisfied by issuing parent company shares.

TAXATION OF CONSOLIDATED COMPANIES

Consolidated companies that do not meet the requirements to be an *affiliated group*, as defined by the tax law, must pay their taxes as separate entities. The tax definition of an affiliated group is less inclusive than that used in accounting theory. Section 1504(a) of the Tax Code does not allow two or more corporations to file a consolidated return or to be considered an affiliated group for tax purposes unless the parent owns:

1. 80% of the voting power of all classes of stock *and*
2. 80% of the fair market value of all the outstanding stock of the other corporation.

For these provisions, preferred stock is not included if it (a) is not entitled to vote, (b) is limited and preferred as to dividends, (c) does not have redemption rights beyond its issue price plus a reasonable redemption or liquidation premium, and (d) is not convertible into the other class of stock. Comparison of these criteria with those required for consolidated financial reporting indicates that many consolidated companies have no choice but to submit to separate taxation of the member companies.

Consolidated companies that do meet the tax law requirements to be an affiliated group may elect to be taxed as a single entity or as separate entities. Once the election is made to file as a single entity, the permission of the Internal Revenue Service is required before the companies can be taxed separately again. Companies that elect to be taxed as a single entity file a consolidated tax return that may provide several tax advantages. For example, a consolidated return generally permits the offset of operating profits and losses and of capital gains and losses. Also, intercompany profits are not taxed until realized in later periods.

When companies that comprise an affiliated group elect not to file a consolidated return, each company within the group computes and pays its taxes independently. All members of the group must use the parent's tax year. However, the members may use different accounting methods.

Members of consolidated groups, when filing separate returns, must sum their incomes when applying graduated corporate tax rates. The lower tax rates available for low income levels can be used only once and cannot be applied by each of the companies individually.

Foreign corporations are not includible in consolidated tax returns. U.S. companies do not pay U.S. tax on foreign business profits of their foreign subsidiaries until the earnings are repatriated to the U.S. parent through a dividend distribution. This is not likely to happen if the U.S. company is trying to grow its business abroad. This policy is known as "deferral." A U.S. company may be motivated to engage in "deferral," when U.S. tax rates exceed those of other countries. The Organization for Economic Cooperation and Development (OECD) tracks average corporate tax rates for 34 countries, including the United States. For 2013, the U.S. average corporate tax rate was 39.1%. The average for the other 32 countries tracked by the OECD was 25.1%. No other country in the database had a higher rate.

3

OBJECTIVE

Calculate and prepare a consolidated worksheet where the consolidated firm is an "affiliated group" and pays a single consolidated tax.

Consolidated Tax Return

When an affiliated group elects to be taxed as a single entity, consolidated income as determined on the worksheet is the basis for the tax calculation. The affiliated companies should not record a provision for income tax based on their own separate incomes. Rather, the income tax expense is calculated as part of the consolidated worksheet process. The tax provision is based on consolidated income; intercompany profits will have been eliminated already. Thus, no special procedures are needed to deal with intercompany transactions when computing the tax provision. Once calculated, the tax provision may be recorded on the books of the separate companies.

As an example of an affiliated group's choosing to be taxed as a single entity, assume Company P acquired an 80% interest in Company S on January 1, 2015, at which time the following determination and distribution of excess schedule was prepared:

Determination and Distribution of Excess Schedule

	Company Implied Fair Value	Parent Price (80%)	NCI Value (20%)
Fair value of subsidiary	$993,750	$795,000	$198,750
Less book value of interest acquired:			
Common stock	$500,000		
Retained earnings	400,000		
Total stockholders' equity	$900,000	$900,000	$900,000
Interest acquired		80%	20%
Book value		$720,000	$180,000
Excess of fair value over book value	$93,750	$ 75,000	$ 18,750

Adjustment of identifiable accounts:

	Adjustment	Life	Amortization per Year	Worksheet Key
Patent	$ 93,750	15	$ 6,250	**debit D**

The following income statements are for Companies P and S for 2017. Since the companies desire to file a consolidated tax return, neither company has recorded a provision for income tax. The corporate tax rate is 30%.

	Company P	Company S
Sales	$600,000	$400,000
Less cost of goods sold	350,000	200,000
Gross profit	$250,000	$200,000
Less expenses:		
Depreciation expense	25,000	20,000
Other operating expenses	75,000	80,000
Operating income	$150,000	$100,000
Subsidiary income	80,000	
Income before tax	$230,000	$100,000

On January 1, 2016, Company P sold a piece of equipment, with a book value of $40,000, to Company S for $60,000. The equipment is depreciated by Company S on a straight-line basis over a 5-year life.

The following applies to 2017 intercompany merchandise sales to Company P by Company S:

Intercompany sales in beginning inventory of Company P	$ 50,000
Intercompany sales in ending inventory of Company P.	$ 70,000
Sales to Company P during 2017	$100,000
Gross profit rate.	50%

A 30% tax rate applies to both companies.

Worksheet 6-1, pages 348 to 349, contains the trial balances of Companies P and S on December 31, 2017. Since the income tax is to be calculated on the worksheet, no provision exists on the separate books. If separate provisions appear in the trial balances, they should be eliminated as an initial procedure in consolidating.

Worksheet 6-1: page 348

The balance of the investment in Company S account results from the use of the simple equity method. All eliminations should be made prior to calculating the provision for tax. This will assure that the consolidated income, upon which the provision is based, is adjusted for all intercompany transactions.

All worksheet entries, other than (T) are unchanged from procedures used in prior worksheets, and the same coding is used. In journal entry form, the entries are as follows:

(CY1)	Eliminate current-year equity income:		
	Subsidiary Income.	80,000	
	Investment in Company S.		80,000
(EL)	Eliminate 80% of subsidiary equity:		
	Common Stock—Company S	400,000	
	Retained Earnings—Company S.	560,000	
	Investment in Company S.		960,000
(D)/(NCI)	Distribute excess to patent:		
	Patent.	93,750	
	Investment in Company S.		75,000
	Retained Earnings—Company S (NCI adjustment)		18,750
(A)	Amortize patent for two prior years and the current year:		
	Patent Amortization Expense.	6,250	
	Retained Earnings—Company P.	10,000	
	Retained Earnings—Company S.	2,500	
	Patent.		18,750
(F1)	Adjust retained earnings for fixed asset profit at start of year:		
	Retained Earnings—Company P.	16,000	
	Accumulated Depreciation—Equipment.	4,000	
	Equipment		20,000
(F2)	Adjust current-year depreciation for gain on fixed asset sale:		
	Accumulated Depreciation—Equipment.	4,000	
	Depreciation Expense		4,000
(IS)	Eliminate intercompany merchandise sales:		
	Sales	100,000	
	Cost of Goods Sold		100,000
(BI)	Adjust January 1 retained earnings for inventory profit recorded by subsidiary:		
	Retained Earnings—Company S.	5,000	
	Retained Earnings—Company P.	20,000	
	Cost of Goods Sold		25,000
(EI)	Adjust cost of goods sold for profit in ending inventory:		
	Cost of Goods Sold	35,000	
	Inventory, December 31, 2017.		35,000

Consolidated net income before tax is calculated on the worksheet and becomes the base for the tax provision. Entry **(T)** is not entered until this calculation is made. In journal entry form, the entry is as follows:

Consolidated Tax Provision	**71,700**	
Income Tax Payable		**71,700**

Explanation:

Consolidated income before tax (from the consolidated worksheet)	$237,750
Nondeductible amortization of patent applicable to NCI (explained below)	1,250
Adjusted reported income	$239,000
Tax rate	× 30%
Tax provision and liability	$ 71,700

In this case, it was assumed that the acquisition was a taxable exchange to the seller. The parent's share of the patent amortization is deductible. However, the portion of the patent amortization applicable to the NCI is not deductible. The portion of the asset adjustment applicable to the NCI was not taxed and thus does not have the stepped-up basis. As indicated in Chapter 1, there are some combinations that are nontaxable exchanges and amortizations of excess are then not deductible.[1]

A new tax schedule is needed to aid the preparation of the subsidiary IDS. The complication is that the amortizations of excess attributable to the NCI are not deductible. The tax schedule is prepared as follows:

Subsidiary Tax Schedule	Controlling	NCI	Total
1. Total adjusted income	$ 67,000[c]	$ 16,750[b]	$ 83,750[a]
2. NCI share of asset adjustments		1,250	1,250
3. Taxable income (1. + 2.)	$ 67,000	$ 18,000	$ 75,000
4. Tax (30% × 3.)	**$20,100**	**$ 5,400**	**$25,500**
Net-of-tax share of income (1. − 4.)	**$46,900**	**$11,350**	**$58,250**

[a]Shown on the subsidiary's IDS as the internally generated income net of adjustments ($100,000 + $25,000 − $35,000 − $6,250). *Note: These are before-tax numbers.*
[b]$83,750 × 20%
[c]$83,750 × 80%

The IDS schedule of the subsidiary reflects the amounts in the above schedule. The parent's IDS schedule has two unique features.

1. The share of subsidiary income is already taxed and is entered on an after-tax basis using the amount shown in the subsidiary IDS schedule.
2. The parent's internally generated net income is taxed as part of the parent's IDS schedule.

It will be necessary for each member company to record its share of the tax provision on its own books. The subsidiary, Company S, would record the following:

Provision for Income Tax	25,500	
Income Tax Payable.		25,500
To record the allocated portion of the tax provision.		

---

1 When there are nondeductible amortizations of excess cost, there also may be a recorded deferred tax liability. Recall that an excess of fair value over cost relative to an identifiable asset requires the recording of a deferred tax liability for the amount of the tax rate times the excess. This deferred tax liability would be amortized to tax expense in proportion to the amortization of the excess.

The parent, Company P, would record the following:

Subsidiary Income (80% × $25,500 tax provision)	20,400	
Investment in Company S.		20,400
To adjust Subsidiary Income for the tax expense recorded by		
Company S.		
Provision for Income Tax (from parent's IDS)	46,200*	
Income Tax Payable.		46,200
To record the allocated portion of the tax provision.		

*$154,000 internally generated income, net of adjustments × 30%

Complications Caused by Goodwill

The distribution of excess purchase price to goodwill creates a tax timing difference. Goodwill is no longer amortized for financial reporting but still is amortized for tax purposes over a 15-year life. Each year, the tax deduction taken for goodwill will result in a *deferred tax liability (DTL)*. The DTL will not be utilized until either the goodwill is impairment adjusted or the company purchased is later sold. For example, assume goodwill amortization is $5,000 per year for tax purposes, and the company has a 40% tax rate. Each year, the following adjustment would be made on the consolidated worksheet and on the parent company books:

Income Tax Payable	2,000	
Deferred Tax Liability.		2,000
To defer tax equal to 40% of $5,000 goodwill amortization for tax		
purposes only.		

After five years, there would be a $10,000 DTL. If, at the end of five years, the goodwill is reduced $20,000 for an impairment loss, the following adjustments would be made on the consolidated worksheet and on the parent company books:

Goodwill Impairment Loss.	20,000	
Goodwill		20,000
To record loss on impairment of goodwill.		
Deferred Tax Liability.	8,000	
Provision for Income Taxes		8,000
To reduce tax provision for realization of tax liability resulting from prior		
amortization of goodwill for tax purposes.		

The amortization of goodwill built a DTL account that is reduced when the goodwill impairment loss is recorded. The DTL could also be removed if the company to which it relates is sold.

Consolidated returns are consistent with consolidated reporting procedures and do not alter in any way the procedures that have been discussed in previous chapters. It is necessary to add only new procedures to the worksheet to provide for income taxes. The procedures were explained in our example assuming the use of the simple equity method. There would not be any impact on the tax entry if the cost or sophisticated equity method were used.

Separate Tax Returns

When separate returns are required or are elected to be filed, each member of the consolidated group must base its provision for tax on its own reported income. For the parent, taxable income may include dividends received from other corporations. When the members of the consolidated company meet the requirements of an affiliated company (this requires at least an 80% ownership interest), 100% of the dividends received is excluded from reported income. For ownership interests of at least 20% but less than 80%, 80% of the dividends received is excluded from reported taxable income.[2] For ownership interests less than 20%, 70% of the

4

OBJECTIVE

Prepare a consolidated worksheet where the parent and subsidiary are separately taxed by employing tax allocation procedures.

2 The exclusion rate is determined by current tax law and is subject to change.

dividends received is excluded from reported income. The full or partial exclusion of dividends applies only to dividends from domestic corporations and is intended to reduce multiple taxation of the same income.

A major complication arises in consolidating. **The provision for tax recorded by each company is based on its reported separate net income prior to eliminating intercompany transactions.** This means that timing differences are created when consolidating. For example, suppose the parent sells inventory to the subsidiary at a price that includes a 25% gross profit. If $40,000 of intercompany sales remains in the subsidiary's ending inventory, consolidation procedures defer $10,000 of intercompany profit. The problem is that the parent already recorded a 30% or $3,000 tax provision on the profit as a separate company. This $3,000 now becomes a *deferred (prepaid) tax asset* (DTA) when the profit to which it attaches is deferred on the consolidated worksheet. In the following period, the intercompany profit on the inventory is realized (assuming the inventory is sold in that period). The deferred tax asset relative to the inventory profit is then expensed as part of the current year's provision for tax. The adjustments required as a result of these tax issues are examples of applying interperiod tax allocation procedures.

The use of separate tax returns for a consolidated group leads to a complicated application of interperiod tax allocation techniques. The calculations may become cumbersome when intercompany sales of plant assets and merchandise are involved. To illustrate, assume Company P purchased a 75% interest in Company S on January 1, 2015, at which time the following determination and distribution of excess schedule was prepared:

Determination and Distribution of Excess Schedule

	Company Implied Fair Value	Parent Price (75%)	NCI Value (25%)
Fair value of subsidiary	$380,000	$285,000	$ 95,000
Less book value of interest acquired:			
Common stock	$250,000		
Retained earnings	100,000		
Total stockholders' equity	$350,000	$350,000	$350,000
Interest acquired		75%	25%
Book value		$262,500	$ 87,500
Excess of fair value over book value	**$ 30,000**	$ 22,500	$ 7,500

Adjustment of identifiable accounts:

	Adjustment	Life	Amortization per Year	Worksheet Key
Patent	$ 30,000	15	$ 2,000	**debit D**

The patent amortization will not appear on the separate statements of the parent or the subsidiary. It will only arise in the consolidation process. Since it has not been included in the parent's determination of income, the parent has taken no tax deduction.

Further assume that on January 1, 2016, the subsidiary sold equipment with a cost of $60,000 to the parent for $100,000. This means that the subsidiary has included the $40,000 gain in 2016 income and has paid the tax on it. Meanwhile, the parent is depreciating the asset over five years on a straight-line basis. The parent is recording depreciation of $20,000 per year using a cost of $100,000. The parent's tax is computed using the $20,000 depreciation deduction.

In 2017 and 2018, the parent sold merchandise to the subsidiary to realize a gross profit of 40%. In 2018, the subsidiary had a beginning inventory of goods purchased from the parent for $60,000. The parent included this amount in its 2017 income and paid the taxes on it. During the 2018 year, sales by the parent to the subsidiary totaled $100,000. Intercompany goods of $40,000 remain in the subsidiary's 2018 ending inventory. Again, the parent has included the profit in its income and paid taxes on it.

The separate income statements of the parent and the subsidiary for 2018 are as follows:

	Company P	Company S
Sales (includes $100,000 intercompany sale by P)	$430,000	$240,000
Less cost of goods sold (includes $100,000 for intercompany purchase by S)	280,000	150,000
Gross profit	$150,000	$ 90,000
Less expenses:		
Depreciation expense (includes parent's $20,000 depreciation of equipment purchased from S)	20,000	10,000
Other operating expenses..................................	50,000	20,000
Operating income.......................................	$ 80,000	$ 60,000

Taxation of Separate Entities. Before Companies P and S can be consolidated, it is necessary to calculate their separate tax liabilities since the 80% test of an affiliated group for tax purposes is not met. The tax provision of the subsidiary is $18,000 (30% × $60,000 Company S income before tax). Company S would record its tax provision as follows:

Provision for Income Tax	18,000	
Income Tax Payable...		18,000

The tax provision for Company P requires consideration of the tax status of subsidiary income. When the conditions for an affiliated group are not met, the parent company must include in its taxable income 20% of the dividends it receives from a subsidiary. According to FASB ASC 740-30-25, subsidiary income included in the pretax income of a parent leads to a temporary difference between the earning of the income and its inclusion in the tax return as dividend income.[3] It is not necessary to account for the temporary difference if the tax law provides a means by which the investment can be recovered tax free. Company P will provide for tax expense equal to its tax rate times 20% of its share of the total subsidiary net income. It is assumed that the parent records its tax provision based on the income it records from the subsidiary. In this example, the parent records the investment under the simple equity method. Thus, the tax accrual is based on 20% of the simple equity income without any reduction for amortization of excesses. A parent using the cost method would record the tax only on dividends received and would need to accrue tax on the worksheet based on the cost-to-equity conversion.

This tax may be viewed as a secondary tax since it is the second taxation of subsidiary income. For 2018, this tax liability would be calculated as follows:

Subsidiary net income ($60,000 − $18,000 tax)	$42,000
Controlling interest (75% × $42,000)	31,500
Provision for tax on subsidiary income (30% × 20% × $31,500)	1,890

Company P would add this amount to the tax it has provided for its internally generated income to arrive at its total tax provision for the period as follows:

Tax on internally generated income (30% × $80,000)	$24,000
Secondary tax provision for subsidiary income..................................	1,890
Total Company P provision for tax...	$25,890

---

3 FASB ASC 740-30-25, *Income Taxes—Other Considerations or Special Areas—Recognition—General* (Norwalk, CT, 2010).

Since Company P has not received its share of the income of Company S, the secondary tax is not immediately payable, and a deferred tax liability for $1,890 is created. Assuming that the tax on internally generated income is currently payable, Company P would make the following entry to record its 2018 tax provision:

Provision for Income Tax	25,890	
Income Tax Payable		24,000
Deferred Tax Liability		1,890

If dividends had been paid by the subsidiary, the secondary tax applicable to the dividends received by Company P would be included in the current tax liability. Note that the secondary tax applies only to consolidated companies that do not qualify as an affiliated group. Companies that do meet the requirements would calculate only a single tax on each company's adjusted net income. When an affiliated group *elects* separate taxation, no dividends are included and no additional tax needs to be calculated.

Worksheet 6-2: page 352

Worksheet Procedures. Worksheet 6-2, on pages 352 to 353, includes the trial balances of Companies P and S. The companies do not qualify as an affiliated group for tax purposes. **Several observations should be made regarding the amounts listed in the trial balance before you study the elimination entries.**

1. The balance in Investment in Company S is computed according to the simple equity method, as follows:

Original cost			$285,000
Subsidiary income, 2015–2017 (*after tax*):			
Company S retained earnings, January 1, 2018	$350,000		
Company S retained earnings, January 1, 2015	100,000		
Net increase	$250,000		
Controlling interest	×	75%	187,500
Controlling interest in subsidiary net income, 2018 (75% × $42,000)			31,500
Equity-adjusted balance, December 31, 2018			$504,000

2. Since the parent's share of subsidiary undistributed income has been recorded from the date of acquisition, a deferred tax liability has been recorded by Company P each year to recognize the secondary tax provision. The total deferred tax liability on December 31, 2018, is calculated as follows:

Deferred tax liability on 2015–2017 income (20% × 30% × $187,500* on 2015–2017 undistributed income)	$11,250
Current year's additional deferment (20% × 30% × $31,500)	1,890
Total deferred tax liability	$13,140

*75% × $250,000 increase in Company S retained earnings

3. The trial balances of both companies include their separate provisions for income tax and the current tax liabilities. **These provisions do not reflect adjustments for intercompany transactions.**

All worksheet entries, other than (T1) and (T2) are unchanged from procedures used in prior worksheets, and the same coding is used. In journal entry form, the entries for Worksheet 6-2 are as follows:

(CY1)	Eliminate current-year equity income:		
	Subsidiary Income	31,500	
	Investment in Company S		31,500

(EL)	Eliminate 75% of subsidiary equity:		
	Common Stock, Company S	187,500	
	Retained Earnings, Company S.	262,500	
	Investment in Company S.		450,000
(D)/(NCI)	Distribute excess to patent:		
	Patent.	30,000	
	Investment in Company S.		22,500
	Retained Earnings—Company S (NCI adjustment)		7,500
(A)	Amortize patent for three prior years and the current year:		
	Patent Amortization Expense.	2,000	
	Retained Earnings—Company P	4,500	
	Retained Earnings—Company S	1,500	
	Patent.		8,000
(F1)	Adjust retained earnings for fixed asset profit at start of year (two prior years):		
	Retained Earnings—Company P	18,000	
	Retained Earnings—Company S	6,000	
	Accumulated Depreciation—Equipment	16,000	
	Equipment		40,000
(F2)	Adjust current-year depreciation for gain on fixed asset sale:		
	Accumulated Depreciation—Equipment	8,000	
	Depreciation Expense		8,000
(IS)	Eliminate intercompany merchandise sales:		
	Sales	100,000	
	Cost of Goods Sold		100,000
(BI)	Adjust January 1 retained earnings for inventory profit recorded by parent:		
	Retained Earnings—Company P	24,000	
	Cost of Goods Sold		24,000
(EI)	Adjust cost of goods sold for profit in ending inventory:		
	Cost of Goods Sold	16,000	
	Inventory, December 31, 2018.		16,000
(T1)	Record deferred tax asset applicable to prior adjustments:		
	Deferred Tax Liability.	16,695	
	Retained Earnings—Company S		1,800
	Retained Earnings—Company P		14,895
(T2)	Record change in deferred tax asset during current period:		
	Provision for Income Tax	4,539	
	Deferred Tax Liability.		4,539

Worksheet entries (T1) and (T2) are explained in the directions that accompany the worksheet, but let us expand on them. Entry (T1) takes the position that both companies have already paid a tax on the income recorded by the companies in prior periods. If consolidation procedures change the income, for example reduce income, then the taxes are considered to have been paid in advance and the taxes paid become a deferred tax asset.

It should be noted that only the controlling portion of excess amortizations are deductible since a tax deduction is allowed only for the interest in the assets that was actually purchased. The increase in the value of the assets attributed to the NCI are not subject to tax adjustments.

The adjustment to beginning retained earnings for taxes paid in prior periods, entry **(T1)**, is explained as follows:

DTA/DTL adjustments:

To beginning retained earnings:

Subsidiary transactions:	Total Tax	Parent Share	Subsidiary Share
Remaining fixed asset profit.	$ 24,000	$ 18,000	$ 6,000
Amortization of excess (patent, 75% × $6,000) . . .	4,500	4,500	
Total.	$ 28,500	$ 22,500	$ 6,000
1. First tax (30%)	8,550	6,750	1,800
Net income after tax	$ 19,950	**$15,750**	$ 4,200
2. 20% × 30% × $15,750.	$ 945	$ 945	
3. Total tax (1. + 2.)	$ 9,495	$ 7,695	$ 1,800
Parent transactions:			
Beginning inventory	$ 24,000	$ 24,000	
4. First tax (30% × $24,000)	$ 7,200	$ 7,200	
Total increase in DTA and retained earnings			
(3. + 4.).	**$16,695**	**$14,895**	**$1,800**

(T2) Adjust current-year tax provision and adjust deferred tax asset for the effects of current-year income adjustments:

Subsidiary transactions:	Total Tax	Parent Share	Subsidiary Share
Realized fixed asset profit	$ (8,000)	$(6,000)	$(2,000)
Amortization of excess (patent, 75% × $2,000) . . .	1,500	1,500	
1. Total	$ (6,500)	$(4,500)	$(2,000)
First tax (30% × 1.)	$ (1,950)	$(1,350)	$ (600)
20% × 30 × ($4,500 − $1,350) first tax.	(189)	(189)	
2. Total tax.	$ (2,139)	$(1,539)	$ (600)
Parent transactions:			
Beginning inventory	$(24,000)		
Ending inventory	16,000		
Total.	$ (8,000)		
3. First tax (30% × $8,000)	$ (2,400)	$(2,400)	
Increase (decrease) in DTA (2. + 3.)	$ (4,539)	$(3,939)	$ (600)

This means that income of prior periods has been reduced by $52,500 ($24,000 + $4,500 + $24,000) and the taxes already paid on these reductions are $16,695. These tax payments now create a deferred tax asset that will be consumed in future periods.

Entry (T2) considers the tax effects of adjustments made to the current-year income. Let us consider an expanded version of the explanation to entry (T2) in the explanations to the worksheet.

When the entries in Worksheet 6-2 are completed, the resulting consolidated net income is $105,571, which is distributed to the controlling and noncontrolling interests.

Complications Caused by Goodwill

Since the firms are taxed separately, goodwill that results from a purchase has not been acknowledged for tax purposes and, thus, does not create a tax deduction for goodwill amortization and a resulting DTL as it did in the case of taxation of the consolidated company.

Let us revisit Worksheet 6-2 to discuss how it would be simplified if the consolidated company met the requirements of an affiliated company. The following procedures would be omitted from the worksheet:

1. Company P would not have recorded the deferred tax liability of $13,140 on its books. If the companies are an affiliated group, there is no tax due on the parent's share of subsidiary income. The parent's current-year provision for income tax would be only $24,000 since there would not be the secondary tax of $1,890 on the parent's share of subsidiary income.
2. Entry (T1) would not include the secondary tax applicable to the patent amortization and the intercompany equipment sale.
3. Entry (T2) would not include the secondary tax of $252 applicable to the patent amortization and the intercompany equipment sale.
4. The parent's income distribution schedule would not deduct the secondary tax on the parent's share of subsidiary income. Instead, the parent would just include 75% of the subsidiary's after-tax income of $46,050, or $34,538.

There are some additional minor worksheet modifications required if the cost or sophisticated equity methods are used by the parent company. If the cost method is used, there needs to be a recording of the deferred tax liability for prior years' subsidiary income. The adjustment would be to multiply the net amount of the cost-to-equity conversion adjustment by the effective tax rate, to debit the parent's retained earnings, and to credit a deferred tax liability account. If the sophisticated equity method is used, the parent company's retained earnings and current-year tax provision are correct and need no adjustment. The only entry needed in consolidating is to adjust the beginning retained earnings of the subsidiary for any intercompany profits on a net-of-tax basis. The adjustment of subsidiary retained earnings on the consolidated worksheet was covered in the partial worksheet on page 223. It still would be necessary to calculate the noncontrolling and controlling interests in combined net income on an after-tax basis when preparing the income distribution schedules. (Note that each income distribution schedule starts with net income *before tax*. This is done so that the tax provision may be recalculated on a consolidated basis.)

REFLECTION

- An "affiliated group" (under tax law) may prepare a consolidated tax return. The tax provision is computed based on the consolidated income computed on the worksheet. The provision is then allocated to the controlling and noncontrolling interests.

- When a consolidated company is subject to separate taxation, each firm has recorded its tax provision based on its own reported income. Taxes have already been paid on intercompany profits. The parent has paid the double tax on its share of subsidiary income.

- A worksheet prepared under separate taxation requires procedures for the adjustment of the separate taxes already present. The taxes applicable to intercompany gains, which are eliminated, become a deferred tax asset. Amortizations of excess (not deductible on separate tax returns) create additional deferred tax assets.

- As intercompany profits are realized through sale to the "outside world" or through amortization, the deferred tax asset is realized as an increase in the provision for taxes.

Worksheet 6-1

Affiliates File Consolidated Income Tax Return
Company P and Subsidiary Company S
Worksheet for Consolidated Financial Statements
For Year Ended December 31, 2017

	(Credit balance amounts are in parentheses.)	Trial Balance	
		Company P	Company S
1	Cash	205,000	380,000
2	Inventory	150,000	120,000
3	Investment in Company S	1,115,000	
4			
5			
6	Patent		
7	Plant and Equipment	900,000	1,100,000
8	Accumulated Depreciation	(440,000)	(150,000)
9			
10	Liabilities		(150,000)
11	Common Stock—Company S		(500,000)
12	Retained Earnings, January 1, 2017—Company S		(700,000)
13			
14			
15	Common Stock—Company P	(800,000)	
16	Retained Earnings, January 1, 2017—Company P	(900,000)	
17			
18			
19	Sales	(600,000)	(400,000)
20	Cost of Goods Sold	350,000	200,000
21			
22	Patent Amortization Expense		
23	Depreciation Expense	25,000	20,000
24	Other Expenses	75,000	80,000
25	Subsidiary Income	(80,000)	
26	Total	0	0
27	**Consolidated Income Before Tax**		
28	**Consolidated Tax Provision**		
29	**Income Tax Payable**		
30	Consolidated Net Income		
31	NCI Share		
32	Controlling Share		
33	NCI		
34	Controlling Retained Earnings		
35	Total		

Worksheet 6-1 (see page 339)

Eliminations & Adjustments				Consolidated Income Statement	NCI	Controlling Retained Earnings	Consolidated Balance Sheet	
Dr.		Cr.						
							585,000	1
		(EI)	35,000				235,000	2
		(CY1)	80,000					3
		(EL)	960,000					4
		(D)	75,000					5
(D)	93,750	(A)	18,750				75,000	6
		(F1)	20,000				1,980,000	7
(F1)	4,000							8
(F2)	4,000						(582,000)	9
							(150,000)	10
(EL)	400,000				(100,000)			11
(EL)	560,000	(NCI)	18,750					12
(A)	2,500							13
(BI)	5,000				(151,250)			14
							(800,000)	15
(A)	10,000							16
(BI)	20,000							17
(F1)	16,000					(854,000)		18
(IS)	100,000			(900,000)				19
		(IS)	100,000					20
(EI)	35,000	(BI)	25,000	460,000				21
(A)	6,250			6,250				22
		(F2)	4,000	41,000				23
				155,000				24
(CY1)	80,000							25
	1,336,500		1,336,500					26
				(237,750)				27
(T)	71,700			71,700				28
		(T)	71,700				(71,700)	29
				(166,050)				30
				11,350	(11,350)			31
				154,700		(154,700)		32
					(262,600)		(262,600)	33
						(1,008,700)	(1,008,700)	34
							0	35

Eliminations and Adjustments:

(CY1) Eliminate the parent's entry recording its share of the current year's subsidiary income. This step returns the investment account to its balance on January 1, 2017.

(EL) Eliminate 80% of the January 1, 2017, subsidiary equity balances against the investment in Company S account.

(D) Record the NCI portion of excess of fair value over book value, distribute excess in investment account, and adjust patent to fair value.

(A) Amortize the patent at an annual amount of $6,250 per year for the current and prior two years. Split retained earnings for prior years—80% controlling retained earnings and 20% NCI.

(IS) Eliminate intercompany merchandise sales of $100,000 to avoid double-counting sale and purchase.

(BI) Reduce the cost of goods sold by the $25,000 of intercompany profit included in the beginning inventory.
Since the sale was made by the subsidiary, the reduction of retained earnings is allocated 20% to the NCI and 80% to the controlling retained earnings.

(EI) Reduce the ending inventory to its cost to the consolidated company by decreasing it $35,000, and increase the cost of goods sold by $35,000.

(F1) Reduce retained earnings for the remaining undepreciated intercompany equipment gain on January 1, 2017.
Since the sale was by the parent, the entire retained earnings adjustment is debited to Controlling Retained Earnings.

(F2) Adjust depreciation expense and accumulated for $4,000 over depreciation of equipment in current year.
This is the added depreciation caused by the $20,000 intercompany gain.

(T) Record the provision for taxes, calculated as follows: ($237,750 + $1,250 adjustment for NCI share of asset adjustments) × 30% = $71,700.

Subsidiary Company S Income Distribution

Ending inventory profit	$35,000	Internally generated net income	$100,000
Amortizations	6,250	Beginning inventory profit	25,000
		Adjusted income before tax....	$ 83,750
		Company S share of taxes (see tax schedule below the parent IDS schedule)	(25,500)
		Net income	$ 58,250
		NCI share (see schedule)......	11,350
		Controlling share...........	$ 46,900

Parent Company P Income Distribution

	Internally generated net income	$150,000
	Realized gain	4,000
	Adjusted income before tax....	$154,000
	Company P share of taxes (30% × $154,000)........	(46,200)
	Company P net income	$107,800
	Controlling share of subsidiary net income (see schedule) ...	46,900
	Controlling interest	$154,700

Subsidiary Tax Schedule	Controlling	NCI	Total
1. Total adjusted income	$ 67,000[c]	$ 16,750[b]	$ 83,750[a]
2. NCI share of asset adjustments		1,250	1,250
3. Taxable income (1. + 2.)	$ 67,000	$ 18,000	$ 75,000
4. Tax (30% × 3.)	**$20,100**	**$ 5,400**	**$25,500**
Net-of-tax share of income (1. − 4.)	**$46,900**	**$11,350**	**$58,250**

[a]Shown on the subsidiary's IDS as the internally generated income net of adjustments ($100,000 + $25,000 − $35,000 − $6,250). *Note: These are before-tax numbers.*
[b]$83,750 × 20%.
[c]$83,750 × 80%.

Worksheet 6-2

Nonaffiliated Group for Tax Purposes
Company P and Subsidiary Company S
Worksheet for Consolidated Financial Statements
For Year Ended December 31, 2018

	(Credit balance amounts are in parentheses.)	Trial Balance	
		Company P	Company S
1	Cash	19,200	80,000
2	Inventory	170,000	150,000
3	Investment in Company S	504,000	
4			
5			
6	Patent		
7	Plant and Equipment	600,000	550,000
8	Accumulated Depreciation	(410,000)	(120,000)
9			
10	Current Tax Liability	(24,000)	(18,000)
11	**Deferred Tax Liability**	**(13,140)**	
12			
13	Common Stock—Company S		(250,000)
14	Retained Earnings, January 1, 2018—Company S		(350,000)
15			
16			
17			
18	Common Stock—Company P	(250,000)	
19	Retained Earnings, January 1, 2018—Company P	(510,450)	
20			
21			
22	Sales	(430,000)	(240,000)
23	Cost of Goods Sold	280,000	150,000
24			
25	Patent Amortization Expense		
26	Depreciation Expense	20,000	10,000
27	Other Expenses	50,000	20,000
28	**Provision for Income Tax**	**25,890**	**18,000**
29	Subsidiary Income	(31,500)	
30	Total	0	0
31	Consolidated Net Income		
32	NCI Share		
33	Controlling Share		
34	NCI		
35	Controlling Retained Earnings		
36	Total		

Worksheet 6-2 (see page 344)

Eliminations & Adjustments				Consolidated Income Statement	NCI	Controlling Retained Earnings	Consolidated Balance Sheet	
Dr.		Cr.						
							99,200	1
		(EI)	16,000				304,000	2
		(CY1)	31,500					3
		(EL)	450,000					4
		(D)	22,500					5
(D)	30,000	(A)	8,000				22,000	6
		(F1)	40,000				1,110,000	7
(F1)	16,000							8
(F2)	8,000						(506,000)	9
							(42,000)	10
(T1)	**16,695**	**(T2)**	**4,539**				(984)	11
								12
(EL)	187,500				(62,500)			13
(EL)	262,500	(NCI)	7,500					14
(A)	1,500	**(T1)**	**1,800**					15
(F1)	6,000							16
					(89,300)			17
							(250,000)	18
(A)	4,500							19
(BI)	24,000	**(T1)**	**14,895**					20
(F1)	18,000					(478,845)		21
(IS)	100,000			(570,000)				22
		(IS)	100,000					23
(EI)	16,000	(BI)	24,000	322,000				24
(A)	2,000			2,000				25
		(F2)	8,000	22,000				26
				70,000				27
(T2)	**4,539**			48,429				28
(CY1)	31,500							29
	728,734		728,734					30
				(105,571)				31
				11,400	(11,400)			32
				94,171		(94,171)		33
					(163,200)		(163,200)	34
						(573,016)	(573,016)	35
							0	36

Eliminations and Adjustments:

(CY1) Eliminate the parent's entry recording its share of the current year's subsidiary income. This step returns the investment account to its balance on January 1, 2018.

(EL) Eliminate 75% of the January 1, 2018, subsidiary equity balances against the investment in Company S account.

(D) Record the NCI portion of excess of fair value over book value, distribute excess in investment account, and adjust patent to fair value.

(A) Amortize the patent at an amount of $2,000 per year for the current and prior three years. Split retained earnings for prior years—75% controlling retained earnings and 25% NCI.

(IS) Eliminate intercompany merchandise sales of $100,000 to avoid double-counting sale and purchase.

(BI) Reduce the cost of goods sold by the $24,000 of intercompany profit included in the beginning inventory. Since the sale was made by the parent, the reduction of retained earnings is allocated only to the parent.

(EI) Reduce the ending inventory to its cost to the consolidated company by decreasing it $16,000, and increase the cost of goods sold by $16,000.

(F1) Reduce retained earnings for the remaining undepreciated intercompany equipment gain on January 1, 2018. Since the sale was by the subsidiary, the adjustment is allocated 25% to NCI and 75% to controlling retained earnings.

(F2) Adjust depreciation expense and accumulated depreciation for $8,000 over depreciation of equipment in current year. This is the added depreciation caused by the $40,000 intercompany gain.

(T1) Adjust beginning retained earnings and create a deferred tax asset on consolidated prior-period adjustments as follows:

DTA/DTL adjustments:
To beginning retained earnings:

	Total Tax	Parent Share	Subsidiary Share
Subsidiary transactions:			
Remaining fixed asset profit.	$ 24,000	$ 18,000	$ 6,000
Amortization of excess (patent, 75% × $6,000) . . .	4,500	4,500	
Total.	$ 28,500	$ 22,500	$ 6,000
1. First tax (30%)	8,550	6,750	1,800
Net income after tax	$ 19,950	**$15,750**	$ 4,200
2. 20% × 30% × $15,750.	$ 945	$ 945	
3. Total tax (1. + 2.)	$ 9,495	$ 7,695	$ 1,800
Parent transactions:			
Beginning inventory	$ 24,000	$ 24,000	
4. First tax (30% × $24,000)	$ 7,200	$ 7,200	
Total increase in DTA and retained earnings (3. + 4.).	**$16,695**	**$14,895**	**$1,800**

(T2) Adjust current-year tax provision and adjust deferred tax asset for the effects of current-year income adjustments:

	Total Tax	Parent Share	Subsidiary Share
Subsidiary transactions:			
Realized fixed asset profit	$ (8,000)	$(6,000)	$(2,000)
Amortization of excess (patent, 75% × $2,000) . . .	1,500	1,500	
1. Total	$ (6,500)	$(4,500)	$(2,000)
First tax (30% × 1.)	$ (1,950)	$(1,350)	$ (600)
20% × 30 × ($4,500 − $1,350) first tax.	(189)	(189)	
2. Total tax.	$ (2,139)	$(1,539)	$ (600)
Parent transactions:			
Beginning inventory	$(24,000)		
Ending inventory	16,000		
Total.	$ (8,000)		
3. First tax (30% × $8,000)	$ (2,400)	$(2,400)	
Increase (decrease) in DTA (2. + 3.)	$ (4,539)	$(3,939)	$ (600)

Subsidiary Company S Income Distribution

Amortizations	$2,000	Internally generated net income	$ 60,000
		Realized gain	8,000
		Adjusted income before tax. . . .	$ 66,000
		Company S share of taxes (see tax schedule below the parent IDS schedule)	(19,950)
		Net income	$ 46,050
		NCI share (see schedule).	11,400
		Controlling share.	$ 34,650

Parent Company P Income Distribution

Ending inventory profit	$16,000	Internally generated net income	$ 80,000
		Beginning inventory profit	24,000
		Adjusted income before tax. . . .	$ 88,000
		Company P share of taxes (30% × $88,000)	(26,400)
		Company P net income	$ 61,600
		Controlling share of subsidiary net income (see schedule) . . .	34,650
		Second tax on subsidiary income (30% × 20% × $34,650). . .	(2,079)
		Controlling interest	$ 94,171

Subsidiary Tax Schedule	Controlling	NCI	Total
1. Total adjusted income	$49,500	$16,500	$66,000
2. NCI share of asset adjustments		500	500
3. Taxable income (1. + 2.)	$49,500	$17,000	$66,500
4. Tax (30% × 3.)	$14,850	$ 5,100	$19,950
Net-of-tax share of income (1. − 4.)	$34,650	$11,400	$46,050

UNDERSTANDING THE ISSUES

1. Par Company acquires 100% of the common stock of Sub Company for an agreed-upon price of $900,000. The book value of the net assets is $700,000, which includes $50,000 of subsidiary cash equivalents. Existing fixed assets have fair values greater than their recorded book values. How will this transaction affect the cash flow statement of the consolidated firm in the period of the purchase, if:

   a. Par Company pays $900,000 cash to purchase the stock?
   b. Par Company pays $500,000 cash and signs 5-year notes for $400,000? All Sub Company shareholders receive notes.
   c. Par Company exchanges only common stock with the shareholders of Sub Company?

2. What will be the effect of the above acquisition on cash flow statements prepared in periods after the year of the purchase?

3. P Company acquires 80% of the common stock of S Company for an agreed-upon price of $640,000. The fair value of the NCI is $160,000. The book value of the net assets is $600,000, which includes $50,000 of subsidiary cash equivalents. Any excess is attributable to goodwill. (A D&D schedule is suggested to properly calculate the NCI.) How will this transaction affect the cash flow statement of the consolidated firm in the period of the purchase, if:

   a. P Company pays $640,000 cash to purchase the stock?
   b. P Company pays $400,000 cash and signs 5-year notes for $240,000? 80% of the Company S shareholders receives notes.
   c. P Company exchanges only common stock with 80% of the shareholders of Company S?

4. Company P has internally generated net income of $250,000 (excludes share of subsidiary income). Company P has 100,000 shares of outstanding common stock. Subsidiary Company S has a net income of $60,000 and 40,000 shares of outstanding common stock. What is consolidated basic EPS, if:

   a. Company P owns 100% of the Company S shares?
   b. Company P owns 80% of the Company S shares?

5. Company P has internally generated net income of $200,000 (excludes share of subsidiary income). Company P has 100,000 shares of outstanding common stock. Subsidiary Company S has a net income of $60,000 and 40,000 shares of outstanding common stock. Company P owns 100% of the Company S shares. What is consolidated diluted EPS, if:

   a. Company S has outstanding stock options for Company S shares, which cause a dilutive effect of 2,000 additional shares of Company S shares?
   b. Company S has outstanding stock options for Company P shares, which cause a dilutive effect of 2,000 additional shares of Company P shares?
   c. Company P has outstanding stock options for Company P shares, which cause a dilutive effect of 2,000 additional shares of Company P shares?

6. Company S is an 80% owned subsidiary of Company P. For 2015, Company P reports internally generated income before tax of $100,000. Company S reports an income before tax of $40,000. A 30% tax rate applies to both companies. Calculate consolidated net income (after taxes) and the distribution of income to the controlling and noncontrolling interests, if:

   a. The consolidated firm meets the requirements of an affiliated firm and files a consolidated tax return.
   b. The consolidated firm does not meet the requirements of an affiliated firm and files separate tax returns. Assume an 80% dividend exclusion rate.

7. Company S is an 80% owned subsidiary of Company P. On January 1, 2015, Company P sells equipment to Company S at a $50,000 profit. Assume a 30% corporate tax rate and an 80% dividend exclusion. The equipment has a 5-year life. The question is, would taxes be paid on this profit and what adjustments (if needed) for the tax would be made, if:

a. Companies P and S are an "affiliated firm" and file a consolidated tax return?
b. Companies P and S are not an "affiliated firm" and file separate tax returns?

EXERCISES

Exercise 1 *(LO 1)* **Cash flow, cash payment, year of acquisition.** Born Company acquires an 80% interest in Roland Company for $660,000 cash on January 1, 2017. The NCI has a fair value of $165,000. Any excess of cost over book value is attributed to goodwill. To help pay for the acquisition, Born Company issues 5,000 shares of its common stock with a fair value of $70 per share. Roland's balance sheet on the date of the purchase is as follows:

Assets		Liabilities and Equity	
Cash	$ 20,000	Current liabilities	$110,000
Inventory	140,000	Bonds payable	100,000
Property, plant, and		Common stock ($10 par)........	200,000
equipment (net)	550,000	Retained earnings	300,000
Total assets	$710,000	Total liabilities and equity	$710,000

Controlling share of net income for 2017 is $150,000, net of the noncontrolling interest of $10,000. Born declares and pays dividends of $10,000, and Roland declares and pays dividends of $5,000. There are no purchases or sales of property, plant, or equipment during the year. Based on the following information, prepare a statement of cash flows using the indirect method for Born Company and its subsidiary for the year ended December 31, 2017. Any supporting schedules should be in good form.

	Born Company December 31, 2016	Consolidated December 31, 2017
Cash	$ 300,000	$ 199,000
Inventory	220,000	454,000
Property, plant, and equipment (net)	800,000	1,230,000
Goodwill		325,000
Current liabilities	(160,000)	(284,000)
Bonds payable	(200,000)	(300,000)
Noncontrolling interest		(174,000)
Controlling common stock ($10 par)..............	(200,000)	(250,000)
Controlling paid-in capital in excess of par	(300,000)	(600,000)
Retained earnings	(460,000)	(600,000)
Totals	$ 0	$ 0

Exercise 2 *(LO 1)* **Cash flow, issue stock, year of purchase.** Duckworth Corporation purchases an 80% interest in Panda Corporation on January 1, 2017, in exchange for 5,000 Duckworth shares (market value of $18) plus $155,000 cash. The fair value of the NCI is proportionate to the price paid by Duckworth for its interest. The appraisal shows that some of Panda's equipment, with a 4-year estimated remaining life, is undervalued by $20,000. The excess is attributed to goodwill. Panda Corporation's balance sheet on December 31, 2016 is shown on page 358.

Assets		Liabilities and Equity	
Cash	$ 30,000	Current liabilities	$ 30,000
Inventory	30,000	Long-term liabilities	40,000
Property, plant, and equipment. . .	300,000	Common stock ($10 par).	150,000
Accumulated depreciation	(90,000)	Retained earnings	50,000
Total assets.	$270,000	Total liabilities and equity	$270,000

Comparative balance sheet data are as follows:

	December 31, 2016 (Parent Only)	December 31, 2017 (Consolidated)
Cash	$ 100,000	$ 95,000
Inventory	60,000	84,200
Property, plant, and equipment.	950,000	1,346,000
Accumulated depreciation	(360,000)	(575,000)
Goodwill		86,250
Current liabilities	(80,000)	(115,000)
Long-term liabilities	(100,000)	(130,000)
Noncontrolling interest		(63,250)
Controlling interest:		
Common stock ($10 par).	(350,000)	(400,000)
Additional paid-in capital in excess of par	(50,000)	(90,000)
Retained earnings	(170,000)	(238,200)
Totals	$ 0	$ 0

The following information relates to the activities of the two companies for 2017:

a. Panda pays off $10,000 of its long-term debt.
b. Duckworth purchases production equipment for $76,000.
c. Consolidated net income is $103,200; the NCI's share is $5,000. Depreciation expense taken by Duckworth and Panda on their separate books is $92,000 and $28,000, respectively.
d. Duckworth pays $30,000 in dividends; Panda pays $15,000.

Prepare the consolidated statement of cash flows for the year ended December 31, 2017, for Duckworth Corporation and its subsidiary, Panda Corporation.

Exercise 3 *(LO 1)* **Cash flow, subsequent to year of purchase.** Paridon Motors purchases an 80% interest in Snap Battery Company on January 1, 2012, for $700,000 cash. At that date, Snap Battery Company has the following stockholders' equity:

Common stock ($10 par).	$100,000
Paid-in capital in excess of par	300,000
Retained earnings	250,000
Total stockholders' equity.	$650,000

Any excess of cost over book value is attributed to goodwill. A statement of cash flows is being prepared for 2015. For each of the following situations, indicate the impact on the cash flow statement for 2015:

1. Adjustment resulting from the original acquisition of the controlling interest.
2. Snap Battery Company issues 2,000 shares of common stock for $90 per share on January 1, 2015. At the time, the stockholders' equity of Snap Battery is $800,000. Paridon Motors purchases 1,000 shares.
3. Paridon Motors purchases at 102, $100,000 of face value, 10% annual interest bonds issued by Snap Battery Company at face value on January 1, 2013. Paridon purchases the bonds on January 1, 2015.

4. Snap Battery purchases a production machine from Paridon Motors on July 1, 2015, for $80,000. Paridon's cost is $60,000, and accumulated depreciation is $20,000.

Exercise 4 *(LO 3)* **Taxation as consolidated company.** On May 1, 2016, Tole Company acquires a 80% interest in Marco Company for $400,000. The fair value of the NCI is $100,000. The following determination and distribution of excess schedule is prepared:

Determination and Distribution of Excess Schedule

	Implied Company Fair Value	Parent Price (80%)	NCI Value (20%)
Fair value of subsidiary	$ 500,000	$400,000	$100,000
Less book value of interest acquired:			
Common stock	$ 300,000		
Retained earnings	100,000		
Total equity	$ 400,000	$400,000	$400,000
Interest acquired		80%	20%
Book value.		$320,000	$ 80,000
Excess of fair value over book value	**$100,000**	$ 80,000	$ 20,000

Adjustment of identifiable accounts:

	Adjustment	Amortization per Year	Life	Worksheet Key
Goodwill.	**$100,000**			**debit D**

Goodwill, applicable to the parent's interest ($80,000), will be amortized over 15 years *for tax purposes only.*

Tole Company and Marco Company have the following separate income statements for the year ended December 31, 2018:

	Tole Company	Marco Company
Sales	$750,000	$600,000
Less cost of goods sold.	440,000	350,000
Gross profit	$310,000	$250,000
Less other expenses	250,000	140,000
Income before dividends	$110,000	$110,000
Dividends received	17,500	
Income before tax	$127,500	$110,000

During 2018, Marco Company pays cash dividends of $25,000.

Prepare the entry to record income tax payable on each company's books. Assume a 30% corporate income tax rate.

Exercise 5 *(LO 3)* **Consolidated taxation, intercompany profits.** Deko Company purchases an 80% interest in the common stock of Farwell Company for $850,000 on January 1, 2017. At the time of the purchase, the total stockholders' equity of Farwell is $968,750. The fair value of the NCI is $212,500. The excess of cost over book value is attributed to a patent with a 10-year life.

During 2019, Deko Company and Farwell Company report the internally generated income before taxes as shown on page 360.

	Deko Company	Farwell Company
Sales	$ 300,000	$120,000
Cost of goods sold.	(200,000)	(90,000)
Gain on machine.	5,000	
Expenses	(40,000)	(20,000)
Income before taxes	$ 65,000	$ 10,000

Farwell Company sells goods to Deko Company for $50,000. Deko Company has $20,000 of Farwell Company's goods in its beginning inventory and $6,000 of Farwell's goods in its ending inventory. Farwell Company sells goods to Deko Company at a gross profit of 40%.

Deko Company sells a new machine to Farwell Company on January 1, 2019, for $30,000. The machine has a 5-year life, and its cost is $25,000. The affiliated group files a consolidated tax return and is taxed at 30%.

Prepare a determination and distribution of excess schedule and a consolidated income statement for 2019. Include income distribution schedules for both companies.

Exercise 6 *(LO 4)* **Separate taxation, intercompany transactions.** *(This is the same as Exercise 5 but with separate taxation.)* Dunker Company purchases an 80% interest in the common stock of Fennig Company for $850,000 on January 1, 2017. The fair value of the NCI is $212,500. At the time of the purchase, the total stockholders' equity of Fennig is $968,750. The price paid is $75,000 in excess of the book value of the controlling portion of Fennig equity. The excess is attributed to a patent with a 10-year life.

During 2019, Dunker Company and Fennig Company report the following internally generated income before taxes:

	Dunker Company	Fennig Company
Sales	$ 300,000	$120,000
Cost of goods sold.	(200,000)	(90,000)
Gain on machine.	5,000	
Expenses	(40,000)	(20,000)
Income before taxes	$ 65,000	$ 10,000

Fennig Company sells goods to Dunker Company for $50,000. Dunker Company has $20,000 of Fennig Company's goods in its beginning inventory and $6,000 of Fennig's goods in its ending inventory. Fennig Company sells goods to Dunker Company at a gross profit of 40%.

Dunker Company sells a new machine to Fennig Company on January 1, 2019, for $30,000. The machine has a 5-year life, and its cost is $25,000. The companies file separate tax returns. Both are subject to a 30% tax rate. Dunker receives an 80% dividend deduction.

Prepare a consolidated income statement for 2019. Include income distribution schedules for both companies.

Exercise 7 *(LO 4)* **Tax allocation with separate taxation.** The separate income statements of Coors Company and its 60% owned subsidiary, Vespa Company, for the year ended December 31, 2017, are as follows:

	Coors Company	Vespa Company
Sales	$520,000	$370,000
Less cost of goods sold.	350,000	180,000
Gross profit	$170,000	$190,000
Less operating expenses	100,000	90,000
Operating income	$ 70,000	$100,000

	Coors Company	Vespa Company
Subsidiary (dividend) income	12,600	
Income before tax	$ 82,600	$100,000
Provision for income tax	21,756	30,000
Net income	$ 60,844	$ 70,000

The following additional information is available:

a. Coors Company acquires its interest in Vespa Company on July 1, 2015. The excess of cost over book value is attributable to machinery which is undervalued by a total amount of $100,000. The remaining life of the machine is 20 years.

b. Vespa Company sells a machine to Coors Company on December 31, 2016, for $10,000. This machine has a book value of $6,000 and an estimated future life of four years at the purchase date. Straight-line depreciation is assumed.

c. Coors Company sells $15,000 worth of merchandise to Vespa Company during 2017. Cooper sells its merchandise at a price that enables it to realize a gross profit of 25%. Vespa Company has $2,000 worth of Coors merchandise in its ending inventory.

d. A corporate income tax rate of 30% is assumed.

Prepare the worksheet adjustments (in journal entry format) pertaining to the purchase cost amortization and the intercompany transactions, and prepare the interperiod tax allocations that result from the elimination of the intercompany transactions. The companies do not qualify as an affiliated group under the tax code.

PROBLEMS

Problem 6-1 *(LO 1)* **Cash flow, year subsequent to purchase.** Marion Company is an 80% owned subsidiary of Lange Company. The interest in Marion is purchased on January 1, 2015, for $680,000 cash. The fair value of the NCI was $170,000. At that date, Marion has stockholders' equity of $650,000. The excess price is attributed to equipment with a 5-year life undervalued by $50,000 and to goodwill.

The following comparative consolidated trial balances apply to Lange Company and its subsidiary, Marion:

	December 31, 2015	December 31, 2016
Cash	16,000	24,500
Inventory	120,000	160,000
Accounts Receivable	200,000	300,000
Property, Plant, and Equipment	3,030,000	3,450,000
Accumulated Depreciation	(1,086,000)	(1,292,000)
Investment in Charles Corporation (30%)		244,500
Goodwill	150,000	150,000
Accounts Payable	(117,000)	(200,000)
Bonds Payable	(100,000)	(450,000)
Noncontrolling Interest	(167,000)	(179,000)
Controlling Interest:		
Common Stock (par)	(1,000,000)	(1,000,000)
Additional Paid-In Capital in Excess of Par	(650,000)	(650,000)
Retained Earnings	(396,000)	(558,000)
Totals	0	0

The 2016 information shown on page 362 is available for the Lange and Marion companies.

a. Marion purchases equipment for $70,000.
b. Marion issues $350,000 of long-term bonds and later uses the proceeds to purchase a new building.
c. On January 1, 2016, Lange purchases 30% of the outstanding common stock of Charles Corporation for $230,000. This is an influential investment. Charles's stockholders' equity is $700,000 on the date of the purchase. Any excess cost is attributed to equipment with a 10-year life. Charles reports net income of $80,000 in 2016 and pays dividends of $25,000.
d. Controlling share of consolidated income for 2016 is $262,000; the noncontrolling interest in consolidated net income is $15,000. Lange pays $100,000 in dividends in 2016; Marion pays $15,000 in dividends in 2016.

Required ▶ ▶ ▶ ▶ ▶ Prepare the consolidated statement of cash flows for 2016 using the indirect method. Any supporting calculations (including a determination and distribution of excess schedule) should be in good form.

Problem 6-2 *(LO 1)* **Cash flow, year of partial noncash purchase.** Billing Enterprises purchases a 90% interest in the common stock of Rush Corporation on January 1, 2015, for an agreed-upon price of $495,000. Billing issues $400,000 of bonds to Rush shareholders plus $95,000 cash as payment. Rush's balance sheet on the acquisition date is as follows:

Assets		Liabilities and Equity	
Cash	$ 60,000	Accounts payable	$ 45,000
Accounts receivable	95,000	Long-term liabilities	120,000
Plant assets (net)...............	460,000	Common stock ($10 par)........	150,000
		Retained earnings	300,000
Total assets................	$615,000	Total liabilities and equity	$615,000

Rush's equipment is understated by $20,000 and has a remaining depreciable life of five years. Any remaining excess is attributed to goodwill.

In addition to the bonds issued as part of the purchase, Billing sells additional bonds in the amount of $100,000.

Consolidated net income for 2015 is $92,300. The controlling interest is $87,700, and the noncontrolling interest is $4,600. Rush pays $10,000 in dividends to all shareholders, including Billing Enterprises.

No plant assets are purchased or sold during 2015.

Comparative balance sheet data are as follows:

	December 31, 2014 (Parent Only)	December 31, 2015 (Consolidated)
Cash	$ 82,000	$ 187,700
Accounts receivable	120,000	161,000
Plant assets (net).............................	870,000	1,277,600
Goodwill		80,000
Accounts payable	(52,000)	(80,000)
Bonds payable		(500,000)
Long-term liabilities	(80,000)	(40,000)
Noncontrolling interest		(58,600)
Controlling interest:		
Common stock ($10 par)......................	(200,000)	(200,000)
Additional paid-in capital in excess of par	(300,000)	(300,000)
Retained earnings	(440,000)	(527,700)
Totals......................................	$ 0	$ 0

Required ▶ ▶ ▶ ▶ ▶ Prepare a consolidated statement of cash flows using the indirect method for the year ended December 31, 2015. Supporting schedules (including a D&D schedule) should be in good form.

Problem 6-3 *(LO 1)* **Comprehensive cash flow, indirect method.** Presented below are the consolidated workpaper balances of Bush, Inc., and its subsidiary, Dorr Corporation, as of December 31, 2016 and 2015:

Assets	2016	2015	Net Change Incr. (Decr.)
Cash	$ 313,000	$ 195,000	$118,000
Marketable equity securities (at cost)	175,000	175,000	0
Allowance to reduce marketable equity securities to market	(13,000)	(24,000)	11,000
Accounts receivable (net)	418,000	440,000	(22,000)
Inventories	595,000	525,000	70,000
Land	385,000	170,000	215,000
Plant and equipment	755,000	690,000	65,000
Accumulated depreciation	(199,000)	(145,000)	(54,000)
Goodwill	60,000	60,000	0
Total assets	$2,489,000	$2,086,000	$403,000

Liabilities and Stockholders' Equity	2016	2015	Net Change Incr. (Decr.)
Current portion of long-term note	$ 150,000	$ 150,000	$ 0
Accounts payable and accrued liabilities	595,000	474,000	121,000
Note payable, long-term	300,000	450,000	(150,000)
Deferred income taxes	44,000	32,000	12,000
Noncontrolling interest in net assets of subsidiary	179,000	161,000	18,000
Common stock ($10 par)	580,000	480,000	100,000
Additional paid-in capital in excess of par	303,000	180,000	123,000
Retained earnings	338,000	195,000	143,000
Treasury stock (at cost)		(36,000)	36,000
Total liabilities and stockholders' equity	$2,489,000	$2,086,000	$ 403,000

Additional information:

a. On January 20, 2016, Bush, Inc., issues 10,000 shares of its common stock for land having a fair value of $215,000.

b. On February 5, 2016, Bush reissues all of its treasury stock for $44,000.

c. On May 15, 2016, Bush pays a cash dividend of $58,000 on its common stock.

d. On August 8, 2016, equipment is purchased for $127,000.

e. On September 30, 2016, equipment is sold for $40,000. The equipment costs $62,000 and has a net book value of $34,000 on the date of the sale.

f. On December 15, 2016, Dorr Corporation pays a cash dividend of $50,000 on its common stock.

g. Deferred income taxes represent timing differences relating to the use of accelerated depreciation methods for income tax reporting and the straight-line method for financial reporting.

h. Net income for 2016 is as follows:

Controlling interest in consolidated net income	$201,000
Dorr Corporation	110,000

i. Bush, Inc., owns 70% of Dorr Corporation. There is no change in ownership interest in Dorr during 2015 and 2016. There are no intercompany transactions other than the dividend paid to Bush by its subsidiary.

Required ▶ ▶ ▶ ▶ ▶ Prepare the statement of cash flows for the consolidated company using the indirect method. A cash analysis worksheet should be prepared to aid in the development of the statement. Any other supporting schedules should be in good form.

Problem 6-4 *(LO 2)* **Consolidated EPS.** On January 1, 2016, Peanut Corporation acquires an 80% interest in Sunny Corporation. Information regarding the income and equity structure of the two companies as of the year ended December 31, 2018, is as follows:

	Peanut Corporation	Sunny Corporation
Internally generated net income	$55,000	$56,000
Common shares outstanding during the year	20,000	12,000
Warrants to acquire Peanut stock, outstanding during the year	2,000	1,000
5% convertible (into Sunny's shares), $100 par preferred shares, outstanding during the year		800
Nonconvertible preferred shares outstanding	1,000	

Additional information is as follows:

a. The warrants to acquire Peanut stock are issued in 2017. Each warrant can be exchanged for one share of Peanut common stock at an exercise price of $12 per share.
b. Each share of convertible preferred stock can be converted into two shares of Sunny common stock. The preferred stock pays an annual dividend totaling $4,000. Peanut owns 60% of the convertible preferred stock.
c. The nonconvertible preferred stock is issued on July 1, 2018, and pays a 6-month dividend totaling $500.
d. Relevant market prices per share of Peanut common stock during 2018 are as follows:

	Average
First quarter	$10
Second quarter	12
Third quarter	13
Fourth quarter	16

Required ▶ ▶ ▶ ▶ ▶ Compute the basic and diluted consolidated EPS for the year ended December 31, 2018. Use quarterly share averaging.

Problem 6-5 *(LO 3)* **Consolidated income statement, affiliated firm for tax.** On January 1, 2015, Dawn Corporation exchanges 12,000 shares of its common stock for an 80% interest in Mercer Company. The stock issued has a par value of $10 per share and a fair value of $25 per share. On the date of purchase, Mercer has the following balance sheet:

Common stock ($2 par)	$ 20,000
Paid-in capital in excess of par	50,000
Retained earnings	100,000
Total equity	$170,000

On the purchase date, Mercer has equipment with an 8-year remaining life that is undervalued by $100,000. Any remaining excess cost is attributed to goodwill.

There are intercompany merchandise sales. During 2016, Dawn sells $20,000 of merchandise to Mercer. Mercer sells $30,000 of merchandise to Dawn. Mercer has $2,000 of Dawn goods in its beginning inventory and $4,200 of Dawn goods in its ending inventory. Dawn has $2,500 of Mercer goods in its beginning inventory and $3,000 of Mercer goods in its ending inventory. Dawn's gross profit rate is 40%; Mercer's is 25%.

On July 1, 2015, Dawn sells a machine to Mercer for $90,000. The book value of the machine on Dawn's books is $50,000 at the time of the sale. The machine has a 5-year remaining life. Depreciation on the machine is included in expenses.

The consolidated group meets the requirements of an affiliated group under the tax law and files a consolidated tax return. The corporate tax rate is 30%. The original purchase is not structured as a nontaxable exchange.

Dawn uses the cost method to record its investment in Mercer. Since Mercer has never paid dividends, Dawn has not recorded any income on its investment in Mercer. The two companies prepare the following income statements for 2016:

	Dawn Corporation	Mercer Company
Sales	$1,000,000	$600,000
Less cost of goods sold	800,000	375,000
Gross profit	$ 200,000	$225,000
Less expenses	80,000	185,000
Income before tax	$ 120,000	$ 40,000

Prepare a determination and distribution of excess schedule. Prepare the 2016 consolidated net income in schedule form. Include eliminations and adjustments. Provide income distribution schedules to allocate consolidated net income (after tax) to the controlling and noncontrolling interests. ◄ ◄ ◄ ◄ ◄ **Required**

Problem 6-6 *(LO 3)* **Worksheet, consolidated taxation, simple equity, inventory, land.** On January 1, 2015, Pepper Company purchases 80% of the common stock of Salty Company for $270,000. On this date, Salty has total owners' equity of $300,000. The excess of cost over book value is due to goodwill. For tax purposes, goodwill is amortized over 15 years.

During 2015, Pepper appropriately accounts for its investment in Salty using the simple equity method.

During 2015, Pepper sells merchandise to Salty for $50,000, of which $10,000 is held by Salty on December 31, 2015. Pepper's gross profit on sales is 40%.

During 2015, Salty sells some land to Pepper at a gain of $10,000. Pepper still holds the land at year-end. Pepper and Salty qualify as an affiliated group for tax purposes and, thus, will file a consolidated tax return. Assume a 30% corporate income tax rate.

The following trial balances are prepared on December 31, 2015:

	Pepper Company	Salty Company
Inventory, December 31	100,000	50,000
Other Current Assets	198,000	200,000
Investment in Salty Company	302,000	
Land	240,000	100,000
Buildings and Equipment	300,000	200,000
Accumulated Depreciation	(80,000)	(60,000)
Current Liabilities	(150,000)	(50,000)
Long-Term Liabilities	(200,000)	(100,000)
Common Stock	(100,000)	(50,000)
Paid-In Capital in Excess of Par	(180,000)	(100,000)
Retained Earnings	(320,000)	(150,000)
Sales	(500,000)	(300,000)
Cost of Goods Sold	300,000	180,000
Operating Expenses	100,000	80,000
Subsidiary Income	(40,000)	
Gain on Sale of Land		(10,000)
Dividends Declared	30,000	10,000
Totals	0	0

Required ▶ ▶ ▶ ▶ ▶ Prepare a consolidated worksheet for Pepper Company and subsidiary Salty Company for the year ended December 31, 2015. Include the determination and distribution of excess schedule and the income distribution schedules.

Problem 6-7 *(LO 3)* **Worksheet, consolidated taxation, simple equity, inventory, fixed asset sale.** On January 1, 2015, Pillar Company purchases an 80% interest in Stark Company for $890,000. On the date of acquisition, Stark has total owners' equity of $800,000. Buildings, which have a 20-year life, are undervalued by $200,000. The remaining excess of cost over book value is attributable to goodwill. For tax purposes only, goodwill is amortized over 15 years.

On January 1, 2015, Stark sells equipment, with a net book value of $60,000, to Pillar for $100,000. The equipment has a 5-year remaining life. Straight-line depreciation is used.

During 2017, Pillar sells $70,000 worth of merchandise to Stark. As a result of these intercompany sales, Stark holds beginning inventory of $40,000 and ending inventory of $30,000. At December 31, 2017, Stark owes Pillar $8,000 from merchandise sales. Pillar has a gross profit rate of 50%.

Neither company has provided for income tax. The companies qualify as an affiliated group and, thus, will file a consolidated tax return based on a 30% corporate tax rate. The original purchase is not a nontaxable exchange.

Trial balances of Pillar and Stark as of December 31, 2017, are as follows:

	Pillar Company	Stark Company
Cash	208,600	380,000
Accounts Receivable	130,000	150,000
Inventory	120,000	80,000
Investment in Stark	1,098,000	
Plant and Equipment	600,000	900,000
Accumulated Depreciation	(350,000)	(300,000)
Liabilities	(205,000)	(150,000)
Deferred Tax Liability (goodwill amortization)	(3,600)	
Common Stock	(500,000)	(300,000)
Retained Earnings, January 1, 2017	(950,000)	(700,000)
Sales	(800,000)	(550,000)
Cost of Goods Sold	430,000	320,000
Depreciation Expense	60,000	50,000
Other Expenses	210,000	120,000
Subsidiary Income	(48,000)	
Totals	0	0

Required ▶ ▶ ▶ ▶ ▶ Prepare a consolidated worksheet based on the trial balances. Include a provision for income tax, a determination and distribution of excess schedule, and income distribution schedules.

Use the following information for Problems 6-8 and 6-9:

On January 1, 2015, Parson Company acquires an 80% interest in Solar Company for $500,000. Solar had the following balance sheet on the date of acquisition:

Solar Company
Balance Sheet
January 1, 2015

Assets		Liabilities and Equity	
Accounts receivable	$ 60,000	Accounts payable	$ 70,000
Inventory	80,000	Bonds payable	100,000

Assets		Liabilities and Equity	
Land......................	120,000	Common stock.............	10,000
Buildings	250,000	Paid-in capital in excess	
Accumulated depreciation	(50,000)	of par.................	190,000
Equipment	120,000	Retained earnings	170,000
Accumulated depreciation	(70,000)		
Goodwill	30,000		
Total assets..............	$540,000	Total liabilities and equity ...	$540,000

Buildings, which have a 20-year life, are undervalued by $70,000. Equipment, which has a 5-year life, is undervalued by $50,000. Any remaining excess of cost over book value is attributable to goodwill, which has a 15-year life for tax purposes only.

Problem 6-8 *(LO 3)* **Worksheet, consolidated taxation, simple equity, inventory, fixed asset sale.** Refer to the preceding facts for Parson's acquisition of Solar common stock. Parson uses the simple equity method to account for its investment in Solar. During 2016, Solar sells $30,000 worth of merchandise to Parson. As a result of these intercompany sales, Parson holds beginning inventory of $12,000 and ending inventory of $16,000 of merchandise acquired from Solar. At December 31, 2016, Parson owes Solar $6,000 from merchandise sales. Solar has a gross profit rate of 30%.

On January 1, 2015, Parson sells equipment having a net book value of $50,000 to Solar for $80,000. The equipment has a 5-year useful life and is depreciated using the straight-line method.

Neither company has provided for income tax. The companies qualify as an affiliated group and, thus, will file a consolidated tax return based on a 40% corporate tax rate. The original purchase is not a nontaxable exchange.

On December 31, 2016, Parson and Solar have the following trial balances:

	Parson Company	Solar Company
Cash	46,080	54,000
Accounts Receivable	150,600	90,000
Inventory	105,000	90,000
Land...	100,000	150,000
Investment in Solar.......................................	567,200	
Buildings	800,000	250,000
Accumulated Depreciation	(250,000)	(70,000)
Equipment..	210,000	120,000
Accumulated Depreciation	(115,000)	(90,000)
Accounts Payable	(70,000)	(40,000)
Bonds Payable..		(100,000)
Deferred Tax Liability (goodwill amortization)	(2,880)	
Common Stock	(100,000)	(10,000)
Paid-In Capital in Excess of Par	(600,000)	(190,000)
Retained Earnings, January 1, 2016.........................	(622,400)	(222,000)
Sales	(890,000)	(350,000)
Cost of Goods Sold	480,000	220,000
Depreciation Expense—Buildings............................	30,000	10,000
Depreciation Expense—Equipment..........................	25,000	10,000
Other Expenses	150,000	60,000
Interest Expense..		8,000
Subsidiary Income..	(33,600)	
Dividends Declared.......................................	20,000	10,000
Totals	0	0

Required ▶ ▶ ▶ ▶ ▶

1. Prepare a determination and distribution of excess schedule.
2. Prepare a consolidated worksheet for the year ended December 31, 2016. Include a provision for income tax and income distribution schedules.

Problem 6-9 *(LO 3)* **Worksheet, consolidated taxation, simple equity, inventory, fixed asset sale, later year.** Refer to the preceding facts for Parson's acquisition of Solar common stock. Parson uses the simple equity method to account for its investment in Solar. During 2017, Solar sells $40,000 worth of merchandise to Parson. As a result of these intercompany sales, Parson holds beginning inventory of $16,000 and ending inventory of $10,000 of merchandise acquired from Solar. At December 31, 2017, Parson owes Solar $8,000 from merchandise sales. Solar has a gross profit rate of 30%.

During 2017, Parson sells $60,000 worth of merchandise to Solar. Solar holds $15,000 of this merchandise in its ending inventory. Solar owes $10,000 to Parson as a result of these intercompany sales. Parson has a gross profit rate of 40%.

On January 1, 2015, Parson sells equipment having a net book value of $50,000 to Solar for $80,000. The equipment has a 5-year useful life and is depreciated using the straight-line method.

On January 1, 2017, Solar sells equipment to Parson at a profit of $25,000. The equipment has a 5-year useful life and is depreciated using the straight-line method.

Neither company has provided for income tax. The companies qualify as an affiliated group and, thus, will file a consolidated tax return based on a 40% corporate tax rate. The original purchase is not a nontaxable exchange.

On December 31, 2017, Parson and Solar have the following trial balances:

	Parson Company	Solar Company
Cash	49,760	80,000
Accounts Receivable	150,600	100,000
Inventory	115,000	120,000
Land.	100,000	150,000
Investment in Solar.	604,000	
Buildings	900,000	250,000
Accumulated Depreciation	(290,000)	(80,000)
Equipment	210,000	120,000
Accumulated Depreciation	(140,000)	(100,000)
Accounts Payable	(50,000)	(40,000)
Bonds Payable.		(100,000)
Deferred Tax Liability (goodwill amortization)	(5,760)	
Common Stock	(100,000)	(10,000)
Paid-In Capital in Excess of Par	(600,000)	(190,000)
Retained Earnings, January 1, 2017.	(747,000)	(238,000)
Sales	(950,000)	(400,000)
Cost of Goods Sold	550,000	250,000
Depreciation Expense—Buildings.	40,000	10,000
Depreciation Expense—Equipment.	25,000	10,000
Other Expenses	176,000	75,000
Interest Expense.		8,000
Gain on Sale of Fixed Asset.		(25,000)
Subsidiary Income.	(57,600)	
Dividends Declared.	20,000	10,000
Totals	0	0

1. Prepare a determination and distribution of excess schedule.
2. Prepare a consolidated worksheet for the year ended December 31, 2017. Include a provision for income tax and income distribution schedules.

◄ ◄ ◄ ◄ ◄ **Required**

Problem 6-10 *(LO 4)* **Worksheet, separate tax, simple equity, inventory, fixed asset sale.** On January, 1, 2015, Perko Company acquires 70% of the common stock of Solan Company for $385,000 in a taxable combination. On this date, Solan has total owners' equity of $422,000, including retained earnings of $222,000. The excess of cost over book value is attributable to goodwill.

During 2015 and 2016, Solan Company reports the following information:

	2015	2016
Net income before taxes	$40,000	$40,000
Dividends.	0	30,000

During 2015 and 2016, Perko appropriately accounts for its investment in Solan using the simple equity method, including income tax effects.

On January 1, 2016, Perko holds merchandise acquired from Solan for $10,000. During 2016, Solan sells merchandise to Perko for $60,000, of which $20,000 is held by Perko on December 31, 2016. Solan's usual gross profit on affiliated sales is 30%.

On December 31, 2015, Perko sells some equipment to Solan, with a cost of $40,000 and a book value of $18,000. The sales price is $39,000. Solan is depreciating the equipment over a 3-year life, assuming no salvage value and using the straight-line method.

Perko and Solan do not qualify as an affiliated group for tax purposes and, thus, will file separate tax returns. Assume a 30% corporate tax rate and an 80% dividends received deduction.

The following trial balances are prepared by Perko and Solan on December 31, 2016:

	Perko Company	Solan Company
Accounts Receivable	282,576	295,000
Inventory	110,000	85,000
Land.	150,000	90,000
Investment in Solan	422,800	
Buildings	200,000	200,000
Accumulated Depreciation	(100,000)	(50,000)
Equipment	120,000	80,000
Accumulated Depreciation	(35,000)	(20,000)
Goodwill		
Accounts Payable	(120,000)	(80,000)
Current Tax Liability.	(31,260)	(24,000)
Bonds Payable.	(200,000)	(100,000)
Discount (premium)		
Deferred Tax Liability.	(2,268)	
Common Stock—Solan		(10,000)
Paid-In Capital in Excess of Par—Solan.		(190,000)
Retained Earnings—Solan.		(250,000)
Common Stock—Perko	(100,000)	
Paid-In Capital in Excess of Par—Perko.	(200,000)	
Retained Earnings—Perko.	(450,000)	
Sales	(590,000)	(370,000)
Cost of Goods Sold	340,000	220,000
Depreciation Expense—Buildings	15,000	8,000
Depreciation Expense—Equipment.	20,000	12,000

(continued)

	Perko Company	Solan Company
Other Expenses	115,000	50,000
Interest Expense		
Provision for Tax	32,352	24,000
Subsidiary Income	(39,200)	
Dividends Declared—Solan		30,000
Dividends Declared—Perko	60,000	
Totals	0	0

Note:

Provision for income taxes (Perko):

Current ($100,000 × 30%)	$30,000
Solan dividends ($21,000 × 20% × 30%)	1,260
	$31,260
Current deferred taxes [($39,200 − $21,000) × 20% × 30%]	1,092
Provision for income taxes	$32,352

Deferred tax liability (Perko):

Current deferred taxes [($39,200 − $21,000) × 20% × 30%]	$1,092
Change in Solan retained earnings [70% × ($250,000 − $222,000) × 20% × 30%]	1,176
Deferred tax liability	$2,268

Required ▶ ▶ ▶ ▶ ▶ Prepare a consolidated worksheet for Perko Company and subsidiary Solan Company for the year ended December 31, 2016. Include the determination and distribution of excess schedule and the income determination schedules.

Use the following information for Problems 6-11 and 6-12:

On January 1, 2015, Penske Company acquires an 80% interest in Stock Company for $450,000. Stock has the following balance sheet on the date of acquisition:

Stock Company
Balance Sheet
January 1, 2015

Assets		Liabilities and Equity	
Accounts receivable	$ 60,000	Accounts payable	$ 70,000
Inventory	80,000	Bonds payable	100,000
Land	120,000	Common stock	10,000
Buildings	250,000	Paid-in capital in excess	
Accumulated depreciation . . .	(50,000)	of par	190,000
Equipment	120,000	Retained earnings	170,000
Accumulated depreciation . . .	(70,000)		
Goodwill	30,000		
Total assets	$540,000	Total liabilities and equity . .	$540,000

Buildings, which have a 20-year life, are undervalued by $100,000. Equipment, which has a 5-year life, is undervalued by $50,000. Any remaining excess of cost over book value is attributable to goodwill.

Problem 6-11 *(LO 4)* **Worksheet, separate tax, simple equity, inventory, fixed asset sale, analyze price.** Refer to the preceding facts for Penske's acquisition of Stock common stock. Penske uses the simple equity method to account for its investment in Stock. During 2016, Stock sells $30,000 worth of merchandise to Penske. As a result of these inter-company sales, Penske holds beginning inventory of $12,000 and ending inventory of $16,000 of merchandise acquired from Stock. At December 31, 2016, Penske owes Stock $6,000 from merchandise sales. Stock has a gross profit rate of 30%.

On January 1, 2015, Penske sells equipment having a net book value of $50,000 to Stock for $90,000. The equipment has a 5-year useful life and is depreciated using the straight-line method.

Penske and Stock do not qualify as an affiliated group for tax purposes and, thus, will file separate tax returns. Assume a 40% corporate tax rate and an 80% dividends received exclusion.

On December 31, 2016, Penske and Stock have the following trial balances:

	Penske Company	Stock Company
Cash	92,400	53,200
Accounts Receivable	150,600	90,000
Inventory	105,000	90,000
Land	100,000	120,000
Investment in Stock	503,120	
Buildings	800,000	250,000
Accumulated Depreciation	(250,000)	(70,000)
Equipment	210,000	120,000
Accumulated Depreciation	(115,000)	(90,000)
Goodwill		30,000
Accounts Payable	(70,000)	(40,000)
Current Tax Liability	(82,640)	(16,800)
Bonds Payable		(100,000)
Deferred Tax Liability (see note below)	(4,250)	
Common Stock	(100,000)	(10,000)
Paid-In Capital in Excess of Par	(600,000)	(190,000)
Retained Earnings, January 1, 2016	(617,683)	(221,200)
Sales	(890,000)	(350,000)
Cost of Goods Sold	480,000	220,000
Depreciation Expense—Buildings	30,000	10,000
Depreciation Expense—Equipment	25,000	10,000
Other Expenses	150,000	60,000
Interest Expense		8,000
Provision for Income Tax (see note below)	83,613	16,800
Subsidiary Income	(20,160)	
Dividends Declared	20,000	10,000
Totals	0	0

Note:

Provision for income taxes (Penske):

Current ($205,000 × 40%)	$82,000
Stock dividends ($8,000 × 20% × 40%)	640
	$82,640
Current deferred taxes [($20,160 − $8,000) × 20% × 40%]	973*
Provision for income taxes	$83,613

Deferred tax liability (Penske):

Current deferred taxes [($20,160 − $8,000) × 20% × 40%]...................	$ 973*
Change in Stock retained earnings [80% × ($221,200 − $170,000) × 20% × 40%]	3,277*
Deferred tax liability	$4,250

*Differences due to rounding.

Required ▶ ▶ ▶ ▶ ▶

1. Prepare a value analysis and a determination and distribution of excess schedule.
2. Prepare a consolidated worksheet for the year ended December 31, 2016. Include a provision for income tax and income distribution schedules.

Problem 6-12 *(LO 4)* **Worksheet, separate tax, simple equity, inventory, fixed asset sale, analyze price, later year.** Refer to the preceding facts for Penske's acquisition of Stock common stock. Penske accounts for its investment in Stock using the simple equity method, including income tax effects. During 2017, Stock sells $40,000 worth of merchandise to Penske. As a result of these intercompany sales, Penske holds beginning inventory of $16,000 and ending inventory of $10,000 of merchandise acquired from Stock. At December 31, 2017, Penske owes Stock $8,000 from merchandise sales. Stock has a gross profit rate of 30%.

During 2017, Penske sells $60,000 worth of merchandise to Stock. Stock holds $15,000 of this merchandise in its ending inventory. Stock owes $10,000 to Penske as a result of these intercompany sales. Penske has a gross profit rate of 40%.

On January 1, 2015, Penske sells equipment having a net book value of $50,000 to Stock for $90,000. The equipment has a 5-year useful life and is depreciated using the straight-line method.

On January 1, 2017, Stock sells equipment to Penske at a profit of $25,000. The equipment has a 5-year useful life and is depreciated using the straight-line method.

Penske and Stock do not qualify as an affiliated group for tax purposes and, thus, will file separate tax returns. Assume a 40% corporate tax rate and an 80% dividends received exclusion.

On December 31, 2017, Penske and Stock have the following trial balances:

	Penske Company	Stock Company
Cash	91,760	78,400
Accounts Receivable	150,600	100,000
Inventory	115,000	120,000
Land...	100,000	120,000
Investment in Stock	529,680	
Buildings	900,000	250,000
Accumulated Depreciation	(290,000)	(80,000)
Equipment	210,000	120,000
Accumulated Depreciation	(140,000)	(100,000)
Goodwill...		30,000
Accounts Payable	(50,000)	(40,000)
Current Tax Liability...	(64,240)	(28,800)
Bonds Payable...		(100,000)
Deferred Tax Liability (see note below)	(6,375)	
Common Stock	(100,000)	(10,000)
Paid-In Capital in Excess of Par	(600,000)	(190,000)
Retained Earnings, January 1, 2017...	(739,230)	(236,400)
Sales	(950,000)	(400,000)
Cost of Goods Sold	550,000	250,000
Depreciation Expense—Buildings...	40,000	10,000
Depreciation Expense—Equipment...	25,000	10,000
Other Expenses	176,000	75,000
Interest Expense...		8,000

	Penske Company	Stock Company
Gain on Sale of Fixed Asset.		(25,000)
Provision for Income Taxes (see note below)	66,365	28,800
Subsidiary Income	(34,560)	
Dividends Declared	20,000	10,000
Totals	0	0

Note:

Provision for income taxes (Penske):

Current ($159,000 × 40%)	$63,600
Stock dividends ($8,000 × 20% × 40%)	640
	$64,240
Current deferred taxes [($34,560 − $8,000) × 20% × 40%]	2,125[a]
Provision for income taxes	$66,365

Deferred tax liability (Penske):

Current deferred taxes [($34,560 − $8,000) × 20% × 40%]	$2,125[a]
Change in Stock retained earnings [80% × ($236,400 − $170,000) × 20% × 40%]	4,250[a]
Deferred tax liability	$6,375

[a]Differences due to rounding.

◀ ◀ ◀ ◀ ◀ Required

1. Prepare a value analysis and a determination and distribution of excess schedule.
2. Prepare a consolidated worksheet for the year ended December 31, 2017. Include a provision for income tax and income distribution schedules.

Chapter 7

Special Issues in Accounting for an Investment in a Subsidiary

CHAPTER

Learning Objectives

When you have completed this chapter, you should be able to

1. Consolidate a subsidiary when a parent purchases stock directly from the subsidiary.

2. Account for purchases of additional shares of a subsidiary by the parent.

3. Demonstrate the accounting procedures for a complete or partial sale of the investment in a subsidiary.

4. Explain the issues surrounding preferred stock in the equity structure of the subsidiary, and follow the procedures used when the parent owns subsidiary preferred stock.

5. Solve balance-sheet-only problems (CPA Exam issue). (Appendix)

This chapter considers several issues concerning the acquisition and sale of a parent's interest in a subsidiary. The first concern is special purchase situations. A parent may purchase its controlling interest directly from the subsidiary at the time of original issue. Procedures also are developed for parent ownership interests that are acquired in a series of separate purchases over time.

    This chapter then will consider the issues involved when a parent company sells all or a portion of its controlling interest in a subsidiary. Not only must the sale be properly recorded, but special care must also be taken in accounting for any portion of the investment retained.

    The final equity concern of the chapter is the procedure needed in consolidation when the subsidiary has preferred stock in its equity structure. An apportionment of retained earnings may be needed in order to properly account for the parent's interest in common stock. If the parent owns any subsidiary preferred stock, it must be treated as retired in the consolidation process.

    The chapter concludes with an appendix that provides the consolidation procedures needed when a worksheet is used to produce only a consolidated balance sheet. These procedures are really only of concern when preparing for the CPA Exam. The Exam may use this approach to save time and space. It is not a worksheet that is used in practice since the accountant must prepare a consolidated income statement, a consolidated statement of retained earnings, and a consolidated balance sheet. There would be no practical reason to use a worksheet for only one of the three statements.

PARENT ACQUISITION OF STOCK DIRECTLY FROM SUBSIDIARY

A parent company may organize a new corporation and supply all of the common stock equity funds in exchange for all of the newly organized company's common stock. Since the newly formed corporation receives the funds directly, there will be no difference between the price paid for the shares and the equity in assets acquired. Thus, the determination and distribution of excess (D&D) schedule will show no excess of cost over book value or excess of book value over cost.

1

OBJECTIVE

Consolidate a subsidiary when a parent purchases stock directly from the subsidiary.

In other cases, the parent company will allow the newly organized subsidiary to sell a portion of the shares to persons outside the consolidated group. If the shares are sold to outsiders at a price equal to the price paid by the parent, the cost and book value again will be equal. However, if a price greater or less than the price paid by the parent is charged to outside parties, an excess of cost or book value will result. This excess occurs because the total price paid by the parent will not equal its ownership interest multiplied by the total subsidiary common stockholders' equity. Normally, the excess of cost is recorded as goodwill, and an excess of book value is recorded as a gain.

An existing corporation might sell a sufficient number of new shares to grant a controlling interest to the buying company. For example, assume Company S had the following equity balances prior to a sale of shares to Company P:

Common stock ($10 par, 10,000 shares).......	$100,000
Paid-in capital in excess of par	150,000
Retained earnings	220,000
Total stockholders' equity.................	$470,000

Assume Company S sells 30,000 additional shares directly to Company P at $50 per share, for a total of $1,500,000. Subsequent to the sale, the equity balances of Company S appear as follows:

Common stock ($10 par, 40,000 shares).......	$ 400,000
Paid-in capital in excess of par	1,350,000
Retained earnings	220,000
Total stockholders' equity.................	$1,970,000

A determination and distribution of excess schedule must be prepared for this investment as it would be for any acquisition of a controlling interest. There is no direct connection between the price paid and the interest in subsidiary equity received. It is assumed that the NCI shares are also worth $40 per share. The monies paid become a part of the subsidiary's total equity. The interest purchased is a 75% interest (30,000 of 40,000 shares) in the total equity after the sale of the new shares, not a 100% interest in the funds provided by the specific sale of the new shares purchased by the parent. The following determination and distribution of excess schedule would be prepared for the interest purchased by the parent:

Determination and Distribution of Excess Schedule

	Company Implied Fair Value	Parent Price (75%)	NCI Value (25%)
Fair value of subsidiary	$2,000,000*	$1,500,000	$ 500,000
Less book value of interest acquired:			
Common stock ($10 par)..................	$ 400,000		
Paid-in capital in excess of par	1,350,000		
Retained earnings	220,000		
Total stockholders' equity.................	$1,970,000	$1,970,000	$1,970,000
Interest acquired		75%	25%
Book value.............................		$1,477,500	$ 492,500
Excess of fair value over book value	$ 30,000	$ 22,500	$ 7,500

Adjustment of identifiable accounts:

	Adjustment	Worksheet Key
Goodwill..............................	$ 30,000	**debit D**

*$1,500,000/75%

The excess would be distributed to identifiable accounts using normal purchase rules. Any remaining excess, as in this example, would be considered goodwill.

REFLECTION

- The purchase of a controlling interest directly from the subsidiary still requires the preparation of a D&D schedule.

Parent Purchase of Additional Subsidiary Shares

Chapter 2 included consideration of a situation where a potential parent company may own less than a controlling interest in another company and then buy additional shares to obtain control. The previously owned shares are adjusted to fair values and are combined with the newly acquired shares to create a single D&D schedule for the combined set of shares.

The current concern is that of a parent company that already owns a controlling interest in a subsidiary Company B and then purchases additional shares. For example, Company P may already own a 60% interest in a subsidiary and already be consolidating its financial statements since it has control over Company S. If Company P acquires another 20% interest, how is it accounted for? The purchase is viewed as the retirement of existing outstanding shares by the consolidated entity. Since the consolidated firm is a single reporting entity, the reacquisition of parent or subsidiary shares is a reduction of total equity.

Applying the retirement theory means that the rules for retirement are the same as for any retirement of shares.

- There can never be an income statement gain or loss.
- If the price paid to reacquire the shares is less than their book value, there is a credit to paid-in capital in excess of par from retirement.
- If the price paid to reacquire the shares exceeds their book value, the debit first is used to reduce existing paid-in capital in excess of par from retirement and the balance is a debit to Retained Earnings.

The guidance for these rules comes form FASB ASC 505-30-30. The complication in applying this approach is that you cannot compare the price paid for the reacquired shares to the subsidiary book value. Instead, **the price paid has to be compared to the NCI value as established on the day control was achieved, less any amortizations of excess calculated on the date of acquisition.**

As an example, assume that Company P purchased its original 60% (6,000 shares) controlling interest in Company S on January 1, 2015, for $126,000. On that date, Company S had the following balance sheet:

Assets		Liabilities and Equity	
Current assets	$ 50,000	Liabilities	$ 40,000
Equipment (net)	150,000	Common stock ($10 par,	
		10,000 shares)	100,000
		Retained earnings	60,000
Total assets.	$200,000	Total liabilities and equity . . .	$200,000

Assume that equipment has a fair value of $180,000 with a 5-year remaining life. Any remaining excess is attributed to goodwill. The D&D schedule shown on page 378 would be prepared for the 60% purchase.

2

OBJECTIVE

Account for purchases of additional shares of a subsidiary by the parent.

Determination and Distribution of Excess Schedule

	Company Implied Fair Value	Parent Price (60%)	NCI Value (40%)
Fair value of subsidiary	$210,000*	$126,000	$ 84,000
Less book value of interest acquired:			
Common stock ($10 par).	$100,000		
Retained earnings	60,000		
Total stockholders' equity.	$160,000	$160,000	$160,000
Interest acquired		60%	40%
Book value.		$ 96,000	$ 64,000
Excess of fair value over book value	**$ 50,000**	$ 30,000	$ 20,000

Adjustment of identifiable accounts:

	Adjustment	Amortization per Year	Life	Worksheet Key
Equipment	$ 30,000	$ 6,000	5	**debit D1**
Goodwill.	**20,000**			**debit D2**
Total	**$ 50,000**			

*$126,000/60% (assumes value of NCI is proportionate to price paid by parent)

On January 1, 2017, Company P acquired another 2,000 shares from NCI shareholders for $25 each, for a total of $50,000. Further assume that the Company S retained earnings on that date was $100,000, a $40,000 increase since the date of the purchase of the original 60% interest. The difference between the $50,000 price paid and the January 1, 2017, NCI balance is the adjustment of parent company equity caused by the acquisition of the shares. The following analysis is prepared for the new 20% interest:

Price paid for 20% interest, 50% of then existing 40% NCI		$50,000
Less book value of NCI interest purchased:		
Common stock ($10 par, 2,000 shares)	$ 20,000	
Retained earnings, January 1, 2017 (20% × $100,000)	20,000	
Total book value of interest purchased		40,000
Excess of cost over book value.		$10,000
Excess attributed to change in NCI:		
Original excess cost for company	$ 50,000	
Amortizations to date (2 years × $6,000)	(12,000)	
Balance	$ 38,000	
NCI adjustment applicable to shares purchased	× 20%	7,600
Balance, adjustment to parent paid-in capital in excess of par (unless there is none, then adjustment is to parent retained earnings)		$ 2,400

This $2,400 adjustment becomes a part the distribution of the excess on future worksheets. This adjustment to the parent's paid-in capital in excess of par would be made on each subsequent consolidated worksheet.

The additional worksheet procedures that arise from this piecemeal acquisition are shown in Worksheet 7-1 on pages 400 to 401. The trial balances of Companies P and S are shown as they would appear on December 31, 2017. The investment in Company S account is based on the use of the simple equity method during the current and previous years. The December 31, 2017, balance was determined as shown on page 379.

Worksheet 7-1: page 400

Cost of **60%** investment (January 1, 2015)		$ 126,000
Add equity share of change in Company S retained earnings as of January 1, 2013:		
Balance, January 1, 2017	**$100,000**	
Balance, January 1, 2015	60,000	
Increase in retained earnings	**$ 40,000 × 60% =**	24,000
Cost of **20%** investment (January 1, 2017)		50,000
Add equity share of Company S 2017 net income (**80%** × $35,000)		28,000
Investment account balance, December 31, 2017		**$228,000**

In journal entry form, the eliminations are as follows:

(CY)	Eliminate current-year entries to record subsidiary income:		
	Subsidiary Income	28,000	
	Investment in Company S.		28,000
(EL)	Eliminate 80% of subsidiary equity against investment account:		
	Common Stock—(Company S)	80,000	
	Retained Earnings, January 1, 2017—Company S	80,000	
	Investment in Company S.		160,000
(D/NCI)	Distribute excess on 2015, 60% investment and the NCI adjustment:		
(D1)	Equipment	30,000	
(D2)	Goodwill	20,000	
	Investment in Company S.		30,000
	Retained Earnings—Company S (for NCI)		20,000
(A1)	Adjust depreciation on equipment for 60% purchase:		
	Retained Earnings—Company P (2 years × 60% × $6,000). .	7,200	
	Retained Earnings—Company S (2 years × 40% × $6,000). .	4,800	
	Expenses	6,000	
	Accumulated Depreciation—Equipment		18,000
(D3)	Distribute excess on 2017, 20% investment:		
	Retained Earnings—Company S (NCI)	7,600	
	Retained Earnings—Company P (adjustment for retirement). . .	2,400	
	Investment in Company S.		10,000

The correctness of the $7,600 debit to NCI is confirmed as follows:

NCI adjustment on January 1, 2015.	$20,000
Depreciation adjustment (2 years × $6,000 × 40% NCI share)	(4,800)
Balance on January 1, 2017.	$15,200
½ of 40% NCI share	× 50%
Applicable to 20% total retired	$ 7,600

The consolidated net income of $79,000 is distributed to the controlling and noncontrolling interests as shown in the income distribution schedules (IDS) that accompany Worksheet 7-1. The $6,000 amortization of excess attributed to equipment depreciation is a debit on the subsidiary's IDS.

When investment blocks are carried at cost, each investment must be converted separately to its simple equity balance as of the beginning of the year. For each investment, the adjustment is based on the change in subsidiary retained earnings between the date of acquisition of the individual investment and the beginning of the current year.

The determination and distribution of excess schedule for the second purchase should consider existing unrealized intercompany profits recorded by the subsidiary. Suppose the subsidiary of the previous example sold merchandise to the parent during 2016, and a $2,000 subsidiary profit is included in the parent's ending inventory of merchandise and in the subsidiary retained earnings. *In theory*, the determination and distribution of excess schedule prepared for the 20% investment purchased on January 1, 2017, should reflect the unrealized gross profit on sales applicable to the 20% interest purchased. Thus, the determination and distribution of excess schedule would be revised to distribute the excess as follows:

Excess of cost over book value.			$10,000
Excess attributed to change in NCI:			
Original excess cost for company	$ 50,000		
Amortizations to date (2 years × $6,000)	(12,000)		
Balance	$ 38,000		
NCI adjustment applicable to shares purchased	× 20%	$7,600	
Adjustment for unrealized inventory profit ($2,000 × 20%).		(400)	7,200
Balance, adjustment to parent paid-in capital in excess of par (unless			
there is none, then adjustment is to parent retained earnings)			$ 2,800

The deferred gross profit on the inventory sale means that the NCI just acquired is overstated since the profit already is included in retained earnings. The decrease in the equity acquired increases the excess of cost over book value and increases the negative impact of the retirement on equity.

The following entry would distribute the revised excess on the 2017 worksheet:

Retained Earnings—Company S (NCI)	7,600	
Retained Earnings—Company P	2,800	
Deferred Gross Profit on Inventory Sale		400
Investment in Company S.		10,000

The following elimination for the $2,000 profit in the beginning inventory then would be made:

Retained Earnings—Controlling Interest (60% interest at time of original sale). . .	1,200	
Retained Earnings—NCI (20%)	400	
Deferred Gross Profit on Inventory Sale.	400	
Cost of Goods Sold (beginning inventory).		2,000

In practice, the concept of materiality often will prevail, and the above procedure may not be followed. The determination and distribution of excess schedule may not recognize the deferred inventory profit, which will result in the lesser debit to Retained Earnings. Under this practical approach, worksheets for periods subsequent to the second purchase will ignore the deferred profit existing on the purchase date and will distribute the retained earnings adjustment according to the ownership percentages existing at the time the worksheet is prepared. In this example, the 20% profit applicable to the inventory on the second purchase date would be allocated to the parent with the following adjustment on the worksheet:

Retained Earnings—Controlling Interest (80%)	1,600	
Retained Earnings—NCI (20%)	400	
Cost of Goods Sold (beginning inventory).		2,000

R E F L E C T I O N

- The acquisition of additional shares of a subsidiary is viewed as the retirement of those shares.

- When control already exists at the time the parent purchases another block of subsidiary stock, a second D&D schedule is prepared. The purpose of the schedule is to determine the impact of the "retirement" on controlling equity.

SALE OF PARENT'S INVESTMENT IN COMMON STOCK

3

OBJECTIVE

Demonstrate the accounting procedures for a complete or partial sale of the investment in a subsidiary.

A parent may sell some or all of its subsidiary interest. When control is lost through the sale of enough shares to fall below the 50% interest generally required for consolidated reporting, a gain or loss on the transaction is recorded. There may be other subsidiary stock sales where the parent reduces its percentage interest but still has control after the sale. Such a sale is considered to be the sale of the shares to NCI shareholders.

Sale of Entire Investment

The sale of the entire investment in a subsidiary terminates the need for consolidated financial statements. In fact, when a sale occurs during the parent's fiscal year, the results of the subsidiary operations prior to the sale date are not consolidated. In recording the sale of the investment in a subsidiary, the accountant's primary concern is to adjust the carrying value of the investment so that the correct dollar effect on the sale can be recorded. The results of the subsidiary's operations up to the date of sale must be reported in one of two ways: (a) the net results of operations as a separate line item in the determination of income from continuing operations or (b) as a disposal of a component of an entity.

The accountant must determine if the sale of the investment in a subsidiary constitutes a disposal of a component of an entity. FASB ASC 205-20-20 states:

> A component of an entity comprises operations and cash flows that can be clearly distinguished, operationally and for financial reporting purposes, from the rest of the entity. A component of an entity may be a reportable segment or an operating segment, a reporting unit, a subsidiary, or an asset group.[1]

Not all subsidiaries qualify as components of an entity. For example, a parent may own several subsidiaries engaged in mining coal. If one subsidiary is sold, that would not constitute a sale of a component on an entity since the parent still is involved in coal mining. When the sale of a subsidiary qualifies as a disposal of a component of an entity, both the gain or loss on the sale and the results of operations for the period are shown net of tax in a separate discontinued operations section of the income statement. When the sale does not qualify as a disposal of a component on an entity, the gain or loss and the results of operations for the period usually are shown on the income statement as a part of the normal recurring operations.

The complexities of properly recording the sale of an entire subsidiary investment are shown in the following example. Suppose Company P purchased an 80% interest in Company S on January 1, 2015, for $250,000, and the determination and distribution of excess schedule was prepared as shown on page 382.

---

1 FASB ASC 205-20-20 *Presentation of Financial Statements—Discontinued Operations—Glossary* (Norwalk, CT).

Determination and Distribution of Excess Schedule

	Company Implied Fair Value	Parent Price (80%)	NCI Value (20%)
Fair value of subsidiary	$312,500	$250,000	$ 62,500
Less book value of interest acquired:			
Common stock	$100,000		
Retained earnings	150,000		
Total equity	$250,000	$250,000	$250,000
Interest acquired		80%	20%
Book value		$200,000	$ 50,000
Excess of fair value over book value	**$ 62,500**	$ 50,000	$ 12,500

Adjustment of identifiable accounts:

	Adjustment	Life	Amortization per Year	Worksheet Key
Equipment	$ 25,000	5	5,000	**debit D1**
Goodwill	**37,500**			**debit D2**
Total	**$ 62,500**			

Company S earned $40,000 in 2015 and $25,000 in 2016. Company P sells the entire 80% interest on January 1, 2017, for $320,000. Assuming the use of the simple equity method, Company P's separate statements reflect the following:

Purchase price	$250,000
Share of subsidiary income, 2015, 80% × $40,000	32,000
Share of subsidiary income, 2016, 80% × $25,000	20,000
Investment in Company S, December 31, 2016	$302,000

The investment account and the parent's January 1, 2017, retained earnings balance reflect a $52,000 increase as a result of subsidiary operations in 2015 and 2016. On this basis, it appears that there is an $18,000 gain on the sale of the investment ($320,000 selling price less $302,000 simple-equity-adjusted cost). This result does not agree, however, with the consolidated financial statements prepared for 2015 and 2016, which included as expenses the amortizations of excess required by the determination and distribution of excess schedule. The parent's share of subsidiary income appeared as follows in the consolidated statements:

	2015	2016	Total
Share of subsidiary income to Company P (80%)	$32,000	$20,000	$52,000
Less amortization of excess of cost of investment over book value:			
Adjustment for depreciation on equipment: ($25,000 ÷ 5 = $5,000 per year) × 80% interest	(4,000)	(4,000)	(8,000)
Net increase in Company P income due to ownership of Company S investment	$28,000	$16,000	$44,000

Thus, while Company P's investment account shows a $52,000 share of Company S income, the consolidated statements reflect only $44,000, the difference being caused by the $8,000 of amortizations indicated by the determination and distribution of excess schedule. Clearly, the recording of the sale of the parent's interest must be based on the $44,000 share of income, since that amount of income is shown on the prior income statements of the consolidated company. Before recording the sale of the investment, Company P must adjust its books to be consistent with prior consolidated statements. In other words, it must adjust its investment to show the balance under the sophisticated equity method. The entry needed will adjust the January 1, 2017, retained earnings account on the separate books of the parent to the December 31, 2016, balance of the controlling interest in retained earnings shown on the consolidated statements. The adjusting entry on the books of Company P is as follows:

Retained Earnings, January 1, 2017.	8,000	
Investment in Company S.		8,000
To adjust the investment account and Company P retained earnings		
account for the parent's share of amortizations made on past		
consolidated statements.		

If the sophisticated equity method was used, the amortizations would be reflected already in the investment account and no adjustment would be needed.

Under either equity method, the entry to record the sale then would be as follows:

Cash	320,000	
Investment in Company S ($302,000 – $8,000)		294,000
Gain on Disposal of Subsidiary		26,000
To record the gain on the sale of the 80% interest in Company S.		

Note that the $8,000 adjusting entry for the past years' amortizations of excess normally would have been made on the consolidated worksheet for 2017. However, since there will be no further consolidations, the adjustment must be made directly on Company P's books. The gain (net of tax) on the disposal of the subsidiary will appear as a separate item on the income statement for 2017 if the sale of the subsidiary meets the criteria for a disposal of a component on an entity.

Since there will no longer be a consolidation, the NCI adjustments will no longer be made. The former subsidiary company will report as an independent entity, and its equity balances will not be affected by the prior adjustments that were required as part of the consolidation process.

In this example, if Company P had used the cost method, the investment account still would be shown at the original cost of $250,000. It then would be necessary to update the investment and retained earnings accounts on the separate books of Company P to include its $44,000 (net of amortizations) share of subsidiary income for 2015 and 2016. This adjustment would allow the accounts of the parent on January 1, 2017, to conform to past consolidated statements. The following entries would be made on the books of Company P to record the sale of the parent's 80% interest:

Investment in Company S	44,000	
Retained Earnings, January 1, 2017.		44,000
To record the parent's share of subsidiary income as shown on		
prior years' consolidated statements.		
Cash	320,000	
Investment in Company S ($250,000 + $44,000).		294,000
Gain on Disposal of Subsidiary		26,000

It also is necessary to adjust the investment account for any unrealized intercompany gains and losses. These profits would have been deferred in the most recent consolidated statement, but under the cost or simple equity method they are not reflected in the investment account. Again, we must adjust the investment account to reflect the income reported in past consolidated statements. Suppose the parent had on hand at the sale date inventory on which the subsidiary recorded a $1,000 profit. Since the parent owns an 80% interest, the adjusting entry on the day the investment is sold would be as follows:

Retained Earnings	800	
Investment in Company S.		800

Assume the investment in the previous example was sold for $320,000 on July 1, 2017, and Company S reported income of $12,000 for the first six months of 2017. Since Company S will not be a part of the consolidated group at the end of the period, the results of its operations will not be consolidated with those of the parent. Therefore, the parent must record its share of subsidiary income for the current period to the date of disposal. The parent's net share of subsidiary income would be calculated on a basis consistent with past consolidated statements, as follows:

Share of subsidiary income for first six months to Company P (80%)	$ 9,600
Less amortization of excess of cost over book value that would have been made on consolidated statements:	
Equipment depreciation adjustment ($5,000 per year × ½ year × 80% interest)	(2,000)
Net share of subsidiary income	$ 7,600

The parent would proceed to record the July 1, 2017, sale of its subsidiary investment as follows:

1. Assuming the past use of the simple equity method, the parent's investment account on January 1, 2017, is adjusted to reflect the amortizations made on past consolidated statements (as calculated on page 382).

Retained Earnings, January 1, 2017.	8,000	
Investment in Company S.		8,000

2. The parent's share of subsidiary income for the partial year is recorded. This amount is the $7,600 income net of amortizations (as calculated above).

Investment in Company S	7,600	
Investment income		7,600

3. The sale of the investment for $320,000 is recorded.

Cash	320,000	
Investment in Company S.		301,600
Gain on Disposal of Subsidiary		18,400

The adjusted cost of the investment is determined as follows:

Original cost, January 1, 2015.	$250,000
Simple equity income adjustments for 2015 and 2016	52,000
Amortization of excess (entry 1)	(8,000)
Share of Company S income for six months (entry 2)	7,600
Net cost, July 1, 2017	$301,600

Sale of Portion of Investment

The sale of a portion of an investment in a subsidiary requires unique treatment, depending on whether effective control is lost as a result of the sale. Special procedures must also be used when a sale of a partial interest occurs during a reporting period.

Loss of Control. A parent may sell a portion of its investment in a subsidiary so that it loses control. This situation may occur for foreign subsidiaries when the foreign government passes a law forbidding control of its companies by nonresidents. Such a sale also may be made to avoid consolidating affiliated companies. For example, a parent company may not want to include in its statements, the results of financing units that have large amounts of debt. If control is lost, consolidation procedures no longer will apply. This situation would require that the parent company books be adjusted to make them consistent with prior consolidated statements. Exactly the same adjusting entries as in the immediately preceding section are needed to adjust the parent's investment account. Note that the adjustments are made for the *entire interest* previously owned, not just the portion sold. If, in the preceding example, Company P sells one-half instead of all of its 80% interest, the investment account should be adjusted for the entire 80% interest in past and current years' subsidiary income, net of amortizations. The 40% interest sold must be adjusted to properly record the sale, and the 40% interest retained also must be adjusted, since it no longer will be consolidated. Past adjustments that would be handled as part of the annual consolidation process now must be made directly to the investment account, so that the investment remaining conforms with FASB ASC 323, *Investments—Equity Method and Joint Ventures.* The sophisticated equity method should be applied to remaining interests of 20% or more.[2]

If one-half of Company P's investment of the preceding section is sold for $160,000 on July 1, 2017, the following entries would be recorded:

1. Assuming the past use of the simple equity method, the parent's investment account on January 1, 2017, is adjusted to reflect the amortizations made on past consolidated statements.

Retained Earnings, January 1, 2017.	8,000	
Investment in Company S.		8,000

2. The parent's share of subsidiary income for the partial year is recorded. This amount is the $7,600 income net of amortizations.

Investment in Company S	7,600	
Operating Income of Former Subsidiary		7,600

3. The sale of one-half of the investment for $160,000 is recorded. The resulting gain is always ordinary income and never a gain from a "discontinued segment."

Cash	160,000	
Investment in Company S (½ of $301,600 adjusted cost		
calculated on page 384)		150,800
Gain on Sale of Investment		9,200

The remaining 40% investment will not be consolidated. It will be accounted for as an "influential" investment under the sophisticated equity method.

Control Retained. A parent company may sell a portion of its investment in a subsidiary but still have an interest that provides control even after the sale. For example, assume that on January 1, 2015, a parent purchased from outside parties 8,000 of the total 10,000 shares of a subsidiary. On January 1, 2017, the parent sold 2,000 shares and thereby lowered its percentage of ownership to 60%. Since the parent still had control, the 2,000 shares were sold, in essence, to NCI shareholders. Such a sell-down is considered to be a sale of additional shares to NCI shareholders. The parent has chosen to sell subsidiary shares, instead of parent shares, to raise additional equity capital. **There can be no income statement gains or losses resulting from any stock issuances by the consolidated entity.** This transaction would impact only paid-in capital in excess of par.

To illustrate the recording of such a partial sale, return to the example for which a determination and distribution of excess schedule was prepared on page 382. Assume that on January 1, 2017, Company P sells 2,000 subsidiary shares to lower its total interest to 60%. **Only the portion of the investment account sold is to be adjusted to the sophisticated equity method** to allow the

---

2 ASC 323-10-15-8, *Investments, Equity Method and Joint Ventures,* FASB (Norwalk, CT).

proper recording of the sale. The 60% remaining interest need not be adjusted on Company P's books since all amortization adjustments on the 60% interest will be made on future consolidated statements. The adjustment of the 20% interest on the separate books of Company P must agree with the treatment of that interest in prior consolidated statements. Assuming the use of the simple equity method, the portion of the investment sold must be adjusted for its share of the past amortizations made on consolidated statements. The annual amortization of the excess attributable to the equipment is $5,000. The amount applicable to the 20% interest sold is 20% of $5,000, or $1,000 per year. The adjustment for the prior two years would be as follows:

Retained Earnings, January 1, 2017.	2,000	
Investment in Company S.		2,000
To adjust for amortizations made on previous consolidated statements for the portion of the subsidiary investment sold.		

To record the sale of the investment, the parent would remove from its books **one-fourth** of the simple-equity-adjusted cost of January 1, 2017, as follows:

Simple equity adjusted cost of investment (page 382).	$302,000
	× 25%
¼ of 80% interest sold.	$ 75,500
Less amortizations of excess on 20% interest	(2,000)
Adjusted investment balance.	$ 73,500

If the sale price is greater than $73,500, then an increase in the paid-in capital in excess of par would be recorded, as shown in the following entry to record the sale of the investment for $80,000:

Cash	80,000	
Investment in Company S [(¼ × $302,000) – $2,000 amortization adjustment].		73,500
Paid-In Capital in Excess of Par, Company P.		6,500

If the sale price is less than $73,500, then a reduction of the paid-in capital in excess of par would be recorded. If there is not an adequate amount of paid-in capital in excess of par, Retained Earnings is debited.

If the parent in the previous example had used the cost method, only the portion of the investment sold would be adjusted to the sophisticated equity method on the parent's books. The analysis on page 382 shows that the parent's 80% share of income for 2015 and 2016 was $44,000 on a consolidated basis, net of amortizations. The interest sold must be adjusted by **one-fourth** (20% out of 80%) of $44,000, or $11,000. The remaining 60% will be adjusted in future worksheets. The entry to adjust the 20% interest would be as follows:

Investment in Company S	11,000	
Retained Earnings, January 1, 2017.		11,000
To adjust for the parent's share of past consolidated income pertaining to the interest sold.		

The parent then would proceed to record the sale of the investment for $80,000 as follows:

Cash	80,000	
Investment in Company S (¼ of original $250,000 cost + $11,000 equity income).		73,500
Paid-In Capital in Excess of Par, Company P.		6,500

Intraperiod Sale of a Partial Interest. When a sale of an interest during the reporting period does not result in loss of control, careful analysis is needed to ensure that the worksheet adheres to consolidation theory. Referring to the situation on pages 385–386, assume Company P sells **one-fourth** of its 80% interest for $80,000 on July 1, 2017, and subsidiary income for the first half of the year is $12,000. Assuming the use of the simple equity method, the parent would adjust its own investment and the beginning-of-year retained earnings accounts for the amortizations of excess cost recorded on the prior years' consolidated worksheets. The adjustment would be recorded as follows:

Retained Earnings, January 1, 2017	2,000	
Investment in Company S		2,000
To record 20% of the $10,000 amortizations for 2015 and 2016.		

A parent using the cost method would adjust the retained earnings for the subsidiary income, net of amortizations, for 2015 and 2016 (1/4 × $44,000 income on a consolidated basis).

Next, the parent would calculate its share of subsidiary income for the first half of 2017 applicable to the 20% interest sold and adjusted for partial-year amortizations of excess relating to that portion of the investment as follows:

Income on 20% interest in Company S sold (20% × $12,000)	$2,400
Less amortizations of excess of cost over book value that would be	
necessary on consolidated statements:	
Equipment depreciation adjustment ($5,000 per year × ½ year ×	
20% interest sold)	(500)
Net share of income on interest sold	$1,900

The parent then would make a sophisticated equity method adjustment for this income and record the sale as follows:

Investment in Company S	1,900	
Subsidiary Income		1,900
To record share of first six months' subsidiary income applicable to the 20% interest sold and adjusted for partial-year amortizations of excess relating to that portion of the investment.		
Cash	80,000	
Investment in Company S [(¼ × $302,000) – $2,000 amortizations + $1,900 income]		75,400
Paid-In Capital in Excess of Par—Company P		4,600
To record sale of 20% interest in subsidiary.		

The sale of a partial interest that does not result in loss of control requires special procedures on the consolidated worksheet for the period in which the sale occurs. Worksheets of later periods would not include any complications resulting from the sale. In Worksheet 7-2 on pages 404 to 405, the following should be noted:

Worksheet 7-2: page 404

1. The investment in Company S account reflects its simple equity balance on December 31, 2017, for the remaining 60% interest held. The balance is computed as follows:

December 31, 2016, balance applicable to remaining (60%) interest held at year-end, ¾ × $302,000	$226,500
Add **60%** of subsidiary reported income of $30,000* for 2017	18,000
Simple equity balance, December 31, 2017	$244,500

*This is for all of 2017 and includes the $12,000 reported in the first half of the year.

2. The balance in Paid-In Capital in Excess of Par—Company P is the increase in equity from the parent's ¼ interest sold.
3. The balance in Subsidiary Income includes **60%** of the subsidiary's $30,000 2017 income, plus the $1,900 earned on the **20%** interest prior to its sale.

In journal entry form, the eliminations are as follows:

(NCI)	Transfer income on interest sold to NCI and record amortizations of excess on interest sold:		
	Subsidiary Income.	1,900	
	Income Sold to NCI		1,900
(CY)	Eliminate current-year entries to record subsidiary income:		
	Subsidiary Income.	18,000	
	Investment in Company S.		18,000
(EL)	Eliminate subsidiary equity against investment account on 60% investment still owned:		
	Common Stock—Company S	60,000	
	Retained Earnings, January 1, 2017—Company S	129,000	
	Investment in Company S.		189,000
(D)/(NCI)	Distribute excess and NCI adjustment:		
(D1)	Equipment	25,000	
(D2)	Goodwill	37,500	
	Investment in Company S (60% of original total excess on D&D)		37,500
	Retained Earnings—Company S (NCI) (40% of original total excess on D&D)		25,000
(A)	Adjust depreciation on equipment:		
	Retained Earnings—Company P (2 years × $5,000 × 60% remaining interest)	6,000	
	Retained Earnings—Company S (2 years × $5,000 × 40% current NCI)	4,000	
	Expenses	5,000	
	Accumulated Depreciation—Equipment		15,000

Carefully study the income distribution schedules for Worksheet 7-2. The NCI receives its 40% interest in subsidiary adjusted income of $25,000 for the entire year, but there is a deduction for the income purchased from the parent for the first six months. The parent company income distribution schedule claims 60% of the subsidiary income for the entire year plus a 20% interest in the first six months' income.

If the parent had used the cost method, there would be few changes in Worksheet 7-2. Entry (NCI) would be unchanged; however, an entry would be needed to convert the remaining 60% interest to the simple equity method at the beginning of the year. Entry (CY) would not be applicable since there would be no current-year equity adjustment to reverse. Remaining entries would remain the same.

Complications Resulting from Intercompany Transactions. When a sale of subsidiary stock results in loss of control, the parent should adjust its investment account on the date of the sale for its share of unrealized subsidiary gains and losses resulting from intercompany transactions. When control is not lost as the result of a sale of subsidiary shares, the adjustment on the consolidated worksheet for unrealized gains and losses resulting from previous intercompany transactions need be recorded only as it applies to the interest sold. The remaining controlling interest's share of these gains and losses can be adjusted on subsequent consolidated worksheets. On these worksheets, retained earnings adjustments for unrealized gains and losses would be distributed according to the relative ownership interests existing on the dates the worksheets are prepared.

REFLECTION

- When the parent's entire investment in a subsidiary is sold, the investment must be adjusted to the sophisticated equity method to properly record the gain or loss. The gain or loss may qualify as a gain or loss on a discontinued operation.

- If a portion of the investment in a subsidiary is sold and control is lost, the entire investment is still adjusted to the sophisticated equity method. This allows the correct gain or loss to be calculated on the interest sold. The remaining investment is also then restated at the sophisticated equity balance.

- If a portion of the investment in a subsidiary is sold, but control is retained, only the block sold is adjusted to the sophisticated equity balance. This allows the correct calculation of the increases or decreases of the parent's paid-in capital in excess of par resulting from the sale of the interest. The remaining investment will still be consolidated and may be accounted for under the cost, equity, or sophisticated equity method. Special procedures are needed for the current-year portion of income on the interest sold.

SUBSIDIARY PREFERRED STOCK

The existence of preferred stock in the capital structure of a subsidiary complicates the calculation of a parent's claim on subsidiary retained earnings, both at the time of acquisition and in the preparation of subsequent consolidated statements. In previous examples, the subsidiary had only common stock outstanding, so that all retained earnings were associated with common stock, and the parent had a claim on subsidiary retained earnings in proportion to its ownership interest. When a subsidiary has preferred stock outstanding, however, the preferred stock also may have a claim on retained earnings. This claim may be caused by a liquidation value in excess of par value and/or by participation and cumulative dividend rights. When these conditions exist, the retained earnings must be divided between the preferred and common stockholder interests.

Once retained earnings are allocated between the common and preferred stockholders, the intercompany investments can be eliminated. The investment in subsidiary common stock account will be eliminated against the total equity claim of the common stockholders. If there is an investment in subsidiary preferred stock account, it will be eliminated against the preferred stockholders' total equity.

4

OBJECTIVE

Explain the issues surrounding preferred stock in the equity structure of the subsidiary, and follow the procedures used when the parent owns subsidiary preferred stock.

Determination of Preferred Shareholders' Claim on Retained Earnings

The allocation of the retained earnings to the preferred and common stockholder interests is accomplished by employing the procedures used to calculate the book value of preferred and common stock. Although typically covered in intermediate accounting, the topic will be reviewed briefly in the following paragraphs.

The preferred shareholders' claim on retained earnings equals the claim they would have if the company was dissolved. In addition to the par value of the preferred shares, there may be a stipulated liquidation value in excess of par and/or dividend preferences. In the rare case of a liquidation value in excess of par, an amount equal to the liquidation bonus (liquidation value less par value) must be segregated from retained earnings as a preferred shareholder claim. Liquidation values should not be confused with paid-in capital in excess of par, which results from the sale of preferred shares. Such paid-in capital is not available to preferred shareholders in liquidation and is not part of the book value of preferred shares. Instead, it becomes part of the total paid-in capital in excess of par that is available to common shareholders.

In addition to a liquidation bonus, there must be an analysis of any cumulative and/or participation clauses applicable to the preferred stock. Other than the effect of a liquidation bonus, if the preferred stock is noncumulative and nonparticipating, the preferred stockholders would have no claim and all the retained earnings attach to the common stock. However, if there are preferred shareholder claims resulting from cumulative and/or participation clauses, these claims reduce the retained earnings applicable to the common stock. For example, if the preferred stock is noncumulative but fully participating, the retained earnings are allocated pro rata according to the total par or stated values of the preferred and common stock. If the preferred stock is cumulative but nonparticipating and, for example, has two years' dividends in arrears, a claim on retained earnings equal to the two years of dividends exists, although there is no liability to pay the preferred dividends until a dividend is declared.

When preferred stock is both cumulative and fully participating, the arrearage for prior periods is met first. The remaining retained earnings are allocated pro rata according to the total par values of the preferred and common stock. When preferred stock is cumulative and participating but no dividends are in arrears, the analysis is the same as if the preferred stock were noncumulative but participating.

When preferred stock is cumulative and limited in participation to a percentage of par value, the arrearage for prior periods is met first and is excluded from the limited participation. The lesser of a pro rata share of the remaining retained earnings or the limiting percentage of the preferred stock's par value is allocated to the preferred claim. Any retained earnings remaining after this allocation are assigned to the common stock.

Apportionment of Retained Earnings

Additional procedures are required when a subsidiary with preferred stock that has liquidation and/or dividend preferences is consolidated, even if none of the preferred shares are owned by the parent. In this situation, allocation of retained earnings to the preferred and common stock is as follows:

1. The determination and distribution of excess schedule prepared as of the date of the parent's investment in common stock must include only that portion of retained earnings that is allocable to the common stock on the purchase date.
2. Periodic equity adjustments for the parent's investment in common stock are made only for the common shareholders' claim on income. The preferred shareholders' claim on the current year's income, including dividends paid or accumulated and any participation rights for the current year, must be deducted to arrive at income available to common shareholders. When the cost method is used, the worksheet's simple equity conversion adjustment is made for the parent's share of change in the retained earnings applicable to common stock since the date of acquisition.
3. Subsidiary retained earnings must be allocated between preferred and common stockholders on consolidated worksheets. The parent's investment in common stock account then is eliminated against the parent's pro rata share of only the equity attaching to common stock.

To illustrate these procedures, assume Company S has the following stockholders' equity on January 1, 2017, the date on which Company P purchases an 80% interest in the common stock for $150,000:

Preferred stock ($100 par, 6% cumulative)	$100,000
Common stock ($10 par)	100,000
Retained earnings	80,000
Total equity	$280,000

The preferred stock has a liquidation value equal to par value, and dividends are two years in arrears as of January 1, 2017. Company S assets have a fair value equal to book value. Any excess purchase price is attributable to goodwill. The determination and distribution of excess schedule would be prepared as shown on page 391.

Determination and Distribution of Excess Schedule

	Company Implied Fair Value	Parent Price (80%)	NCI Value (20%)
Fair value of subsidiary	$187,500	$150,000	$ 37,500
Less book value of interest acquired:			
Common stock	$100,000		
Retained earnings	80,000		
Preferred dividends in arrears (2 yrs. × $6,000).	(12,000)		
Total common equity	$168,000	$168,000	$168,000
Interest acquired		80%	20%
Book value.		$134,400	$ 33,600
Excess of fair value over book value	**$ 19,500**	$ 15,600	$ 3,900

Adjustment of identifiable accounts:

	Adjustment	Worksheet Key
Goodwill.	**$ 19,500**	**debit D**

Assume that income is exactly $25,000 per year in future years and no dividends are paid. Each year, the following entry would be made by Company P using the simple equity method of accounting for its subsidiary investment:

```
Investment in Company S . . . . . . . . . . . . . . . . . . . . . . . . . . . . . . . . . . . . . . . . . .   15,200
    Subsidiary Income. . . . . . . . . . . . . . . . . . . . . . . . . . . . . . . . . . . . . . . . . .              15,200
        To adjust for 80% of Company S income applicable to common stock
        ($25,000 reported income – $6,000 cumulative claim of preferred stock)
```

Worksheet 7-3, pages 408 to 409, is a consolidated financial statements worksheet for the year ended December 31, 2019 (3 years subsequent to the purchase). The investment in Company S common stock account includes the original cost of the investment plus three years (3 × $15,200 = $45,600) of simple equity adjustments for income and dividends. The worksheet is unique in that it subdivides the subsidiary retained earnings into two parts: one for the common portion and one for the preferred portion of retained earnings. Entry (PS) of Worksheet 7-3 accomplishes this apportionment.

Worksheet 7-3: page 408

In journal entry form, the eliminations are as follows:

(PS) Distribute portion of retained earnings to preferred stockholders as of January 1, 2019 (original arrearages totaling $12,000 plus $12,000 for 2017 and 2018):

```
    Retained Earnings, January 1, 2019—Company S . . . . . . . . . . . . . .   24,000
        Retained Earnings Allocated to Preferred Stock, January 1,
        2019—Company S. . . . . . . . . . . . . . . . . . . . . . . . . . . . . . . . . . .              24,000
```

(CY) Eliminate current-year entries to record subsidiary income:

```
    Subsidiary Income. . . . . . . . . . . . . . . . . . . . . . . . . . . . . . . . . . . . . .   15,200
        Investment in Company S. . . . . . . . . . . . . . . . . . . . . . . . . . . . . .              15,200
```

(continued)

(EL) Eliminate subsidiary common stock equity against investment in
        common stock account:
        Common Stock, Company S   80,000
        Retained Earnings, January 1, 2019—Company S 84,800*
            Investment in Common Stock of Company S   164,800
        *(Retained earnings of $130,000 – $24,000 allocated to preferred stock) × 80%.

(D)   Distribute excess on 80% investment in common stock:
        Goodwill   19,500
            Investment in Common Stock of Company S   15,600
            Retained Earnings—Company S (NCI)   3,900

This division of retained earnings is only for worksheet purposes; the subsidiary will maintain only one retained earnings account.

After the eliminations and adjustments are completed, the resulting consolidated net income of $175,000 is allocated as shown in the income distribution schedules. Since none of the preferred stock is owned by controlling shareholders, the NCI receives all applicable preferred income plus 20% of the income allocable to common stock. It should be observed that the NCI column, as well as the NCI shown on a formal balance sheet, includes the NCI in both preferred and common shares.

The worksheet just analyzed can handle all types of subsidiary preferred stockholder claims. Once the claim is determined, with supporting calculations, it can be isolated in a separate worksheet account, *Retained Earnings Allocated to Preferred Stock.*

When a parent uses the cost method to record its investment in a subsidiary, slightly different worksheet procedures are used. In the previous illustration, if Company P had used the cost method, the investment account still would be at the $150,000 original cost. In addition, there would be no subsidiary income shown, and the January 1, 2019, retained earnings of Company P would not reflect the 2017 and 2018 simple equity adjustments. As described earlier, a conversion to the simple equity method is made on the worksheet. Since the beginning-of-the-period investment balance is needed for elimination, the equity adjustment converts the investment account to the January 1, 2019, balance, as follows:

Retained earnings, January 1, 2019—Company S $130,000
Less four years' arrearage of preferred dividends   24,000

**Retained earnings applicable to common stock,
January 1, 2019** **$106,000**
Retained earnings, January 1, 2017—Company S . . . . $ 80,000
Less two years' arrearage of preferred dividends   12,000

**Retained earnings applicable to common stock,
January 1, 2017** **68,000**
Increase in common stock portion of retained earnings . . . . $ 38,000
Controlling interest (80%) . . . . $ 30,400

The conversion (CV) entry for $30,400 would debit the investment account and credit the Company P retained earnings account. The investment account now would be stated at its simple-equity-adjusted, January 1, 2019, balance. Worksheet entries (PS), (EL), (D), and (NCI) would be made just as in Worksheet 7-3. Only entry (CY) would be omitted, since it is not applicable to the cost method. The following partial worksheet includes the conversion and subsequent eliminations and adjustments under the cost method. All remaining procedures for this example would be identical to those used in Worksheet 7-3.

Subsidiary Preferred Stock, None Owned by Parent
Cost Method Used for Investment in Common Stock

	Partial Trial Balance		Eliminations & Adjustments			
	Company P	Company S	Dr.		Cr.	
Investment in Common Stock of Company S	150,000		(CV)	30,400	(EL)	164,800
					(D)	15,600
Goodwill			(D)	19,500		
Retained Earnings, January 1, 2015—Company P	(309,600)				(CV)	30,400
Preferred Stock ($100 par)—Company S		(100,000)				
Retained Earnings, Allocated to Preferred Stock, January 1, 2019, Company S					(PS)	24,000
Common Stock ($10 par)—Company S		(100,000)	(EL)	80,000		
Retained Earnings, January 1, 2019—Company S		(130,000)	(PS)	24,000	(NCI)	3,900
			(EL)	84,800		
Expenses	100,000	25,000				

Eliminations and Adjustments:

(CV) The cost-to-equity conversion entry was explained prior to the partial worksheet.
(PS) Distribute the beginning-of-period subsidiary retained earnings into the portions allocable to common and preferred stock. The typical procedure would be to consider the stated subsidiary retained earnings as applicable to common and to remove the preferred portion. This distribution reflects four years of arrearage (as of January 1, 2019) at $6,000 per year.
(EL) Eliminate the pro rata subsidiary common stockholders' equity at the beginning of the period against the investment account. This entry includes elimination of the 80% of subsidiary retained earnings applicable to common stock.
(D)/(NCI) Distribute the excess of cost and the NCI adjustment according to the determination and distribution of excess schedule.

Parent Investment in Subsidiary Preferred Stock

A parent may purchase all or a portion of the preferred stock of a subsidiary. Normally, preferred stock is nonvoting; therefore, it is not considered in determining whether the parent owns a controlling interest in the subsidiary. Thus, a 100% ownership of nonvoting preferred stock and a 49% interest in voting common stock may not require the preparation of consolidated statements.

From a consolidated viewpoint, the parent's purchase of subsidiary preferred stock is viewed as a retirement of the stock.[3] The amount paid is compared to the sum of the original proceeds resulting from the issuance of the shares and any claim the shares have on retained earnings, and an increase or decrease in equity as a result of the retirement is calculated. When the price paid is less than the preferred equity retired, the resulting increase in equity is credited to the controlling paid-in capital in excess of par account, not the retained earnings account, because it results from a transaction with the consolidated company's shareholders. A decrease in equity, which occurs when the price paid exceeds the preferred equity, would offset against the paid-in capital in excess of par applicable to the preferred stock. If not enough of the preferred stock paid-in capital in excess of par exists, the remaining decrease would be taken from the controlling retained earnings and viewed as a retirement dividend.

---

3 It also would be possible to view the investment as treasury shares, in which case they would appear as a contra account to the preferred stock in the minority interest section of the consolidated balance sheet. This approach, however, does not have popular support. It could be justified only if there were intent to reissue the shares.

To illustrate this type of investment, assume Company P in the previous example purchased 600 shares (60%) of Company S preferred stock on January 1, 2017, for $65,000. The increase or decrease in equity resulting from the retirement would be calculated as follows:

Price paid		$65,000
Less **preferred** interest acquired:		
Preferred stock ($100 par)..	$100,000	
Claim on dividends (2 years in arrears × $6,000 per year)	12,000	
Total preferred interest...	$112,000	
Interest acquired	× 60%	67,200
Increase in equity (credit parent's Paid-In Capital in Excess of Par) .		**$ 2,200**

Though viewed as retired, the preferred stock investment account will continue to exist on the books of the parent in subsequent periods. At the end of each period, the investment must be "retired" on the consolidated worksheet. The procedures used depend on whether the parent accounts for the investment in preferred stock under the equity method or the cost method. Under the equity method, the parent adjusts the investment in preferred stock account each period for any additional claim on the subsidiary retained earnings, including any continued arrearage or participation privilege. In this example, the arrearage of dividends would be recorded each year, 2017 to 2019, as follows:

Investment in Company S Preferred Stock	3,600	
Subsidiary Income..		3,600
To acknowledge 60% of the annual increase in the Company S preferred stock dividend arrearage.		

Assuming the equity adjustments are properly made, any original discrepancy between the price paid for the preferred shares and their book value would be maintained. The equity method also acknowledges that, even though the shares are viewed as retired in consolidated reports, the controlling interest is entitled to its proportionate share of consolidated net income based on both its common and preferred stock holdings.

Worksheet 7-4: page 410 Worksheet 7-4, pages 410 to 411, displays the consolidation procedures that would be used for the ownership interest in preferred stock described above. This worksheet parallels Worksheet 7-3 except that the parent owns 60% of the subsidiary preferred stock. The investment is listed at its $65,000 cost plus three years of equity adjustments to reflect the increasing dividend arrearage.

All of the eliminations from Worksheet 7-3 are repeated in Worksheet 7-4. The following additional eliminations are added in Worksheet 7-4:

(CYP) Eliminate the income reported during the current year on the interest in preferred stock:		
Subsidiary Income—Preferred...........................	3,600	
Investment in Company S Preferred Stock		3,600
(ELP) Eliminate investment in preferred stock against equity applicable to parent's share of subsidiary preferred stock equity; excess of equity over investment is an increase in parent's paid-in capital in excess of par:		
Preferred Stock ($100 par)—Company S...................	60,000	
Retained Earnings Allocated to Preferred Stock, January 1, 2019—Company S	14,400*	
Investment in Company S Preferred Stock		72,200
Paid-In Capital in Excess of Par—Company P		2,200

*$24,000 × 60%

Consolidated net income is distributed as shown in the income distribution schedules that accompany the worksheet. The distributions respect the controlling/NCI ownership of both common and preferred shares. The common and preferred equity interests of the NCI again are summarized on the worksheet and for presentation on the formal balance sheet.

If a parent uses the cost method for its investment in subsidiary preferred stock, the investment should be converted to its equity balance as of the beginning of the period. In this example, if the cost method is used for the investment in preferred stock, the following conversion adjustment would be made on the worksheet:

(CVP)	Preferred stock cost-to-equity conversion:		
	Investment in Company S Preferred Stock	7,200	
	Retained Earnings, January 1, 2019—Company P.		7,200

The adjustment reflects two years of arrearage at $6,000 per year times the 60% ownership interest. Eliminations and adjustments would proceed as in Worksheet 7-4, except that there would be no need for entry (CY).

This example contains only cumulative preferred stock. However, the same principles would apply to participating preferred stock, and the allocation procedures outlined earlier in this chapter would be used. Only the subdivision of the subsidiary retained earnings and the amounts of the equity adjustments would differ.

REFLECTION

- If a subsidiary has preferred stock with a claim on retained earnings (because it is cumulative and/or participating), the subsidiary retained earnings must be allocated between the preferred and common stock. The investment in common stock is eliminated only against the retained earnings allocated to the common stock.

- In addition, if the parent owns subsidiary preferred stock, the investment is eliminated on the worksheet against the applicable subsidiary preferred stock.

APPENDIX: WORKSHEET FOR A CONSOLIDATED BALANCE SHEET

5

OBJECTIVE

Solve balance-sheet-only problems (CPA Exam issue).

Previous chapters displayed procedures applicable to worksheets that produced a consolidated income statement, retained earnings statement, and balance sheet. However, there may be occasions when only consolidated balance sheets are required, and the separate balance sheets of the affiliates form the starting point for consolidation procedures. Such occasions are rare in practice but are of concern to students desiring to take the CPA Exam. Past examinations have used balance-sheet-only consolidation problems as an expedient method for testing purposes. This type of problem requires less time to solve while still testing the candidates' knowledge of consolidations.

A balance sheet worksheet requires only adjustments to balance sheet accounts. No adjustments for nominal accounts are required. Your past experience often will lead you to consider the impact of an elimination on the nominal accounts, but you must adjust your thinking to cover only the remaining impact of an elimination on the balance sheet. For example, intercompany merchandise sales no longer will require an elimination of the sales and cost of goods sold relative to the transaction. The only balance sheet adjustment would be for intercompany profit on the ending inventory. The following sections examine the simplified procedures that are used on a consolidated balance sheet worksheet.

Investment Account

When the investment account is maintained under the simple equity method, it will reflect the same point in time as do the subsidiary equity balances. There is no need to eliminate the parent's entry for its share of subsidiary income. Instead, the pro rata share of subsidiary equity balances may be eliminated directly against the investment account.

Investments maintained under the sophisticated equity method are also at a common point in time and, thus, can be eliminated directly against the underlying subsidiary equity. The distributable excess, however, will be only that which remains net of the amortizations made in the current and previous periods.

Investments maintained at cost should be converted to the simple equity method as of the *end of the year* to agree in time with the subsidiary equity balances. The entire conversion adjustment is carried to the controlling retained earnings.

Excesses and the NCI adjustment are distributed according to the determination and distribution of excess schedules. Once distributed, the excesses are amortized to the balance sheet date and the entire amortization is carried to the controlling retained earnings and the NCI.

Merchandise Sales

Only the intercompany profit in the ending inventory needs adjustment. The profit is eliminated from the inventory and from retained earnings. The adjustment to retained earnings is allocated according to the NCI/controlling ownership percentages in effect when the subsidiary made the intercompany sale. If the parent made the sale, the adjustment is made only to the controlling retained earnings. The intercompany profit in the beginning inventory either has been realized through the subsequent sale of the merchandise to an outside party, or, if the units in the beginning inventory are still on hand at year-end, they would be included in the adjustment for intercompany profit in the ending inventory.

Plant Asset Sales

The only matter for concern in the case of intercompany plant asset sales is the adjustment of the asset and retained earnings accounts for the undepreciated portion of the intercompany gain or loss as of year-end. The asset account is adjusted to its cost to the consolidated firm; accumulated depreciation is adjusted for all periods to date; and retained earnings are adjusted for the undepreciated profit or loss that is to be deferred to future periods. If the subsidiary sold to the parent, the retained earnings adjustment is allocated to the NCI and controlling interests that existed at the time of the sale.

Investment in Bonds

The amortized balance in Investment in Company S Bonds is eliminated against the bonds payable and any related discount or premium balance. The net disparity in amounts is the net retirement gain or loss remaining at year-end, which is carried to retained earnings. When the subsidiary is the issuer, the retained earnings adjustment is allocated to the NCI and controlling interests.

Leases

For operating leases, it is necessary only to reclassify the asset and accumulated depreciation as owned assets rather than assets under operating leases. Where direct financing leases exist, the intercompany debt resulting from the capitalized lease must be eliminated. Also, it is necessary to reclassify the asset and accumulated depreciation as owned assets rather than assets under capital leases. An intercompany sales-type lease requires the same procedures as a direct-financing lease plus an additional adjustment to defer the remaining undepreciated intercompany profit on the lease. If the subsidiary leased the asset to the parent, the retained earnings adjustment is allocated to the NCI and controlling interest that existed at the inception of the lease.

Illustration

To illustrate the procedures used for the balance sheet worksheet, assume Company P purchased an 80% interest in Company S on January 1, 2015. Company P uses the cost method to record its investment in Company S. The determination and distribution of excess schedule prepared for this purchase is as follows:

Determination and Distribution of Excess Schedule

	Company Implied Fair Value	Parent Price (80%)	NCI Value (20%)
Fair value of subsidiary	$ 937,500	$750,000	$187,500
Less book value of interest acquired:			
Common stock	$ 200,000		
Retained earnings	600,000		
Total stockholders' equity	$ 800,000	$800,000	$800,000
Interest acquired		80%	20%
Book value		$640,000	$160,000
Excess of fair value over book value	**$137,500**	$110,000	$ 27,500

Adjustment of identifiable accounts:

	Adjustment	Life	Amortization per Year	Worksheet Key
Building	$ 37,500	10	$ 3,750	**debit D1**
Goodwill	**100,000**			**debit D2**
Total	**$137,500**			

The facts pertaining to intercompany sales by Company S to Company P are as follows:

	2017	2018
Intercompany sales	$80,000	$100,000
Gross profit	30%	40%
Intercompany sales in ending inventory	$20,000	$ 40,000
Unpaid balance, end of the year	$30,000	$ 35,000

On January 1, 2016, Company P sold a new piece of equipment that cost $10,000 to Company S for $15,000. Company S is depreciating the equipment over five years on a straight-line basis.

Company S has outstanding $100,000 of 20-year, 5% bonds due January 1, 2023. Interest is payable on January 1 for the previous year. The bonds originally were sold to yield 6%. On January 1, 2017, Company P purchased the bonds on the open market at a price to yield 8%.

Worksheet 7-5: page 414   Worksheet 7-5, pages 414 to 415, contains the balance sheets and eliminations and adjustments for Companies P and S on December 31, 2018. After the worksheet entries are completed, the amounts are combined to produce the consolidated balance sheet.

In journal entry form, the eliminations for Worksheet 7-5 are as follows:

(CV)   Convert investment to simple equity balance on
            December 31, 2018 (end of year):
            Investment in Company S Stock 240,000
                Retained Earnings, December 31, 2018—Company P   240,000
            Adjustment = 80% × $300,000 increase in retained earnings of
                Company S.

(EL)   Eliminate 80% of subsidiary equity against the investment account:
            Common Stock—Company S 160,000
            Retained Earnings, December 31, 2018—Company S 720,000
                Investment in Company S Stock   880,000

(D)/(NCI)   Distribute excess and NCI adjustment to buildings and goodwill:
            Buildings   37,500
            Goodwill 100,000
                Investment in Company S Stock   110,000
                Retained Earnings, December 31, 2018—Company S (NCI) . .   27,500

(A)   Adjust depreciation on buildings through end of year:
            Retained Earnings, December 31, 2018—Company P (4 years ×
                $3,750 × 80%)   12,000
            Retained Earnings, December 31, 2018—Company S (4 years ×
                $3,750 × 20%)   3,000
                Accumulated Depreciation—Buildings (4 × $3,750)   15,000

(IA)   Eliminate intercompany trade balances:
            Accounts Payable   35,000
                Accounts Receivable   35,000

(EI)   Defer ending inventory profit (40% × $40,000):
            Retained Earnings, December 31, 2018—Company P   12,800
            Retained Earnings, December 31, 2018—Company S (20%)   3,200
                Inventory, December 31, 2018   16,000

(F)   Defer remaining profit on equipment sale (2/5 of $5,000):
            Retained Earnings, December 31, 2018—Company P   2,000
            Accumulated Depreciation (3 years × $1,000)   3,000
                Equipment   5,000

(B)   Retire intercompany bonds on the worksheet:

Bonds Payable	100,000	
Discount on Bonds Payable		3,465
Investment in Company S Bonds		90,064
Retained Earnings, December 31, 2018—Company P		
(80% × $6,471*)		5,177
Retained Earnings, December 31, 2018, Company S		
(20% × $6,471)		1,294

*($100,000 – $3,465) – $90,064

The time savings from the balance sheet worksheet stems from the fact that there is no consolidated net income to calculate and distribute.

Worksheet 7-1

Acquisition of Additional Shares of Subsidiary

Company P and Subsidiary Company S
Worksheet for Consolidated Financial Statements
For Year Ended December 31, 2017

	(Credit balance amounts are in parentheses.)	Trial Balance	
		Company P	Company S
1	Current Assets	60,000	130,000
2	Investment in Company S	228,000	
3			
4			
5			
6	Building	400,000	80,000
7	Accumulated Depreciation—Building	(100,000)	(5,000)
8	Equipment		150,000
9			
10	**Accumulated Depreciation—Equipment**		(90,000)
11			
12	Goodwill		
13			
14	Liabilities	(100,000)	(30,000)
15	Common Stock—Company P	(200,000)	
16	**Retained Earnings, January 1, 2017—Company P**	**(210,000)**	
17			
18	Common Stock—Company S		(100,000)
19	**Retained Earnings, January 1, 2017—Company S**		(100,000)
20			
21			
22	Sales	(400,000)	(200,000)
23	Cost of Goods Sold	300,000	120,000
24	**Expenses**	**50,000**	**45,000**
25			
26	Subsidiary Income	(28,000)	
27		0	0
28	Consolidated Net Income		
29	To NCI (see distribution schedule)		
30	Balance to Controlling Interest (see distribution schedule)		
31	Total NCI		
32	Retained Earnings, Controlling Interest, December 31, 2017		
33			

Worksheet 7-1 (see page 378)

Eliminations & Adjustments Dr.		Eliminations & Adjustments Cr.		Consolidated Income Statement	NCI	Controlling Retained Earnings	Consolidated Balance Sheet	
							190,000	1
		(CY)	28,000					2
		(EL)	160,000					3
		(D)	**30,000**					4
		(D3)	**10,000**					5
							480,000	6
							(105,000)	7
(D1)	**30,000**						180,000	8
								9
		(A1)	**18,000**				(108,000)	10
								11
(D2)	**20,000**						20,000	12
								13
							(130,000)	14
							(200,000)	15
(A1)	**7,200**					(200,400)		16
(D3)	**2,400**							17
(EL)	80,000				(20,000)			18
(EL)	80,000	**(NCI)**	**20,000**		(27,600)			19
(A1)	**4,800**							20
(D3)	**7,600**							21
				(600,000)				22
				420,000				23
(A1)	**6,000**			101,000				24
								25
(CY)	28,000							26
	266,000		266,000					27
				(79,000)				28
				5,800	(5,800)			29
				73,200		(73,200)		30
					(53,400)		(53,400)	31
						(273,600)	(273,600)	32
							0	33

Eliminations and Adjustments:

(CY)   Eliminate the parent's entry recognizing 80% of the subsidiary net income for the current year. This entry restores the investment account to its balance at the beginning of the year, so that it can be eliminated against Company S beginning-of-year equity balances.

(EL)   Eliminate the 80% controlling interest in beginning-of-year subsidiary accounts against the investment account. The 60% and 20% investments could be eliminated separately if desired.

(D1/NCI) The $30,000 excess of cost on the original 60% investment and the NCI adjustment on the purchase date is distributed to the equipment (D1) and goodwill (D2) accounts according to the determination and distribution of excess schedule prepared on January 1, 2015.

(A1)   Since the equipment has a 5-year remaining life on January 1, 2015, the depreciation should be increased $6,000 per year for three years. This entry corrects the controlling retained earnings for the past two years by $7,200 (60%) and the NCI for $4,800 (40%) and adjusts the current depreciation expense by $6,000.

(D3)   The $10,000 excess of cost on the 20% block is distributed to the NCI for $7,600, which was the portion of the NCI adjustment applicable to the 20% interest on January 1. The $2,400 is the adjustment to parent retained earnings resulting from the retirement of the subsidiary shares.

Subsidiary Company S Income Distribution

Equipment depreciation	$6,000	Internally generated net income	$35,000
		Adjusted income	$29,000
		NCI share	× 20%
		NCI	$ 5,800

Parent Company P Income Distribution

Internally generated net income	$50,000
80% × Company S adjusted income of $29,000. . . .	23,200
Controlling interest	$73,200

Worksheet 7-2

Sale of Subsidiary Interest During Period; No Loss of Control
Company P and Subsidiary Company S
Worksheet for Consolidated Financial Statements
For Year Ended December 31, 2017

	(Credit balance amounts are in parentheses.)	Trial Balance	
		Company P	Company S
1	Investment in Company S (60%)	244,500	
2			
3			
4	Equipment	600,000	100,000
5	Accumulated Depreciation—Equipment	(100,000)	(60,000)
6	Other Assets	581,500	305,000
7	Goodwill		
8	Common Stock—Company P	(500,000)	
9	Retained Earnings, January 1, 2017—Company P	(701,500)	
10			
11	Common Stock—Company S		(100,000)
12	Retained Earnings, January 1, 2017—Company S		(215,000)
13			
14	Sales	(500,000)	(200,000)
15	Cost of Goods Sold	350,000	140,000
16	Expenses	50,000	30,000
17			
18	**Paid-In Capital in Excess of Par—Company P**	**(4,600)**	
19	**Subsidiary Income**	**(19,900)**	
20			
21	**Income Sold to NCI (second 20% block)**		
22		0	0
23			
24	Consolidated Net Income		
25	To NCI (see distribution schedule)		
26	Balance to Controlling Interest (see distribution schedule)		
27	Total NCI		
28	Retained Earnings, Controlling Interest, December 31, 2017		
29			

Worksheet 7-2 (see page 387)

Eliminations & Adjustments		Consolidated Income Statement	NCI	Controlling Retained Earnings	Consolidated Balance Sheet	
Dr.	Cr.					
	(CY) 18,000					1
	(EL) 189,000					2
	(D) 37,500					3
(D1) 25,000					725,000	4
	(A) 15,000				(175,000)	5
					886,500	6
(D2) 37,500					37,500	7
					(500,000)	8
(A) 6,000				(695,500)		9
						10
(EL) 60,000			(40,000)			11
(EL) 129,000	(NCI) 25,000		(107,000)			12
(A) 4,000						13
		(700,000)				14
		490,000				15
		85,000				16
(A) 5,000						17
					(4,600)	18
(NCI) 1,900						19
(CY) 18,000						20
	(NCI) 1,900		(1,900)			21
286,400	286,400					22
						23
		(125,000)				24
		8,100	(8,100)			25
		116,900		(116,900)		26
			(157,000)		(157,000)	27
				(812,400)	(812,400)	28
					0	29

Eliminations and Adjustments:

(NCI)   The income earned by the parent on the 20% interest sold on July 1, though earned by the controlling interest, now belongs to the NCI. The NCI owns 20% of the reported subsidiary income for the half-year ($12,000), which is $2,400. Note that this entry credits the account, Income Sold to NCI, to accomplish the transfer of the income to the NCI. The offsetting debit is explained as follows:

20% of subsidiary income for the first six months, adjusted for one-fourth of the parent's half-year amortization of excess or $(20\% \times \$12,000) - (20\% \times \frac{1}{2} \times \$5,000) = \$1,900$.

(CY)   Eliminate the parent's entry recording its 60% share of subsidiary net income of $30,000. This entry restores the 60% interest to its simple-equity-adjusted cost at the beginning of the year so that the investment can be eliminated against subsidiary equity balances at the beginning of the year.

(EL)   Eliminate 60% of the subsidiary equity balances at the beginning of the year against the investment account. An excess cost of $37,500 remains. This amount is 60% of the original $62,500 total excess shown on page 382, since only a 60% interest is retained.

(D)/(NCI)   Distribute $62,500 total adjustment to equipment (D1) and goodwill (D2) according to the D&D schedule. 60% of the excess ($37,500) applies to the remaining investment and 40% ($25,000) now applies to the 40% NCI.

(A)   Amortize equipment $5,000 for two prior years and the current year. Prior-year amortization is distributed 60% to controlling interest and 40% to the NCI.

Subsidiary Company S Income Distribution

Depreciation adjustment . . . . (A)	$5,000	Internally generated net income	$ 30,000
		Adjusted income	$ 25,000
		NCI share	× 40%
		NCI for full year	$ 10,000
		Less income purchased.	**1,900**
		NCI	$ 8,100

Parent Company P Income Distribution

		Internally generated net income	$100,000
		60% × Company S adjusted income of $25,000.	15,000
		20% × Company S adjusted income for first six months (net of amortization)	**1,900**
		Controlling interest	$116,900

Worksheet 7-3

Subsidiary Preferred Stock, None Owned by Parent
Company P and Subsidiary Company S
Worksheet for Consolidated Financial Statements
For Year Ended December 31, 2019

	(Credit balance amounts are in parentheses.)	Trial Balance	
		Company P	Company S
1	Current Assets	259,600	150,000
2	Property, Plant, and Equipment (net)	400,000	250,000
3	Investment in Company S Common Stock	195,600	
4			
5			
6	Goodwill		
7	Liabilities	(150,000)	(45,000)
8	Common Stock—Company P	(200,000)	
9	Retained Earnings, January 1, 2019—Company P	(340,000)	
10	Preferred Stock ($100 par)—Company S		(100,000)
11	**Retained Earnings Allocated to Preferred Stock, January 1, 2019—Company S**		
12	Common Stock ($10 par)—Company S		(100,000)
13	Retained Earnings, January 1, 2019—Company S		(130,000)
14			
15	Sales	(450,000)	(200,000)
16	Cost of Goods Sold	200,000	150,000
17	Expenses	100,000	25,000
18	Subsidiary Income	(15,200)	
19		0	0
20			
21	Consolidated Net Income		
22	To NCI (see distribution schedule)		
23	Balance to Controlling Interest (see distribution schedule)		
24	Total NCI		
25	Retained Earnings, Controlling Interest, December 31, 2019		
26			

Eliminations and Adjustments:

(PS) Distribute the beginning-of-period subsidiary retained earnings into the portions allocable to common and preferred stock. The typical procedure would be to consider the stated subsidiary retained earnings as applicable to common and to remove the preferred portion. This distribution reflects four years of arrearage (as of January 1, 2019) at $6,000 per year.

(CY) Eliminate the parent's entry recording its share of subsidiary current income.

(EL) Eliminate the pro rata subsidiary common stockholders' equity at the beginning of the period against the investment account. This entry includes elimination of the 80% of subsidiary retained earnings applicable to common stock.

(D)/(NCI) Distribute the excess of cost and the NCI adjustment according to the determination and distribution of excess schedule.

Worksheet 7-3 (see page 391)

Eliminations & Adjustments				Consolidated Income Statement	NCI	Controlling Retained Earnings	Consolidated Balance Sheet	
Dr.		Cr.						
							409,600	1
							650,000	2
		(CY)	15,200					3
		(EL)	164,800					4
		(D)	15,600					5
(D)	19,500						19,500	6
							(195,000)	7
							(200,000)	8
						(340,000)		9
					(100,000)			10
		(PS)	**24,000**		(24,000)			11
(EL)	80,000				(20,000)			12
(PS)	**24,000**	(NCI)	3,900		(25,100)			13
(EL)	84,800							14
				(650,000)				15
				350,000				16
				125,000				17
(CY)	15,200							18
	223,500		223,500					19
								20
				(175,000)				21
				9,800	(9,800)			22
				165,200		(165,200)		23
					(178,900)		(178,900)	24
						(505,200)	(505,200)	25
							0	26

Subsidiary Company S Income Distribution

Internally generated net income (no adjustments) . . .	$	25,000
Less preferred cumulative claim to NCI		**(6,000)**
Common stock income	$	19,000
NCI share	×	20%
NCI in common income.	$	3,800
Total NCI ($6,000 + $3,800)	**$**	**9,800**

Parent Company P Income Distribution

Internally generated net income		$ 150,000
80% × Company S adjusted income on common stock of $19,000		15,200
Controlling interest		$ 165,200

Worksheet 7-4

Subsidiary Preferred Stock Owned by Parent
Company P and Subsidiary Company S
Worksheet for Consolidated Financial Statements
For Year Ended December 31, 2019

	(Credit balance amounts are in parentheses.)	Trial Balance	
		Company P	Company S
1	Current Assets	194,600	150,000
2	Property, Plant, and Equipment (net)	400,000	250,000
3	Investment in Company S Common Stock	195,600	
4			
5			
6	**Investment in Company S Preferred Stock**	75,800	
7			
8	Goodwill		
9	Liabilities	(150,000)	(45,000)
10	Common Stock—Company P	(200,000)	
11	**Paid-In Capital in Excess of Par—Company P**		
12	Retained Earnings, January 1, 2019—Company P	(347,200)	
13	Preferred Stock ($100 par)—Company S		(100,000)
14	Retained Earnings Allocated to Preferred Stock, January 1, 2019—Company S		
15	Common Stock ($10 par)—Company S		(100,000)
16	Retained Earnings, January 1, 2019—Company S		(130,000)
17			
18	Sales	(450,000)	(200,000)
19	Cost of Goods Sold	200,000	150,000
20	Expenses	100,000	25,000
21	Subsidiary Income—Common	(15,200)	
22	**Subsidiary Income—Preferred**	**(3,600)**	
23		0	0
24			
25	Consolidated Net Income		
26	To NCI (see distribution schedule)		
27	Balance to Controlling Interest (see distribution schedule)		
28	Total NCI		
29	Retained Earnings, Controlling Interest, December 31, 2019		
30			

Worksheet 7-4 (see page 394)

Eliminations & Adjustments				Consolidated Income Statement	NCI	Controlling Retained Earnings	Consolidated Balance Sheet	
Dr.		Cr.						
							344,600	1
							650,000	2
		(CY)	15,200					3
		(EL)	164,800					4
		(D)	15,600					5
		(CYP)	**3,600**					6
		(ELP)	**72,200**					7
(D)	19,500						19,500	8
							(195,000)	9
							(200,000)	10
		(ELP)	**2,200**				(2,200)	11
						(347,200)		12
(ELP)	**60,000**				(40,000)			13
(ELP)	**14,400**	(PS)	24,000		(9,600)			14
(EL)	80,000				(20,000)			15
(PS)	24,000	(NCI)	3,900		(25,100)			16
(EL)	84,800							17
				(650,000)				18
				350,000				19
				125,000				20
(CY)	15,200							21
(CYP)	**3,600**							22
	301,500		301,500					23
								24
				(175,000)				25
				6,200	(6,200)			26
				(168,800)		(168,800)		27
					(100,900)		(100,900)	28
						(516,000)	(516,000)	29
							0	30

Eliminations and Adjustments:

(PS), (CY), (EL), and (D)	Same as Worksheet 7-3; the common stock investment elimination procedures are unaffected by the investment in preferred stock.
(CYP)	Eliminate the entry recording the parent's share of income allocable to preferred stock. If declared, intercompany preferred dividends would also have been eliminated. This adjustment restores the investment account to its beginning-of-period equity balance.
(ELP)	The parent's ownership portion of the par value and beginning-of-period retained earnings applicable to preferred stock is eliminated against the balance in the investment in preferred stock account. The difference in this case was an increase in equity, and it was carried to the controlling paid-in capital in excess of par.

Subsidiary Company S Income Distribution		
Internally generated net income (no adjustments) .	$	25,000
Less preferred cumulative claim:		
to NCI, 40% × $6,000		(2,400)
to controlling, 60% × $6,000		**(3,600)**
Common stock income	$	19,000
NCI share	×	20%
NCI in common income.	$	3,800
Total NCI ($2,400 + $3,800)	$	6,200

Parent Company P Income Distribution		
Internally generated net income		$150,000
60% × Company S income attributable		
to preferred stock		**3,600**
80% × Company S adjusted income on		
common stock of $19,000.		15,200
Controlling interest		$168,800

Worksheet 7-5

Balance Sheet Only
Company P and Subsidiary Company S
Worksheet for Consolidated Balance Sheet
December 31, 2018

| | (Credit balance amounts are in parentheses.) | Trial Balance | |
		Company P	Company S
1	Cash	61,936	106,535
2	Accounts Receivable	80,000	200,000
3	Inventory, December 31, 2018	60,000	150,000
4	Land	300,000	250,000
5	Building	800,000	600,000
6	Accumulated Depreciation—Building	(400,000)	(100,000)
7	Equipment	120,000	95,000
8	Accumulated Depreciation—Equipment	(70,000)	(30,000)
9	Investment in Company S Bonds	90,064	
10	Investment in Company S Stock	750,000	
11			
12	Goodwill		
13	Accounts Payable	(92,000)	(75,000)
14	Bonds Payable		(100,000)
15	Discount on Bonds Payable		3,465
16	Common Stock—Company P	(500,000)	
17	Retained Earnings, December 31, 2018—Company P	(1,200,000)	
18			
19			
20	Common Stock—Company S		(200,000)
21	Retained Earnings, December 31, 2018—Company S		(900,000)
22			
23			
24		0	0
25	Total NCI		
26			

Eliminations and Adjustments:

(CV) Investment in Company S Stock is converted to the simple equity method as of December 31, 2018, as follows: 80% × $300,000 increase in retained earnings = $240,000.

(EL) 80% of the subsidiary equity balances is eliminated against the investment in stock account.

(D)/(NCI) The $110,000 excess of cost and $27,500 NCI adjustment is distributed according to the determination and distribution of excess schedule. Entry (D1) adjusts the building account and (D2) adjusts goodwill.

(A) The excess attributable to the building is amortized for four years at $3,750 per year. The retained earnings adjustment is allocated 80% to Company P retained earnings and 20% to Company S retained earnings.

(IA) The intercompany trade balance is eliminated.

(EI) The gross profit of $16,000 (40% × $40,000) recorded by Company S and applicable to merchandise in Company P's ending inventory is deferred by reducing the inventory and retained earnings. Since the sale was made by Company S, the adjustment is allocated to the NCI and controlling retained earnings.

(F) As of December 31, 2018, $2,000 ($5,000 × 2/5) of the profit on the equipment sale is still to be deferred. Since the sale was made by Company P, the controlling retained earnings absorb this adjustment, and the equipment and accumulated depreciation accounts are adjusted.

(B) Investment in Company S Bonds is eliminated against the net book value of the bonds. The remaining gain on the worksheet retirement is allocated to the NCI and controlling retained earnings, since the subsidiary originally issued the bonds.

Worksheet 7-5 (see page 398)

Eliminations & Adjustments				NCI	Consolidated Balance Sheet	
Dr.		Cr.				
					168,471	1
		(IA)	35,000		245,000	2
		(EI)	16,000		194,000	3
					550,000	4
(D1)	37,500				1,437,500	5
		(A)	15,000		(515,000)	6
		(F)	5,000		210,000	7
(F)	3,000				(97,000)	8
		(B)	90,064			9
(CV)	**240,000**	(EL)	880,000			10
		(D)	110,000			11
(D2)	100,000				100,000	12
(IA)	35,000				(132,000)	13
(B)	100,000					14
		(B)	3,465			15
					(500,000)	16
(A)	12,000	**(CV)**	**240,000**		(1,418,377)	17
(EI)	12,800	(B)	5,177			18
(F)	2,000					19
(EL)	160,000			(40,000)		20
(EL)	720,000	(B)	1,294	(202,594)		21
(EI)	3,200	(NCI)	27,500			22
(A)	3,000					23
	1,428,500		1,428,500			24
				(242,594)	(242,594)	25
					0	26

UNDERSTANDING THE ISSUES

1. Company S has 4,000 shares outstanding and a total stockholders' equity of $200,000. It is about to issue 6,000 new shares to the prospective parent company. The shares will be sold for a total of $650,000. Will there be an excess of cost over book value? If so, how will it likely be accounted for?

2. Company P purchases an 80% interest in Company S on January 1, 2015, for $480,000. Company S had equity of $450,000 on that date. Any excess of cost over book value was attributed to equipment with a 10-year life. On July 1, 2020, Company P purchased another 10% interest for $160,000. Company S's equity was $550,000 on January 1, 2020, and it earned $50,000 evenly during 2020. Company P had internally generated net income of $120,000 during 2020. Calculate consolidated income for 2020 and the distribution of consolidated income to the noncontrolling and controlling interests.

3. Company P purchased an 80% interest (8,000 shares) in Company S for $800,000 on January 1, 2015. Company S's equity on that date was $900,000. Any excess of cost over book value was attributed to equipment with a 10-year life. On January 1, 2019, Company S's equity was $1,200,000. Company S earned $200,000, evenly, during 2019. In December 2019, Company S paid $10,000 in dividends. Company P had internally generated net income of $150,000. On July 1, 2019, there was a sale of Company S stock, for $150 per share, to outside interests by Company P. Consider these situations:

   ◆ Company P sells all 8,000 shares.
   ◆ Company P sells 2,000 shares.
   ◆ Company P sells 6,000 shares.

   For each of these situations:

   a. How will the sale be recorded?
   b. Will consolidated statements be prepared for 2019? If so, what will be consolidated net income, and what will be the distribution to the NCI?
   c. If consolidated statements will not be prepared, what will be reported by the parent for its income from Company S?

4. Company S has the following stockholders' equity on January 1, 2019:

Common stock ($1 par, 100,000 shares)	$100,000
6% preferred stock ($100 par, 2,000 shares)	200,000
Paid-in capital in excess of par	900,000
Retained earnings	500,000

   The preferred stock is cumulative and has dividends one year in arrears on January 1, 2019.

   Company P purchased an 80% interest in the common stock of Company S on January 1, 2019, for $1,400,000. Any excess of cost over book value was attributed to goodwill. Company S earned $80,000 during 2019 and paid no dividends. Company P had internally generated net income of $120,000.

   What is consolidated net income for 2019, and how is it distributed to the controlling and noncontrolling interests?

   How would the answer differ if Company P also purchases one-half of the preferred stock of Company S for $120,000?

EXERCISES

Exercise 1 *(LO 1)* **Purchase of shares directly from subsidiary.** Prior to January 2, 2018, Prestar and Saturn are separate corporations. Saturn Corporation is contemplating a major expansion and seeks to be purchased by a larger corporation with available cash. Prestar Corporation issues $1,350,000 of bonds and uses the proceeds to buy 30,000 newly issued Saturn shares for $45 per share. The price reflects a control premium since the fair value of the NCI shares is $40. Just prior to the issue of the bonds and the issue and purchase of Saturn stock, Prestar and Saturn have the following separate balance sheets:

Assets	Prestar Corporation	Saturn Corporation
Current assets	$ 600,000	$100,000
Land	150,000	60,000
Property, plant, and equipment	700,000	400,000
Total assets	$1,450,000	$560,000
Liabilities and Stockholders' Equity		
Current liabilities	$ 250,000	$100,000
Common stock ($5 par)	400,000	100,000
Retained earnings	800,000	360,000
Total liabilities and equity	$1,450,000	$560,000

Purchasing the 30,000 new shares gives Prestar Corporation a 60% controlling interest (30,000 of a total 50,000 common shares). On the purchase date, Saturn's property is undervalued by $200,000 and has a remaining life of 20 years. Any remaining excess cost can be attributed only to goodwill.

Prepare a determination and distribution of excess schedule for Prestar Corporation's investment in Saturn. Prepare a consolidated balance sheet for the consolidated firm immediately after the acquisition by Prestar Corporation.

Exercise 2 *(LO 2)* **Block purchase, control with first block.** Baker Corporation purchases a 60% interest in Hardee Company on January 1, 2015, for $135,000. On that date, Hardee Company has the following stockholders' equity:

Common stock ($10 par)	$100,000
Retained earnings	20,000
	$120,000

Any excess of cost over fair value is due to equipment with a 10-year life.

Baker Corporation purchases another 20% interest in Hardee Company for $40,000 on January 1, 2017, when Hardee Company has the following stockholders' equity:

Common stock ($10 par)	$100,000
Retained earnings	50,000
	$150,000

On December 31, 2019, Baker Corporation and Hardee Company have the following balance sheets:

Assets	Baker Corporation	Hardee Company
Current assets	$ 285,000	$ 80,000
Investment in Hardee Company	175,000	
Property, plant, and equipment	740,000	240,000
Total assets	$1,200,000	$320,000

Liabilities and Stockholders' Equity	Baker Corporation	Hardee Company
Current liabilities	$ 400,000	$100,000
Stockholders' equity:		
Common stock ($10 par).	500,000	100,000
Retained earnings	300,000	120,000
Total liabilities and stockholders' equity	$1,200,000	$320,000

Prepare a determination and distribution of excess schedule for the January 1, 2015, acquisition and analysis of the 20% acquisition on January 1, 2017. Prepare the consolidated balance sheet of Baker Corporation and subsidiary Hardee Company on December 31, 2019.

Exercise 3 *(LO 3)* **Sale of interest, loss of control.** Rob Company purchases a 90% interest in Venus Company for $418,500 on January 1, 2017. Any excess of cost over book value is attributed to equipment, which is being depreciated over 20 years. Both companies end their reporting periods on December 31. Since the investment in Venus Company is consolidated, Rob Company chooses to use the cost method to maintain its investment.

On December 31, 2020, Rob Company sells 8,000 shares of Venus Company for $700,000. The following stockholders' equity balances of Venus Company are available:

	January 1, 2017	January 1, 2020
Common stock ($10 par).	$100,000	$100,000
Retained earnings	250,000	420,000
Total equity	$350,000	$520,000

Venus Company earns $70,000 during 2020. Prepare a determination and distribution of excess schedule. Record the sale of the shares of Venus Company and any other adjustments needed to the investment account.

Exercise 4 *(LO 3)* **Sale of interest, control maintained.** Carpenter Company has the following balance sheet on December 31, 2015:

Assets		Liabilities and Equity		
Current assets	$150,000	Liabilities		$100,000
Investment in Hinckley		Equity:		
Company	160,000	Common stock ($10 par)	$500,000	
Property, plant, and		Retained earnings	100,000	600,000
equipment (net)	390,000			
Total assets.	$700,000	Total liabilities and equity		$700,000

The investment in Hinckley Company account reflects the original cost of an 80% interest (40,000 shares) purchased on January 1, 2012. On the date of the purchase, Hinckley stockholders' equity has a book value of $150,000. Hinckley's other book values approximate fair values, except for a machine with a 5-year remaining life that is undervalued by $20,000. Any additional excess is attributed to goodwill.

A review of Hinckley's past financial statements reveals the following:

	Income	Dividends Paid
2012.	$ 10,000	$ 5,000
2013.	25,000	5,000

	Income	Dividends Paid
2014....................	40,000	5,000
2015....................	35,000	5,000
Total....................	$110,000	$20,000

Carpenter sells 2,000 shares of Hinckley common stock on January 1, 2016, for $40,000.

Prepare the necessary entries on Carpenter's books to account accurately for the sale of the 2,000 Hinckley shares. Provide a determination and distribution of excess schedule along with all other necessary computations as support.

Exercise 5 *(LO 3)* **Sale of interest, alternative remaining interests.** Center, Inc., purchases 24,000 shares of Bruce Corporation, which equates to an 80% interest, on January 1, 2015. The following determination and distribution of excess schedule is prepared:

Determination and Distribution of Excess Schedule

	Company Implied Fair Value	Parent Price (80%)	NCI Value (20%)
Fair value of subsidiary	$1,000,000	$800,000	$200,000
Less book value of interest acquired:			
Common stock ($10 par)...................	$ 300,000		
Retained earnings	400,000		
Total stockholders' equity................	$ 700,000	$700,000	$700,000
Interest acquired		80%	20%
Book value.............................		$560,000	$140,000
Excess of fair value over book value	**$ 300,000**	$240,000	$ 60,000

Adjustment of identifiable accounts:

	Adjustment	Amortization per Year	Life	Worksheet Key
Building	$ 50,000	$ 5,000	10	**debit D1**
Goodwill..............................	**250,000**			**debit D2**
Total	**$ 300,000**			

Bruce Corporation reports net income of $35,000 for the six months ended July 1, 2018. Center's simple-equity-adjusted investment balance is $864,000 as of December 31, 2017.

Prepare all entries for the sale of the Brown Corporation shares on July 1, 2018, for each of the following situations:

1. 24,000 shares are sold for $890,000.
2. 12,000 shares are sold for $455,000.
3. 6,000 shares are sold for $232,500.

Exercise 6 *(LO 4)* **D&D with preferred stock.** On January 1, 2016, Boelter Company purchases 80% of the outstanding common stock of Mill Corporation for $280,000. On this date, Mill Corporation stockholders' equity is as follows:

6% Preferred stock (1,000 shares, $100 par).......................................	$100,000
Common stock (20,000 shares, $10 par)...	200,000
Retained earnings	90,000
Total stockholders' equity...	$390,000

Prepare a determination and distribution of excess schedule under each of the following situations (any excess of cost over book value is attributable to goodwill):

1. The preferred stock is cumulative, with dividends one year in arrears at January 1, 2016, and has a liquidation value equal to par.
2. The preferred stock is noncumulative but fully participating.
3. The preferred stock is cumulative, with dividends two years in arrears as of January 1, 2016, and has a liquidation value equal to 110% of par.

Exercise 7 *(LO 4)* **Equity adjustments with preferred stock.** Brian Construction Company has the following stockholders' equity on January 1, 2015, the date on which Roller Company purchases an 80% interest in the common stock for $720,000:

8% cumulative preferred stock (5,000 shares, $100 par)	$ 500,000
Common stock (40,000 shares, $20 par)	800,000
Retained earnings	200,000
Total stockholders' equity	$1,500,000

Brian Construction Company did not pay preferred dividends in 2014.

1. Prepare a determination and distribution of excess schedule. Assume that the preferred stock's liquidation value is equal to par and that any excess of cost is attributable to goodwill.
2. Assume Ace Construction has the following net income (loss) for 2015 and 2016 and does not pay any dividends:

2015 income	$70,000
2016 income	40,000

Roller maintains its investment account under the cost method. Prepare the cost-to-equity conversion entries necessary on Roller Company's books to adjust its investment account to the simple equity balance as of January 1, 2017.

Exercise 8 *(LO 4)* **Cost-to-equity conversion with preferred stock.** On December 31, 2014, Zigler Corporation purchases an 80% interest in the common stock of Kim Company for $420,000. The stockholders' equity of Kim Company on December 31, 2014, is as follows:

8% Cumulative preferred stock (2,000 shares, $100 par)	$200,000
Common stock (30,000 shares, $10 stated value)	300,000
Retained earnings	160,000
Total stockholders' equity	$660,000

Any excess of cost over book value is attributable to goodwill. The common stock investment is accounted for under the cost method.

Zigler Corporation purchases 1,000 shares of the cumulative preferred stock of Kim Company on January 1, 2015, for $90,000. Kim Company issues a total of 2,000 preferred shares on January 1, 2011. Dividends on preferred stock are paid in 2011 and 2012, but not in subsequent years. Zigler Corporation accounts for its investment using the cost method.

During 2015 and 2016, Kim Company pays no dividends, and its retained earnings balance on December 31, 2016, is $210,000. Kim Company income during 2017 is $60,000.

1. Calculate the preferred and common stockholders' equity claim on Kim Company's retained earnings balance at January 1, 2017.
2. Prepare the cost-to-simple-equity conversion and the elimination as of January 1, 2017, that would be made on the December 31, 2017, consolidated trial balance worksheet for the investment in preferred stock.

3. Prepare the cost-to-simple-equity conversion and the eliminations that would be made on the December 31, 2017, consolidated trial balance worksheet for the investment in common stock. Provide a determination and distribution of excess schedule as support.

PROBLEMS

Problem 7-1 *(LO 2)* **Worksheet, blocks, control with first block.** The following determination and distribution of excess schedule is prepared on January 1, 2012, the date on which Palmer Company purchases a 60% interest in Sharon Company:

Determination and Distribution of Excess Schedule

	Company Implied Fair Value	Parent Price (60%)	NCI Value (40%)
Fair value of subsidiary	$ 300,000	$180,000	$120,000
Less book value of interest acquired:			
Common stock	$ 100,000		
Retained earnings	60,000		
Total equity.	$ 160,000	$160,000	$160,000
Interest acquired		60%	40%
Book value.		$ 96,000	$ 64,000
Excess of fair value over book value	**$140,000**	$ 84,000	$ 56,000

Adjustment of identifiable accounts:

	Adjustment	Amortization per Year	Life	Worksheet Key
Equipment	$50,000	$5,000	10	**debit D1**
Goodwill	90,000			**debit D2**

On December 31, 2013, Palmer Company purchases an additional 20% interest in Sharon Company for $70,000. Sharon's stockholders' equity is determined to be the following at that date:

Common stock	$100,000
Retained earnings	85,000
Total stockholders' equity.	$185,000

On December 31, 2015, the following trial balances are available:

	Palmer Company	Sharon Company
Current Assets	160,000	80,000
Investment in Sharon Company.	301,000	
Property, Plant, and Equipment (net)	450,000	170,000
Current Liabilities.	(110,000)	(20,000)
Common Stock ($10 par)	(500,000)	(100,000)
Retained Earnings, January 1, 2015.	(198,000)	(100,000)
Sales	(400,000)	(110,000)
Subsidiary Income.	(28,000)	
Cost of Goods Sold	200,000	60,000
Other Expenses	100,000	15,000
Dividends Declared.	25,000	5,000
Totals	0	0

Required ▶ ▶ ▶ ▶ ▶

1. Prepare an analysis for the second purchase of Sharon stock by Palmer Company on December 31, 2013.
2. Prepare the worksheet necessary to produce the consolidated financial statements of Palmer Company and its subsidiary as of December 31, 2015. Include an income distribution schedule.

Problem 7-2 *(LO 2)* **Worksheet, blocks, control with first block, merchandise sales.** On January 1, 2015, James Company purchases 70% of the common stock of Craft Company for $245,000. On this date, Craft has common stock, other paid-in capital in excess of par, and retained earnings of $50,000, $100,000, and $150,000, respectively.

On May 1, 2016, James Company purchases an additional 20% of the common stock of Craft Company for $92,000.

Net income and dividends for two years for Craft Company are as follows:

	2015	2016
Net income for year.	$60,000	$90,000
Dividends, declared in December	20,000	30,000

In 2016, the net income of Craft from January 1 through April 30 is $30,000.

On January 1, 2015, the only tangible asset of Craft that is undervalued is equipment, which is worth $20,000 more than book value. The equipment has a remaining life of four years, and straight-line depreciation is used. Any remaining excess is goodwill.

In the last quarter of 2016, Craft sells $50,000 in goods to James, at a gross profit rate of 30%. On December 31, 2016, $10,000 of these goods are in James's ending inventory.

The trial balances for the companies on December 31, 2016, are as follows:

	James Company	Craft Company
Inventory, December 31	100,000	50,000
Other Current Assets	126,000	180,000
Investment in Craft Company	*	
Land.	50,000	50,000
Buildings and Equipment.	350,000	320,000
Accumulated Depreciation	(100,000)	(60,000)
Other Intangibles.	20,000	
Current Liabilities.	(120,000)	(40,000)
Bonds Payable.		(100,000)
Other Long-Term Liabilities	(200,000)	
Common Stock—James.	(200,000)	
Other Paid-In Capital in Excess of Par—James	(100,000)	
Retained Earnings—James	(214,000)	
Common Stock—Craft.		(50,000)
Other Paid-In Capital in Excess of Par—Craft		(100,000)
Retained Earnings—Craft		(190,000)
Net Sales.	(520,000)	(450,000)
Cost of Goods Sold	300,000	260,000
Operating Expenses	121,000	100,000
Subsidiary Income.	*	
Dividends Declared.	50,000	30,000
Totals	0	0

* To be calculated and inserted.

Required ▶ ▶ ▶ ▶ ▶

1. Using this information, prepare a determination and distribution of excess schedule. Prepare an analysis of the later purchase of a 20% interest.
2. James Company carries the investment in Craft Company under the simple equity method. In general journal form, record the entries that would be made to apply the equity method in 2015 and 2016.

3. Compute the balance that should appear in Investment in Craft Company and in Subsidiary Income on December 31, 2016 (the second year). Fill in these amounts on James Company's trial balance on the worksheet for 2016.
4. Complete the worksheet for consolidated financial statements for 2016.

Problem 7-3 *(LO 2)* **Worksheet, blocks, control with first block, loans, fixed asset sales, intercompany merchandise.** During 2017, Away Company acquires a controlling interest in Stallward, Inc. Trial balances of the companies at December 31, 2017, are as follows:

	Away Company	Stallward, Inc.
Cash	99,500	78,000
Notes Receivable.	100,000	
Accounts Receivable	200,000	100,000
Interest Receivable.	3,000	
Dividends Receivable	4,500	
Inventories	924,000	125,000
Investment in Stallward, Inc.	469,200	
Property, Plant, and Equipment	1,250,000	500,000
Accumulated Depreciation	(500,000)	(150,000)
Deferred Charges	25,000	
Patents and Licenses		50,000
Accounts Payable	(425,000)	(80,000)
Notes Payable.		(75,000)
Dividends Payable.		(5,000)
Capital Stock.	(300,000)	(100,000)
Retained Earnings, January 1, 2017.	(1,605,000)	(400,000)
Sales and Services.	(1,800,000)	(750,000)
Subsidiary Income.	(43,200)	
Interest Income.	(3,000)	
Cost of Goods Sold	1,350,000	525,000
Administrative and Selling Expenses.	251,000	174,000
Interest Expense.		3,000
Dividends Declared		5,000
Totals	0	0

The following information is available regarding the transactions and accounts of the two companies:

a. An analysis of the investment in Stallward, Inc., account follows:

	Description	Amount	Interest Acquired
January 1, 2017	Investment	$325,000	70%
September 30, 2017	Investment	105,000	20%
Total.		$430,000	90%
December 31, 2017	90% of Stallward income for 2017	43,200	
December 31, 2017	90% of Stallward dividends for 2017	(4,500)	
Total.		$468,700	

b. The net income of Stallward, Inc., for the nine months ended September 30, 2017, is $25,000.

c. The price paid by the parent on January 1, 2017, to achieve control is considered to be a bargain and will result in a gain (only for the parent).

d. On September 30, 2017, Away Company loans its subsidiary $100,000 on a 1-year, 12% note. Interest and principal are payable in quarterly installments beginning December 31, 2017. The December 31, 2017, payment is made by Stallward but is not received by Away. Away Company has no other notes receivable outstanding.

e. Stallward, Inc.'s sales principally are engineering services billed at cost plus 50%. During 2017, Away Company is billed for $40,000, of which $16,500 is treated as a deferred charge at December 31, 2017.

f. During the year, parent company sales to the subsidiary total $60,000, of which $10,000 remains in the inventory of Stallward, Inc., at December 31, 2017.

g. In 2017, Away constructs certain tools at a cost of $15,000 and sells them to Stallward, Inc., for $25,000. Stallward, Inc., depreciates such tools using the straight-line method over a 5-year life. One-half year's depreciation is taken in the year of acquisition.

Required ▶ ▶ ▶ ▶ ▶   Prepare the worksheet necessary to produce the consolidated financial statements of Away Company and its subsidiary for the year ended December 31, 2017. Include the determination and distribution of excess and income distribution schedules.

(AICPA adapted)

Problem 7-4 *(LO 3)* **Sale of partial, then balance of interest.** On January 1, 2013, Carlos Corporation purchases 90% (18,000 shares) of the outstanding common stock of Dower Company for $504,000. Just prior to Carlos Corporation's purchase, Dower Company has the following stockholders' equity:

Common stock ($5 par)	$100,000
Paid-in capital in excess of par	300,000
Retained earnings	100,000
Total stockholders' equity	$500,000

At this time, Dower Company's book values approximate fair values except for buildings with a 20-year life.

On January 1, 2017, Dower Company's retained earnings balance amounts to $200,000. No changes have taken place in the paid-in capital in excess of par accounts since the original sale of common stock on July 10, 2010.

On July 1, 2017, Carlos Corporation sells 2,000 of its Dower Company shares to Tanner Corporation for $100,000. At the time of this sale, Carlos has no intention of selling the balance of its holding in Dower Company.

In an unexpected move on December 31, 2017, Carlos Corporation sells its remaining 80% interest in Dower Company to Tanner Corporation for $540,000.

Dower Company's reported income and dividends for 2017 are as follows:

	Income	Dividends
January 1, 2017–July 1, 2017	$30,000	$0.50/share
July 1, 2017–December 31, 2017	40,000	0.50/share

Required ▶ ▶ ▶ ▶ ▶   Prepare the determination and distribution of excess schedule for Carlos Corporation's purchase of Dower Company common stock on January 1, 2013. Then, prepare all the entries on Carlos's books needed to reflect the changes in its investment account from January 1, 2017, to December 31, 2017. (Assume Carlos uses the cost method to report its investment in Dower Company.)

Problem 7-5 *(LO 2, 3, 4)* **Analysis of block acquisitions, sale of interest, preferred stock.** The information shown on page 425 is available regarding the investments of Billings Corporation in Channel Company for the years 2011–2015.

Date	Transaction	Interest	Price
January 1, 2011	Purchased common	10%	$ 25,000
January 1, 2012	Purchased preferred	60	30,000
January 1, 2013	Purchased common	50	140,000
January 1, 2015	Purchased common	20	60,000
December 31, 2015	Sold common	10	(35,000)

The stockholders' equity section of Channel Company's balance sheet has not changed since the January 1, 2010, original sale of preferred stock to the public, except for the balance in the retained earnings account. The stockholders' equity as of January 1, 2013, is as follows:

6% Cumulative preferred stock ($50 par, liquidation value equals par value)	$ 50,000
Common stock ($10 par)...	100,000
Paid-in capital in excess of par	20,000
Retained earnings	103,000
Total stockholders' equity..	$273,000

Other relevant facts are as follows:

a. On January 1, 2011, Channel has a $60,000 retained earnings balance and there are no dividends in arrears on the preferred stock.
b. Any excess of cost over book value on the investment in common stock is viewed as goodwill.
c. The 10% interest sold on January 1, 2016, is the interest purchased on January 1, 2011.
d. Channel Company income and dividends are as follows for 2011–2015:

	Net Income	Preferred Dividends	Common Dividends
2011.......................	$25,000	$3,000	None
2012.......................	30,000	3,000	$6,000
2013.......................	30,000	3,000	5,000
2014.......................	25,000	None	None
2015.......................	20,000	None	None

Billings's investment account balances for its interests in Channel Company are calculated as follows on December 31, 2015:

Investment in preferred stock:

Original cost	$ 30,000
Plus dividends in arrears for 2014......................................	1,800
Balance, December 31, 2015..	$ 31,800

Investment in common stock:

January 1, 2011, purchase...	$ 25,000
January 1, 2013, purchase...	140,000
2013 Channel income ($30,000 × 60%)	18,000
2013 Channel dividends ($5,000 × 60%)...............................	(3,000)
2014 Channel income ($25,000 × 60%)	15,000
January 1, 2015 purchase	60,000
2015 Channel income ($20,000 × 80%)	16,000
December 31, 2015, sale..	(35,000)
Balance, December 31, 2015..	$236,000

Assume the investment accounts are to be properly maintained under the simple equity ◀ ◀ ◀ ◀ ◀ **Required** method. Prepare all necessary correcting entries on the books of Billings Corporation as of

January 1, 2016. (Assume nominal accounts are open.) All supporting computations and schedules should be in good form.

Problem 7-6 *(LO 4)* **Worksheet, preferred stock, fixed asset sale.** Marsha Corporation purchases an 80% interest in the common stock of Transam Corporation on December 31, 2013, for $720,000, when Transam has the following condensed balance sheet:

Assets		Liabilities and Stockholders' Equity	
Current assets	$ 500,000	Liabilities	$ 600,000
Land.	100,000	Preferred stock (8% cumulative,	
		$100 par)	100,000
Building (net)	400,000	Common stock ($20 par).	750,000
Equipment (net)	500,000	Retained earnings	50,000
Total assets.	$1,500,000	Total liabilities and equity	$1,500,000

On the December 31, 2013, purchase date, the dividends on the preferred stock are two years in arrears. Also on this date, the book values of Transam's assets approximate fair values, except for the building which is undervalued by $28,000 and has a 20-year remaining life. Any remaining excess is considered to be goodwill.

For 2014–2016, earnings and dividends for Transam Corporation are as follows:

	Income	Preferred Dividends	Common Dividends
2014.	$40,000		
2015.	50,000	$16,000	
2016.	80,000	24,000	$26,750

The following trial balances of the two companies are prepared on December 31, 2016:

	Marsha Corporation	Transam Corporation
Current Assets	806,400	463,250
Investment in Transam Corporation.	720,000	
Land.	400,000	210,000
Building	950,000	500,000
Accumulated Depreciation—Building.	(200,000)	(160,000)
Equipment	1,500,000	740,000
Accumulated Depreciation—Equipment.	(400,000)	(200,000)
Liabilities	(800,000)	(550,000)
Preferred Stock, 8%.		(100,000)
Common Stock ($20 par)	(2,000,000)	(750,000)
Retained Earnings, January 1, 2016.	(860,000)	(124,000)
Sales	(2,100,000)	(1,000,000)
Subsidiary Dividend Income	(21,400)	
Cost of Goods Sold	1,155,000	600,000
Other Expenses	650,000	320,000
Dividends Declared.	200,000	50,750
Totals	0	0

On January 1, 2015, Marsha sells production equipment to Transam for $55,000 with a 5-year remaining life. Marsha's original cost is $80,000, and accumulated depreciation on the date sold is $50,000.

Required ▶ ▶ ▶ ▶ ▶   Prepare the worksheet necessary to produce the consolidated financial statements of Marsha Corporation and its subsidiary as of December 31, 2016. Include the determination and distribution of excess and income distribution schedules.

Problem 7-7 *(LO 4)* **Worksheet, two subsidiaries, preferred stock, intercompany merchandise and fixed assets, bonds.** The following information pertains to Titan Corporation and its two subsidiaries, Boat Corporation and Engine Corporation:

a. The three corporations are all in the same industry and their operations are homogeneous. Titan Corporation exercises control over the boards of directors of Boat Corporation and Engine Corporation and has installed new principal officers in both.

b. Boat Corporation has a retained earnings balance of $92,000 at January 1, 2017, and has income of $15,000 for the first three months of 2017 and $20,000 for the first six months of 2018.

c. Titan Corporation acquires 250 shares of fully participating Engine preferred stock for $7,000 and 14,000 shares of Engine common stock for $196,000 on January 2, 2018. Engine Corporation has a net income of $20,000 in 2018 and does not declare any dividends.

d. Engine Corporation's inventory includes $22,400 of merchandise acquired from Boat Corporation subsequent to July 2018, for which no payment has been made. Boat Corporation marks up the merchandise 40% on cost.

e. Titan Corporation acquires in the open market twenty-five $1,000, 6% bonds of Boat Corporation for $21,400 on January 1, 2015. Boat Corporation bonds mature December 31, 2020. Interest is paid each June 30 and December 31. Straight-line amortization is allowed on the basis of materiality.

f. The 2018 year-end balance in the investment in Boat Corporation stock account is composed of the items shown in the following schedule:

Date	Description	Amount
April 1, 2017	Cost of 5,000 shares of Boat Corporation stock	$ 71,400
December 31, 2017	20% of the dividends declared in December 2017 by Boat Corporation	(9,000)
December 31, 2017	20% × 2017 annual net income of $60,000 for Boat Corporation.	12,000
July 1, 2018	Cost of 15,000 shares of Boat Corporation	226,200
December 31, 2018	80% of the dividends declared in December 2018 by Boat Corporation	(24,000)
December 31, 2018	80% of the 2018 June–December net income of Boat Corporation.	16,000
December 31, 2018	Total.	$292,600

g. Titan Corporation does not properly adjust the prior 20% investment when it acquires the 60% interest on July 1, 2018.

h. The December 31, 2018, trial balances for the three corporations appear as follows:

	Titan Corporation	Boat Corporation	Engine Corporation
Cash	100,000	87,000	95,000
Accounts Receivable	158,200	210,000	105,000
Inventories	290,000	90,000	115,000
Advance to Boat Corporation	17,000		
Dividends Receivable	24,000		
Property, Plant, and Equipment.	777,600	325,000	470,000
Accumulated Depreciation	(180,000)	(55,000)	(160,000)
Investment in Boat Corporation:			
6% Bonds.	23,800		
Common Stock.	292,600*		
Investment in Engine Corporation:			
Preferred Stock.	7,400		

(continued)

	Titan Corporation	Boat Corporation	Engine Corporation
Common Stock..........................	207,200		
Notes Payable........................	(45,000)	(14,000)	(44,000)
Accounts Payable	(170,000)	(96,000)	(86,000)
Bonds Payable........................	(285,000)	(150,000)	(125,000)
Discount on Bonds Payable	8,000		
Dividends Payable.....................	(22,000)	(30,000)	
Preferred Stock ($20 par)	(400,000)		(50,000)
Common Stock ($10 par)	(600,000)	(250,000)	(200,000)
Retained Earnings, January 1, 2018........	(154,600)	(107,000)	(100,000)
Sales	(1,050,000)	(500,000)	(650,000)
Other Revenue........................	(2,100)		
Subsidiary Income:			
Common Stock—Boat	(16,000)		
Preferred Stock—Engine	(400)		
Common Stock—Engine	(11,200)		
Cost of Goods Sold	650,000	300,000	400,000
Other Expenses	358,500	160,000	230,000
Dividends Declared....................	22,000	30,000	
Totals	0	0	0

*Correction required.

Required ▶ ▶ ▶ ▶ ▶

1. Prepare any adjustment needed to the investment account as a result of the July 1, 2018, acquisition.

2. Prepare the worksheet necessary to produce the consolidated financial statements of Titan Corporation and its subsidiaries as of December 31, 2018. Correct the trial balances prior to consolidating. Consolidated retained earnings should be allocated to Titan Corporation, and the NCIs should be shown separately in the Consolidated Balance Sheet column. All supporting computations and schedules should be in good form.

(AICPA adapted)

Problem 7-8 *(LO 4)* **Worksheet, preferred stock, intercompany fixed assets and merchandise, sale of interest.** On January 1, 2017, Black Jack Corporation purchases all of the preferred stock and 60% of the common stock of Zeppo Company for $56,000 and $111,000, respectively. Immediately prior to the purchases, Zeppo Company has the following stockholders' equity:

8% Cumulative preferred stock ($100 par, two years in arrears)	$ 50,000
Common stock ($10 par)...	100,000
Paid-in capital in excess of par (common stock)................................	20,000
Retained earnings	30,000
Total stockholders' equity.......................................	$200,000

The December 31, 2018, trial balances of the two companies are as follows:

	Black Jack Corporation	Zeppo Company
Cash	30,400	10,000
Accounts Receivable (net)	80,000	76,000
Inventories.................................	230,000	44,000
Other Current Assets	20,000	8,000

	Black Jack Corporation	Zeppo Company
Property, Plant, and Equipment	1,450,000	122,000
Accumulated Depreciation	(420,000)	(25,000)
Investment in Zeppo Preferred Stock	56,000	
Investment in Zeppo Common Stock	121,200	
Liabilities	(350,000)	(18,000)
Common Stock—Black Jack	(1,000,000)	
Retained Earnings—Black Jack	(195,000)	
Preferred Stock—Zeppo ($100 par)		(50,000)
Common Stock—Zeppo		(100,000)
Paid-In Capital in Excess of Par—Zeppo		(20,000)
Retained Earnings—Zeppo		(41,000)
Sales	(420,000)	(96,000)
Cost of Goods Sold	300,000	60,000
Other Expenses	80,000	26,000
Dividends Declared	25,000	4,000
Subsidiary Income—Preferred	(4,000)	
Subsidiary Income—Common	(3,600)	
Totals	0	0

Additional information is as follows:

a. Any excess of cost over book value on the investment in common stock is attributed to equipment with an 8-year life.
b. On December 30, 2017, and December 30, 2018, Zeppo Company pays preferred stock dividends of $8 per share.
c. Zeppo Company has a net income of $15,000 in 2017 and $10,000 for 2018.
d. Zeppo Company sells a piece of equipment with a book value of $8,000 to Black Jack Corporation for $13,000 on January 2, 2017. The machine has an estimated future life of five years, and straight-line depreciation is being used.
e. During 2018, Black Jack sells $20,000 of goods to Zeppo for cost plus 40%. Zeppo has $2,800 of such purchases in its beginning inventory and $7,000 of such purchases in its ending inventory. Zeppo owes Black Jack $2,000 for purchases at year-end. During 2018, Zeppo sells $8,000 of goods to Black Jack at cost plus 60%. Of these goods, $1,200 are in Black Jack's beginning inventory, and $1,600 of such goods are in its ending inventory. Black Jack owes Zeppo $6,000 for purchases at year-end.
f. On January 1, 2019, Black Jack Corporation sells its 60% interest in Zeppo Company common stock for $130,000.

1. Prepare the worksheet necessary to produce the consolidated financial statements of Black Jack Corporation and its subsidiary for the year ended December 31, 2018. Include the determination and distribution of excess and income distribution schedules. ◄ ◄ ◄ ◄ ◄ **Required**
2. Prepare the entries on Black Jack Corporation's books to reflect the sale of its investment in Zeppo Company common stock on January 1, 2019.

APPENDIX PROBLEMS

Problem 7A-1 *(LO 5)* **Balance sheet worksheet, blocks, control with first, inventory, fixed asset sales.** The December 31, 2019, post-closing trial balances of Marley Corporation and its subsidiary, Foster Corporation, are as follows:

	Marley Corporation	Foster Corporation
Cash	167,250	101,000
Accounts Receivable	170,450	72,000
Notes Receivable	87,500	28,000
Dividends Receivable	36,000	
Inventories	122,000	68,000
Property, Plant, and Equipment	487,000	252,000
Accumulated Depreciation	(117,000)	(64,000)
Investment in Foster Corporation	248,800	
Accounts Payable	(222,000)	(76,000)
Notes Payable	(79,000)	(89,000)
Dividends Payable		(40,000)
Common Stock ($10 par)	(400,000)	(100,000)
Retained Earnings	(501,000)	(152,000)
Totals	0	0

The following additional information is available:

a. Marley initially acquires 60% of the outstanding common stock of Foster in 2017. There is no difference between the cost and book value of the net assets acquired. As of December 31, 2019, the percentage owned is 90%. An analysis of the investment in Foster Corporation account is as follows:

Date	Description	Amount
December 31, 2017	Acquired 6,000 shares	$ 70,800
December 31, 2018	60% of 2018 net income of $78,000	46,800
September 1, 2019	Acquired 3,000 shares	100,000
December 31, 2019	Subsidiary income for 2019	67,200*
December 31, 2019	90% of dividends declared	(36,000)
	Investment balance, December 31, 2019	$248,800

*Subsidiary income for 2019:

60% × $96,000	$57,600
30% × $96,000 × 33½%	9,600
Total	$67,200

Foster net income is earned ratably during the year.

On December 15, 2019, Foster declares a cash dividend of $4 per share of common stock, payable to shareholders on January 7, 2020.

b. During 2019, Marley sells merchandise to Foster. Marley has a 25% gross profit, and the sale is made at $80,000. Foster's inventory at December 31, 2019, includes merchandise purchased from Marley for $40,000.

c. On October 1, 2019, Marley sells excess equipment to Foster for $45,000. Data relating to this equipment are as follows:

Book value on Marley's records	$36,000
Method of depreciation...	Straight-line
Estimated remaining life on October 1, 2019............................	10 years

d. Near the end of 2019, Foster reduces the balance of its intercompany account payable to zero by transferring $8,000 to Marley. This payment is still in transit on December 31, 2019.

    Prepare the worksheet necessary to produce the consolidated balance sheet of Marley Corporation and its subsidiary as of December 31, 2019. Include an analysis for Marley's purchase of Foster common stock on September 1, 2019. ◀ ◀ ◀ ◀ ◀ **Required**

(AICPA adapted)

Problem 7A-2 *(LO 5)* **Balance sheet worksheet, mid-year purchase, intercompany bonds and inventory.** Book, Inc., acquires all of the outstanding $25 par common stock of Cray, Inc., on June 30, 2014, in exchange for 40,000 shares of its $25 par common stock. On June 30, 2014, Book, Inc., common stock closes at $65 per share on a national stock exchange. Any excess of cost over book value is attributed to goodwill. Both corporations continue to operate as separate businesses, maintaining separate accounting records with years ending December 31.

    Additional information is as follows:

a. Book, Inc., uses the simple equity method to account for its investment in Cray.
b. On June 30, 2014, Cray pays cash dividends of $4 per share on its common stock.
c. On December 10, 2014, Book pays a cash dividend totaling $256,000 on its common stock.
d. On June 30, 2014, immediately before the combination, the stockholders' equities are as follows:

	Book, Inc.	Cray, Inc.
Common stock......................................	$2,200,000	$1,000,000
Additional paid-in capital in excess of par	1,660,000	190,000
Retained earnings	3,036,000	980,000
Totals	$6,896,000	$2,170,000

e. Cray's long-term debt consists of 10-year, 10% bonds issued at face value on March 31, 2011. Interest is payable semiannually on March 31 and September 30. Book purchases Cray's bonds at the face value of $320,000 in 2011, and there is no change in ownership.
f. During October 2014, Book sells merchandise to Cray at a total invoice price of $720,000, which includes a profit of $180,000. At December 31, 2014, one-half of the merchandise remains in Cray's inventory, and Cray has not paid Book for the merchandise purchased.
g. The 2014 net income amounts per the separate books of Book and Cray are $890,000 (exclusive of equity in Cray earnings) and $580,000 ($320,000 in the first six months and $260,000 in the second six months), respectively.
h. The retained earnings balances at December 31, 2013, are $2,506,000 and $820,000 for Book and Cray, respectively.
i. On December 31, 2014, the companies have the following post-closing trial balances:

	Book, Inc.	Cray, Inc.
Cash	825,000	330,000
Accounts and Other Current Receivables	2,140,000	835,000
Inventories.......................................	2,310,000	1,045,000
Land...	650,000	300,000
Depreciable Assets (net)	4,575,000	1,980,000
Investment in Cray, Inc..........................	2,860,000	
Long-Term Investments and Other Assets....................	865,000	385,000
Accounts Payable and Other Current Liabilities	(2,465,000)	(1,145,000)
Long-Term Debt	(1,900,000)	(1,300,000)

(continued)

	Book, Inc.	Cray, Inc.
Common Stock ($25 par)	(3,200,000)	(1,000,000)
Additional Paid-In Capital in Excess of Par	(3,260,000)	(190,000)
Retained Earnings	(3,400,000)	(1,240,000)
Totals	0	0

Required ▶ ▶ ▶ ▶ ▶

1. Prepare the worksheet necessary to produce the consolidated balance sheet of Book, Inc., and its subsidiary for the year ended December 31, 2014. Include a determination and distribution of excess schedule.
2. Prepare the formal consolidated statement of retained earnings for December 31, 2014.

Problem 7A-3 *(LO 5)* **Balance sheet worksheet, intercompany inventory, bonds and capital lease.** On January 1, 2015, Press Company acquires 90% of the common stock of Soap Company for $324,000. On this date, Soap has total owners' equity of $270,000, including retained earnings of $100,000.

On January 1, 2015, any excess of cost over book value is attributable to the undervaluation of land, building, and goodwill. Land is worth $20,000 more than cost. Building is worth $40,000 more than book value. It has a remaining useful life of 20 years and is depreciated using the straight-line method.

During 2015 and 2016, Press has appropriately accounted for its investment in Soap using the simple equity method.

During 2016, Soap sells merchandise to Press for $40,000, of which $15,000 is held by Press on December 31, 2016. Soap's usual gross profit on affiliated sales is 40%. On December 31, 2016, Press still owes Soap $8,000 for merchandise acquired in December.

On October 1, 2014, Soap sells $100,000 par value of 10-year, 10% bonds for $102,000. The bonds pay interest semiannually on April 1 and October 1. Straight-line amortization is used. On October 2, 2015, Press repurchases $60,000 par value of the bonds for $59,100. Straight-line amortization is used.

On January 1, 2016, Press purchases equipment for $111,332 and immediately leases the equipment to Soap on a 3-year lease. The minimum lease payments of $40,000 are to be made annually on January 1, beginning immediately, for a total of three payments. The implicit interest rate is 8%. The useful life of the equipment is three years. The lease has been capitalized by both companies. Soap is depreciating the equipment using the straight-line method and assuming a salvage value of $6,332. A lease amortization schedule, applicable to both companies, follows:

Carrying Value on	Carrying Value	Interest Rate	Interest	Payment	Principal Reduction
January 1, 2015	111,332				
	(40,000)				
January 1, 2016	71,332	8%	$5,707	$40,000	$34,293
	(34,293)				
January 1, 2017	37,039	8%	2,961*	40,000	37,039
	(37,039)				
January 1, 2018	0				

*Adjusted for rounding error.

The balance sheet for the companies on December 31, 2016, is as follows:

Assets	Press Company	Soap Company
Accounts receivable	$ 65,000	$ 50,000
Bond interest receivable	1,500	
Minimum lease payments receivable	80,000	
Unearned interest income	(2,961)	
Inventory	86,000	80,000
Other current assets	60,236	183,668
Investment in Soap Company	351,000	
Investment in Soap bonds	59,225	
Land	60,000	30,000
Building and equipment	300,000	230,000
Accumulated depreciation	(100,000)	(50,000)
Equipment under capital lease		111,332
Accumulated depreciated equipment under lease		(35,000)
Totals	$ 960,000	$600,000

Liabilities and Equity	Press Company	Soap Company
Accounts payable	$ 78,000	$ 70,000
Bond interest payable		2,500
Lease interest payable		5,707
Other current liabilities	57,000	48,911
Lease obligation payable		71,332
Bonds payable	150,000	100,000
Premium on bonds		1,550
Common stock—Press	200,000	
Other paid-in capital in excess of par—Press	150,000	
Retained earnings—Press	325,000	
Common stock—Soap		100,000
Other paid-in capital in excess of par—Soap		70,000
Retained earnings—Soap		130,000
Totals	$960,000	$600,000

Complete the worksheet for a consolidated balance sheet as of December 31, 2016. Include ◄◄◄◄◄ **Required** a determination and distribution of excess schedule. Round all computations to the nearest dollar.

Chapter 8

Subsidiary Equity Transactions, Indirect Subsidiary Ownership, and Subsidiary Ownership of Parent Shares

CHAPTER

Learning Objectives

When you have completed this chapter, you should be able to

1. Explain the effect of subsidiary stock dividends on elimination procedures.

2. Account for the effect of the subsidiary's sale of its own common stock on the parent's investment in the subsidiary.

3. Account for the effect of subsidiary treasury stock transactions on the parent's investment in the subsidiary.

4. Demonstrate accounting procedures for multilevel holdings.

5. Demonstrate an understanding of the alternatives used for accounting for investments in the parent company owned by the subsidiary.

This chapter is concerned with subsidiary equity transactions and complicated parent ownership arrangements that affect the recording and consolidations of the parent's investment in a subsidiary. First, we will consider the impact of subsidiary equity transactions on the parent's recording and consolidation of the investment in the subsidiary. We will consider the subsidiary declaration of stock dividends, subsidiary sales of additional shares of stock, and the subsidiary repurchase of its outstanding shares.

Second, this chapter will deal with more complex ownership structures. Accounting procedures will be developed for indirect holdings and ownership of parent shares by a subsidiary. Indirect holdings are situations where a parent holds a controlling interest in a subsidiary and the subsidiary is, in turn, a parent of another company. A mutual holding exists when the subsidiary also owns voting common stock of the parent company.

SUBSIDIARY STOCK DIVIDENDS

A subsidiary may issue stock dividends to convert retained earnings into paid-in capital. The minimum amount to be removed from retained earnings is the par value or stated value of the shares distributed. However, according to accounting principles, when the distribution does not exceed 20% to 25% of the previously outstanding shares, an amount equal to the fair value of the shares should be removed from retained earnings and transferred to paid-in capital in excess of par. The recording of stock dividends at fair value is defended by FASB ASC 505-20-05-2:

> Many recipients of stock dividends look upon them as distributions of corporate earnings, and usually in an amount equivalent to the fair value of the additional shares received. If the issuances of stock dividends are so small in comparison with the shares previously outstanding,

1

OBJECTIVE

Explain the effect of subsidiary stock dividends on elimination procedures.

such issuances generally do not have any apparent effect on the share market price and, consequently, the market value of the shares previously held remains substantially unchanged.

Accounting theory, however, is not consistent when it comes to recording the receipt of dividends by an investor. Even though the false impression of the "typical" investor is sufficient reason to allow the issuing corporation to record the market value of the shares distributed, the investor is not permitted to do likewise. In fact, the investor must not record income when stock dividends are received but must acknowledge the true impact of the transaction, which is that nothing of substance has been given or received. Thus, the investor merely makes a memo entry indicating that the cost of the original investment now is allocated to a greater number of shares. The revised number of shares is important in computing cost per share if there is a subsequent partial sale of the investment.

To review the recording of a stock dividend and to provide a basis for worksheets, assume that Company P acquired an 80% interest in Company S on January 1, 2015, at which time the following determination and distribution of excess schedule was prepared:

Determination and Distribution of Excess Schedule

	Company Implied Fair Value	Parent Price (80%)	NCI Value (20%)
Fair value of subsidiary	$250,000	$200,000	$ 50,000
Less book value of interest acquired:			
Common stock	$100,000		
Retained earnings	80,000		
Total equity.	$180,000	$180,000	$180,000
Interest acquired		80%	20%
Book value.		$144,000	$ 36,000
Excess of fair value over book value	$ 70,000	$ 56,000	$ 14,000

Adjustment of identifiable accounts:

	Adjustment	Life	Amortization per Year	Worksheet Key
Equipment	$ 70,000	10	$ 7,000	**debit D**

On January 2, 2017, Company S declared and distributed a 10% stock dividend. Prior to declaration of the dividend, its stockholders' equity appeared as follows:

Common stock ($10 par).	$100,000
Retained earnings	120,000
Total stockholders' equity.	$220,000

In the following entry to record the stock dividend, Company S acknowledged the $25 fair value of the 1,000 shares distributed:

Retained Earnings (or Stock Dividends Declared) ($25 fair value × 1,000 shares) . . .	25,000	
Common Stock ($10 par × 1,000 shares)		10,000
Additional Paid-In Capital in Excess of Par from Stock Dividend (1,000 shares × $15 excess over par)		15,000

Parent Using the Simple Equity Method

Continuing the example, on January 1, 2017 (prior to the dividend), Company P has a simple-equity-adjusted balance of $232,000 in its investment in Company S account, derived as shown on page 437.

Original cost		$200,000
Share of undistributed income:		
Company S retained earnings, January 1, 2017	$120,000	
Company S retained earnings, January 1, 2015	80,000	
Increase in retained earnings.	$ 40,000	
Ownership interest.	× 80%	32,000
Simple-equity-adjusted balance, January 1, 2017		$232,000

During 2017, Company S earned $20,000 and made no other dividend declarations. Company P would make the following entries during 2017, under the simple equity method:

Receipt of stock dividend:

Jan. 2, 2017   Memo: Investment in Company S now includes 800 added shares for a total of 8,800 shares. The parent's interest remains at 80%.

Recording of equity income:

Dec. 31, 2017   Investment in Company S 16,000
                 Subsidiary Income 16,000
                 To record the 80% interest in Company S
                 $20,000 reported net income for 2017.

The partial worksheet below lists the investment in Company S account at the December 31, 2017, simple-equity-adjusted cost of $248,000. Note that the partial worksheet includes the redistributed capital structure of Company S, which resulted from the stock dividend. It should be clear that the complications arising from stock dividends pertain primarily to their recording by the separate affiliated firms. There is only a minimal effect on the consolidated worksheet.

	Trial Balance		Eliminations & Adjustments			
	Company P	Company S	Dr.		Cr.	
Investment in Company S	248,000				(CY)	16,000
					(EL)	176,000
					(D)	56,000
Equipment			(D)	70,000	(A)	21,000
Common Stock—Company P	(500,000)					
Retained Earnings—Company P	(420,000)		(A)	11,200		
Common Stock ($10 par)—Company S		(110,000)	(EL)	88,000		
Additional Paid-In Capital in Excess of Par from Stock						
Dividend—Company S		(15,000)	(EL)	12,000		
Retained Earnings—Company S (reduced $25,000 for stock dividend)		(95,000)	(EL)	76,000	(NCI)	14,000
			(A)	2,800		
Subsidiary Income	(16,000)		(CY)	16,000		
Expenses	30,000	18,000	(A)	7,000		

Eliminations and Adjustments:

(CY)   Eliminate the parent's entry recording its share of subsidiary income for the current year. There is no complication caused by the stock dividend since it does not constitute income to Company P.

(EL)   Eliminate 80% of Company S equity balances as restructured by the stock dividend. If the subsidiary recorded the stock dividend with a debit to Stock Dividends Declared, 80% of that account would be eliminated in this step.

(D)/NCI   Distribute the excess cost and NCI adjustment to the equipment account as required by the determination and distribution of excess schedule.

(A)   Depreciate the equipment for three years. Depreciation for the two prior years reduces the controlling and noncontrolling interest in retained earnings (80%/20%), while the current-year depreciation reduces current consolidated net income.

Parent Using the Sophisticated Equity Method

Using the sophisticated equity method, the parent would have a balance in its investment in Company S account of $220,800, derived as follows:

Original cost		$200,000
Share of undistributed income:		
Company S retained earnings, January 1, 2017	$120,000	
Company S retained earnings, January 1, 2015	80,000	
Increase in retained earnings.	$ 40,000	
Ownership interest.	× 80%	32,000
Equipment depreciation, 2 years × 80% × $7,000.		(11,200)
Sophisticated-equity-adjusted balance, January 1, 2017.		$220,800

During 2017, Company P would make the same memo entry as under the simple equity method to record the stock dividend. The following entry would be made to record equity income for 2017:

Dec. 31, 2017	Investment in Company S	10,400	
	Subsidiary Income		10,400
	To record the 80% interest in Company S reported		
	income for 2017 less 80% × $7,000 equipment		
	depreciation.		

The following partial worksheet would apply to the investment maintained under the sophisticated equity method:

	Trial Balance		Eliminations & Adjustments			
	Company P	Company S	Dr.		Cr.	
Investment in Company S	231,200				(CY)	10,400
					(EL)	176,000
					(D)	44,800
Equipment			(D)	56,000	(A)	7,000
Common Stock—Company P	(500,000)					
Retained Earnings, January 1, 2017—Company P	(408,800)					
Common Stock ($10 par)—Company S		(110,000)	(EL)	88,000		
Additional Paid-In Capital in Excess of Par from Stock						
Dividend—Company S		(15,000)	(EL)	12,000		
Retained Earnings (reduced $25,000 for stock dividend), January 1, 2017—Company S		(95,000)	(EL)	76,000	(NCI)	11,200
Subsidiary Income	(10,400)		(CY)	10,400		
Expenses	30,000	18,000	(A)	7,000		

Eliminations and Adjustments:

(CY)   Eliminate the parent's entry recording its share of subsidiary income for the current year. There is no complication caused by the stock dividend since it does not constitute income to Company P.

(EL)   Eliminate 80% of Company S equity balances as restructured by the stock dividend. If the subsidiary recorded the stock dividend with a debit to Stock Dividends Declared, 80% of that account would be eliminated in this entry.

(D)/(NCI)   Distribute the excess cost and NCI adjustment to the equipment account as required by the determination and distribution of excess schedule. Since the parent is amortizing the excess on its books, this is the remaining balance at the start of the year ($70,000 less two years' amortization at $7,000 per year).

(A)   Depreciate the equipment for the current year. The parent retained earnings is already adjusted for prior-year depreciation. The NCI adjustment is the net amount remaining at the start of the year; no depreciation for prior years is needed.

Note the following special features:

1. The investment is at the sophisticated equity balance of $231,200 ($220,800 balance on January 1, 2017, plus $10,400 equity income for 2017).

2. The retained earnings of Company P are $408,800. This is $11,200 less than under the simple equity method since there is $5,600 per year of equipment depreciation subtracted for 2015 and 2016.

3. Subsidiary income is the sophisticated equity amount of $10,400.

4. Only the equipment adjustment remaining on January 1, 2017, is entered when distributing the excess in entry (D). Recall that the prior years' depreciation has already reduced the investment account and the parent retained earnings. Note that only the current-year depreciation is made in entry (A).

Parent Using the Cost Method

In the preceding example, if the parent, Company P, had used the cost method to record its investment in Company S, no adjustments would have been made to the investment account. The investment in Company S still would be carried at its original cost of $200,000 on the December 31, 2017, worksheet.

The declaration of a stock dividend by a subsidiary requires a more difficult process for the conversion of the parent's investment account from a cost to a simple-equity basis. The conversion must reflect all the changes in subsidiary retained earnings since acquisition, including the retained earnings transferred to paid-in capital in excess of par as a result of a stock dividend. The correct simple-equity conversion would be made as follows for the preceding example:

Retained earnings, January 2, 2017 (after stock dividend)	$95,000
Retained earnings, January 1, 2015	80,000
Change in retained earnings balance	$15,000
Retained earnings transferred to paid-in capital in excess of par ($25 × 1,000 shares)	
as a result of stock dividend	25,000
Total change in retained earnings	$40,000
Ownership interest	× 80%
Simple-equity conversion	$32,000

A faster approach to the simple-equity conversion is to consider the change in total subsidiary stockholders' equity available to common stockholders as follows:

Subsidiary total equity, January 1, 2017	$220,000
Subsidiary total equity, January 1, 2015	180,000
Net change	$ 40,000
Ownership interest	× 80%
Simple-equity conversion	$ 32,000

Normally, a parent will maintain a permanent file with the needed information for this adjustment. This faster method, however, could be useful in later years if facts surrounding the stock dividend were not readily available. The faster procedure will work well, provided in the interim periods there have been no other changes in subsidiary paid-in capital in excess of par, such as a subsidiary sale or retirement of its shares.

The $32,000 simple-equity conversion would be the first step on a worksheet when the cost method is used for the subsidiary investment. This step converts the investment in subsidiary account to its simple-equity balance at the beginning of 2017. The entry would be as follows:

Investment in Company S	32,000	
Retained Earnings, January 1, 2017		32,000

The remaining worksheet procedures would not include the elimination of the current year's subsidiary income, but otherwise it would be identical to entries (D), (NCI), (EL), and (A) of the partial worksheet on page 438.

REFLECTION

- The receipt of subsidiary stock dividends requires no entry by the parent.
- Care needs to be taken when converting from cost to equity. The adjustment for the increase in equity includes amounts moved from retained earnings to paid-in capital in excess of par as a result of subsidiary stock dividends.

2

OBJECTIVE

Account for the effect of the subsidiary's sale of its own common stock on the parent's investment in the subsidiary.

SUBSIDIARY SALE OF ITS OWN COMMON STOCK

In virtually all cases where the subsidiary issues additional shares of stock, the transaction impacts the parent's investment in the subsidiary account. Even though the parent purchases none of the newly issued shares, its share of subsidiary equity has changed, and consolidation procedures must acknowledge the change. When the parent purchases some of the newly issued shares, the adjustment needed depends on whether the ownership interest after the purchase is equal to, less than, or greater than the ownership interest prior to the purchase. The adjustments resulting from a subsidiary stock sale are made at the time of the sale when the equity method is used, or they are part of the cost-to-equity conversion process when the cost method is used. In all cases, a comparison is made of the parent's position before and after the subsidiary transaction occurs. Thus, the term that will be used is "before and after" analysis.

Sale of Subsidiary Stock to Noncontrolling Shareholders

A parent may allow a subsidiary to sell additional shares of stock in order to raise additional equity. A sale of stock by the subsidiary to new or existing noncontrolling shareholders results in an increase in the total subsidiary stockholders' equity against which the controlling interest has a claim. However, the effect of increasing the number of subsidiary shares in the hands of noncontrolling stockholders is to lower the controlling interest ownership percentage. Thus, the controlling ownership receives a smaller percentage of a larger subsidiary equity. The net effect on the value of the controlling interest depends on the price at which the shares are sold.

A change in the equity of the subsidiary is recorded as a capital transaction, and it never has an impact on income. In most cases, the subsidiary equity change would be recorded as a change in the paid-in capital in excess of par of the parent company (debit effect could impact retained earnings when no paid-in capital in excess of par exists).[1]

Parent Using the Equity Method. A parent company using either the simple or sophisticated equity method usually will need to make an adjustment to its investment account when its subsidiary sells additional shares of stock to NCI shareholders. To illustrate, assume Company P has a 90% interest in Company S. The interest was purchased on January 1, 2015, at which time the determination and distribution of excess schedule was prepared, as shown on page 441.

---

1 FASB ASC 810-10-45-23.

Determination and Distribution of Excess Schedule

	Company Implied Fair Value	Parent Price (90%)	NCI Value (10%)	
Fair value of subsidiary	$160,000	$144,000	$ 16,000	
Less book value of interest acquired:				
Common stock	$100,000			
Retained earnings	50,000			
Total equity.	$150,000	$150,000	$150,000	
Interest acquired		90%	10%	
Book value.		$135,000	$ 15,000	
Excess of fair value over book value	**$ 10,000**	$ 9,000	$ 1,000	

Adjustment of identifiable accounts:

	Adjustment	Life	Amortization per Year	Worksheet Key
Equipment	$ 10,000	10	$ 1,000	**debit D**

Assume that Company S will issue additional shares on January 1, 2018. The equity of Company S is based on the recorded equity amounts as adjusted by the fair value adjustments made on the acquisition date. That amount is calculated as follows:

Common stock ($10 par).	$100,000
Retained earnings, January 1, 2018.	140,000
Company S equity.	$240,000
Remaining fair value adjustment [$10,000 − (3 years × $1,000)]	7,000
Equity adjusted for fair value adjustment on acquisition date	$247,000

The "before and after" analysis will be applied to the following example. On January 1, 2018, 2,000 shares of previously unissued common stock are sold to the noncontrolling interest. As a result, the parent's interest is reduced to 75% ($9,000 ÷ $12,000). An analysis of the controlling interest before and after the sale of 2,000 new subsidiary shares to noncontrolling shareholders follows. The "before and after" analysis shows the three possibilities: shares sold at book value (Case 1), at more than book value (Case 2), and at less than book value (Case 3).

	Case 1 (sold at book value)	Case 2 (sold at price greater than book value)	Case 3 (sold at price less than book value)
Sale price per share.	$ 24.70	$ 30.00	$ 20.00
Company S shareholders' equity prior to sale			
Adjusted for fair value adjustments (see above)	$247,000	$247,000	$247,000
Add to common stock ($10 par × 2,000 shares)	20,000	20,000	20,000
Add to paid-in capital in excess of par	29,400	40,000	20,000
Company S shareholders' equity after the sale	$296,400	$307,000	$287,000
Controlling interest after the sale (75%).	$222,300	$230,250	$215,250
Controlling interest before the sale (90% × $247,000) .	222,300	222,300	222,300
Net increase (decrease) in controlling interest.	$ 0	$ 7,950	$ (7,050)

Based on the results of the three cases in the above table, it should be noted that no change in controlling interest occurs when a subsidiary sells new stock to noncontrolling shareholders at adjusted book value (as adjusted for fair value adjustments on acquisition date). An increase occurs when the stock is sold above adjusted book value, and a decrease results when the stock is sold below adjusted book value.

The parent would adjust its investment in subsidiary account to record the effect on controlling interest in each of the three cases as follows:

Case 1: Memo entry only to record a change from a 90% to a 75% interest.

Case 2: Investment in Company S   7,950
        Paid-In Capital in Excess of Par   7,950
        To record increase in ownership interest and change from 90%
        to 75% interest.

Case 3: Paid-In Capital in Excess of Par*   7,050
        Investment in Company S   7,050
        To record decrease in ownership interest. It is assumed that
        parent additional paid-in capital in excess of par exists to offset
        the decrease. Also record change from 90% to 75% interest.

*Or Retained Earnings if there is no paid-in capital in excess of par.

Note that when the equity method is used, these entries would be made directly on the books of the parent; they are not worksheet adjustments.

To illustrate the effect of Case 2 on consolidation, assume subsidiary income for 2018 was $40,000 and no dividends were declared. The investment account balance under the simple equity method would be determined as follows:

Original cost	$144,000
Simple-equity income adjustments (2015 through 2017, 90% × $90,000	
increase in retained earnings).	81,000
Increase from stock sale to NCI on January 1, 2018.	7,950
Simple-equity adjustment for 2018 subsidiary income (75% × $40,000 income)	30,000
Balance, December 31, 2018	$262,950

In the partial worksheet shown below, for the year ended December 31, 2018, the trial balances of Company P and Company S reflect the sale of 2,000 additional shares at $30 per share (Case 2).

	Trial Balance		Eliminations & Adjustments			
	Company P	Company S	Dr.		Cr.	
Investment in Company S (75%)	262,950				(CY)	30,000
					(EL)	225,000
					(D)	7,500
					(adj)	450
Equipment			(D)	10,000	(A)	4,000
Common Stock—Company P	(400,000)					
Paid-In Capital in Excess of Par—Company P	(7,950)					
Retained Earnings—Company P	(320,000)		(A)	2,250		
			(adj)	450		
Common Stock—Company S		(120,000)	(EL)	90,000		
Paid-In Capital in Excess of Par—Company S		(40,000)	(EL)	30,000		
Retained Earnings, January 1, 2018—Company S		(140,000)	(EL)	105,000	(NCI)	2,500
			(A)	750		
Subsidiary Income	(30,000)		(CY)	30,000		
Expenses	40,000	27,000	(A)	1,000		

Eliminations and Adjustments:

(CY)   Eliminate the parent's entry recording subsidiary income for the current year. The parent's share is now **75%** of the subsidiary undistributed net income. If the sale had occurred during the year, the old percentage of ownership would be applied to income earned prior to the sale date.

(EL)   Eliminate the parent's **75%** share of subsidiary equity balances at the beginning of the year against the investment account.

(D)/(NCI) Distribute to the equipment account the original excess of cost over book value and NCI adjustment, as required by the January 1, 2015, determination and distribution of excess schedule. The adjustment is now allocated 75%/25% to the investment account and to the NCI.

(A)   Depreciate equipment for the past three years and the current year. The prior-year amortizations are allocated 75%/ 25% to controlling and noncontrolling retained earnings.

(adj)   The "amortization adjustment" is to adjust parent retained earnings for the fact that the amortization in prior years was allocated 90% to the parent, as opposed to the current 75% allocation. It is calculated as (15% change × $1,000 annual depreciation × 3 years).

The consolidated worksheet may require the adjustment of both the controlling and non-controlling interests in beginning retained earnings for intercompany transactions originating in previous periods. When such adjustments are necessary, the current, not the original, ownership interest percentages are used.

Parent Using the Cost Method. A parent using the cost method records only dividends received from a subsidiary. Usually, no adjustment is made for any other changes in the subsidiary stockholders' equity, including changes caused by sales of subsidiary stock. As a result, the entry to convert from the cost method to the equity method on future worksheets must consider not only the equity adjustments for the subsidiary undistributed income but also adjustments in the parent's ownership interest caused by subsidiary stock sales. A parent using the cost method still would list the subsidiary investment at its original cost.

The partial worksheet on page 444 demonstrates the consolidation procedures needed for Case 2 when the cost method is used.

To review this process, the cost-to-simple-equity conversion amount for Case 2 is determined as it would apply to the December 31, 2018, worksheet.

Undistributed income:		
90% of change in retained earnings of Company S from		
January 1, 2015, to January 1, 2018 (90% × $90,000)		$81,000
Adjustment to paid-in capital in excess of par:		
Controlling interest in Company S equity subsequent to sale on		
January 1, 2018 (75% × $307,000).	$230,250	
Controlling interest in Company S equity prior to sale on		
January 1, 2018 (90% × $247,000).	222,300	
Net increase in paid-in capital in excess of par		7,950
Total increase in investment account		$88,950

This adjustment becomes (CV) in the cost method worksheet. In later years, the conversion entry would include only 75% of the change in subsidiary retained earnings that occurs after the January 1, 2018, sale of stock.

Company P and Subsidiary Company S
Partial Worksheet (Cost Method)
For Year Ended December 31, 2018

	Trial Balance		Eliminations & Adjustments			
	Company P	Company S	Dr.		Cr.	
Investment in Company S (75%)	144,000		(CV)	88,950	(EL)	225,000
					(D)	7,500
					(adj)	450
Equipment			(D)	10,000	(A)	4,000
Common Stock—Company P	(400,000)					
Paid-In Capital in Excess of Par—Company P					(CV)	7,950
Retained Earnings ($81,000 less since no equity income was recorded), January 1, 2018—Company P	(239,000)		(A)	2,250	(CV)	81,000
			(adj)	450		
Common Stock—Company S		(120,000)	(EL)	90,000		
Paid-In Capital in Excess of Par—Company S		(40,000)	(EL)	30,000		
Retained Earnings, January 1, 2018—Company S		(140,000)	(EL)	105,000	(NCI)	2,500
			(A)	750		
Expenses	40,000	27,000	(A)	1,000		

Eliminations and Adjustments:

(CV) The simple-equity conversion is recorded:
(EL) Eliminate the parent's **75%** share of subsidiary equity balances at the beginning of the year against the investment account.
(D)/(NCI) Distribute to the equipment account the original excess of cost over book value and NCI adjustment, as required by the January 1, 2015, determination and distribution of excess schedule. The adjustment is now allocated 75%/25% to the investment account and to the NCI.
(A) Depreciate equipment for the past three years and the current year. The prior-year amortizations are allocated 75%/25% to controlling and noncontrolling retained earnings.
(adj) The "amortization adjustment" is to adjust parent retained earnings for the fact that the amortization in prior years was allocated 90% to the parent, as opposed to the current 75% allocation. It is calculated as (15% change × $1,000 annual depreciation × 3 years).

A dangerous shortcut might be attempted whereby the net change in the controlling ownership interest is calculated by comparing 90% of the total subsidiary equity (adjusted for fair value adjustments) on January 1, 2015, to 75% of the total subsidiary equity (adjusted for fair value adjustments) on January 1, 2019. This shortcut will produce the correct adjustment to the investment in subsidiary account, but it will not provide the analysis needed to distribute the adjustment to the parent's paid-in capital in excess of par and retained earnings.

Parent Purchase of Newly Issued Subsidiary Stock

A parent may purchase all or a portion of the newly issued stock. The general approach in such cases is to compare the change resulting from the sale to the price paid for the additional interest:

◆ When the ownership interest remains the same, there will be no adjustment.
◆ When the ownership interest increases or decreases, the difference between the change in equity and the price paid is viewed as a change in paid-in capital in excess of par. (In some cases, there may be a debit to Retained Earnings.)

Presented in the following table are three cases based on the previous example for which the determination and distribution of excess schedule was shown on page 441. Recall that the subsidiary is issuing 2,000 new shares of common stock for $30 per share.

		Case A (maintain interest)	Case B (increase interest)	Case C (decrease interest)
1	Shares purchased by parent	1,800	2,000	1,000
2	Total shares owned by parent after purchase	10,800	11,000	10,000
3	Total subsidiary shares outstanding after issue	12,000	12,000	12,000
4	Subsidiary equity after the sale (includes fair value adjustment from Case 2, page 441)	$307,000	$307,000	$307,000
5	Parent's ownership percent after purchase (2 ÷ 3).	× 90%	× 91.67%	× 83.33%
6	Parent's new equity interest after purchase (4 × 5)	$276,300	$281,427	$255,823
7	Subsidiary equity before the sale (from page 441).	$247,000	$247,000	$247,000
8	Parent's ownership percent before the purchase	× 90%	× 90%	× 90%
9	Parent's equity interest before the purchase (7 × 8)	222,300	222,300	222,300
10	Change in parent's equity interest due to purchase (6 − 9)	$ 54,000	$ 59,127	$ 33,523
11	Price paid ($30 × 1)	54,000	60,000	30,000
12	Increase (decrease) in parent's equity interest over price paid (10 − 11)	$ 0	$ (873)	$ 3,523

In Case A, the parent maintains its ownership interest by purchasing 90% of the newly issued shares. Note that there is no difference between the price paid by the parent for the new shares and the dollar change in the parent's ownership interest due to the purchase. Thus, no entry is needed other than to record the purchase of the shares as follows:

Investment in Company S (1,800 shares × $30)	54,000	
Cash		54,000

No new disparity between cost and underlying equity is created. As a result, **no additional equity adjustment is needed when the parent maintains its ownership interest and the same price is paid by all buyers**.

In Case B, the parent has increased its ownership interest to 91.67%. The price paid in excess of the additional interest is a reduction of equity that is charged against existing parent paid-in capital in excess of par, unless it does not exist. In that case, it is a debit to the parent's Retained Earnings.

The entry at the time of the purchase of the additional shares would be as follows:

Investment in Company S	59,127	
Retained Earnings—Parent (assumes no paid-in capital in excess of par) . . .	873	
Cash (2,000 shares × $30)		60,000
Future eliminations would be based on the 91.67% interest		

In Case C, the parent did not buy enough shares to maintain its ownership interest. However, the parent's investment account increased by $3,523 more than the price paid for the new interest. The increase would be an addition to paid-in capital in excess of par. A decrease would be a debit to existing Paid-In Capital in Excess of Par. If there is no existing paid-in capital in excess of par on the parent's books, retained earnings would be reduced. In Case C, the investment account increased $33,523, and the price paid was only $30,000. In addition to recording the purchase of the shares, the entry records the $3,523 increase in the parent's ownership interest. The entry for the transactions discussed would be as follows:

Investment in Company S	33,523	
Cash (1,000 shares × $30)		30,000
Paid-In Capital in Excess of Par—Parent		3,523

This entry is made at the time of the purchase and assumes the use of the equity method. If the cost method were used, it would be made as part of the cost-to-equity conversion process.

REFLECTION

- The subsidiary may increase its equity by issuing additional shares to noncontrolling shareholders.

- A "before and after" analysis is used to calculate the effect of stock issuance by the subsidiary on the parent's interest.

- The adjustment is made to the paid-in capital in excess of par account of the parent. (A decrease in equity would be a reduction of the parent's retained earnings if no paid-in capital in excess of par is available.)

3

OBJECTIVE

Account for the effect of subsidiary treasury stock transactions on the parent's investment in the subsidiary.

SUBSIDIARY PURCHASE OF ITS OWN COMMON STOCK

When a subsidiary acquires some of its own shares from the noncontrolling interest, the subsidiary equity is reduced. The parent will now own a larger percentage of a smaller equity. As is the case when subsidiary equity increases, a "before and after" analysis is needed. When the parent's interest increases, the increase is credited to the parent's Paid-In Capital in Excess of Par. When the parent's interest is reduced, the decrease is debited to the parent's Paid-In Capital in Excess of Par, if available. If paid-in capital in excess of par is not available, then the parent's retained earnings is reduced.

Purchase of Shares as Treasury Stock

To illustrate a subsidiary treasury stock purchase, assume the parent, Company P, owned a 70% interest in Company S. On January 1, 2015, Company S had the following stockholders' equity:

Capital stock ($10 par)	$100,000
Paid-in capital in excess of par	50,000
Retained earnings	90,000
Total stockholders' equity	$240,000

Further assume that the remaining fair value adjustment resulting from the original acquisition is $15,000. Thus, the adjusted equity of the subsidiary was as follows:

Total stockholder's equity from above	$240,000
Remaining fair value adjustment	15,000
Adjusted subsidiary equity	$255,000

On this date, the subsidiary purchased 2,000 of its 10,000 outstanding shares. The entry (shown on page 447) then was recorded by Company S as a result of this purchase from noncontrolling shareholders at a cost of $26 each.

Treasury Stock (at cost)	52,000	
Cash		52,000

As a result of the purchase, Company S had the following stockholders' equity:

Capital stock ($10 par)	$100,000
Paid-in capital in excess of par	50,000
Retained earnings	90,000
Total..	$240,000
Less treasury stock (at cost)	52,000
Total stockholders' equity......................................	$188,000
Add remaining fair value adjustment...............................	15,000
Adjusted subsidiary equity after treasury stock purchase	$203,000

The parent now owns 7,000 of 8,000 outstanding subsidiary shares (87.5% interest). The "before and after" analysis is as follows:

Parent interest after treasury stock purchase (87.5% × $203,000)	$177,625
Parent interest prior to treasury stock purchase (70% × $255,000)	178,500
Increase (decrease) in parent company equity	$ (875)

An increase would be credited to the parent's Paid-In Capital in Excess of Par. A decrease is debited to the available parent Paid-In Capital in Excess of Par, otherwise to the parent's Retained Earnings. In this case (assuming no parent paid-in capital in excess of par), the entry for a parent using either equity method would be as follows:

Retained Earnings—Parent	875	
Investment in Subsidiary		875

Eliminations in future periods would be based on the resulting 87.5% parent interest. Eliminations would include eliminating 87.5% of the subsidiary treasury stock account.

A parent using the cost method would include the above adjustment in its cost-to-equity conversion worksheet adjustment (CV).

Resale of Shares Held in Treasury

The purchase and resale of treasury stock by a subsidiary would be handled as two separate events using the previously described "before and after" comparison method. Alternative procedures might be used if there is any intent to resell the treasury shares in the near future. When, for example, the treasury stock is purchased and resold within the consolidated company's fiscal period, a shortcut is possible. Since there would be no change in the parent's percentage of ownership by the end of the period, the parent only needs to make an adjustment equal to its ownership interest multiplied by the subsidiary's increase or decrease in equity as a result of the treasury stock transaction. This adjustment should be carried to the additional paid-in capital in excess of par of the parent and is not viewed as an operating gain or loss since it results from dealings with the company's own shareholders. Using the same reasoning, a decrease in equity reduces the parent's retained earnings only when no additional paid-in capital in excess of par is available.

R E F L E C T I O N

- The repurchase of shares by a subsidiary is treated as a change in subsidiary equity that is accounted for by employing "before and after" analysis.

<table>
<tr><td>

4

―――――――

OBJECTIVE

―――――――

Demonstrate accounting procedures for multilevel holdings.

</td></tr>
</table>

INDIRECT HOLDINGS

A parent company may own a controlling interest in a subsidiary that, in turn, owns a controlling interest in another company. For example, Company A may own a 75% interest in Company B, which owns an 80% interest in Company C. Thus, A has indirect holdings in C. This situation could be diagrammed as follows:

The treatment of the *level one* investment in B and the *level two* investment in C can be mastered with the methods we have used, but the procedures must be applied carefully. The procedures are applied easily to indirect holdings when the level one investment already exists at the time of the level two acquisition. Complications arise in preparing the determination and distribution of excess schedule for the new investment when the level two investment exists prior to the time that the parent achieves control over the subsidiary (level one investment). These complications result because the level two investment held by the subsidiary represents one of the subsidiary's assets that may require adjustment to fair value on the determination and distribution of excess schedule prepared at the time of the parent's level one acquisition. **The use of separate and distinct determination and distribution of excess schedules for each level of investment should facilitate the maintaining of proper accounting when two or more levels are involved.**

Level One Holding Acquired First

Assume Company A purchased a 75% interest in Company B on January 1, 2015, at which time the following determination and distribution of excess schedule was prepared:

Determination and Distribution of Excess Schedule

	Company Implied Fair Value	Parent Price (75%)	NCI Value (25%)
Fair value of subsidiary	$ 550,000	$412,500	$137,500
Less book value of interest acquired			
Common stock	$ 200,000		
Retained earnings	100,000		
Total equity	$ 300,000	$300,000	$300,000
Interest acquired		75%	25%
Book value		$225,000	$ 75,000
Excess of fair value over book value	**$250,000**	$187,500	$ 62,500

Adjustment of identifiable accounts:

	Adjustment	Life	Amortization per Year	Worksheet Key
Equipment	$ 250,000	10	$ 25,000	**debit D_b**

On January 1, 2016, the subsidiary, Company B, purchased an 80% interest in Company C, and the following schedule was prepared:

Determination and Distribution of Excess Schedule

	Company Implied Fair Value	Parent Price (80%)	NCI Value (20%)
Fair value of subsidiary	$ 337,500	$270,000	$ 67,500
Less book value of interest acquired:			
Common stock.	$ 100,000		
Retained earnings	120,000		
Total equity.	$ 220,000	$220,000	$220,000
Interest acquired		80%	20%
Book value.		$176,000	$ 44,000
Excess of fair value over book value	**$117,500**	$ 94,000	$ 23,500

Adjustment of identifiable accounts:

	Adjustment	Life	Amortization per Year	Worksheet Key
Building	$ 117,500	20	$ 5,875	**debit Dc**

Equity adjustments must be made carefully. Company A must be sure that Company B has included its equity income from Company C in its net income before Company A records its percentage share of Company B income.

Assume the following internally generated net incomes:

	Company A	Company B	Company C
2015	$100,000	$100,000	$20,000
2016	70,000	76,000	30,000
2017	90,000	100,000	30,000

On this basis, the following simple-equity adjustments would be required:

Date	Company B's Books			Company A's Books		
2015 Dec. 31	None (interest in Company C not yet acquired)			Investment in Company B . . . . Subsidiary Income. . . . . To adjust for 75% of Company B reported income.	75,000	75,000
2016 Dec. 31	Investment in Company C . . . . Subsidiary Income. . . . . To adjust for 80% of Company C reported income.	24,000	24,000	Investment in Company B . . . . Subsidiary Income. . . . . To adjust for 75% of Company B total income ($76,000 plus $24,000 subsidiary income).	75,000	75,000
2017 Dec. 31	Investment in Company C . . . . Subsidiary Income. . . . . To adjust for 80% of Company C reported income.	24,000	24,000	Investment in Company B . . . . Subsidiary Income. . . . . To adjust for 75% of Company B total income ($100,000 plus $24,000 subsidiary income).	93,000	93,000

Worksheet 8-1, pages 458 and 459, is based on the trial balances of the three separate companies on December 31, 2017. The investment account balances reflect the equity adjustments previously shown. The additional information for 2017, shown on page 450, is assumed.

Worksheet 8-1: page 458

	Intercompany Sales by B to A	Intercompany Sales by C to B
Selling company goods in buyer's January 1, 2017, inventory	$ 8,000	$ 6,000
Sales during 2017	$50,000	$40,000
Selling company goods in buyer's December 31, 2017, inventory	$10,000	$10,000
Gross profit on all sales	25%	30%

The investment accounts must be handled carefully when any eliminations are made in order to ensure that the NCI accounts are available to receive applicable amortizations of excess. It is suggested that the level one investment be eliminated first, thereby reducing Company B retained earnings to the NCI. Then, it will be possible to allocate the amortizations of excess resulting from the level two (Company C) holding to the controlling interest (Company A) and the Company B NCI. Since Company B owns the interest in Company C, the Company B NCI must share in the amortizations of excess resulting from the investment in Company C.

The eliminations for Worksheet 8-1 in journal entry form are as follows:

Entries to eliminate investment in Company B:

(CYb)	Eliminate current-year equity income:		
	Subsidiary Income	93,000	
	Investment in Company B		93,000

(ELb)	Eliminate subsidiary B equity:		
	Common Stock ($10 par)—Company B	150,000	
	Retained Earnings, January 1, 2017—Company B	225,000	
	Investment in Company B		375,000

(Db)/(NCIb)	Distribute excess to buildings and equipment:		
	Buildings and Equipment	250,000	
	Investment in Company B		187,500
	Retained Earnings, January 1, 2017—Company B (NCI)		62,500

(Ab)	Amortize excess:		
	Retained Earnings, January 1, 2017—Company A	37,500	
	Retained Earnings, January 1, 2017—Company B	12,500	
	Expenses	25,000	
	Accumulated Depreciation		75,000

Entries to eliminate investment in Company C:

(CYc)	Eliminate current-year equity income:		
	Investment Income	24,000	
	Investment in Company C		24,000

(ELc)	Eliminate subsidiary C equity:		
	Common Stock ($10 par)—Company C	80,000	
	Retained Earnings, January 1, 2017—Company C	120,000	
	Investment in Company C		200,000

(Dc)/(NCIc)	Distribute excess and NCI adjustment to buildings and equipment:		
	Buildings and Equipment	117,500	
	Investment in Company C		94,000
	Retained Earnings, January 1, 2017—Company C (NCI)		23,500

(Ac)	Amortize excess:		
	Retained Earnings, January 1, 2017—Company A	3,525	
	Retained Earnings, January 1, 2017—Company B	1,175	
	Retained Earnings, January 1, 2017—Company C	1,175	
	Expenses	5,875	
	Accumulated Depreciation		11,750
(IS)	Eliminate intercompany sales:		
	Sales	90,000	
	Cost of Goods Sold		90,000
(BIb)	Beginning inventory profit, Company B sales:		
	Retained Earnings, January 1, 2017—Company A	1,500	
	Retained Earnings, January 1, 2017—Company B	500	
	Cost of Goods Sold		2,000
(EIb)	Ending inventory profit, Company B sales:		
	Cost of Goods Sold	2,500	
	Inventory, December 31, 2017.		2,500
(BIc)	Beginning inventory profit, Company C sales:		
	Retained Earnings, January 1, 2017—Company A	1,080	
	Retained Earnings, January 1, 2017—Company B	360	
	Retained Earnings, January 1, 2017—Company C	360	
	Cost of Goods Sold		1,800
(EIc)	Ending inventory profit, Company C sales:		
	Cost of Goods Sold	3,000	
	Inventory, December 31, 2017.		3,000

In Worksheet 8-1, the consolidated net income is $187,425, which must be distributed to the two NCIs and to the controlling interest. Distribution must proceed from the lowest level (level two) to ensure proper distribution. Company B adjusted income includes 80% of Company C adjusted income. Thus, the Company C IDS must be completed first, followed by the distribution schedules for Companies B and A. These schedules accompany Worksheet 8-1.

If the cost method was used in the previous example, the investment account balances still would contain the January 1, 2015, $412,500 cost of the Company B investment and the January 1, 2016, $270,000 cost of the Company C investment. Conversion entries would be made on the consolidated worksheet to update both investment accounts to their January 1, 2017, simple-equity balances. It is advisable to make equity adjustments at the lowest level of investment first, because the retained earnings of the mid-level firm must be adjusted for its share of investment income before the parent can adjust for the change in its subsidiary's retained earnings. The following simple-equity conversion entry would be made first for Company B's investment in Company C:

Investment in Company C	24,000	
Retained Earnings—Company B.		24,000
To record 80% of $30,000 increase in Company C retained earnings between January 1, 2016, and January 1, 2017.		

The following conversion entry then would be made for Company A's investment in Company B:

Investment in Company B	150,000	
Retained Earnings—Company A.		150,000
To record 75% of $200,000 increase in Company B retained earnings (including previous equity adjustment for Company B) between January 1, 2015, and January 1, 2017.		

Eliminations and adjustments would be made as on Worksheet 8-1, except that there would be no need to eliminate the current year's equity adjustment.

Level Two Holding Exists at Time of Parent's Purchase

When a parent acquires a controlling interest in another parent company, the determination and distribution of excess schedule must compare the price paid with the interest in the parent acquired. For example, assume that in a period before January 1, 2015, Company Y purchased an 80% interest in Company Z for a price equal to book value. Also assume that on January 1, 2015, Company Z's book value is $200,000 and its fair value is $300,000. The $100,000 is attributable to one of Company Z's buildings. On January 1, 2015, Company X purchased a 70% interest in Company Y for $700,000. On that date, Company Y had a stockholders' equity of $740,000 (including its interest in Company Z), and it had equipment that was understated by $40,000. Based on these facts, the following determination and distribution of excess schedule would be prepared:

Determination and Distribution of Excess Schedule

	Company Implied Fair Value	Parent Price (70%)	NCI (Y) Value (30%)
Fair value of subsidiary	$1,000,000	$700,000	$300,000
Less book value of interest acquired:			
Common stock	$ 400,000		
Retained earnings	340,000		
Total equity.	$ 740,000	$740,000	$740,000
Interest acquired		70%	30%
Book value.		$518,000	$222,000
Excess of fair value over book value	$ 260,000	$182,000	$ 78,000

Adjustment of identifiable accounts:

	Adjustment	Life	Amortization per Year	Worksheet Key
Company Z building (80%)	$ 80,000	20	$ 4,000	**debit D1**
Company Y equipment	40,000	5	8,000	**debit D2**
Goodwill.	**140,000**			**debit D3**
Total	**$ 260,000**			

The distribution of the excess and NCI adjustments would be made on the worksheet as follows:

Company Z Building ($80,000 parent share + $20,000 NCI –
    Company Z share) 100,000
Company Y Equipment 40,000
Company Y Goodwill 140,000
    Investment in Company Y (excess remaining after elimination) 182,000
    NCI—Company Y 78,000
    NCI—Company Z (for building) 20,000

In future years, amortization adjustments would be distributed to retained earnings in the following percentages:

	Controlling	NCI Company Y	NCI Company Z
(A1) Building	70% × 80% = 56%	30% × 80% = 24%	20%
(A2) Equipment	70%	30%	

The above example assumes that the investment in Company Z was acquired at book value. If that were not the case, the Company Z equity would be adjusted for the remaining excess, prior to multiplying by the Company X ownership interest.

When the simple equity method is used for the investments, the procedures illustrated in Worksheet 8-1 apply without modification. When the cost method is used, simple-equity conversion adjustments again proceed from the lowest level. Be sure to note, however, that in this example Company X would convert to the equity basis for the change in Company Y retained earnings after January 1, 2017.

Connecting Affiliates

A business combination involving connecting affiliates exists when a parent company has a direct (level one) investment in a company and an indirect (level two) investment in the same company sufficient to result in control. For example, the following diagram illustrates a connecting affiliate structure:

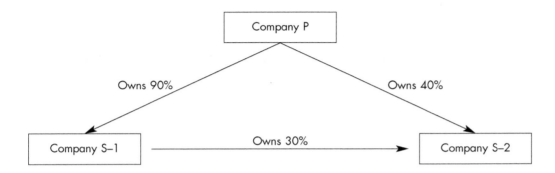

Not only does Company P have a 90% interest in Company S–1, but it also has, in effect, a 67% interest in Company S–2, calculated as follows:

Direct............................	40%
Indirect (90% × 30%)	27%
Total...........................	67%

This type of structure is consolidated more readily once the determination and distribution of excess schedule has been prepared. Referring to the diagram, the special concerns in consolidating connecting affiliates are as follows:

1. Company S–2 generally is not included in the consolidation process until the total percentage of S–2 shares held by the parent and its subsidiaries (70% in this example) exceeds 50%. Prior to that time, an investment of 20% or more is accounted for under the sophisticated equity method, and a less-than-20% investment is accounted for under the cost method.

2. Company S–2 accounts are adjusted to fair value on the date that control of Company S–2 is achieved. The amortizations resulting from the D&D schedule would be distributed to the ownership groups by including them in the Company S–2 IDS schedule. Prior-period amortizations on the worksheet would be distributed as follows:
   - 30% (NCI %) to S–2 retained earnings
   - 3% (10% NCI × 30% interest) to S–1 retained earnings
   - 67% [(90% interest × 30% Company S–1 interest) + 40% interest in Company S–2] to the controlling interest.

   The above percentages are also used for prior-period intercompany profits originated by Company S–2.

3. Company S–1 accounts are adjusted to fair value on the date that control of Company S–1 is achieved. The amortizations resulting from the D&D schedule would be distributed to the ownership groups by including them in the Company S–1 IDS schedule. Prior-period amortizations on the worksheet would be distributed as follows:
   - 10% to S–1 retained earnings
   - 90% to the controlling interest

The percentages shown on page 453 are also used for prior-period intercompany profits originated by Company S–2.

4. Income distributions would begin with Company S–2: 30% of its income would go to NCI S–2, 30% would flow to the Company S–1 distribution schedule, and 40% would flow to the Company P schedule. Company P will receive 90% of the Company S–1 adjusted income (including the 30% share of Company S–2).

5. When either equity method is used, Companies P and S–1 each must adjust for their interest in Company S–2, even though neither company's interest by itself would merit consolidation techniques.

6. When the cost method is used, each investment is converted to the simple equity method from the purchase date forward. Again, equity conversions must begin at the lowest level. For example, the Company S–1 investment in Company S–2 must be converted first, so that Company S–1 retained earnings are updated before the Company P investment in Company S–1 is converted to the simple equity method.

R E F L E C T I O N

- Indirect holdings have three or more ownership tiers and create the ownership of the shares of one subsidiary by another subsidiary.

- Equity adjustments must proceed from the lowest level to the highest to ensure that upper-level investments include the effect of income earned by the subsidiary being analyzed.

- Eliminations should begin at the highest level. This makes the NCI available to receive adjustments from the elimination of lower-level investments.

- Retained earnings and IDS adjustments must be made carefully to assign adjustments to the appropriate ownership group.

5
OBJECTIVE

Demonstrate an understanding of the alternatives used for accounting for investments in the parent company owned by the subsidiary.

PARENT COMPANY SHARES PURCHASED BY SUBSIDIARY

The subsidiary may use its resources to purchase shares of the parent. When this occurs, the subsidiary is viewed as the parent's agent purchasing treasury shares for the parent. The shares purchased are recorded at cost. When the shares are resold, an excess received over cost is carried to additional paid-in capital in excess of par. If cost exceeds proceeds on resale, the difference is offset against existing paid-in capital in excess of par. If there is no additional paid-in capital in excess of par, retained earnings are reduced. There is never an income statement effect, and the resulting capital account adjustments fall entirely upon the parent

An important requirement of the treasury stock approaches is that the subsidiary investment in the parent be maintained at its original cost. Since the stock is not to be viewed as outstanding, it has no claim on income. If equity adjustments have been made in error, they must be reversed on the consolidated worksheet.

To illustrate the treasury stock method, consider the following example. Suppose Company P acquired an 80% interest in Company S on January 1, 2015, at which time the following determination and distribution of excess schedule was prepared:

Determination and Distribution of Excess Schedule

	Company Implied Fair Value	Parent Price (80%)	NCI Value (20%)
Fair value of subsidiary	$ 250,000	$200,000	$ 50,000
Less book value of interest acquired:			
Common stock	$ 100,000		
Retained earnings	50,000		
Total equity	$ 150,000	$150,000	$150,000
Interest acquired		80%	20%
Book value.		$120,000	$ 30,000
Excess of fair value over book value	**$100,000**	$ 80,000	$ 20,000

Adjustment of identifiable accounts:

	Adjustment	Life	Amortization per Year	Worksheet Key
Equipment	$ 100,000	20	$ 5,000	**debit D**

Further assume that on January 1, 2017, Company S purchases a 10% interest (1,000 shares) in the parent for $80,000. There would be no need for a determination and distribution of excess schedule for the subsidiary investment, since no excess of cost or book value is acknowledged or distributed. For 2017, the parent will make the normal simple-equity adjustment to acknowledge its 80% interest in subsidiary income of $20,000 as follows:

Investment in Company S	16,000	
Subsidiary Income.		16,000
To record 80% of subsidiary reported income of $20,000.		

There is no equity adjustment for the Company S investment in the parent since it must remain at cost.

The trial balances of the two companies on December 31, 2017, are contained in the first two columns of Worksheet 8-2 on pages 462 and 463. The investment in Company S account on Worksheet 8-2 is computed as follows:

Worksheet 8-2: page 462

Original cost	$200,000
80% × 2015 and 2016 undistributed income of $40,000	32,000
2013 simple-equity adjustment	16,000
Balance, December 31, 2017	$248,000

The eliminations for Worksheet 8-2 in journal entry form are as follows:

(CY)	Eliminate current-year equity income:		
	Subsidiary Income......................................	16,000	
	Investment in Company S............................		16,000
(EL)	Eliminate subsidiary S equity:		
	Common Stock—Company S	80,000	
	Retained Earnings, January 1, 2017—Company S	72,000	
	Investment in Company S.............................		152,000
(D)/(NCI)	Distribute excess and NCI adjustment to equipment:		
	Equipment	100,000	
	Investment in Company S.............................		80,000
	Retained Earnings—Company S.......................		20,000
(A)	Amortize excess:		
	Retained Earnings, January 1, 2017—Company P	8,000	
	Retained Earnings, January 1, 2017—Company S	2,000	
	Expenses	5,000	
	Accumulated Depreciation		15,000
(TS)	Restate investment in Company P as treasury stock:		
	Treasury Stock (at cost)	**80,000**	
	Investment in Company P (10%, at cost)		**80,000**

Examination of the formal statements of the consolidated company reveals that the treasury shares are held by the consolidated company and no income accrues to them. These statements, based on Worksheet 8-2, are as follows:

Company P and Subsidiary Company S
Consolidated Income Statement
For Year Ended December 31, 2017

Sales	$500,000
Less cost of goods sold.....................................	300,000
Gross profit	$200,000
Less expenses	145,000
Consolidated net income....................................	$ 55,000
Noncontrolling interest of Company S	$ 3,000
Controlling interest	$ 52,000

Company P and Subsidiary Company S
Retained Earnings Statement
For Year Ended December 31, 2017

	Noncontrolling Interest	Controlling Interest
Balance, January 1, 2017..............................	$36,000	$192,000
Net income	3,000	52,000
Balance, December 31, 2017	$39,000	$244,000

Company P and Subsidiary Company S
Consolidated Balance Sheet December 31, 2017

Assets		Stockholders' Equity		
Equipment	$888,000	Noncontrolling interest		$ 59,000
Less accumulated		Controlling interest:		
depreciation	165,000	Common stock	$500,000	
		Retained earnings	244,000	744,000
		Total		$803,000
		Less treasury stock (at cost)		80,000
Total assets	$723,000	Net stockholders' equity		$723,000

REFLECTION

- If a subsidiary purchases parent company shares, the transaction is viewed as the purchase of parent company treasury shares.

- The treasury stock method allows the parent shares, owned by the subsidiary, to remain on the balance sheet as treasury stock.

Worksheet 8-1

Indirect Holdings; Intercompany Sales
Company A and Subsidiary Companies B and C

Worksheet for Consolidated Financial Statements
For Year Ended December 31, 2017

	(Credit balance amounts are in parentheses.)	Trial Balance		
		Company A	Company B	Company C
1	Inventory, December 31, 2017	80,000	20,000	30,000
2				
3	Other Assets	47,500	146,000	130,000
4	Building and Equipment	300,000	200,000	150,000
5				
6	Accumulated Depreciation	(100,000)	(60,000)	(30,000)
7				
8	Investment in Company B	655,500		
9				
10				
11	Investment in Company C		318,000	
12				
13				
14	Common Stock ($10 par)—Company A	(300,000)		
15	**Retained Earnings, January 1, 2017—Company A**	**(500,000)**		
16				
17				
18				
19	Common Stock ($10 par)—Company B		(200,000)	
20	**Retained Earnings, January 1, 2017—Company B**		**(300,000)**	
21				
22				
23				
24				
25	Common Stock ($10 par)—Company C			(100,000)
26	**Retained Earnings, January 1, 2017—Company C**			**(150,000)**
27				
28				
29	Sales	(400,000)	(300,000)	(150,000)
30	Cost of Goods Sold	250,000	160,000	80,000
31				
32				
33	Expenses	60,000	40,000	40,000
34				
35	Subsidiary or Investment Income	(93,000)	(24,000)	
36				
37		0	0	0
38	Consolidated Net Income			
39	To NCI, Company C (see distribution schedule)			
40	To NCI, Company B (see distribution schedule)			
41	To Controlling Interest (see distribution schedule)			
42	Total NCI			
43	Retained Earnings, Controlling Interest, December 31, 2017			
44				

Worksheet 8-1 (see page 449)

Eliminations & Adjustments Dr.		Eliminations & Adjustments Cr.		Consolidated Income Statement	NCI	Controlling Retained Earnings	Consolidated Balance Sheet	
		(Elb)	2,500				124,500	1
		(Elc)	3,000					2
							323,500	3
(Db)	250,000						1,017,500	4
(Dc)	117,500							5
		(Ab)	75,000				(276,750)	6
		(Ac)	**11,750**					7
		(CYb)	93,000					8
		(ELb)	375,000					9
		(Db)	187,500					10
		(CYc)	24,000					11
		(ELc)	200,000					12
		(Dc)	94,000					13
							(300,000)	14
(Ab)	37,500					(456,395)		15
(Ac)	**3,525**							16
(Blb)	1,500							17
(Blc)	**1,080**							18
(ELb)	150,000				(50,000)			19
(ELb)	225,000	(NClb)	62,500		(122,965)			20
(Ab)	12,500							21
(Ac)	**1,175**							22
(Blb)	500							23
(Blc)	**360**							24
(ELc)	80,000				(20,000)			25
(ELc)	120,000	(NClc)	23,500		(51,965)			26
(Ac)	**1,175**							27
(Blc)	**360**							28
(IS)	90,000			(760,000)				29
(Elb)	2,500	(IS)	90,000	401,700				30
(Elc)	3,000	(Blb)	2,000					31
		(Blc)	**1,800**					32
(Ac)	**5,875**							33
(Ab)	25,000			170,875				34
(CYb)	93,000							35
(CYc)	24,000							36
	1,245,550		1,245,550					37
				(187,425)				38
				4,585	(4,585)			39
				23,210	(23,210)			40
				159,630		(159,630)		41
					(272,725)		(272,725)	42
						(616,025)	(616,025)	43
							0	44

Eliminations and Adjustments:

(CYb)	Eliminate the entry made by Company A to record its share of Company B income. This step returns the investment in the Company B account to its January 1, 2017, balance to aid the elimination process.
(ELb)	Eliminate 75% of the January 1, 2017, Company B equity balances against the investment in Company B.
(Db)/(NCIb)	Distribute the $187,500 excess of cost and $62,500 NCI adjustment to the building and equipment account according to the determination and distribution of excess schedule applicable to the level one investment.
(Ab)	Amortize the excess (added depreciation) according to the determination and distribution of excess schedule. This step requires adjustment of Company A and B retained earnings for 2015 and 2016, plus adjustment of 2017 expenses.
(CYc)	Eliminate the entry made by Company B to record its share of Company C income. This returns the investment in Company C account to its January 1, 2017, balance to aid elimination.
(ELc)	Eliminate 80% of the January 1, 2017, Company C equity balances against the investment in Company C.
(Dc)/(NCIc)	Distribute the $94,000 excess of cost and the $23,500 NCI adjustment to the building and equipment account according to the determination and distribution of excess schedule applicable to the level two investment.
(Ac)	Amortize the excess (added depreciation) according to the determination and distribution of excess schedule. Since it is created by actions of subsidiary Company B, the 2016 amortization must be prorated 20% ($1,175) to the Company B NCI, 20% ($1,175) to the Company C NCI and 75% × 80% = 60% ($3,525) to the controlling interest. Note that the Company B NCI appears on the worksheet only after the first level investment has been eliminated, again pointing to the need to eliminate the level one investment first.
(IS)	Eliminate intercompany sales to prevent double counting in the consolidated sales and cost of goods sold.
(BIb)	Eliminate the Company B profit contained in the beginning inventory. Since Company B generated the sale, the correction of beginning retained earnings is split 75% to the controlling interest and 25% to the noncontrolling interest. The cost of goods sold is decreased since the beginning inventory was overstated.
(EIb)	The cost of goods sold is adjusted and the ending inventory is reduced by the $2,500 of Company B profit contained in the ending inventory.
(BIc)	Eliminate the Company C profit contained in the beginning inventory. Since Company C generated the retained earnings adjustment, it is apportioned as follows:

To NCI in Company C (20%)	$ 360
To NCI in Company B (25% of 80%).	360
To controlling interest (75% of 80%)	1,080
Total	$1,800

(EIc)	The cost of goods sold is adjusted, and the ending inventory is reduced by the $3,000 of Company C profit.

Company C Income Distribution

Ending inventory profit .... (EIc)	$ 3,000	Internally generated net income	$30,000
Building depreciation .... **(Ac)**	**5,875**	Beginning inventory profit .... **(BIc)**	**1,800**
		Adjusted income	$22,925
		Company C NCI share	× 20%
		Company C NCI	$ 4,585

Company B Income Distribution

Ending inventory profit .... (EIb)	$ 2,500	Internally generated net income	$100,000
Equipment depreciation .... (Ab)	25,000	Beginning inventory profit .... (BIb)	2,000
		80% of Company C adjusted income	18,340
		Adjusted income	$ 92,840
		Company B NCI share	× 25%
		Company B NCI	$ 23,210

Company A Income Distribution

		Internally generated income	$ 90,000
		75% of Company B adjusted income	69,630
		Controlling interest	$159,630

Worksheet 8-2

Treasury Stock Method for Parent Shares Owned by Subsidiary
Company P and Subsidiary Company S
Worksheet for Consolidated Financial Statements
For Year Ended December 31, 2017

	(Credit balance amounts are in parentheses.)	Trial Balance	
		Company P	Company S
1	Investment in Company S (80%)	248,000	
2			
3			
4	**Investment in Company P (10%, at cost)**		**80,000**
5	Equipment	608,000	180,000
6	Accumulated Depreciation	(100,000)	(50,000)
7	Common Stock—Company P	(500,000)	
8	Retained Earnings, January 1, 2017—Company P	(200,000)	
9	Common Stock—Company S		(100,000)
10	Retained Earnings, January 1, 2017—Company S		(90,000)
11			
12	Sales	(300,000)	(200,000)
13	Cost of Goods Sold	180,000	120,000
14	Expenses	80,000	60,000
15	Subsidiary Income	(16,000)	
16	**Treasury Stock (at cost)**		
17		0	0
18	Consolidated Net Income		
19	To NCI (see distribution schedule)		
20	Balance to Controlling Interest (see distribution schedule)		
21	Total NCI		
22	Retained Earnings, Controlling Interest, December 31, 2017		
23			

Eliminations and Adjustments:

(CY)	Eliminate the entry made by the parent during the current year to record its share of Company S income.
(EL)	Eliminate 80% of the January 1, 2017, subsidiary equity balances against the investment in Company S account.
(D)/(NCI)	Distribute the excess of cost over book value and the NCI adjustment to the equipment account as specified by the determination and distribution of excess schedule applicable to the Investment in Company S.
(A)	Amortize the excess of $100,000 for the past two years and the current year at the rate of $5,000 per year.
(TS)	The investment in Company P must be at cost. If any equity adjustments have been made, they must be reversed and the investment in the parent returned to cost. If the shares are to be reissued, as is the case in this example, the investment is then transferred to the treasury stock account, a contra account to total consolidated stockholders' equity.

As an alternative to entry **(TS)**, the cost of the treasury shares could be used to retire them on the worksheet as follows:

Common Stock—Company P	50,000	
Retained Earnings—Company P	30,000	
Investment in Company P		80,000

Worksheet 8-2 (see page 455)

| Eliminations & Adjustment | | Consolidated Income Statement | NCI | Controlling Retained Earnings | Consolidated Balance Sheet | |
Dr.	Cr.					
	(CY) 16,000					1
	(EL) 152,000					2
	(D) 80,000					3
	(TS) 80,000					4
(D) 100,000					888,000	5
	(A) 15,000				(165,000)	6
					(500,000)	7
(A) 8,000				(192,000)		8
(EL) 80,000			(20,000)			9
(EL) 72,000	(NCI) 20,000		(36,000)			10
(A) 2,000						11
		(500,000)				12
		300,000				13
(A) 5,000		145,000				14
(CY) 16,000						15
(TS) 80,000					80,000	16
363,000	363,000					17
		(55,000)				18
		3,000	(3,000)			19
		52,000		(52,000)		20
			(59,000)		(59,000)	21
				(244,000)	(244,000)	22
					0	23

Subsidiary Company S Income Distribution

Depreciation of excess for current year . . . . (A) $5,000	Internally generated net income	$20,000
	Adjusted income	$15,000
	NCI share	× 20%
	NCI	$ 3,000

Parent Company P Income Distribution

Internally generated net income	$40,000
80% × Company S adjusted income of $15,000. . .	12,000
Controlling interest	$52,000

UNDERSTANDING THE ISSUES

1. Subsidiary Company S had the following stockholders' equity on December 31, 2017, prior to distributing a 10% stock dividend:

Common stock ($1 par), 100,000 shares issued and outstanding	$ 100,000
Paid-in capital in excess of par	1,900,000
Retained earnings	2,000,000
Total equity	$4,000,000

The fair value of the shares distributed is $50 each. What is the effect of this dividend on the subsidiary equity, the investment account, and the December 31, 2017, elimination procedures? Assume the parent uses the simple equity method to account for its investment in the subsidiary.

2. Subsidiary Company S had the following stockholders' equity on January 1, 2018, prior to issuing 20,000 additional new shares to noncontrolling shareholders:

Common stock ($1 par), 100,000 shares issued and outstanding	$ 100,000
Paid-in capital in excess of par	1,900,000
Retained earnings	2,000,000
Total equity	$4,000,000

At that time, the parent company owned 90,000 Company S shares. Assume that the parent acquired the shares at a price equal to their book value. What is the impact on the parent's investment account of the sale of 20,000 additional shares by the subsidiary for $45 per share?

3. Subsidiary Company S had the following stockholders' equity on January 1, 2018, prior to issuing 5,000 additional new shares:

Common stock ($1 par), 100,000 shares issued and outstanding	$ 100,000
Paid-in capital in excess of par	1,900,000
Retained earnings	2,000,000
Total equity	$4,000,000

Prior to the sale of additional shares, the parent owned 90,000 shares. Assume that the parent acquired the shares at a price equal to their book value. Assume that the new shares are sold for $45 each. Describe the general impact (no calculations required) the sale will have on the parent's investment account if:

  a. The parent buys less than 90% of the new shares.
  b. The parent buys 90% of the new shares.
  c. The parent buys all the new shares.

4. Company A owns 80% of Company B. Company B owns 60% of Company C. From a consolidated viewpoint, does A control C? How will $10,000 of Company C income flow to the members of the consolidated firms when it is distributed at year-end?

5. Company P owns 90% of Company S's shares. Assume Company S then purchases 2% of Company P's outstanding shares of common stock. When consolidating, what happens to the 2% holding in the consolidated financial statements?

EXERCISES

Exercise 1 *(LO 1)* **Subsidiary stock dividend.** On January 1, 2015, Talbot Company acquires 90% of the outstanding stock of Lego Company for $810,000. At the time of the acquisition, Lego Company has the following stockholders' equity:

Common stock ($10 par)................	$300,000
Paid-in capital in excess of par	150,000
Retained earnings	200,000
Total stockholders' equity..............	$650,000

It is determined that Lego Company's book values approximate fair values as of the purchase date. Any excess of cost over book value is attributed to goodwill.

On July 1, 2015, Lego Company distributes a 10% stock dividend when the fair value of its common stock is $40 per share. A cash dividend of $0.50 per share is distributed on December 31, 2015. Lego Company's net income for 2015 amounts to $108,000 and is earned evenly throughout the year.

1. Prepare the entry required on Lego Company's books to reflect the stock dividend distributed on July 1, 2015. Prepare the stockholders' equity section of the Lego Company balance sheet as of December 31, 2015.
2. Prepare the simple equity method entries that Talbot Company would make during 2015 to record its investment in Lego Company.
3. Prepare the eliminations that would be made on the December 31, 2015, consolidated worksheet. (Assume the use of the simple equity method.) Prepare a determination and distribution of excess schedule to support the elimination.

Exercise 2 *(LO 2)* **Subsidiary sale of shares to noncontrolling interest.** Truck Company owns a 90% interest in Trailer Company on January 1, 2015, when Trail has the following stockholders' equity:

Common stock ($10 par)....................	$100,000
Paid-in capital in excess of par	250,000
Retained earnings	200,000
Total stockholders' equity..................	$550,000

The investment is purchased for book value, $495,000.

On July 1, 2015, Trail sells 2,000 additional shares to noncontrolling shareholders in a private offering for $75 per share. Trailer's net income for 2015 is $70,000, and the income is earned evenly during the year.

Truck uses the simple equity method to record the investment in Trailer. Summary entries are made each December 31 to record the year's activity.

Prepare Truck's equity adjustments for 2015 that result from the above activities of Trailer Company during 2011. Assume Truck has $500,000 of paid-in capital in excess of par.

Exercise 3 *(LO 2)* **Subsidiary sale of shares, alternative amounts purchased by parent.** On January 1, 2015, Artic Company acquires an 80% interest in Calco Company for $400,000. On the acquisition date, Calco Company has the following stockholders' equity:

Common stock ($10 par).................	$200,000
Paid-in capital in excess of par	100,000
Retained earnings	150,000
Total stockholders' equity...............	$450,000

Assets and liabilities have fair values equal to book values. Goodwill totals $50,000.

Calco Company has net income of $60,000 for 2015. No dividends are paid or declared during 2015.

On January 1, 2016, Calco Company sells 10,000 shares of common stock at $60 per share in a public offering.

Assuming the parent uses the simple equity method, prepare all parent company entries required for the issuance of the shares.

Assume the following alternative situations:

1. Artic Company purchases 8,000 shares.
2. Artic Company purchases 9,000 shares.
3. Artic Company purchases 5,000 shares.

Suggestion: It is helpful to use a 3-column table which, for each case, organizes the changes in ownership interest. See the schedule on page 441.

Exercise 4 *(LO 3)* **Subsidiary treasury stock.** The following comparative statements of stockholders' equity are prepared for Nolan Corporation:

	Jan.1,2015	Jan.1,2017	Jan.1,2019
Common stock ($10 par).	$300,000	$300,000	$300,000
Paid-in capital in excess of par	60,000	60,000	60,000
Retained earnings		42,000	120,000
Total.	$360,000	$402,000	$480,000
Less treasury stock (at cost)		(75,000)	(75,000)
Total stockholders' equity.	$360,000	$327,000	$405,000

Tarman Corporation acquires 60% of Nolan Corporation common stock for $12 per share on January 1, 2015, when the latter corporation is formed.

On January 1, 2017, Nolan Corporation purchases 5,000 shares of its own common stock from noncontrolling interests for $15 per share. These shares are accounted for as treasury stock at cost.

Assuming Tarman Corporation uses the cost method to record its investment in Nolan Corporation, prepare the necessary cost-to-simple-equity conversion and the eliminations and adjustments required on the consolidated worksheet as of December 31, 2019. Include all pertinent supporting calculations in good form.

Exercise 5 *(LO 4)* **Three-level acquisition.** You have secured the following information for Companies A, B, and C concerning their internally generated net incomes (excluding subsidiary income) and dividends paid:

		A	B	C
2015	Internally generated net income	$30,000	$20,000	$10,000
	Dividends declared and paid	10,000	5,000	
2016	Internally generated net income	50,000	30,000	25,000
	Dividends declared and paid	10,000	5,000	5,000
2017	Internally generated net income	40,000	40,000	30,000
	Dividends declared and paid	10,000	5,000	5,000

1. Assume Company A acquires an 80% interest in Company B on January 1, 2015, and Company B acquires a 60% interest in Company C on January 1, 2016. Prepare the simple equity method adjusting entries made by Companies A and B for subsidiary investments for the years 2015 through 2017.
2. Assume Company B acquires a 70% interest in Company C on January 1, 2015, and Company A acquires a 90% interest in Company B on January 1, 2017. Prepare the simple equity method adjusting entries made by Companies A and B for subsidiary investments for the years 2015 through 2017.

Exercise 6 *(LO 4)* **Three-level acquisition, intercompany asset sale.** Baker Company acquires an 80% interest in the common stock of Cain Company for $440,000 on January 1, 2015. The price is equal to the book value of the interest acquired. Baker Company maintains its investment in Cain Company under the cost method.

Able Company acquires a 60% interest in the common stock of Baker Company on January 1, 2019, for $2,700,000. Any excess of cost is attributable to Cain Company equipment, which is understated by $80,000, and a Baker Company building, which is understated by $200,000. Any remaining excess is considered goodwill. Relevant stockholders' equities are as follows:

	Baker Company	Cain Company	
	Jan.1, 2019	Jan.1, 2015	Jan.1, 2019
Common stock............................	$ 400,000	$100,000	$100,000
Paid-in capital in excess of par	1,100,000	150,000	150,000
Retained earnings	2,000,000	300,000	450,000

1. Prepare a determination and distribution of excess schedule for Able Company's investment in Baker Company.
2. On January 1, 2020, Cain Company sells a machine with a net book value of $35,000 to Able Company for $60,000. The machine has a 5-year life. Prepare the eliminations and adjustments needed on the December 31, 2021, trial balance worksheet that relate to this intercompany sale.

Exercise 7 *(LO 4)* **Three-level acquisition, inventory and fixed asset sales.** Companies A, B, and C produce the following separate internally generated net incomes during 2015:

	A	B	C
Sales	$300,000	$400,000	$100,000
Less cost of goods sold.....................	200,000	300,000	60,000
Gross profit	$100,000	$100,000	$ 40,000
Expenses	60,000	30,000	10,000
Internally generated net income	$ 40,000	$ 70,000	$ 30,000

Company A acquires an 80% interest in Company B on January 1, 2012, and Company B acquires a 60% interest in Company C on January 1, 2013. Each investment is acquired at a price equal to the book value of the stock purchased.

Additional information is as follows:

a. Company A purchases goods billed at $30,000 from Company C during 2015. The price includes a 40% gross profit. One-half of the goods are held in Company A's year-end inventory.
b. Company B purchases goods billed at $30,000 from Company A during 2015. Company A always bills Company B at a price that includes a 30% gross profit. Company B has $6,000 of Company A goods in its beginning inventory and $2,400 of Company A goods in its ending inventory.
c. Company C purchases goods billed at $15,000 from Company B during 2015. Company B bills Company C at a 20% gross profit. At year-end, $7,500 of the goods remains unsold. The goods are inventoried at $5,000, under the lower-of-cost-or-market procedure.
d. Company B sells a machine to Company C on January 1, 2014, for $50,000. Company B's cost is $70,000, and accumulated depreciation on the date of sale is $40,000. The machine is being depreciated on a straight-line basis over five years.

Prepare the consolidated income statement for 2015, including the distribution of consolidated net income supported by distribution schedules.

Exercise 8 *(LO 4)* **Acquisition of a company with a subsidiary.** On January 1, 2015, Bell Company acquires an 80% interest in Carter Company for $140,000. The purchase price results in a $30,000 (including NCI adjustment) increase in the patent which has a 10-year life. The investment is recorded under the simple equity method.

On January 1, 2017, Ace Company purchases a 60% interest in Bell Company for $420,000. Ace Company believes that the patent value remaining on the investment by Bell in Carter is stated correctly. Comparative equities of Bell Company and Carter Company immediately prior to the purchase reveal the following:

Stockholders' Equity	Bell Company	Carter Company
Common stock ($5 par)	$200,000	
Common stock ($10 par)		$100,000
Paid-in capital in excess of par	100,000	20,000
Retained earnings	150,000	80,000
Total stockholders' equity	$450,000	$200,000

An analysis of the separate accounts of Bell and Carter on January 1, 2017, reveals that Carter's inventory is undervalued by $20,000 and that Bell's equipment with a 5-year future life is undervalued by $30,000. All other book values approximate fair values for Bell and Carter.

Prepare the determination and distribution of excess schedule for Ace's purchase of Bell Company on January 1, 2017.

Exercise 9 *(LO 4)* **Direct and indirect holdings.** The following diagram depicts the investment affiliations among Companies M, N, and O:

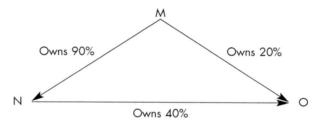

The following facts apply to 2017 operations:

	M	N	O
Internally generated net income	$200,000	$90,000	$40,000
Dividends declared and paid	40,000	10,000	5,000

All investments are made at a price equal to book value.

1. Prepare the simple equity method adjustments that would be made for the investments owned by Companies M and N during the year 2017.
2. Intercompany inventory transactions affecting 2017 are as follows:

	Sold by N to O	Sold by O to M
Profit on sales	25%	30%
Beginning inventory of intercompany goods	$10,000	$15,000
2017 sales	$50,000	$75,000
Ending inventory of intercompany goods	$12,000	$20,000

Using the facts given, determine the consolidated income of the consolidated company, the noncontrolling interest, and the controlling interest net income. Income distribution schedules may be used for support.

Exercise 10 *(LO 5)* **Treasury stock method.** Myles Corporation and its subsidiary, Downer Corporation, have the following trial balances as of December 31, 2017:

	Myles Corporation	Downer Corporation
Current Assets	402,000	182,000
Investment in Downer Corporation	396,000	
Investment in Myles Corporation		150,000
Property, Plant, and Equipment (net)	850,000	400,000
Liabilities	(200,000)	(100,000)
Common Stock ($10 par)	(1,000,000)	(500,000)
Retained Earnings, January 1, 2017	(400,000)	(100,000)
Sales	(800,000)	(350,000)
Dividend Income		(2,000)
Subsidiary Income	(18,000)	
Cost of Goods Sold	600,000	240,000
Expenses	150,000	80,000
Dividends Declared	20,000	
Totals	0	0

Myles Corporation acquires its 60% interest in Downer Corporation for $348,000 on January 1, 2015. At that time, Downer's retained earnings balance is $50,000. Any excess of cost over book value is attributed to equipment and given a 20-year life.

Downer Corporation purchases a 10% interest in Myles Corporation on January 1, 2017, for $150,000.

No intercompany transactions occur during 2017.

1. Prepare determination and distribution of excess schedules for the investment in Downer.
2. Prepare the 2017 consolidated income statement, including the consolidated net income distribution, using the treasury stock method for mutual holdings. Prepare the supporting income distribution schedules.

PROBLEMS

Problem 8-1 *(LO 1)* **Stock dividend, subsidiary stock sales, equity method.** On January 1, 2015, Wells Corporation acquires 8,000 shares of Towne Company stock and 18,000 shares of Sara Company stock for $176,000 and $240,000, respectively. Each investment is acquired at a price equal to the subsidiary's book value, resulting in no excesses.

Towne Company and Sara Company have the following stockholders' equities immediately prior to Wells's purchases:

	Towne Company	Sara Company
Common stock ($5 par)	$ 50,000	
Common stock ($10 par)		$300,000
Paid-in capital in excess of par	100,000	
Retained earnings	70,000	100,000
Total stockholder's equity	$220,000	$400,000

Additional information is as follows:

a. Net income for Towne Company and Sara Company for 2015 and 2016 follows (income is assumed to be earned evenly throughout the year):

	2015	2016
Towne Company......................................	$50,000	$50,000
Sara Company	40,000	40,000

b. No cash dividends are paid or declared by Towne or Sara during 2015 and 2016.
c. Towne Company distributes a 10% stock dividend on December 31, 2015. Towne stock is selling at $25 per share when the stock dividend is declared.
d. On July 1, 2016, Towne Company sells 2,750 shares of stock at $35 per share. Wells Corporation purchases none of these shares.
e. Sara Company sells 5,000 shares of stock on July 1, 2015, at $25 per share. Wells Corporation purchases 3,700 of these shares.
f. On January 1, 2016, Sara Company purchases 5,000 shares of its common stock from noncontrolling interests at $20 per share.

Required ▶ ▶ ▶ ▶ Assume Wells Corporation uses the simple equity method for its investments in subsidiaries. For 2015 and 2016, record each of the adjustments to the investment accounts. Provide all supporting calculations in good form.

Problem 8-2 *(LO 1)* **Stock dividend, subsidiary stock sales, cost method.** On January 1, 2015, Bear Corporation acquires a 60% interest in Kelly Company and an 80% interest in Samco Company. The purchase prices are $225,000 and $250,000, respectively. The excess of cost over book value for each investment is considered to be goodwill.

Immediately prior to the purchases, Kelly Company and Samco Company have the following stockholders' equities:

	Kelly Company	Samco Company
Common stock ($10 par).......................................	$200,000	
Common stock ($20 par).......................................		$200,000
Paid-in capital in excess of par	50,000	
Retained earnings	100,000	100,000
Total stockholder' equity	$350,000	$300,000

Additional information:

a. Kelly Company and Samco Company have the following net incomes for 2015 through 2017 (incomes are earned evenly throughout the year):

	2015	2016	2017
Kelly Company	$50,000	$60,000	$60,000
Samco Company..................................	40,000	30,000	55,000

b. Kelly Company has the following equity-related transactions for the first three years after it becomes a subsidiary of Bear Corporation:

July 1, 2015	Sells 5,000 shares of its own stock at $20 per share. Bear purchases 3,000 of these shares.
December 31, 2016......	Pays a cash dividend of $1 per share.
July 1, 2017	Purchases 5,000 shares of NCI-owned stock as treasury shares at $27 per share.

c. Samco Company has the following equity-related transactions for the first three years after it becomes a subsidiary of Bear Corporation:

December 31, 2015 . . Issues a 10% stock dividend. The estimated fair value of Samco common stock is $30 per share on the declaration date.

October 1, 2016 . . . . . Sells 4,000 shares of its own stock at $30 per share. Of these shares, 200 are purchased by Bear.

d. Bear Corporation has $200,000 of additional paid-in capital in excess of par on December 31, 2017.

Bear Corporation uses the cost method to account for its investments in subsidiaries. ◄ ◄ ◄ ◄ ◄ **Required** Convert its investments to the simple equity method as of December 31, 2017, and provide adequate support for the entries. Assume that the 2017 nominal accounts are closed. Prepare D&D schedules for each investment.

Problem 8-3 *(LO 2)* **Worksheet, subsidiary stock sale, intercompany merchandise.** On January 1, 2016, Palo Company acquires 80% of the outstanding common stock of Sheila Company for $700,000.

On January 1, 2018, Sheila Company sells 25,000 shares of common stock to the public at $12 per share. Palo Company does not purchase any of these shares. No entry has been made by the parent. Sheila Company has the following stockholders' equity at the end of 2015 and 2017:

	December 31,	
	2015	2017
Common stock ($2 par).	$200,000	$200,000
Paid-in capital in excess of par	400,000	400,000
Retained earnings	100,000	180,000
Total stockholders' equity.	$700,000	$780,000

On the January 1, 2016, acquisition date, Sheila Company's book values approximate fair values, except for a building that is undervalued by $80,000. The building has an estimated future life of 20 years. Any additional excess is attributed to goodwill.

Trial balances of the two companies as of December 31, 2018, are as follows:

	Palo Company	Sheila Company
Cash	179,040	105,000
Accounts Receivable (net)	280,000	190,000
Inventory	325,000	175,000
Investment in Sheila Company	700,000	
Property, Plant, and Equipment	2,450,000	1,400,000
Accumulated Depreciation	(1,256,000)	(536,000)
Liabilities	(750,000)	(210,000)
Common Stock ($10 par)	(1,500,000)	
Common Stock ($2 par)		(250,000)
Paid-In Capital in Excess of Par		(650,000)
Retained Earnings, January 1, 2018.	(375,000)	(180,000)
Sales	(1,600,000)	(750,000)
Subsidiary Dividend Income	(23,040)	
Cost of Goods Sold	1,120,000	450,000
Other Expenses	405,000	220,000
Dividends Declared.	45,000	36,000
Totals	0	0

During 2018, Sheila Company sells $50,000 of merchandise to Palo Company at a price that includes a 20% gross profit. This is their first intercompany sale. $10,000 of the goods remains in Palo's ending inventory.

Required ▶ ▶ ▶ ▶ ▶   Prepare the worksheet necessary to produce the consolidated financial statements of Palo Company and its subsidiary as of December 31, 2018. Include the determination and distribution of excess and income distribution schedules.

Problem 8-4 *(LO 2)* **Worksheet, subsidiary stock sale with parent purchase, intercompany merchandise.** On January 1, 2016, Mitta Corporation acquires a 60% interest (12,000 shares) in Train Company for $156,000. Train stockholders' equity on the purchase date is as follows:

Common stock ($5 par)............................	$100,000
Paid-in capital in excess of par	50,000
Retained earnings	80,000
Total stockholders' equity.........................	$230,000

At the purchase date, Train's book values for assets and liabilities closely approximate fair values. Any excess of cost over book value is attributed to goodwill.

On January 1, 2017, Train Company sells 5,000 shares of common stock in a public offering at $20 per share. Mitta Corporation purchases 4,000 shares.

During 2017, Mitta sells $30,000 of goods to Train at a gross profit of 25%. There are $6,000 of Mitta goods in Train's beginning inventory and $8,000 of Mitta goods in Train's ending inventory.

Merchandise sales by Train to Mitta are $20,000 during 2017 at a gross profit of 30%. There are $6,000 of Train goods in Mitta's beginning inventory and $2,000 of Train goods in Mitta's ending inventory.

Intercompany gross profit rates have been constant for many years. There are no intercompany payables/receivables.

Mitta's investment in Train Company balance is determined as follows:

Original cost	$156,000
60% of Train 2016 income ($40,000 × 60%)................................	24,000
Subtotal	$180,000
Less 60% of Train dividends declared in 2016 (60% × $8,000)	(4,800)
Subtotal	$175,200
Cost to acquire additional shares (new issue)	80,000
64% of Train 2017 income ($50,000 × 64%)................................	32,000
Subtotal	$287,200
Less 64% of Train dividends declared in 2017 (64% × $10,000)	(6,400)
Investment balance, December 31, 2017...................................	$280,800

The trial balances of the two companies as of December 31, 2017, are as follows:

	Mitta Corporation	Train Company
Cash	106,200	63,500
Accounts Receivable	113,600	60,000
Inventory	350,000	80,000
Investment in Train Company	280,800	
Property, Plant, and Equipment.............................	1,800,000	360,000
Accumulated Depreciation	(600,000)	(89,500)
Accounts Payable	(180,000)	(64,000)
Other Current Liabilities....................................	(26,000)	(8,000)
Bonds Payable..	(500,000)	

(continued)

	Mitta Corporation	Train Company
Common Stock ($10 par)	(1,000,000)	
Common Stock ($5 par)		(125,000)
Paid-In Capital in Excess of Par		(125,000)
Retained Earnings, January 1, 2017	(212,600)	(112,000)
Sales	(1,950,000)	(600,000)
Subsidiary Income	(32,000)	
Cost of Goods Sold	1,170,000	420,000
Other Expenses	630,000	130,000
Dividends Declared	50,000	10,000
Totals	0	0

Prepare the worksheet necessary to produce the consolidated financial statements of Mitta ◀ ◀ ◀ ◀ ◀ **Required** Corporation and its subsidiary as of December 31, 2017. Include the determination and distribution of excess and income distribution schedule.

Problem 8-5 *(LO 2)* **Worksheet, two subsidiaries, subsidiary stock sales, inter-company merchandise, fixed assets, bonds.** The audit of Barns Company and its subsidiaries for the year ended December 31, 2016, is completed. The working papers contain the following information:

a. Barns Company acquires 4,000 shares of Webo Company common stock for $320,000 on January 1, 2015. Webo Company purchases 500 shares of its own stock from NCI shareholders as treasury shares for $48,000 on January 1, 2016.

b. Barns Company acquires all 8,000 outstanding shares of Elcam Company stock on January 1, 2015, for $600,000. On January 1, 2016, Elcam Company issues through a private sale 2,000 additional shares to new noncontrolling shareholders at $85 per share. Barns has no investments other than the stock of Webo and Elcam.

c. Elcam Company originally issues $200,000 of 10-year, 8% mortgage bonds at 98, due on January 1, 2019. On January 1, 2016, Webo Company purchases $150,000 of these bonds in the open market at 98. Interest on the bonds is paid each June 30 and December 31.

d. Condensed balance sheets of Webo and Elcam on January 1, 2015, and January 1, 2016, are as follows:

	Webo Company		Elcam Company	
	Jan. 1, 2015	Jan. 1, 2016	Jan. 1, 2015	Jan. 1, 2016
Current assets	$195,000	$225,000	$280,400	$205,000
Property, plant, and equipment	305,000	350,000	613,000	623,800
Unamortized bond discount			1,600	1,200
Total	$500,000	$575,000	$895,000	$830,000
Current liabilities	$100,000	$125,000	$ 95,000	$105,000
Bonds payable			200,000	200,000
Capital stock ($50 par)	250,000	250,000	400,000	400,000
Retained earnings	150,000	200,000	200,000	125,000
Total	$500,000	$575,000	$895,000	$830,000

e. Total dividends declared and paid during 2016 are as follows:

Barns Company	$24,000
Webo Company	22,500
Elcam Company	10,000

f. On June 30, 2016, Barns sells equipment with a book value of $8,000 to Webo for $10,000. Webo depreciates equipment by the straight-line method based on a 10-year life.

g. Barns Company consistently sells to its subsidiaries at prices that realize a gross profit of 25% on sales. Webo and Elcam companies sell to each other and to Barns Company at cost. Prior to 2016, intercompany sales are negligible, but the following sales are made during 2016:

	Total Sales	Included in Purchaser's Inventory at December 31, 2016
Barns Company to Webo Company...............	$172,000	$20,000
Barns Company to Elcam Company	160,000	40,000
Webo Company to Elcam Company	25,000	5,000
Webo Company to Barns Company.............	28,000	8,000
	$385,000	$73,000

h. At December 31, 2016:

Barns Company owes Webo Company	$24,000
Webo Company owes Elcam Company......	16,000
Elcam Company owes Barns Company	12,000
Total	$52,000

i. The following trial balances as of December 31, 2016, are prepared:

	Barns Company	Webo Company	Elcam Company
Cash	110,000	26,000	165,200
Accounts Receivable	85,000	73,500	105,000
Inventories..........................	138,000	163,000	150,000
Investment in Webo Company Stock........	320,000		
Investment in Elcam Company Stock........	600,000		
Investment in Elcam Company Bonds		148,000	
Property, Plant, and Equipment............	700,000	525,000	834,000
Accumulated Depreciation	(402,000)	(325,000)	(240,000)
Accounts Payable	(202,000)	(150,500)	(86,900)
Dividends Payable....................	(12,000)		
Bonds Payable.......................	(400,000)		(200,000)
Unamortized Bond Discount			800
Capital Stock ($50 par).................	(600,000)	(250,000)	(500,000)
Paid-In Capital in Excess of Par			(70,000)
Retained Earnings, January 1, 2016........	(302,200)	(200,000)	(125,000)
Dividends declared	24,000	22,500	10,000
Treasury Stock (at cost)		48,000	
Gain on Sale of Equipment	(2,000)		
Sales	(2,950,000)	(1,550,000)	(1,750,000)
Interest Income on Bonds.................		(13,000)	
Dividend Income	(28,000)		
Cost of Goods Sold	2,500,000	1,200,000	1,400,000
Operating Expenses	405,000	280,000	290,500
Interest Expense......................	16,200	2,500	16,400
Totals.............................	0	0	0

◀ ◀ ◀ ◀ ◀ Required

Prepare the worksheet necessary to produce the consolidated financial statements of Barns Company and its subsidiaries for the year ended December 31, 2016. Include the determination and distribution of excess and income distribution schedules. Any excess of cost over book value is attributable to goodwill. All bond discounts are assumed to be amortized on a straight-line basis.

(AICPA adapted)

Problem 8-6 *(LO 4)* **Worksheet, direct and indirect holding, intercompany merchandise, machine.** The following diagram depicts the relationships among Mary Company, John Company, and Joan Company on December 31, 2018:

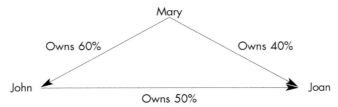

Mary Company purchases its interest in John Company on January 1, 2016, for $204,000. John Company purchases its interest in Joan Company on January 1, 2017, for $75,000. Mary Company purchases its interest in Joan Company on January 1, 2018, for $72,000. All investments are accounted for under the equity method. Control over Joan Company does not occur until the January 1, 2018, acquisition. Thus, a D&D schedule will be prepared for the investment in Joan as of January 1, 2018.

The following stockholders' equities are available:

	John Company December 31,	Joan Company December 31,	
	2015	2016	2017
Common stock ($10 par).	$150,000		
Common stock ($10 par).		$100,000	$100,000
Paid-in capital in excess of par	75,000		
Retained earnings	75,000	50,000	80,000
Total equity	$300,000	$150,000	$180,000

On January 2, 2018, Joan Company sells a machine to Mary Company for $20,000. The machine has a book value of $10,000, with an estimated life of five years and is being depreciated on a straight-line basis.

John Company sells $20,000 of merchandise to Joan Company during 2018 to realize a gross profit of 30%. Of this merchandise, $5,000 remains in Joan Company's December 31, 2018, inventory. Joan owes John $3,000 on December 31, 2018, for merchandise delivered during 2018.

Trial balances of the three companies prepared from general ledger account balances on December 31, 2018, are as follows:

	Mary Company	John Company	Joan Company
Cash	62,500	60,000	30,000
Accounts Receivable	200,000	55,000	30,000
Inventory	360,000	80,000	50,000
Investment in John Company	270,000		
Investment in Joan Company	86,000	107,500	
Property, Plant, and Equipment	2,250,000	850,000	350,000
Accumulated Depreciation	(938,000)	(377,500)	(121,800)

(continued)

	Mary Company	John Company	Joan Company
Intangibles.....................................	15,000		
Accounts Payable	(215,500)	(61,000)	(22,000)
Accrued Expenses	(12,000)	(4,000)	(1,200)
Bonds Payable................................	(500,000)	(300,000)	(100,000)
Common Stock ($5 par)	(500,000)		
Common Stock ($10 par)		(150,000)	
Common Stock ($10 par)			(100,000)
Paid-In Capital in Excess of Par	(700,000)	(75,000)	
Retained Earnings, January 1, 2018...............	(290,000)	(130,000)	(80,000)
Sales	(1,800,000)	(500,000)	(300,000)
Gain on Sale of Equipment			(10,000)
Subsidiary Income............................	(58,000)	(20,000)	
Cost of Goods Sold	1,170,000	350,000	180,000
Other Expenses	525,000	100,000	90,000
Dividends Declared............................	75,000	15,000	5,000
Totals	0	0	0

Required ▶ ▶ ▶ ▶ ▶

Prepare the worksheet necessary to produce the consolidated financial statements of Mary Company and its subsidiaries as of December 31, 2018. Include the determination and distribution of excess and income distribution schedules. Any excess of cost is assumed to be attributable to goodwill.

Problem 8-7 *(LO 4)* **Worksheet, three-level holding, intercompany merchandise, plant assets.** Shelby Corporation purchases 90% of the outstanding stock of Borner Company on January 1, 2015, for $603,000 cash. At that time, Borner Company has the following stockholders' equity balances: common stock, $200,000; paid-in capital in excess of par, $80,000; and retained earnings, $300,000.

All book values approximate fair values except for the plant assets (undervalued by $50,000 and with an estimated remaining life of 10 years). Any remaining excess is goodwill.

DeNoma Company acquires a 60% interest in Shelby on January 1, 2017, for $750,000. At this time, Shelby has consolidated shareholders' equity of common stock, $500,000; paid-in capital in excess of par, $150,000; and controlling retained earnings, $500,000 (not including amortization of excess price applicable to investment in Borner).

At that time, it is also determined that Shelby's plant assets are undervalued by $50,000 and have a 10-year remaining life. Any remaining excess is goodwill.

Intercompany merchandise sales from Borner to Shelby for 2018 are (1) seller's goods in buyer's beginning inventory, $7,500; (2) sales during 2018, $125,000; (3) seller's goods in buyer's ending inventory, $10,000; and (4) gross profit on intercompany sales, 80%.

On January 1, 2017, Shelby sells plant assets with a cost of $80,000 and accumulated depreciation of $45,000 to DeNoma for $50,000. Remaining life on the date of sale is estimated to be five years.

Shelby and DeNoma use the simple equity method to account for their investments. The trial balances on December 31, 2018, are as follows:

	DeNoma Company	Shelby Corporation	Borner Company
Inventory	75,000	60,000	40,000
Other Current Assets	900,000	2,000	390,000
Plant Assets	1,200,000	800,000	600,000
Accumulated Depreciation	(450,000)	(300,000)	(200,000)
Investment in Shelby Corporation	894,000		
Investment in Borner Company		828,000	
Common Stock	(1,500,000)	(500,000)	(200,000)

(continued)

	DeNoma Company	Shelby Corporation	Borner Company
Paid-In Capital in Excess of Par		(150,000)	(80,000)
Retained Earnings	(922,000)	(620,000)	(500,000)
Sales	(900,000)	(700,000)	(600,000)
Cost of Goods Sold	570,000	425,000	400,000
Expenses	205,000	200,000	150,000
Subsidiary Income.	(72,000)	(45,000)	
Totals	0	0	0

Prepare the determination and distribution of excess schedule for Shelby's investment in ◀ ◀ ◀ ◀ ◀ **Required** Borner and DeNoma's investment in Shelby. Prepare the December 31, 2018, consolidated worksheet and income distribution schedules.

Suggestion: The determination and distribution of excess schedule must show an adjustment to Shelby's retained earnings for the amortization of excess applicable to Shelby's investment in Borner. [*Hint* (for consolidated balance sheet): The reduced retained earnings in the determination and distribution of excess schedule must be adjusted before eliminating the pro rata share of equity balances.]

Problem 8-8 *(LO 5)* Worksheet, subsidiary owns parent shares, merchandise. On January 1, 2015, Parson Company purchases 80% of the common stock of Salary Company for $450,000. On this date, Salary has common stock, other paid-in capital in excess of par, and retained earnings of $50,000, $140,000, and $220,000, respectively.

Any excess of cost over book value is due to goodwill.

In both 2015 and 2016, Parson has accounted for the investment in Salary using the cost method.

On January 1, 2016, Salary purchases 1,000 shares (10%) of the common stock of Parson Company from outside investors for $100,000 cash. It is expected that the shares may be resold later. Salary uses the cost method in accounting for the investment.

During the last quarter of 2016, Parson sells merchandise to Salary for $48,000, one-fourth of which is still held by Salary on December 31, 2016. Parson's usual gross profit on intercompany sales is 40%.

The trial balances for Parson and Salary on December 31, 2016, are as follows:

	Parson Company	Salary Company
Inventory	170,000	120,000
Other Current Assets	166,000	196,000
Investment in Salary Company	450,000	
Investment in Parson Company		100,000
Land.	80,000	70,000
Buildings and Equipment.	400,000	280,000
Accumulated Depreciation	(180,000)	(90,000)
Current Liabilities.	(98,000)	(74,000)
Long-Term Liabilities	(250,000)	(100,000)
Common Stock—Parson Company ($10 par).	(100,000)	
Paid-In Capital in Excess of Par—Parson Company	(200,000)	
Retained Earnings—Parson Company	(350,000)	
Common Stock—Salary Company ($10 par).		(50,000)
Paid-In Capital in Excess of Par—Salary Company.		(140,000)
Retained Earnings—Salary Company.		(260,000)
Net Sales.	(640,000)	(350,000)
Cost of Goods Sold	360,000	200,000
Operating Expenses	160,000	90,000
Dividend Income	(8,000)	(2,000)
Dividends Declared.	40,000	10,000
Totals	0	0

Required ▶ ▶ ▶ ▶ ▶   Complete the worksheet for consolidated financial statements for the year ended December 31, 2016. Shares of Parson owned by Salary are to be treated as treasury stock. Round all computations to the nearest dollar. Include a determination and distribution of excess schedule and income distribution schedule.

(AICPA adapted)

Problem 8-9 *(LO 5)* **Worksheet, purchase in blocks, subsidiary stock dividend, subsidiary purchase of parent shares, machinery sale, merchandise.** On January 1, 2017, Heckert Company purchases a controlling interest in Aker Company. The following information is available:

a. Heckert Company purchases 1,600 shares of Aker Company outstanding stock on January 1, 2016, for $48,000 and purchases an additional 1,400 shares on January 1, 2017, for $51,800.

b. An analysis of the stockholders' equity accounts at December 31, 2016, and 2015, follows:

	Heckert Company December 31,		Aker Company December 31,	
	2016	2015	2016	2015
Common stock ($10 par)...........	$150,000	$150,000		
Common stock ($5 par)............			$ 20,000	$ 20,000
Paid-in capital in excess of par	36,000	36,000	10,000	10,000
Retained earnings	378,000	285,000	112,000	82,000
Total	$564,000	$471,000	$142,000	$112,000

c. Aker Company's marketable securities consist of 1,500 shares of Heckert Company stock purchased on June 15, 2017, in the open market for $18,000. The securities are purchased as a temporary investment and are sold on January 15, 2018, for $25,000.

d. On December 10, 2017, Heckert Company declares a cash dividend of $0.50 per share, payable January 10, 2018, to stockholders of record on December 20, 2017. Aker Company pays a cash dividend of $1 per share on June 30, 2017, and distributes a 10% stock dividend on September 30, 2017. The stock is selling for $15 per share ex-dividend on September 30, 2017. Aker Company pays no dividends in 2016.

e. Aker Company sells machinery, with a book value of $4,000 and a remaining life of five years, to Heckert Company for $4,800 on December 31, 2017. The gain on the sale is credited to the other income account.

f. Aker Company includes all intercompany receivables and payables in its trade accounts receivable and trade accounts payable accounts.

g. During 2017, the following intercompany sales are made:

	Net Sales	Included in Purchaser's Inventory at December 31, 2017
Heckert Company to Aker Company....................	$ 78,000	$24,300
Aker Company to Heckert Company..................	104,000	18,000
	$182,000	$42,300

Heckert Company sells merchandise to Aker Company at cost. Aker Company sells merchandise to Heckert at the regular selling price to make a normal profit margin of 30%. There were no intercompany sales in prior years.

The trial balances of the two companies at December 31, 2017, are as follows:

	Heckert Company	Aker Company
Cash	38,100	29,050
Marketable Securities	33,000	18,000
Trade Accounts Receivable	210,000	88,000
Allowance for Doubtful Accounts	(6,800)	(2,300)
Intercompany Receivables	24,000	
Inventories	275,000	135,000
Machinery and Equipment	514,000	279,000
Accumulated Depreciation	(298,200)	(196,700)
Investment in Aker Company (at cost)	99,800	
Patents	35,000	
Dividends Payable	(7,500)	
Trade Accounts Payable	(195,500)	(174,050)
Intercompany Payables	(8,000)	
Common Stock ($10 par)	(150,000)	
Common Stock ($5 par)		(22,000)
Paid-In Capital in Excess of Par	(36,000)	(14,000)
Retained Earnings	(378,000)	(106,000)
Dividends Declared (cash)	7,500	4,000
Sales and Services	(850,000)	(530,000)
Dividend Income	(3,000)	
Other Income	(9,000)	(3,700)
Cost of Goods Sold	510,000	374,000
Depreciation Expense	65,600	11,200
Administrative and Selling Expenses	130,000	110,500
Totals	0	0

Prepare the worksheet necessary to produce the consolidated financial statements of Heckert ◄ ◄ ◄ ◄ ◄ **Required** Company and its subsidiary for the year ended December 31, 2017. Include the determination and distribution of excess and income distribution schedules. Assume any excess of cost over book value is attributable to goodwill.

(AICPA adapted)

Accounting for Influential Investments

In practical terms, an influential investment is generally an investment of 20% or more in the voting common stock of a company, but not more than 50%, which would require consolidation. *Influence* is defined as follows by the FASB:

> *The equity method tends to be most appropriate if an investment enables the investor to influence the operating or financial decisions of the investee. The investor then has a degree of responsibility for the return on its investment, and it is appropriate to include in the results of operations of the investor its share of the earnings or losses of the investee. Influence tends to be more effective as the investor's percent of ownership in the voting stock of the investee increases. Investments of relatively small percentages of voting stock of an investee tend to be passive in nature and enable the investor to have little or no influence on the operations of the investee.*[1]

The use of the sophisticated equity method is required for the following types of investments:

1. **Influential investments.** The FASB defines influence as "representation on the board of directors, participation in policy-making processes, material intercompany transactions, interchange of managerial personnel, or technological dependency."[2] When the investor holds 20% or more of the voting shares of an investee, influence is assumed and the sophisticated equity method is required unless the investor takes on the burden of proof to show that influence does not exist, in which case the cost method would be used.[3] When the investment falls below 20%, the presumption is that influence does not exist, and the cost method is to be used unless the investor can show that influence does exist despite the low percentage of ownership. Since the most common use of the sophisticated equity method is for influential (20% to 50%) investments, such investments are used in subsequent illustrations.

2. **Corporate joint ventures.** A corporate joint venture is a separate, specific project organized for the benefit of several corporations. An example would be a research project undertaken jointly by several members of a given industry. The member corporations typically participate in the management of the venture and share the gains and losses. Since such an arrangement does not involve passive investors, the sophisticated equity method is required.

3. **Unconsolidated subsidiaries.** A parent may own over 50% of the shares of a subsidiary but may meet one of the exceptions (control is temporary or does not rest with the majority owner) to the requirement that subsidiaries be consolidated. However, if influence does exist, the sophisticated equity method would be used for the investment.

---

1 FASB ASC 323-10-05-5.
2 FASB ASC 323-10-15-6.
3 FASB ASC 323-10-15-8.

The use of the equity method requires that the investment in common stock appear as a single, equity-adjusted amount on the balance sheet of the investor. The investor's income statement will include the investor's share of the investee ordinary income as a single amount in the ordinary income section. The investor's share of investee discontinued operations, extraordinary items, and cumulative effects of changes in accounting principles will appear as single amounts in the sections of the investor's income statement that correspond to the placement of these items in the investee's statement.

In 2007, the FASB allowed investors to opt for the use of the fair value method for influential investments that would normally be accounted for under the equity method. This option will be discussed after our study of the equity method.

CALCULATION OF EQUITY INCOME

The equity method requires the investor to recognize its pro rata share of investee reported income. Dividends, when received, do not constitute income but are viewed instead as a partial liquidation of the investment. In reality, however, the price paid for the investment usually will not agree with the underlying book value of the investee, which requires that any amortization of an excess of cost or book value be treated as an adjustment of the investor's pro rata share of investee income. It is very likely that the reported income of the investee will include gains and losses on transactions with the investor. As was true in consolidations, these gains and losses must be deferred until they are confirmed by a transaction between the affiliated group and unrelated parties. The proper application of the sophisticated equity method will mean that the income recognized by the investor will be the same as it would be under consolidation procedures. In fact, the sophisticated equity method sometimes is referred to as "one-line consolidation."

In the next two sections, the sophisticated equity method will be presented without consideration of the tax implications. Following that, the tax effect on such an investment will be addressed.

Amortization of Excesses

A determination and distribution of excess schedule is prepared for a sophisticated equity method investment. It compares the price paid for the investment to only the equity interest that was purchased. **In the absence of control, there is no fair value adjustment for the shares not purchased.** For example, assume the following schedule was prepared by Excel Corporation for a 25% interest in Flag Company acquired on January 1, 2015:

Price paid		$250,000
Less interest acquired:		
Common stock ($10 par)	$200,000	
Retained earnings, January 1, 2015	600,000	
Total stockholders' equity	$800,000	
Interest acquired	× 25%	200,000
Excess of cost over book value		$ 50,000
Less excess attributable to equipment with a 5-year remaining		
life and undervalued by $80,000 (25% × $80,000)		20,000
Goodwill		$ 30,000

As a practical matter, it may not be possible to relate the excess to specific assets, in which case the entire excess may be considered goodwill. However, an attempt should be made to allocate the excess in the same manner as would be done for the purchase of a controlling interest in a subsidiary.[4]

The determination and distribution of excess schedule indicates the pattern of amortization to be followed. The required amortizations must be made directly through the investment account since the distributions shown on the schedule are not recorded in the absence of consolidation procedures. Assuming Flag Company reported net income of $60,000 for 2015, Excel Corporation would make the following entry for 2015:

Investment in Flag Company	11,000	
Investment Income		11,000

Income is calculated as follows:

25% × Flag reported net income of $60,000	$15,000
Less amortizations of excess cost:	
Equipment ($20,000 ÷ 5)	4,000
Investment income, net of amortizations	$11,000

If an investment is acquired for less than book value, the excess of book value over cost would be amortized based on the life of assets to which it pertains. This procedure would increase investment income in the years of amortization.

Intercompany Transactions by Investee

The investee may sell inventory to the investor. As would be true if the investment were consolidated, the share of the investee's profit on goods still held by the investor at the end of a period cannot be included in income of that period. Instead, the profit must be deferred until the goods are sold by the investor. Since the two firms are separate reporting entities, the intercompany sales and related debt cannot be eliminated. Only the investor's share of the investee's profit on unsold goods in the hands of the investor is deferred. In a like manner, the investor may have plant assets that were purchased from the investee. The investor's share of the investee's gains and losses on these sales also must be deferred and allocated over the depreciable life of the asset. Profit deferments should be handled in an income distribution schedule similar to that used for consolidated worksheets. To illustrate, assume the following facts for the example of the 25% investment in Flag by Excel. Again, note that income tax is not being considered in this illustration:

1. Excel had the following merchandise acquired from Flag Company in its ending inventories:

Year	Amount	Gross Profit of Flag Company
2015	$30,000	40%
2016	40,000	45

2. Excel purchased a truck from Flag Company on January 1, 2015, for $20,000. The truck is being depreciated over a 4-year life on a straight-line basis with no salvage value. The truck had a net book value of $16,000 when it was sold by Flag.
3. Flag Company had an income of $60,000 in 2015 and $70,000 in 2016.
4. Flag declared and paid $10,000 in dividends in 2016.

Based on these facts, Excel Corporation would prepare the income distribution schedules shown on page 484.

---

4 FASB ASC 323-10-35-34.

2015 Income Distribution for Investment in Flag Company

Gain on sale of truck, to be amortized over 4 years	$ 4,000	Reported income of Flag Company	$60,000
Profit in Excel ending inventory (40% × $30,000)	12,000	Realization of ¼ of profit on sale of truck	1,000
		Adjusted income of Flag Company	$45,000
		Ownership interest (25%)	$11,250
		Less amortization of excess cost:	
		Equipment	4,000
		Investment income, net of amortizations	$ 7,250

2016 Income Distribution for Investment in Flag Company

Profit in Excel ending inventory (45% × $40,000)	$18,000	Reported income of Flag Company	$70,000
		Profit in Excel beginning inventory (40% × $30,000)	12,000
		Realization of ¼ of profit on sale of truck	1,000
		Adjusted income of Flag Company	$65,000
		Ownership interest (25%)	$16,250
		Less amortization of excess cost:	
		Equipment	4,000
		Income from investment	$12,250

The schedules would lead to the following entries to record investment income:

2015	Investment in Flag Company	7,250	
	Investment Income		7,250
2016	Investment in Flag Company	12,250	
	Investment Income		12,250

In addition, the following entry would be made in 2016 to record dividends received:

Cash	2,500	
Investment in Flag Company		2,500

It should be noted that only the investor's share of intercompany gains and losses is deferred. The investee's remaining stockholders are not affected by the Excel Corporation investment.

TAX EFFECTS OF EQUITY METHOD

The investor not meeting the requirements of affiliation as defined by tax law pays income taxes on dividends received. In the case of a domestic corporation, 20% of the dividends are includable in taxable income. However, a temporary difference is created through the use of the equity method for financial reporting.[5] As a result, **the provision for tax is based on the equity income, and a deferred tax liability is created for undistributed investment income.**

_____

5 FASB ASC 740-20-20.

The provision may be based on the assumption that investment income will be distributed in dividends, or it will be realized via the sale of the investment. In the latter case, it is likely that the income would be taxed in the form of a capital gain. The assumption used will determine the rate to be applied to the undistributed income. The provision for tax is based on the investor's net investment income after adjustments and amortizations. However, **amortizations of excess cost are not deductible** since they have no impact on the income that could be distributed to the investor and, thus, must be added back to the net investment income to compute the tax.

The following entries are based on the previous example of Flag Company and Excel Corporation, but it is assumed that each company is subject to a 30% income tax. Excel Corporation's share of Flag Company net income would now be calculated as follows:

	2015	2016
Adjusted income of Flag Company (before tax)*	$45,000	$65,000
Tax provision (30%)	13,500	19,500
Adjusted net income of Flag Company	$31,500	$45,500
Ownership interest in adjusted net income (25%)	$ 7,875	$11,375
Less amortizations of excess*	4,000	4,000
Net income from investment	$ 3,875	$ 7,375

*See the income distribution schedules in the previous section.

Note that the tax provision calculated by the investor will not agree with the provision for tax on the books of the investee. This is due to the adjustments made in the income distribution schedules to recognize the profit deferrals.

The 2015 and 2016 entries to record investment income and the applicable tax provision would be as follows:

2015	Investment in Flag Company	3,875	
	Investment Income		3,875
	Provision for Income Tax [20% included × 30% tax rate ×		
	($3,875 net income + $4,000 nondeductible		
	amortizations of excess)]	473	
	Deferred Tax Liability		473
2016	Investment in Flag Company	7,375	
	Investment Income		7,375
	Cash	2,500	
	Investment in Flag Company		2,500
	Provision for Income Tax [20% included × 30% tax rate ×		
	($7,375 net income + $4,000 nondeductible		
	amortizations of excess)]	683	
	Income Tax Payable (20% included × 30% tax rate ×		
	$2,500 dividends)		150
	Deferred Tax Liability ($683 – $150)		533

UNUSUAL EQUITY ADJUSTMENTS

There are several unusual situations involving the investee that require special procedures for the proper recording of investment income. These situations are described in the following paragraphs.

Investee with Preferred Stock

In the absence of consolidation, an investment in preferred stock does not require elimination. However, the existence of preferred stock in the capital structure of the investee requires that the investor's equity adjustment be based on only that portion of investee income available for common stockholders. Dividends declared on preferred stock must be subtracted from income of the investee. When the preferred stock has cumulative or participation rights, the claim of preferred stockholders must be subtracted from the investee income each period to arrive at the income available for common stockholders. The procedures for calculating this income are contained in Chapter 7.

Investee Stock Transactions

The investee corporation may engage in transactions with its common stockholders, such as issuing additional shares, retiring shares, or engaging in treasury stock transactions. Each of these transactions affects the investor's equity interest. A comparison is made of the investor's ownership interest before and after the investee stock transaction. An increase in the investor's interest is treated as a gain, while a decrease is recorded as a loss.

Write-Down to Market Value

The investment in another company is subject to reduction to a lower market value if it appears that a relatively permanent fall in value has occurred. The fact that the current market value of the shares is temporarily less than the equity-adjusted cost of the shares is not sufficient cause for a write-down. When the sophisticated equity method is used and a permanent decline in value occurs, a reduction would be made to the equity-adjusted cost. The equity method would continue to be applied subsequent to the write-down. There can be no subsequent write-ups, however, other than through normal equity adjustments.

Zero Investment Balance

It is possible that an investee will suffer losses to the extent that the continued application of the equity method could produce a negative balance in the investment account. Equity adjustments are to be discontinued when the investment balance becomes zero. Further losses are acknowledged only by memo entries, which are needed to maintain the total unrecorded share of losses. If the investee again becomes profitable, the investor must not record income on the investment until its subsequent share of income equals the previously unrecorded share of losses.

To illustrate these procedures, assume Grate Corporation has a 35% investment in Dittmar Company, with a sophisticated equity-adjusted cost of $30,000 on January 1, 2015, and Dittmar reports the following results:

Period	Income (Loss)
2015	$(80,000)
2016	(50,000)
2017	(20,000)
2018	90,000

The following T account summarizes entries for 2015 through 2018 (taxes are ignored):

Investment in Dittmar Company			
Equity-adjusted balance, January 1, 2015..............................	$30,000	Equity loss for 2015 (35% × $80,000 Dittmar loss)............................	$28,000
		Recorded equity loss for 2016 (35% × $50,000 Dittmar loss = $17,500; loss limited to investment balance).........	2,000
Balance, January 1, 2016..............	$ 0	Memo entries:	
Memo entry:		Unrecorded 2016 loss ($17,500 – $2,000) ..	$15,500
Unrecorded share of 2018 Dittmar		Unrecorded loss for 2017 (35% ×	
income	22,500	$20,000 Dittmar loss)...................	7,000
Actual entries resumed:			
Recorded equity income, 2018 [35% × $90,000 Dittmar income = $31,500, less amount to cover unrecorded losses ($15,500 + $7,000)].........................	9,000		
Balance, December 31, 2018	$ 9,000		

Intercompany Asset Transactions by Investor

An investor may sell merchandise and/or plant assets to an investee at a gain or loss. When influence is deemed to exist, it might seem appropriate to defer the entire gain or loss until the asset is resold or depreciated by the investee. However, the entire gain or loss is to be deferred only when the transaction is with a controlled (over 50% owned) investee and is not at arm's length. In all other cases, it is appropriate to defer only a gain or loss that is in proportion to the investor's ownership interest.[6]

To illustrate, assume Grant Corporation, which owns a 35% interest in Hartwig Company sold $50,000 of merchandise to Hartwig at a gross profit of 40%. Of this merchandise, $20,000 is still in Hartwig's 2015 ending inventory. Grant needs to defer only profit equal to the $8,000 (40% × $20,000) unrealized gross profit multiplied by its 35% interest, or $2,800. Grant would make the following entry on December 31, 2015:

Sales	2,800	
Deferred Gross Profit on Sales to Investee		2,800

Assuming the investor recorded the provision for income tax prior to this adjustment, the tax applicable to the unrealized gain would be deferred by the following entry, which is based on a 30% tax rate:

Deferred Tax Expense (30% × $2,800)	840	
Provision for Income Tax		840

The deferred gross profit and the related tax deferment would be realized in the period in which the goods are sold to outside parties. The deferred profit and related tax effects on plant asset sales would be realized in proportion to the depreciation recorded by the investee company.

Intercompany Bond Transactions by Investor

Unlike consolidation procedures, when the investor purchases outstanding bonds of the investee, the bonds are not assumed to be retired since the investor and investee are separate reporting entities.

---

6 FASB ASC 323-10-35 & 36.

Similarly, a purchase of investor bonds by the investee is not a retirement of the bonds. Thus, no adjustments to income are necessary as a result of intercompany bond holdings.

Gain or Loss of Influence

An investor may own less than a 20% interest in an investee, in which case the cost method or fair value method would be used to record the investment. If the investor subsequently buys sufficient additional shares to have its total interest equal or exceed 20%, the investor must *retroactively* apply the sophisticated equity method to the total holding period of the investment.

It is possible that an investor will own 20% or more of the voting shares of the investee but will sell a portion of the shares so that the ownership interest falls below 20%. In such a case, the sophisticated equity method is discontinued as of the sale date. However, there is no adjustment back to the cost method. The balance of the investment account remains at its equity-adjusted balance on the sale date. Should influence be attained again, a retroactive ("catch-up") equity adjustment would be made.

When all or part of an investment recorded under the sophisticated equity method is sold, the gain or loss is based on the equity-adjusted balance as of the sale date. An adjustment also would be necessary for deferred tax balances applicable to the investment.

DISCLOSURE REQUIREMENTS

Since a significant portion of the investor's income may be derived from investments, added disclosures are required in order to properly inform the readers of the financial statements. For investments of 20% or more, the investor must disclose the name of each investee, the percentage of ownership in each investee, and the disparity between the cost and underlying book value for each investment. If the sophisticated equity method is not being applied, the reasons must be given. When investments are material with respect to the investor's financial position or income, the financial statements of the investees should be included as supplemental information.

When a market value for the investment is available, it should be disclosed. However, if the investor owns a relatively large block of a subsidiary's shares, quoted market values would have little relevance because the sale of an entire controlling interest would involve different motivations and would result in a unique value.

REFLECTION

- The sophisticated equity method is used for "influential" investments.

- The sophisticated equity income is based on the investee's adjusted (for intercompany profits) income less amortizations of excess from the D&D. Note that this process includes adjustment for only investee-generated intercompany transactions.

- The investor is liable for the tax on its share of investee income.

- The investor must make a separate adjustment for its share of unrealized profits on sales to the investee. These adjustments also create a deferred tax asset.

- The investor cannot adjust its investment below a zero balance by recording its share of investee losses. If the investee becomes profitable, income equal to the unrecorded losses must be excluded from income.

- An initial ownership interest may not be "influential." If a second block is purchased, so as to make the total interest "influential," the prior block is retroactively converted to the sophisticated equity method.

- If an interest is sold down to a level that is no longer influential, the remaining interest stays at its equity-adjusted cost. The use of the equity method is discontinued in future periods.

FAIR VALUE OPTION

The investor may elect to record an influential investment using fair value at each recording date. The election is made on the date the investment is purchased. The election once made, may not be revoked.

The fair value option is applied as follows:

1. The investment is recorded at the price paid.
2. At the end of each accounting period, the investment is adjusted to fair value, and the adjustment is recorded as income.
3. Dividends are recorded as income when declared by the investee.

The following example applies the fair value option to the investment in Flag Company that starts on page 482. Assume that the fair value of the investment is $270,000 on December 31, 2015, and $310,000 on December 31, 2016.

2015	Purchase Date	Investment in Flag Company	250,000	
		Cash		250,000
		To record purchase of investment		
2015	Year-end adjustment	Investment in Flag Company	20,000	
		Unrealized Gain on Investment		20,000
2016	Year-end adjustment	Investment in Flag Company	40,000	
		Unrealized Gain on Investment		40,000
	Dividend declared	Cash	2,500	
		Dividend Income		2,500

The unrealized gain is recorded as income as is the investor's share of dividends. There would be no adjustments for unrealized intercompany gains and losses. The unrealized gains will require the recording of a deferred income tax liability since the income is not taxable.

UNDERSTANDING THE ISSUES

1. Company R pays $170,000 for a 30% interest in Company E on January 1, 2015. Company E's total stockholders' equity on that date is $500,000. The excess price is attributed to equipment with a 5-year life. During 2015, Company E reports net income of $35,000 and pays total dividends of $10,000. Answer the following questions assuming the investment is recorded under the equity method:

   a. What is Company R's investment income for 2015?
   b. What is Company R's investment balance on December 31, 2015?
   c. Explain, in words, the investment balance on December 31, 2015.

2. Assume the same facts as for Question 1 above. The fair value of the investment in Company E is $220,000 on December 31, 2015. Answer the following questions assuming the investment is recorded using the fair value option:

   a. What is Company R's investment income for 2015?
   b. What is Company R's investment balance on December 31, 2015?
   c. Explain in words the investment balance on December 31, 2015.

3. Company R owns a 30% interest in Company E, which it acquires at book value. Company E reports net income of $50,000 for 2015 (ignore taxes). There is an intercompany sale of equipment at a gain of $20,000 on January 1, 2015. The equipment has a 5-year life. What is Company R's investment income for 2015, and what adjusting entry (if any) does Company R need to make as a result of the equipment sale, if:

   a. Company E made the sale?
   b. Company R made the sale?

4. Company E reports net income of $100,000 for 2015. Assume the income is earned evenly throughout the year. Dividends of $10,000 are paid on December 31. What will Company R report as investment income under the following ownership situations, if:

   a. Company R owns a 10% interest from July 1 to December 31?
   b. Company R owns a 10% interest from January 1 to June 30 and a 25% interest from July 1 to December 31?
   c. Company R owns a 30% interest from January 1 to June 30 and a 10% interest from July 1 to December 31?

5. Company R purchases a 25% interest in Company E on January 1, 2014, at its book value of $20,000. From 2014 through 2018, Company E earns a total of $200,000. From 2019 through 2023, it loses $300,000. In 2024, Company E reports net income of $30,000. What is Company R's investment income for 2024, and what is its balance in the investment in Company E account on December 31, 2024?

EXERCISES

Exercise SA1-1 Income recording. Tucker Corporation purchases a 25% interest in Lincoln Company for $120,000 on January 1, 2017. The following determination and distribution of excess schedule is prepared:

Price paid		$120,000
Less interest acquired:		
Common stock ($10 par)	$200,000	
Retained earnings	100,000	
Total stockholders' equity	$300,000	
Interest acquired	× 25%	75,000
Excess of cost over book value		$ 45,000
Less excess attributable to equipment [25% × $40,000 (5-year life)] .		10,000
Goodwill		$ 35,000

Lincoln Company earns income of $25,000 in 2017 and $30,000 in 2018. Lincoln Company declares a 25-cent per-share cash dividend on December 22, 2018, payable January 12, 2019, to stockholders of record on December 30, 2018.

During 2018, Lincoln sells merchandise costing $10,000 to Tucker for $15,000. Twenty percent of the merchandise is still in Tucker's ending inventory on December 31, 2018. The fair value of the investment is $135,000 on December 31, 2017, and $145,000 on December 31, 2018.

1. Assuming the use of the equity method, prepare the adjustment on Tucker's books on December 31, 2017, and December 31, 2018, to account for its investment in Lincoln Company. Assume Tucker Corporation makes no adjustment except at the end of each calendar year. Ignore income tax considerations.
2. Assuming the use of the fair value option, prepare the adjustment on Tucker's books on December 31, 2017, and December 31, 2018, to account for its investment in Lincoln Company. Assume Tucker Corporation makes no adjustment except at the end of each calendar year. Ignore income tax considerations.

Exercise SA1-2 Equity method investment with intercompany profits. Turf Company purchases a 30% interest in Minnie Company for $90,000 on January 1, 2015, when Minnie has the following stockholders' equity:

Common stock ($10 par)	$100,000
Paid-in capital in excess of par	20,000
Retained earnings	130,000
Total	$250,000

The excess cost was due to a building that is being amortized over 20 years.

Since the investment, Minnie has consistently sold goods to Turf to realize a 40% gross profit. Such sales total $50,000 during 2017. Turf has $10,000 of the goods in its beginning inventory and $40,000 in its ending inventory.

On January 1, 2017, Turf sells a machine with a book value of $15,000 to Minnie for $20,000. The machine has a 5-year life and is being depreciated on a straight-line basis. Minnie reports a net income of $60,000 for 2017 and pays $5,000 in dividends in 2017.

Prepare all 2017 entries caused by Turf's investment in Minnie. Assume that Turf has recorded the tax on its internally generated income. Turf has properly recorded the investment using the equity method in previous periods. Ignore income tax considerations.

Exercise SA1-3 Equity income with intercompany profits. Spancrete Corporation acquires a 30% interest in the outstanding stock of Werl Corporation on January 1, 2015. At that time, the following determination and distribution of excess schedule is prepared:

Price paid		$125,000
Less interest acquired:		
Common stock.....................................	$150,000	
Retained earnings	160,000	
Total stockholders' equity...........................	$310,000	
Interest acquired	× 30%	93,000
Excess of cost over book value attributable to equipment (10-year life)		$ 32,000

During 2015, Spancrete purchases $200,000 of goods from Werl. $20,000 of these purchases are in the December 31, 2015, ending inventory. During 2016, Spancrete purchases $250,000 of goods from Werl. $30,000 of these purchases are in the December 31, 2016, ending inventory. Werl's gross profit rate is 30%. Also, Spancrete purchases a machine from Werl for $15,000 on January 1, 2016. The machine has a book value of $10,000 and a 5-year remaining life. Werl reports net income of $90,000 and pays $20,000 on dividends during 2016.

Prepare an income distribution schedule for Werl, and record the entries to adjust the investment in Werl for 2016 using the equity method.

Exercise SA1-4 Equity method, change in interest. Hanson Corporation purchases a 10% interest in Novic Company on January 1, 2016, and an additional 15% interest on January 1, 2018. These investments cost Hanson Corporation $80,000 and $110,000, respectively.

The following stockholders' equities of Novic Company are available:

	December 31, 2015	December 31, 2017
Common stock ($10 par)....................	$500,000	$500,000
Retained earnings	250,000	300,000
Total equity	$750,000	$800,000

Any excess of cost over book value on the original investment is attributed to goodwill. Any excess on the second purchase is attributable to equipment with a 4-year life.

Novic Company has income of $30,000, $30,000, and $40,000 for 2016, 2017, and 2018, respectively. Novic pays dividends of $0.20 per share in 2017 and 2018.

Ignore income tax considerations, and assume equity method adjusting entries are made at the end of the calendar year only.

1. Prepare the cost-to-equity conversion entry on January 1, 2018, when Hanson's investment in Novic Company first exceeds 20%. Any supporting schedules should be in good form.
2. Prepare the December 31, 2018, equity adjustment on Hanson's books. Provide supporting calculations in good form.

Exercise SA1-5 Sale of equity method investment. On January 1, 2017, Lund Corporation purchases a 30% interest in Aluma-Boat Company for $200,000. At the time of the purchase, Aluma-Boat has total stockholders' equity of $400,000. Any excess of cost over the equity purchased is attributed in part to machinery worth $50,000 more than book value with a remaining useful life of five years. Any remaining excess would be allocated to goodwill.

Aluma-Boat reports the following income and dividend distributions in 2017 and 2018:

	2017	2018
Income...	$50,000	$45,000
Dividends declared and paid	10,000	10,000

Lund sells its investment in Aluma-Boat Company on January 2, 2019, for $230,000. Record the sale of the investments assuming the use of the equity method. You may ignore income taxes. Carefully schedule the investment account balance at the time of the sale.

PROBLEMS

Problem SA1-1 Equity income, inventory, fixed asset sale. Schinzer Company purchases an influential 25% interest in Fowler Company on January 1, 2016, for $300,000. At that time, Fowler's stockholders' equity is $1,000,000.

Fowler Company assets have fair value similar to book value except for a building that is undervalued by $40,000. The building has an estimated remaining life of 10 years. Any remaining excess is attributed to goodwill.

The following additional information is available:

a. On July 1, 2016, Schinzer sells a machine to Fowler for $25,000. The cost of the machine to Schinzer is $16,000. The machine is being depreciated on a straight-line basis over five years.
b. Schinzer provides management services to Fowler at a billing rate of $15,000 per year. This arrangement starts in 2016.
c. Fowler has sold merchandise to Shinzer since 2017. Sales are $15,000 in 2017 and $20,000 in 2018. The merchandise is sold to provide a gross profit rate of 25%. Schinzer has $2,000 of these goods in its December 31, 2017, inventory and $3,000 of such goods in its December 31, 2018, inventory.
d. The income earned and dividends paid by Fowler are as follows:

Year	Income	Dividends
2016	$52,000	$60,000
2017	50,000	10,000
2018	65,000	10,000

Required ▶ ▶ ▶ ▶ ▶ Prepare all entries required by Schinzer's investment in Fowler Company for 2016 through 2018 using the equity method. Supporting schedules should be in good form. Ignore taxes.

Problem SA1-2 Fair value option for influential investment. Assume the same information as for Problem SA1-1. Instead of using the equity method, Schinzer uses the fair value option to record the investment in Fowler. The fair value of the investment in Fowler is as follows:

Date	Fair Value
December 31, 2016	$360,000
December 31, 2017	425,000
December 31, 2018	410,000

Required ▶ ▶ ▶ ▶ ▶ Prepare all entries required by Schinzer's investment in Fowler Company for 2016 through 2018 using the fair value option.

Problem SA1-3 Equity income, taxation, inventory, fixed asset sale. On January 1, 2016, Ashland Company purchases a 25% interest in Cramer Company for $195,000. Ashland Company prepares the following determination and distribution of excess schedule:

Price paid for investment		$195,000
Less book value of interest acquired:		
Common stock ($5 par)	$100,000	
Paid-in capital in excess of par	200,000	
Retained earnings	150,000	
Total stockholders' equity.	$450,000	
Interest acquired	× 25%	112,500
Excess of cost over book value (debit)		$ 82,500
Equipment [25% × $30,000 (10-year life)]		7,500 Dr
Goodwill		$ 75,000 Dr

The following additional information is available:

a. Cramer Company sells a machine to Ashland Company for $30,000 on July 1, 2017. At this date, the machine has a book value of $25,000 and an estimated future life of five years. Straight-line depreciation (to the nearest month) is being used. For income tax purposes, the gain on the sale is taxable in the year of the sale.

b. The following applies to Ashland Company sales to Cramer Company for 2017 and 2018:

	2017	2018
Intercompany merchandise in beginning inventory		$ 4,000
Sales for the year.	$10,000	$15,000
Intercompany merchandise in ending inventory	$ 4,000	$ 5,000
Gross profit on sales	40%	40%

c. Internally generated income (before tax) for the two companies is as follows:

	2016	2017	2018
Ashland Company.	$140,000	$150,000	$155,000
Cramer Company	60,000	80,000	100,000

d. Cramer pays dividends of $5,000, $10,000, and $10,000 in 2016, 2017, and 2018, respectively.

e. The corporate income tax rate of 30% applies to both companies. Assume an 80% dividend exclusion.

◄ ◄ ◄ ◄ ◄ **Required** Prepare all equity method adjustments for Ashland Company's investment in Cramer Company on December 31, 2016, 2017, and 2018. Consider income tax implications. Supporting calculations and schedules should be in good form.

Variable Interest Entities

Consolidation procedures are applied to controlling ownership interests in Variable Interest Entities (VIE). The unusual feature of consolidating a VIE is that control is not based on owning a controlling percentage of voting common stock, rather it is based on the ability to direct the operations of the VIE and the obligation to absorb the majority of the losses or the majority of the economic benefits of the VIE. Where control exists, the entity having control is called the "Primary Beneficiary" rather than the parent company.

DEFINING A VIE

VIE's are often created primarily to serve the primary beneficiary that controls them. They may lease assets, make investments, provide financing, perform research, or provided products and services. There have been abusive situations where the controlled entity borrowed money for the controlling primary beneficiary and the primary beneficiary did not disclose the debt; Enron was such a case. Keeping debt off the primary beneficiary's balance sheet is referred to as "off-balance sheet financing". A driving force behind the consolidation of VIE's was to include VIE debt for which the primary beneficiary is responsible on the primary beneficiary's balance sheet.

A VIE possesses one or more of the following characteristics:

1. The entity has very little residual equity – typically common stock. The issue is that the equity is insufficient to permit the entity to finance its activities without financial support provided by the primary beneficiary. Often this would take the form of guaranteeing the payment of debt or being subordinate to all other creditors. FASB ASC 810-10-25-45/46 provides guidance on assessing this test

2. The residual interest stockholders do not control the entity. The primary beneficiary directs or controls the activities that are most important to economic performance through contractual provisions.

3. The majority of losses or income flow to the primary beneficiaries, not the residual interest shareholders shareholder. The distribution of income is not based on common stock ownership. Instead, it is based on contractual agreements which could include interest on loans, management fees or a defined percentage of revenue or income.

PRIMARY BENEFICIARY

The primary beneficiary is the entity that has effective control of the VIE. In terms of prior chapter terminology, it is the parent company. The primary beneficiary must consolidate its interest in a VIE into its consolidated financial statements. An entity is deemed to have a controlling interest in a VIE if it has both of the following characteristics:

1. The power to direct the activities of the VIE that most significantly impact the VIE's economic performance.

2. The obligation to absorb losses of the VIE that could potentially be significant to the VIE or the right to receive benefits from the VIE that could potentially be significant to the VIE.[1]

---

1 ASC 810-10-25-38A

There can only be one primary beneficiary of a VIE. More than one entity could meet the second criteria, but only one entity can have the most significant impact on the economic performance of a VIE.

CONSOLIDATION PROCEDURES, DATE OF ACQUIRING CONTROL

The primary beneficiary may not have any investment in the VIE. It may, instead guarantee the debt of the VIE or subordinate its claim to those of other creditors. The primary beneficiary may also loan funds to the VIE or purchase the VIE's preferred stock. The investment is recorded at the dollar value of the assets conveyed to the VIE. Assume that the VIE is a functioning company and that on December 31, 2015 Primary Company Loaned the VIE, $500,000 at 11% annual interest. The Primary Company would make the entry:

Loan receivable from VIE Company	$500,000	
Cash		$500,000

The loan is subordinate to the other liabilities of the VIE Company. The primary beneficiary also guarantees the payment of the 6% bonds which are held by outside parties. The loan gives the Primary Company the decision making authority on all transactions by the VIE Company. The Primary Company will also receive a fee equal to 5% of VIE revenues to cover joint marketing expenditures made by the Primary Company.

Assume that on that date, the VIE had the following balance sheet after receipt of the loan and the use of the proceeds to finance The Primary Company's customers:

Balance Sheet
VIE Company

Assets		Liabilities and Equity	
Cash	$100,000	Loan from Primary Company	$500,000
Accounts receivable	650,000	6% Bond payable	300,000
Equipment (net)	120,000	Common stock, $1 par	5,000
		Paid-in Excess of par	45,000
		Retained earnings	20,000
Total assets	$870,000	Total liabilities and equity	$870,000

Fair values differed from book values as follows:

- Equipment was valued at $150,000 and has a 10 year remaining life
- The bond payable had a fair value of $298,000. It is payable to a nonaffiliated owner. It has a 5 year remaining term.
- The common stock had a fair value of $122,000

As a part of the consolidation process, VIE Company's accounts will be adjusted to fair value as follows

- Increase the equipment $30,000
- Decrease the Bond payable by $2,000
- Record goodwill calculated as follows:

Fair value of common stock	$122,000
Less book value of equity	(70,000)
Excess of fair value over book value	52,000
Less amounts assigned to:	
Equipment	(30,000)
Bond payable	(2,000)
Goodwill	20,000

If the VIE was not a business as defined by ASC 819-10-20 which means it is likely a not for profit entity, there is no goodwill recorded. Instead, a gain would be recorded for the excess of the fair value of the assets over the fair value of the liabilities (and preferred stock if it existed). If the fair value of the assets was less than the fair value of the liabilities, a loss would be recorded.

Let us first consider consolidation procedures for a balance sheet prepared immediately after the above transaction occurs. Eliminations are made as follows on Worksheet SA2-1: Worksheet SA2-1: page SA2-9

(EL) Eliminate Loan receivable from the VIE Company on Primary books against Loan from Primary Company on VIE books:

| Loan from Primary Company | 500,000 | |
| Loan receivable from VIE Company | | 500,000 |

(D) Distribute asset and liability adjustments including goodwill to VIE Company accounts. The net amount of the adjustment is a credit to the NCI (using paid-in capital on reevaluation).

Equipment	30,000	
Goodwill	20,000	
Discount on Bonds Payable	2,000	
Paid-in Capital on Revaluation—VIE Co.		52,000

Based on Worksheet SA2-1, the following consolidated balance sheet would be prepared on December 31, 2015:

Consolidated Balance Sheet, December 31, 2015
Primary Company

Assets		Liabilities and Equity	
Cash	$ 150,000	Accounts payable	$ 60,000
Inventory	300,000	Liabilities of VIE:	
Building	400,000	Bond payable	300,000
Accumulated depreciation	(150,000)	Discount on bond payable	(2,000)
Equipment	300,000	Common stock $1 par	100,000
Accumulated depreciation	(100,000)	Paid-in excess of par	900,000
Assets of VIE:		Retained earnings	340,000
Cash	100,000	Noncontrolling interest	122,000
Accounts receivable	650,000		
Equipment	150,000		
Goodwill	20,000		
Total assets	$1,820,000	Total liabilities and equity	$1,820,000

FASB ASC 810-10-45-25 requires that VIE assets and liabilities be shown separately on the balance sheet as shown in the above balance sheet. To date, it is not common to see this separation on published balance sheets. In many cases there is no disclosure of VIE assets and liabilities, and in other cases there is disclosure of VIE assets and liabilities only in the notes to the financial statements.

CONSOLIDATION PROCEDURES, SUBSEQUENT PERIODS

Worksheet SA2-2 illustrates the consolidation of the VIE at the end of the first year of control. Worksheet SA2-2: page SA2-10 The primary beneficiary will likely record its share of VIE interest revenue on its books. In our example, it would record the 11% interest revenue earned on its loan to the VIE. The worksheet trial balances show both the interest revenue recorded by the primary beneficiary and the interest expense recorded by the VIE.

Eliminations are made as follows on Worksheet SA2-2:

(EL)   Eliminate Loan receivable from the VIE Company on Primary books against Loan from Primary
       Company on VIE books:

Loan from Primary Company.	500,000	
Loan receivable from VIE Company.		500,000

(D)   Distribute asset and liability adjustments including goodwill to VIE Company accounts. The net
       amount of the adjustment is a credit to the NCI (using paid-in capital on revaluation).

Equipment	30,000	
Goodwill	20,000	
Discount on Bonds Payable	2,000	
Paid-in Capital on Revaluation—VIE Co.		52,000

(A1)   Increase depreciation by $30,000 divided by 10 year life = $3,000

Depreciation expense	3,000	
Accumulated depreciation (equipment).		3,000

(A3)   Amortize bond discount, straight line method, $2,000 divided by 5 year life = $400.

Interest Expense.	400	
Discount on Bonds Payable		400

(I)   Eliminate interest on intercompany loan

Interest Revenue.	55,000	
Interest Expense		85,000

Income distributions would be prepared as follows:

VIE Company Income Distribution

(A1) Depreciation adjustment	3,000	Internally generated net income	$17,000
(A2) Bond amortization.	400		
		Adjusted income	$13,600
		5% revenues to Primary Co.	5,750
		NCI interest	$ 7,850

Note: The $55,000 interest charged to VIE Company by the Primary Company is not adjusted out of the schedule since it
is an agreed distribution of VIE Company income

Primary Company Income Distribution

	Internally generated net income	$150,000
	5% of VIE Company revenues	5,750
	Controlling interest	$155,750

Based on Worksheet SA2-2, the following consolidated income statement would be prepared on December 31, 2016:

Consolidated Income Statement for Year Ending December 31, 2016
Primary Company

Sales revenue		$950,000
Cost of goods sold.		650,000
Gross profit		300,000
Processing revenue		20,000
Depreciation expense	$ 60,000	
Selling expenses	110,000	
Administrative expenses	63,000	233,000
Operating income		87,000
Interest revenue	95,000	
Interest expense.	(18,400)	76,600
Consolidated net income.		$163,600
Distributed to noncontrolling interest		$ 7,850
Distributed to controlling interest		155,750

Based on Worksheet SA2-2, the following consolidated balance sheet would be prepared on December 31, 2016:

Consolidated Balance Sheet, December 31, 2016
Primary Company

Assets		Liabilities and Equity	
Cash	$ 250,000	Accounts payable	$ 115,000
Inventory	450,000	Liabilities of VIE:	
Building	400,000	Bond payable	300,000
Accumulated depreciation	(170,000)	Discount on bond payable	(1,600)
Equipment	300,000	Common stock $1 par	100,000
Accumulated depreciation	(125,000)	Paid-in excess of par	900,000
Assets of VIE:		Retained earnings	495,750
Cash	99,000	Noncontrolling interest	129,850
Accounts receivable	680,000		
Equipment	150,000		
Accumulated depreciation	(15,000)		
Goodwill	20,000		
Total assets	$2,039,000	Total liabilities and equity	$2,039,000

The consolidation process for VIE's includes the elimination of all inter-entity transactions as would be the case for control based on stock ownership, as explained in chapters 4 and 5.

The major differences between consolidating a VIE versus a subsidiary are:

♦ The equity of the VIE is not eliminated. The entire shareholder equity becomes the noncontrolling interest.

♦ Intercompany debt between a parent and a subsidiary is an elimination made separately from the elimination of the equity investment in the subsidiary. Debt due to the primary beneficiary by the VIE is often the investment in VIE which is eliminated as the intercompany investment.

♦ The controlling company's share of consolidated net income is based on contractual terms, not its percentage of stock ownership.

REFLECTION

- The primary beneficiary has control of the variable interest entity (VIE) based on its power to control the activities of the VIE and the obligation to absorb losses and receive benefits from the VIE.

- The accounts of the VIE are adjusted to fair value on the date control is achieved. The total of the adjustments is an adjustment of the VIE equity.

- Income of the consolidated company is distributed based on contractual terms, not the Primary Company ownership of VIE common stock.

UNDERSTANDING THE ISSUES

1. The Vary Company has total assets with a book value of $3,000,000 and a fair value of $4,000,000. A potential primary beneficiary company has guaranteed the debt of the Vary Company and will receive a share of income of the Vary Company based on contractual terms. The primary beneficiary will also have decision power.

   a. Will the primary beneficiary company record an investment in the equity of the Vary Company?
   b. Will the Vary Company need to be consolidated. If it is to be consolidated, what adjustments would be needed in the consolidation process?

2. Since a primary beneficiary's share of VIE income is not based on common stock ownership, how might it be calculated?

EXERCISES

1. A primary beneficiary company has established control over a VIE by guaranteeing its long term debt and by establishing an income distribution contract. The balance sheet of the VIE on the acquisition date was as follows:

Current assets	100,000	Current liabilities	70,000
Land and buildings	600,000	Long term note payable	700,000
Accumulated depreciation	(100,000)	Common stock, $1 par	5,000
Equipment	300,000	Paid-in excess of par	45,000
Accumulated depreciation	(50,000)	Retained earnings	30,000
Total assets	850,000	Total liabilities and equity	850,000

The fair values of the land and buildings are $800,000. The fair value of the equipment is $400,000. The fair value of the company's net (of debt) assets is estimated to be $600,000.

Prepare the distribution of excess schedule.

2. The following nominal accounts apply to a primary beneficiary company and a VIE:

	Primary Company	VIE Company
Sales	(800,000)	(240,000)
Service fees		(150,000)
Interest revenue	(90,000)	
Interest expense		50,000
Operating expenses	550,000	230,000
Depreciation expense	100,000	40,000

The fair value of the VIE assets had a fair value $100,000 higher than book value on the date control was achieved. The asset adjusted had a 5 year life.

The VIE agrees to distribute a share of its income to the primary beneficiary equal to 10% of sales revenue and service fees.

Prepare income distribution schedules for the Primary and VIE Companies.

PROBLEMS

Problem SA2-1 Consolidate balance sheet, date control is achieved The Primary Company and the VIE Company had the following balance sheet on December 31, 2015, the date control was achieved:

	Primary Company		VIE Company	
Cash	200,000		80,000	
Accounts receivable			400,000	
Inventory	400,000			
Loan receivable from VIE Co.	300,000			
Land	50,000			
Building	500,000			
Accumulated depreciation	(150,000)			
Equipment	400,000		360,000	
Accumulated depreciation	(50,000)		(60,000)	
Accounts payable		80,000		
Loan from Primary Company				300,000
5% Bond Payable				400,000
Common stock, $1 par—Primary Co.		100,000		
Paid in capital in excess of par—Primary Co.		900,000		
Retained earnings—Primary Co.		570,000		
Common stock, $1 par—VIE Co.				10,000
Paid in capital in excess of par—VIE Co.				50,000
Retained earnings—VIE Co.				20,000
Totals	1,650,000	1,650,000	780,000	780,000

The Primary Company guaranteed the 5% bond payable issued by the VIE Company. The Primary Company also loaned the VIE Company $300,000 on a subordinated note at 10% annual interest.

The fair value of the VIE Company's equity is $170,000. Equipment, with a 5 year life has a value $50,000 greater than book value.

1. Prepare a determination and determination of excess schedule.
2. Prepare a worksheet for a consolidated balance as of December 31, 2015.

Problem SA2-2 Consolidate Worksheet, Subsequent Period The Primary Company and the VIE Company had the balance sheet shown in Problem SA2-1 above on the date control was achieved. The Primary Company guaranteed the 5% bond payable issued by the VIE Company. The Primary Company also loaned the VIE Company $300,000 on a subordinated note at 10% annual interest.

The fair value of the VIE Company's assets (without deduction for debt) is $870,000. Equipment, with a 5 year life is $50,000 greater than book value.

The VIE company will pay 10% annual interest to the Primary Company on the intercompany loan. The VIE will also pay a fee of 5% on its sales revenue to the Primary Company.

The Primary Company and the VIE Company had the following trail balances on December 31, 2016:

	Trial Balances, Dec. 31, 2016	
	Primary Company	VIE Company
Cash	305,000	110,000
Accounts receivable		425,000
Inventory	425,000	
Loan receivable from VIE Co.	300,000	
Land	50,000	(*continued*)

	Trial Balances, Dec. 31, 2016	
	Primary Company	VIE Company
Building	500,000	
Accumulated depreciation	(175,000)	
Equipment	400,000	360,000
Accumulated depreciation	(100,000)	(90,000)
Accounts payable	30,000	
Loan from Primary Company.		300,000
6% Bond Payable		400,000
Common stock, $1 par—Primary Co.	100,000	
Paid in capital in excess of par—Primary Co. .	900,000	
Retained earnings—Primary Co.	570,000	
Common stock, $1 par—VIE Co.		10,000
Paid in capital in excess of par—VIE Co.		50,000
Retained earnings—VIE Co.		20,000
Sales	800,000	220,000
Interest revenue	30,000	5,000
Processing revenue		20,000
Cost of goods sold.	500,000	133,000
Depreciation expense	75,000	30,000
Selling expenses	90,000	20,000
Administrative expense	60,000	3,000
Interest expense.		34,000
Totals	2,430,000 2,430,000	1,025,000 1,025,000

1. Prepare a determination and distribution of excess schedule for the schedule. (If problem SA12-1 was completed, the same schedule applies)
2. Prepare a consolidate worksheet for the Primary and VIE Companies as of December 31, 2016. Include the income distribution schedules.

Worksheet SA2-1

Primary Company and VIE Company
Consolidated Balance Sheet
December 31, 2015

Worksheet SA2-1 (see page SA2-3)

		Balance Sheets, Dec. 31, 2015		Eliminations		NCI	Consolidated Balance Sheet	
		Primary Company	VIE Company	Dr	Cr			
1	Cash	150,000	100,000				250,000	1
2	Accounts receivable		650,000				650,000	2
3	Inventory	300,000					300,000	3
4	Loan receivable from VIE Co.	500,000			EL 500,000			4
5	Land							5
6	Building	400,000					400,000	6
7	Accumulated depreciation	(150,000)					(150,000)	7
8	Equipment	300,000	120,000	D1 30,000			450,000	8
9	Accumulated depreciation	(100,000)					(100,000)	9
10	Goodwill			D2 20,000			20,000	10
11	Accounts payable	60,000					(60,000)	11
12	Loan from Primary Company		500,000	EL 500,000				12
13	6% Bond payable		300,000				(300,000)	13
14	Discount on bond payable			D3 2,000			2,000	14
15	Common stock, $1 par—Primary Co.	100,000					(100,000)	15
16	Paid in capital in excess of par—Primary Co.	900,000					(900,000)	16
17	Retained earnings—Primary Co.	340,000					(340,000)	17
18	Common stock, $1 par—VIE Co.		5,000			(5,000)		18
19	Paid in capital in excess of par—VIE Co.		45,000			(45,000)		19
20	Paid-in capital on revaluation—VIE Co.				D 52,000	(52,000)		20
21	Retained earnings—VIE Co.		20,000			(20,000)		21
22	Totals	1,400,000	870,000	552,000	552,000			22
23	Total NCI					(122,000)	(122,000)	23

EL Eliminte loan from Primary Company to VIE Company
D Distribute excess to equipment (D1), goodwill (D2) and discount on bonds payable (D3)

Worksheet SA2-2

Primary Company and VIE Company
Consolidated Trial Balance
December 31, 2016

		Trial Balances, Dec. 31, 2016			
		Primary Company		VIE Company	
1	Cash	250,000		99,000	
2	Accounts receivable			680,000	
3	Inventory	450,000			
4	Loan receivable from VIE Co.	500,000			
5	Land				
6	Building	400,000			
7	Accumulated depreciation	(170,000)			
8	Equipment	300,000		120,000	
9	Accumulated depreciation	(125,000)			12,000
10	Goodwill				
11	Accounts payable		115,000		
12	Loan from Primary Company				500,000
13	6% Bond payable				300,000
14	Discount on bond payable				
15	Common stock, $1 par—Primary Co.		100,000		
16	Paid in capital in excess of par—Primary Co.		900,000		
17	Retained earnings—Primary Co.		340,000		
18	Common stock, $1 par—VIE Co.				5,000
19	Paid in capital in excess of par—VIE Co.				45,000
20	Paid-in capital on revaluation—VIE Co.				
21	Retained earnings—VIE Co.				20,000
22	Sales		950,000		
23	Interest revenue		55,000		95,000
24	Processing revenue				20,000
25	Cost of goods sold	650,000			
26	Depreciation expense	45,000		12,000	
27	Selling expenses	110,000			
28	Administrative expense	50,000		13,000	
29	Interest expense			73,000	
30	Totals	2,460,000	2,460,000	997,000	997,000
31	Consolidated net income				
32	To NCI				
33	To controlling interest				
34	NCI				
35	Retained earnings, controlling interest, December 31, 2016				

EL   Eliminte loan from Primary Company to VIE Company
D   Distribute excess to equipment (D1), goodwill (D2)and discount on bonds payable (D3)
A1   Increase depreciation $3,000 for current year
A3   Amortize discount on bonds, $400 for current year
I   Eliminate $55,000 intercompany interest

Worksheet SA2-2 (see page SA2-3)

	Eliminations			Income Statement	NCI	Controlling Retained Earnings	Consolidated Balance Sheet	
	Dr.		Cr.					
							349,000	1
							680,000	2
							450,000	3
		EL	500,000					4
								5
							400,000	6
							(170,000)	7
D1	30,000						450,000	8
		A1	3,000				(140,000)	9
D2	20,000						20,000	10
							(115,000)	11
EL	500,000							12
							(300,000)	13
D3	2,000	A3	400				1,600	14
							(100,000)	15
							(900,000)	16
						(340,000)		17
					(5,000)			18
					(45,000)			19
								20
		D	52,000		(72,000)			21
				(950,000)				22
I	55,000			(95,000)				23
				(20,000)				24
				650,000				25
A1	3,000			60,000				26
				110,000				27
				63,000				28
A3	400	I	55,000	18,400				29
	610,400		610,400					30
				(163,600)			-	31
				7,850	(7,850)			32
				155,750		(155,750)	-	33
					(129,850)		(129,850)	34
						(495,750)	(495,750)	35

Multinational Accounting and Other Reporting Concerns

I n today's evolving global economy, companies buy goods and services from foreign sources, manufacture goods in a number of different countries, and sell their products to customers throughout the world. The complexities of the many international transactions have required accounting to become more international in nature. Efforts are underway to develop accounting principles that are comparable or harmonious between trading nations.

As international trading expands, accounting principles must address how to account for transactions involving different currencies. Since changes in currency exchange rates expose trading parties to potential gains or losses, the economic consequences of such rate changes must be measured. Also, companies often use different strategies to reduce risk. Hedging strategies, including the use of such derivatives as forward contracts, options, and currency swaps, add complexity to accounting for these transactions.

Companies also invest in foreign entities. These investments create a need to translate foreign entity financial statements from one currency to another. Specialized accounting procedures are used for the required translation or remeasurement from the foreign currency into the domestic currency of the investor.

Interim reporting and segmental reporting are designed to provide timely and relevant information for decision making. Both types of reporting involve the application of special accounting principles. Timely reporting of interim information serves as an indicator of annual results. Segmental reports, arising from growing diversification in companies domestically and globally, communicate useful financial information about segmental assets and performance.

Chapter 9

The International Accounting Environment

CHAPTER

Learning Objectives

When you have completed this chapter, you should be able to

1. **Describe the international business environment.**

2. **Describe the accounting issues associated with foreign currency transactions.**

3. **Describe the accounting issues associated with foreign currency translation.**

4. **Describe the factors and parties influencing the development of International Financial Reporting Standards (IFRS).**

5. **Understand the U.S. initiatives to converge with International Accounting Standards (IAS).**

Jacob Corporation (a fictitious company) began with a small facility in central Wisconsin, where it manufactured precision measuring equipment to be used primarily in the food industry. As the company began to grow, its sales extended throughout the continental United States. While attending a trade show in Atlanta, Georgia, company representatives had the opportunity to arrange a sale to a foreign customer in Germany, and that was the beginning of the company's venture into export sales. The sale to the German company was collected in U.S. dollars, and the company began to expand its sales to other foreign customers. However, as these sales increased, a number of customers settled their accounts by payment in foreign currencies, such as the euro, rather than U.S. dollars. The company quickly realized that this could be good news or bad news, depending on how the U.S. dollar performed against the respective foreign currencies. For example, if the dollar strengthened against the euro, the euros collected by Jacob when the customer paid their account were actually worth fewer dollars than their value at the time of sale. Assume a dollar was equal to 1.5 euros at the time of the sale and goods were sold for 1,500 euros or $1,000. If the customer paid its balance due of 1,500 euros when a dollar was equal to 2.0 euros, the 1,500 euros collected would only be worth $750 at the time of collection. Jacob Corporation recognized that steps might have to be taken that would reduce the risk associated with settling accounts in a currency other than the U.S. dollar.

As sales continued to grow, the company decided to construct a manufacturing facility in France. This new facility was established as a separate French company subject to the laws of France but owned 90% by the U.S. company. The social, language, legal, taxation, and cultural differences of operating in a foreign country were just a few of the challenges with which the company was now dealing. In order to finance the construction of the French facility, Jacob sought financing from both French and German banks. Recognizing that financial statements would have to be submitted as part of any loan application, Jacob became aware of the fact that its financial statements followed generally accepted accounting principles (GAAP) that were recognized in the United States but may not account for transactions the same way that French or German accounting principles would. The French facility sells approximately 40% of its production to a Brazilian company that is a wholly owned subsidiary of Jacob. The pricing of sales between the French and Brazilian companies is designed to take advantage of the higher tax rate in France without violating any tax laws that discourage the manipulation of taxable income through intercompany pricing policies. Both the French and Brazilian company measure their operations in terms of the euro and follow the accounting principles established in their respective countries. However, Jacob prepares consolidated financial statements, in conformity with U.S. GAAP as measured in dollars, that reflect its ownership in these foreign companies. Therefore, Jacob must first make sure that the foreign company's transactions are recorded in conformity with U.S. GAAP and then translate the euro-based financial statements of its foreign subsidiaries into dollars before such statements can be consolidated with those of the U.S. parent company.

Today, we find our U.S. company constructing its sixth manufacturing facility—this one in Africa. As part of its agreement with the government of the African country, the U.S. company will be constructing a health clinic and school in the community and guaranteeing a minimum employment level for the next five years. Thus, Jacob Corporation has come a long way from central Wisconsin. It may be a fictitious company, but the scenario described is common in companies today. Welcome to international business and the global economy. All of this is possible when a commercial activity transcends national boundaries or borders.

In this chapter, the Derivatives Module, and the following two chapters, several issues relating to international accounting will be explored, including the following:

1. Derivative instruments and their use in hedge transactions
2. Accounting for transactions denominated or settled in foreign currencies
3. The translation and remeasurement of financial statements prepared in a foreign currency
4. The international standard-setting process.

THE SCOPE OF INTERNATIONAL BUSINESS ACTIVITIES

1

OBJECTIVE

Describe the international business environment.

An entity's involvement in international business can range from export or import activity to that of a multinational or transnational enterprise with a global approach to manufacturing, distribution, and sales. Trade between different nations certainly is not new. It has existed before biblical times and has provided the means by which certain nations have evolved into world powers. The United Kingdom and the Netherlands are just two examples of countries that have been active in international trade for centuries. However, it has been since World War II that international trade has increased significantly, and many more goods and services are becoming part of a global economy.

Dramatic changes occurring in recent times have allowed a global economy to become a reality for an increasing number of entities. The restructuring of Eastern Europe and the former Soviet Union has opened the door for free enterprise. The growth of the European Union (EU) has been responsible for reducing the economic barriers between nations by forming a single market with its own common currency, the euro. Comprehensive free trade agreements such as the North American Free Trade Agreement (NAFTA) and the American Free Trade Agreement (AFTA) as well as the World Trade Organization (WTO) are committed to reducing trade barriers through multilateral agreements.

As the barriers to world trade are reduced, the world becomes smaller in a number of ways. For example, modern communications technology makes it much easier to transact business between countries. The credit card purchase you made today may be processed in a center located in Ireland, and tomorrow you will be able to inquire about your account balance which will include your recent purchase. The Internet also is proving to be a significant tool through which entities make their goods and services available to consumers on an international scale.

Not only are goods and services trading in international markets, but the stocks of these companies are also traded internationally. International securities trading has increased rapidly due to a number of forces. As companies expand into different international markets, they need to acquire the factors of production in those markets and, thus, need to raise additional capital. International securities trading also offers investors the opportunity to diversify their portfolios against loss from currency fluctuations, political instabilities, and economic downturns.

REFLECTION

- The increasing international business activity includes trading in goods, services, and securities.

FOREIGN CURRENCY TRANSACTIONS

There are many businesses of all sizes within a country that operate on an international scale by exporting and/or importing goods and services. For example, in 2013 the United States exported approximately $1,579 billion of goods and imported approximately $2,267 billion of goods (reported on a seasonally adjusted, census basis). The United States exported $262 billion of goods to European Union countries alone and $184 billion to South/Central American countries. On the other hand, we imported $387 billion from European Union countries, $158 billion from South/Central American countries, and $153 billion from the Organization of Petroleum Exporting Countries (OPEC). During this period of time, trading levels with the top five trading nations were as follows:

2

OBJECTIVE

Describe the accounting issues associated with foreign currency transactions.

	Exports			Imports	
Nation	(in millions)	% of Total	Nation	(in millions)	% of Total
Canada	$ 300,347	19.0	China	$ 440,434	19.4
Saudi Arabia	226,153	14.3	Canada	332,078	14.6
China	122,016	7.7	Saudi Arabia	280,456	12.4
Japan	65,145	4.1	Japan	138,534	6.1
Germany	47,442	3.0	Germany	114,644	5.1
Total all nations	1,578,954	100.0	Total all nations	2,266,855	100.0

Today, there are almost 200 countries in the world and almost as many different currencies in use throughout the world (even the Vatican has its own currency). It is simplistic to think that business activities within a given country are only settled or denominated within their domestic currency (home country). In fact, in some instances, businesses within a country may prefer to settle transactions in a currency other than their domestic currency. Business transactions that are settled in a currency other than that of the domestic currency are referred to, in this text, as *foreign currency transactions*. One of the transacting parties will settle the transaction in its own domestic currency and also measure the transaction in its domestic currency. For example, a German company may sell inventory to a U.S. company and require payment in euros. The currency used to settle the transaction is referred to as the *denominated currency* and would be the euro in this case. The other transacting party will settle the transaction in a foreign currency but will need to measure the transaction in its domestic currency. For example, a U.S. company that purchases inventory from a German company must settle the resulting accounts payable in euros and yet must measure the purchase of inventory and the accounts payable in terms of U.S. dollars. The currency used to measure or record the transaction is referred to as the *measurement currency* and would be the U.S. dollar in this case. Whenever a transaction is denominated in a currency different from the measurement currency, exchange rate risk exists, and exchange rates must be used for measurement purposes. The process of expressing a transaction in the measurement currency when it is denominated in a different currency is referred to as a *foreign currency translation*.

Continuing with our example involving a purchase of inventory from a German company, assume that inventory was purchased for 13,200 euros when $1 was equal to 1.20 euros. At the time of the purchase, the respective parties would recognize the following:

German company	
Sales revenue of.................	€13,200
Accounts receivable of............	€13,200
U.S. company	
Inventory of	$11,000
Accounts payable of	$11,000

Assume that $1 was equal to 1.10 euros at the time of settling the transaction. At that time, the German company would still receive 13,200 euros in settlement of its receivable. However, the U.S. company would have to spend $12,000 (13,200 euros divided by 1.10) in order to settle its account payable rather than the $11,000 that was recorded at the time of the purchase. The U.S. company has experienced an economic loss due to changes in the exchange rates over time. Whenever a transaction is denominated in a currency different than the measurement currency, one of the parties to the transaction is exposed to either economic gain or loss if exchange rates change between the date of the transaction and the date of settlement. The change in exchange rates over time did not expose the German company to exchange risk because the transaction is both denominated and measured in its domestic currency. However, the U.S. company was exposed to exchange risk because the transaction was denominated in euros but measured in dollars. The above example brings to light two issues: first, business strategies may need to be developed to reduce or hedge against this economic impact and second, accounting principles must be developed to account for the economic impact of changing exchange rates. Both of these issues will be explored in the following Derivative Module and in Chapter 10.

REFLECTION

- Strategies may be developed to reduce or hedge against the economic impact associated with changes in rates of exchange between currencies.

- Specialized accounting principles must be developed to account for the economic impact associated with changes in rates of exchange between currencies.

3

OBJECTIVE

Describe the accounting issues associated with foreign currency translation.

FOREIGN CURRENCY TRANSLATION

Foreign currency transactions are not dependent on the domestic entity having an ownership interest in a foreign entity. However, as a company's international activities increase in scale and scope, they often acquire some form of ownership interest or control over a foreign entity and truly become multinational companies, also known as *transnational companies*. The magnitude of U.S. investment abroad has increased significantly in response to a more global economy, a reduction in trade barriers, and the growth of international capital markets. Similarly, these same factors have encouraged an increase in foreign investment in the United States. The size and growth of these investment patterns are suggested by the following statistics.

U.S. Direct Investment Position Abroad and Foreign Direct Investment Position in the United States

	U.S. Direct Investment Position Abroad[a] (in millions)	Foreign Direct Investment Position in the United States[b] (in millions)
2008	$3,232,493	$ 15,369
2009	3,565,020	224,220
2010	3,741,910	393,518
2011	4,084,659	330,491
2012	4,453,307	248,074

[a]U.S. Direct Investment Position Abroad—Value of U.S. direct investors' equity in, and net outstanding loans to, their foreign affiliates. Values are not adjusted to reflect current costs or the replacement costs.

[b]Foreign Direct Investment Position in the United States—Value of foreign direct investors' equity in, and net outstanding loans to, their U.S. affiliates. Values are not adjusted to reflect current costs or the replacement costs.

Source: U.S. Department of Commerce, Bureau of Economic Analysis.

The accounting treatments of domestic and foreign entity relationships that involve some degree of ownership are summarized as follows:

Domestic Entity	Foreign Entity	Accounting Treatment
Home office	Branch	Branch accounting
Parent	Subsidiary	Consolidated financial statements or separate financial statements
Investor	Investee	Investment in foreign entity using cost or equity method, or consolidate if it qualifies as a variable interest entity (VIE)

The above relationships suggest the need to combine or consolidate the foreign entity financial statements with those of the domestic entity. The financial statements of a foreign entity typically are measured in the currency of that foreign country. This currency usually is different from the reporting currency of the domestic entity. Therefore, a methodology must be developed to express the foreign entity's financial statements in the reporting currency of the domestic entity. The process of expressing amounts denominated or measured in foreign currencies into amounts measured in the reporting currency (dollars) of the domestic entity (U.S.) is referred to as foreign currency translation.

Continuing the example from earlier in the chapter, assume that a U.S. company (the domestic entity) has a 100% interest in a German company (the foreign entity) and that the German company conducts business in euros and also records those transactions in euros. In order for the domestic company to prepare consolidated financial statement that reflect its 100% interest in the foreign subsidiary, the domestic company must translate the financial statement amounts from the euro into the U.S. dollar using rates of exchange between the two respective currencies. Several issues come to mind concerning this translation process: first, what impact will changes in exchange rates between the currencies have on the parent company's cash flows and second, what rates of exchange should be used to properly capture the impact of exchange rate changes? For example, should the equipment of the foreign company be translated from euros into dollars using the rate of exchange when the equipment was acquired or at the exchange rate at the date of the balance sheet? These issues will be addressed in Chapter 11 of this text. In addition to these issues, what about the possibility that the accounting principles used by the foreign entity are not the same as those of the domestic entity? If the principles were different, it would seem that the recorded transactions would have to be adjusted to reflect the domestic GAAP. Perhaps a more fundamental question should be whether a common transaction such as the recording of cost of goods sold should have a different recorded impact depending on what country is recording the transaction. Given the global economy, would it not be better to have a single set of global accounting standards?

REFLECTION

- Certain investment and/or control relationships require that a foreign entity's financial statements be consolidated with the statements of a domestic entity.

- The translation of foreign currency financial statements into a domestic entity's currency should capture the economic impact of exchange rate changes on the domestic entity's cash flows.

- Selection of the appropriate rate of exchange is necessary to properly capture the economic impact on cash flows.

4

OBJECTIVE

Describe the factors and parties influencing the development of International Financial Reporting Standards (IFRS).

HARMONIZATION OF ACCOUNTING STANDARDS

It seems that life would be simpler if there were more consistency and uniformity in certain respects. Why doesn't my cell phone charger plug into the outlet in South America as it does when I travel in the United States? Why don't all 2-cycle engines use the same size spark plug? Why don't two identical economic transactions, one occurring in the United States and one occurring in China, receive identical accounting treatment? In a perfect world, identical transactions should receive identical accounting treatment regardless of where the transactions occur, whether it is the United States or China. In reality, this has not been the case and a number of factors have and continue to influence the development of accounting. Harmonization of accounting standards has as its goal the development of consistent accounting standards that will improve comparability of financial information.

Multinational companies must have comparable accounting standards with which to measure the effectiveness and efficiency of their various international subsidiaries, branches, and/or other equity investments. Also, in order to efficiently allocate and regulate the exchange of capital, international capital markets need to evaluate the adequacy of financial statements and disclosures made by those companies seeking to raise capital. Comparable standards of accounting and financial disclosure for companies competing for capital on an international scale are critical to the functioning of such markets. Finally, other users, such as suppliers and customers, exposed to opportunities on an international scale need comparable financial information upon which to base their decisions. Evaluating the profitability or financial position of two competing business opportunities will have meaning only if comparable accounting standards are in place. The international growth of business and investing naturally creates a need for the international development of accounting. Thus, the development of International Accounting Standards must be based on an understanding of international business and markets and the factors that affect accounting in various countries.

Factors Influencing the Development of Accounting

Accounting is not defined by nature but, rather, is made by humans. It evolves from the environment in which humans exist and defines itself in a way which serves the needs of that environment. Given the differences in various environments, it is not surprising that accounting principles may differ between nations. The development of accounting principles and standards is an extremely complex process involving a social and cultural environment, various special interest groups, and varying degrees of due process. By studying the standard-setting process in the United States, one realizes how complex the process can be. This complexity holds true in the development of accounting principles and standards in other nations, too. It is the factors influencing the process, however, that vary from nation to nation.

A number of environmental factors such as the following may explain these differences to varying degrees:

1. Social and cultural values
2. Political and legal systems
3. Business activities and economic conditions
4. Standard-setting processes
5. Forms of ownership and capital markets
6. Cooperative efforts between nations

For example, consider the impact that political and legal systems have had on the development of accounting over time. Nations that previously were ruled or colonized by another country tend to have developed principles similar to those of the ruling nation. Nations such as the United States, Canada, and the Bahamas have accounting principles that historically were patterned after those found in the United Kingdom. Those nations that have more democratic political environments tend to develop principles more through private standard-setting groups than through government decree or regulation. The tax laws and legal requirements of a country also may influence the development of accounting to the extent that differences between accounting income and taxable income are rare or nonexistent.

Although a number of environmental factors have influenced the development of accounting standards throughout the world, there is growing momentum to move toward a single set of International Accounting Standards. A number of professional organizations throughout the world have cooperated in this initiative with the International Accounting Standards Board (IASB) being the major force.

The International Accounting Standards Board

It is understandable that a variety of users of accounting information would be interested in ensuring that the accounting for particular types of transactions is consistent between nations for the purpose of improving comparability. Several approaches to harmonization have been pursued including bilateral agreements between nations and international standard setting on a worldwide scale. The initiatives of the European Union to harmonize accounting standards among member nations are an example of a bilateral approach to harmonization. Standard setting on a worldwide scale obviously represents a monumental task. The leaders of this movement must be sensitive to the variety of cultural, ethical, and economic differences that exist among countries. This approach to harmonization is the dominant approach and major forces behind the effort have been the International Accounting Standards Board and the International Federation of Accountants (IFAC). The IASB is concerned with the promulgation and harmonization of International Accounting Standards. The IFAC is concerned with a variety of issues affecting the professional practice of accounting on a worldwide basis, including quality control standards and international auditing standards.

The IASB was created in 2001 as a result of a restructuring of its predecessor, the International Accounting Standards Committee (IASC). The IASC was formed in 1973 and had two primary objectives: (1) formulate and publish standards on financial accounting and reporting and promote their worldwide acceptance and (2) work for the harmonization of accounting standards and procedures relating to the presentation of financial statements. Rather than each nation establishing its own accounting standards, the IASC recognized the importance of taking a global approach toward standard setting in order to best serve the global economy. The IASC issued 41 International Accounting Standards of which the majority are still in effect.

In the late 1990s, the IASC engaged in a strategy review that resulted in its restructuring. In early 2001, the restructured IASC became the International Accounting Standards Board. The IASB assumed responsibility for establishing a single set of International Financial Reporting Standards and achieving convergence of national accounting standards and IFRS.

The International Accounting Standards Committee (IASC) Foundation. The IASC Foundation was formed in 2001 as the parent entity of the IASB, which is based in London. The structure of the Foundation consists of the Trustees, the Board, the Standing Interpretations Committee, and the Standards Advisory Council. Objectives of the Foundation as set forth in its constitution are:

a. To develop, in the public interest, a single set of high quality, understandable and enforceable global accounting standards that require high quality, transparent and comparable information in financial statements and other financial reporting to help participants in the world's capital markets and other users make economic decisions;
b. To promote the use and rigorous application of those standards;
c. To fulfill the objectives associated with (a) and (b), to take account of, as appropriate, the special needs of small and medium-sized entities and emerging economies; and
d. To bring about convergence of national accounting standards and International Accounting Standards and International Financial Reporting Standards to high quality solutions.

The trustees of the IASC Foundation are the ultimate governing body and appoint the members of the IASB, the Standing Interpretations Committee, and the Standards Advisory Council. The 22 trustees come from a variety of countries (6 from North America, 6 from Europe, 6 from Asia/Oceania region, 4 from any area being sensitive to geographical balance) and have diverse professional backgrounds. Although not responsible for setting international standards, the trustees are responsible for developing and implementing the strategy and operating policies of the IASB and other committees. The trustees also appoint members of the IASB and other committees.

The chairperson of the IASB serves as the chief executive of the Foundation and is supervised by the trustees. Decisions are made by simple majority except for certain actions (e.g., amendments to the constitution) which require a three-fourths majority of all trustees.

International Accounting Standards Board. Appointed by the trustees of the IASC Foundation, the Board consists of 16 members; normally this includes four members from the Asia/Oceania region, four from North America, one from both Africa and South America, and two from any area. The Board must consist of competent individuals with practical experience as auditors, preparers, users, and academics. Each Board member has one vote and may serve a term of up to five years, renewable once for a three-year term subject to certain exceptions for the Chair and Vice-Chairs. The Board has full discretion over the technical agenda and complete responsibility for all technical matters including preparing and issuing International Financial Reporting Standards and Exposure Drafts and approving Interpretations presented by the International Financial Reporting Interpretations Committee.

The Board has responsibility for establishing a single set of International Accounting Standards now designated as International Financial Reporting Standards. However, the International Accounting Standards issued by the IASC have been adopted by the IASB and continue to be referred to as IAS. The IASB has followed a conceptual accounting framework, "Framework for the Preparation and Presentation of Financial Statements," which was approved in 1989 by the IASC and adopted by the IASB in 2001. The framework sets forth the concepts that underlie the preparation and presentation of financial statements for external users and serves as a platform against which future standards are developed and existing standards are reviewed. The Board follows a rigorous due process leading to the issuance of IFRS. This process includes open meetings, webcasts, the possible use of an Advisory Committee, and the publication of Discussion Documents and Exposure Drafts for public comment. The Board has the discretion to use field tests and to hold public hearings regarding proposed standards. The publication of IFRS, Exposure Drafts, or Interpretations requires approval by at least 10 members of the Board. Other decisions of the Board require a simple majority of the members present at a meeting (at least 60% of the members must be present in person or by telecommunication link).

International Financial Reporting Standards (IFRS) Interpretations Committee. The trustees also appoint 14 individuals to the Interpretations Committee. The Committee is responsible for reviewing accounting issues that arise in the context of IFRS and to provide authoritative guidance in the form of interpretations known as IFRIC.

REFLECTION

- A number of factors may explain why accounting principles between nations differ. Factors include social/cultural values, political/legal systems, types of business activities, economic conditions, the standard-setting process, forms of ownership, the extent of capital markets, and cooperation among nations.

- Harmonization is concerned with developing a single set of high-quality worldwide accounting standards that result in comparable information in financial statements and reports.

- The IASB and the IFAC are critical international organizations involved in the harmonization of accounting and professional standards.

CONVERGENCE TO INTERNATIONAL ACCOUNTING STANDARDS

5

OBJECTIVE

Understand the U.S. initiatives to converge with International Accounting Standards (IAS).

The factors that have influenced the development of accounting standards within nations continue to exist and yet there is a recognized need to move toward a single set of International Accounting Standards. The goals of the international standard-setting organizations are ambitious, and it is clear that the harmonization of accounting standards is a complex process that will challenge accountants and professional accountancy organizations within nations. Accountants may be asked to learn new standards and reporting formats that may replace tried and true past practice. Without question, accountants will resist or reject change in certain instances based on theoretical and/or practical considerations. Issuers of financial information will have to modify their accounting systems and educate users of such information regarding new standards and reporting formats. Fortunately, a significant number of national accountancy organizations recognize the importance of harmonization and nearly 120 countries have either adopted IFRS, allowed the optional use of IFRS, or substantially converged with IFRS. The United States continues to use national accounting standards, subject to the areas in which its standards have converged with IFRS. The use of IFRS by various jurisdictions is being "profiled" by the IFRS Foundation and can be accessed at http://www.ifrs.org/Use-around-the-world/Pages/Jurisdiction-profiles.aspx.

Initiatives of the Financial Accounting Standards Board. The FASB believes in the ultimate goal of a single set of International Accounting Standards that would be used worldwide for domestic and international financial reporting. In keeping with this commitment, the FASB and the IASB in 2002 signed a memorandum of understanding (MoU), known as the Norwalk Agreement, formalizing their commitment to the convergence of U.S. GAAP and International Accounting Standards. Convergence means that the FASB and IASB will work together to develop standards rather than the FASB merely agreeing to adopt IFRS. In essence, this will be a collaborative effort whereby IFRS may converge with U.S. GAAP, U.S. GAAP may converge with IFRS, or an entirely new standard may be generated. The parties have agreed to move toward common standards in areas that are not in need of significant improvement.

In 2006, the FASB and the IASB published a MoU that reaffirmed their mutual commitment, set forth a "roadmap" identifying convergence topics, and encouraged the Securities and Exchange Commission (SEC) to allow public foreign companies to file statements according to IFRS without reconciliation to U.S. GAAP. Joint projects between the FASB and the IASB are in place, with full sharing of staff and research resources. In 2010, both parties reaffirmed their earlier commitment to the 2006 MoU and also expanded their efforts to create new accounting standards where existing standards were deemed to be in need of significant improvement.

U.S. GAAP has historically been more rules based than IFRS, which is more principles based; this will certainly introduce much more subjectivity into financial reporting. The impact that the adoption of certain IFRS will have on U.S. companies varies, in part, depending on what industry the company is in. Adoption of international standards will also come at significant cost to some companies. There may also be certain areas where convergence might not be achieved. For example, the LIFO inventory method is a common and popular method within the United States. However, IFRS does not allow LIFO. Will this become the subject of an "adopted in U.S." qualification, or will the United States fully converge? Although it is certain that convergence to International Accounting Standards will not be seamless and many challenges certainly lay ahead, the FASB and the IASB have pledged to make their accounting standards fully compatible and maintain such compatibility over time.

Initiatives of the Securities and Exchange Commission. In 2010, the SEC adopted a timeline that anticipated 2015 as the earliest date the SEC would require U.S. companies to use IFRS in filings with the SEC. However, since that time, the SEC's position regarding the adoption of IFRS has become less clear. The SEC is committed to promoting quality financial reporting worldwide and will consider whether a common set of such financial standards is achievable. However, uncertainty still exists on whether the United States and the SEC will fully accept IFRS as the common denominator. It spite of this uncertainty, it is interesting to note that the SEC has agreed to accept financial statements from foreign registrants to be prepared in accordance with IFRS without reconciliation to U.S. GAAP.

The question of whether the SEC will require the use of IFRS by U.S. registrants is an open question. Currently, there is not a strong clear majority of constituents who favor moving to IFRS. Many believe that U.S. GAAP is better than IFRS, not to mention the concern of significant costs that would be incurred in making a change.

The SEC supports the completion of convergence projects between the FASB and the IASB. It is possible that the SEC will encourage the FASB to endorse selected IFRS and incorporate them into U.S. GAAP, resulting in a partial adoption of IFRS. Regardless of what position the SEC takes, a large number of U.S. companies are already accepting and complying with IFRS as a result of their investments in foreign companies whose country of origin have adopted, fully or partially, IFRS. Regardless of the uncertainty, which may be frustrating to some, a careful and well-thought-out approach to the question of how IFRS will be integrated into the United States is in the best interest of all parties involved.

REFLECTION

- The IASB and the IFAC are critical international organizations involved in the convergence of accounting principles.

- Convergence to International Accounting Standards has already taken place on a worldwide scale, and the FASB, IASB, and SEC are actively involved in the process.

UNDERSTANDING THE ISSUES

1. Identify several environmental factors that may explain why accounting principles differ among countries.

2. What are the objectives of the International Accounting Standards Committee Foundation, and does the FASB support those objectives?

3. Identify the unique accounting issues associated with consolidating a foreign subsidiary with the operations of its U.S. parent company.

EXERCISES

Exercise 1 *(LO 4, 5)* **Convergence.** One of your clients has recently read about the goal of converging to International Accounting Standards and they are concerned about what impact it may have on their company.

1. Discuss some of the costs that a company might incur as part of its converging with International Accounting Standards.
2. Discuss why it might be important to your client to adopt International Accounting Standards even though they are currently only operating domestically throughout the central part of the United States.

Exercise 2 *(LO 3)* **The accounting issues associated with foreign currency transactions.** Assume that a U.S. company has made three purchases of inventory from three different foreign vendors. One of the purchases is denominated in U.S. dollars, and the other two purchases are denominated in foreign currency, FC-A and FC-B, respectively. Furthermore, between the time of the purchase and payment to the vendor, the U.S. dollar has strengthened relative to FC-A and weakened relative to FC-B.

Discuss how exchange rate changes would impact each of the three purchases.

Exercise 3 *(LO 5)* **Harmonization effect.** Harmonization of accounting standards through a private standard-setting process will have both advantages and disadvantages to American investors and businesses.

1. Discuss the advantages of harmonization to American investors.
2. Discuss why differences in accounting principles and disclosure requirements may place American businesses at a competitive disadvantage.
3. Discuss how the U.S. accounting profession can influence the process of harmonization.

Exercise 4 *(LO 4)* **International accounting organizations.** Several organizations are actively involved in international standard setting.

1. Discuss the relationship between the IASB and the International Accounting Standards Committee Foundation.
2. Discuss the position of the SEC with respect to convergence to International Accounting Standards.

Derivatives and Related Accounting Issues

Learning Objectives

When you have completed this module, you should be able to

1. State the general characteristics of a derivative instrument, and define *underlying* and *notional amount*.

2. Explain the basic features of common derivative instruments, including forward contracts, futures contracts, options, and interest rate swaps.

3. Determine and account for the change in value over time of forward and futures contracts.

4. Determine and account for the intrinsic and time value components of an option.

5. Appreciate the basic objectives of an interest rate swap.

6. Explain how a derivative instrument may be used to reduce or avoid the exposure to risk associated with other transactions.

7. Demonstrate how a fair value hedge is used, and account for such hedges.

8. Demonstrate how a cash flow hedge is used, and account for such hedges.

9. Identify the various types of information that should be included in disclosures regarding derivative instruments and hedging activities.

The use of derivative instruments has increased significantly among both financial and non-financial corporations. These instruments derive their value from changes in the price or rate of a related asset or liability. For example, the option or right to buy a share of stock at a fixed price derives its value from the price of the related stock. If you could buy the stock at a fixed price of $50 when the stock is trading at $55, the option has value.

Derivative instruments may be held as: (a) investments or (b) part of a strategy to reduce or hedge against exposure to risk associated with some other transaction. The use of derivatives is most common among large corporations with foreign currency exchange and interest rate exposures. Derivatives received a lot of attention during the mid-1990s due to their use as an investment instrument by large governmental units. These investments were extremely volatile and resulted in huge losses for a number of entities. At that time, derivative instruments were not recorded on the balance sheets. This *off-balance-sheet* treatment made financial analysis even more difficult. Since that time, the Financial Accounting Standards Board (FASB) has issued multiple standards for derivatives that require them to be recorded as assets or liabilities at fair value. These standards are extremely complex and are contained in the FASB Accounting Standards Codification (ASC) Topic 815 (Derivatives and Hedging). These standards are developed from two critical underpinnings: (1) derivatives represent assets or liabilities, and (2) derivatives are to be measured at fair value.

DERIVATIVES: CHARACTERISTICS AND TYPES

1

O B J E C T I V E

State the general characteristics of a derivative instrument, and define *underlying* and *notional amount*.

A financial instrument represents a right, through a contractual agreement between two opposite parties called *counterparties*, to receive or deliver cash or another financial instrument on potentially favorable or unfavorable terms. Financial instruments include cash, equity and debt investments, and derivatives. A derivative is a type of financial instrument that has several distinguishing characteristics that have been set forth by the FASB. These characteristics are that a derivative:

1. Derives its value from changes in the rate or price of a related asset or liability. The rate or price is known as an *underlying*.
2. The quantity or number of units specified by a derivative is known as the *notional amount*.
3. Requires little or no initial investment upon inception.
4. Allows for *net settlement* in that the derivative contract can be settled in exchange for cash, without having to actually buy or sell the related asset or liability.

Characteristics of Derivatives

A critical characteristic of a derivative and the basis for its name is that the instrument derives its value from changes in the value of a related asset or liability. The rates or prices that relate to the asset or liability underlying the derivative are referred to as *underlyings*. The underlying may take a variety of forms, including a commodity price, stock price, foreign currency exchange rate, or interest rate. **It is important to note that the underlying is not the asset or liability itself, but rather its price or rate.** For example, the underlying in an option to buy a share of stock at a fixed price of $50 is not the stock itself; it is the $50 price of the stock, and it determines the value of the derivative. Changes in the underlying price or rate cause the value of the derivative to change. For example, if the price of a stock underlies the value of an option to buy that stock, changes in the price of the stock relative to the option price will cause the value of the option to change. If the underlying price of the stock changes from $50 to $52, then the option to buy at $50 has increased in value by $2 (one could buy the stock for $50 when it has a fair value of $52).

In order to fully value a derivative, one must know the number of units (quantity) that is specified in the derivative instrument. This is called the *notional amount*, and it determines the total dollar value of a derivative, traceable to movement or changes in the underlying. For example, if the option to buy stock for $50 increases in value because the underlying price of the stock moves from $50 to $52, the total magnitude of this increase in value depends on how many shares can be purchased under the terms of the option. If the option applies to 1,000 shares, then the total intrinsic value of the option is $2,000 (a $2 change in the underlying price of $50 to $52 times a notional amount of 1,000 shares). The notional amount of a derivative might refer to so many bushels of a commodity, number of shares, foreign currency units, or principal amount of debt. **Both the underlying price or rate and the notional amount are necessary in order to determine the total value of a derivative at any point in time.**

Typically, a derivative requires little or no initial investment because it is *an investment in a change* in value traceable to an underlying, rather than an investment in the actual asset or liability to which the underlying relates. For example, if the price of a stock increases, the value of an option to buy that stock also increases. If one actually owned the stock, an increase in the price of the stock would also result in increased value. However, the important difference is that in order to experience the increase in value an option holder needs to make little or no initial investment, whereas the owner of the stock has to make a significant investment to acquire the stock in the first place.

Many derivatives do not require the parties to the contract, the counterparties, to actually deliver an asset that is associated with the underlying in order to realize the value of a derivative. For example, the option to buy a share of stock at a fixed price would allow the holder to sell the option rather than requiring the other counterparty to actually transfer stock to them at the option price. Assume that a stock is trading at $52 per share and that one holds an option to buy stock at $50 per share. The holder could sell the option for $2 or require the counterparty to sell them stock at $50. If the stock were purchased for $50, it could readily be converted into cash by selling at $52, thereby realizing a gain of $2. The ability to settle the contract in exchange for cash, without actually buying or selling the related asset or liability, is referred to as *net settlement*.

A derivative may be a separate, distinct financial instrument, or it may be *embedded* in another financial instrument. An embedded derivative has economic characteristics and risks that are not clearly and closely related to those of the host instrument. For example, a convertible bond is a host contract that also contains an embedded derivative. That derivative represents the option to convert the bond into common stock; its underlying is the price of the respective stock. The conversion feature's economic value is more closely related to the underlying stock than the bond. If the embedded derivative meets certain criteria, it may be separated, or *bifurcated*, from the host contract and be accounted for as a separate instrument. The discussion of bifurcation is beyond the scope of this text.

Common Types of Derivatives

The number of financial instruments that have the characteristics of a derivative has continued to expand, and, in turn, these instruments have become increasingly complex. In spite of the diversity and/or complexity that characterizes them, most derivatives are variations of four basic types, including forwards, futures, options, and swaps. Other more complex derivative instruments are not described here.

Derivatives are often part of a trading portfolio and are held primarily for sale in the short term. As with other trading investments, derivatives are marked-to-market, and the resulting gain or loss is recognized currently in earnings. A specific discussion of each type of derivative follows. In this section, we cover derivatives as investments made for speculative purposes. The use of derivatives as a hedging instrument is discussed in a separate section. Transaction costs (e.g., brokers' fees), which are typically included as part of the original cost or basis of the derivative as with all investments, are ignored for purposes of discussion.

Forward Contracts. A *forward contract* is an executory contract to buy or sell a specified amount of an asset, such as foreign currency, at a specified fixed price with delivery at a specified future point in time. The party that agrees to sell the asset is said to be in a *short position,* and the party that agrees to buy the asset is said to be in a *long position.* The specified fixed price in the contract is known as a *forward price* or *forward rate.* The current price or rate for the asset is known as the *spot rate.* The specified future point is referred to as the *forward date.* The difference between the spot rate and the forward rate at inception is referred to as the *premium* or *discount* and represents the time value of the contract. The difference between the spot rate and the remaining forward rate represents the remaining premium or discount at that point in time. Forward contracts are not formally regulated on an organized exchange, and the parties are exposed to a risk that default of the contract could occur. However, the lack of formal regulation means that such contracts can be customized in response to specialized needs regarding notional amounts and forward dates.

The value of a forward contract is zero at inception and typically does not require an initial cash outlay. However, over time, movement in the price or rate of the underlying results in a change in value of the forward contract. **The total change in the value of a forward contract is measured as the difference between the forward rate "at inception of the contract" and the spot rate "at the forward date."**

For example, on April 1, a party (called the *writer*) writes a contract in which she/he agrees to sell (short position) to another party (called the *holder*) who agrees to buy (long position) 1,000,000 foreign currencies (for example, euros) at a specific price of $0.16 per foreign currency (FC) with delivery in 90 days (June 29). The relationship between the parties is as follows:

OBJECTIVE 2

Explain the basic features of common derivative instruments, including forward contracts, futures contracts, options, and interest rate swaps.

OBJECTIVE 3

Determine and account for the change in value over time of forward and futures contracts.

If the spot rate at the end of the forward period is $0.18, the total change in value is determined as follows:

1,000,000 FC at a forward rate (on April 1) of $0.16 (1,000,000 × $0.16)	$160,000
1,000,000 FC at a spot rate (on June 29) of $0.18 (1,000,000 × $0.18).............	180,000
Gain in value to holder	$ 20,000

This is a gain because on June 29 the holder received something with a fair value greater than the fair value given up that day. (Conversely, this would be a loss to the writer.) The holder of the forward contract could buy foreign currencies for $160,000 on the forward date compared to the spot value of $180,000 at that time and experience an immediate $20,000 gain. It is important to note that the value of the currency at the final spot rate could have been less than $160,000. In that case, the holder would have experienced a loss and the writer a gain. When the value of a derivative can change in both directions (gain or loss), it is said to have a *symmetric return profile*. It is also important to note that in the case of a forward contract, if the holder of the contract experiences a gain (loss) in value, then the writer of the contract simultaneously experiences a loss (gain) in value.

The forward price or rate is a function of a number of variables, including the length of the forward period and the current spot rate. As these variables change over the life of the contract, the value of the forward contract also changes. Also, because *the forward prices or rates represent values in the future, the current value is represented by the present value of the future rates.* Continuing with the example involving foreign currencies, assume the following forward rates information throughout the 90-day term of the contract:

Remaining Term of Contract	Forward Rate	Notional Amount	Total Forward Value	Change in Forward Value
90 days	$0.160	1,000,000	$160,000	
60 days	0.170	1,000,000	170,000	$10,000
30 days	0.170	1,000,000	170,000	10,000
0 days	0.180	1,000,000	180,000	20,000

Assuming a 6% discount rate, the change in value of the forward contract over time is as follows:

	60 Days Remaining	30 Days Remaining	Total Life of Contract
Cumulative change in forward value.................	$10,000	$10,000	$20,000
Present value of cumulative change:			
60 days at 6%	$ 9,901		
30 days at 6%		$ 9,950	
0 days at 6%			$20,000
Previously recognized gain or loss	0	(9,901)	(9,950)
Current period gain or loss	$ 9,901	$ 49	$10,050

Note that the total change in the value of the forward contract is $20,000 ($9,901 + $49 + $10,050), which is recognized over the term of the contract as the net present value of changes in the forward rates. Even if the forward rates did not change between two valuation dates (there was no change between 60 and 30 days here), the value of the contract would change because the remaining term of the forward contract continues to decrease and the present value of the forward value increases. Also, note that *the stated forward rate at the expiration date of the contract is equal to the spot rate at that date.* This is due to the fact that at expiration of the contract the forward date is the same as the current date.

Investors could acquire forward contracts to purchase foreign currencies, even though they have no need for the foreign currencies, hoping that the value of the contract increases and results in investment income. Of course, holding the contract as an investment could also expose them to the risk that the value would decrease over time. As previously stated, the value of a forward contract can move in both directions resulting in a symmetric return profile. Investors in forward contracts would typically settle them by selling prior to the forward date because they do not actually need to buy or sell the foreign currencies. If the above forward contract were held as an investment and settled with 30 days remaining, the entries to account for the contract would be as shown below.

Event	Entry		
Initial acquisition.	A memo entry to record acquisition of the contract. At inception, the value of the contract is zero.		
60 days remaining.	Investment in Forward Contract...............................	9,901	
	Gain on Contract..		9,901
	To record the change in value of the contract. (This entry is necessary only when financial statements are being prepared.)		
30 days remaining.	Cash	9,950	
	Investment in Forward Contract............................		9,901
	Gain on Contract..		49
	To record the settlement of the contract.		

Futures Contracts. A *futures contract* is exactly like a forward contract in that it too provides for the receipt or payment of a specified amount of an asset at a specified price with delivery at a specified future point in time. However, the futures contract has the following distinguishing characteristics:

- Unlike forward contracts, futures are traded on organized exchanges. The exchanges help ensure that the trading partners honor their obligations. The exchange clearinghouse actually becomes an intermediary between the buyer and seller of the contract. In essence, the clearinghouse becomes the seller for each buyer and the buyer for each seller.

- The formal regulation of futures contracts results in contracts that are standardized in nature versus customized. For example, the exchange specifies the quantity and quality of commodities traded, as well as the delivery place and date.

- A futures contract requires an initial deposit of funds with the transacting broker. This deposit is referred to as a *margin account*; it serves as collateral to help ensure that the parties to the contract are able to perform. Each day, the contract is valued and marked-to-market. If the contract loses too much value, the holder will have to contribute additional cash to the margin account. If the margin account balance falls below a minimum balance, called the *maintenance margin*, the investor is required to replenish the account through what is called a *margin call*.

- Forward contracts represent cash amounts settled only at delivery and therefore represent future amounts that must be discounted to yield a current present value. However, future prices are marked-to-market each day. At the close of each trading day, a new futures price or settlement price is established. Therefore, the futures price represents a current versus future value, and no discounting is necessary. This new futures price is used to compute the gain or loss on the contract over time.

- The party that has written a futures contract is said to be *short*, and the party that owns the contract is said to be *long*.

For example, assume one buys 50 contracts on the Chicago Board of Trade (CBT) to receive November delivery of corn to a certified warehouse. Each contract is in units of 5,000 bushels at a *futures* price of $2.50 per bushel. Notice that the terms of the contract are standardized. Obviously, a second party must agree to sell corn at a November futures price of $2.50. Acting as an intermediary between the counterparties, the CBT, in essence, writes a contract to sell a corn future to the first party and buys a contract to purchase a corn future from the second party. The relationship between the parties is as follows:

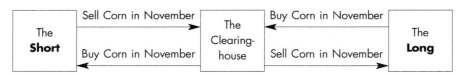

Assume that the initial margin on the above contract is set at $20,000, with a maintenance margin of $15,000, and that future prices are as follows:

Day 1	Day 2	Day 3	Day 4
$2.50	$2.51	$2.49	$2.47

The following entries illustrate the valuation of the futures contracts and the use of a margin account for the long (the owner of the contract).

Day 1	Futures Contract—Margin Account.........................		20,000	
	Cash			20,000
	To record establishment of margin account.			
Day 2	Futures Contract—Margin Account.........................		2,500	
	Gain on Contract....................................			2,500
	To record gain in fair value of contract [50 contracts × 5,000 bushels × ($2.51 vs. $2.50)].			
Day 3	Loss on Contract		5,000	
	Futures Contract—Margin Account.......................			5,000
	To record loss in fair value of contract [50 contracts × 5,000 bushels × ($2.49 vs. $2.51)].			
Day 4	Loss on Contract		5,000	
	Futures Contract—Margin Account.......................			5,000
	To record loss in fair value of contract [50 contracts × 5,000 bushels × ($2.47 vs. $2.49)].			
	Futures Contract—Margin Account.........................		7,500	
	Cash			7,500
	To meet margin call and reestablish initial margin balance of $20,000 (balance before call = $20,000 + $2,500 − $5,000 − $5,000 = $12,500, which is less than $15,000 maintenance margin).			

The value of the futures contract is influenced by either positive or negative movements in the underlying price. Therefore, the risk associated with the contract is symmetrical. Unlike forward contracts, the value of futures contracts, which typically change on a daily basis, can be easily monitored since such contracts are traded on the open market. Futures prices can be found in several different places such as *The Wall Street Journal* or online at http://www.wsjmarkets.com.

4

OBJECTIVE

Determine and account for the intrinsic and time value components of an option.

Option Contracts. An *option* represents a right, rather than an obligation, to either buy or sell some quantity of a particular underlying. Common examples include options to buy or sell stocks, a stock index, an interest rate, foreign currency, oil, metals, and agricultural commodities. The option is valid for a specified period of time and calls for a specified buy or sell price, referred to as the *strike price* or *exercise price*. If an option allows the holder to *buy* an underlying, it is referred to as a *call option*. An option that allows the holder to *sell* an underlying is referred to as a *put option*. Options are actively traded on organized exchanges or may be negotiated on a case-by-case basis between counterparties (over-the-counter contracts). Option contracts require the holder to make an initial nonrefundable cash outlay, known as the *premium,* as represented by the option's current value. The premium is paid, in part, because the writer of the option takes more risk than the holder of the option. The holder can allow the option to expire, while the writer must comply if the holder chooses to exercise it.

During the option period, the strike price of the option on the underlying is generally different from the current value of an underlying. The following terms are used to describe the relationship between the strike price and the current price (note that the premium is not considered in these relationships):

Option Type	Strike Price Is Equal to Current Price	Strike Price Is Greater Than Current Price	Strike Price Is Less Than Current Price
Call (buy) option	At-the-money	Out-of-the-money	In-the-money
Put (sell) option	At-the-money	In-the-money	Out-of-the-money

As the table suggests, in-the-money is a favorable condition as compared to being out-of-the-money, which is an unfavorable condition. The original premium is not considered when describing whether an option is or is not in-the-money. However, it is important to note that the original premium certainly is considered when determining whether an investment in an option has experienced an overall profit. The holder of an option has a right, rather than an obligation, and will not exercise the option unless it is in-the-money. In that case, the holder will experience a gain, and the writer will experience a loss. However, if the option is not in-the-money, the option will not be exercised, the holder will limit her/his loss to the amount of the option premium, and the writer will limit her/his gain to the amount of the premium. Therefore, in theory, the opportunities for gain and loss are characterized as follows:

	Potential for	
	Gain	Loss
Holder of option	Unlimited	Limited to amount of premium
Writer of option	Limited to amount of premium	Unlimited

Because the counterparties do not have equal opportunity for both upside and downside changes in value, options are said to have an *asymmetric* or one-sided *return profile*.

Options are traded on an organized exchange and over the counter; therefore, their current value is quoted in terms of present dollars on a frequent basis. The current value of an option depends on forward periods and spot prices. The difference between the strike and spot price, at any point in time, measures the *intrinsic value* of the option, so changes in spot prices will change the intrinsic value of the option. Changes in the length of the remaining forward period will affect the *time value* of the option. The time value is measured as the difference between an option's current value and its intrinsic value as in the following illustration:

◆ If the option is in-the-money, the option has intrinsic value. For example, if an investor has an April call (buy) option to buy IBM stock at a strike price of $110 and the current stock price is $112, the option is in-the-money and has an intrinsic value of $2. An option that is out-of-the-money or at-the-money has no intrinsic value.

◆ The difference between the current value of an option and its intrinsic value represents time value. For example, if the IBM April call (buy) option has a current value of $8 and an intrinsic value of $2, the time value component is $6 (the current value of $8, less the intrinsic value of $2). The time value of an option represents a discounting factor and a volatility factor.

◆ The *discounting factor* relates to the fact that the strike price does not have to be paid currently, but rather at the time of exercise. Therefore, the holder of an option to buy stock could benefit from an appreciation in stock value without actually having to currently pay out the cash to purchase the stock. For example, assume that a 30-day, at-the-money option has a strike price of $100 and that a discount rate of 12% is appropriate. The ability to use the $100 for 30 days at an assumed discount rate of 12%, rather than having to buy the stock at the current price of $100, is worth $1 ($100 × 12% × $1/12$ year). Thus, the ability to have the alternative use of the cash equal to the strike price until exercise date of the option has value.

◆ The *volatility factor* relates to the volatility of the underlying relative to the fixed strike price and reflects the potential for gain on the option. Underlyings with more price volatility present greater opportunities for gains if the option is in-the-money. Therefore, higher volatility increases the value of an option. Note that volatility could also lead to an out-of-the-money situation. However, this possibility can be disregarded because, unlike forward or futures contracts, the risk for an option is asymmetric since the holder can avoid unfavorable outcomes by allowing the option to expire.

To illustrate the value components of an option, assume that a put (sell) option allows for the sale of a share of stock in 60 days at a strike or exercise price of $50 per share. The value of the option would consist of the following:

	Initial Date of Purchase	End of 30 Days	End of 60 Days
Market value of stock	$51	$49	$48
Assumed total value of option	1.30	1.65	2.00
Intrinsic value (never less than zero)	0 (option is out-of-the-money)	1 (in-the-money = $50 − $49)	2 (in-the-money = $50 − $48)
Time value (total value less intrinsic value)	1.30	0.65	0

The value of an option can be realized either through exercise of the option or through cash settlement. If the option can be exercised any time during the specified period, it is referred to as an *American option*; if it is exercisable only at the maturity date/expiration of the contract, it is referred to as a *European option*.

To illustrate the use of an option, assume that a call (buy) option on 10,000 bushels of corn with delivery in April is purchased in February for a premium of $1,000 and has a strike price of $2.20 per bushel. The values of the option at the end of February and March are $1,050 and $700, respectively. It is sold in early April, prior to expiration, for $750. The relationship between the parties is as follows:

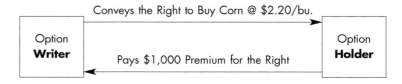

The following entries account for the holder's investment in the option, given various values over time:

Feb. 1	Investment in Call Option	1,000	
	Cash		1,000
	To record purchase of call option.		
28	Investment in Call Option	50	
	Gain on Option		50
	To record change in total value of option ($1,050 − $1,000).		
Mar. 31	Loss on Option.......................................	350	
	Investment in Call Option...............................		350
	To record change in total value of option ($700 − $1,050).		
Apr. 2	Cash	750	
	Investment in Call Option (book value)		700
	Gain on Call Option		50
	To record sale of option.		

The basic concepts related to both call (buy) and put (sell) options are set forth in Exhibit M-1.

Exhibit M-1
Basic Concepts Related to Options

Call Options	Holder	Holder
Rights	Right to buy an underlying asset at a set exercise or strike price.	Obligation to sell an underlying asset at a set exercise or strike price.
Type	European or American—European can be exercised only at maturity date. American can be exercised any time up to and including maturity date.	European or American—European can be exercised only at maturity date. American can be exercised any time up to and including maturity date.
Cost	Pays an initial fixed cost referred to as a premium.	Receives an initial premium.
Value of the call option:		
Net gain	Experienced when the strike price is less than fair value of the underlying asset. In theory, the gain is unlimited. This is referred to as being in-the-money. The value of this difference must exceed the initial premium to produce a net gain.	Experienced when the strike price is more than or equal to the fair value of the underlying asset. The gain is limited to the initial premium.
Net loss	Experienced when the strike price is more than or equal to the fair value of the underlying asset. The loss is limited to the initial premium.	Experienced when the strike price is less than fair value of the underlying asset. In theory, the loss is unlimited. The value of this difference must exceed the initial premium to produce a net loss.
Components of value	The value consists of intrinsic value and time value.	The value consists of intrinsic value and time value.

Put Options	Holder	Writer
Rights	Right to sell an underlying asset at a set exercise or strike price.	Obligation to buy an underlying asset at a set exercise or strike price.
Type	European or American—European can be exercised only at maturity date. American can be exercised any time up to and including maturity date.	European or American—European can be exercised only at maturity date. American can be exercised any time up to and including maturity date.
Cost	Pays an initial fixed cost referred to as a premium.	Receives an initial premium.
Value of the put option:		
Net gain	Experienced when the strike price is more than fair value of the underlying asset. In theory, the gain is unlimited. This is referred to as being in-the-money. The value of this difference must exceed the initial premium to produce a net gain.	Experienced when the strike price is less than or equal to the fair value of the underlying asset. The gain is limited to the initial premium.
Net loss	Experienced when the strike price is less than or equal to the fair value of the underlying asset. The loss is limited to the initial premium.	Experienced when the strike price is more than fair value of the underlying asset. The value of this difference must exceed the initial premium. The maximum loss is limited to the strike price, less the initial premium.
Components of value	The value consists of intrinsic value and time value.	The value consists of intrinsic value and time value.

Swaps. A *swap* is a type of forward contract represented by a contractual obligation, arranged by an intermediary that requires the exchange of cash flows between two parties. Swaps are customized to meet the needs of the specific parties and are not traded on regulated exchanges. Most often, swaps are used to hedge against unfavorable outcomes and are explained more fully in the later discussion of hedging. However, it is important to understand the basic format of a swap. Common examples include foreign currency swaps and interest rate swaps. For example,

5

OBJECTIVE

Appreciate the basic objectives of an interest rate swap.

assume a U.S. company has an opportunity to invest in a German joint venture that is expected to last six months. The U.S. company must invest euros in the venture, and its investment will be returned in euros at the end of the 6-month period. Through an intermediary, the U.S. company could contract with a German company that needs U.S. dollars for a similar period of time. Each of the companies would have available or borrow their respective currencies and then swap the currencies, dollars for euros and euros for dollars. At the end of the 6-month investment period, the U.S. company would return euros to the German company, and the German company would return dollars to the U.S. company.

Rather than involving the swap of different currencies, an interest rate swap involves exchanging variable or floating (fixed) interest rates for fixed (variable or floating) rates. For example, assume a Company issued $10,000,000 of variable interest debt when rates were 6% and is now concerned that interest rates will increase. In order to protect against rising rates, the Company contracts with a Bank and agrees to pay a fixed rate of interest of 6.5% to the Bank in exchange for receiving variable rates. The Company is referred to as the *pay fixed* or *receive floating* party, and the Bank is referred to as the *pay floating* or *receive fixed* party. In essence, the Company has converted its floating or variable rate debt into fixed rate debt. The relationship between the parties is as follows:

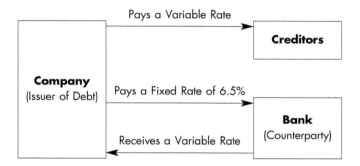

If the variable rate increased to 6.7% on the $10,000,000 of variable interest debt, the Company's semiannual net interest expense would be determined as follows:

Variable interest paid to creditors (6.7% × $10,000,000 × ½ year) . . . . $ 335,000
Fixed interest paid to the Bank (6.5% × $10,000,000 × ½ year) 325,000*
Variable interest received from the Bank (6.7% × $10,000,000 × ½ year)* . . . . (335,000)
Net interest paid [(−6.7% − 6.5% + 6.7%) × $10,000,000 × ½ year] . . . . $ 325,000

*Rather than actually paying and receiving, the entities exchange the net difference between the rates (fixed vs. variable) in the amount of $10,000 ($325,000 vs. $335,000). This results in a net interest expense of $325,000 ($335,000 paid to creditors less $10,000 received from the Bank).

The interest swap was entered into because the Company feared that variable rates would increase. In essence, the swap allowed the Company to exchange a variable interest rate for a fixed interest rate as though it had actually issued fixed debt. As the swap continues, new variable rates will be determined and applied to subsequent semiannual interest payments. This process of determining a new rate for the swap is referred to as *resetting* the rate. Generally, the variable interest rate is reset at each interest date and is applied to the subsequent period's interest calculations.

In the above example, if the variable rate increased to more than the 6.5% fixed rate paid to the Bank, the Company received a net cash amount from the bank and realized a gain as a result of entering into the swap. Therefore, the value of the swap, represented by the payment of a fixed rate in exchange for a higher variable rate, has increased. If the variable rate had decreased below the 6.5% fixed rate paid to the Bank, the Company would have made a net cash settlement payment to the Bank, and the swap would have lost value. Changes in the variable interest rates expose one party to potential loss and the other party to potential gain. Therefore, swaps, like other forward contracts, are characterized by symmetric risk. In the above example, the Bank is acting as the counterparty and lost value on the swap. However, acting as a counterparty, the Bank will attempt to match the notional amount of the current swap with the notional amount of another swap with a party that is seeking to pay floating/receive fixed. This results in the counterparty Bank having one swap where it pays floating (receive fixed) and another swap where it pays fixed (receive floating). The counterparty will have a spread between the pay and receive floating rate or the pay and receive fixed rate that compensates it for its services. For example, assume a notional amount of $10,000,000. If the counterparty has a pay floating rate of 3.5% and a receive floating rate of 3.7%, then the spread will result in compensation of $20,000 [(−3.5% + 3.7%) × $10,000,000].

The valuation of swaps is complex and dependent on assumptions regarding future rates or prices. For example, if a fixed interest payment is swapped for a variable interest payment, the value of the swap is a function of how future variable rates are expected to compare to the fixed rate. Therefore, an estimate of future variable rates is required. Furthermore, the differences between the future variable rates and the fixed rate represent future differences that need to be discounted in order to produce a present value of the differences.

The above example involved a swap of fixed interest payments to a counterparty in exchange for the receipt of a variable rate of interest. It is also possible to swap a variable interest payment in exchange for a fixed rate of interest. The use of these swaps and the resulting accounting will be discussed in greater detail in a subsequent section of this chapter.

Summary of Derivative Instruments

Exhibit M-2 presents a summary and comparison of the four basic types of derivative instruments discussed in the preceding sections. The most important differences are between options and the other three types of derivatives. Futures, forwards, and swaps each provide symmetric risk to a holder because the value of the derivative can change in both directions (gains or losses) without limits. This symmetric risk profile requires both counterparties to execute the contract whether the effect is favorable or unfavorable. In contrast, the holder of an option is not required or obligated to exercise the option and, in fact, will not do so if the option is at- or out-of-the-money. This provides asymmetric risk for the holder who may want to avoid downside risk. Options also differ from the other derivative instruments described here in the requirement for an initial cash outlay, which represents the initial intrinsic and time values of the option.

Exhibit M-2
Basic Concepts Related to Selected Derivative Instruments

	Forward Contracts	**Futures Contracts**	**Options**	**Swaps**
Basic design	An obligation to buy or sell an asset at a specified forward price/rate with delivery at a specified forward date.	An obligation to buy or sell an asset at a specified forward price/rate with delivery at a specified future date.	A right to buy or sell an asset at a specified strike price. The strike price is valid for a specified period of time.	A contract that exchanges cash flows between two parties. In substance, a type of forward contract.
Trading and regulation	Not traded on an organized exchange. Trading is not formally regulated.	Traded on an organized exchange (e.g., Chicago Board of Trade). Trading is formally regulated.	Traded on an organized exchange (e.g., Chicago Board Options Exchange) and in the over-the-counter (OTC) market. Trading is formally regulated.	Not traded on an organized exchange. Trading is not formally regulated.
Counterparty default risk	Parties are exposed to default risk.	The exchange clearinghouse acts as an intermediary between the counterparties. It helps to ensure that the parties honor their obligations.	Because of the involvement of the exchange, there is no default risk.	Parties are exposed to default risk.

(continued)

Exhibit M-2 *(concluded)*

	Forward Contracts	Futures Contracts	Options	Swaps
Derivative form	Customized contracts to meet the specialized needs of the counterparties.	The formal regulation of contracts results in standardized contracts.	The formal regulation of options results in standardized contracts.	Swaps are customized to meet the needs of the specific parties.
Initial cash outlay	No initial cash outlay required.	Typically, no initial cash outlay. However, holders of a contract must establish a cash margin account.	Holders are required to make an initial cash outlay known as a premium.	No initial cash outlay required.
Return profile	Symmetric.	Symmetric.	Asymmetric.	Symmetric.

REFLECTION

- An underlying, a notional amount, and the opportunity for net settlement characterize derivatives.

- Major types of derivative instruments include forward contracts, futures contracts, options, and swaps.

- Derivative instruments may be held as an investment, and changes in their value should be recognized in current earnings. The value of a derivative is a function of the movement or changes in the underlying and the notional amount.

6

OBJECTIVE

Explain how a derivative instrument may be used to reduce or avoid the exposure to risk associated with other transactions.

ACCOUNTING FOR DERIVATIVES THAT ARE DESIGNATED AS A HEDGE

Changes in the value of a derivative held as an investment are recognized currently in earnings, and the derivative is carried on the balance sheet at its current value. Aside from holding derivatives as an investment, derivatives may be used to hedge against changes in the value of existing assets or liabilities, as well as changes in the value of commitments or forecasted transactions. For example, assume that a commercial feed company is committed to buy corn as an ingredient. In order to protect against increasing corn prices, the company could buy a futures contract in order to hedge against this risk. If the hedged item, the commitment to buy corn in this example, experiences an unfavorable change in value, a properly structured hedge (the hedging instrument) could be effective in providing a change in value in the opposite direction such that there is no adverse effect. If a derivative is properly structured for this purpose, it seems that the change in the value of the derivative (the hedging instrument) should be recognized in the same accounting period as is the change in the value of the hedged item. Hedges are generally designated as either *fair value* or *cash flow*. A **fair value** hedge is used to offset changes in the fair value of items with fixed prices or rates. Fair value hedges include hedges against a change in the fair value of:

- A recognized asset or liability.
- An unrecognized firm commitment.

A **cash flow hedge** is used to establish fixed prices or rates when future cash flows could vary due to changes in prices or rates. Cash flow hedges include hedges against the change in cash flows associated with:

- A forecasted transaction.
- The variability in the cash flows associated with a recognized asset or liability.

Derivative instruments are frequently used as hedges with respect to the exposure to risk associated with foreign currency transactions and investments in foreign companies. The use of derivatives in this context is discussed in Chapter 10, which deals with multinational accounting. The following sections deal with the accounting for hedges employed in other contexts.

Special Accounting for Fair Value Hedges

The hedged item in a fair value hedge is either a recognized asset or liability or a firm commitment. Recognized assets or liabilities in a fair value hedge result from actual past transactions such as a purchase of inventory or a note payable. Commitments relate to transactions that have not yet occurred, such as a contract to purchase inventory or incur debt. A commitment is a binding agreement between two parties that specifies all significant terms related to the prospective transaction. The price of the prospective transaction is fixed or it may involve a specified fixed rate such as a rate of interest. The agreement also includes a large enough disincentive to make performance of the contract probable.

Because the prices or rates are fixed, subsequent changes in prices or rates affect the value of a recognized asset, liability, or commitment. For example, if a company holds an inventory of crude oil, changes in the price of crude oil will affect the fair value of the asset. Similarly, if a company has committed to acquire crude oil for a fixed price, changes in the price of crude oil will affect the value of the commitment. If the price of crude oil increased, the value of the asset or commitment would increase favorably. The existing inventory would be worth more, or the commitment to acquire crude at previously fixed lower prices would have more value. However, if crude oil prices decreased, the resulting effect would be unfavorable.

To avoid the potential unfavorable effect associated with changes in prices or rates on recognized transactions or commitments with fixed terms, an entity could acquire a derivative instrument as a hedge against unfavorable outcomes. For example, in order to hedge against a decrease in the value of an inventory (asset) of crude oil, an entity could acquire a futures contract to sell crude and thereby lock into a selling price for the crude oil. Many accounting principles do not allow for the *recognition in current earnings of both increases and decreases* in the value of recognized assets, liabilities, or firm commitments. However, if the risk of such changes in value is covered by a fair value hedge, special accounting treatment is allowed that provides for the recognition of such changes in earnings. In a qualifying fair value hedge, the gain or loss on the derivative hedging instrument and the offsetting loss or gain on the hedged item are both recognized currently in earnings. For instance, assume an existing liability has a fixed interest rate. A decrease in interest rates will result in a higher fair value of the debt (lower interest rates result in larger present values). If the debt is not hedged, the increase in the value of the debt is not recognized in earnings. However, if the liability is hedged with an interest rate swap, both the increase in the value of the debt and the change in the value of the derivative instrument used as a hedge are recognized in earnings.

It is important to note that if both increases and decreases in the value of a recognized asset or liability are recognized in current earnings according to existing accounting principles, special hedge accounting is not necessary. For example, if a trading portfolio consisted of debt instruments, such investments would be marked-to-market, and both increases and decreases in value would be recognized in current earnings. Therefore, if the portfolio were hedged, special accounting treatment would not be necessary. Changes in the value of both the hedged item and the hedging instrument are already being recognized in earnings. However, if a debt instrument is part of an *available-for-sale portfolio* and the debt is marked-to-market, the resulting changes in value are not recognized in current earnings. Therefore, if the portfolio were hedged, special accounting treatment would be allowed and would result in recognizing in earnings the change in value of the debt instrument.

Qualifying Criteria for Fair Value Hedges. In order to qualify for special fair value hedge accounting, the derivative hedging instrument and the hedged item must satisfy a number of criteria. A critical criterion is that an entity must have formal documentation of the hedging relationship and the entity's risk-management objective and strategy. The entity must indicate the reason for undertaking the designated hedge, identify the hedged item and the derivative hedging instrument, and explain the nature of the risk being hedged. This criterion must be satisfied at inception and cannot be retroactively applied after an entity has determined whether hedging would be beneficial.

7

OBJECTIVE

Demonstrate how a fair value hedge is used, and account for such hedges.

Another important criterion is that the hedging relationship must be assessed both at inception and on an ongoing basis to determine if it is highly effective in offsetting the identified risks. Although specific quantitative guidelines are not available to define *highly effective,* the FASB expects a high correlation to exist between changes in the value of the derivative instrument and in the fair value of the hedged item such that the respective changes in value would be substantially offset. Generally speaking, a hedge would be totally effective if the terms (such as notional amount, maturity dates, quality/condition, delivery locations) of the hedging instrument and the hedged item are the same. This approach is known as *critical terms analysis.* It is important to note that in practice the terms of a derivative do not always align with the terms of the related asset or liability. For example, a corn future may call for delivery at a different location than where the related inventory of hedged corn is located.

Another approach to assessing effectiveness is known as *statistical analysis.* This approach statistically measures the correlation between the value of the derivative and the related asset or liability. For example, if you are hedging an inventory of 200 tons of flour with a wheat future for 5,000 bushels of wheat, you would measure the correlation between prices for flour and wheat. You could also examine the relationship between changes in the value of the wheat future derivative and the changes in the value of flour over a period of time. This approach is known as *frequency analysis,* and the ratio between these price changes is known as the *delta ratio.* Although the FASB requires that the hedge be highly effective, it has not set specific quantitative levels of effectiveness that must be satisfied by the hedging relationship. However, practical standards have developed, which suggest target values that must be satisfied in order to be considered highly effective. For example, if the change in the value of a derivative is 80% to 125% of the change in the value of the hedged item, the hedge is considered to be highly effective.

Management must also describe how it will assess hedge effectiveness. Generally, hedge ineffectiveness is the difference between the gains or losses on the derivative and the hedged item. However, the portion of the gain or loss representing time value may be excluded from the assessment of effectiveness and included in current earnings. For example, the hedge of an inventory of corn with an option might only consider changes in the intrinsic value of the option for purposes of assessing effectiveness. The exclusion of a portion of the change in the value of a derivative instrument from the assessment of effectiveness will be illustrated in subsequent discussions.

Although set out in greater detail in the Accounting Standards Codification,[1] selected qualifying criteria for fair value hedges are listed in Exhibit M-3.

Accounting for a Fair Value Hedge. If the derivative instrument and the hedged item satisfy the above criteria, then the fair value hedge will qualify for special accounting. The gain or loss on the derivative hedging instrument will be recognized currently in earnings, along with the change in value on the hedged item, and an appropriate adjustment to the basis of the hedged item will be recorded. If the cumulative change in the value of the derivative instrument does not exactly offset the cumulative change in the value of the hedged item, the difference is recognized currently in earnings. Because both hedge effectiveness and ineffectiveness are recognized currently in earnings, it is not necessary to separately account for that portion of the hedge that is considered to be ineffective.

Examples of fair value hedges against inventory, a firm commitment, and a fixed interest notes payable follow. Entries for the transaction/commitment are presented side by side with entries for the hedges. All transaction costs are ignored. The examples include the use of derivatives in the form of a futures contract, forward contract, and swap. Note, however, that other types of derivatives could have been used in some of these examples.

The special accounting treatment given a fair value hedge should continue unless:

◆ The criteria necessary for special accounting treatment are no longer satisfied,

◆ The derivative instrument expires or is sold, terminated, or exercised,

◆ The entity no longer designates the derivative instrument as a fair value hedge, or

◆ The hedging relationship is no longer considered highly effective based on management's policies.

---

1 FASB ASC Section 815-25-25, *Derivatives and Hedging—Fair Value Hedges—Recognition.*

Exhibit M-3
Selected Qualifying Criteria for Fair Value Hedges

1. At inception of the hedge, there must be formal documentation of the hedging relationship and the entity's risk-management objective and strategy. Documentation should also identify the hedging instrument, the hedged transaction, the nature of the risk being hedged, and a plan for assessing the effectiveness of the hedge.

2. Both at inception and on an ongoing basis, the hedging relationship must be assessed to determine if it is highly effective in offsetting the risk exposure associated with changes in the hedged item's fair value. The effectiveness of the hedging instrument must be assessed whenever financial statements or earnings are reported and at least every three months.

3. The hedged item is specifically identified as part or all of a recognized asset, recognized liability, or unrecognized firm commitment. The hedged item may be a single asset or liability or a portfolio of similar assets or liabilities.

4. The hedged item has exposure to changes in fair value, due to the hedged risk, that could affect earnings. For example, decreasing prices could affect an existing inventory of materials and result in lower gross profits.

5. The hedged item is not an asset or a liability that is being measured at fair value, with changes in fair value, both positive and negative, being currently recognized in earnings. For example, an investment in securities, classified as a trading portfolio, would not qualify for special hedge accounting. The unrealized gains and losses on the portfolio would already be recognized in earnings, and changes in the value of a designated derivative would also be recognized currently in earnings. Therefore, special hedge accounting would only be allowed if generally accepted accounting principles (GAAP) do not already require the hedged item to be measured at fair value.

6. For nonfinancial assets (such as inventory) or liabilities, the risk being hedged against is the change in value of the entire item at its actual location rather than a change in value due to a different location or a component part. Therefore, you could not hedge an inventory of butter by designating price changes of milk as the risk being hedged.

7. Financial assets or liabilities and nonfinancial commitments with a financial component can be designated as hedged items if certain types of risks, such as those related to benchmark interest rate risk, foreign currency exchange rates, and creditworthiness are being hedged. Two or more of the above risks may be hedged simultaneously. Prepayment risk may not be designated as the risk being hedged.

An Example of a Fair Value—Inventory Transaction Hedge Using a Futures Contract

Assume that a Midwest hog producer has an inventory of hogs. On April 1, the producer decides to hedge the fair value of the hog inventory by acquiring two July futures contracts to sell hogs (each contract has a notional amount of 40,000 pounds) at $0.65 per pound. Assume the contracts are settled on July 15. It is assumed that the terms of the futures contracts and the hedged assets match with respect to the delivery location, quantity, and quality of hogs. (Margin amounts and brokers' fees are ignored for purposes of discussion.) On July 20, the producer sells 80,000 pounds of hogs at the current market price of $0.611 per pound and offsets the contract. Assume that the producer's carrying basis (book value) of the hogs is $40,000 before any adjustments related to the hedging transaction. The producer designates the futures contracts as a hedge against changes in the fair value of hogs.

The fair value of the futures contracts will be based on changes in the futures prices over the life of the contract. As previously stated, this difference represents current marked-to-market value and no discounting is required. Effectiveness of the hedging relationship will be assessed by comparing changes over time in the current spot prices for hogs and changes in the value of the futures contracts attributable to changes in spot prices. The time value of the futures contract will be excluded from the assessment of hedge effectiveness. The time value component of the futures contract is the difference between the original spot rate and the original futures rate and is referred to as the *spot-forward difference*. The time value will periodically be recognized over the life of the contract and is measured in one of two ways. The change in the time value, spot-forward difference, may be calculated as either (1) the difference between the change in fair value of the contract and the change in spot rates or (2) directly as the change in spot-forward rates over time. Relevant values are as follows:

	April 1	May 1	June 1	July 15
Number of lbs.	80,000	80,000	80,000	80,000
Spot price/lb.	$0.640	$0.628	$0.622	$0.610
Futures price/lb.	$0.650	$0.635	$0.624	$0.610
Fair value of contract		$1,200 = ($0.650 − $0.635) × 80,000	$2,080 = ($0.650 − $0.624) × 80,000	$3,200 = ($0.650 − $0.610) × 80,000
(a) Current period change in above fair value of contract – gain (loss)		$1,200 = $1,200 − $0	$880 = $2,080 − $1,200	$1,120 = $3,200 − $2,080
(b) Current period change in intrinsic (spot rates) – gain (loss)		$960 = ($0.640 − $0.628) × 80,000	$480 = ($0.628 − $0.622) × 80,000	$960 = ($0.622 − $0.610) × 80,000
(a) − (b) = Current period change in time value, (spot-forward difference) – gain (loss)		$240 = ($0.650 − $0.640) − ($0.635−$0.628) × 80,000 or $1,200 − $960	$400 = ($0.635 − $0.628) − ($0.624 − $0.622) × 80,000 or $880 − $480	$160 = ($0.624 − $0.622) − ($0.610 − $0.610) × 80,000 or $1,120 − $960

The following entries to record the hedging relationship are on the producer's books:

Accounting for Hog Inventory			Accounting for Derivative Hedge		
Apr. 1			Memo entry to record the acquisition of the futures contracts.		
May 1 Loss on Inventory	960		Futures Contract*	960	
Inventory of Hogs		960	Gains on Futures Contract		960
To record the change in the value of the inventory.			To record the change in the value of the contract included in hedge effectiveness.		
			Futures Contract*	240	
			Gains on Futures Contract		240
			To record the change in time value excluded from hedge effectiveness.		
			*Note: The two previous entries regarding the change in the value of the futures contract could be combined into one single entry.		
June 1 Loss on Inventory	480		Futures Contract	480	
Inventory of Hogs		480	Gains on Futures Contract		480
To record the change in the value of the inventory.			To record the change in the value of the contract included in hedge effectiveness.		
			Futures Contract	400	
			Gains on Futures Contract		400
			To record the change in time value excluded from hedge effectiveness.		
July 15 Loss on Inventory	960		Futures Contract	960	
Inventory of Hogs		960	Gains on Futures Contract		960
To record the change in the value of the inventory.			To record the change in the value of the contract included in hedge effectiveness.		
			Futures Contract	160	
			Gains on Futures Contract		160
			To record the change in time value excluded from hedge effectiveness.		

(continued)

Accounting for Hog Inventory			Accounting for Derivative Hedge		
July 20 Cash	48,880		Cash	3,200	
Sales Revenue		48,880	Futures Contract.		3,200
To record the sale of 80,000 pounds of hogs at $0.611 per pound.			To record settlement of the futures contract.		
Cost of Sales	37,600				
Inventory of Hogs.		37,600			
To record the cost of sales consisting of original carrying value of $40,000 less decline in value of $2,400 [($0.640 − $0.610) × 80,000] due to price changes.					

In this example, the hedge totally offsets the adverse effect of price changes on the fair value of the hog inventory. The hedge was highly effective because:

1. The terms of the futures contract and the hedged inventory match regarding quantity, location, and quality.
2. The assessment of the effectiveness of the hedge excludes the time value of the futures contract.

The benefit of the hedge can best be understood by evaluating the situation as follows:

	Desired Position	Without the Hedge	With the Hedge
Sales price of hogs	$ 51,200	$ 48,880	$ 48,880
Cost of sales.	(40,000)	(40,000)	(37,600)
Gross profit	$ 11,200	$ 8,880	$ 11,280
Hedging gain on derivative ($960 + $480 + $960)			2,400
Loss on inventory ($960 + $480 + $960)			(2,400)
Subtotal	$ 11,200	$ 8,880	$ 11,280
Gain excluded from hedge effectiveness ($240 + $400 + $160)			800
Net effect on earnings	$ 11,200	$ 8,880	$ 12,080

The hedge was highly effective in achieving the desired position which was to maintain the sales value of the inventory at the April 1 spot rate (80,000 pounds × $0.64 = $51,200) and realize a gross profit of at least $11,200. The hedge allowed the producer to avoid the exposure to decreases in the value of the inventory due to adverse price changes (decreasing spot rates). Excluding the $800 gain from the time value component, the net effect on earnings of $11,280 ($12,080 − $800) resulting from the use of the hedge was basically the same as the desired position of $11,200. The $80 difference was due to the increase in the spot rate from the expiration date of the futures contracts (July 15) to the actual sale date (July 20).

An Example of a Fair Value—Firm Commitment Hedge Using a Forward Contract

The special accounting treatment given a fair value hedge is also applicable to a hedge on a firm commitment. By way of example, assume that on April 14, when the current spot rate is $172, a company makes a firm commitment to sell 3,000 tons of inventory at the end of June for $172 per ton. It is estimated that the cost of inventory sold under the contract will be $430,000. Concerned that prices may increase and that the firm commitment will prevent the company from realizing even a higher sales value, on April 14 the company enters into a forward contract to buy 3,000 tons of identical inventory at the current forward rate of $173 per ton. The forward contract expires on June 30. The forward contract will gain in value if prices increase, because the holder will be able to buy inventory at the lower price of $173 per ton. Therefore, if prices increase, the loss associated with the firm commitment will be offset by the gain traceable to the forward contract.

Changes in the value of the commitment may be measured in several ways. One way to measure the change in value is to measure changes in the spot rates over time and then discount that value at an appropriate discount rate. It is also possible to measure the change in the value of a commitment based on changes in forward rates over time and then discount that value.

Changes in the fair value of the contract that are attributable to changes in the time value, that is changes in the spot-forward difference, are excluded from the assessment of hedge effectiveness and reported directly in current earnings.[2] Because changes in the time value are reported in earnings along with changes in the intrinsic value of the hedging instrument, it is not necessary to separately account for the change in time value.

The change in the value over time of the forward contract used to hedge the firm commitment is calculated as follows:

	April 14	April 30	May 31	June 30
Notional amount in tons	3,000	3,000	3,000	3,000
Spot rate per ton	$172	$174	$174	$176
Forward rate per ton for remaining time	$173	$175	$174	$176
Initial forward rate		$173	$173	$173
Change from original forward rate		$2	$1	$3
Fair value of forward contract in future dollars:				
Original forward value		$519,000	$519,000	$519,000
Current forward value		525,000	522,000	528,000
Change – gain (loss) in forward value		$ 6,000	$ 3,000	$ 9,000
Discount rate		6%	6%	6%
Present value of the fair value of the contract:				
FV = $6,000, n = 2, i = 0.5%		$ 5,940		
FV = $3,000, n = 1, i = 0.5%			$ 2,985	
FV = $9,000, n = 0, i = 0.5%				$ 9,000
Change in above fair value of the contract – gain (loss):				
Current present value		$ 5,940	$ 2,985	$ 9,000
Prior present value		0	5,940	2,985
Change in present value		$ 5,940	$ (2,955)	$ 6,015

Assume that management has decided to measure changes in the value of the commitment based on changes in the forward rates over time and that the suggested change in value is then discounted. Therefore, the change in value of the commitment will equal the change in the value of the forward contract. Based on the above relevant information, the entries to record the commitment, hedge, and sales transaction follow on page 527.

---

2 Management has the discretion to either include or exclude the time value of the futures contract from the assessment of effectiveness. However, excluding the time value of the contract increases the likelihood that there will be no ineffectiveness in the hedge. Generally speaking, if the terms of the forward contract and the commitment are the same (in terms of notional amount, expiration date, location, etc.) and the time value is excluded, there will be no hedge ineffectiveness.

Apr. 30	Loss on Firm Commitment	5,940		Forward Contract*	5,940	
	Firm Commitment		5,940	Gain on Forward Contract		5,940
	To record change in fair value of firm commitment.			To record the change in value of forward contract.		

*Note: The above entry records the total change in the value of the contract including both the intrinsic value and the time value.

May 31	Firm Commitment	2,955		Loss on Forward Contract	2,955	
	Gain on Firm Commitment		2,955	Forward Contract		2,955
	To record change in fair value of firm commitment.			To record the change in value of forward contract.		
June 30	Loss on Firm Commitment	6,015		Forward Contract	6,015	
	Firm Commitment		6,015	Gain on Forward Contract		6,015
	To record change in value forward.			To record the change in value of contract.		
	Cash	516,000		Cash	9,000	
	Firm Commitment	9,000		Forward Contract		9,000
	Sales		525,000	To record settlement of forward contract.		
	To record the sale of inventory covered by the firm commitment (3,000 tons sold at $172).					
	Cost of Sales	430,000				
	Inventory		430,000			
	To record the cost of sales.					

The concern with the firm commitment was that prices would increase above the firm sales price and reduce the value of the commitment. A forward contract to buy is an appropriate strategy if prices are expected to increase, because as prices increase, the value of the forward contract would increase. After excluding the time value of the contract, the forward contract was expected to be highly effective as a hedge because the derivative instrument had the same type of inventory, notional amount, and forward rate as the hedged commitment. The effectiveness of the hedge is as follows:

	Desired Position	Without the Forward Contract	With the Forward Contract
Sales value of firm commitment	$ 528,000	$ 516,000	$ 525,000
Cost of sales	(430,000)	(430,000)	(430,000)
Gross profit	$ 98,000	$ 86,000	$ 95,000
Loss on firm commitment			(9,000)
Gain in value of forward contract			9,000
Net effect on earnings	$ 98,000	$ 86,000	$ 95,000

The hedge on the firm commitment was highly effective in that the loss in the value of the firm commitment was totally offset by the gain in the value of the forward contract. This resulted in establishing a sales value that reflected the rate at the actual date of the sale (3,000 tons at $176 = $528,000) less the $3,000 [3,000 × ($172 − $173)] spot forward difference rather than the lower value (3,000 tons at $172 = $516,000) that was established at the date of the commitment. Note that the account Firm Commitment serves the purpose of adjusting the sales value of the commitment. In essence, through the use of a hedge, the firm commitment did not prevent the company from realizing even a higher sales value.

An Example of a Fair Value—Hedge against a Fixed Interest Notes Payable Using an Interest Rate Swap

If a company has borrowed at a fixed rate of interest, the fair value of the resulting liability will change if benchmark interest rates change.[3] Although the cash flows are fixed, the discount (current interest) rate changes, resulting in a change in present value. For example, if interest rates decrease, the net present value of the cash flows and the liability will increase. Furthermore, if the debtor company anticipates that variable rates will fall below the original fixed rate, it would have preferred to structure the debt with a variable rate rather than a fixed rate of interest. An interest rate swap would allow the company to accomplish this if it paid a variable rate of interest to a counterparty in exchange for the receipt of a fixed rate of interest. In essence, the debt with a fixed rate of interest is converted into debt with a variable rate of interest.

For example, assume that on January 1, 2015, a company had taken out an 18-month, $20,000,000 note from a bank at a fixed rate of 7% with interest due on a semiannual basis. On January 1, 2015, believing that interest rates are likely to drop, the company arranged to receive a 7% fixed rate of interest from another financial institution in exchange for the payment of variable rates. Differences between the fixed and variable rates are to be settled on a semiannual basis. The variable rates are based on the London Interbank Offered Rate (LIBOR) rate + 1.25% (125 basis points) and are reset semiannually in order to determine the interest rate to be used for the next semiannual payment. The notional amount of the interest rate swap is $20,000,000, and the expiration date of the swap matches the maturity date of the original bank loan. Relevant values are as follows:

Reset Dates	LIBOR +1.25% Rates for Next Period	Assumed Fair Value of Swap	Change in Fair Value
Jan. 1, 2015	7.0%		
June 30, 2015	6.8	$38,000	$38,000
Dec. 31, 2015	6.7	29,000	(9,000)

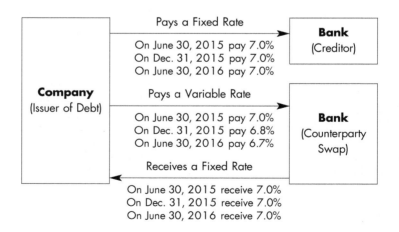

---

3 Currently, the interest rates on direct Treasury obligations of the U.S. government, the London Interbank Offered Rate (LIBOR) swap rate, and the Overnight Index Swap Rate (also referred to as the Fed Funds Effective Swap Rate) are considered to be benchmark interest rates.

Based on the above relevant information, the entries to record the note payable and the interest rate swap are as follows:

2015

Jan. 1   Cash   20,000,000

         7% Note Payable..........   20,000,000

         To record receipt of note proceeds.

June 30   Interest Expense.............   700,000

         Cash   700,000

         To record semiannual interest payment

         ($20,000,000 × 7% × ½ year).

Loss on Debt............... 38,000	Interest Rate Swap Asset 38,000
7% Note Payable.......... 38,000	Gain on Swap 38,000
To recognize the change in the value of the debt.	To recognize the change in the value of the swap.

Dec. 31   Interest Expense............. 700,000   Cash 20,000

         Cash 700,000   Interest Expense........... 20,000

         To record semiannual interest payment   To record settlement of interest rate difference on

         ($20,000,000 × 7% × ½ year).   swap (6.8% vs. 7% on $20,000,000 × ½ year).

         7% Note Payable 9,000   Loss on Swap............... 9,000

         Gain on Debt............. 9,000   Interest Rate Swap Asset 9,000

         To recognize the change in the value of the debt.   To recognize the change in the value of the swap.

2016

June 30   Interest Expense............. 700,000   Cash 30,000

         Cash 700,000   Interest Expense........... 30,000

         To record semiannual interest payment   To record settlement of interest rate difference on

         ($20,000,000 × 7% × ½ year).   swap (6.7% vs. 7% on $20,000,000 × ½ year).

         7% Note Payable 29,000   Loss on Swap............... 29,000

         Gain on Debt............. 29,000   Interest Rate Swap Asset 29,000

         To recognize the change in the value of the debt.   To write down swap value to zero at end of contract.

         7% Note Payable 20,000,000

         Cash   20,000,000

         To record repayment of debt.

During the period covered by the interest rate swap, the carrying amount of the debt was adjusted to reflect changes in the value traceable to movement in benchmark interest rates. In essence, these adjustments represent a discount or premium on the debt. However, while the hedge is in effect, the discount or premium does not have to be amortized. After termination of the swap, any remaining discount or premium must be amortized over the remaining life of the debt.

The interest rate swap was highly effective in replacing a 7.0% fixed rate of interest on the debt with a variable or floating rate of interest equal to LIBOR + 1.25%. The variable rate of interest is derived as follows:

Rate paid on original debt.......................................	−7.00%
Receive fixed rate on swap	+7.00%
Pay floating rate on swap	− LIBOR + 1.25%
Net pay rate [− 7.00% + 7.00% − (LIBOR +1.25%)]	= LIBOR + 1.25%

Given the decreasing pattern of the floating rates, the company experienced a reduction in interest expense and cash outflows as follows:

Total interest expense at fixed rate.................................	$2,100,000
Total interest expense at floating rate	2,050,000
Reduction in interest expense and cash flows	$ 50,000

The change in the value of the swap offsets the change in the value of the debt. The fair value hedge was expected to be highly effective (in this case perfectly effective) in offsetting changes in the fair value of the debt due to the fact that:

◆ The notional amount of the swap matches that of the debt.

◆ The maturity date of the swap matches that of the debt.

◆ The fair value of the swap at inception is zero.

◆ The fixed rate is the same over the life of the note, and the variable rate is based on the same index (LIBOR) over the life of the note.

◆ The debt is not prepayable.

◆ There is no floor or ceiling on the variable interest rate.

◆ The intervals between reset dates are frequent enough to justify an assumption that the settlement amounts are based on market rates.

<table>
<tr><td>

8

O B J E C T I V E

Demonstrate how a cash flow hedge is used, and account for such hedges.

</td></tr>
</table>

Special Accounting for Cash Flow Hedges

The hedged item in a cash flow hedge is one in which future cash flows could be affected due to a particular risk. These hedges involve cash flows associated with a forecasted transaction, forecasted cash flows associated with a recognized asset or liability, or an unrecognized firm commitment. A forecasted transaction is one that is expected to occur in the future at a market price that will be in existence at the time of the transaction. This is in contrast to a commitment, which involves market prices that have been previously determined at the time of the commitment. Unlike a commitment, a forecasted transaction does not provide an entity with any present rights or obligations and therefore does not have any fixed prices or rates. Because fixed prices or rates are not present in a forecasted transaction, an entity is exposed to the risk that future cash flows may vary due to changes in prices/rates. In order to reduce the risk associated with unfavorable cash flow variability, a strategy is developed to hedge the variable cash flows. These hedges are known as cash flow hedges. For example, assume that a food processor forecasts that it will need to purchase corn in 60 days. Absent a fixed commitment, the producer is exposed to the risk that corn prices may increase and more cash will be needed to acquire the inventory. In order to reduce the risk associated with uncertain variable cash flows, the producer could acquire a futures contract to buy corn or perhaps a call option to buy corn. The objective of the hedge is to allow the entity to fix the price or rate and reduce the variability of cash flows.

Qualifying Criteria for Cash Flow Hedges. As is the case with a fair value hedge, special hedge accounting is not available for a cash flow hedge unless a number of criteria are satisfied. Cash flow hedges must also meet the criteria regarding documentation and assessment of effectiveness. Although set forth in greater detail in the FASB's Accounting Standards Codification, selected qualifying criteria for a cash flow hedge are set forth in Exhibit M-4.[4]

Accounting for a Cash Flow Hedge. If the derivative instrument and the hedged item satisfy the criteria, then the cash flow hedge will qualify for special accounting. The gain or loss on the derivative instrument will be reported in **other comprehensive income (OCI)**, and the ineffective portion, if any, will be recognized currently in earnings.[5] As with fair value hedges, a portion of the derivative instrument's gain or loss may be excluded from the assessment of effectiveness. That portion of the gain or loss will be recognized currently in earnings rather than as a component of other comprehensive income.

The gain or loss on a cash flow hedge is reported as OCI, rather than recognized currently in earnings, because the hedged forecasted cash flows have not yet occurred or been recognized in the financial statements. The hedge is intended to establish the values that will be recognized once the forecasted transaction occurs and is recognized. Once the forecasted transaction has actually occurred, the OCI gain or loss will be reclassified into earnings in the same period(s) as the

---

4 FASB ASC 815-20-25.

5 Other comprehensive income is not included in the income statement; it bypasses the traditional income statement but is shown as a component of equity.

forecasted transaction affects earnings. For example, assume that a forecasted sale of inventory is hedged. Once the inventory is sold and recognized in earnings, the applicable amount, the OCI gain or loss, will also be recognized in earnings. If the forecasted transaction were a purchase of a depreciable asset, the applicable portion of the OCI would be recognized in earnings when the asset's depreciation expense is recognized.

Exhibit M-4
Selected Qualifying Criteria for Cash Flow Hedges

1. At inception of the hedge, there must be formal documentation of the hedging relationship and the entity's risk-management objective and strategy. Documentation should also identify the hedging instrument, the hedged transaction, the nature of the risk being hedged, and a plan for assessing the effectiveness of the hedge.

2. Both at inception and on an ongoing basis, the hedging relationship must be assessed to determine if it is highly effective in achieving offsetting cash flows attributable to the hedged item's fair value. The effectiveness of the hedging instrument must be assessed whenever financial statements or earnings are reported and at least every three months.

3. If a hedging instrument is used to modify variable interest rates on a recognized asset or liability to another variable interest rate (such instruments are known as basis swaps), the hedging instrument must be a link between a recognized asset with variable rates and a recognized liability with variable rates. For example, an entity with a variable rate loan receivable (e.g., prime rate + 1%) and a variable rate loan payable (e.g., LIBOR) may use a hedging instrument (e.g., swap prime rate + 1% for LIBOR) to link the two variable rate instruments.

4. The forecasted transaction is specifically identified as a single transaction or a group of individual transactions.

5. The forecasted transaction is with an external party, probably will occur, and presents exposure to variability in cash flows that could affect earnings.

6. The forecasted transaction is not the acquisition of an asset or incurrence of a liability that will subsequently be measured at fair value with changes in fair value being currently recognized in earnings. If the forecasted transaction relates to a recognized asset or liability, such asset or liability is not remeasured with changes in fair value being reported in current earnings.

7. For the forecasted purchase or sale of a nonfinancial item (such as inventory), the risk being hedged against is the change in cash flows due to price/rate changes rather than a change in cash flows due to a different location or a component part.

8. The forecasted purchase or sale of a financial asset or liability (or the interest payments on that asset or liability) or the variable cash flows associated with an existing financial asset or liability can be designated as a hedged item if certain types of risks, such as those related to changes in cash flows, benchmark interest rates, foreign currency exchange rates, and creditworthiness are being hedged. Two or more of the above risks may be hedged simultaneously. Prepayment risk may not be designated as the risk being hedged.

The deferral of a loss on a cash flow hedge as a component of OCI is not appropriate if it is likely to result in a combined basis/cost that exceeds the fair value of the resulting asset or liability. For example, assume a derivative loss associated with a forecasted purchase of equipment will, when combined with the expected cost of the equipment, result in a total cost in excess of the item's fair value. If this is expected, the derivative's loss should be recognized immediately in earnings, to the extent that it exceeds the equipment's fair value.

The change in the value of a derivative instrument that equals the change in the value of the forecasted cash flows is recognized as OCI. If the change in the value of the derivative is less than the change in forecasted cash flows, only the lesser amount is recorded. However, if the change in the value of the derivative exceeds the change in forecasted cash flows, the excess (ineffective portion of the derivative) is recognized in current earnings. For example, if a derivative instrument increases $1,000 in value and the forecasted cash flows decrease in value by $900, a $900 gain will be shown as OCI, and a $100 gain will be recognized in current earnings.

If the change in value of a derivative instrument is less than the change in value of the forecasted transaction, all of the change in value of the derivative instrument is recognized as a component of other comprehensive income. However, the excess change in value of the forecasted transaction is not recognized. To do so would allow partial recognition of a transaction that has not yet occurred. For example, assume a derivative instrument changes $1,000 in value and the forecasted cash flows change in value by $1,200. Only $1,000 of the change in value is recognized as a component of other comprehensive income and the $200 difference is not accounted for.

If all or part of a transaction is still forecasted, there may be some gain or loss on a corresponding derivative that is still being classified as a component of OCI. On an ongoing basis, it is important to make sure that the gain (loss) on a derivative that remains as a component of OCI does not more than offset the cumulative loss (gain) in the value of the remaining forecasted transaction. If excessive amounts are classified as OCI, such excess amounts must be reclassified as a component of current earnings. By way of illustration, consider the following independent cases:

	Case A	Case B	Case C
Amount of gain (loss) on derivative that is still being classified as OCI...............	$ 10,000	$10,000	$(10,000)
Cumulative gain (loss) on remaining forecasted transaction........................	(12,000)	(8,000)	8,000
Extent to which OCI gain (loss) more than offsets the cumulative loss (gain) in the value of the remaining forecasted transaction	Not applicable	2,000	(2,000)
Amount of OCI to be reclassified as a component of current earnings................	Not applicable	2,000	(2,000)

The accounting treatment given a cash flow hedge should continue unless:

♦ The criteria identified above are no longer satisfied,

♦ The derivative instrument expires or is sold, terminated, or exercised,

♦ The entity no longer designates the derivative instrument as a cash flow hedge, or

♦ The hedging relationship is no longer considered highly effective based on management's policies.

If any of the above conditions occur, the cumulative balance remaining in other comprehensive income should be reclassified into earnings in the same period or periods as the forecasted transaction affects earnings. Furthermore, if it is probable that a forecasted transaction will not occur by the end of the original anticipated time or within an additional 2-month period thereafter, the cumulative balance remaining in other comprehensive income should generally be immediately reclassified into earnings.

Examples of cash flow hedges against a forecasted transaction and a variable interest notes payable follow. Entries for the transactions are presented side by side with entries for the hedges for clarity. All transaction costs are ignored. The examples include the use of derivatives in the form of an option and a swap.

An Example of a Cash Flow—Hedge against a Forecasted Transaction Using an Option

Assume that in March, a processor of cereals and other food forecasts a purchase of 300 tons of soybean meal for June delivery. Concerned that prices may increase, the processor purchases three at-the-money, June call options on March 10. On the Chicago Board of Trade, the options are trading at $800 per option with a strike price of $165 per ton. Note that the option was trading at-the-money, which means that the strike price ($165) and current spot price ($165) are equal and that the option has no intrinsic value. The $800 paid for the option reflects time value. Each option is for a 100-ton unit with delivery at a warehouse specified by the CBT and a settlement date of June 25. Effectiveness of the hedge is measured by comparing changes in the option's intrinsic value with changes in the forecasted cash flows based on spot rates for soybean meal. Therefore, the change in time value of the option is excluded from the assessment of hedge effectiveness. In addition to the information given above, the data shown on page 533 are relevant to the hedging strategy.

Given:	March 10	March 31	April 30	May 31	June 25
Spot price per ton	$165	$167	$164	$172	$178
Strike price	$165	$165	$165	$165	$165
Number of tons per option	100	100	100	100	100
Fair value per option (given)	$800	$920	$700	$1,100	$1,300
Calculations per Option:					
Intrinsic value (Spot minus strike × number of tons)[a]	$ 0	$200	$ 0	$ 700	$ 1,300
Time value	800	720	700	400	0
Total (intrinsic + time)	$800	$920	$700	$1,100	$ 1,300
Value of expected cash flows [change in spot rates – gain (loss)]		$(200)[b]	$100[c]	$(700)[d]	$ (1,300)[e]
OCI balance after adjustments Dr (Cr) (lesser of intrinsic value or expected cash flows		(200)	0	(700)	(1,300)
Adjustment to OCI – Dr (Cr) (change in OCI balance)		(200)	200	(700)	(600)
Adjustment to income – Dr (Cr) (change in time value)		80	20	300	400

[a]The intrinsic value is never less than zero because the holder does not have to exercise the option if it is not in-the-money.
[b]($165 – $167) × 100 = $(200)
[c]($165 – $164) × 100 = $100
[d]($165 – $172) × 100 = $(700)
[e]($165 – $178) × 100 = $(1,300)

The following entries relate only to the hedge because no transaction has yet occurred. The recorded amounts are based on the above calculations:

Mar. 10	Investment in Call Option	2,400	
	Cash		2,400
	To record purchase of three options at $800 each.		
31	Investment in Call Option [($920 – $800) × 3]	360	
	Loss on Option ($80 × 3)	240	
	Other Comprehensive Income ($200 × 3)		600
	To record the change in the value of the option. The change in time value is excluded from the assessment of hedge effectiveness.		
Apr. 30	Loss on Option ($20 × 3)	60	
	Other Comprehensive Income [($0 – $200) ×3]	600	
	Investment in Call Option [($700 – $920) × 3]		660
	To record the change in the value of the option (note the absence of intrinsic value).		
May 31	Investment in Call Option [($1,100 – $700) × 3]	1,200	
	Loss on Option ($300 × 3)	900	
	Other Comprehensive Income [($700 – $0) × 3]		2,100
	To record the change in the value of the option.		
June 25	Investment in Call Option [($1,300 – $1,100) × 3]	600	
	Loss on Option ($400 × 3)	1,200	
	Other Comprehensive Income [($1,300 – $700) × 3]		1,800
	To record the change in the value of the option.		
	Cash ($1,300 × 3)	3,900	
	Investment in Call Option		3,900
	To record settlement of option.		
	Inventory—Soybean Meal	53,400	
	Cash		53,400
	To record purchase of 300 tons at the spot rate of $178 per ton.		

When the inventory of soybean meal is recognized as a component of cost of sales and thereby affects earnings, the applicable amount of other comprehensive income will also be recognized in earnings. Entries to reflect this are as follows:

```
Cost of Sales—Soybean Meal....................................  53,400
   Inventory—Soybean Meal.....................................           53,400
      To recognize cost of sales.

Other Comprehensive Income......................................  3,900
   Cost of Sales—Soybean Meal.................................            3,900
      To adjust cost of sales by the gain accumulated in other
      comprehensive income.
```

There are several important points to note about the above entries regarding the cash flow hedge.

◆ Changes in the time value of the option (from $800 to $0 on three options) are recognized currently in earnings, not OCI, as an unrealized loss of $2,400 ($240 + $60 + $900 + $1,200) on the hedge.

◆ At the end of April, the cumulative change in the value of the expected cash flows associated with the forecasted purchase of inventory was a $300 gain ($100 × 3), but the intrinsic value of the derivative hedge was $0. Therefore, the balance in OCI must be the lesser of the absolute value of these two values. At the end of April, the OCI balance is zero even though there is a cumulative loss due to changes in the spot rates.

◆ The cumulative balance in OCI will be reclassified into earnings in the same periods(s) in which the inventory of soybean meal affects earnings (as cost of sales). As shown above, this occurred through the entry that reduced the cost of goods sold by the OCI balance amount.

Note that this example contained no hedge ineffectiveness because of the following:

1. The terms of the derivative option and the forecasted transaction match in terms of commodity, quantities, qualities, location, and timing.
2. The time value of the option was excluded from an assessment of the hedge effectiveness.
3. The call option was in-the-money;, therefore, the changes in intrinsic value could offset the changes in the forecasted cash flows based on spot rates. If an option is out-of-the-money, it has no intrinsic value and cannot offset the changes in the forecasted cash flows.

The hedge was effective against adverse effects of increases in the spot price. By entering into the hedging relationship, the cost of the inventory, and ultimately the resulting cost of sales, was fixed at the strike price of $49,500 (300 tons at the strike price of $165 per ton). This was accomplished by incurring a cost of $2,400, represented by the initial premium on the three options (3 × $800 = $2,400). The effect the cash flow hedge had on the forecasted transaction is summarized as follows:

	Without the Call Option	With the Call Option
Cost of inventory to be included in cost of sales based on spot prices (300 tons @ $178 per ton)	$53,400	$53,400
Gain included in other comprehensive income and reclassified as an adjustment to cost of sales [300 tons × ($165 − $178)]		(3,900)
Adjusted basis of inventory to be included in cost of sales........	$53,400	$49,500
Time value of the option recognized as a loss on hedge equal to the premium (3 options @ $800)		2,400
Net cost to be recognized in income statement...............	$53,400	$51,900

Although this hedge was effective, it is important to note that if the spot rate on June 25 had been less than the strike price, the hedge would not have been effective.

An Example of a Cash Flow—Hedge against a Variable Interest Notes Payable Using an Interest Rate Swap

If an entity has a note receivable or payable that is based on a variable rate of interest, the entity may hedge the variable interest cash flows. Note that a hedge of an asset or liability involving a fixed rate of interest would be a fair value hedge, but if the interest rate is variable, it is a cash flow hedge. The purpose of the cash flow hedge is to offset the risk associated with uncertain variable cash flows by establishing a fixed interest rate.

For example, assume that on January 1, 2015, an entity has loaned $10,000,000 for two years with semiannual interest due based on a variable rate of LIBOR + 1% (100 basis points). On June 30, 2015, concerned that variable interest rates will decline, the entity enters into a swap to receive a fixed rate of 7% in return for payment of a variable LIBOR + 1.25% (125 basis points) rate. The notional amount of the swap is $10,000,000. At each semiannual period, the swap is settled, and the variable rate is reset for the following semiannual interest payment. Relevant values are as follows:

Reset Dates	Receive LIBOR + 1% for Next Period	Pay LIBOR + 1.25% for Next Period	Fair Value of Swap	Change in Fair Value
June 30, 2015	6.75%	7.0%		
Dec. 31, 2015	6.65%	6.9	$ 9,505	$9,505
June 30, 2016	6.35%	6.6	19,361	9,856*

*Note that the loan is for two years and matured on December 31, 2016. Therefore, the swap does not exist after that point in time.

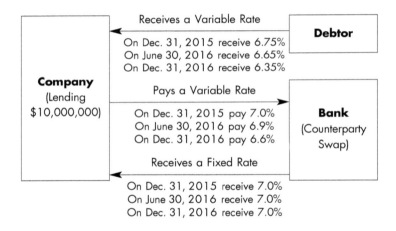

The swap was not a hedge against changing values of the debt, but rather a hedge against the changing cash values of the variable interest payments. The interest rate swap was highly effective in replacing a LIBOR + 1% variable or floating rate of interest on the note receivable with a fixed rate of interest equal to 6.75%. The fixed rate of interest is derived as follows:

Rate received on original debt.	LIBOR + 1.00%
Pay floating rate on swap	− LIBOR + 1.25%
Receive fixed rate on swap	+ 7.00%
Net receive rate [(LIBOR + 1.00%) − (LIBOR + 1.25%) + 7.00%]	= 6.75%

The net receive rate of 6.75% on the $10,000,000 loan, or $337,500 (6.75% × $10,000,000 × ½ year), per six months is the amount of interest income that will be recognized each period. This will be accomplished by recording the interest income at the variable interest rate of LIBOR + 1% and transferring from OCI to income the amount necessary to yield total interest income of $337,500 per period of the hedge. The amount transferred from OCI each period is done when the hedged item impacts earnings and represents the cash received each period as settlement of the swap.

The entries to record the interest rate swap are as follows:

2015

Dec. 31	Cash	337,500	
	Interest Income......................................		337,500
	To record interest income at the variable rate ($10,000,000 × 6.75% × ½ year).		
	Interest Rate Swap Asset	9,505	
	Other Comprehensive Income*......................		9,505
	To record settlement of the swap [$10,000,000 × (7.0% − 7.0%) × ½ year] plus the change in the value of the swap.		

2016

June 30	Cash	332,500	
	Interest Income......................................		332,500
	To record interest income at the variable rate ($10,000,000 × 6.65% × ½ year).		
	Cash	5,000	
	Interest Rate Swap Asset	9,856	
	Other Comprehensive Income.......................		14,856
	To record settlement of the swap [$10,000,000 × (7.0% − 6.9%) × ½ year] plus the change in the value of the swap.		
	Other Comprehensive Income*	5,000	
	Interest Income......................................		5,000
	To reclassify other comprehensive income to earnings (equal to the cash settlement associated with interest currently being recognized in earnings).		

Dec. 31	Cash	317,500	
	Interest Income......................................		317,500
	To record interest income at the variable rate ($10,000,000 × 6.35% × ½ year).		
	Cash	20,000	
	Interest Rate Swap Asset		19,361
	Other Comprehensive Income.......................		639
	To record settlement of the swap [$10,000,000 × (7.0% − 6.6%) × ½ year] plus the change in the value of the swap.		
	Other Comprehensive Income........................	20,000	
	Interest Income......................................		20,000
	To reclassify other comprehensive income to earnings.		

*The two previous entries could be combined into one entry. However, it is important to note that other comprehensive income is reclassified into earnings only in the period in which the forecasted transaction affects earnings (i.e., interest income is recognized).

Given the decreasing pattern of the floating rates, the company experienced an increase in interest income and cash inflows with a swap to pay floating for receive fixed as follows:

Total interest income from receive fixed rate swap (net rate of 6.75% × $10,000,000 × 1.5 years)	$1,012,500
Total interest income at floating rate	987,500
Increase in interest income and cash inflows.	$ 25,000

The $25,000 increase in interest income was initially recorded in OCI and was then reclassified into earnings when interest on the loan receivable affected earnings. In each of the three interest periods accounted for with the above entries, the interest income was $337,500. This represents the fixed rate of interest of 6.75% on $10,000,000 for one-half of a year. In each of the three interest periods, the interest income at the floating rate was increased by reclassifying OCI in order to net interest income of $337,500.

REFLECTION

- Fair value hedges apply to recognized assets and liabilities or firm commitments. The terms, prices, and/or rates for these items are fixed. However, market changes in the prices or rates affect the fair value of the recognized item or commitment.

- Cash flow hedges apply to existing assets or liabilities with variable future cash flows and to forecasted transactions. The prices or rates for these items are not fixed, and, therefore, future cash flows may vary due to changes in prices or rates.

- In a fair value hedge, both the derivative instrument and the hedged item are measured at fair value. Changes in the fair value of the respective items are recognized currently in earnings.

- In a cash flow hedge, the derivative instrument is measured at fair value with changes in value being recognized in other comprehensive income. The amounts in other comprehensive income are recognized in current earnings in the same period(s) as are the earnings impact of the hedged cash flow.

IASB PERSPECTIVES

In late 2013, the IASB issued new hedge accounting principles as an amendment to IFRS 9. These new principles differ from U.S. accounting for hedge transactions as set forth in ASC 815 in a number of ways. Although there are numerous differences, some of the differences are as follows: IFRS allows the risk component of both financial and nonfinancial items as a hedged item. ASC does not allow hedging of nonfinancial items, except in the case of foreign currency cash flow hedges. IFRS allows nonderivative financial instruments to be used as hedging instruments, whereas this is not permitted per ASC 815 except in the case of certain foreign currency hedges.

IASB *standards*

- ◆ IFRS does not require a quantitative assessment of hedging effectiveness, but rather relies more on a qualitative assessment. ASC 815 typically focuses on a quantitative assessment of effectiveness.

- ◆ ASC 815 requires both a prospective and retrospective assessment of hedge effectiveness, whereas IFRS does not require a retroactive assessment.

- ◆ In the case of cash flow hedges, IFRS requires that amounts accumulated in OCI be included in the cost or carrying amount of the hedged nonfinancial item. Per ASC 815, amounts accumulated in OCI are not recorded as basis adjustments, but rather reclassified to earnings when the hedged item affects earnings.

DISCLOSURES REGARDING DERIVATIVE INSTRUMENTS AND HEDGING ACTIVITIES

The FASB requires entities that hold or issue derivative instruments that are designated and qualify as hedging instruments to disclose information that allows users to understand:

1. How and why the reporting entity uses derivative instruments.
2. In the case of both fair value and cash flow hedges, how to account for the derivative instruments and the related hedged items.

9

OBJECTIVE

Identify the various types of information that should be included in disclosures regarding derivative instruments and hedging activities.

3. In the case of both fair value and cash flow hedges, how the derivative instruments and the related hedged items affect the reporting entity's financial position, financial performance, and cash flows.

The above disclosures must be made on an annual basis as well as on an interim reporting basis when a statement of financial position and a statement of financial performance are presented. The complete disclosure requirements are contained in FASB ASC 815-10-50.

Certain other disclosures are required for hedges relating to the foreign currency exposure of a net investment in a foreign operation. These disclosures will be discussed in Chapter 11.

REFLECTION

- The FASB requires general and specific financial statement disclosures by companies holding or issuing derivative instruments.

UNDERSTANDING THE ISSUES

1. Explain how both the intrinsic value and the time value are measured for a forward contract to sell and for a put option.

2. What is the exposure to risk associated with a firm commitment to sell inventory that a fair value hedge is intended to reduce?

3. A regional bakery is forecasting a major purchase of flour and is considering the use of a cash flow hedge. Explain how a cash flow hedge affects operating income currently and in the future as well as how such amounts are calculated.

4. Why might an option be preferred over a futures contract?

5. Using an example, explain how an interest swap works.

EXERCISES

Exercise 1 *(LO 4, 5)* **Impact on earnings of an option and an interest rate swap.** Millikin Corporation decided to hedge two transactions. The first transaction is a forecasted transaction to buy 500 tons of inventory in 60 days. The company was concerned that selling prices might increase, and it acquired a 60-day option to buy inventory at a price of $1,200 per ton. Upon acquiring the option, the company paid a premium of $10 per ton when the spot price was $1,201. At the end of 30 days, the option had a value of $19 per ton and a current spot price of $1,214 per ton. Upon expiration of the option, the spot price was $1,216 per ton.

In another transaction, the company borrowed $3,000,000 at a fixed rate of 8%; after three months, the company became concerned that variable rates would be lower than 8%. In response, the company entered into an interest rate swap whereby it paid variable rates to a counterparty in exchange for a fixed rate of 8%. The reset rate for the first 30 days of the swap was 8.1% and was 7.8% for the second 30 days of the swap. The fair value of the swap was $3,000 after the first 30 days and $3,300 after 60 days.

Determine the impact on earnings of the above hedges for the first and second 30-day period.

Exercise 2 *(LO 3)* **Fair value hedges using futures.** A large corporate farming operation is holding an inventory of corn and wheat and is concerned that excess harvests this season will lower the value of the commodities. In order to hedge against adverse market changes, the corporation acquired the following contracts on June 1:

◆ 30 contracts to sell 5,000 bushels of corn in December at a future price of $3.56 per bushel.

◆ 30 contracts to sell 5,000 bushels of wheat in December at a future price of $6.35 per bushel.

Spot and future prices are as follows:

| | Corn—Dollars per Bushel | | Wheat—Dollars per Bushel | |
	Spot Price	Future Price	Spot Price	Future Price
June 1	$3.42	$3.56	$6.20	$6.35
June 30	3.41	3.53	6.19	6.33
July 31	3.43	3.54	6.175	6.32

For each of the fair value hedges, determine, by month, the change in the value of the respective inventories and the gain or loss on the futures contracts.

Exercise 3 *(LO 3, 7)* **Fair value hedge—an interest rate swap's effect on interest and the carrying value of a note.** On July 1, 2016, Hargrove Corporation issued a 2-year note with a face value of $4,000,000 and a fixed interest rate of 9%, payable on a semiannual basis. On January 15, 2017, the company entered into an interest rate swap with a financial institution in anticipation of lower variable rates. At the initial date of the swap, the company paid a premium of $9,200. The swap had a notional amount of $4,000,000 and called for the payment of a variable rate of interest in exchange for a 9% fixed rate. The variable rates are reset semiannually beginning with January 1, 2017, in order to determine the next interest payment. Differences between rates on the swap will be settled on a semiannual basis. Variable interest rates and the value of the swap on selected dates are as follows:

Reset Date	Variable Interest Rate	Value of the Swap
January 1, 2017	8.75%	
June 30, 2017.	8.50	$14,000
December 31, 2017	8.85	3,500

For each of the above dates June 30 and December 31, determine:

1. The net interest expense.
2. The carrying value of the note payable.
3. The net unrealized gain or loss on the swap.

Exercise 4 *(LO 6, 7)* **Evaluating a hedge of a firm commitment with a put option.** A major cattle feeding operation has entered into a firm commitment to buy 100,000 bushels of corn to be delivered to its feed lot in Kansas. The corn is expected to be delivered in 90 days. The company is committed to pay $1.50 per bushel. If corn yields are greater than expected, the price of corn could decline and the company would experience higher operating costs than necessary as a result of the commitment.

In order to protect itself against falling corn prices, the company purchased an option to sell corn in 90 days at a strike price of $1.51 per bushel delivered to a facility in Nebraska.

1. Assuming that the company designated the swap as a fair value hedge, identify several critical criteria that would need to be satisfied in order to justify this classification.
2. Identify several factors that would suggest that the company's hedge would qualify as being highly effective in reducing the risk associated with the firm's commitment to buy 100,000 bushels of corn.
3. Explain why an option to sell corn rather than corn futures may provide the company with more flexibility.

4. Assume that at the time of acquiring the put option, the price of corn was more than $1.51. Explain why the option had a value of more than zero at inception.

5. Assume that one of your colleagues made the following comment: "An option can never have a negative value; therefore, you can never lose money on an option." Discuss whether or not you agree with your colleague.

6. Assuming that only the intrinsic value is used to assess effectiveness, explain how the option's time value affects earnings prior to the end of the commitment.

Exercise 5 *(LO 4, 8)* **Evaluating the impact of hedging a forecasted transaction with an option.** Casper Enterprises is forecasting two significant transactions and is concerned that adverse price movements could negatively impact these transactions. In order to hedge against adverse movements, Casper has acquired two options as described below.

The first forecasted transaction involves the purchase of a commodity with the concern being that commodity prices could increase prior to the transaction actually taking place. As a defensive move, Casper acquired Option A. The option is a call option involving 200 tons of a commodity with a strike price of $1,500 per ton with delivery of the commodity in 90 days.

The other forecasted transaction involves the sale of 100,000 bushels of a harvested commodity with the concern that the price of the commodity may decrease prior to the transaction actually taking place. As a defensive move, Casper acquired Option B. The option is a put option involving 100,000 bushels of the commodity with a strike price of $2.50 per bushel and delivery in 90 days.

Effectiveness of the hedge is measured by comparing the changes in the intrinsic value of the option with changes in the forecasted cash flows based on spot rates. The time value is to be expensed over the life of the option. Information concerning the options is as follows:

	At Inception of Option	30 Days Later	60 Days Later
Option A:			
Spot price per ton	$1,490	$1,498	$1,510
Strike price per ton	$1,500	$1,500	$1,500
Number of tons per option	200	200	200
Fair value of option	$900	$700	$2,500
Option B:			
Spot price per bushel	$2.52	$2.48	$2.45
Strike price per bushel	$2.50	$2.50	$2.50
Number of bushels per option	100,000	100,000	100,000
Fair value of option	$1,200	$3,300	$5,200

For each option, determine the following balances at both 30 days and 60 days after inception of the option: Investment in Option, Other Comprehensive Income, and Gain or Loss on Option (the change in time value).

Exercise 6 *(LO 4, 8)* **Entries to record a hedge of a forecasted purchase with an option.** A Midwest food processor forecasts purchasing 300,000 pounds of soybean oil in May. On February 20, the company acquires an option to buy 300,000 pounds of soybean oil in May at a strike price of $1.60 per pound. Information regarding spot prices and option values at selected dates is as follows:

	February 20	February 28	March 31	April 20
Spot price per pound	$ 1.61	$ 1.59	$ 1.62	$ 1.64
Fair value of option	3,800	1,200	6,800	12,500

The company settled the option on April 20 and purchased 300,000 pounds of soybean oil on May 3 at a spot price of $1.63 per pound. During May, the soybean oil was used to produce food. One-half of the resulting food was sold in June. The change in the option's time value is excluded from the assessment of hedge effectiveness.

1. Prepare all necessary journal entries through June to reflect the above activity.
2. What would the effect on earnings have been had the forecasted purchase not been hedged? Assume that half of the food was sold for $300,000.

Exercise 7 *(LO 5, 7)* **Interest rate swap with variable for fixed.** At the beginning of the current year, Skeeba Manufacturing borrowed $10 million to be repaid over the next five calendar quarters with quarterly payments of $2,090,893.23 based on a fixed annual interest rate of 6.0%. Concerned that variable interest rates would be lower than the 6.0% fixed interest rate, on March 31 Skeeba secured an interest rate swap whereby it would receive a 6.0% fixed rate of interest in exchange for the payment of a variable rate. The notional amount of the swap is $10 million, and the maturity date of the swap matches the maturity date of the original borrowing.

Reset dates are March 31, June 30, September 30, and December 31, with variable rates for the next quarter of 5.8%, 5.5%, 5.6%, and 5.4%, respectively. Assumed fair values of the swap are $14,954, $6,037, and $3,049, as of June 30, September 30, and December 31, respectively.

Determine the basis of the 6% note payable on June 30, September 30, and December 31 along with the interest expense for each of those calendar quarters.

PROBLEMS

Problem M-1 *(LO 4, 7)* **Entries to record a commitment and the impact on earnings.** On March 17, Kennedy Baking, Inc., committed to buy 1,000 tons of commodity A for delivery in May at a cost of $118 per ton. Concerned that the price of commodity A might decrease, on March 29 the company purchased a May put option for 1,000 tons of commodity A at a strike price of $119 per ton. The change in the time value of the option is excluded from the assessment of hedge effectiveness, and the option was settled on May 18. After processing all 1,000 tons of commodity A at a cost of $25 per ton, one-half of the resulting inventory was sold for $180 per ton on June 16. Relevant values are as follows:

	March 29	March 31	April 30	May 18
Number of tons per option...............	1,000	1,000	1,000	1,000
Spot price per ton	$118	$118	$116	$115
Strike price per ton.....................	$119	$119	$119	$119
Value of option	$2,400	$2,200	$3,300	$4,000

1. Prepare all applicable entries for the months of March through June regarding the inventory and the hedging instrument assuming qualification as a fair value hedge. Record the changes in the intrinsic value and time value of the option with separate entries.
2. For the entire 1,000 tons of processed commodity A, prepare a schedule regarding the cost of the processed commodity available for sale in terms of the desired cost, the cost without the hedge, and the cost with the hedge.

Problem M-2 *(LO 3, 8)* **Cash flow hedge of a forecasted purchase of wheat.** Custom Brand Bakeries, Inc. (CBBI), located in Erie, Pennsylvania, bakes a variety of products for various parties on a contract basis. For example, a food company may contract with CBBI to make energy bars that are then sold under the food company's private label. Contracts are typically signed several months in advance of actual production and set forth a fixed sales price. Because sales prices are fixed by contact, CBBI is concerned that materials costs do not increase and further reduce profits. However, CBBI does not want to guard against increasing costs by purchasing materials in advance of their scheduled production. Corn and wheat flour are two major ingredients used in the production process where increasing costs are of concern. CBBI wants to hedge against these costs increasing but cannot buy flour futures. However, buying corn and wheat futures can provide an effective hedge against changing flour prices. Changes in the price of corn flour and wheat flour often correlate highly with changes in the price of corn and wheat.

On September 1, 2015, the company purchased, on the Chicago Board of Trade, futures for delivery of the commodities in November. The CBT required a deposit of $70,000 toward a margin account.

	Corn Futures		
Date	Spot Price per Bushel	Futures Price per Bushel	Notional Amount
September 1	$2.5000	$2.5100	1,000,000 bushels
September 30	2.5380	2.5420	1,000,000
October 31	2.5680	2.5700	1,000,000
November 5	2.5685	2.5710	1,000,000

	Wheat Futures		
Date	Spot Price per Bushel	Futures Price per Bushel	Notional Amount
September 1	$3.5150	$3.5210	2,000,000 bushels
September 30	3.5480	3.5520	2,000,000
October 31	3.5700	3.5710	2,000,000
November 5	3.5700	3.5705	2,000,000

CBBI properly documents the hedging relationship, and all criteria for special accounting as a hedge are satisfied. The hedging instruments are determined to be highly effective as a hedge against changing flour prices. The changes in the time value of the futures contracts are to be excluded from the assessment of hedge effectiveness.

In early November, CBBI actually purchased both corn flour and wheat flour used in products sold to contracting parties on November 21. The futures contracts are settled net on November 5.

Required ▶ ▶ ▶ ▶ ▶

1. Prepare all monthly entries to record hedging activity.
2. Identify and discuss several factors that might cause the futures contracts to not be perfectly effective as a hedge against changes in the price of flour used by CBBI.

Problem M-3 *(LO 3, 4, 7, 8)* **Impact on earnings of various hedged relationships.** The chief financial officer (CFO) of Baxter International has employed the use of hedges in a variety of contexts over the first quarter of the current calendar year as follows:

Futures Contract—The company hedged against a possible decline in the value of inventory represented by commodity A. At the beginning of February, an April futures contract to sell 10,000 units of commodity A for $3.50 per unit was acquired. It is assumed that the terms of the futures contract and the hedged assets match with respect to delivery location, quantity, and quality. The fair value of the futures contract will be measured by changes in the futures prices over time, and the time value component of the futures contract will be excluded from the assessment of hedge effectiveness. Relevant values are as follows:

	February 28	March 31
Number of units per contract	10,000	10,000
Spot price per unit	$3.45	$3.40
Futures price per unit	$3.50	$3.44

Forward Contract—On January 15, the company committed to sell 5,000 units of inventory for $90 per unit on March 15. Concerned that selling prices might increase over time, the company entered into a March 15 forward contract to buy 5,000 units of identical inventory at a forward rate of $92 per unit. Changes in the value of the commitment are measured based on the changes in the forward rates over time discounted at 6%. On March 15, the inventory, with a cost of $360,000, was sold, and the forward contract was settled. Relevant values are as shown on page 543.

	January 15	January 31	February 28	March 15
Number of units per contract	5,000	5,000	5,000	5,000
Spot price per unit	$90.00	$90.20	$90.50	$90.60
Forward rate per unit	$92.00	$91.50	$91.20	$90.60

Option—In January, the company forecasted the purchase of 100,000 units of commodity B with delivery in February. Upon receipt, the commodity was processed further and sold for $12 per unit on March 17. On January 15, the company purchased a February 20 call option for 100,000 units of commodity B at a strike price of $8 per unit. Changes in the time value of the option are excluded from the assessment of hedge effectiveness. Relevant values are as follows:

	January 15	January 31	February 20	March 17
Number of units per option	100,000	100,000	100,000	
Spot price per unit	$8.05	$8.02	$7.95	
Strike price per unit	$8.00	$8.00	$8.00	
Fair value of option	$6,000	$2,400	$—	
Processing costs per unit				$1.10

For each of the above hedged events and the related hedging instruments, prepare a schedule to ◀ ◀ ◀ ◀ ◀ **Required**
reflect the effect on earnings for each of the months of January through March of the current year. Clearly identify each component account impacting earnings.

Problem M-4 *(LO 5)* **Hedging both fixed and floating interest rates.** Pasu International purchased a plant in Louisiana on December 31, 2015, and financed $20,000,000 of the purchase price with a 5-year note. The note bears interest at the fixed rate of 5%, and payments on the note are made quarterly in the amount of $1,136,408. The note has a balance of $12,590,619 as of December 31, 2017. At the beginning of 2018, Pasu became concerned that variable or floating interest rates would be less than its fixed rate on the above note. Given this concern, Pasu arranged an interest rate swap on a notional amount equal to the outstanding balance of the note at the beginning of each quarter beginning with the January 1, 2018, balance of the note. The swap calls for the payment of a variable or floating interest rate on the principal balance of the note to a counterparty in exchange for a fixed rate of 4.75%. The floating rate is LIBOR plus 1.5% and is reset at the beginning of each quarter for that quarter's calculations.

In an unrelated transaction, on June 30, 2018, Pasu sold its plant in Europe and as part of the transaction received an 18-month $10,000,000 note receivable from the buyer. The note bears interest at a rate of LIBOR plus 2.0%, and interest-only payments are made each quarter during 2018. The floating rate is reset at the beginning of each quarter. Concerned that declining floating interest rates will decrease the value of the note, Pasu has arranged an interest rate swap with a counterparty effective July 1, 2018. The swap calls for the payment by Pasu of floating rate of LIBOR plus 1.7% in exchange for a fixed rate of 4.5%.

LIBOR rates at the beginning of each calendar quarter of 2018 are as follows:

January 1	3.25%
April 1	3.15
July 1	2.90
October 1	2.65

All interest rates are stated as annual interest rates. As of December 31, 2018, calculate each of ◀ ◀ ◀ ◀ ◀ **Required**
the following:

1. Annual fixed interest paid on the note resulting from the purchase of the Louisiana plant.
2. Annual floating interest paid to the counterparty on the note resulting from the sale of the European plant.
3. Annual net interest expense on the note resulting from the purchase of the Louisiana plant.
4. Annual net interest income on the note receivable.

5. Assuming that the LIBOR rate at October 1, 2018, will continue into the future, determine the December 31, 2018, value of the interest rate swap associated with the note receivable. (*Hint*: Compare the year-end present value of paying a floating rate on the notional amount with the year-end present value of receiving a fixed rate on the notional amount.)

6. If the note receivable had been denominated in euros versus U.S. dollars, determine to what additional risks Pasu would have been exposed.

Problem M-5 *(LO 8)* **Prepare entries to account for a cash flow hedge involving an option.** Industrial Plating Corporation coats manufactured parts with a variety of coatings such as Teflon, gold, and silver. The company intends to purchase 100,000 troy ounces of silver in September. The purchase is highly probable, and the company has become concerned that the prices of silver may increase, and, therefore, the forecasted purchase will become even more expensive. In order to reduce the exposure to rising silver prices, on July 10 the company purchased 20 September call (buy) options on silver. Each option is for 5,000 troy ounces and has a strike price of $5.00 per troy ounce. The company excludes from hedge effectiveness changes in the time value of the option. Spot prices and option value per troy ounce of silver are as follows:

	July 10	July 31	August 31	September 10
Spot price	$5.10	$5.14	$5.35	$5.32
Option value	0.20	0.23	0.37	0.33

On September 10, the company settled the option and on September 15 purchased 100,000 troy ounces of silver on account at $5.33 per ounce. The silver was used in the company's production process over the next three months. In September and October, plating services were provided as follows:

	September	October
Units of silver used	15,000	50,000
Other costs.	$105,000	$350,000
Plating revenues	$225,000	$750,000

Required ▶ ▶ ▶ ▶ ▶ Prepare all necessary entries to account for the above activities through October. Assume that the hedge satisfies all necessary criteria for special hedge accounting.

Problem M-6 *(LO 4)* **Prepare a schedule to determine the earnings effect of various hedging relationships.** During the third quarter of the current year, Beamer Manufacturing Company invested in derivative instruments for a variety of reasons. The various investments and hedging relationships are as follows:

a. Call Option A—This option was purchased on July 10 and provided for the purchase of 10,000 units of commodity A in October at a strike price of $45 per unit. The company designated the option as a hedge of a commitment to sell 10,000 units of commodity A in October at a fixed price of $45 per unit. Information regarding the option and commodity A is as follows:

	July 10	July 31	August 31	September 30
Spot price	$ 45	$ 46	$ 44	$ 46.50
Value of option	2,000	12,400	1,000	16,000

b. Call Option B—This option provided for the purchase of 10,000 units of commodity B in October at a strike price of $30 per unit. The company designated the option as a hedge of a forecasted purchase of commodity B in October. Information regarding the option and commodity B is as follows:

	July 1	July 31	August 31	September 30
Spot price	$ 29	$29.50	$ 29	$28.75
Value of option	1,100	900	600	200

c. Put Option C—This option provided for the sale of 10,000 units of commodity C in September at a strike price of $30 per unit. The company designated the option as a hedge of a forecasted sale of 10,000 units of commodity C on September 10. Information regarding the option and commodity C is as follows:

	July 1	July 31	August 31	September 10
Spot price	$ 30	$29.50	$ 29	$ 28.75
Value of option	500	5,600	10,200	12,600

The company settled the option on September 10 and sold 10,000 units of commodity C at the spot price. The manufacturing cost of the units sold was $20 per unit.

d. Futures Contract D—The contract calls for the sale of 10,000 units of commodity D in October at a future price of $10 per unit. The company designated the contract as a hedge on a forecasted sale of commodity D in October. Information regarding the contract and commodity D is as follows:

	July 1	July 31	August 31	September 10
Spot price	$9.95	$9.92	$9.89	$9.85
Futures price	9.94	9.90	9.87	9.84

e. Interest Rate Swap—The company has a 12-month note receivable with a face value of $10,000,000 that matures on June 30 of next year. The note calls for interest to be paid at the end of each month based on the LIBOR variable interest rate at the beginning of each month. On July 31, the company entered into an agreement to receive a 7% fixed rate of interest beginning in August in exchange for payment of a variable rate based on LIBOR. The reset date is at the beginning of each month, and net settlement occurs at the end of each month. LIBOR rates and swap values are as follows:

	July	August	September
LIBOR for month	6.8%	6.8%	6.7%
Swap value at end of month	$17,729	$24,249	$21,884

In all of the above cases, the change in the time value of the derivative instrument is excluded from the assessment of hedge effectiveness. Furthermore, the company assesses hedge effectiveness on a continuing basis. Such an assessment at the end of June concluded that call option B was not effective.

Prepare a schedule to reflect the effect on current earnings of the above hedging relationships. ◀ ◀ ◀ ◀ ◀ **Required** The schedule should show relevant amounts for each month from July through September.

Problem M-7 *(LO 4)* **Prepare entries to record a variable for fixed interest rate swap.** Hauser Corporation has $20,000,000 of outstanding debt that bears interest at a variable rate and matures on June 30, 2018. At inception of the debt, the company had a lower credit rating, and most available financing carried a variable rate. The company's variable rate is the LIBOR rate plus 1%. However, the company's credit rating has improved, and the company feels that a fixed, lower rate of interest would be most appropriate. Furthermore, the company is of the opinion that variable rates will increase over the next 24 months. In May 2016, the company negotiated with First Bank of Boston an interest rate swap that would allow the company to pay a fixed rate of 7% in exchange for receiving interest based on the LIBOR rate. The terms of the swap call for settlement at the end of June and December, which coincides with the company's interest payment dates. The variable rates are reset at the end of each 6-month period for the following 6-month period. The terms of the swap are effective for the 6-month period beginning July 2016.

The hedging relationship has been properly documented, and management has concluded that the hedge will be highly effective in offsetting changes in the cash flows due to changes in interest rates. The criteria for special accounting have been satisfied.

Relevant LIBOR rates and swap values are as follows:

	June 30, 2016	Dec. 31, 2016	June 30, 2017	Dec. 31, 2017
LIBOR rate	7.0%	7.1%	6.9%	6.8%
Swap value		$27,990	$(19,011)	$(19,342)

Required ▶ ▶ ▶ ▶ ▶

1. Prepare the necessary entries to record the activities related to the debt and the hedge from July 1, 2016, through June 30, 2018.
2. Prepare a schedule to evaluate the positive or negative impact the hedge had on each 6-month period of earnings.
3. What would the LIBOR rate on December 31, 2017, have had to be in order for the interest expense to be the same whether or not there was a cash flow hedge?

Chapter 10

Foreign Currency Transactions

Learning Objectives

When you have completed this chapter, you should be able to

1. Explain the floating international monetary system, and identify factors that influence rates of exchange between currencies.

2. Define the various terms associated with exchange rates, including spot rates, forward rates, premiums, and discounts.

3. Account for a foreign currency transaction, including the measurement of exchange gain or loss.

4. Identify the contexts in which a company may be exposed to foreign currency exchange risk.

5. Understand the characteristics of derivatives and the common types used to hedge foreign currency exchange rate risk.

6. Explain the accounting treatment given various types of foreign currency hedges.

As discussed in Chapter 9, companies in the United States are engaged in significant export and import activity. Such transactions must be denominated or settled in a currency agreed upon by the transacting parties. Each party would often like to use its own national currency. Since it is impossible to use more than one currency as the medium of exchange, a currency must be selected, and rates of exchange must be established between the two competing currencies. For example, if a U.S. footwear manufacturer purchases leather from a German supplier, the transaction would usually be settled in either U.S. dollars or euros. If euros are chosen, a rate of exchange between the U.S. dollar and the euro must be determined in order to record the transaction on the American company's books in dollars. Given that rates of exchange vary, the number of U.S. dollars needed to acquire the necessary euros also could change between the time the goods are received and when payment is made for the goods. If, during this time, more dollars are needed to acquire the necessary euros to pay for the leather, the U.S. purchaser is exposed to an additional business risk. The more volatility there is in exchange rates, the more risk to which the party is exposed. Similarly, if the dollar is used as the medium of exchange, this risk would still exist, but it would be transferred to the German vendor.

It is readily apparent that the currency decision becomes an important factor in negotiating such transactions. Due to the volatility of currency exchange rates, companies transacting business in foreign markets should aggressively control and measure exchange risk. Management should develop a model that enables them to forecast the direction, magnitude, and timing of exchange rate changes. This model, in turn, can be used to develop a strategy to minimize foreign exchange losses and maximize foreign exchange gains.

Business transactions that are settled in a currency other than that of the domestic (home country) currency are referred to, in this text, as *foreign currency transactions*. One of the transacting parties will settle the transaction in its own domestic currency and also measure the transaction in its domestic currency. For example, a German company may sell inventory to a U.S. company and require payment in euros. The currency used to settle the transaction is referred to as the *denominated currency* and would be the euro in this case. The other transacting party will settle the transaction in a foreign currency but will need to measure the transaction in its domestic currency. For example, a U.S. company that purchases inventory from a German company must settle the resulting accounts payable in euros and yet must measure the purchase of inventory and the accounts payable in terms of U.S. dollars. The currency used to measure or record the transaction is referred to as the *measurement currency* and would be the U.S. dollar in this case. Whenever a transaction is denominated in a currency different from the measurement currency, exchange rate risk exists, and exchange rates must be used for measurement purposes. The process of expressing a transaction in the measurement currency when it is denominated in a different currency is referred to as a *foreign currency translation*.

<table>
<tr><td>

1

O B J E C T I V E

Explain the floating international monetary system, and identify factors that influence rates of exchange between currencies.

</td></tr>
</table>

THE INTERNATIONAL MONETARY SYSTEM

Denominating a transaction in a currency other than the entity's domestic currency requires the establishment of a rate of exchange between the currencies. The international monetary system establishes rates of exchanges between currencies through the use of a variety of systems. The selection of a particular monetary system and the resulting exchange rates have a significant effect on international business and the risk associated with such business.

Alternative International Monetary Systems

Several major international monetary systems have been employed over time, and previous systems have occasionally been reestablished. Prior to 1944, the *gold system* provided a strict apolitical system based on gold. The currencies of nations were backed by or equivalent to some physical measure of gold. To illustrate, suppose Nation A has 1 million currency units backed by 1,000 ounces of gold and Nation B has 2 million currency units also backed by 1,000 ounces of gold. With gold as the common denominator, exchange rates between currencies could be established. In the above example, one unit of Nation A's currency could be exchanged for two units of Nation B's currency. A nation's supply of gold, therefore, influenced its money supply, rates of exchange, prices, and international trading levels (imports and exports).

In 1944, the *Bretton Woods Agreement*, which created the International Monetary Fund (IMF) and a *fixed rate exchange system*, was signed. The fixed rate system required each nation to set a par value for its currency in terms of gold or the U.S. dollar. In turn, the U.S. dollar's value was defined in terms of gold. Modest variations from a currency's par value were allowed, and each nation could adjust its money supply in order to maintain its par value. The IMF could provide support to a nation in order to maintain its par value. Changes in a currency's par value were referred to as *devaluations* and *revaluations*.

As pressures to maintain the par values established by the fixed rate system increased, pressure was placed on the U.S. dollar. The ability of the dollar to support the system became questionable, and fears arose that countries with dollar surpluses might seek to convert these dollars into gold. In 1971, the U.S. government, for all practical purposes, terminated the Bretton Woods Agreement by suspending the convertibility of the dollar into gold.

Currencies temporarily became part of a *floating system* where rates of exchange were in response to the supply and demand factors affecting a currency. Shortly thereafter, the IMF accepted the *Smithsonian Agreement* which devaluated the U.S. dollar and did not allow for the convertibility of the dollar into gold. Par values of currencies were established along with a wider margin of acceptable values around the par value. The Smithsonian Agreement was short-lived, and in response to increasing pressures on the U.S. dollar, the fixed rate system was abandoned in 1973.

Today, the international monetary system is a floating system whereby the factors of supply and demand primarily define currency exchange rates. Each nation's central bank may intervene in order to move its currency toward a target rate of exchange. This intervention results in a managed, or "dirty" float, versus an unmanaged, or "clean" float. Supply and demand factors along with possible central bank intervention result in much more uncertainty and risk than that experienced in a fixed rate system. A number of factors beyond supply and demand affect exchange rates including but not limited to a nation's trade balances, money supply, economic stability, interest rates, and governmental intervention.

Although the present international monetary system is best described as a floating system, there are a number of special variations within the system. Some nations still maintain a fixed system whereby the rate of exchange is established by their central bank. However, because these fixed rates are changed frequently, sometimes daily, they may be viewed as a controlled or "dirty" float. A currency that is frequently adjusted downward, such as those in less-developed nations, is referred to as a "crawling peg" currency. Tiered systems also exist whereby special rates are established for certain types of transactions, such as import and export sales and dividend payments, to accomplish desired political and economic objectives. For example, to encourage exports and to discourage capital withdrawal, a foreign government may establish favorable official rates for export sales and less favorable exchange rates for the payment of dividends to investors in other countries. The forces of supply and demand, however, occasionally make it difficult for a government to maintain an official exchange rate. In response, the government either devalues or revalues its currency.

The Mechanics of Exchange Rates

An exchange rate is a measure of how much of one currency may be exchanged for another currency. These rates may be in the form of either *direct* or *indirect quotes* made by a foreign currency trader who is usually employed by a large commercial bank. A direct quote measures how much of the domestic currency must be exchanged to receive one unit of the foreign currency (1 FC). Direct quotes allow the party using the quote to understand the price of the foreign currency in terms of its own "base" or domestic currency. This method is frequently used in the United States, and direct quotes are published daily in financial papers such as *The Wall Street Journal* or on Web sites such as http://www.x-rates.com/. Indirect quotes, also known as European terms, measure how many units of foreign currency will be received for one unit of the domestic currency. Thus, if the direct quote for a foreign currency (FC) is $0.25, then 1 FC would cost $0.25. The indirect quote would be the reciprocal of the direct quote, or 4 FC per dollar ($1.00 divided by $0.25).

	Exchange Rate Quotes	
Direct Quote	Indirect Quote
1 FC = $0.25	$1 = 4 FC

The business news often reports that a currency has strengthened (gained) or weakened (lost) relative to another currency. Assuming a direct quote system, such changes measure the difference between the new rate and the old rate, as a percentage of the old rate. For example, if the dollar strengthened or gained 20% against a foreign currency from its previous rate of $0.25, the dollar would now command more FC (i.e., the FC would be cheaper to buy). To be exact, the new exchange rate would be $0.20 [$0.25 − (20% × 0.25)]. Therefore, *the strengthening currency would be evidenced by a reduction in the directly quoted amount and an increase in the indirectly quoted amount.* The opposite would be true for a weakening of the domestic currency. Reaction to the strengthening or weakening of a currency depends on what type of transaction is contemplated. For example, an American exporter would want a weaker dollar because the foreign importer would need fewer of its currency units to acquire a dollar's worth of U.S. goods. Thus, U.S. goods would cost less in terms of the foreign currency. If the dollar strengthened so that one could acquire more foreign currency units for a dollar, importers would benefit. Therefore, U.S. companies and citizens would have to spend fewer U.S. dollars to buy the imported goods.

2

OBJECTIVE

Define the various terms associated with exchange rates, including spot rates, forward rates, premiums, and discounts.

Changes Relative to Another Currency

A Strengthening U.S Currency		A Weakening U.S. Currency	
Before:	1 FC = $0.25	Before:	1 FC = $0.25
After:	1 FC = $0.20	After:	1 FC = $0.30
Result:	The dollar gained 20%.	Result:	The dollar lost 20%.
	($0.25 − $0.20 = $0.05;		($0.25 − $0.30 = −$0.05;
	$0.05 ÷ $0.25 = 20%)		−$0.05 ÷ $0.25 = −20%)

Exchange rates often are quoted in terms of a buying rate (the bid price) and a selling rate (the offered price). The buying and selling rates represent what the currency broker (normally a large commercial bank) is willing to pay to acquire or sell a currency. The difference or spread between these two rates represents the broker's commission and is often referred to as the points. The spread is influenced by several factors, including the supply of and demand for the currency, the number of transactions taking place, currency risk, and the overall volatility of the market. For example, assume a currency broker agrees to pay $0.20 to a holder of a foreign currency and agrees to sell that currency to a buyer of foreign currency for $0.22. In this case, the broker will receive a commission of $0.02 ($0.22 − $0.20). In the United States, rates generally are quoted between the U.S. dollar and a foreign currency. However, rates between two foreign currencies are also quoted and are referred to as cross rates.

Exchange rates fall into two primary groups. A *spot rate* is the current rate of exchange between two currencies. In addition to current exchange rates governing the immediate delivery of currency, *forward rates* apply to the exchange of different currencies at a future point in time. An agreement to exchange currencies at a specified price with delivery at a specified future point in time is a *forward contract*. Although not all currencies are quoted in forward rates, virtually all major trading nations have forward rates.

Although future exchange dates typically are quoted in 30-day intervals, contracts can be written to cover any number of days. To illustrate a forward contract, assume the forward rate to buy one FC to be delivered in 90 days is $1.650. This means that, after the specified time from the inception of the contract date (90 days), one FC will be exchanged for $1.650, regardless of what the spot rate is at that time.

Inception of Contract	⟵ 90 Days ⟶	Settlement of Contract
Forward Rate		Exchange Rate
1 FC = $1.650		1 FC = $1.650 (Regardless of what the spot rate is on that day.)
Spot Rate		Spot Rate
1 FC = $1.640		1 FC = $1.655

Several aspects of spot rates and forward rates are noteworthy. First, typically, both rates are constantly changing. Spot rates are revised daily; as they change, forward rates for the *remaining time* covered by a given forward contract also change even though the forward rate at inception is fixed. At the expiration date of the contract, the forward date is the current date and, therefore, the forward rate at that time is the current spot rate. Thus, the value of a forward contract changes over the forward period. For instance, in the above example, if the forward rate is 1 FC = $1.652 with 30 days remaining, the right to *buy* FC at the original fixed forward rate of 1 FC = $1.650 suggests that the value of the forward contract has increased. Rather than paying a forward rate of $1.652 to acquire FC in 30 days, the holder of the original forward contract must only pay the fixed rate of $1.650. Second, the ultimate value of the forward contract must be assessed by comparing the original fixed forward rate against the spot rate at the settlement date. In the above example, at the settlement date, the holder of the contract will pay the fixed rate of 1 FC = $1.650 to buy an FC rather than the spot rate of 1 FC = $1.655. The total change in value is represented by the difference between the original fixed forward rate and the spot rate at settlement date ($1.650 vs. $1.655). Finally, the difference between the original forward rate and the spot rate at inception of the contract ($1.650 vs. $1.640) represents a premium or discount which is traceable to a number of factors. This difference between the spot and original fixed forward rate represents the time value of the forward contract.

If the original fixed forward rate is greater than the spot rate at inception of the contract, the contract is said to be at a *premium* (as in the above example). The opposite situation results in a discount. Quoting premiums or discounts (known as forward differentials) relative to the spot rate, rather than forward rates, is common industry practice.

Forward Rates
Employ a Forward Exchange Contract

At a Premium	At a Discount
Forward Rate > Spot Rate (At inception of contract)	Forward Rate < Spot Rate (At inception of contract)

At inception, the difference between the forward and spot rates represents a contract expense or contract income to the purchaser of the forward contract. A number of factors influence forward rates and, thus, account for the difference between a forward rate and a spot rate. A primary factor is the interest rate differential between holding an investment in foreign currency and holding an investment in domestic currency over a period of time. It is for this reason that the difference between a forward rate is referred to as the *time value* of the forward contract. For example, if a broker sold a contract to deliver foreign currency in 30 days, the interest differential would be the difference between:

1. The interest earned on investing foreign currency for the 30 days prior to delivery date and
2. The 30 days of interest lost on the domestic currency that was not invested but was used to acquire the foreign currency needed for delivery.

Assume that the spot rate is 1 FC = $0.60 and that you want to determine a 6-month forward rate for 1,000 FC. Further, assume that the dollar could be invested at 4.5% and the FC could be invested at 7.25%. The forward rate would be calculated as follows:

	U.S. Dollars	Foreign Currency (FC)
Value today	$600.00	1,000 FC
Interest rate	4.5%	7.25%
Six months of interest	$ 13.50	36.25 FC
Value in six months	$613.50	1,036.25 FC

6-month forward rate = $613.50 ÷ 1,036.25 FC = 1 FC = $0.592

The forward rate for a currency can also be derived by the following formula:

$$\text{Forward Rate} = \text{Direct Spot Rate at the Beginning of Period } t \times \frac{1 + \text{Interest Rate for Domestic Investment During Period } t}{1 + \text{Interest Rate for Foreign Country Investment During Period } t}$$

Using the formula to solve the previous example results in the following, based on 6-month interest rates:

$$\text{Forward rate of } \$0.592 = \$0.60 \times \frac{1 + 0.0225}{1 + 0.03625}$$

If the interest yield on the FC is greater than the yield on the U.S. dollar, the forward rate will be less than the spot rate (contract sells at a discount). The forward contract will sell at a premium if the opposite is true. The forward rate based on interest differentials will be slightly different from the quoted forward rate because the quoted rate includes a commission to the foreign currency broker. Furthermore, other factors in addition to interest differentials could be incorporated into the forward rate. These other factors include the volatility of the spot rates, the time period covered by the contract, expectations of future exchange rate changes, and the political and economic environments of a given country.

The student of international accounting should have an understanding of the international monetary system and exchange rates. As previously mentioned, changes in exchange rates represent an additional business risk when transactions are denominated in a foreign currency. The accounting for foreign currency transactions measures this risk and demonstrates the use of both spot and forward rates.

REFLECTION

- The current international monetary system is a floating system in which rates of exchange between currencies change in response to a variety of factors including trade balances, interest rates, money supply, and other economic factors.

- Spot rates represent the current rate of exchange between two currencies. A forward rate represents a future rate of exchange at a future point in time. If the forward rate exceeds the spot rate, the contract is at a premium rather than a discount.

3

OBJECTIVE

Account for a foreign currency transaction, including the measurement of exchange gain or loss.

ACCOUNTING FOR FOREIGN CURRENCY TRANSACTIONS

Assume a U.S. company sells mining equipment to a foreign company and the equipment must be paid for in 30 days with U.S. dollars. This transaction is denominated in dollars and will be measured by the U.S. company in dollars. Changes in the exchange rate between the U.S. dollar and the foreign currency from the transaction date to the settlement date will not expose the U.S. company to any risk of gain or loss from exchange rate changes. Now assume that the same transaction occurs except that the transaction is to be settled in the foreign currency. Because this transaction is denominated in the foreign currency and will be measured by the U.S. company in dollars, changes in the exchange rate subsequent to the transaction date expose the U.S. company to the risk of an exchange rate loss or gain. If the U.S. dollar strengthens, relative to the foreign currency, the U.S. company will experience a loss because it is holding an asset (a receivable of foreign currency) whose price and value have declined. If the dollar weakens, the opposite effect would be experienced. For example, assume the U.S. company sells the mining equipment for 1,000,000 FC when the spot rate is 1 FC = $0.50 and that the dollar subsequently strengthens 10% (1 FC = $0.45).

Time	Spot Rate	Value of Receivable
Originally	1 FC = $0.50	$500,000
Subsequent strengthening	1 FC = $0.45	$450,000
Decline in value of receivable resulting in a loss ..		$ 50,000

Whether a transaction is settled in dollars versus a foreign currency is a matter that is negotiated between the transacting parties and is influenced by a number of factors. For one of the parties, the currency will be a foreign currency; for the other party, the currency will be its domestic currency. A bank wire transfer is generally used to transfer currency between parties in different countries. When a bank wire transfer is used, the owing party instructs its bank to reduce its bank account by the appropriate amount. Its bank, in turn, notifies the receiving party's bank to add a corresponding translated amount to the receiving party's bank account. Therefore, the bank wire transfer, through the use of electronic means, eliminates the need to physically transfer currencies between transacting parties.

To summarize, *changes in exchange rates do not affect transactions that are both denominated and measured in the reporting entity's currency.* Therefore, these transactions require no special accounting treatment. However, if a transaction is denominated in a foreign currency and measured in the reporting entity's currency, changes in the exchange rate between the transaction date and settlement date result in a gain or loss to the reporting entity. These gains or losses are referred to as exchange gains or losses, and their recognition requires special accounting treatment.

Effect of Rate Changes	
No Exchanges Gain or Loss	Exchange Gain or Loss
Transactions are denominated and measured in the reporting entity's currency.	Transactions are denominated in the foreign currency and measured in the reporting entity's currency.

Originally, two methods were proposed for the treatment of exchange gains or losses arising from foreign currency transactions. After considering the merits of these two methods, the FASB adopted the *two-transactions method* which views the initial foreign currency transaction as one transaction. The effect of any subsequent changes in the exchange rates and the resulting exchange gain or loss are viewed as a second transaction. Therefore, the initial transaction is recorded independently of the settlement transaction. This method is consistent with accepted accounting techniques, which normally account for the financing of a transaction as a separate and distinct event. (The required two-transactions method is used in all instances with one exception. The exception relates to a hedge on a foreign currency commitment that is discussed later in this chapter. Therefore, unless otherwise stated, the two-transactions method will be used throughout the chapter.)

In order to illustrate the two-transactions method, assume that a U.S. company sells mining equipment on June 1 of the current year to a foreign company, with the corresponding receivable to be paid or settled on July 1 of the current year. The equipment has a selling price of $306,000 and a cost of $250,000. On June 1, the foreign currency is worth $1.70, and on July 1, the foreign currency is worth $1.60. Illustrations 10-1 and 10-2 present the entries to record the sale of the mining equipment, assuming that the transaction is denominated in dollars ($306,000) and then in foreign currency (180,000 FC = $306,000/$1.70). Note that, when the transaction is denominated in dollars (in Illustration 10-1), the U.S. company does not experience an exchange gain or loss. However, because the foreign company measures the transaction in foreign currency but denominates the transaction in dollars, it experiences an exchange loss. In substance, the value of the foreign company's accounts payable changed because it was denominated in a foreign currency (dollars, in this case), that is, in a currency other than its own. In order to emphasize that the value of certain asset or liability balances is not fixed and will change over time, these changing accounts are identified in **boldface type** throughout the text.

When the transaction is denominated in foreign currency, as in Illustration 10-2, the U.S. company experiences an exchange loss (or gain). The exchange loss (or gain) is accounted for separately from the sales transaction and does not affect the U.S. company's gross profit on the sale. This separately recognized exchange gain or loss is not viewed as an extraordinary item, but should be included in determining income from continuing operations for the period and, if material, should be disclosed in the financial statements or in a note to the statements. Finally, it is important to note in Illustration 10-2 that the foreign company does not experience an exchange gain or loss. This is because the foreign company both measured and denominated the transaction in foreign currency.

Unsettled Foreign Currency Transactions

If a foreign currency transaction is unsettled at year-end, an unrealized gain or loss should be recognized to reflect the change in the exchange rate occurring between the transaction date and the end of the reporting period (e.g., year-end). This treatment focuses on accrual accounting and the fact that exchange gains and losses occur over time rather than only at the date of settlement or payment. Therefore, at any given time the asset or liability arising from a foreign currency transaction that is denominated in a foreign currency *should be measured at its fair value* as suggested by current spot rates. The changes in fair value, both positive and negative, are recognized in current earnings. In essence, the asset or liability is *marked-to-market*.

Illustration 10-1
Transaction Denominated in **Dollars:** Two-Transactions Method

U.S. Company (dollars)			Foreign Company (foreign currency—FC)		
June 1					
Accounts Receivable	306,000		Equipment	180,000*	
Sales Revenue		306,000	**Accounts Payable—FC**		**180,000**
Cost of Goods Sold	250,000				
Inventory		250,000			
July 1					
Cash	306,000		**Accounts Payable—FC**	**180,000**	
Accounts Receivable		306,000	Exchange Loss	11,250	
			Cash		191,250**

Note: The U.S. company experienced no exchange gain or loss because its transaction was both denominated and measured in dollars. However, under the two-transactions method, the foreign company did experience an exchange loss since its transaction was measured in foreign currency and denominated in dollars. The decrease in the value of the foreign currency relative to the U.S. dollar means more foreign currency must be paid to cover the liability.

*$306,000 \div \$1.70 = 180,000$ FC
**$306,000 \div \$1.60 = 191,250$ FC

Illustration 10-2
Transaction Denominated in **Foreign Currency (FC):** Two-Transactions Method

U.S. Company (dollars)			Foreign Company (foreign currency)		
June 1					
Accounts Receivable—FC	**306,000**		Equipment	180,000	
Sales Revenue		306,000	Accounts Payable		180,000
Cost of Goods Sold	250,000				
Inventory		250,000			
July 1					
Cash	288,000*		Accounts Payable	180,000	
Exchange Loss	18,000**		Cash		180,000
Accounts Receivable—FC		**306,000**			

Note: The loss is considered to be part of a separate financing decision and unrelated to the original sales transaction.

*The company received 180,000 FC when the exchange rate was 1 FC = $1.60 (180,000 FC × $1.60 = $288,000). Normally, the company would not physically receive FC but would have the dollar equivalent wired to its bank account. Through the use of a bank wire transfer, the foreign company's account would be debited for the number of FC, and the U.S. company's bank account would be credited for the applicable number of dollars, given the exchange rate.
**The decrease in the value of the FC from $1.70 to $1.60 results in an exchange loss to the U.S. company since the FC it received is less valuable than it was at the transaction date [180,000 × ($1.60 − $1.70) = −$18,000].

To illustrate the accounting for unsettled transactions, assume a U.S. company purchases goods from a foreign company on November 1, 2015. The purchase in the amount of 1,000 foreign currencies (FC) is to be paid for on February 1, 2016, in foreign currency. To record or measure the transaction, the domestic company would make the following entry, assuming an exchange rate of 1 FC = $0.50:

Inventory	500	
Accounts Payable—FC		500
Purchase of inventory for 1,000 FC when the exchange rate is 1 FC = $0.50.		

Assuming the exchange rate on the December 31, 2015, year-end is 1 FC = $0.52, the following entry would be necessary:

Exchange Loss [1,000 × ($0.52 − $0.50)]*	20	
Accounts Payable—FC		20
To accrue the exchanges loss on the unperformed portion of the foreign currency transaction when 1 FC = $0.52.		

*The increase in the value of each FC from $0.50 to $0.52 results in a loss to the domestic company since, as of year-end, the company would have to pay out more dollars than originally recorded in order to eliminate the liability.

If the transaction had been settled at year-end, the domestic company would have had to expend $520 to acquire 1,000 FC. Therefore, a loss of $20 is traceable to the unperformed portion of the transaction. Some theorists have suggested that an exchange gain or loss should not be recognized prior to settlement because the gain or loss has not been "realized" through settlement. This position fails to recognize the merits of accrual accounting and is in conflict with the position of the FASB, which requires that the assets or liabilities that are denominated in a foreign currency be measured at fair value with the recognition of resulting unrealized gains or losses being recognized in current earnings.

Finally, assuming an exchange rate of 1 FC = $0.55 on the settlement date (February 1, 2016), the domestic entity would make the following entry to record the settlement:

Accounts Payable—FC ($500 + $20)	520	
Exchange Loss [1,000 × ($0.55 − $0.52)]	30	
Cash		550
To accrue payment of liability for 1,000 FC, when 1 FC = $0.55.		

Note that the company experiences a $50 loss due to changes in the exchange rate. This is allocated between 2015 and 2016 in accordance with accrual accounting.

REFLECTION

- If a transaction is denominated in a foreign currency, there is exposure to risk associated with exchange rate changes.

- Assets or liabilities that are denominated in foreign currency are to be measured at fair value using spot exchange rates at the date of measurement. In essence, such accounts are marked-to-market. Exchange gains and losses are recorded in current earnings even if not yet realized.

4

OBJECTIVE

THE EXPOSURE TO FOREIGN CURRENCY EXCHANGE RISK AND THE USE OF DERIVATIVES

Identify the contexts in which a company may be exposed to foreign currency exchange risk.

When business transactions are measured in one currency and settled in another currency, one of the transacting parties will be exposed to the exchange rate risk associated with having a transaction denominated in a foreign currency. Companies may be exposed to foreign currency exchange risk in several situations including the following:

1. *An actual existing foreign currency transaction that results in the recognition of assets or liabilities.* As previously illustrated, the risk to be hedged against is the risk that exchange rates may change between the transaction date and the settlement date.

2. *A firm commitment to enter into a foreign currency transaction.* Such a commitment is an agreement between two parties that specifies all significant terms related to the prospective transaction including prices or amounts of consideration stated in foreign currency units. Beginning at the date of the commitment, the risk to be hedged against is the risk that the value of the commitment, which is fixed in a foreign currency amount, could be adversely affected by subsequent changes in exchange rates. For example, a commitment to purchase inventory for a fixed amount of foreign currency could have a value of $100,000 at the commitment date but, due to exchange rate changes, have a value of $110,000 at the transaction date thus resulting in a higher inventory cost than anticipated.

3. *A forecasted foreign currency transaction that has a high probability of occurrence.* Such a forecasted transaction, unlike a commitment or an existing transaction, does not provide an entity with any present rights or obligations and does not have any fixed prices or rates. Because fixed prices or rates are not present, an entity is exposed to the risk that future cash flows may vary due to changes in prices and exchange rates. The risk being hedged against is the risk associated with exchange rate changes. For example, if a manufacturer forecasted needing raw materials to meet future production, even if material prices to be paid in foreign currency did not change in the future, the dollar equivalent cash flows associated with the forecasted purchase could change over time due to changes in exchange rates.

4. *An investment in a foreign subsidiary.* Translating the financial statements of a foreign subsidiary expressed in foreign currency into the domestic currency of the investor entity can affect the equity of the investor entity. The risk being hedged against is the risk that the translation will reduce the investor's equity due to adverse changes in exchange rates. Such a hedge is known as a *hedge of a net investment.*

The risk associated with (4) above will be discussed in the next chapter. However, the risk associated with the first three situations above is traceable to the risk of changes in exchange rates over the time periods prior to when payment is made on a transaction as shown in the following illustration:

Situation 3	Situation 2	Situation 1	
Company forecasts a transaction	Company commits to a transaction	Transaction occurs	Payment is made on the transaction

Characteristics of Derivatives

5

OBJECTIVE

Understand the characteristics of derivatives and the common types used to hedge foreign currency exchange rate risk.

As stated, a company can be exposed to the risk associated with changes in currency exchange rates in a number of contexts. Common strategies to hedge against such risks involve the use of derivative financial instruments. A financial instrument represents a right, through a contractual agreement between two opposite parties called *counterparties*, to receive or deliver cash or another financial instrument on potentially favorable or unfavorable terms. Financial instruments include cash, equity and debt investments, and derivatives. A derivative is a type of financial instrument that has several distinguishing characteristics that have been set forth by the FASB. These are the characteristics of a derivative.

1. It derives its value from changes in the rate or price of a related asset or liability. The rate or price is known as an underlying.

2. The quantity or number of units specified by a derivative is known as the notional amount.

3. It requires little or no initial investment upon inception.
4. It allows for net settlement in that the derivative contract can be settled in exchange for cash, without having to actually buy or sell the related asset or liability.

A critical characteristic of a derivative and the basis for its name is that the instrument derives its value from changes in the value of a related asset or liability. The rates or prices that relate to the asset or liability underlying the derivative are referred to as *underlyings*. The underlying may take a variety of forms, including a commodity price, stock price, foreign currency exchange rate, or interest rate. **It is important to note that the underlying is not the asset or liability itself, but rather its price or rate**. For example, the underlying in a forward contract is not the foreign currency itself but rather the currency exchange rate. Changes in the underlying price or rate cause the value of the derivative to change. For example, if the forward exchange rate underlies the value of the forward contract, an increase in the forward rate will cause a forward contract to buy foreign currency to increase in value.

In order to fully value a derivative, one must know the number of units (quantity) that is specified in the derivative instrument. This is called the *notional amount*, and it determines the total dollar value of a derivative, traceable to movement or changes in the underlying. For example, if the forward contract to buy foreign currency increases in value, the total magnitude of this increase in value depends on how many foreign currency units, for example 100,000 units, can be sold under the terms of the contract. **Both the underlying price or rate and the notional amount are necessary in order to determine the total value of a derivative at any point in time.**

Typically, a derivative requires little or no initial investment because it is an investment in a change in value traceable to an underlying, rather than an investment in the actual asset or liability to which the underlying relates. The holder of a forward contract to buy foreign currency to be used at a future date involves no initial investment, whereas the holder of actual foreign currency to be used at a future date has already made an investment in the currency.

Many derivatives do not require the parties to the contract, the counterparties, to actually deliver an asset that is associated with the underlying in order to realize the value of a derivative. For example, the holder of a forward contract to buy foreign currency could sell the contract. The ability to settle the contract in exchange for cash, without actually buying or selling the related asset or liability, is referred to as *net settlement*.

Common Types of Derivatives

The number of financial instruments that have the characteristics of a derivative has continued to expand, and, in turn, these instruments have become increasingly complex. However, within the context of hedging the risk associated with foreign currency exchange rate risk, two common types of derivatives are forward contracts and options (the use of foreign currency swaps are beyond the scope of this chapter).

Foreign Currency Forward Contract. A *foreign currency forward contract* is an executory contract to buy or sell a specified amount of foreign currency, at a specified fixed rate with delivery at a specified future point in time. The party that agrees to sell the asset is said to be in a *short position*, and the party that agrees to buy the asset is said to be in a *long position*. The specified fixed rate in the contract is known as a *forward rate*. The specified future date is referred to as the *forward date*. Forward contracts are not formally regulated on an organized exchange, and the parties are exposed to a risk that default of the contract could occur. However, the lack of formal regulation means that such contracts can be customized in response to specialized needs regarding notional amounts and forward dates.

The value of a forward contract is zero at inception and typically does not require an initial cash outlay. However, over time, movement in the rate of the underlying results in a change in value of the forward contract. **The total change in the value of a forward contract is measured as the difference between the forward rate and the spot rate at the forward date**. For example, on April 1, a party (called the *writer*) writes a contract in which she/he agrees to sell (short position) to another party (called the *holder*) who agrees to buy (long position) 1,000,000 FC (for example, euros) at a specific price of $0.16 per FC with delivery in 90 days (June 29). The relationship between the parties is as shown on page 558.

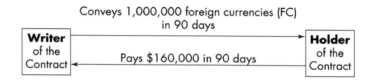

If the spot rate at the end of the forward period is $0.18, the total change in value is determined as follows:

1,000,000 FC at a forward rate (on April 1) of	
$0.16 (1,000,000 × $0.16)	$160,000
1,000,000 FC at a spot rate (on June 29) of	
$0.18 (1,000,000 × $0.18)	180,000
Gain in value to holder	$ 20,000

This is a gain because on June 29 the holder received something with a fair value greater than the fair value given up that day. (Conversely, this would be a loss to the writer.) The holder of the forward contract could buy foreign currencies for $160,000 on the forward date compared to the spot value of $180,000 at that time and experience an immediate $20,000 gain. It is important to note that the value of the currency at the final spot rate could have been less than $160,000. In that case, the holder would have experienced a loss and the writer a gain. When the value of a derivative can change in both directions (gain or loss), it is said to have a *symmetric return profile*. It is also important to note that in the case of a forward contract, if the holder of the contract experiences a gain (loss) in value, then the writer of the contract simultaneously experiences a loss (gain) in value.

The forward rate is a function of a number of variables and as these variables change over the life of the contract, the value of the forward contract also changes. Also, because the forward rates represent values in the future, the current value is represented by the present value of the future rates. Continuing with the example involving foreign currencies, assume the following forward rate information throughout the 90-day term of the contract:

Remaining Term of Contract	Forward Rate	Notional Amount	Total Forward Value	Cumulative Change in Forward Value
90 days	$0.160	1,000,000	$160,000	
60 days	0.170	1,000,000	170,000	$10,000
30 days	0.170	1,000,000	170,000	10,000
0 days	0.180	1,000,000	180,000	20,000

Assuming a 6% discount rate, the change in value of the forward contract over time is as follows:

	60 Days Remaining	30 Days Remaining	Total Life of Contract
Cumulative change in forward value.	$10,000	$10,000	$20,000
Present value of cumulative change:			
60 days at 6%	$ 9,901		
30 days at 6%		$ 9,950	
0 days at 6%			$20,000
Previously recognized gain or loss.	0	(9,901)	(9,950)
Current period gain or loss	$ 9,901	$ 49	$10,050

Note that the total change in the value of the forward contract is $20,000 ($9,901 + $49 + $10,050), which is recognized over the term of the contract as the net present value of changes in the forward rates. Even if the forward rates did not change between two valuation dates (as is the case here between 60 and 30 days), the value of the contract would change because the remaining term of the forward contract continues to decrease and the present value of the forward value increases. *Also, note that the stated forward rate at the expiration date of the contract is equal to the spot rate at that date.* This is due to the fact that at expiration of the contract the forward date is the same as the current date.

Foreign Currency Option. A *foreign currency option* represents a right, rather than an obligation, to either buy or sell some quantity of a particular foreign currency. The option is valid for a specified period of time and calls for a specified buy or sell rate or price, referred to as the *strike price* or *exercise price*. If an option allows the holder to *buy* an underlying, it is referred to as a *call option*. An option that allows the holder to *sell* an underlying is referred to as a *put option*. Options are actively traded on organized exchanges or may be negotiated on a case-by-case basis between counterparties (over-the-counter contracts). Option contracts require the holder to make an initial nonrefundable cash outlay, known as the *premium*, as represented by the option's current value. The premium is paid, in part, because the writer of the option takes more risk than the holder of the option. The holder can allow the option to expire, while the writer must comply if the holder chooses to exercise it.

During the option period, the strike price of the option on the underlying is generally different from the current value of an underlying. The following terms are used to describe the relationship between the strike price and the current price (note that the premium is not considered in these relationships):

Option Type	Strike Price Is Equal to Current Price	Strike Price Is Greater Than Current Price	Strike Price Is Less Than Current Price
Call (buy) option	At-the-money	Out-of-the-money	In-the-money
Put (sell) option	At-the-money	In-the-money	Out-of-the-money

As the above table suggests, in-the-money is a favorable condition as compared to being out-of-the-money, which is an unfavorable condition. The original premium is not considered when describing whether an option is or is not in-the-money. However, it is important to note that the original premium certainly is considered when determining whether an investment in an option has experienced an overall profit. The holder of an option has a right, rather than an obligation, and will not exercise the option unless it is in-the-money. In that case, the holder will experience a gain, and the writer will experience a loss. However, if the option is not in-the-money, the option will not be exercised, the holder will limit her/his loss to the amount of the option premium, and the writer will limit her/his gain to the amount of the premium. Therefore, in theory, the opportunities for gain and loss are characterized as follows:

	Potential for	
	Gain	Loss
Holder of option	Unlimited	Limited to amount of premium
Writer of option	Limited to amount of premium	Unlimited

Because the counterparties do not have equal opportunity for both upside and downside changes in value, options are said to have an *asymmetric* or one-sided return profile.

Options are traded on an organized exchange and over the counter; therefore, their current value is quoted in terms of present dollars on a frequent basis. The current value of an option depends on forward periods and spot prices. The difference between the strike and spot prices, at any point in time, measures the intrinsic value of the option, so changes in spot prices will change the intrinsic value of the option. Changes in the length of the remaining forward period will affect the time value of the option. The time value is measured as the difference between an option's current value and its intrinsic value as in the following illustration:

◆ If the option is in-the-money, the option has intrinsic value. For example, if an investor has a 90-day call (buy) option to buy 100,000 FC at a strike price of $1.10 per FC and the current spot rate is $1.12 FC, the option is in-the-money and has an intrinsic value of $2,000 (100,000 × $0.02). An option that is out-of-the-money or at-the-money has no intrinsic value.

◆ The difference between the current value of an option and its intrinsic value represents time value. For example, if the 90-day call (buy) option has a current value of $2,200 and an intrinsic value of $2,000, the time value component is $200 (the current value of $2,200, less the intrinsic value of $2,000). The time value of an option represents a discounting factor and a volatility factor.

◆ The discounting factor relates to the fact that the strike price does not have to be paid currently, but rather at the time of exercise. Therefore, the holder of an option to buy FC could benefit from an appreciation in the value of FC without actually having to currently pay out the cash to purchase the FC. Thus, the ability to have the alternative use of the cash equal to the strike price until exercise date of the option has value and is a component of the time value.

◆ The volatility factor relates to the volatility of the underlying relative to the fixed strike price and reflects the potential for gain on the option. Underlyings with more price volatility present greater opportunities for gains if the option is in-the-money. Therefore, higher volatility increases the value of an option and this is a component of the time value. Note that volatility could also lead to an out-of the-money situation. However, this possibility can be disregarded because, unlike forward contracts, the risk for an option is asymmetric since the holder can avoid unfavorable outcomes by allowing the option to expire.

To illustrate the value components of an option, assume that a put (sell) option allows for the sale of 100,000 FC in 60 days at a strike or exercise price of $0.50 per FC. The value of the option would consist of the following:

	Initial Date of Purchase	End of 30 Days	End of 60 Days
Value of 100,000 FC at the current spot rate	$51,000	$49,000	$48,000
Assumed total value of option	$ 1,300	$ 1,650	$ 2,000
Intrinsic value (never less than zero)	0 (option is out-of-the-money)	1,000 [in-the-money ($50,000 vs. $49,000)]	2,000 [in-the-money ($50,000 vs. $48,000)]
Time value (total value less intrinsic value)	$ 1,300	$ 650	$ 0

REFLECTION

- Derivatives have a number of characteristics including: value derived from a change in the rate or price of a related asset or liability, a notional amount, little or no initial investment, and allowance for net settlement.

- Common types of derivatives include a foreign currency forward contract and a foreign currency option.

ACCOUNTING FOR DERIVATIVES THAT ARE DESIGNATED AS A HEDGE

If an item is denominated in a foreign currency, it is exposed to risk associated with changes in exchange rates. The risk may be traceable to a number of situations including a recognized asset or liability, forecasted transactions, or firm commitments. Regardless of the type of situation, the critical concern is the exposure to foreign currency exchange risk. This exposure can be hedged through the use of a fair value hedge or a cash flow hedge. It is possible that a hedge could either qualify as a fair value hedge or a cash flow hedge. Therefore, it is important that the hedging relationship be clearly defined so that the appropriate accounting will occur.

A **fair value hedge** is used to offset changes in the fair value of items with fixed exchange prices or rates. Fair value hedges include hedges against a change in the fair value of:

- A recognized foreign-currency-denominated asset or liability.
- An unrecognized foreign currency firm commitment.

A **cash flow hedge** is used to establish fixed prices or rates when future cash flows could vary due to changes in prices or rates. Cash flow hedges include hedges against the change in cash flows (variable cash flows) associated with:

- A forecasted foreign currency transaction.
- The forecasted functional-currency-equivalent cash flows associated with a recognized asset or liability.
- An unrecognized foreign currency firm commitment.

Special Accounting for Fair Value Hedges

The hedged item in a fair value hedge is either a recognized asset or liability or a firm commitment. Recognized assets or liabilities in a fair value hedge result from actual past transactions such as a purchase of inventory denominated in foreign currency. Commitments relate to transactions that have not yet occurred, such as a contract to purchase inventory denominated in foreign currency. A commitment is a binding agreement between two parties that specifies all significant terms related to the prospective transaction. Such terms include the quantity to be exchanged, the timing of the transaction, and a fixed price (e.g., the number of foreign currency units). The agreement also includes a large enough disincentive to make performance of the contract probable.

Because the number of foreign currency units in an existing transaction or a firm commitment is fixed, subsequent changes in currency exchange rates affect the value of a recognized asset, liability, or commitment. For example, if an entity has purchased inventory and has a recognized accounts payable to be settled in FC, changes in exchange rates will change the value of the payable. Similarly, if an entity has a firm commitment to purchase inventory, changes in the exchange rates will change the value of the commitment.

Many accounting principles do not allow for the recognition in current earnings of both increases and decreases in the value of recognized assets, liabilities, or firm commitments. However, if the risk of such changes in value is covered by a fair value hedge, special accounting treatment is allowed that provides for the recognition of such changes in earnings. In a qualifying fair value hedge, the gain or loss on the derivative hedging instrument and the offsetting loss or gain on the hedged item are both recognized currently in earnings. For instance, assume a recognized account payable is to be settled in FC. If the domestic currency weakens relative to the FC, it will require more domestic currency to settle the account payable than previously thought, resulting in an exchange loss. If the payable is hedged, both the exchange loss on the payable and the change in the value of the derivative instrument used as a hedge are recognized in earnings.

In order to qualify for special fair value hedge accounting, the derivative hedging instrument and the hedged item must satisfy a number of criteria. A critical criterion is that an entity must have formal documentation of the hedging relationship and the entity's risk-management objective and strategy. The entity must indicate the reason for undertaking the designated hedge, identify the hedged item and the derivative hedging instrument, and explain the nature of the risk being hedged. This criterion must be satisfied at inception and cannot be retroactively applied after an entity has determined whether hedging would be appropriate. Another important criterion is that the hedging relationship must be assessed both at inception and on an ongoing basis to determine if it is highly effective in offsetting the identified risks. Generally speaking, a hedge would be totally effective if the terms (such as notional amount, maturity dates, quality/condition, delivery locations, etc.) of the hedging instrument and the hedged item are the same. This approach is known as *critical terms analysis*. It is important to note that in practice the terms of a derivative do not always align with the terms of the related asset or liability, and, therefore, other approaches to assessing effectiveness must be employed. Management must also describe how it will assess hedge effectiveness. Generally, hedge ineffectiveness is the difference between the gains or losses on the derivative and the hedged item.

Assuming the necessary criteria are satisfied for treatment as a fair value hedge, the hedge will qualify for special accounting treatment. The gain or loss on the derivative hedging instrument will be recognized currently in earnings, along with the change in value on the hedged item, and an appropriate adjustment to the basis of the hedged item will be recorded. If the cumulative change in the value of the derivative instrument does not exactly offset the cumulative change in the value of the hedged item, the difference is recognized currently in earnings. Because both hedge effectiveness and hedge ineffectiveness are recognized currently in earnings, it is not necessary to separately account for that portion of the hedge which is considered to be ineffective.

Special Accounting for Cash Flow Hedges

The hedged item in a cash flow hedge is one in which future cash flows could be affected due to a particular risk such as the change in foreign currency exchange rates. A forecasted transaction is well suited to the use of a cash flow hedge. Because fixed prices or rates are not present in a forecasted transaction, an entity is exposed to the risk that future cash flows may vary due to changes in prices/rates. For example, if an entity forecasted purchasing raw materials from a foreign vendor with the invoice payable in FC, the cash flows needed to acquire the materials could change because the price of the materials could change between the forecast date and the purchase date. However, even if that did not occur, the necessary cash flows could also be affected because of changes in the exchange rate between the foreign and domestic currencies. Another application of a cash flow hedge could involve an existing liability, denominated in FC, which bears interest at a variable rate of interest. The cash flows associated with interest could be affected due to not only the variability of interest rates but also changes in the exchange rate.

A nonderivative financial instrument may not be used as the hedging instrument in a foreign currency cash flow hedge. Furthermore, as is the case with a fair value hedge, special hedge accounting is not available for a cash flow hedge unless a number of criteria are satisfied. Cash flow hedges must also meet the criteria regarding documentation and assessment of effectiveness. If the derivative instrument and the hedged item satisfy the criteria, then the cash flow hedge will qualify for special accounting. The effective portion of the gain or loss on the derivative instrument will be reported in *other comprehensive income (OCI)*, which is a separate component of shareholders' equity.[1] As with fair value hedges, a portion of the derivative instrument's gain or loss may be excluded from the assessment of effectiveness. That portion of the gain or loss will be recognized currently in earnings rather than as a component of other comprehensive income. The amounts reported in OCI will be reclassified into recognized earnings in the same period in which the hedged item affects earnings. For example, assume that a forecasted sale of inventory is hedged. Once the inventory is sold and recognized in earnings, the applicable amount, the OCI gain or loss, will also be recognized in earnings. If the forecasted transaction were a purchase of a depreciable asset, the applicable portion of the OCI would be recognized in earnings when the asset's depreciation expense is recognized.

Type of Hedge	Fair Value	Cash Flow
The hedged item.	◆ A recognized foreign currency denominated asset or liability. ◆ An unrecognized foreign currency firm commitment.	◆ A forecasted foreign currency transaction. ◆ The forecasted functional-currency-equivalent cash flows associated with a recognized asset or liability. ◆ An unrecognized foreign currency firm commitment.

(continued)

---

1 Other comprehensive income is not included in the income statement; it bypasses the traditional income statement but is shown as a component of equity.

Type of Hedge	Fair Value	Cash Flow
Objective of hedge.	To protect the value of asset, liabilities, and firm commitments against negative changes in value related to foreign currency exchange rate risk.	To protect against the uncertain risk that changes in foreign currency exchange rates could negatively impact future cash flows.
Accounting for changes in the value of the hedged item.	Changes in the value of the hedged item are recognized currently as a component of earnings (net income).	If the hedged item is a forecasted transaction, no changes in value are recognized until after the transaction actually occurs. In the case of a hedge of forecasted cash flows associated with a recognized asset or liability, or in the case of an unrecognized foreign currency firm commitment, changes in value are recognized currently as the value of the cash flows changes.
Accounting for changes in the value of the hedging instrument (derivative).	Derivatives are marked to market and carried at fair value. Changes in value are recognized currently as a component of earnings (net income).	Changes in value are recognized currently in other comprehensive income (a separate component of shareholders' equity) and are subsequently recognized as a component of income when the hedged item affects earnings.
Effective portion of a hedge.	If effective, the gain or loss on the hedged item will be offset by the gain or loss on the derivative.	If effective, the gain or loss on the hedged item will be offset by the gain or loss on the derivative.
Ineffective portion of a hedge.	The ineffective portion of the hedge will be recognized currently as a component of earnings (net income).	The ineffective portion of the hedge will be recognized currently as a component of earnings (net income).

REFLECTION

- Hedges are generally designated as either fair value or cash flow hedges.

- The hedged item in a fair value hedge is either a recognized asset or liability or a firm commitment. The value of the hedged item changes over time and such changes in value are recognized currently in earnings.

- The hedged item in a cash flow hedge is either a forecasted foreign currency transaction, forecasted cash flows associated with a recognized asset or liability, or an unrecognized foreign currency commitment. The effective portion of the gain or loss on the derivative instrument will be reported in other comprehensive income and subsequently reclassified into earnings.

EXAMPLES OF THE ACCOUNTING FOR FAIR VALUE HEDGES

As previously stated, fair value hedges may be used to hedge against changes in the fair value of either a recognized foreign-currency-denominated asset or liability or an unrecognized foreign currency firm commitment. Assuming the necessary criteria are satisfied, the fair value hedge will be given special accounting treatment. This special treatment allows for the recognition in current earnings of both the gain or loss on the derivative hedging instrument and the offsetting loss or gain on the hedged item.

6
OBJECTIVE

Explain the accounting treatment given various types of foreign currency hedges.

Hedging an Existing Foreign-Currency-Denominated Asset or Liability

The gain or loss associated with the foreign currency exposure of a recognized, foreign-currency-denominated asset or liability as measured by changes in the spot rate is generally recognized in earnings. However, this recognition does not prevent such exposed positions from being hedged with a fair value hedge. It is important to note that only derivative instruments can be designated as a hedge of a foreign-currency-denominated asset or liability.

Illustration of Hedging with a Forward Contract. Assume that a U.S. company purchases inventory from a foreign vendor with subsequent payment due in FC, a foreign-currency-denominated liability, and that the company acquires a forward contract to buy FC. If prior to settlement, the dollar weakens relative to the FC, the accounts payable will increase in value resulting in an exchange loss. However, the forward contract to buy FC (an asset) will increase in value if the dollar weakens.

Additional information supporting this illustration is as follows:

1. On November 1, 2015, the company bought inventory from a foreign vendor with payment due on February 1, 2016, in the amount of 100,000 FC.

2. On November 1, 2015, the company purchased a forward contract to buy 100,000 FC on February 1, 2016, at a forward rate of 1 FC = $0.506.

3. The entire change in the value of the derivative is based on changes in the forward rate and is used to assess effectiveness. If effectiveness were assessed by measuring changes in the spot rate over time, then the difference between the spot rate and forward rate at inception of the contract (the premium or discount) representing time value would be related to ineffectiveness and be recognized in earnings (net income) over the term of the contract.

4. Selected spot and forward rates are as follows:

Date	Spot Rate	Forward Rate for Remaining Term of Contract
November 1, 2015	1 FC = $0.500	1 FC = $0.506
December 31, 2015	1 FC = 0.520	1 FC = 0.530
February 1, 2016	1 FC = 0.550	1 FC = 0.550

5. Changes in the value of the forward contract are to be discounted at a 6% rate.

6. Changes in the value of the forward contract over time are as follows:

	November 1— 90 Days Remaining	December 31— 30 Days Remaining	Transaction Date
Number of FC	100,000	100,000	100,000
Spot rate — 1 FC	$0.500	$0.520	$0.550
Forward rate for remaining time — 1 FC	$0.506	$0.530	$0.550
Initial forward rate — 1 FC		$0.506	$0.506
Fair value of forward contract:			
Original forward value		$50,600	$50,600
Current forward value		53,000	55,000
Change—gain (loss) in forward value		$ 2,400	$ 4,400

(continued)

Present value of change:		
n = 1, i = 6%/12...........	$2,388	
n = 0, i = 6%/12...........		$4,400
Change in value from prior period:		
Current present value.........	$2,388	$4,400
Prior present value...........	0	2,388
Change in present value	$2,388	$2,012

Illustration 10-3 presents the entries to record the foreign currency transaction and the related forward contract. Once again, in order to emphasize that the value of certain account balances is not fixed and will change over time, these accounts are identified in boldface type.

Illustration 10-3
Hedging a Foreign-Currency-Denominated Liability

Relating to the Purchase of Inventory			Relating to the Forward Contract		
November 1, 2015					
Inventory	50,000		Memo: Company acquires a forward		
Accounts Payable—FC		50,000	contract to buy 100,000 FC at a forward		
Purchase of inventory			rate of 1 FC = $0.506.[a]		
for 100,000 FC when					
1 FC = $0.500.					
December 31, 2015					
Exchange Loss	2,000		**Forward Contract**......................	2,388	
Accounts Payable—FC		2,000	Gain on Contract......................		2,388
To accrue the exchange loss on			To record change in the value		
the FC denominated payable			of the forward contract.		
when the spot rate is $0.520.					
			Note that the above entry includes the entire		
			change in the value of the contract.[b]		
February 1, 2016					
Accounts Payable—FC	52,000		**Forward Contract**......................	2,012	
Exchange Loss	3,000		Gain on Contract......................		2,012
Foreign Currency.............		55,000	To record change in value		
To record settlement			of the forward contract.		
of the liability when					
1 FC = $0.550.					
			Foreign Currency[c]......................	55,000	
			Forward Contract....................		4,400
			Cash		50,600
			To record settlement of contract.		

[a]Noting the executory nature of the contract, a memo entry is made to describe the derivative.
[b]Given that the hedge is a fair value hedge, the entire change in value of the contract is recorded in earnings (net income). If the initial spot-forward difference were chosen to represent hedge ineffectiveness, the gain or loss related to the ineffectiveness would also have been reported in earnings. Therefore, there is no need to separately account for the ineffective portion of the hedge.
[c]Generally, the company would not physically receive the foreign currency. Instead, a bank wire transfer would be used to settle the transaction. The currency broker would debit the domestic company's bank account for the necessary number of dollars and credit the foreign company's bank account for the necessary number of foreign currencies.

To summarize, the accounting for the fair value hedge of a foreign-currency-denominated asset or liability is characterized as follows:

1. The accounting for the hedging instrument is separate from the accounting for the foreign-currency-denominated asset or liability.
2. The hedging instrument will be carried at fair value, and changes in value over time will be recognized as an unrealized gain or loss and be reported in earnings.
3. The change in value of the hedging instrument consists of a change in the instrument's intrinsic value and its time value. The total change in value of the instrument, including both hedge effectiveness and hedge ineffectiveness, is reported currently in earnings.
4. Changes in the value of the hedging instrument should be accrued at the end of a reporting period.
5. The gains (losses) on the hedging instrument will offset or net against the losses (gains) on the foreign currency asset or liability (the hedged item).
6. A hedge would be fully effective or "perfect" if the critical terms (nature of the underlying, notional amount, delivery dates, settlement date, type of currency, etc.) of the hedging instrument matched the terms of the hedged item. In a perfect hedge, the net difference between the change in value of the hedged item and the change in value of the hedging instrument will merely equal the change in the time value of the hedging instrument.
7. How hedge effectiveness will be assessed must be set forth and documented. The spot-forward difference at inception of the contract can either be included or excluded in the assessment of effectiveness.
8. In the case of a forward contract, technically there is no need to record the contract at inception because it is an executory contract. In reality, most companies follow this no recording practice but do keep supporting schedules detailing contracts. Even if this practice is followed, the forward contract is marked-to-market in order to reflect changes in the value of the underlying foreign currency. These changes in fair value are recorded by the company.

The hedge accounted for in Illustration 10-3 was effective in that the losses associated with the changing value of the FC-denominated account payable were offset by the positive changes in the value of the forward contract. Instead of a $5,000 exchange loss, the company incurred only a $600 loss, which represents the premium on the forward rate of $0.506 versus the spot rate of $0.500 on the inception date of the forward contract (100,000 FC × ($0.506 − $0.500). The net loss of $600 consists of the $5,000 exchange loss ($2,000 + $3,000) offset by the gain on the derivative of $4,400 ($2,388 + $2,012). The $600 loss is the ineffective portion of the hedge. If financial statements were presented on December 31, 2015, the purchase and hedge would be reported as follows:

Income Statement		Balance Sheet	
		Assets:	
Exchange loss	$(2,000)	Inventory	$50,000
Unrealized gain on contract	2,388	Forward contract	$ 2,388
Net gain	$ 388		
		Liabilities:	
		Accounts payable—FC	$52,000

The overall effect of the hedge presented in Illustration 10-3 is summarized as follows:

	Without the Hedge	With the Hedge
Exchange gain (loss) on foreign-currency-denominated asset or liability [100,000 FC × ($0.550 − $0.500)]	$(5,000)	$(5,000)
Gain on forward contract [100,000 FC × ($0.550 − $0.506)]		4,400
Net income effect	$(5,000)	$ (600)

The net effect on income represents the original spot-forward difference (premium) at inception of the forward contract of $600 [100,000 × (forward rate of $0.506 versus original spot rate of $0.500)].

It is important to note that a hedge may also eliminate exchange gains associated with a foreign-currency-denominated asset or liability. For instance, when a forward contract establishes a forward rate, it is possible that changes in the spot rate may not move in the same direction or may not move as much as had been expected. Considering the previous transactions, assume the same facts except that the spot rates are as follows:

Date	Spot Rate
November 1, 2015	1 FC = $0.50
December 31, 2015	1 FC = $0.49
February 1, 2016	1 FC = $0.48

In effect, the hedge eliminated potential exchange gains, and the company paid the same $600 premium for the forward contract:

	Without the Hedge	With the Hedge
Exchange gain (loss) on foreign currency transaction		
[100,000 FC × ($0.480 − $0.500)]	$2,000	$ 2,000
Loss on forward contract [100,000 FC × ($0.480 − $0.506)]		(2,600)
Net income effect	$2,000	$ (600)

Although this hedge had a negative impact on earnings, it did eliminate the uncertainty associated with exchange rate risk. By entering into a forward contract on the date of the transaction, the company established a known payment amount of $50,600. Illustration 10-3 involved the use of a forward contract to buy FC in order to settle the FC-denominated accounts payable. A forward contract may also be used to sell FC when an FC-denominated receivable is settled. For example, if a U.S. company sold inventory to a foreign customer and the resulting account receivable was denominated in FC, the company would receive FC. The company could acquire a forward contract to sell FC upon receipt from the foreign customer. If the dollar strengthened relative to the FC, the U.S. company's receivable would decrease in value. However, a forward contract to sell FC in this scenario would increase in value and serve as a hedge against the losses on the receivable.

Illustration of Hedging with a Foreign Currency Option. Assume that a U.S. company sold inventory to a foreign customer with subsequent collection due in FC, a foreign-currency-denominated asset, and that the company acquired a put option to sell FC.

Additional information supporting this illustration is as follows:

1. On November 1, 2015, the company sold inventory, with a cost of $32,000, to a foreign customer with payment due on February 1, 2016, in the amount of 100,000 FC.

2. On November 1, 2015, the company purchased an out-of-the-money put option to sell 100,000 FC on February 1, 2016, at a strike price of 1 FC = $0.510. An option premium of $400 was paid.

3. Spot rates, option values, and changes in value over time are as follows:

	November 1, 2015	December 31, 2015	February 1, 2016
Strike price 1 FC	$0.510	$0.510	$0.510
Spot rate 1 FC	$0.515	$0.498	$0.495
Fair value of options	$ 400	$1,300	$1,500
Intrinsic value of option	0	1,200	1,500
Time value of option	$ 400	$ 100	$ 0

4. In the case of an option, the company can choose to either include or exclude the time value of the option from the assessment of effectiveness. In this example, assume that the changes in the time value are excluded from the assessment of effectiveness.

Illustration 10-4 presents the entries to record the foreign currency transaction and the related option. Once again, in order to emphasize that the value of certain account balances is not fixed and will change over time, these accounts are identified in boldface type.

Illustration 10-4
Hedging a Foreign-Currency-Denominated Asset

Relating to the Sale of Inventory			Relating to the Put Option		
November 1, 2015					
Accounts Receivable—FC ...	51,500		Investment in Put Option. ...	400	
Sales Revenue ...		51,500	Cash. ...		400
			To record purchase of option.		
Cost of Sales ...	32,000				
Inventory ...		32,000			
To record sale of inventory.					
December 31, 2015					
Exchange Loss ...	1,700		**Investment in Put Option** ...	900	
Accounts Receivable—FC ...		1,700	Gain on Option ...		900
To accrue the exchange loss on the FC-denominated receivable when the spot rate is $0.498.			To record change in the value of the put option.		
			Note that the above entry includes the entire change in the value of the option including both the $1,200 effective gain (intrinsic value) and $300 ineffective loss (time value) portion.		
February 1, 2016					
Foreign Currency. ...	49,500		Investment in Put Option ...	200	
Exchange Loss ...	300		Gain on Option ...		200
Accounts Receivable—FC ...		49,800	To record change in the value of the put option.		
To record settlement of the receivable when 1 FC = $0.495.					
			Cash ...	51,000	
			Foreign Currency. ...		49,500
			Investment in Put Option. ...		1,500
			To record settlement of the option.		

The overall effect of the hedge presented in Illustration 10-4 is summarized as follows:

	Without the Hedge	With the Hedge
Exchange gain (loss) on foreign-currency-denominated asset or liability [100,000 FC × ($0.515 − $0.495)] ...	$(2,000)	$(2,000)
Gain on option ($1,500 − $400). ...		1,100
Net income effect ...	$(2,000)	$ (900)

As a result of the hedge, the net effect on income represents two components: (a) the fact that the option's intrinsic value of $1,500 only offsets $2,000 of the exchange loss on the receivable (traceable to the fact that the option was originally out-of-the-money) and (b) the $400 cost of the original premium on the option.

Special Hedging Complications

The previous examples assumed that the term of the hedging instrument covered the same period of time as the settlement period, which is defined as the period of time between the transaction date and the settlement date of the foreign-currency-denominated asset or liability. However, it is possible that a hedging instrument could cover a period of time different from the settlement period. The previous examples also assumed that the hedging instrument was for the same number of foreign currency units as required by the foreign currency transaction. It also is possible that a hedging instrument could be for a number of foreign currency units different from the number of units required by the transaction.

Hedging Instrument Expires Before Settlement Date. Prior to the expiration date of a hedging instrument, it is possible for the holder of the contract to settle the contract in exchange for cash. Net settlement is a characteristic of all derivatives such as a forward contract. However, if the contract expires before the settlement date of the underlying hedged transaction, the holder of the hedging instrument has several alternatives for dealing with the contract. For example, assuming that a forward contract to sell foreign currency expires before the customer remits the foreign currency, the seller may: (a) roll over the forward contract, (b) purchase the necessary foreign currency to satisfy the contract and acquire a new forward contract to sell the foreign currency when the customer pays, or (c) simply purchase the necessary foreign currency to satisfy the contract and deal with the foreign currency when it is received.

Transactions and hedging instruments may be settled on different dates. For example, some currency brokers will extend a forward contract for a short time at the original forward rate as a courtesy to their clients. However, if settlement is not expected soon, the original contract may be rolled over into a new contract to settle on the anticipated date of payment. Rather than rolling over a forward contract, the needed FC can be purchased to settle the forward contract. When the hedged transaction is ultimately settled, the FC received could then be sold at the spot rate. Obviously, this route creates exposure to the risk that spot rates will change between the time of purchasing FC and receiving FC from the customer. In order to avoid this exposure, a new forward contract to sell FC could be employed.

Hedging Instrument Expires After Settlement Date. Hedging instruments can also expire after the settlement date. For example, suppose a customer paying in foreign currency accelerates the payment date in order to improve his/her current ratio. Assuming the seller has hedged the transaction with a forward contract, they once again have several options: (a) hold the foreign currency until the date of the original forward contract, (b) roll the contract back and sell the foreign currency immediately, (c) sell the foreign currency immediately and sell the forward contract to another party, and (d) sell the foreign currency immediately and acquire FC at the spot rate when the forward contract is settled. Alternative (d) results in a speculative position. (There is no hedged transaction, and it is discouraged by many company policy statements.) If a forward contract expires after the settlement date, any gain or loss that accrues on the forward contract after the transaction settlement date is recognized as a component of current operating income.

Hedging Instrument's Notional Amount Different from Transaction Amount. If a hedging instrument is for a smaller number of foreign currency units than the foreign currency transaction, the contract gain or loss is recognized as a partial hedge on the exposed position. However, if the forward contract is for a greater number of foreign currency units than the exposed asset or liability position, special treatment is required. That portion of the hedging instrument which exceeds the exposed position is considered to be a speculative hedge and is accounted for as an investment. The gain or loss on that portion of the contract which exceeds the exposed position is accordingly accounted for as an investment gain or loss.

Hedging an Identifiable Foreign Currency Firm Commitment

An identifiable firm commitment is a binding agreement between two parties that specifies all significant terms related to a yet-to-be-executed transaction. If the commitment requires ultimate settlement in a fixed amount of FC, then exposure to exchange rate risk exists. Because the terms and prices of the commitment in FC are fixed, changes in FC exchange rates affect the value of the commitment or the cash flows associated with the commitment. For example, assume a commitment to buy inventory in 60 days for 500,000 FC. If at the date of the commitment the spot rate is 1 FC = $0.250 and the 60-day forward rate is 1 FC = $0.258, changes in these rates could be used to suggest the change in the relative dollar value of the commitment. If 30 days after the commitment date the spot rate is 1 FC = $0.254 and the remaining 30-day forward rate is 1 FC = $0.264, it would appear that the commitment has lost value. Clearly, it appears that the commitment will require more dollars to settle than previously estimated. Using spot rates to suggest that the commitment has lost value, consider the following:

Number of dollars needed to satisfy commitment at commitment date equals	$125,000 (500,000 FC × $0.250)
Number of dollars needed to satisfy commitment 30 days later equals	$127,000 (500,000 FC × $0.254)

As suggested above, given changes in the spot rate it will take more U.S. dollars to satisfy the commitment than anticipated; therefore, the commitment has lost value. Furthermore, because the commitment terms (e.g., pay 500,000 FC) are fixed, the commitment cannot be renegotiated to take into consideration the fact that the dollar has weakened relative to the FC. Changes in the value of a commitment can be suggested by either changes in spot rates or forward rates over time. In either case, the suggested change reflects value at the transaction date, versus commitment date, and therefore must be discounted to reflect the change in value at the present time. Using the above example and a discount rate of 6%, the change in value of the above commitment after the first 30 days would be measured as follows:

	Based on Spot Rates	Based on Forward Rates
Rate at:		
Commitment date.	$0.250	$0.258
30 days later	$0.254	$0.264
Change in rate.	$0.004	$0.006
Number of FC	500,000	500,000
Change in value	$2,000	$3,000
Present value of change where n = 1 month and i = 6%/12	$1,990	$2,985

In order to avoid the unfavorable effect of exchange rate changes on the firm commitment, an entity could designate a derivative instrument as a hedge against unfavorable outcomes. The hedge of a firm commitment can be designated as either a fair value hedge or a cash flow hedge assuming the necessary respective criteria are satisfied. At inception of the hedge, management must specify whether the hedge will be accounted for as a fair value hedge or a cash flow hedge. For purposes of illustration the following example will assume a fair value hedge.

The special accounting for a fair value hedge of a firm foreign currency commitment is characterized as follows:

1. The accounting for the hedge (the hedging instrument) is separate from the accounting for the foreign currency commitment (the hedged item). If the commitment were not hedged, no special accounting treatment would be given the commitment.

2. The hedging instrument will be carried at fair value, and changes in value over time will be recognized as an unrealized gain or loss and be reported currently in earnings.

3. The change in the value of the hedging instrument consists of a change in the instrument's intrinsic value and its time value. Because the hedge is classified as a fair value hedge, changes in both the intrinsic and time values are reported currently in earnings and therefore will not be separately accounted for.

4. Changes in the value of the hedging instrument should be accrued at the end of a reporting period.

5. A hedge would be fully effective or "perfect" if the critical terms (nature of the underlying, notional amount, delivery dates, settlement date, type of currency, etc.) of the hedging instrument matched the terms of the hedged item. At inception of the hedge, management must choose whether or not to exclude the time value of the derivative instrument from the assessment of hedge effectiveness.

6. Management must set forth how the gain or loss on the firm commitment will be measured. The resulting gain or loss in value will be reported currently in earnings. The change in the value of the firm commitment from the time of the commitment to the transaction date is recognized as a firm commitment asset or liability. This recognized change in value will result in an adjustment to the basis of the committed item. The gains (losses) on the hedging instrument will offset or net against the losses (gains) on the commitment (the hedged item).

7. If the hedge is perfectly effective, the change in the value of the firm commitment will result in an adjustment, at the date of the transaction, to the basis of the committed item so that the effect of exchange rate changes on fixed prices can be offset. The result is that the dollar basis of the transaction is established at the commitment date rather than the later transaction date, and the targeted values at the date of the commitment can be realized.

8. That portion of the hedging instrument which exceeds the notional amount of the commitment is considered to be a speculative hedge and is accounted for accordingly. Therefore, the special accounting treatment given a fair value hedge is not extended to the portion of the hedge which is deemed to be ineffective.

To illustrate, assume that on March 31, a U.S. company commits to selling specialty equipment to a foreign customer with delivery and payment in 90 days. The firm commitment calls for a selling price of 100,000 FC, and it is estimated that the cost to manufacture the equipment will be $55,000. Assume that the spot rate at the date of the commitment is 1 FC = $0.850. If the spot rate were to remain constant over time, management would be able to realize a target gross profit on the sale of $30,000 [(100,000 FC × $0.850) − $55,000]. However, management fears that the FC could weaken relative to the dollar and the target gross profit margin could be reduced. For example, if the rate of exchange at the transaction date were 1 FC = $0.800, the gross profit would be reduced to $25,000 [(100,000 FC × $0.800) − $55,000]. Recognizing that it may be desirable to establish the dollar basis of a transaction at the commitment date rather than the later transaction date, management could enter into a hedge.

To continue the above example, assume that at the date of the commitment, management decides to hedge the commitment by acquiring a forward contract to sell FC in 90 days. Management has elected to include both the change in intrinsic value and time value in the measurement of hedge effectiveness. The change in the value of the firm commitment will be measured by changes in the forward rates. Assume that a 6% discount rate is to be used.

Selected rates and changes in value are presented in the table below. It is important to note the following:

1. The forward contract calls for the sale of FC. Therefore, as remaining forward rates fall below the original forward rate (FC can be sold forward for fewer dollars), the forward contract increases in value and gains are experienced.

2. The difference between the initial spot and forward rates, referred to as the spot-forward difference, represents the time value of the contract and is either a premium or discount. In the present case, the spot-forward difference is a discount that represents a loss. The initial forward rate to sell is less than the initial spot value of the FC. This loss is included in the assessment of hedge effectiveness as so elected at inception of the hedge although management could have elected to exclude it from hedge effectiveness. The hedge is expected to be fully effective or "perfect" because the critical terms (nature of the underlying, notional amount,

delivery dates, settlement date, type of currency, etc.) of the hedging instrument match the terms of the hedged item.

3. Changes in the value of the firm commitment are measured as changes in the forward rate over time. As the forward rates decrease over time, the commitment to sell becomes less valuable.

	March 31— 90 Days Remaining	60 Days Remaining	30 Days Remaining	Transaction Date
Number of FC	100,000	100,000	100,000	100,000
Spot rate 1 FC	$0.850	$0.840	$0.820	$0.800
Forward rate for remaining time — 1 FC	$0.845	$0.838	$0.814	$0.800
Initial forward rate — 1 FC		$0.845	$0.845	$0.845
Fair value of forward contract:				
Original forward value		$ 84,500	$ 84,500	$ 84,500
Current forward value		83,800	81,400	80,000
Change—gain (loss)—in forward value		$ 700	$ 3,100	$ 4,500
Present value of change:				
$n=2, i=6\%/12$		$ 693		
$n=1, i=6\%/12$			$ 3,085	
$n=0, i=6\%/12$				$ 4,500
Change in value from prior period:				
Current present value		$ 693	$ 3,085	$ 4,500
Prior present value		0	693	3,085
Change in present value		$ 693	$ 2,392	$ 1,415

Entries by the U.S. company to record the fair value hedge are set forth in Illustration 10-5. An analysis of the entries in Illustration 10-5 reveals that the fair value hedge was effective in accomplishing the concerns of the U.S. company. At the commitment date, the commitment to receive FC had a value of $85,000 (ignoring the time value of money), represented by 100,000 FC at a then spot rate of 1 FC = $0.850. Nevertheless, the company was concerned that the FC would weaken, resulting in a reduction of the targeted gross profit. In fact, the value of the commitment to receive FC did lose value over time as evidenced by a declining spot rate. However, by hedging the commitment, the company was able to ultimately adjust the basis of the sales transaction and, with the exception of the forward contract discount, attain the targeted gross profit. Note that the account "Firm Commitment" serves the purpose of fixing the basis of the sale by the amount of the loss on the firm commitment recognized during the commitment period. The effect of the above fair value hedge on reported income can be summarized as follows:

	Targeted Position	Without the Hedge	With the Hedge
Sales price	$85,000	$80,000	$84,500
Cost of sales	55,000	55,000	55,000
Gross profit	$30,000	$25,000	$29,500

Illustration 10-5
Hedge of an Identifiable Foreign Currency Commitment

Relating to the Commitment and Sale of Equipment			Relating to the Forward Contract		

March 31
Memo: Company commits to sell equipment.

Memo: Company acquires a forward contract to sell 100,000 FC at a forward rate of 1 FC = $0.845

60 days remaining

Loss on Firm Commitment	693		**Forward Contract**.	693	
Firm Commitment.		693	Gain on Contract.		693
To record the loss on commitment measured by change in the forward rates.			To record change in value due to forward rate changes.		

30 days remaining

Loss on Firm Commitment	2,392		**Forward Contract**.	2,392	
Firm Commitment.		2,392	Gain on Contract.		2,392
To record the loss on commitment.			To record change in value due to forward rate changes.		

0 days remaining

Loss on Firm Commitment	1,415		**Forward Contract**.	1,415	
Firm Commitment.		1,415	Gain on Contract.		1,415
To record the loss on commitment.			To record change in value due to forward rate changes.		

Foreign Currency.	80,000		**Cash**.	84,500	
Firm Commitment.	4,500		Foreign Currency.		80,000
Sales Revenue		84,500	**Forward Contract**		4,500
To record sale and adjustment to basis of sale.			To record settlement of contract.		

Cost of Sales	55,000	
Equipment Inventory		55,000
To record cost of sales.		

If the commitment had not been hedged, the actual gross profit on the sale would have been reduced from the targeted gross profit of $30,000 to $25,000. However, the fair value hedge was effective in maintaining the targeted gross profit. This was accomplished at a cost of $500, which represents the time value (the original discount – a forward rate less than the spot rate) on the forward contract [($0.845 – $0.850) × 100,000 FC]. This hedge was highly effective in that the loss on the commitment ($4,500) was perfectly offset by the gain on the forward contract ($4,500). Although this hedge was highly effective in offsetting losses on the commitment, it is important to remember that forward rates could have increased over time, and the hedge would have effectively eliminated gains on the commitment.

If financial statements were presented on April 30, with 60 days remaining on the hedge, the sale and hedge would be reported as follows:

Income Statement		Balance Sheet	
		Assets:	
Loss on firm commitment	$(693)	Forward contract	$693
Gain on contract	693		
Net loss	$ (0)	Liabilities:	
		Firm commitment	$693

The special accounting treatment given a fair value hedge of a firm commitment continues during the commitment period unless:

◆ The necessary criteria to qualify as a fair value hedge are no longer satisfied,

◆ The derivative instrument expires or is sold, terminated, or exercised,

◆ The entity no longer designates the derivative as a fair value hedge, or

◆ The hedging relationship is no longer considered highly effective based on management's policies.

Furthermore, note that the treatment given a fair value hedge does not continue beyond the point in time where the commitment actually becomes a transaction. If the term of the derivative instrument extends beyond the transaction date, any exchange gains or losses after the transaction date are treated, as shown in Illustration 10-3, as a hedge of an existing foreign-currency-denominated asset or liability assuming proper documentation.

Foreign currency commitments are frequently hedged through the use of forward contracts. However, other forms of derivative and nonderivative instruments may be effective. For example, in the above illustration, management could have acquired a put option to sell foreign currency at the transaction date. Alternatively, management could have borrowed dollars for a short term with a promise to repay the loan with a fixed number of FC. The FC received from the sales transaction could have been used to settle the loan denominated in FC. Regardless of the instrument used, the goal of a hedge of a commitment is to reduce the exposure that exchange rate changes may have on the value or amount of the U.S. (domestic) currency to be received or paid. Although the above illustration focused on a commitment involving the receipt of FC in connection with a sale, it is also possible that a commitment might involve the payment of FC. For example, if a company was committed to acquire inventory to be paid for in FC, changes in exchange rates could result in the inventory costing more than anticipated. Such increases in the cost of inventory could reduce gross profits associated with the subsequent sale of the inventory.

R E F L E C T I O N

- In a hedge of an existing foreign currency transaction, both the hedging instrument and the hedged transaction are measured at fair value with resulting gains or losses being recognized currently in earnings.

- A hedge of a foreign currency commitment is a fair value hedge that is given special accounting treatment. Changes in the fair value of both the hedging instrument and the commitment are recognized currently in earnings. When the transaction occurs, the hedged item is adjusted for the accumulated gain or loss on the commitment.

EXAMPLES OF THE ACCOUNTING FOR CASH FLOW HEDGES

As previously stated, cash flow hedges may be used to hedge against changes in the cash flows of either a forecasted foreign currency transaction, the forecasted functional currency equivalent cash flows associated with a recognized asset or liability, and an unrecognized foreign currency firm commitment. It is important to note that regarding a recognized asset or liability, standards allow for the hedge of such an item to be accounted for as either a fair value hedge or a cash flow hedge. This is a special exception in the case of foreign-currency-denominated transactions. Furthermore, in order to qualify for hedge accounting, *all of the variability* in the asset's or liability's foreign currency cash flows must be eliminated by the hedging instrument. Assuming the necessary criteria are satisfied, the cash flow hedge will be given special accounting treatment. This special treatment is characterized as follows:

1. The effective portion of the gain or loss on the derivative instrument will be reported in other comprehensive income.
2. Although not required, a portion of the derivative instrument's gain or loss represented by the time value may be excluded from the assessment of hedge effectiveness. If the time value is excluded, changes in time value will be recognized currently in earnings rather than as a component of other comprehensive income.
3. The amounts reported in OCI will be reclassified into recognized earnings in the same period in which the hedged item affects earnings.
4. Given a hedge of a forecasted transaction, special rules relate to how much of the change in the value of the derivative instrument can be recognized in OCI relative to the change in the forecasted transaction. These rules will be discussed in a subsequent section.

Hedging a Foreign Currency Forecasted Transaction

A forecasted transaction is one that is expected to occur in the future at market prices that will be in existence at the time of the transaction. This is in contrast to a foreign currency commitment, which involves market prices that have been previously determined or committed to at the time of the commitment. Because the transaction is forecasted and has not yet occurred, a forecasted transaction does not provide an entity with any present rights or obligations and therefore does not have any fixed prices or rates. Because, unlike a firm commitment, no terms are fixed, an entity is exposed to the risk that future cash flows associated with the forecasted transaction could change. For example, if a company forecasted a purchase of inventory, the cost of the inventory could change. Furthermore, if the forecasted transaction were denominated in FC, not only could the FC price change, but the number of dollars needed to acquire the necessary FC could also change. To illustrate, assume that a company forecasts purchasing inventory for 100,000 FC and that the current spot rate is 1 FC = \$1.100. The entity is exposed to the risk that the actual cost of the inventory could exceed 100,000 FC and that the FC could strengthen relative to the dollar. For example, if it turned out that the inventory actually cost 105,000 FC and that 1 FC = $1.140, then the transaction that was forecasted to cost $110,000 (100,000 FC × $1.100) would actually cost $119,700 (105,000 FC × $1.140).

The objective of a hedge of a forecasted transaction is to reduce the variability of cash flows associated with the transaction by fixing exchange rates. As previously stated, qualifying cash flow hedges are given special accounting treatment and in the case of a forecasted transaction it is important to note the following:

1. The accounting for the hedge (the hedging instrument) is separate from the accounting for the forecasted foreign currency transaction (the hedged item). Furthermore, since the hedged item is a forecasted transaction, which obviously has not yet occurred or been firmly committed to, no accounting is necessary until the forecasted transaction actually takes place. Therefore, there are no recognized gains or losses in the value of the forecasted transaction being concurrently recognized along with changes in the value of the hedging instrument.

2. The cumulative amount of OCI, resulting from changes in the value of the hedging instrument, cannot exceed the cumulative change in the value of expected/forecasted cash flows. If the cumulative amount of OCI exceeds the cumulative change in the value of expected/forecasted cash flows, the difference is removed from OCI and recognized currently as earnings. For example, if a derivative instrument increases $1,000 in value and the forecasted cash flows decrease in value by $900, a $900 gain will be shown as OCI, and a $100 gain will be recognized in current earnings. In essence, if the hedge is over effective, that amount will be taken to earnings rather than OCI.

3. If the change in value of a derivative instrument is less than the change in value of the forecasted transaction, all of the change in value of the derivative instrument is recognized as a component of other comprehensive income.

4. Changes in the value of the hedging instrument should be accrued at the end of a reporting period.

5. When the forecasted transaction actually affects earnings (versus occurs), the change in the hedging instrument's value recognized as a component of OCI is reclassified into current earnings.

6. If the hedge is perfectly effective, the variability of forecasted cash flows due to changes in exchange rates will be reduced. The component of OCI that is reclassified into current earnings, when the forecasted transaction actually affects earnings, will reduce the effect that changes in exchange rates have had on the underlying cash flows. The result of the hedge is that resulting cash flows are fixed at an exchange rate rather that being allowed to vary as would be the case without a hedge.

7. The deferral of a loss on a cash flow hedge as a component of OCI is not appropriate if it is likely to result in a combined basis/cost that exceeds the fair value of the resulting asset or liability. For example, assume a derivative loss associated with a forecasted purchase of equipment will, when combined with the expected cost of the equipment, result in a total cost in excess of the item's fair value. If this is expected, the derivative's loss should be recognized immediately in earnings, to the extent that it exceeds the equipment's fair value.

8. If all or part of a transaction is still forecasted, there may be some gain or loss on a corresponding derivative that is still being classified as a component of OCI. On an ongoing basis, it is important to make sure that the gain (loss) on a derivative that remains as a component of OCI does not more than offset the cumulative loss (gain) in the value of the remaining forecasted transaction. If excessive amounts are classified as OCI, such excess amounts must be reclassified as a component of current earnings. For example, if the balance in OCI related to a forecasted transaction represents a gain on the hedging

instrument of $10,000 and the loss in value of the remaining forecasted transaction is $8,000, the excess OCI balance of $2,000 must be reclassified as a component of current earnings.

Illustration of Hedging a Forecasted Transaction with an Option. To illustrate the special accounting for a cash flow hedge of a forecasted transaction, assume the following:

1. On June 1, a company forecasted the purchase of 5,000 units of inventory from a foreign vendor. The purchase would probably occur on September 1 and is forecasted to require the payment of 100,000 FC.

2. Upon purchase of the inventory, it is anticipated that the inventory could be further processed and delivered to customers by early October.

3. On June 1, the company purchased an out-of-the-money call option to buy 100,000 FC at a strike price of 1 FC = $0.550 during September. An option premium of $900 was paid.

4. Effectiveness of the hedge is measured by comparing changes in the option's intrinsic value with changes in the forecasted cash flows based on changes in the spot rates for FC. Changes in the time value of the option will be excluded from the assessment of hedge effectiveness and recognized currently in earnings rather than as a component of other comprehensive income. The hedge is expected to be fully effective because the critical terms (nature of underlying, notional amounts, delivery dates, settlement date, type of currency, etc.) of the hedging instrument match the terms of the hedged item.

5. Spot rates, option values, and changes in value over time are as follows:

	June 1	June 30	July 31	September 1
Strike price — 1 FC	$0.550	$ 0.550	$ 0.550	$ 0.550
Spot rate — 1 FC	$0.530	$ 0.552	$ 0.570	$ 0.575
Fair value of options	$ 900	$ 1,350	$ 2,400	$ 2,600
Intrinsic value of option	0	200	2,000	2,500
Time value of option	$ 900	$ 1,150	$ 400	$ 100
Gain (loss) in time value	$ 0	$ 250	$ (750)	$ (300)
Gain (loss) in intrinsic value	$ 0	$ 200	$ 1,800	$ 500
Cumulative change — gain/(loss) in:				
(a) Intrinsic value		$ 200	$ 2,000	$ 2,500
(b) Value of forecasted cash flows (change in spot rates over time)		$(2,200)	$(4,000)	$(4,500)
Lesser (in absolute amount) of (a) or (b) above		$ 200	$ 2,000	$ 2,500

6. On September 1, the company purchased 5,000 units of inventory at a cost of 103,000 FC. The option was settled/sold on September 1 at its fair value of $2,600.

7. After incurring further processing costs of $20,000, the inventory was sold for $95,000 on October 5.

Illustration 10-6 presents the necessary entries to account for the cash flow hedge of the above forecasted transaction and the subsequent actual transactions.

Illustration 10-6
Using an Option as a Cash Flow Hedge of a Forecasted Transaction

The following entries relate to the hedge. There is no corresponding transaction.

June 1

Investment in Call Option	900	
Cash		900
To record purchase of option.		

June 30

Investment in Call Option ($1,350 − $900).	450	
Gain on Option (change in time value)		250
OCI [($0.552 − $0.550) × 100,000 FC]		200
To record change in the value of the option.		

The change in the time value is excluded from the assessment of hedge effectiveness. The portion of the gain recorded in OCI equals the change in the option's intrinsic value, which was zero on June 1 because the strike price of $0.550 was greater than the spot rate of $0.530.

July 31

Investment in Call Option ($2,400 − $1,350)	1,050	
Loss on Option (change in time value).	750	
OCI [($0.570 − $0.552) × 100,000 FC]		1,800
To record change in the value of the option.		

September 1

Investment in Call Option	200	
Loss on Option (change in time value).	300	
OCI		500
To record change in value of the option.		

Cash	2,600	
Investment in Call Option.		2,600
To record net settlement of option.		

The remaining entries relate to the inventory purchase and subsequent sale. There is no hedge outstanding.

Inventory	59,225	
Cash		59,225
To record payment of 103,000 FC × $0.575.		

Inventory	20,000	
Cash		20,000
To record additional processing costs.		

October 5

Cash	95,000	
Sales Revenue		95,000
To record sale of inventory.		

Cost of Sales ($59,225 + $20,000)	79,225	
Inventory		79,225
To recognize cost of sales.		

OCI (balance)	2,500	
Cost of Sales		2,500
To adjust cost of sales by the gain accumulated in OCI.		

An analysis of the entries in Illustration 10-6 reveals that the cash flow hedge was effective in accomplishing the concerns of the U.S. company. At the time of the forecasted transaction, the company anticipated purchasing inventory for 100,000 FC. At a current spot rate of 1 FC = $0.530, the cash outflow would have been $53,000. However, as the spot rate began to increase, the cost of the inventory would increase, and the potential gross profit on its eventual sale would decrease. At the date of the transaction, the spot rate was 1 FC = $0.575. If the price of the inventory had remained at 100,000 FC, the cost of the inventory would have been $57,500. Acquiring an option to buy FC allowed the company to reduce the variability of cash flows and acquire FC at a fixed strike price of 1 FC = $0.550. The effect of the cash flow hedge of the forecasted transaction can be summarized as follows:

	Without the Call Option	With the Call Option
Sales price of inventory	$ 95,000	$ 95,000
Cost of sales—Raw materials	(59,225)	(59,225)
Cost of sales—Processing costs	(20,000)	(20,000)
Gross profit	$ 15,775	$ 15,775
Adjustment to cost of sales due to change in the intrinsic value of the option		2,500
Adjusted gross profit	$ 15,775	$ 18,275
Unrealized loss on hedge excluded from assessment of hedge effectiveness (change in time value)		(800)
Net income effect	$ 15,775	$ 17,475

The adjusted gross profit resulting from the use of a hedge results from the following:

Sales revenue	$ 95,000
Locked in cost of sales on 100,000 FC at the strike price of $0.550	(55,000)
No hedge on the additional cost of 3,000 FC at the transaction date spot rate of $0.575	(1,725)
Processing costs	(20,000)
Adjusted gross profit	$ 18,275

An analysis of the entries also shows that the balance in OCI at any point in time never exceeded the lesser (in absolute amounts) of the derivative's cumulative gain (loss) in intrinsic value or the loss (gain) in the value of the expected/forecasted cash flows (as measured by changes in spot rates).

The cash flow hedge was effective in reducing the variability of cash flows and was accomplished at a cost of $800, which represents the change in the time value of the option over the holding period ($900 – $100). Once again, remember that the variability of cash flows may also produce a positive effect. For example, if the spot rate had decreased, the purchase of inventory would have required even less cash flow than originally forecasted, and additional gross profit may have resulted. However, an option is a useful derivative to employ in such situations. Remember that the option represents a right, rather than an obligation, to buy FC. If spot rates had declined below the strike price, the holder of the out-of-the-money option would have elected not to exercise the option and merely recognize the option premium of $900 as a loss. If a forward contract to buy FC had been employed, the holder would have been obligated to exercise or settle the contract. In that case, the hedging instrument would have had an unfavorable effect, offsetting the positive effects associated with variable cash flows.

If financial statements were presented at June 30, the hedge would be reported as follows:

Income Statement		Balance Sheet	
		Assets:	
Gain on option	$250	Investment in options	$1,350
		Stockholders' Equity:	
		Other comprehensive income—Gain on option	$ 200

The special accounting treatment given a cash flow hedge of a forecasted transaction continues unless:

◆ The necessary criteria to qualify as a cash flow hedge are no longer satisfied,
◆ The derivative instrument expires or is sold, terminated, or exercised,
◆ The derivative instrument is no longer designated as a hedge on a forecasted transaction, or
◆ The hedging relationship is no longer highly effective based on management's policies.

If a forecasted transaction is no longer probable, the gain or loss accumulated in OCI should be recognized immediately in earnings. Once a forecasted transaction actually occurs, however, it is possible at that time to designate the original derivative, if not expired, or a new derivative as a hedge on any exposed asset or liability resulting from the actual transaction.

Illustration of Hedging a Forecasted Transaction with a Forward Contract. To illustrate the special accounting for a cash flow hedge of a forecasted transaction with a forward contract, assume the same facts as presented above in the case of hedging with an option except the following:

1. On June 1, the company purchased a forward contract to buy 100,000 FC at a forward rate of 1 FC = $0.542 on September 1.
2. Effectiveness of the hedge is measured by comparing changes in the spot rates (intrinsic value) with changes in the forecasted cash flows based on changes in the spot rates for FC. Changes in the time value of the forward will be excluded from the assessment of hedge effectiveness and recognized currently in earnings rather than as a component of other comprehensive income.

   Straight-line amortization of the time value of the hedging instrument is no longer acceptable. There are several ways to amortize the spot-forward difference over the life of the instrument. In this current example, the implicit interest rate method will be applied. At inception of the contract, the difference between the notional amount at the spot rate of $53,000 (100,000 FC × $0.530) and the notional amount at the forward rate of $54,200 (100,000 FC × $0.542) represents a contract premium (interest expense) of $1,200 to be recognized over the three months of the contract. Solving for the periodic implicit interest rate where n is 3 periods, the present value is $53,000, and the future value is $54,200 results in a period rate of 0.7491%. Based on this rate, the periodic amortization of the contract premium is as follows:

Period	Beginning Balance	Interest at 0.7491%	Ending Balance
1	$53,000	$ 397	$53,397
2	$53,397	$ 400	$53,797
3	$53,797	$ 403	$54,200
		$1,200	

3. The hedge is expected to be fully effective because the critical terms (nature of underlying, notional amounts, delivery dates, settlement date, type of currency, etc.) of the hedging instrument match the terms of the hedged item.
4. Spot rates, forward rates, and changes in value over time are as follows:

	June 1	June 30	July 31	September 1
Number of FC	100,000	100,000	100,000	100,000
Spot rate — 1 FC	$0.530	$0.552	$0.570	$0.575
Forward rate for remaining time — 1 FC	$0.542	$0.560	$0.572	$0.575
Initial forward rate — 1 FC		$0.542	$0.542	$0.542
Value of spot-forward difference on 100,000 FC	$1,200	$ 800	$ 200	$ 0
Change in spot-forward difference between time periods	$ 0	$ 400	$ 600	$ 200

Fair value of forward contract:

Original forward value	$54,200	$54,200	$ 54,200
Current forward value	56,000	57,200	57,500
Change—gain (loss)—in forward value	$ 1,800	$ 3,000	$ 3,300
Present value of change:			
$n = 2, i = 6\%/12$........................	$ 1,782		
$n = 1, i = 6\%/12$........................		$ 2,985	
$n = 0, i = 6\%/12$........................			$ 3,300
Change in value from prior period:			
Current present value........................	$ 1,782	$ 2,985	$ 3,300
Prior present value	0	1,782	2,985
Change in present value	$ 1,782	$ 1,203	$ 315
Amortization of time value	397	400	403
Increase (decrease) in OCI	$ 2,179	$ 1,603	$ 718

Using a forward contract as the hedging instrument, Illustration 10-7 presents the necessary entries to account for the cash flow hedge of the above forecasted transaction and the subsequent actual transactions.

Illustration 10-7
Using a Forward Contract as a Cash Flow Hedge of a Forecasted Transaction

The following entries relate to the hedge. There is no corresponding transaction.

June 1
Memo: Company acquires a forward contract to buy 100,000 FC at a forward rate of 1 FC = $0.542.

June 30

Forward Contract...	1,782	
Premium Expense	397	
OCI		2,179
To record change in value of the forward contract and record the amortization of the contract premium.		

July 31

Forward Contract...	1,203	
Premium Expense	400	
OCI		1,603
To record change in value of the forward contract and record the amortization of the contract premium.		

September 1

Forward Contract...	315	
Premium Expense	403	
OCI		718
To record change in value of the forward contract and record the amortization of the contract premium.		

Foreign Currency..	57,500	
Forward Contract...		3,300
Cash		54,200
To record settlement of the forward contract.		(continued)

The remaining entries relate to the inventory purchase and subsequent sale. There is no hedge outstanding.

Inventory	59,225	
Cash		1,725
Foreign currency		57,500
To record payment of 103,000 FC × $0.575.		

Inventory	20,000	
Cash		20,000
To record additional processing costs.		

October 5

Cash	95,000	
Sales Revenue		95,000
To record sale of inventory.		

Cost of Sales ($59,225 + $20,000)	79,225	
Inventory		79,225
To recognize cost of sales.		

OCI (balance)	4,500	
Cost of Sales		4,500
To adjust cost of sales by the gain accumulated in OCI.		

In the example set forth in Illustration 10-7, the time value of the forward contract, measured by the spot-forward difference at inception, was excluded from hedge effectiveness. This resulted in the recognition of a premium expense of $1,200 over the life of the contract and a total of $4,500 recognized as OCI. Had the time value of the contract been included in the assessment of effectiveness, there would have been no separate expensing of the contract premium. Rather it would have been included as part of the adjustment to OCI. A comparison of the two approaches is as follows:

Over the Life of the Contract	Time Value Is Excluded from Assessment of Effectiveness	Time Value Is Included from Assessment of Effectiveness
Premium expense	$1,200	$ 0
Other comprehensive income	4,500	3,300
Change in the value of the forward contract	3,300	3,300
Actual savings in the cost of inventory (100,000 FC × $0.542 or $54,200 rather than 100,000 FC × $0.575 or $57,500)	3,300	3,300
Final adjustment to cost of sales	4,500	3,300

The accounting for the spot-forward difference will definitely be simplified, if the time value of the forward contract is not excluded from the assessment of hedge effectiveness. If it is included in the assessment of effectiveness, the change in the value of the hedged item will be perfectly offset by the change in the value of the forward contract. Not only is the need to separately account for the spot-forward difference avoided, but generally volatility in earnings can be minimized. Given this simplification, unless otherwise stated, *the spot-forward difference on forward contracts will be included in the assessment of effectiveness.*

An analysis of the entries in Illustration 10-7 reveals that the cash flow hedge was effective in accomplishing the concerns of the U.S. company. Given the use of a forward contract, the effect of the cash flow hedge of the forecasted transaction can be summarized as follows:

	Without the Forward Contract	With the Forward Contract
Sales price of inventory	$ 95,000	$ 95,000
Cost of sales—Raw materials	(59,225)	(59,225)
Cost of sales—Processing costs	(20,000)	(20,000)
Gross profit	$ 15,775	$ 15,775
Adjustment to cost of sales		4,500
Adjusted gross profit	$ 15,775	$ 20,275
Unrealized loss on hedge excluded from assessment of hedge effectiveness		(1,200)
Net income effect	$ 15,775	$ 19,075

The adjusted gross profit resulting from the use of a hedge results from the following:

Sales revenue	$ 95,000
Locked in cost of sales on 100,000 FC at the spot rate of $0.530	(53,000)
No hedge on the additional cost of 3,000 FC at the transaction date spot rate of $0.575	(1,725)
Processing costs	(20,000)
Adjusted gross profit	$ 20,275

The above gross profit of $20,275 based on the use of a forward contract is $2,000 greater than the gross profit of $18,275 traceable to the earlier hedge of a forecasted transaction using an option (Illustration 10-5). The difference is traceable to the fact that the forward contract was able to lock in the purchase of inventory at a cost of $53,000 (100,000 × $0.530 spot rate) compared to the option that locked in a cost of inventory of $55,000 (100,000 × $0.550 strike price).

Illustration of Hedging the Cash Flows Associated with a Recognized Asset or Liability. As previously discussed in the section dealing with fair value hedges, the risk associated with recognized assets or liabilities can be hedged with a fair value hedge. However, the cash flows associated with a recognized asset or liability denominated in foreign currency may also be designated as a cash flow hedge. However, in order to be designated as a cash flow hedge, all of the variability in the hedged item's foreign currency cash flows must be eliminated by the hedging instrument. In the case of a cash flow hedge, the risk is that the cash flows associated with the recognized asset or liability could be affected due to changes in the foreign currency exchange rates. In order to demonstrate the treatment as a cash flow hedge, the facts of the illustration involving the hedge of a foreign currency asset with a fair value hedge set forth on page 564 will be used. Those facts are as follows:

1. On November 1, 2015, the company bought inventory from a foreign vendor with payment due on February 1, 2016, in the amount of 100,000 FC.
2. On November 1, 2015, the company purchased a forward contract to buy 100,000 FC on February 1, 2016, at a forward rate of 1 FC = $0.506.
3. Selected spot and forward rates are as follows:

Date	Spot Rate	Forward Rate for Remaining Term of Contract
November 1, 2015	1 FC = $0.500	1 FC = $0.506
December 31, 2015	1 FC = 0.520	1 FC = 0.530
February 1, 2016	1 FC = 0.550	1 FC = 0.550

4. Changes in the value of the forward contract are to be discounted at a 6% rate.
5. The contract premium is included in the assessment of hedge effectiveness. Therefore, changes in the value of the forward contract based on changes in the forward rate are used to assess effectiveness. There is no separate accounting for the contract premium.
6. Changes in the value of the forward contract over time are as follows:

	November 1— 90 Days Remaining	December 31— 30 Days Remaining	Transaction Date
Number of FC	100,000	100,000	100,000
Spot rate — 1 FC	$0.500	$0.520	$0.550
Forward rate for remaining time — FC	$0.506	$0.530	$0.550
Initial forward rate — FC		$0.506	$0.506
Fair value of forward contract:			
Original forward value		$50,600	$50,600
Current forward value		53,000	55,000
Change—gain (loss)—in forward value		$ 2,400	$ 4,400
Present value of change:			
n = 1, i = 6%/12		$ 2,388	
n = 0, i = 6%/12			$ 4,400
Change in value from prior period:			
Current present value		$ 2,388	$ 4,400
Prior present value		0	2,388
Change in present value		$ 2,388	$ 2,012

Illustration 10-8 presents the entries to record the foreign currency transaction and the related forward contract as a cash flow hedge. Once again, in order to emphasize that the value of certain account balances is not fixed and will change over time, these accounts are identified in boldface type.

Illustration 10-8
Using a Cash Flow Hedge to Hedge a Foreign-Currency-Denominated Liability

Relating to the Purchase of Inventory	Relating to the Forward Contract

November 1, 2015

Inventory 50,000
   Accounts Payable—FC 50,000
   To record purchase of inventory for
   100,000 FC when 1 FC = $0.500.

Memo: Company acquired a forward
contract to buy 100,000 FC at a forward rate
of 1 FC = $0.506.

December 31, 2015

Exchange Loss 2,000
   Accounts Payable—FC 2,000
   To accrue exchange loss on the
   FC-denominated payable when
   the spot rate is $0.520.

Forward Contract 2,388
   OCI 2,388
   To record change in the value of the forward
   contract and premium expense.

OCI 2,000
   Gain on Contract 2,000
   To offset impact on earnings of exchange loss
   on accounts payable.

(continued)

February 1, 2016

Accounts Payable—FC	52,000			
Exchange Loss	3,000			
Foreign Currency		55,000		
To record settlement of the liability when 1 FC = $0.550.				

Forward Contract	2,012	
OCI		2,012
To record change in the value of the forward contract and premium expense.		
OCI	2,400	
Gain on Contract		2,400
To offset impact on earnings of exchange loss on accounts payable.		
Foreign Currency	55,000	
Forward Contract		4,400
Cash		50,600
To record settlement of contract.		

In order to understand the impact of treating a hedge on an existing foreign-currency-denominated asset or liability as a fair value hedge versus a cash flow hedge, the financial statement impact of Illustration 10-3 is compared to Illustration 10-8 as follows:

Debit (Credit)	Fair Value Hedge (Illustration 10-3)	Cash Flow Hedge (Illustration 10-8)
December 31, 2015, balance sheet values:		
Inventory	$ 50,000	$ 50,000
Forward contract	2,388	2,388
Accounts payable	(52,000)	(52,000)
Other comprehensive income	0	(388)
2015 income statement values:		
Exchange loss	2,000	2,000
Gain on contract	(2,388)	(2,000)
Premium expense	0	0
Impact on net earnings	(388)	0
February 1, 2016, balance sheet values	No balances	No balances
2016 income statement values:		
Exchange loss	3,000	3,000
Gain on contract	(2,012)	(2,400)
Premium expense	0	0
Impact on net earnings	988	600
Total impact on net earnings—2015 and 2016	600	600

Based on the above table, the balance sheet difference between the alternative hedging classifications relates only to the balance in other comprehensive income resulting from the cash flow treatment. However, the big differences in classifications relate to the income statement. Under the fair value classification, there is significantly more volatility in reported earnings between periods than under the cash flow treatment. In fact, under the cash flow treatment, the only periodic net impact on earnings will be traceable to the amortization of the contract premium or discount that is excluded from hedge effectiveness. In fact, the periodic impact on net earnings will be known in advance because the contract premium or discount is known at inception of the contract. Although the overall impact on net earnings is the same ($600) regardless of the classification of the hedge, the predictability of the periodic impact on net earnings associated with the cash flow treatment is a clear advantage.

Summary of Hedging Transactions

When transactions are denominated in one currency and measured in another, changes in currency exchange rates can expose the transacting party to potential exchange gains or losses. In order to reduce the uncertainty associated with exchange rate changes, forward contracts and other derivatives are often used to hedge against the exposure associated with:

- A forecasted foreign currency transaction,
- An unrecognized foreign currency commitment, or
- A recognized foreign currency denominated asset or liability.

The following table summarizes some of the details relating to these risk-management techniques:

	Transaction Is Forecasted	Commit to Transaction	Transaction Occurs
	Hedge of a Forecasted Transaction	Hedge of an Identifiable Firm Commitment	Hedge of a Denominated FC Asset or Liability
1. Type of hedge.	Cash flow hedge.	Fair value hedge or cash flow hedge.	Fair value hedge or cash flow hedge.
2. Basic purpose of hedge.	Hedge against changes in the cash flows due to exchange rate risk occurring between the time of the probable forecasted transaction and the resulting actual transaction.	Hedge against exchange rate risk occurring between the commitment date and the transaction date.	Hedge the exchange rate risk between the transaction date and the payment/settlement date.
3. Measurement of the value of a forward contract at a point in time.	Measured as the net present value of the difference between the notional amount at the forward rate at inception and the notional amount at the now current forward rate.	Measured as the net present value of the difference between the notional amount at the forward rate at inception and the notional amount at the now current forward rate.	Measured as the net present value of the difference between the notional amount at the forward rate at inception and the notional amount at the now current forward rate.
4. Measurement of the value of an option at a point in time.	Measured as the quoted option value.	Measured as the quoted option value.	Measured as the quoted option value.
5. Recognition over time of changes in the value of the derivative.	Changes in value are recognized as a component of other comprehensive income. When the resulting transaction affects earning, an offsetting amount of OCI is also recognized currently in earnings.	Changes in value are recognized currently as a component of income.	Changes in value are recognized currently as a component of income in the case of a fair value hedge and as a component of OCI in the case of a cash flow hedge.
6. Measurement of the time value of a derivative at inception.	For a forward contract, the difference between the initial forward rate and the initial spot rate times the notional amount. For an option, the total value of the option at inception less the intrinsic value at inception.	For a forward contract, the difference between the initial forward rate and the initial spot rate times the notional amount. For an option, the total value of the option at inception less the intrinsic value at inception.	For a forward contract, the difference between the initial forward rate and the initial spot rate times the notional amount. For an option, the total value of the option at inception less the intrinsic value at inception.
7. Portion of the time value of a derivative that is excluded from assessment of hedge effectiveness.	May elect to exclude that portion traceable to the time value of the derivative.	May elect to exclude that portion traceable to the time value of the derivative.	May elect to exclude that portion traceable to the time value of the derivative.

(continued)

	Transaction Is Forecasted	Commit to Transaction	Transaction Occurs
	Hedge of a Forecasted Transaction	Hedge of an Identifiable Firm Commitment	Hedge of a Denominated FC Asset or Liability
8. If excluded from the assessment of hedge effectiveness, recognition of the change in time value.	Recognized currently in earnings with an offsetting amount being recorded in OCI.	Recognized currently in earnings. There is no need to separately account for the ineffective portion.	Recognized currently in earnings if a fair value hedge. If a cash flow hedge, recognized currently in earnings with an offsetting amount being recorded in OCI.
9. Recognition of the gain or loss on the hedged item.	No gain or loss—forecasted transaction is not recorded.	Recognized currently in earnings and results in an adjustment to the basis of the hedged transaction.	Recognized currently in earnings.
10. Measurement of the gain or loss on the hedged item.	No gain or loss—forecasted transaction is not recorded.	Measured as the change in spot or forward rates between the date of the commitment and the transaction date.	Measured as the change in spot rates between the date of the transaction date and the settlement date.
11. Effect on the basis of the resulting transaction.	Fixes the dollar basis of the actual transaction.	Fixes the dollar basis of the actual transaction.	None.

Disclosures Regarding Hedges of Foreign Currency Exposure

Disclosures regarding foreign currency hedges are required as part of the broader disclosure requirements for derivative instruments and hedging activity. More specific disclosure requirements also exist for fair value and cash flow hedges. Exhibit 10-1 contains an example of certain disclosures regarding the hedging of foreign currency transactions.

Exhibit 10-1
Johnson Controls, Inc.
Fiscal Year Ended September 30, 2013 SEC Form 10-K
Selected Notes to the Financial Statements

NOTE 11. FAIR VALUE MEASUREMENTS

VALUATION METHODS

Foreign currency exchange derivatives—The Company selectively hedges anticipated transactions that are subject to foreign exchange rate risk primarily using foreign currency exchange hedge contracts. The foreign currency exchange derivatives are valued under a market approach using publicized spot and forward prices. As cash flow hedges under ASC 815, the effective portion of the hedge gains or losses due to changes in fair value are initially recorded as a component of accumulated other comprehensive income and are subsequently reclassified into earnings when the hedged transactions occur and affect earnings. Any ineffective portion of the hedge is reflected in the consolidated statement of income. These contracts were highly effective in hedging the variability in future cash flows attributable to changes in currency exchange rates at September 30, 2013 and 2012. The fair value of foreign currency exchange derivatives not designated as hedging instruments under ASC 815 are recorded in the consolidated statements of income.

(continued)

NOTE 14. EQUITY AND NONCONTROLLING INTERESTS

The following schedules present changes in accumulated other comprehensive income (AOCI) attributable to Johnson Controls, Inc. (in millions, net of tax):

	Year Ended September 30, 2013	Year Ended September 30, 2012	Year Ended September 30, 2011
Foreign currency translation adjustments			
Balance at beginning of period...................	$413	$634	$743
Aggregate adjustment for the period [net of tax effect of $19, $(15), and $(3)]	21	221	109
Balance at end of period.......................	$392	$413	$634

REFLECTION

- A hedge of a forecasted foreign currency transaction is a cash flow hedge that is given special accounting treatment. Changes in the fair value of the hedging instrument are recognized as a component of other comprehensive income. Components of OCI are subsequently recognized in earnings in the same period(s) as the actual transaction affects earnings.

- The risk associated with a recognized asset or liability may be hedged with either a fair value hedge or a cash flow hedge. Hedging with a cash flow hedge results in less volatility in reported earnings over time as compared to if a fair value hedge were used.

- A company may be exposed to foreign currency exchange risk in several contexts including forecasted transactions, commitments, and foreign currency transactions. The hedge used in each area of risk has a unique purpose and requires special measurement principles.

UNDERSTANDING THE ISSUES

1. If the U.S. dollar was expected to strengthen relative to a foreign currency (FC), what effect might this have on a U.S. exporter?

2. A U.S. company purchases inventory from a foreign vendor, and purchases are denominated in the foreign currency (FC). The U.S. dollar is expected to weaken against the FC. Explain how a forward contract might be employed as a hedge against exchange rate risk.

3. Explain how a U.S. company's commitment to purchase inventory with settlement in foreign currency (FC) might become less attractive over time and how adverse effects on earnings could be reduced.

4. A company is forecasting the purchase of inventory from an overseas vendor with payment to be made in a foreign currency (FC). Assume an option were used as a hedging instrument for this forecasted transaction. Explain how changes in the time value of the option would be measured and accounted for.

EXERCISES

Exercise 1 *(LO 3, 6)* **Hedging a foreign currency liability with an option designated as a fair value hedge.** Williams Corporation imports, from a number of German manufacturers, large machining equipment used in the tooling industry. On June 1, the company received delivery of a piece of machinery with a cost of 450,000 euros when the spot rate was 1 euro equals $1.370. Williams had already paid 50,000 euros, when the spot rate was 1 euro equals $1.350, to the German company at the time of placing the order, and the balance of the invoice was due in 60 days after delivery. On June 15, the company became concerned that the dollar would weaken relative to the euro and proceeded to purchase an option to buy euros on July 31 at a strike price of 1 euro equals $1.375. The hedge was designated as a fair value hedge. At the time of purchase, the out-of-the-money option had a value of $1,400 and a value of $2,600 at June 30. Euro spot rates are as follows:

	1 euro =
June 15	$1.373
June 30	1.381
July 31	1.385

On July 31, the option was settled and the foreign currency was remitted to the German vendor.

Assuming that financial statements are prepared for June and July, identify all relevant income statement and balance sheet accounts for the above transactions and determine the appropriate monthly balances.

Exercise 2 *(LO 2)* **Spot rates and forward rates.** On January 1, one U.S. dollar can be exchanged for eight foreign currencies (FC). The dollar can be invested short term at a rate of 4%, and the FC can be invested at a rate of 5%.

1. Calculate the direct and indirect spot exchange rates as of January 1.
2. Calculate the 180-day forward rate to buy FC (assume 365 days per year).
3. If the spot rate is 1 FC = $0.740 and the 90-day forward rate is $0.752, what does this suggest about interest rates in the two countries?
4. Explain why a weak dollar relative to the FC would likely increase U.S. exports.
5. Discuss what would happen to the forward rate if the dollar strengthened relative to the FC.

Exercise 3 *(LO 5, 6)* **Measuring changes in the value of derivatives and accounting for such changes.** A company has acquired two derivatives: an option to buy foreign currency (FC) and a forward contract to buy FC. Both derivatives were acquired on the same day, for the same notional amount and expire on May 31. Relevant information involving the derivatives is as follows:

	February 1	April 30	May 31
Notional amount in FC ...	100,000	100,000	100,000
Spot rate	$ 2.05	$ 2.08	$ 2.10
Forward rate	$ 2.07	$ 2.09	$ 2.10
Strike price.............	$ 2.05	$ 2.05	$ 2.05
Value of option	$ 1,000	$ 3,400	$ 5,000

1. Calculate the intrinsic and the time value of the option for each of the above dates and indicate how the changes in each of these values would be accounted for if the option hedged: (a) a forecasted FC transaction and (b) a recognized FC-denominated liability.
2. Calculate the value of the forward contract at each of the above dates and indicate how the changes in each of these values would be accounted for if the contract hedged: (a) an unrecognized FC firm commitment (b) a recognized FC-denominated liability. Assume a 6% interest rate for any discounting purposes.
3. In part (2), assume that the two hedged items involved the purchase of inventory. Explain how the changes in value of the hedging instruments would affect the basis of the inventory.

Exercise 4 *(LO 3, 6)* **Fair value hedge with forward contract.** Stark, Inc., placed an order for inventory costing 500,000 FC with a foreign vendor on April 15 when the spot rate was 1 FC = $0.683. Stark received the goods on May 1 when the spot rate was 1 FC = $0.687. Also on May 1, Stark entered into a 90-day forward contract to purchase 500,000 FC at a forward rate of 1 FC = $0.693. Payment was made to the foreign vendor on August 1 when the spot rate was 1 FC = $0.696. Stark has a June 30 year-end. On that date, the spot rate was 1 FC = $0.691, and the forward rate on the contract was 1 FC = $0.695. Changes in the current value of the forward contract are measured as the present value of the changes in the forward rates over time and no separate accounting is given the time value of the contract. The relevant discount rate is 6%.

1. Prepare all relevant journal entries suggested by the above facts assuming that the hedge is designated as a fair value hedge.
2. Prepare a partial income statement and balance sheet as of the company's June 30 year-end that reflect the above facts.

Exercise 5 *(LO 3, 6)* **Hedging a commitment with an option.** Wellington Manufacturing manufactures industrial ovens used primarily in the process of coating or painting metals. The ovens are sold throughout the world, and units are manufactured to customers' specifications. On June 15, the company committed to sell two ovens to a major transnational customer. One of the ovens has a selling price of $549,600 and is to be paid for with foreign currency A (FCA). The other unit has a selling price of $297,975 and is to be paid for with foreign currency B (FCB). Both units were shipped, FOB shipping point, on September 15, and payment is due within 30 days of shipment. In order to hedge against exchange rate risks, Wellington acquired two put options on June 15 with notional amounts equal to the respective foreign currency selling prices. The options expire on October 15, and customer remittances are also received on October 15. Relevant information concerning the options and exchange rates is as shown:

Fair Value of Option	June 15	September 15	October 15
FCA option (strike price = $1.200).....	$5,000	$21,000	
FCB option (strike price = $0.700).....	$8,500	$ 4,300	

Spot Rates			
FCA.........................	$1.200	$1.160	$1.170
FCB.........................	$0.685	$0.692	$0.720

1. Assuming that the time value of the options is excluded from the determination of hedge effectiveness, determine the gain or loss to be recognized on each of the commitments. The firm commitment is measured based on changes in the spot rate over time.
2. Assuming that the costs of the FCA unit and the FCB unit are $440,000 and $235,000, respectively, calculate the gross profit margin on each of the units that would have been experienced with and without the hedge.

Exercise 6 *(LO 4, 5)* **Hedging a commitment; forecasted transaction—forward contract vs. option.** Jackson, a U.S. company, acquires a variety of raw materials from foreign vendors with amounts payable in foreign currency (FC). The company needs to acquire 20,000 units of raw materials, and the goods are expected to have a price of 100,000 FC. Assume that the inventory can be subsequently sold to U.S. customers for $160,000.

Jackson is contemplating committing to the purchase of the inventory on September 1 with delivery on November 1. However, rather than making a commitment, the company could forecast a probable purchase of inventory with delivery on November 1. In either case, assume that on September 1 the company would either (a) acquire a forward contract to buy 100,000 FC with a forward date of November 1 or (b) acquire an option to buy FC in November at a strike price of $1.250. The option premium is expected to cost $2,100.

Various spot rates, forward rates, and option values are as follows:

	Spot Rate	Forward Rate for November 1	Time Value of Option
September 1	1 FC = $1.250	1 FC = $1.270	$2,100
November 1	1 FC = $1.320	1 FC = $1.320	0

1. Prepare a schedule that would compare the effect on current earnings of the two alternatives (commit or forecast), given the alternative hedging instruments. Show the effect on earnings for the period prior to the transaction date separately from the effect after the transaction date. The time value component of the hedging instruments is excluded from the assessment of hedge effectiveness. Changes in the value of the commitment are measured by changes in the spot rates.
2. Discuss your conclusion, and explain to Jackson why one alternative might be preferable over the other.

Exercise 7 *(LO 3)* **Foreign currency transactions involving a building and loan payable.** Regber International is building an addition to one of its overseas manufacturing facilities with all construction costs being paid in foreign currency (FC) as follows: 200,000 FC, 300,000 FC, 400,000 FC, and 100,000 FC on March 1, June 30, August 31, and September 30, respectively.

The initial payment was financed by a 2-month note in the amount of 200,000 FC. The note bears interest at the rate of 4.8% and principal and interest are to be paid on April 30. On April 30, the company secured a 6-month note in order to finance ongoing construction costs. This 300,000 FC note bears interest at 6% and calls for quarterly interest payments. On June 1, the company forecasted remaining construction payments and acquired a forward contract to buy 400,000 FC at a forward rate of $1.53 with settlement on August 31. Various spot and forward rates are as shown:

	Spot Rate	Forward Rate			Spot Rate	Forward Rate
March 1	$1.50			June 30	$1.55	$1.57
April 30	$1.48			July 31	$1.58	$1.59
June 1	$1.52	$1.53		August 31	$1.60	$1.60
				September 30 . . .	$1.65	

Calculate the basis of the building addition including capitalized interest and financing costs associated with the forward contract. Assume that the construction was completed on September 30.

Exercise 8 *(LO 4, 5)* **Income statement effects with and without hedging.** In the past, Baxter Manufacturing has engaged in a number of foreign currency transactions but has never before attempted to hedge these transactions. Baxter has given you three past events and asked you to illustrate how hedging could have been employed. The events are as follows:

Event A: Purchased raw materials from a foreign supplier for 100,000 FC when 1 FC = $1.100. The supplier was paid 60 days later when 1 FC = $1.150. When the goods were purchased, a 60-day forward contract to buy FC had a forward rate of 1 FC = $1.110.

Event B: Committed to sell inventory (with a cost of $120,000) to a foreign buyer for 200,000 FC when 1 FC = $1.130. Sixty days later, when the inventory was shipped, 1 FC = $1.170, and 90 days later, when the customer paid, 1 FC = $1.180. At the date of the commitment, the 90-day forward rate to sell was 1 FC = $1.150, and at the date of shipment, a 30-day forward rate was 1 FC = $1.172. Changes in the value of the commitment are based on changes in forward rates. Assume a 6% discount rate.

Event C: Forecasted needing to buy inventory with a cost of 60,000 FC in 60 days in order to meet a sale in the amount of $100,000. When the inventory was actually purchased, it had a cost of 68,000 FC. At the time of the forecast, the spot rate was 1 FC = $1.160, and a 60-day forward contract to buy FC was 1 FC = $1.150. At the time the goods were actually purchased, the spot rate was 1 FC = $1.170.

For each of the above events, indicate how income would have been affected with and without the accompanying hedge.

PROBLEMS

Problem 10-1 *(LO 5)* **FC transactions, commitments, forecasted transactions—earnings impact.** Jarvis Corporation transacts business with a number of foreign vendors and customers. These transactions are denominated in FC, and the company uses a number of hedging strategies to reduce the exposure to exchange rate risk. Several such transactions are as follows:

Transaction A: On November 30, the company purchased inventory from a vendor in the amount of 100,000 FC with payment due in 60 days. Also on November 30, the company purchased a forward contract to buy FC in 60 days. Assume a fair value hedge.

Transaction B: On November 1, the company committed to provide services to a foreign customer in the amount of 100,000 FC. The services will be provided in 30 days. On November 1, the company also purchased a forward contract to sell 100,000 FC in 30 days. Changes in the value of the commitment are based on changes in forward rates.

Transaction C: On November 1, the company forecasted a purchase of equipment in 30 days. The forecasted cost is 100,000 FC, and the equipment is to be depreciated over five years using the straight-line method of depreciation. On November 1, the company acquired a forward contract to buy 100,000 FC in 30 days.

Transaction D: On November 30, the company purchased an option to sell 100,000 FC in 60 days to hedge a forecasted sale to a customer in 60 days. The option sold for a premium of $1,200 and had a strike price of $1.155. The value of the option on December 31 was $2,000.

Relevant spot and forward rates are as shown below.

	Spot Rate	Forward Rate for 30 Days from November 1	Forward Rate for 60 Days from November 30
November 1	1 FC = $1.120	1 FC = $1.132	
November 15	1 FC = $1.130		
November 30	1 FC = $1.150		1 FC = $1.146
December 31.............	1 FC = $1.140		1 FC = $1.138

Required ▶ ▶ ▶ ▶ ▶ Assuming that the company's year-end is December 31, for each of the above transactions determine the current-year effect on earnings. All necessary discounting should be determined by using a 6% discount rate. For transactions C and D, the time value of the hedging instrument is excluded from hedge effectiveness and is to be separately accounted for.

Problem 10-2 *(LO 3, 6)* **Hedge with forward contract a commitment and subsequent transaction.** Kaiser Exporters buys used medical equipment and sells it to various foreign health care institutions. On June 15, the company committed to sell medical equipment to a foreign hospital for 800,000 FC. The equipment, with a cost of $325,000, was shipped to the customer on August 15 with terms FOB shipping point and payment due on October 15. At the time of the commitment, Kaiser acquired a forward contract to sell 800,000 FC in 120 days. Selected spot and forward rates are as follows:

	June 15	June 30	August 15	September 30
Spot rate	$0.500	$0.485	$0.480	$0.470
Forward rate	0.510	0.490	0.475	0.468

The relevant discount rate is 6% and changes in the value of the firm commitment are measured as changes in the forward rate over time. Assume that the hedge is accounted for as a fair value hedge and that the time value of the hedge is included in the assessment of effectiveness.

Required ▶ ▶ ▶ ▶ ▶ Assuming that financial statements are prepared for the second and third quarters, identify all relevant income statement and balance sheet accounts for the above transactions and determine the appropriate quarterly balances.

Problem 10-3 *(LO 3, 5)* **Income statement effects of transactions, commitments, and hedging.** Clayton Industries sells medical equipment worldwide. On March 1 of the current year, the company sold equipment, with a cost of $160,000, to a foreign customer for 200,000 euros payable in 60 days. At the same time, the company purchased a forward contract to sell 200,000 euros in 60 days. In another transaction, the company committed, on March 15, to deliver equipment in May to a foreign customer in exchange for 300,000 euros payable in June. This equipment is anticipated to have a completed cost of $210,000. On March 15, the company hedged the commitment by acquiring a forward contract to sell 300,000 euros in 90 days. Changes in the value of the commitment are based on changes in forward rates, and all discounting is based on a 6% discount rate. Assume all hedges are accounted for as fair value hedges and that the spot-forward difference is included in the assessment of hedge effectiveness.

Various spot and forward rates for the euro are as follows:

	Spot Rate	Forward Rate for 60 Days from March 1	Forward Rate for 90 Days from March 15
March 1	$1.180	$1.181	
March 15	1.181	1.180	$1.179
March 31	1.179	1.178	1.177
April 30	1.175		1.174

For individual months of March and April, calculate the income statement effect of: ◄ ◄ ◄ ◄ ◄ **Required**

1. The foreign currency transaction.
2. The hedge on the foreign currency transaction.
3. The foreign currency commitment.
4. The hedge on the foreign currency commitment.

Problem 10-4 *(LO 3, 6)* **Hedging foreign currency transactions and commitments.** Medical Distributors, Inc., is a U.S. company that buys and sells used medical equipment throughout the United States and Canada. During the month of June, the company had the following transactions with Canadian parties:

1. Purchased used equipment on June 1 from a hospital located in Toronto for 220,000 Canadian dollars (CA$) payable in 45 days. On the same day, the company paid $1,000 for a call option to buy 220,000 Canadian dollars during July at a strike price of 1 CA$ = $0.726. The option had a fair value of $3,200 on June 30. The hedge was designated as a fair value hedge.
2. Sold equipment on June 1 for 300,000 Canadian dollars to be paid in 30 days. At the same time, the company purchased a forward contract to sell the Canadian dollars in 30 days and the hedge was designated as a fair value hedge.
3. Committed to buy equipment on June 15 from a Montreal health care provider for 400,000 Canadian dollars in 45 days. At the same time, the company purchased a forward contract to buy 400,000 Canadian dollars in 45 days.
4. Paid 30,000 Canadian dollars on June 20 to refurbish the equipment purchased on June 1.
5. Sold the equipment purchased on June 1 on June 20 for 310,000 Canadian dollars to be received in 30 days.
6. Collected the 300,000 Canadian dollars on June 30 from the sale on June 1.

Selected spot and forward rates are as follows:

	Spot Rate 1 CA$	Forward Rate 1 CA$ =
June 1	$0.720	30-day sell rate = $0.729
June 15	0.729	45-day buy rate = $0.731
June 20	0.732	
June 30	0.735	30-day buy rate = $0.737

Required ▶ ▶ ▶ ▶ ▶ Prepare all of the necessary journal entries to record the above activities during the month of June. Changes in the value of the commitment are based on changes in forward rates. All necessary discounting should be determined using a 6% discount rate. The time value of all derivatives is included in the assessment of hedge effectiveness.

Problem 10-5 *(LO 6)* **Cash flow hedges of a commitment, a forecasted transaction and a recognized liability.** On March 1, a company committed to acquire 10,000 units of inventory to be delivered on May 31. The purchase price is to be paid in foreign currency (FC) in the amount of 200,000 FC. Assume that the commitment's negative values are $7,960 and $14,000 as of March 31 and May 31, respectively. Also assume that the inventory will be processed further during the month of June at a cost of $12.50 per unit and will be sold on July 10 to a customer for $90 per unit. On March 1, the company also forecasted the purchase of a piece of equipment to be delivered on May 31 with a cost of 200,000 FC. The equipment was placed into service at the beginning of July and has a useful life of 10 years and a salvage value of $74,000. On March 1, the company borrowed 200,000 FC from a foreign bank at an interest rate of 6.0% with interest and principal to be repaid on May 31.

Assume that on March 1 the company acquired three identical options to buy FC on May 31 with each option to be designated as a hedge for each of the three situations described above. Information relating to each option is as follows:

For each option	March 1	March 31	May 31
Notional amount	200,000	200,000	200,000
Strike price.	$ 2.52	$ 2.52	$ 2.52
Spot price	$ 2.50	$ 2.54	$ 2.57
Value of option	$ 1,300	$ 5,000	$ 10,000

Required ▶ ▶ ▶ ▶ ▶ For each of the three hedged situations, prepare a schedule to show the impact on earnings for each of the first three calendar quarters of the year noting that all hedges are to be considered cash flow hedges.

Problem 10-6 *(LO 5, 6)* **The impact of no hedging versus hedging.** In several instances, Neibler Corporation has been engaged in transactions that were denominated or settled in foreign currencies (FC). Given recent volatility in exchange rates between the U.S. dollar and the FC, the company is considering using FC derivatives in a number of instances. In order to communicate to management the impact of hedging, you have been asked to develop a schedule relating to several hypothetical situations.

Hypothetical A involves the purchase of inventory in the amount of 100,000 FC with payment due in 60 days. Assume that the hedge would involve: (a) an option to buy 100,000 FC in 60 days and (b) a forward contract to buy 100,000 FC in 60 days. In both cases, the hedge is to be considered a fair value hedge.

Hypothetical B involves the same facts as Hypothetical A except that the hedge is to be considered a cash flow hedge.

Hypothetical C involves a commitment to sell inventory in 90 days for 100,000 FC. Assume that the hedge would involve: (a) an option to sell 100,000 FC in 90 days and (b) a forward contract to sell 100,000 FC in 90 days. In both cases, the hedge is to be considered a cash flow hedge. In the case of the option, changes in the value of the commitment are to be measured by changes in spot rates over time, whereas in the case of the forward contract, changes in the value of commitment are measured based on changes in forward rates. The inventory sold has a cost of $100,000.

Hypothetical D involves a 90-day 100,000 FC note receivable bearing interest at 6%. Both principal and interest are payable at maturity, and it is assumed that an option to sell 100,000 FC will be employed as a cash flow hedge.

Hypothetical E involves a forecasted sale of inventory in 90 days for 100,000 FC. Assume that the inventory has a cost of $110,000 and a forward contract to sell 100,000 FC in 90 days is the hedging instrument.

Selected rate information is as follows:

	At Inception	After 60 days	After 90 days
Derivatives to buy FC			
Spot rate	$ 1.50	$ 1.55	
Forward rate	$ 1.52	$ 1.55	
Strike price	$ 1.51	$ 1.51	
Option value	$ 800	$4,000	
Derivates to sell FC			
Spot rate	$ 1.50		$ 1.40
Forward rate	$ 1.48		$ 1.40
Strike price	$ 1.50		$ 1.50
Option value	$1,000		$10,000

In all hypotheticals, the time value of the derivative is to be excluded from the assessment of ◄ ◄ ◄ ◄ ◄ **Required** effectiveness. For each of the above hypothetical situations, prepare a schedule to show the activity in balance sheet accounts and income statement accounts over the course of the events assuming: (1) no hedging and (2) hedging. With respect to the balance sheet accounts, show the balance in the derivative just prior to settlement and ignore an analysis of cash or foreign currency balances.

Problem 10-7 *(LO 6)* **Hedging a forecasted transaction with a forward contract.** In the process of preparing a budget for the second quarter of the current fiscal year, Anderson Welding, Inc., has forecasted foreign sales of 1,200,00 foreign currency (FC). The company is concerned that the dollar will strengthen relative to the FC and has decided to hedge one-half of the forecasted foreign sales with a forward contract to sell FC in 90 days. Assume that all 1,200,000 of the forecasted sales are shipped 60 days after acquiring the contract and that payment of the sales invoices occurs 30 days after shipment, with terms FOB shipping point. Selected rate information is as shown below.

Days remaining on forward contract	90 days	60 days	30 days	0 days
Spot rate	$1.900	$1.920	$1.880	$1.850
Forward rate	1.890	1.910	1.900	1.850

Assume that contract premiums or discounts are to be amortized over the term of the contract using the implicit interest rate of 0.1757% per 30-day period. This results in amortization of $2,004, $2,000, and $1,996 for the three consecutive periods. All discounting is to be based on a 6% interest rate.

1. Prepare all entries to record the forecasted sales and the related hedging activity. Assume that ◄ ◄ ◄ ◄ ◄ **Required** financial statements are prepared every month and that entries should be made monthly.
2. Prepare a schedule to compare the impact on earnings of hedging half of the forecasted sales versus not hedging the other half. Assume that the total cost of goods sold was $1,800,000, evenly divided among the sales.

PRESENT VALUE TABLES

Present Value of $1 Due in n Periods

$$PV = A\left[\frac{1}{(1+i)^n}\right] = A(PVF_{\overline{n}|i})$$

n	2%	3%	4%	5%	6%	8%	10%	12%	16%	20%
1	0.9804	0.9709	0.9615	0.9524	0.9434	0.9259	0.9091	0.8929	0.8621	0.8333
2	0.9612	0.9426	0.9246	0.9070	0.8900	0.8573	0.8264	0.7972	0.7432	0.6944
3	0.9423	0.9151	0.8890	0.8638	0.8396	0.7938	0.7513	0.7118	0.6407	0.5787
4	0.9238	0.8885	0.8548	0.8227	0.7921	0.7350	0.6830	0.6355	0.5523	0.4823
5	0.9057	0.8626	0.8219	0.7835	0.7473	0.6806	0.6209	0.5674	0.4761	0.4019
6	0.8880	0.8375	0.7903	0.7462	0.7050	0.6302	0.5645	0.5066	0.4104	0.3349
7	0.8706	0.8131	0.7599	0.7170	0.6651	0.5835	0.5132	0.4523	0.3538	0.2791
8	0.8535	0.7894	0.7307	0.6768	0.6274	0.5403	0.4665	0.4039	0.3050	0.2326
9	0.8368	0.7664	0.7026	0.6446	0.5919	0.5002	0.4241	0.3606	0.2630	0.1938
10	0.8203	0.7441	0.6756	0.6139	0.5584	0.4632	0.3855	0.3220	0.2267	0.1615
11	0.8043	0.7224	0.6496	0.5847	0.5268	0.4289	0.3505	0.2875	0.1954	0.1346
12	0.7885	0.7014	0.6246	0.5568	0.4970	0.3971	0.3186	0.2567	0.1685	0.1122
13	0.7730	0.6810	0.6006	0.5303	0.4688	0.3677	0.2897	0.2292	0.1452	0.0935
14	0.7579	0.6611	0.5775	0.5051	0.4423	0.3405	0.2633	0.2046	0.1252	0.0779
15	0.7430	0.6419	0.5553	0.4810	0.4173	0.3152	0.2394	0.1827	0.1079	0.0649
16	0.7284	0.6232	0.5339	0.4581	0.3936	0.2919	0.2176	0.1631	0.0930	0.0541
17	0.7142	0.6050	0.5134	0.4363	0.3714	0.2703	0.1978	0.1456	0.0802	0.0451
18	0.7002	0.5874	0.4936	0.4155	0.3503	0.2502	0.1799	0.1300	0.0691	0.0376
19	0.6864	0.5703	0.4746	0.3957	0.3305	0.2317	0.1635	0.1161	0.0596	0.0313
20	0.6730	0.5537	0.4564	0.3769	0.3118	0.2145	0.1486	0.1037	0.0514	0.0261
25	0.6095	0.4776	0.3751	0.2953	0.2330	0.1460	0.0923	0.0588	0.0245	0.0105
30	0.5521	0.4120	0.3083	0.2314	0.1741	0.0994	0.0573	0.0334	0.0116	0.0042
40	0.4529	0.3066	0.2083	0.1420	0.0972	0.0460	0.0221	0.0107	0.0026	0.0007
50	0.3715	0.2281	0.1407	0.0872	0.0543	0.0213	0.0085	0.0035	0.0006	0.0001

Present Values of an Annuity of $1 per Period

$$PV_n = R \left[\frac{1 - \dfrac{1}{(1+i)^n}}{i} \right] = R(PVAF_{\overline{n}|})$$

n	2%	3%	4%	5%	6%	8%	10%	12%	16%	20%
1	0.9804	0.9709	0.9615	0.9524	0.9434	0.9259	0.9091	0.8929	0.8621	0.8333
2	1.9416	1.9135	1.8861	1.8594	1.8334	1.7833	1.7355	1.6901	1.6052	1.5278
3	2.8839	2.8286	2.7751	2.7232	2.6730	2.5771	2.4869	2.4018	2.2459	2.1065
4	3.8077	3.7171	3.6299	3.5460	3.4651	3.3121	3.1699	3.0373	2.7982	2.5887
5	4.7135	4.5797	4.4518	4.3295	4.2124	3.9927	3.7908	3.6048	3.2743	2.9906
6	5.6014	5.4172	5.2421	5.0757	4.9173	4.6228	4.3553	4.1114	3.6847	3.3255
7	6.4720	6.2303	6.0021	5.7864	5.5824	5.2064	4.8684	4.5638	4.0386	3.6016
8	7.3255	7.0197	6.7327	6.4632	6.2098	5.7466	5.3349	4.9676	4.3436	3.8372
9	8.1622	7.7861	7.4353	7.1078	6.8017	6.2469	5.7590	5.3282	4.6065	4.0310
10	8.9826	8.5302	8.1109	7.7217	7.3601	6.7101	6.1446	5.6502	4.8332	4.1925
11	9.7868	9.2526	8.7605	8.3064	7.8869	7.1390	6.4951	5.9377	5.0286	4.3271
12	10.5753	9.9540	9.3851	8.8633	8.3838	7.5361	6.8137	6.1944	5.1971	4.4392
13	11.3484	10.6350	9.9856	9.3936	8.8527	7.9038	7.1034	6.4235	5.3423	4.5327
14	12.1062	11.2961	10.5631	9.8986	9.2950	8.2442	7.3667	6.6282	5.4675	4.6106
15	12.8493	11.9379	11.1184	10.3797	9.7122	8.5595	7.6061	6.8109	5.5755	4.6755
16	13.5777	12.5611	11.6523	10.8378	10.1059	8.8514	7.8237	6.9740	5.6685	4.7296
17	14.2919	13.1661	12.1657	11.2741	10.4773	9.1216	8.0216	7.1196	5.7487	4.7746
18	14.9920	13.7535	12.6593	11.6896	10.8276	9.3719	8.2014	7.2497	5.8178	4.8122
19	15.6785	14.3238	13.1339	12.0853	11.1581	9.6036	8.3649	7.3658	5.8775	4.8435
20	16.3514	14.8775	13.5903	12.4622	11.4699	9.8181	8.5136	7.4694	5.9288	4.8696
25	19.5235	17.4134	15.6221	14.0939	12.7834	10.6748	9.0770	7.8431	6.0971	4.9476
30	22.3965	19.6004	17.2920	15.3725	13.7648	11.2578	9.4269	8.0552	6.1772	4.9789
40	27.3555	23.1148	19.7928	17.1591	15.0463	11.9246	9.7791	8.2438	6.2335	4.9966
50	31.4236	25.7298	21.4822	18.2559	15.7619	12.2335	9.9148	8.3045	6.2463	4.9995

Index